D1738216

THE COLLECTED WORKS OF W. B. YEATS

George Bornstein, George Mills Harper,
and Richard J. Finneran, General Editors

VOLUME I THE POEMS
ed. Richard J. Finneran

VOLUME II THE PLAYS
ed. David R. Clark and Rosalind E. Clark

VOLUME III AUTOBIOGRAPHIES
ed. William H. O'Donnell and Douglas N. Archibald

VOLUME IV EARLY ESSAYS
ed. Richard J. Finneran and George Bornstein

VOLUME V LATER ESSAYS
ed. William H. O'Donnell with Elizabeth Bergmann Loizeaux

VOLUME VI PREFACES AND INTRODUCTIONS
ed. William H. O'Donnell

VOLUME VII LETTERS TO THE NEW ISLAND
ed. George Bornstein and Hugh Witemeyer

VOLUME VIII THE IRISH DRAMATIC MOVEMENT
ed. Mary FitzGerald and Richard J. Finneran

VOLUME IX EARLY ARTICLES AND REVIEWS
ed. John P. Frayne and Madeleine Marchaterre

VOLUME X LATER ARTICLES AND REVIEWS
ed. Colton Johnson

VOLUME XI MYTHOLOGIES
ed. Jonathan Allison

VOLUME XII JOHN SHERMAN AND DHOYA
ed. Richard J. Finneran

VOLUME XIII A VISION (1925)
ed. Catherine E. Paul and Margaret Mills Harper

VOLUME XIV A VISION (1937)
ed. Margaret Mills Harper and Catherine E. Paul

THE COLLECTED WORKS OF W. B. YEATS

VOLUME XIV

W. B. YEATS

A Vision:
The Revised 1937 Edition

EDITED BY
Margaret Mills Harper
and Catherine E. Paul

Scribner
NEW YORK LONDON TORONTO SYDNEY NEW DELHI

Scribner
An Imprint of Simon & Schuster, Inc.
1230 Avenue of the Americas
New York, NY 10020

This Scribner hardcover edition May 2015

Manufactured in the United States of America

3 5 7 9 10 8 6 4 2

Library of Congress Cataloging-in-Publication Data
Yeats, W. B. (William Butler), 1865–1939, author.
A Vision: The Revised 1937 Edition : the Collected Works of W. B. Yeats Volume XIV / William Butler Yeats ; edited by Margaret Mills Harper and Catherine E. Paul. — Scribner hardcover edition.
pages cm. — (The Collected Works of W. B. Yeats ; Volume XIV)
Includes bibliographical references and index.
1. Yeats, W. B. (William Butler), 1865–1939—Knowledge—Occultism.
2. Occultism—Ireland. 3. Mysticism. I. Harper, Margaret Mills, 1957– editor.
II. Paul, Catherine E., 1971– editor. III. Title.
PR5904.V5 2014
828'.807—dc23
2014017856

ISBN 978-0-684-80734-8
ISBN 978-1-4767-9211-8 (ebook)

For Connie K.
and
Walter Kelly Hood

CONTENTS

A Vision (1937)

EDITORS' PREFACE AND ACKNOWLEDGMENTS

The editors gratefully acknowledge the extraordinary generosity of the Yeats family, the late Michael, Gráinne, and Anne Yeats, and Caitríona Yeats, who, along with her siblings Siobhán, the late Síle, and Padraig Yeats, continues a legacy of unwavering support of those who "cough in ink" or pixels to edit and annotate the work of W. B. Yeats. Such magnanimity is rare, and all Yeats scholars are in their debt.

We also extend the first order of thanks to Walter and Connie Kelly Hood, the first designated editors of the 1937 *A Vision* for this series. To observe that this edition would not have been possible without their extensive archival and contextual work is to understate drastically, and we are deeply in their debt. Other scholars who have contributed generously include Jonathan Allison, Brian Arkins, George Bornstein, Ronald Bush, Wayne K. Chapman, Patricia Coughlan, Alex Davis, John Dillon, Wayne Erickson, Sr. Mary de Lourdes Fahy, Matthew Gibson, Warwick Gould, Mark Patrick Hederman OSB, Michael G. Kelly, Sr. Maria Kiely, Peter Liebregts, Neil Mann, Bernadette McCarthy, Gillian McIntosh, Mary Kathryn Mishler, Mitsuko Ohno, James Pethica, Laura Mernie Pomeroy, LeeAnne Richardson, Ronald Schuchard, Sanghita Sen, William David Soud, Deirdre Toomey, Wim Van Mierlo, and Tom Walker. We thank for superb research assistance Paula McGeever, Niall Jordan, Niamh O'Hehir, and Stephanie O'Riordan (University of Limerick); Zachary Cromie and George DuBose (Clemson University); and Nancy Kojima and Jim Shimkus (Georgia State University).

Librarians who have given of their time and expertise include Tom Desmond, Catherine Fahy, Colette O'Daly, and Pat Sweeney at the National Library of Ireland; Pattie Punch at the Glucksman Library, University of Limerick; Rebecca Drummond at the

University Library, Georgia State University; Elizabeth Chase and colleagues at MARBL (Manuscripts, Archives, and Rare Book Library), Emory University; Kristen Nyitray at Special Collections, Frank Melville, Jr., Memorial Library, Stony Brook University Libraries; staff of the Manuscript Reading Room and the Humanities Reading Rooms at the British Library (Macmillan archives); and staff at Thompson Library, Ohio State University; Harvard University Library; Trinity College Library; and the McClay Library, Queen's University Belfast.

We are grateful for the financial support of the College of Architecture, Arts and Humanities and Department of English, Clemson University; the School of Languages, Literatures, Culture and Communication, University of Limerick; and the Department of English, Georgia State University. We extend special thanks to Richard W. Stoops, Jr., for unstinting technical support; George Bornstein, upon whom we have relied for clearheaded advice and assistance; and Samantha Martin and Ashley Gilliam, our patient and thoroughly helpful editors at Scribner.

ABBREVIATIONS

Arkins Brian Arkins. *Builders of My Soul: Greek and Roman Themes in Yeats.* Gerrards Cross, UK: Colin Smythe, 1990.

AS Automatic Script [see *YVP* 1, 2].

Au *Autobiographies.* Ed. William H. O'Donnell and Douglas N. Archibald. *The Collected Works of W. B. Yeats.* Vol. 3, gen. eds. Richard J. Finneran and George Mills Harper. New York: Scribner, 1999.

AVA W. B. Yeats. *A Vision: The Original 1925 Edition.* Ed. Catherine E. Paul and Margaret Mills Harper. *The Collected Works of W. B. Yeats.* Vol. 13, gen. ed. George Bornstein. New York: Scribner, 2008.

AVA-Laurie W. B. Yeats. *A Vision: An Explanation of Life Founded upon the Writings of Giraldus and upon Certain Doctrines attributed to Kusta Ben Luka.* London: T. Werner Laurie, 1925.

AVB W. B. Yeats. *A Vision.* London: Macmillan, 1937.

BL Add Additional Manuscript, The British Library, London [holdings cited by number].

Blake *The Complete Poetry and Prose of William Blake.* Ed. David V. Erdman. Rev. ed. New York: Anchor, 1988.

Burnet John Burnet. *Early Greek Philosophy.* London: Adam and Charles Black, 1892. (YL 308)

Cantos Ezra Pound. *The Cantos.* Thirteenth Printing. New York: New Directions, 1995 [cited by Canto number and page number].

Chapman Wayne K. Chapman. *The W. B. and George*

Yeats Library: A Short-Title Catalog. Clemson, SC: Clemson University Digital Press, 2006. http://www.clemson.edu/cedp/cudp/pubs/YeatsSTC/index.htm

CL *The Collected Letters of W. B. Yeats*. 4 vols. Vol. 1 (1865–95), gen. ed. John Kelly, co-ed. Eric Domville. Vol. 2 (1896–1900), gen. ed. John Kelly, co-eds. Warwick Gould and Deirdre Toomey. Vol. 3 (1901–4), gen. ed. John Kelly, co-ed. Ronald Schuchard. Vol. 4 (1905–7), gen. ed. John Kelly, co-ed. Ronald Schuchard. Oxford: Oxford University Press, 1986, 1994, 1997, 2005.

CL InteLex # *The Collected Letters of W. B. Yeats*, InteLex Electronic Edition. Gen. ed. John Kelly. Oxford: Oxford University Press [cited by accession number].

Diary 1930 *Pages from a Diary Written in Nineteen Hundred and Thirty*. In *Explorations* 287–340 [first publication, Dundrum: Cuala Press, 1944; complete manuscript, NLI 30354].

DMR-MS "The Discovery of Michael Robartes" manuscript [see *YVP* 4].

DMR-TS "The Discovery of Michael Robartes" typescript [see *YVP* 4].

Duhem Pierre Duhem. *Le système du monde: Histoire des doctrines cosmologiques de Platon à Copernic*. 10 vols. Paris: Librairie Scientifique A. Hermann et Fils, 1913–59.

E&I *Essays and Introductions*. London and New York: Macmillan, 1961.

EAR *Early Articles and Reviews*. Ed. John P. Frayne and Madeleine Marchaterre. *The Collected Works of W. B. Yeats*. Vol. 9, gen. eds. Richard J. Finneran and George Mills Harper. New York: Scribner, 2004.

EE *Early Essays*. Ed. George Bornstein and Richard J. Finneran. *The Collected Works of W. B.*

Yeats. Vol. 4, gen. eds. George Bornstein and George Mills Harper. New York: Scribner, 2007.

Ex *Explorations*. Selected by Mrs. W. B. Yeats. New York: Macmillan, 1962.

Foster R. F. Foster. *W. B. Yeats: A Life*. 2 vols. Oxford and New York: Oxford University Press, 1997, 2003.

FPS Richard Taylor, *Frank Pearce Sturm: His Life, Letters, and Collected Work*. Urbana, Chicago, London: University of Illinois Press, 1969.

Gallup Donald Gallup. *Ezra Pound: A Bibliography*. Charlottesville: University Press of Virginia, 1983 [cited by bibliographic entry numbers].

Gibbon Edward Gibbon. *The History of the Decline and Fall of the Roman Empire*. Ed. J. B. Bury. 7 vols. London: Methuen, 1909–14. (YL 746)

GY George Yeats

Hastings *Encyclopaedia of Religion and Ethics*. Ed. James Hastings. 13 vols. Edinburgh: T. & T. Clark, 1908–26. (YL 855)

Hood, "Remaking" Connie K. Hood. "The Remaking of *A Vision*." *Yeats: An Annual of Critical and Textual Studies*. Vol. 1, ed. Richard J. Finneran (1983): 33–67.

Hood, "Search" Connie K. Hood. "A Search for Authority: Prolegomena to a Definitive Critical Edition of W. B. Yeats's *A Vision* (1937)." Ph.D. diss., University of Tennessee, 1983.

IDM *The Irish Dramatic Movement*. Ed. Mary FitzGerald and Richard J. Finneran. *The Collected Works of W. B. Yeats*. Vol. 8, gen. eds. Richard J. Finneran and George Mills Harper. New York and London: Scribner, 2003.

L *The Letters of W. B. Yeats*. Ed. Allan Wade. London: Rupert Hart-Davis, 1954; New York: Macmillan, 1955.

LE *Later Essays*. Ed. William H. O'Donnell with

Elizabeth Bergmann Loizeaux. *The Collected Works of W. B. Yeats*. Vol. 5, gen. eds. Richard J. Finneran and George Mills Harper. New York and London: Scribner, 1994.

Liebregts P. Th. M. G. Liebregts. *Centaurs in the Twilights: W. B. Yeats's Use of the Classical Tradition*. Amsterdam and Atlanta: Rodopi, 1993.

Loeb The Loeb Classical Library. London: William Heinemann (1912–89). Co-published Cambridge, MA: Harvard University Press (1934–89). Cambridge, MA: Harvard University Press (1989–).

LNI *Letters to the New Island*. Ed. George Bornstein and Hugh Witemeyer. London: Macmillan, 1989.

LTSM *W. B. Yeats and T. Sturge Moore: Their Correspondence 1901–1937*. Ed. Ursula Bridge. New York: Oxford University Press, 1953.

LWBY *Letters to W. B. Yeats*. Ed. Richard J. Finneran, George Mills Harper, and William M. Murphy. 2 vols. (continuous pagination). New York: Columbia University Press, 1977.

LWBY/GY *W. B. Yeats and George Yeats: The Letters*. Ed. Ann Saddlemyer. Oxford: Oxford University Press, 2011.

Mann Neil Mann. The System of W. B. Yeats's *A Vision*. Website. http://www.yeatsvision.com

Mann et al. Neil Mann, Matthew Gibson, and Claire V. Nally, eds. *W. B. Yeats's* A Vision: *Explications and Contexts*. Clemson, SC: Clemson University Digital Press, 2012.

Mem *Memoirs: Autobiography—First Draft, Journal*. Transcribed and ed. Denis Donoghue. London: Macmillan, 1972.

Myth1 *Mythologies*. New York: Macmillan, 1959.

Myth2 *Mythologies*. Ed. Warwick Gould and Deirdre Toomey. London: Palgrave Macmillan, 2005.

MYV George Mills Harper. *The Making of Yeats's* A Vision: *A Study of the Automatic Script*. 2 vols. Carbondale and Edwardsville: Southern Illinois University Press, 1987.

NLI National Library of Ireland / Leabharlann Náisiúnta na hÉireann [holdings cited by manuscript number].

O'Shea Edward O'Shea. *A Descriptive Catalog of W. B. Yeats's Library*. New York and London: Garland, 1985 [cited by item number].

OBMV *The Oxford Book of Modern Verse 1892–1935*. Chosen by W. B. Yeats. Oxford: Clarendon Press, 1936.

P&I *Prefaces and Introductions*. Ed. William H. O'Donnell. *Collected Works of W. B. Yeats*. Vol. 6, gen. eds. Richard J. Finneran and George Mills Harper. New York: Macmillan, 1989.

Packet *A Packet for Ezra Pound*. Dundrum: Cuala Press, 1929.

PASL *Per Amica Silentia Lunae*. London: Macmillan; New York: Macmillan, 1918. *LE* 1–33.

Paul Catherine E. Paul. "Compiling *A Packet for Ezra Pound*," *Paideuma* 38 (2011), 29–53.

Personae Ezra Pound. *Personae: The Collected Poems of Ezra Pound*. New York: Boni & Liveright, 1926.

Plays *The Plays*. Ed. David R. Clark and Rosalind E. Clark. *Collected Works of W. B. Yeats*. Vol. 2, gen. eds. Richard J. Finneran and George Mills Harper. New York and London: Scribner, 2001.

Plotinus *Plotinus*. Trans. Stephen MacKenna. 5 vols. London: P. L. Warner for the Medici Society, 1917–30. (YL 1589–93)

Poems *The Poems*. Ed. Richard J. Finneran. 2nd edition. *Collected Works of W. B. Yeats*. Vol. 1, gen. eds. Richard J. Finneran and George Mills Harper. New York: Scribner, 1997.

Saddlemyer — Ann Saddlemyer. *Becoming George: The Life of Mrs W. B. Yeats*. Oxford: Oxford University Press, 2002.

Shelley — *The Poems of Percy Bysshe Shelley*. Ed. C. D. Locock. 2 vols. London: Methuen, 1911. (YL 1905).

Stories — *Stories of Michael Robartes and his Friends: An Extract from a Record Made by his Pupils: And a Play in Prose*. Dublin: Cuala Press, 1931.

Sutherland — Alexander Charles Sutherland. "Yeats's Revisions of *A Vision*: A Study of the Text, with Appendices of Textual Variants and Annotations." Ph.D. diss., New York University, 1978.

TS carbon — NLI 36,272/6, identified by Connie K. Hood as a carbon of the setting-copy typescript sent to Macmillan for production of *A Vision*.

UP 1 — *Uncollected Prose by W. B. Yeats: First Reviews & Articles, 1886–1896*. Vol. 1, edited by John P. Frayne. New York: Columbia University Press, 1970.

UP 2 — *Uncollected Prose by W. B. Yeats: Reviews, Articles and Other Miscellaneous Prose, 1897–1939*. Vol. 2, edited by John P. Frayne and Colton Johnson. New York: Columbia University Press, 1976.

VP — *The Variorum Edition of the Poems of W. B. Yeats*. Ed. Peter Allt and Russell K. Alspach. Sixth printing. New York: Macmillan, 1973.

VPl — *The Variorum Edition of the Plays of W. B. Yeats*. Ed. Russell K. Alspach with Catharine C. Alspach. New York: Macmillan, 1966.

Wade — Allan Wade. *A Bibliography of the Writings of W. B. Yeats*. 3rd ed. Rev. ed. by Russell K. Alspach. London: Rupert Hart-Davis, 1968 [cited by item number].

WBY — William Butler Yeats

WWB *The Works of William Blake*. Ed. Edwin John Ellis and William Butler Yeats. 3 vols. London: Bernard Quaritch, 1893. (YL 220)

YA *Yeats Annual*. Ed. Warwick Gould. London: Macmillan, 1982–2012; Open Book Publishers, 2013– .

YAACTS *Yeats: An Annual of Critical and Textual Studies*. Ed. Richard J. Finneran. Ithaca and London: Cornell University Press, 1983–85; Ann Arbor: UMI Research Press, 1986–87; Ann Arbor: University of Michigan Press, 1988–99.

YL The Yeats Library, housed in the National Library of Ireland. Full listings are available in O'Shea (which numbering system the library follows) and Chapman (which includes some items not in O'Shea).

YO George Mills Harper (ed.). *Yeats and the Occult*. Yeats Studies Series. Toronto: Macmillan, 1975.

YVP 1 *The Automatic Script: 5 November 1917–18 June 1918*. Ed. Steve L. Adams, Barbara J. Frieling, and Sandra L. Sprayberry. *Yeats's* Vision *Papers*. Vol. 1, gen. ed. George Mills Harper, assisted by Mary Jane Harper. London: Macmillan, 1992.

YVP 2 *The Automatic Script: 25 June 1918–29 March 1920*. Ed. Steve L. Adams, Barbara J. Frieling, and Sandra L. Sprayberry. *Yeats's* Vision *Papers*. Vol. 2, gen. ed. George Mills Harper, assisted by Mary Jane Harper. London: Macmillan.

YVP 3 *Sleep and Dream Notebooks,* Vision *Notebooks 1 and 2, Card File*. Ed. Robert Anthony Martinich and Margaret Mills Harper. *Yeats's* Vision *Papers*. Vol. 3, gen. ed. George Mills Harper, assisted by Mary Jane Harper. London: Macmillan, 1992.

YVP 4 *"The Discoveries of Michael Robartes," Version B ["The Great Wheel" and "The Twenty-Eight Embodiments"]*. Ed. George Mills Harper and Margaret Mills Harper. *Yeats's* Vision *Papers*. Vol. 4, gen. ed. George Mills Harper, assisted by Mary Jane Harper. London: Palgrave, 2001.

ILLUSTRATIONS

EDITORS' INTRODUCTION

A Vision was impossible to finish, much to WBY's dismay, and despite repeated claims of near or final completion. But he never stopped trying. Having published a first, limited edition with T. Werner Laurie, a version he regarded as seriously flawed, WBY immediately began revising. Even after a second edition was published by Macmillan a dozen years after the first, WBY found it incomplete, imperfect, inadequate. The present volume presents that second edition while offering some sense of both posthumous editions and ways that *A Vision* might have continued to evolve.

On December 31, 1934, Harold Macmillan wrote to A. P. Watt and Sons, WBY's literary agent:

> Mr. Yeats called in here just before Christmas and wants us to produce a new edition of a book entitled "A Vision" which I think he printed privately many years ago, and which has also been published in another form in the past. I believe it now to be out of print, and Mr. Yeats has largely re-written it. I do not know whether he spoke to you about it, but I assume he had done so. If so, you will realise that the subject matter of the book is one that makes a very limited appeal. To most ordinary minds it appears to be quite mad, and I cannot believe that the sale will be anything but a very small one. I rather gathered from Mr. Yeats that he shared this view.[1]

Between the appearance of the Laurie edition in January 1926 (despite the date of 1925 on its title page) and Macmillan's much larger run of the second edition on October 7, 1937, WBY made extensive changes—removing and rewriting large swathes of text, adding new prefatory material, and completely rethinking parts of the system. The 1937 version had become effectively a new work.

The first edition had received limited and critical reviews. An anonymous reviewer in *The New Statesman* called the book "a dark and difficult study." Ernest de Selincourt acknowledged its "accomplishment, its genius of intuition, its fleeting beauty," but suggested that WBY has not "struck the system which will free his imagination for the unrolling of final poetic truth," concluding that the book "is tiresome because of the conviction it leaves with us that he knows this as well as anyone and yet cannot detach himself from the delights of dalliance." Three years later, Edmund Wilson wondered whether WBY, who shrouded the revelations of *AVA* in fictions, "intends us to take it seriously" and whether the poet was "really attempting, in a sense, to eat his cake and have it, too?"[2] G. R. S. Mead, on the other hand, aimed to get to the bottom of the fictions, saying that the book would be of greater value had WBY "told us quite frankly how he became possessed of the information." Like Frank Pearce Sturm, he found fault with the "inferior Latin" of the title of the fictitious source, the "Speculum Angelorum et Homenorum," concluding that spelling to be "a 'howler' for which Smith Minor at a Preparatory School would receive condign punishment." Making a comparison that WBY would also make, he noted that "Oswald Spengler might have helped Mr. Yeats to a more plausible survey," concluding that "when we are asked to subscribe 3 3s. for a copy of a book, we expect it to be either one that contains some very valuable reliable information or a literary masterpiece; and it cannot be said that *A Vision* as a whole comes up to either expectation."[3]

It is no surprise, then, that WBY would want to improve *A Vision*. His ambitions for the new version were high; he noted in a letter to his old friend Olivia Shakespear in September 1929 that "this new edition will be a new book, all I hope clear and as simple as the subject permits." He hoped, he told her, that his book would have a real power beyond ratiocination: "I have constructed a myth, but then one can believe in a myth—one only assents to philosophy. Heaven is an improvement of sense—one listens to music, one does not read Hegel's logic."[4]

This introduction offers a sense of how the 1937 version of *A Vision* came to be. We treat WBY's recasting of text from the first version of *A Vision* and his writing and initial publication of new material.[5] Turning to the 1937 publication, we attend to the setting materials sent to Macmillan, revisions made even at proof stages, the product issued in London in 1937 and in New York in 1938, and reception of the new edition. And because WBY could not stop rethinking *A Vision*, we note corrections made by WBY and GY (equally responsible for the construction of the system of *A Vision*) after the publication of the second edition—made mostly in anticipation of an Edition De Luxe of the poet's work, of which *A Vision* was to have been a part. Work on this collected edition continued after WBY's death, as GY and Thomas Mark of Macmillan tried to produce a corrected edition of the text, taking into consideration corrections made by WBY and corrections they deemed necessary based on their understanding of the system and *A Vision*. Although World War II and ensuing economic limitations meant that the revised version of *A Vision* is only now part of a collected edition, there were later "corrected" editions issued in the United States (in 1956 and 1961) and in the United Kingdom (in 1962). We treat the editing process for those editions, which rather than producing the definitive editions they advertised introduced further errors. After the complicated history of the text, we offer our editorial principles for the current edition. In all, this introduction offers a compact treatment of how *A Vision* was made.

MATERIAL FROM *AVA* AND NEW EXPOSITION (1926 TO 1937)

In April 1925, WBY celebrated finishing *A Vision*, declaring himself free to "write letters again & idle," but that feeling would not last.[6] He explains in his "Introduction to the Great Wheel" that his instructors had told him not to read philosophy "until their exposition was complete," and that his "ignorance of philosophy" made him fail "to understand distinctions upon which the coherence of the whole depended."[7] However, WBY continues, "When the proof sheets came I felt myself relieved from my promise not to read philosophy and began with Berkeley."[8] As elsewhere in that "Introduction," WBY more or less speaks the truth, and the evidence of his self-imposed course in reading offers important clues to his revising of his book.[9]

On May 22, 1925, well before *AVA-Laurie* was published on January 15, 1926, WBY wrote to GY that he was reading Plato's *Timaeus*, works by Sir William Matthew Flinders Petrie on the Egyptian origin of mystical thought, and the texts of Hermes Trismegistus. All through 1926 and into 1927, WBY corresponded with his fellow poet T. Sturge Moore about his readings in European philosophy, including Vico, Hegel, Kant, Hartmann, Schopenhauer, Berkeley, G. E. Moore, Bertrand Russell, Bergson, Gentile, Croce, Spengler, Whitehead, and Henry James—as well as Greek and Latin classics and scholarly works on them, from A. E. Taylor on Plato to the translation of Plotinus by Stephen MacKenna. Letters to GY, friends, and others also mention religious texts from Pauline Christianity to Zen Buddhism.[10] Among modern currents and figures, WBY discovered an affinity with the writings of Wyndham Lewis, especially *The Art of Being Ruled* (1926) and *Time and Western Man* (1927).[11]

Indeed, in the years between 1926 and 1937, WBY was concerned with a number of readerly projects, all attacked with considerable energy (so much so that he at times made himself ill and needed to be stopped by doctor's orders). He renewed an old interest in art history, and he undertook detailed research in comparative religion, history (especially of Rome and the eighteenth century, as well as particular writers such as Henry Adams and Arnold Toynbee), and political thought (from a wide range of ideological leanings), not to mention such specialized topics as the history of calendars. His work with Shri Purohit Swāmi in the early 1930s led to an extensive course in Hindu philosophy, including (besides the principal Upanishads) readings in Vedānta, classical Yoga, Tantra, and bhakti (especially Vaishnavism).[12]

As always, WBY read widely in contemporary literature in English. Particularly after agreeing to edit the *Oxford Book of Modern Verse* in 1934, he tried to uncover what might characterize his cultural moment. Happily for our purposes, WBY's efficient habits of composition, which involved using similar thoughts and sources for multiple projects, give multiple contexts in which to understand the sometimes eccentric interpretations he brought to bear on his reading. Thus, for example, rereading Plotinus, with the help of the superb translation by Stephen MacKenna, helped him explain the *Principles* in *A Vision*, as well as the "timeless individuality" that accounts for spirits in séances or the "stream of souls" of reincarnation, described in the introductions that accompany the plays *The Words upon the Window-Pane* and *The Resurrection.*[13]

One of the most important sources for *AVB* is the magisterial multivolume *Système du monde* of the French physicist and historian of science Pierre Duhem, a work that both traces and argues for the importance of premodern and medieval science. It helped WBY understand a system that depends much on astronomical (and astrological) data.[14] On November 16, 1937, he explained to the British writer Helen Beauclerk (whom WBY knew through her lover Edmund Dulac) that "Pierre Duhem 'Systeme du Monde' (4 vols. Librairie Scientifique A. Hermann et Fils, Paris. 1917) was essential to anybody who wanted to get a grasp of the myth and philosophy of the Greeks, Romans, and of our own Middle Ages. It summarises the physics, cosmogony, and the philosophical bearings of both through all the centuries up to the Rennaissance."[15] WBY's French was shaky, and Duhem's prose is very dense; Duhem's influence on *AVB* testifies to the continuing importance of GY, who almost certainly translated for her husband. Although the AS had more or less tapered off by the mid-1920s, GY continued to be an essential consultant on the ideas she and WBY had developed together (occasionally still in conjunction with the supernatural communicators of the automatic experiments).

Although we cannot date WBY's work on sections of *AVB* with precision by following his reading, it is possible to make inferences. To give just one example, we note that Section II of Book IV (178–79) was revised in autumn 1931, when WBY asked GY to look up passages for him in the work of the Cambridge Platonist Ralph Cudworth. Other sections, such as Section XIV of Book II (154–55), may also have been reworked at about this time, in late 1931 and early 1932, when WBY was staying at Coole with his old friend Lady Gregory, during her last illness. This period occurs between one of several of WBY's announcements that he had finished "The Vision" and the realization that there was more to do: "I shall spend the spring & summer . . . getting 'the Vision' into final shape."[16] His thinking on such topics from Book II as the *Daimon*, destiny, light, and a universal self, in this instance, suggest his reading or rereading of several sources in close succession or simultaneously:

1. Shelley (whose *Prometheus Unbound* he reread in December 1931 and about whose not altogether positive influence on his early life he wrote an essay in 1932);

2. the Asclepius dialogue from the Hermetic fragments in the Walter Scott edition published in 1924 (studied for purposes of rethinking the *Daimon*, as a marginal note on "daimon not phasal" makes clear);
3. George Berkeley (M. M. Rossi, who co-edited Berkeley in an edition for which WBY had written an introduction in 1931, had been a guest at Coole in August 1931);
4. Balzac's novel *Louis Lambert* (WBY was, he told GY on December 22, 1931, "reading Balzac with all my old delight," and he wrote an essay on this novel in 1933); and
5. Vedantic philosophy (WBY had received Robert Ernest Hume's translation of the *Thirteen Principal Upanishads* for Christmas in 1931 and had begun to read the autobiography of Shri Purohit Swāmi in the early months of 1932).[17]

WBY's reading and revision are largely interrelated. Even in *AVA*, WBY warned, "I could I daresay make the book richer, perhaps immeasurably so, if I were to keep it by me for another year, and I have not even dealt with the whole of my subject, perhaps not even with what is most important . . . ; but I am longing to put it out of reach that I may write the poetry it seems to have made possible," and "Doubtless I must someday complete what I have begun."[18] The Yeatses' marks in their four copies of *AVA-Laurie* suggest an early eye toward a corrected version.[19] Indeed, many sections of the 1937 published text follow that of 1926 quite closely; see the table in this introduction (xl).

These retentions do not mean that WBY intended simple corrections: he was convinced that the first version of *A Vision* was deeply flawed. His conversation with the poet and translator Frank Pearce Sturm—who shared WBY's interest in esoterica and read the first version of *A Vision* quite carefully—began almost immediately after its release. On January 19, 1926, Sturm wrote with numerous specific corrections, saying, "Until some dull dog with an eye for detail & accuracy goes over book II, it will remain incomprehensible simply because of inaccuracies in the text."[20] From then through early March, the two corresponded frequently, with WBY trying to clarify lunar and solar movement, the importance of gyres to St. Thomas Aquinas and Virgil, relationships between the Yeatses' system and astronomical movement, Macrobius's *Commentary on the Dream of Scipio*, the Syrian gnostic poet Bardesanes, the "dog Latin" of the fictional title *Speculum Angelorum et Hominorum*, and the writings of the Elizabethan mathematician and occultist Dr. John Dee. On March 1, WBY asked, "Have you found any more errors?"[21]

Plans for "major revisions" of the book are mentioned in a notebook begun in 1921, in a long diary entry from March 14, 1926.[22] As early as May 1926, WBY was recommending against buying the book, which he described as "horribly expensive" and "only a first draft of a book & intended for students of Plotinus, the Hermetic fragments & unpopular literature of that kind."[23] By mid-1926—during the same time that the poem "The Tower" ponders choosing "Plato and Plotinus for a friend" (*Poems* 198)—WBY began revising *A Vision*. By June, he was making extensive notes in the 1921 notebook of material to add to *A Vision*, should there be another edition.[24] In a diary entry that could not have been written before March 1927, he notes, "I see now that section XII Book IV in 'A Vision' should have been the most important in the book, & it is the slightest and worst." A page later, in what may be a continuation of the same entry or a separate entry, he observes, "The part of 'Vision' about the Beatitude is also poor."[25] Increasingly the pages of this notebook, as well as the "Rapallo" notebooks, are filled with rewritings of various sections. Some entries look very much like sections in *AVA*.[26]

Some revisions seem to come out of his rereading of his own text. "Error in Vision – pages 159, 160," he notes in the 1921 notebook, referring to the passage about "The Cones of Individual Life."[27] Others begin as answers to questions from readers. On May 25, 1926, he told Olivia Shakespear that he was "writing answers to a long series of questions sent me by a reader of a 'Vision' & Plotinus helps me there."[28] An undated entry in the 1921 notebook is organized around questions from Mary Devenport O'Neill: "How is will affected by 26000 year cycle?"; "How is civilization upheld in 2000 year gyre?"; "Has a daimon any separate masters apart from human being to whom it belongs?"; "How do Four Principles affect us during life?"; "What sort of ghosts are Daimons & Demigods?"; "What accounts for out burst, literature all lower northern Europe in 19th century?" His drafted answers extend over many manuscript pages.[29] In all cases, there is a concern with the terminology, diagrams, geometry, and the interrelationships of various parts of the system.

Throughout are expressions of concern and frustration at the published text. "The old statement is probably wrong and certainly confusing," WBY comments at one point, going on to rethink the cones of the *Faculties*.[30] He makes a series of notes labeled "Important," and they seem to be reminders not just of how to change the text but of where his central focus should be. The series culminates in a declaration of "Important" written in a particularly large and loopy hand, as if in haste or with great emotion: "All I have written about great year a muddle. Dionertes first statements correct. Great Year begun at Lunar East (Lunar ♈)."[31] Each attempt to clarify opened new puzzles and raised new questions, requiring further revision of the text and its diagrams.

WBY's correspondence offers further evidence. In October 1927, two letters to Maud Gonne include possible drafts of his thinking about victimage, love, and hate. On March 12, 1928, WBY tells Lady Gregory that he alternates between revising *A Vision* and writing the material for *A Packet*. On April 2, WBY notes to Jack Lindsay that he has "just finished a long essay on what I called 'The Four Principles' & am now passing on to 'The Four Faculties'. There are two or three bad errors in the geometrical symbolism itself to correct." He writes to GY on July 23, 1929, "I have done all the troubl some [*sic*] part of the system now—after a little tidying up tomorrow I shall begin to copy out what I have done. The other night I tried to get some instruction on the religeous [*sic*] side of it all in my dreams. Result—a magnificent Cathedral & a man in it who started to prey [*sic*] for my conversion. I got perfectly furious & told him that such a preyer [*sic*] was an insult. I hope he was not Dionurtes [*sic*]." On September 13, WBY tells his dear friend Olivia Shakespear, "I am taking to Rapallo what will be I hope a clear typed script of the whole book. I will work at it here & there free at last, now that all is constructed to sharpen definitions & enrich descriptions. I should go to press with it next Spring." In early October, a similar prediction of completion is sent to Frank Pearce Sturm: "The Vision, now 'The Great Wheel' requires another six months simplification, but it is already fairly simple."[32] During this same year, he finished, proofed, and published *A Packet for Ezra Pound*.

By 1930, WBY was again declaring the book finished and thinking ahead to the published volume, while at the same time working on *The Winding Stair*, *The Words upon the Window-Pane*, *The Resurrection*, and plans for the new Macmillan Edition de Luxe. In February 1931, he declares to Olivia Shakespear, "I have really finished 'A VISION'—I turn over the pages & find nothing to add. I am still at Coole but go to Dublin to morrow to dictate 'A Vision' from my MSS to a certain young man, a friend of McGreavys who has come from Paris for the purpose." Months later, on October 13, he informs GY, "I have now finished—all but the bit from Cicero—the section of the Great Year. All that remains is some revision of 'A Packet for Ezra Pound' and a few final paragraphs to wind up the book." In another letter to Shakespear from December 1931, he mentions dictating corrections and additions to GY—and that "Two days ago she went back to Dublin taking it with her. I asked her to take it that I might return to verse." He did not relinquish it altogether, however: on April 14, 1932, he tells GY that he plans to "spend the spring & summer with proofs [for the Edition De Luxe] & getting 'the Vision' into final shape." These claims of completion continue.[33]

As the text of *A VB* moved from manuscript drafts to typescripts, some sections got closer to their published form more quickly than others. Most drafts are undated, but we have benefited from materials compiled by Connie and Walter Kelly Hood in their research on *A Vision*, and from the knowledge laid out by Connie Hood, from which the chronology of revision presented here primarily derives.[34] WBY began making typescripts for the new material in what became Book I in 1928. The earliest was titled "The Symbol of the Double Vortex," and later drafts change the title to "Principal Symbols," and then "The Double Vortex" and "Dramatis Personae." The material for Books I and II was commingled in early typescripts, and WBY did not sort the books out until after 1932. The numbering of books was generally unclear at early stages: one draft of what would become Book III is labeled "Book IV," and an earlier version "Notes upon Life after Death." Rejected typescripts for what would become Book IV approach the published version earlier than other sections. And while WBY mostly used material from *A VA* for Book V, the ending, what he calls in the 1937 version "The End of the Cycle," went through seven draft stages, largely composed from 1931 to 1933, though one radically different rejected draft is dated "January 7, 1934."[35] On January 27 of that year, WBY wrote to Olivia Shakespear that he had "faced at last & finished the prophesy [*sic*] of the next hundred years. Now Georges [*sic*] work begins—to draw the diagrams & the book is done." On January 7, 1935, he wrote to Sturm that he had "left the new version of The Vision with Macmillan. They have handed it over to their excellent reader [presumably Thomas Mark], who is probably, poor man, trying to understand it."[36] Meanwhile, WBY had been working on two sections of material that would form fascinating new prefaces to *A Vision*.

A PACKET FOR EZRA POUND (1929)

The same notebooks in which WBY was revising *A Vision* contain the early drafts of *A Packet for Ezra Pound* (Cuala, 1929). The American poet Ezra Pound and his wife, Dorothy (née Shakespear), both of them friends of both WBY and GY, had settled in the Ligurian Riviera town of Rapallo in 1924, and the Yeatses moved there in February 1928, searching for rest, sun, and warmth necessary to help WBY recuperate from illness. Almost immediately, WBY began imagining an essay about Rapallo as a new introduction to *A Vision*. By this time, Pound had taken up residence at via Marsala 20, and the balcony of Pound's top-floor apartment, with its view over the Gran Caffè Rapallo to the Golfo di Tigullio, became the setting for numerous conversations between the poets—and subject matter for *Packet*. The Yeatses lived for many months in the Albergo Rapallo, along the sea, before moving to a flat at via Americhe 12-8, now Corso Colombo. As WBY wrote to Lady Gregory shortly after his arrival, "This is an indescribably lovely place—some little Greek town one imagines—there is a passage in Keats describing just such a town. Here I shall put off the bitterness of Irish quarrels, and write my most amiable verses. They are already, though I dare not write, crowding my head."[37]

Of course, Pound's company was a huge part of the appeal of Rapallo. WBY wrote to GY on February 25, "To night Ezra & Dorothy bring me to dine with a Mrs Stein & her daughter & her son in law who is an Italian Prince of the Holy Roman Empire,

& descended from Charlemagne." Pound connected WBY with numerous modernist artists at Rapallo, including Basil Bunting, George Antheil, Gerhart Hauptmann, and Max Beerbohm. Two days after meeting the Steins mentioned above—and the son-in-law who would be described in *A Packet* as "an Italian prince descended from Charlemagne and no richer than the rest of us"—WBY noted, "Ezra explains his Cantos & reads me Cavalcanti & we argue about it quite amicably."[38] WBY's letters and manuscripts show that he and Pound talked and argued about poetry, politics, the ethnographic writings of Leo Frobenius, modern music, and Wyndham Lewis's theories of modernism.

Within the first month of his time in Rapallo, WBY began to envisage a new book about his literary community there. As he explained to Lennox Robinson, WBY's collaborator at the Abbey Theatre, in early March 1928:

> I am now working again (though only on alternate days) & what I am doing is a comment on a philosophical poem of Guido Cavalcantis, translated by Ezra Pound, which I hope to make a book of to follow your Anthology. I think of calling the book "Siris"; it is about Rapallo, Ezra & the literary movements of our time all deduced from Guido's poem, as Berkeley in his "Siris" deduced all from tar-water.[39]

This essay became "Rapallo," and in early drafts WBY writes at greater length about Pound's long work, *The Cantos*, than is presented in either the Cuala or Macmillan published texts. Almost immediately, WBY connected this new piece to *A Vision* and was referring to it as "my notes on Ezra for Cuala."[40]

During this same period, WBY was trying to explain the origin of the system, writing what would become "Introduction to 'A Vision.'" He worked in September 1928 to date the first appearance of elements of the system. "Script began Oct 24, 1917. (Four days after my marriage)," he wrote, adding and then crossing out that the first cones appeared in November or December. He traced the appearance of the Great Wheel, the Four Principles, and the relationship between the spiritual cycle and the Christian Era.[41] The first draft opens:

> On the afternoon of October the 24, four days after my marriage my wife ~~suggested proposed that said~~ said she would like to attempt automatic writing. She told me afterwards that she ~~intended to amuse me by some invented message~~ had meant to make up messages, & having amused me for an afternoon say what she had done. She ~~went out of her way~~ did invent a few lines, some names & some imaginary address when her hand was, as it were, grasped by another & this came ~~in an almost illegible in disjointed sentence~~ in disjointed sentences in almost illegible handwriting ~~certain startling sentences disjointed sentences~~ in imagined his what was at first that was a ~~development of~~ comment about my little book "Per Amica Silentia Lunae," . . .[42]

Removed from this first version and never reintroduced is the sense that GY's first automatic writing after their wedding began as a ruse—an amusement—as if even the merest mention of such a possibility might have diminished the very real transmission invoked by a grasp of the hand. This notebook draft of the introduction does not contain the famous line "we have come to give you metaphors for poetry"—the very line that would be most quoted in early reviews of *A Vision*—though the line does appear in all extant subsequent autograph and typescript drafts.[43]

By November 1928, WBY was calling the book "either 'A Packet' or 'A Packet for Ezra Pound.'" WBY describes the contents:

> It contains first a covering letter to Ezra saying that I offer him the contents, urging him not to be elected to the Senate of his country and telling him why. Then comes a long essay already finished, the introduction to the new edition of *A Vision* and telling all about its origin, and then I shall wind up with a description of Ezra feeding the cats ("some of them are so ungrateful" T. S. Eliot says), of Rapallo and Ezra's poetry—some of which I greatly admire, indeed his collected edition is a great excitement to me.[44]

As published, this order is reversed to begin with "Rapallo," followed by the poem "Meditations Upon Death" (not included in *A Vision*), then "Introduction to the Great Wheel," and finally the letter "To Ezra Pound," which closes by quoting Pound's poem "The Return" (1912).[45] "Meditations Upon Death" was a late addition.[46]

Written in early February 1929, the parts of this poem would later be split into two separate poems—"At Algeciras—a Meditation upon Death" and "Mohini Chatterjee."[47] In later printings the two (separated) poems are dated "November 1928" and "1928" respectively, effectively occluding the extent to which their writing, like their subject matter, was linked to the rethinking of *A Vision*. *A Packet for Ezra Pound* was published in August 1929, in a run of 425 copies, with the usual Cuala Press blue paper boards and buff linen spine, black lettering on the front cover and on the spine of the white paper label.[48]

Although *A Packet* ostensibly focuses on Pound and WBY's literary relationship to him, the revelations about *A Vision* caught reviewers' attention. G. W. Russell (Æ) attempted to rationalize the Instructors to whom WBY attributed the system of *A Vision*:

> The most important part of this book is that which the poet has named "Introduction to the Great Wheel," and in this he tells how the geometrical philosophy of the book, *The Vision*, came to be written. It is a collaboration between the dreaming consciousness of his wife and his own, with possibly other entities not of this plane of being. The poet speaks of them as if he believed they were external to consciousness, but when we enter into the dream world there is a dramatic sundering of the ego, and while we dream we are persuaded of the existence of many people which, when we wake, we feel were only part of our own protean nature. I do not suggest that these philosophic entities who communicated to the poet and his wife the substance of *The Vision* may be simply some submerged part of the soul, because I am skeptical of the possibility. I merely say that the poet has not given me enough material to decide.[49]

Writing in *Commonweal*, Seán Ó Faoláin expressed skepticism that the poems deriving from WBY's spiritual experiments—especially those in *The Cat and the Moon* (1924)—could match his earliest verse, where "there was an air of the other world that was far more charming and far more persuasive," concluding that "[t]here is a great gap between spirits and spirituality, and none of Mr. Yeats's spiritistic verse has succeeded in bridging it." Similarly, in *The Nation*, he described WBY as "exchanging the fairies of Sligo for the spooks of Soho" and suggested that WBY's account would be "of some interest to the psychologist if of none to the literary man." His harsh review speaks to the conundrum WBY concocts for his readers:

> It is hard on Yeats's admirers: he invents a world of unattractive spooks, then invents stories about it to give it color, then writes poems that are only intelligible when read with these invented stories, and for the sake of the verse we put up with the story and the spooks only to be told of a sudden that it was a foolish story anyway and that the spooks had misled him.[50]

These same concerns and questions about *A Vision* and its relationship to WBY's other writings would permeate reviews of the 1937 edition. Given the extent to which the poems of such volumes as *The Tower* and *The Winding Stair*, and indeed much of WBY's late poetry, builds on the system of *A Vision*, Ó Faoláin's assessment seems limited indeed.

STORIES OF MICHAEL ROBARTES AND HIS FRIENDS (1931)

By 1930 or so, WBY was also writing what would become *Stories of Michael Robartes and his Friends: An Extract from a Record Made by his Pupils: And a Play in Prose* (Cuala, 1931). In a notebook, WBY drafted the stories of Denise de L'Isle Adam, Huddon, Duddon, and Daniel O'Leary; Michael Robartes and Owen Aherne; and Mary Bell and John Bond. He played around with framing fictions:

> Stories of Michael Robartes his Friends a letter
> ~~from Daniel O'Leary + John Aherne edited by WBYeats~~
> an extract from a manuscript book compiled by
> May 1924
> Dear Mr. ~~Duddon~~ Aherne,

WBY imagined an epistolary story—but would it be told by Daniel O'Leary or John Aherne? Sent to Duddon or Owen Aherne? And what was WBY's role to be—editor? compiler? possessor of a manuscript book? At the end of what would become the letter to WBY by John Aherne (see 38–40), WBY wrote and then struck through a potential postscript:

> PS. I enclose some photographs Duddon took of Wood Cuts in Speculum. He says that Gyraldus is in portrait so like you that he may have been one of your incarnations. I cannot myself see the resemblance.[51]

Like the fictions of *AVA*, these framing devices play with notions of authorship and trouble the lines between fiction and reality, always with humor.

Published in March 1932, *Stories* saw a run of 450 copies.[52] The illustration of the unicorn and star, made for *AVA-Laurie* by Edmund Dulac and retained in *AVB*, appears on the title page. As with *A Packet*, the Cuala *Stories* differs somewhat from *A Vision*. It opens with "Huddon, Duddon and Daniel O'Leary," printed in red. Then follows John Duddon's story that incorporates the finding of Giraldus' *Speculum Angelorum et Hominum* as narrated in Owen Aherne's "Introduction" to *A Vision* (1925).[53] This story introduces an array of other characters, all of whom have some relationship to Aherne and Robartes, and whose fantastical stories echo the material in *A Vision* and of the framing material of *AVA*. In *Stories*, Denise de L'Isle Adam is interrupted before she can tell her own story (see 30–31). Next comes a letter from John Aherne (brother of Owen) to WBY, disputing "the facts" in "The Gift of Harun Al-Rashid," attempting to understand the automatic script in terms of Platonic notions of memory, and noting his brother Owen's bitterness about his depiction in WBY's stories. John Aherne compares the two versions of WBY's "diagrams and explanations" to find no essential difference, leading WBY, acting as a sort of editor, to note: "*I published in 1925 an inaccurate, obscure, incomplete book, called 'A Vision.' It lies beside me now, corrected, clarified and completed after five years' work and thought.*"[54] Perhaps recognizing the additional seven years' work needed to complete *A Vision*, and perhaps wanting to minimize his own intrusion, WBY removed this note from the 1937 text. Otherwise, all these texts appear in *AVB*. *Stories* concludes with WBY's play *The Resurrection*, not included in *AVB*.

As Connie K. Hood notes, plans by Macmillan for a multivolume Edition de Luxe of WBY's works may have made the *Stories* material part of *A Vision*. In December 1930, WBY proposed a volume containing

1. The two little volumes of "Diaries" published at Cuala.
2. A collection of philosophic stories about to be published at Cuala.
3. "A Packet for Ezra Pound" published at Cuala two years ago.
4. "A Vision" published privately by Werner Laurie in, I think, 1922 or 23.

> These four sections support each other. "A Vision" is not the crude book published by Laurie; I have worked years on it since then. The philosophic stories, which were written this summer and are amongst the best things I have written, expound its fundamental ideas. "A Packet for Ezra Pound" is the introduction to "A Vision" and the "Diaries" which are probably my best critical writings have sufficient relation to it not to seem out of harmony. I don't want to publish "A Vision" by itself for various reasons.[55]

Hood identifies the two "little volumes of 'Diaries'" as *Estrangement* (Cuala, 1926) and *The Death of Synge, and Other Passages from an Old Diary* (Cuala, 1928). She consulted the setting copy of *Stories* in Michael B. Yeats's collection, but that volume has not become a part of the Yeatses' library in the NLI, and we have not consulted it. Most of the markings in this copy pertain to changes in house style, meaning that most of the differences between *Stories* and *A Vision* unfolded at some galley or proof stage.[56]

If the new "Introduction to 'A Vision'" from *A Packet* clears away the old fictions of *AVA*, *Stories* and its "strange disorderly people" (as WBY called the characters in a letter to Dorothy Wellesley) bring them back.[57] Reviewers of *Stories* recognized the connections to *AVA*. Charles Powell noted that with this book, "Mr. Yeats returns to his unresting inquiry into the truth about the life of the mind and the life of the soul, and treads again the mystic, psychic, magic ground of the earlier stories of Michael Robartes and Owen Traherne [*sic*]." And Austin Clarke observed an irony, that "The obscurity of Mr. Yeats's thought has taken refuge nowadays in his prose, and it is noteworthy that we must turn to his poetry for explanation," adding that here "the curious will find matter for ingenious speculation."[58] The incorporation of these stories into *A Vision* only multiplied this speculation.

PUBLICATION PROCESS FOR THE 1937 EDITION

The materials sent to Macmillan in December 1935 as the basis of this new version of *A Vision* convey how the volume was pieced together from previously published and new material. These included copy no. 498 of *AVA-Laurie*, marked on its cover "Book A," to serve as setting copy for those parts of the text copied from the first version. Also included were copies of the *Packet* and *Stories* to serve as setting copy for the material from these volumes. Finally, there was a typescript for the new material, to replace what was cut from the first version of *A Vision*. Not all of these materials are still in existence. The Yeats Library in the National Library of Ireland retains the copy of *AVA-Laurie* sent to Macmillan; the printer's copy of *Packet* is in the Yeats Collection in the Manuscript, Archives and Rare Book Library at Emory University.[59] As noted above, the copy of *Stories* used as setting copy was once held in the collection of Michael B. Yeats, but its current location is unknown. The setting typescript for the new material has largely been lost, although the first twelve pages were unearthed at Basingstoke by Warwick Gould, who sent a photocopy of them to Connie K. Hood. Her research revealed that these pages correspond to NLI 36,272/6.[60] This carbon typescript is mostly complete, though it does not include text for sections X–XVIII of "Book IV: The Great Year of the Ancients" (186–92). The Basingstoke typescript includes numerous manuscript additions and changes, which were not copied to the carbon typescript; nor were the diagrams, for which spaces were left in the typescript. Additionally, the galleys and page proofs for this edition are lost. That there is not a complete extant setting copy for *A Vision* (1937) creates editorial problems that we enumerate later in this introduction.

Some sections were more complete at the time of the mailing of the typescript than others. Judging from the section of carbon typescript available for "Book IV," that book was hardly revised after submission to Macmillan. By contrast, the addition to "Dove or Swan" entitled "The End of Cycle" bears only small resemblance to that of the carbon typescript.

The Basis of the 1937 Edition

Pages in this edition	Pages in 1937 edition	Section description	Textual basis
3–22	1–30	"A Packet for Ezra Pound"	*Packet*; MARBL copy
23–40	31–38, 40–55	"Stories of Michael Robartes and his Friends: An Extract from a Record Made by his Pupils"	*Stories*; copy previously in collection of Michael B. Yeats
28	39	illustration: "Portrait of Giraldus"	*AVA-Laurie* #498 (YL 2433c)
41–47	57–64	"The Phases of the Moon"	*AVA-Laurie* #498 (YL 2433c)
48	66	illustration: "The Great Wheel"	*AVA-Laurie* #498 (YL 2433c)
49–66	67–89	"Book I: The Great Wheel": Part I, Part II sec. I–V	Basingstoke TS [NLI 36,272/6/1a]
66–136	90–184	"Book I: The Great Wheel": Part II sec. VI–XVII, Part III	*AVA-Laurie* #498 (YL 2433c)
137–58	185–215	"Book II: The Completed Symbol"	lost TS [NLI 36,272/6/1b]
159–75	217–40	"Book III: The Soul in Judgment"	lost TS [NLI 36,272/6/2a]
177–85	241–54	"Book IV: The Great Year of the Ancients": sec. I–IX	lost TS [NLI 36,272/6/2b]
186–92	255–63	"Book IV: The Great Year of the Ancients": sec. X–XVIII	lost TS, no carbon in NLI
193–218	265–300	"Book V: Dove or Swan"	*AVA-Laurie* #498 (YL 2433c)
219–20	301–2	"The End of the Cycle"	lost TS [NLI 36,272/6/2c?]
221–24	303–5	"All Souls' Night: An Epilogue"	*AVA-Laurie* #498 (YL 2433c)

WBY began reading proofs for *A Vision* in early 1935.[61] Given his propensity for revision on galleys, it is particularly regrettable that these have not been preserved. In part because of WBY's weakness due to illness, Macmillan offered to have some proofs read in house, and WBY accepted. There were numerous concerns about the placement of diagrams. Paged proofs came in early 1936, and again WBY's illness interfered, so that on February 11 GY sent a telegraph to Watt: "TELL MACMILLAN IMPOSSIBLE YEATS CORRECT PROOFS STOP ASK MR MARKS [*sic*] PASS THEM FOR PRESS = YEATS +."[62] Despite continuing difficulties with proofs, by early September 1937 all proofs were reviewed, and the book was published by Macmillan of London on October 7, 1937, in decorated black and brown paper boards bound in a black cloth spine with gold lettering, in an edition of 1,500 copies. On its frontispiece is a portrait of WBY by Augustus John. Illustrations of Giraldus, the unicorn, and the Great Wheel by Edmund Dulac remain from the first edition, as does the two-color design of the Historical Cones. The American edition, published on February 23, 1938, by Macmillan of New York, was prepared from the pages of the London edition, with some small stylistic changes. With a cover of black cloth with a light green cloth spine, lettering blind on the front cover and in silver on the spine, it appeared in an edition of 1,200 copies.[63] The Yeatses had copies of both these printings in their library, and textual corrections have been marked in both (YL 2434 and 2435). Even so, about a year after the book was published, WBY complained to the novelist Ethel Mannin that *A Vision* still had not encompassed all that he had come to understand from his communicators.[64] Given the chance, WBY would no doubt have further revised, perhaps producing a third edition.

RECEPTION OF THE 1937 EDITION

The new 1937 edition was not particularly well received. Most reviewers did not try to make sense of the Yeatses' system but focused on the materials from *Packet*, occasionally noting which famous writers were assigned to which phase. Searching for antecedents for WBY's endeavor, reviewers compared his work to the prophetic works of William Blake, *The Anatomy of Melancholy* of Robert

Burton, the revelations of Emanuel Swedenborg and Thomas Lake Harris, the shorter works of Sir Thomas Browne, *The Caprices* and *Disasters of War* by Francisco Goya, and the encyclopedic tendency of Oswald Spengler. The occult novelist and theologian Charles Williams was one of the few to grapple with the book as a whole, seeing its matter as inseparable from a style that "imposes attention on his readers; no other living writer arouses so easily a sense of reverie moving into accurate power."[65]

Most reviewers commented on the difficulty of *A Vision*. Geoffrey Grigson wrote in his own *New Verse* that the book "remains an entirely impossible monster." Michael Roberts (whose nominal likeness to Michael Robartes we must take as coincidence) worried that WBY wrote "in terms that many readers will find distracting and confusing." Kerker Quinn opened by claiming, "Mr. Yeats's new volumes will convince many that he has gone unquestionably, though perhaps serviceably, mad." Mary M. Colum agreed: "If we did not know Mr. Yeats to be a very sane man, we should regard his revelations as having come over from that other region where the mind is no longer in control and where what little individual consciousness we mortals have becomes more and more diminished." She acknowledged, "I understand very little of this book," noting with amazement that "Mr. Yeats undoubtedly believes that a number of readers will devote their whole intellectual lives to a study of *A Vision* and its conclusions." Horace Reynolds suggested that WBY "seems to crave and demand the stimulation of difficulty as some other poets have demanded drink and drugs," and he could not be sure whether the book reveals that "Yeats hasn't a stime of a sense of humor, or—a Gargantuan one."[66] Was the book a joke or an admission of insanity, a challenge to readers or an expression of disdain?

Reviewers worried about the implication in the system that there is no free will. In a review entitled "Doom," Michael Williams read *A Vision* as of "the literature of pessimism," noting its emphasis on "one of the oldest and most ruinous illusions of humanity—the awful nightmare of doom, the idea of 'Eternal Recurrence.'" He described *A Vision* as

> the utter denial of the Christian revelation, the negation, indeed, of all belief in God. Man's free will is banished in such a system. The

> "great wheel" of life merely turns and re-turns, forever, through cycle after cycle, so that each and every human soul, born again and again without cessation into different environments, will go on doing so eternally.

Reynolds claimed that the system disallows free will in individual or communal life, noting that "[b]oth man and civilization are as fated and destiny determined as a tragic character in the mind of Shakespeare." Seán Ó Faoláin lamented, "There is no ethic, no morality."[67]

The story of the communication with spirits featured in most reviews. William Rose Benét called WBY "the most psychic of Celts." Stephen Spender wrote: "The spirit which made this remark deserves a literary prize, for not only is it responsible for some of the greatest poetry in the English language, but also it has provided a valuable hint towards the critical attitude which the reader may perhaps—fortified by that voice from the 'other world'—take up towards *A Vision*." E. A. Cazamian noted that "the uninitiated reader will find much to pique his curiosity in these pages, where the poet retraces the history of his engagement with the spirit world, thanks to the aptitude for automatic writing first revealed in his young wife."[68] So central is this material to the book, Edmund Wilson suggested, that *A Vision* "will be of relatively little interest to anybody but spiritualists and theosophists." Michael Roberts similarly acknowledged the difficulty of explaining "poetic inspiration" in terms of automatic writing, spirit instructors, and frustrators, since such material reminds most readers "of spiritualistic claptrap and bogus religions," but was a rare reviewer to acknowledge GY's role as "perhaps the most significant revelation of the book."[69]

Of great interest was WBY's discussion of his own belief in the system he had created (see 19). Roberts distinguished WBY's own "personal myths" from "scientific theories," concluding that "if [these myths] are to be effective, there must be moments when the poet takes them as being true in every sense." Wilson worried that WBY might "be thought to take his 'vision' too literally." Grigson proclaimed that despite whatever WBY might have gained from the instructors, "quack remains quack."[70]

Given the importance of both poets by this time, it is not surprising that WBY's commentary on Pound and his *Cantos* would matter. Wilson noted that the volume "throws some light on Pound's design in his 'Cantos,'" and Babette Deutsch called WBY's comments on *The Cantos* one of the most valuable parts of a book she largely dismissed as "tedious." Eda Lou Walton described the book as containing "the most complete account, received directly from Pound, of what he is doing with his *Cantos*." The reviewer for *The Illustrated London News* took consolation that just as he had been baffled by *A Vision* and "[j]ust as Æ was disconcerted by Yeats' visionary philosophy, so Yeats himself appears puzzled by another poet's *magnum opus*, continued in *The Fifth Decad of Cantos*."[71]

Many wondered how to understand *A Vision* as a description of a wider political reality. Quinn highlighted "any number of piercing comments of men and times," though he wondered "[h]ow much or how little 'A Vision' may eventually be found to contribute to study of complex human nature and changing society." Grigson similarly asked, "[H]ow much hold of reality and justice is there in Yeats *now*?" adding that "[r]espect for an able and aged poet does not preclude scepticism about his opinions." Grigson used WBY's own complicated political stances—his celebration of his Anglo-Irish background, his tendency to admire fascism—to offer his own views:

> The value of Yeats is nothing but the sum of his expressed moments of reality: the value of Communism, or the value of Fascism, is the sum of its working truths or realities. What is shocking about Yeats is asking us to declare only for Reality, in general, in the singular. *All things fall and are built again.* How comfortable! We have no right to listen to Yeats, no right at least to stay outside. To be free as a poet, to be free and to be allowed to have Reality in view, enjoins upon us, that, as clearly as we can with our imperfections of reason and sensibility, we must recognise, and not evade, realities of the present. We must risk (this is for Eliot as well as Yeats) having bad press with posterity; or else Beauty in view becomes a beast.[72]

Perhaps following WBY's own lead (see 14, 189–91), several reviewers considered connections between *A Vision* and Oswald Spengler's writings. Roberts called the book "a stranger version of

Spengler," and J. Bronowski acknowledged the book's likeness to "Spengler's shabby system of history." For Stephen Spender, however, the parallel had implications beyond mere literary likeness:

> Spengler, Stefan George, D'Annunzio, Yeats: is it really so impossible to guess at the "instructors" who speak behind these mystic veils? It is interesting, too, to speculate whether Fascism may not work out through writers such as these a mystery which fills its present yawning void of any myth, religion, law, or even legal constitution, which are not improvised.[73]

Given WBY's insistence on connections among these various elements of his *Vision*, reviewers' concerns testify to the seriousness with which this new version was read, as well as to the complicated motives that could underlie the explanation WBY attempted.

For most reviewers, however, the only way to assess the value of the book was through WBY's poetry. R. C. Bald, in a brief note in the *Philosophical Review*, concluded that "the symbolism has a validity, if only because it has provided a mould for the thought of one of the most sensitive minds of modern times." For Bronowski, the superiority of the poetry over anything in *A Vision* called into question the usefulness of, say, the exposition of "the mystic meanings of the twenty-eight phases of the moon" since "nothing in the book gives these meanings as richly as the poem *The Phases of the Moon*." An anonymous reviewer in *The New Statesman and Nation* agreed, concluding that "prolonged struggles with the 'system' and comparisons with those poems in which the same symbols are used suggest that their significance is not increased by the confused notions of gyres and phases, lunar cycles and zodiacal houses, in which Mr. Yeats' psychic dictators materialise their mediaeval doctrine of fundamental antinomies and revolutions."[74] William Rose Benét confessed similar preferences, admitting that "[p]erhaps it is a limitation of my mind that it can consign the diagram of the Historical Cones to limbo since, on the facing page, stands that superb poem concerning Leda—and I had rather read 'All Souls' Night' at the end of the book than the thorough-going explication of all the symbolism of the 'Vision.'" Spender judged that *A Vision* can "only assume shape and significance in Mr. Yeats's poetry." H. T. Hunt Grubb put these propositions to a test, reading the "wonderful mechanism" of *A Vision* through WBY's wide corpus of writings. And although he had raised concerns about the exposition of the system in *A Vision*, Seán Ó Faoláin concluded that "nobody who would read these poems in mood with the poet, extract from them the ultimate pleasure of the implications and overtones, can afford not to wind his way, with this book, into their cavern-sources in one of the most complex and solitary minds among lyric poets since the death of Keats."[75]

EDITIONS AFTER 1937

Editions of *A Vision* pursued and published after the death of WBY have become a part of its history. Beginning in 1930, Macmillan planned an Edition de Luxe of the works of WBY, an edition that at GY's suggestion came to be called "the Coole Edition."[76] During the last years of WBY's life, plans were made for the volumes' contents, and while WBY read proofs for some volumes, numerous delays kept Macmillan of London from releasing any. After WBY's death, work restarted in earnest. The edition by this point was to have eleven volumes, and volume IX, "Discoveries," would include *A Vision*.[77] On June 26, 1939, Thomas Mark mailed GY proofs for VIII, IX, and X, "Mythologies," "Discoveries," and "Essays," noting that only the proofs for Volume VIII had been read by WBY. She read them and replied to his questions and suggestions, and on July 14, 1939, Mark acknowledged return of the proofs for Volume IX. These proofs, housed in the Macmillan archive at the British Library (BL Add. 55893), contain a number of corrections marked by GY and Mark, aimed toward perfecting the 1937 text of *A Vision*.[78]

These proofs contain various types of changes. A few were authorized by WBY before his death and marked in his own hand in the Yeatses' copies of *A Vision*. Some are changes noted in GY's hand in these same printed copies. Others are changes suggested by Thomas Mark and accepted by GY. Some changes attempt to make the headnotes for the descriptions of the phases in Part III of Book I (79–136) correspond to the descriptions of the same phases in the Table of the Four Faculties (71–73). Others correct errors, such as the spelling of authors' names, foreign words, and the rendering of quotations from other works. Some recognize shifts in the wider historical context, as when "the present Pope" was to be changed to "Pope Pius XI" (157). The texts of poems are made to match the definitive edition, that is, the first volume of the Coole Edition. Other changes facilitate reading: for instance, parenthetical page references are inserted beside mentions of diagrams. A few changes improve or correct the description of the system itself. For instance, in 1937, an often-quoted and frequently puzzling sentence describes the concept closest to the idea of God: "The particulars are the work of the *thirteenth sphere* or cycle which is in every man and called by every man his freedom." In the Coole proofs and here, the sphere (which according to the system is beyond human comprehension) is replaced by the cone, that is, its shape when apprehended from a mortal perspective: "The particulars are the work of the *Thirteenth Cone* or cycle which is in every man and called by every man his freedom" (219–20). Finally, there are changes aiming to bring the text into alignment with Macmillan house style. Mark prepared a second pull of Coole proofs (BL Add. 55886), incorporating most but not all of the corrections. Most of these changes were never incorporated into a published version of *A Vision*, but as they remain a part of its textual history, we have included them in Appendix 1, Table 3, so that readers can compare this imagined version of *A Vision* with those published.

By the autumn of 1939, plans for the Coole Edition were put on hold. On October 17, 1939, Harold Macmillan wrote to GY, noting that "the present state of the publishing world is so difficult that I feel it would be in the best interest of Mr. Yeat's [*sic*] poems and plays if we postpone publication until early 1940."[79] Thomas Mark similarly acknowledged the effect of the onset of the war on the book market, writing to GY two days later that "[t]he Coole edition has to wait for better times," but wondering if it might be possible nonetheless for GY to continue with the proofs for Volume XI. Even after the war, however, the full Coole edition was never produced, with the *Poems* (1949) volume the only published result of this endeavor.[80]

In the 1950s, Macmillan of New York planned for a corrected reissue of *A Vision*. When GY corrected the first-pull Coole proofs, she had also marked a number of corrections in her copy of *A Vision* (1937, YL 2434), labeling it "Partially | corrected copy | July

1939." Connie K. Hood notes that on April 17, 1956, GY sent a copy of the 1938 New York text, with these same corrections marked, as setting copy for this partially corrected reissue of the text; all these corrections are noted in our Appendix 1, Tables 1–2.[81] Issued in dark blue cloth binding, with white endpapers and silver lettering on the spine, this edition was printed in 1,500 copies. Macmillan of London then used the New York sheets to print its own edition on December 7, 1961.[82]

In the early 1960s, interest in a corrected reissue of *A Vision* returned. On the second-pull Coole proofs, Mark made a fresh set of corrections, ignoring many of the corrections from the first pull of proofs (see Appendix 1, Table 3). These proofs begin at page 59 (41 of the current edition), thereby excluding "A Packet for Ezra Pound" and "Stories of Michael Robartes and his Friends."[83] Thomas Mark seems to have compared these proofs with the 1956 New York reissue, aiming to reconcile this text with that edition. Mark kept a notebook (see Appendix 1, Table 3), in which he noted changes made for the new 1962 edition; it includes only a small fraction of those imagined at the Coole proof stage. In 1962, Macmillan of London issued a new version of *A Vision*. These proofs were not its basis, because the text was a "corrected" printing of the 1937 edition. Some had been agreed on by Mark and George Yeats in their work on the Coole proofs. Others brought the volume into line with Macmillan house style. As Connie K. Hood summarizes:

> Thus, the 1962 reissue was a syncretic text, based partly on Mark's re-editing of Mrs. Yeats's editing of the 1956 reissue and partly on their joint editing of the Coole proofs; the 1956 reissue was itself based on Mrs. Yeats's re-editing of Yeats's editing of the 1937 edition and possibly on the editing of the Scribner edition by Mrs. Yeats, Yeats, or both; and Mrs. Yeats's re-editing of Yeats's editing of the 1937 edition was based on the editing by Mrs. Yeats and Thomas Mark of the Coole proofs: *A Vision* had become a modern palimpsest.[84]

By this point, we are many textual stages away from the 1937 edition of *A Vision*, the final version of the text over which W. B. Yeats had "authorial" control.

EDITORIAL PRINCIPLES AND APPARATUS FOR THIS VOLUME

The current edition of *A Vision* faces two large sets of challenges in a series invested in the authorial intentions of WBY. First is the difficulty of ascertaining his intentions in the last version of the text published in his lifetime. Second is the question of what to do with emendations made to that text by trusted collaborators after his death. When combined, these challenges make the ideal of a perfected text impossible.

First, we struggle with the difficulty of critical assessment of authorial intentions. As noted (xxxix), we do not have a complete setting copy for the 1937 printing of *A Vision*. Some parts survive: the NLI has copy #498 of *AVA-Laurie* (YL 2433c), and the copy of *Packet* used for setting is held in the Manuscript and Rare Book Library at Emory, and thanks to Connie K. Hood and Warwick Gould we have a photocopy of the first twelve pages of the setting-copy typescript from Basingstoke. Some parts exist in imperfect form: NLI 36,272/6 has been identified as a carbon of the setting-copy typescript, and although it lacks all inked corrections, additions, and diagrams, it offers some impression of the setting typescript. While the copy of *Stories* used as setting copy cannot be located, we have Connie Hood's notes and other copies of that text. Other parts, however, are completely lost: no galleys or proofs survive (typically the locus of many revisions), and even the carbon of the setting typescript for sections X–XVIII of Book IV is lost. Establishing WBY's real "intentions," therefore, is difficult at best. More important, there are numerous significant and often lengthy disparities between the carbon of the setting-copy typescript and the text as it appears in the 1937 edition, likely because of WBY's late-stage revisions. For our edition, we have had to rely on the text as printed by Macmillan in 1937, but it is frequently impossible to ascertain where printers' errors might have been introduced into the text—that is to say, where WBY's intentions were not followed. While we have not attempted to give full account of the many manuscript and typescript draft stages of this revised *Vision*, we have noted disparities between the printed text of 1937 and the carbon of the setting typescript in our annotations, reserving the most substantial variants for Appendix II, so that readers of this edition may reflect on relationships among the extant testaments to WBY's intentions and process.

Second, there is the problem of the corrections made to the text after WBY's death. There are three corrections marked in his hand in the Yeatses' copies of *A Vision* (1937), and presumably these may be taken as authoritative. But to what degree are changes marked in those same copies in GY's hand a reflection of WBY's wishes, or of her profound understanding of the system of *A Vision*, which she helped create? Are we to accept GY as an author of equal standing? She was, of course, the main "writer" of the original materials for the book, although her contributions were almost entirely mediumistic; by the 1930s, automatic sessions were rare, though WBY still relied on her (and to some extent also the spirit instructors) for consultation about details of the system. Her marking of corrections in the same copies as WBY argues for her semi-authorial status. And as for Thomas Mark, does his "permission" to correct *A Vision* expire with WBY's death, or could we take his corrections as well?

We have charted a conservative course, keeping our emendations minimal, noting all in Appendix 1, Table 4. In that same Appendix, Tables 1 and 2 compile changes marked by the Yeatses in their copies of *A Vision* (1937, YL 2434; and 1938, YL 2435), and these tables also note changes made in the copy of *A Vision* (1938) in the Alspach collection. Table 3 compiles corrections proposed for or made in posthumous editions of *A Vision*, comparing them with the 1937 text. These apparatuses allow readers both to reconstruct different published and imagined states of the text, and to consider our own editorial practice, and thereby to ruminate over the textual authority of Thomas Mark and GY while seeing what text WBY left behind. Just as our edition of *AVA* aimed to represent that text's appearance at publication in January 1926, the current volume offers insight into the reimagining of the work and its later states of presentation. We hope that in these two volumes, readers of WBY and the Yeatses' system will have the tools needed to understand the changes in the system and its textual representation, and what kind of framing WBY believed it requires.

Although all our emendations are noted in Appendix 1, Table 4, we explain our principles here. As Connie K. Hood has rightly noted,

WBY's texts were wildly inconsistent: despite his desire for internal consistency, he revised continually, meaning that "some problems with consistency in meaning in the 1937 edition arise because the materials represent several stages of the creative process captured simultaneously in print." Additionally, errors were introduced by his typists attempting to represent accurately his dictation and his nearly illegible manuscript drafts.[85] And unfortunately for all his editors, WBY resisted proofreading. We have accepted most corrections that appear in the Yeatses' copies of *A Vision* (1937, YL 2434; and 1938, YL 2435) and those noted in the copy of *A Vision* (1938) in the Alspach collection (see Appendix 1, Tables 1 and 2). Because of GY's co-authorship of the system of *A Vision*, we have accepted her corrections as well as WBY's. In keeping with established series policy, we have not incorporated Thomas Mark's corrections, but because WBY frequently deferred to Mark on matters of mechanics, we have included his corrections to the Coole proofs, the corrections marked in his notebook, and the text as printed in 1962 in Table 3.[86]

Some terminology has been standardized, as in *AVA*. Readers are often reminded that these are precise technical terms, and we have honored that aim by standardizing the capitalization and italicization of the following terms: *antithetical, Daimon, Ghostly Self, Head, Heart, Hodos Chameliontos,* Phase (when referring to a specifically numbered phase) and phase (when being used generally), *primary,* the *Four Principles* (*Celestial Body, Husk, Passionate Body, Spirit*), and True and False when they are used with respect to *Faculties. Will,* one of the *Four Faculties* (*Body of Fate, Creative Mind, Mask,* and *Will*), is not regularized with the others. Since WBY also uses the word "will" in its ordinary sense, and it is not always clear whether he refers to the common concept or the specialized term, we have yielded to the authority of the copy text for this word. Where typically italicized terminology occurs in italicized passages, we have not romanized. Additionally, and in keeping with our practice in *AVA*, we have several other minor emendations, standardizing the punctuation of titles, the spelling of proper names, the Anglicization of Cyrillic names, and reference marks for WBY's notes. We have kept the punctuation of the Macmillan copy text and WBY's drafts, though we use U.S. conventions for editorial text, including notes. All emendations are noted in Appendix 1, Table 4.

A Vision (1937)

W. B. Yeats, 1907
From an etching by Augustus John, R. A.[1]

A PACKET FOR EZRA POUND[2]

RAPALLO

I

Mountains that shelter the bay from all but the south wind, bare brown branches of low vines and of tall trees blurring their outline as though with a soft mist; houses mirrored in an almost motionless sea; a verandahed gable a couple of miles away bringing to mind some Chinese painting.[3] Rapallo's thin line of broken mother-of-pearl along the water's edge. The little town described in the "Ode on a Grecian Urn."[4] In what better place could I, forbidden Dublin winters and all excited crowded places, spend what winters yet remain? On the broad pavement by the sea pass Italian peasants or working people, people out of the little shops, a famous German dramatist, the barber's brother looking like an Oxford don, a British retired skipper, an Italian prince descended from Charlemagne and no richer than the rest of us, a few tourists seeking tranquillity.[5] As there is no great harbour full of yachts, no great yellow strand, no great ballroom, no great casino, the rich carry elsewhere their strenuous lives.

II

I shall not lack conversation. Ezra Pound, whose art is the opposite of mine, whose criticism commends what I most condemn, a man with whom I should quarrel more than with anyone else if we were not united by affection, has for years lived in rooms opening on to a flat roof by the sea.[6] For the last hour we have sat upon the roof which is also a garden, discussing that immense poem of which but seven and twenty cantos are already published.*[7] I have often found there brightly printed kings, queens, knaves, but have never discovered why all the suits could not be dealt out in some quite different order.[8] Now at last he explains that it will, when the hundredth canto is finished, display a structure like that of a Bach Fugue.[9] There will be no plot, no chronicle of events, no logic of discourse, but two themes, the Descent into Hades from Homer, a Metamorphosis from Ovid, and, mixed with these, mediaeval or modern historical characters.[10] He has tried to produce that picture Porteous commended to Nicholas Poussin in *Le chef d'œuvre inconnu* where everything rounds or thrusts itself without edges, without contours—conventions of the intellect—from a splash of tints and shades; to achieve a work as characteristic of the art† of our time as the paintings of Cézanne, avowedly suggested by Porteous, as *Ulysses* and its dream association of words and images, a poem in which there is nothing that can be taken out and reasoned over, nothing that is not a part of the poem itself.[12] He has scribbled on the back of an envelope certain sets of letters that represent emotions or archetypal events—I cannot find any adequate definition—A B C D and then J K L M, and then each set of letters repeated, and then A B C D inverted and this repeated, and then a new element X Y Z, then certain letters that never recur, and then all sorts of combinations of X Y Z and J K L M and A B C D and D C B A, and all set whirling together. He has shown me upon the wall a photograph of a Cosimo Tura decoration in three compartments, in the upper the Triumph of Love and the Triumph of Chastity, in the middle Zodiacal signs, and in the lower certain events in Cosimo Tura's day.[13] The Descent and the Metamorphosis—A B C

*There are now forty-nine.

†Mr. Wyndham Lewis, whose criticism sounds true to a man of my generation, attacks this art in *Time and Western Man*. If we reject, he argues, the forms and categories of the intellect there is nothing left but sensation, "eternal flux". Yet all such rejections stop at the conscious mind, for as Dean Swift says in a meditation on a woman who paints a dying face,

> Matter as wise logicians say
> Cannot without a form subsist;
> And form, say I as well as they,
> Must fail, if matter brings no grist.[11]

D and J K L M—his fixed elements, took the place of the Zodiac, the archetypal persons—X Y Z—that of the Triumphs, and certain modern events—his letters that do not recur—that of those events in Cosimo Tura's day.

I may, now that I have recovered leisure, find that the mathematical structure, when taken up into imagination, is more than mathematical, that seemingly irrelevant details fit together into a single theme, that here is no botch of tone and colour, all *Hodos Chameliontos*, except for some odd corner where one discovers beautiful detail like that finely modelled foot in Porteous' disastrous picture.[14]

III

Sometimes about ten o'clock at night I accompany him to a street where there are hotels upon one side, upon the other palm-trees and the sea, and there, taking out of his pocket bones and pieces of meat, he begins to call the cats.[15] He knows all their histories—the brindled cat looked like a skeleton until he began to feed it; that fat grey cat is an hotel proprietor's favourite, it never begs from the guests' tables and it turns cats that do not belong to the hotel out of the garden; this black cat and that grey cat over there fought on the roof of a four-storied house some weeks ago, fell off, a whirling ball of claws and fur, and now avoid each other. Yet now that I recall the scene I think that he has no affection for cats—"some of them so ungrateful", a friend says—he never nurses the café cat, I cannot imagine him with a cat of his own.[16] Cats are oppressed, dogs terrify them, landladies starve them, boys stone them, everybody speaks of them with contempt. If they were human beings we could talk of their oppressors with a studied violence, add our strength to theirs, even organise the oppressed and like good politicians sell our charity for power. I examine his criticism in this new light, his praise of writers pursued by ill-luck, left maimed or bedridden by the War; and thereupon recall a person as unlike him as possible, the only friend who remains to me from late boyhood, grown gaunt in the injustice of what seems her blind nobility of pity: "I will fight until I die", she wrote to me once, "against the cruelty of small ambitions".[17] Was this pity a characteristic of his generation that has survived the Romantic Movement, and of mine and hers that saw it die—I too a revolutionist—some drop of hysteria still at the bottom of the cup?

IV

I have been wondering if I shall go to church and seek the company of the English in the villas. At Oxford I went constantly to All Souls Chapel, though never at service time, and parts of *A Vision* were thought out there. In Dublin I went to Saint Patrick's and sat there, but it was far off; and once I remember saying to a friend as we came out of Sant'Ambrogio at Milan, "That is my tradition and I will let no priest rob me".[18] I have sometimes wondered if it was but a timidity come from long disuse that keeps me from the service, and yesterday as I was wondering for the hundredth time, seated in a café by the sea, I heard an English voice say: "Our new Devil-dodger is not so bad. I have been practising with his choir all afternoon. We sang hymns and then 'God Save the King,' more hymns and 'He's a Jolly Good Fellow.' We were at the hotel at the end of the esplanade where they have the best beer." I am too anaemic for so British a faith; I shall haunt empty churches and be satisfied with Ezra Pound's society and that of his travelling Americans.

V

All that is laborious or mechanical in my book is finished; what remains can be added as a momentary rest from writing verse. It must be this thought of a burden dropped that made me think of attending church, if it is not that these mountains under their brilliant light fill me with an emotion that is like gratitude. Descartes went on pilgrimage to some shrine of the Virgin when he made his first philosophical discovery, and the mountain road from Rapallo to Zoagli seems like something in my own mind, something that I have discovered.[19]

March and October 1928

INTRODUCTION TO "A VISION"

"This way of publishing introductions to books, that are God knows when to come out, is either wholly new, or so long in practice that my small reading cannot trace it."

—SWIFT[20]

I

The other day Lady Gregory said to me: "You are a much better educated man than you were ten years ago and much more powerful in argument". And I put *The Tower* and *The Winding Stair* into evidence to show that my poetry has gained in self-possession and power.[21] I owe this change to an incredible experience.

II

On the afternoon of October 24th 1917, four days after my marriage, my wife surprised me by attempting automatic writing.[22] What came in disjointed sentences, in almost illegible writing, was so exciting, sometimes so profound, that I persuaded her to give an hour or two day after day to the unknown writer, and after some half-dozen such hours offered to spend what remained of life explaining and piecing together those scattered sentences. "No," was the answer, "we have come to give you metaphors for poetry."[23] The unknown writer took his theme at first from my just published *Per Amica Silentia Lunae*. I had made a distinction between the perfection that is from a man's combat with himself and that which is from a combat with circumstance, and upon this simple distinction he built up an elaborate classification of men according to their more or less complete expression of one type or the other. He supported his classification by a series of geometrical symbols and put these symbols in an order that answered the question in my essay as to whether some prophet could not prick upon the calendar the birth of a Napoleon or a Christ.[24] A system of symbolism, strange to my wife and to myself, certainly awaited expression, and when I asked how long that would take I was told years. Sometimes when my mind strays back to those first days I remember that Browning's Paracelsus did not obtain the secret until he had written his spiritual history at the bidding of his Byzantine teacher, that before initiation Wilhelm Meister read his own history written by another, and I compare my *Per Amica* to those histories.[25]

III

When the automatic writing began we were in a hotel on the edge of Ashdown Forest, but soon returned to Ireland and spent much of 1918 at Glendalough, at Rosses Point, at Coole Park, at a house near it, at Thoor Ballylee, always more or less solitary, my wife bored and fatigued by her almost daily task and I thinking and talking of little else.[26] Early in 1919 the communicator of the moment—they were constantly changed—said they would soon change the method from the written to the spoken word as that would fatigue her less, but the change did not come for some months. I was on a lecturing tour in America to earn a roof for Thoor Ballylee when it came.[27] We had one of those little sleeping compartments in a train, with two berths, and were somewhere in Southern California. My wife, who had been asleep for some minutes, began to talk in her sleep, and from that on almost all communications came in that way. My teachers did not seem to speak out of her sleep but as if from above it, as though it were a tide upon which they floated. A chance word spoken before she fell asleep would sometimes start a dream that broke in upon the communications, as if from below, to trouble or overwhelm, as when she dreamed she was a cat lapping milk or a cat curled up asleep and therefore dumb. The cat returned night after night, and once when I tried to drive it away by making the sound one makes when playing at being a dog to amuse a child, she awoke trembling, and the shock was so violent that I never dared repeat it.[28] It was plain therefore that, though the communicators' critical powers were awake, hers slept, or that she was aware of the idea the sound suggested but not of the sound.

IV

Whenever I received a certain signal (I will explain what it was later), I would get pencil and paper ready. After they had entranced my wife suddenly when sitting in a chair, I suggested that she must always be lying down before they put her to sleep. They seemed ignorant of our surroundings and might have done so at some inconvenient time or place; once when they had given their signal in a restaurant they explained that because we had spoken of a garden they had thought we were in it. Except at the start of a new topic, when they would speak or write a dozen sentences unquestioned, I had always to question, and every question to rise out of a previous answer and to deal with their chosen topic. My questions must be accurately worded, and, because they said their thought was swifter than ours, asked without delay or hesitation. I was constantly reproved for vague or confused questions, yet I could do no better, because, though it was plain from the first that their exposition was based upon a single geometrical conception, they kept me from mastering that conception. They shifted ground whenever my interest was at its height, whenever it seemed that the next day must reveal what, as I soon discovered, they were determined to withhold until all was upon paper. November 1917 had been given to an exposition of the twenty-eight typical incarnations or phases and to the movements of their *Four Faculties*, and then on December 6th a cone or gyre had been drawn and related to the soul's judgment after death; and then just as I was about to discover that incarnations and judgment alike implied cones or gyres, one within the other, turning in opposite directions, two such cones were drawn and related neither to judgment nor to incarnations but to European history. They drew their first symbolical map of that history, and marked upon it the principal years of crisis, early in July 1918, some days before the publication of the first German edition of Spengler's *Decline of the West*, which, though founded upon a different philosophy, gives the same years of crisis and draws the same general conclusions, and then returned to the soul's judgment.[29] I believe that they so changed their theme because, had I grasped their central idea, I would have lacked the patience and the curiosity to follow their application of it, preferring some hasty application of my own. They once told me not to speak of any part of the system, except of the incarnations which were almost fully expounded, because if I did the people I talked to would talk to other people, and the communicators would mistake that misunderstanding for their own thought.

V

For the same reason they asked me not to read philosophy until their exposition was complete, and this increased my difficulties. Apart from two or three of the principal Platonic Dialogues I knew no philosophy. Arguments with my father, whose convictions had been formed by John Stuart Mill's attack upon Sir William Hamilton, had destroyed my confidence and driven me from speculation to the direct experience of the Mystics. I had once known Blake as thoroughly as his unfinished confused Prophetic Books permitted, and I had read Swedenborg and Boehme, and my initiation into the "Hermetic Students" had filled my head with Cabbalistic imagery, but there was nothing in Blake, Swedenborg, Boehme or the Cabbala to help me now.[30] They encouraged me, however, to read history in relation to their historical logic, and biography in relation to their twenty-eight typical incarnations, that I might give concrete expression to their abstract thought. I read with an excitement I had not known since I was a boy with all knowledge before me, and made continual discoveries, and if my mind returned too soon to their unmixed abstraction they would say, "We are starved".

VI

Because they must, as they explained, soon finish, others whom they named Frustrators attempted to confuse us or waste time.[31] Who these Frustrators were or why they acted so was never adequately explained, nor will be unless I can finish "The Soul in Judgment" (Book III of this work), but they were always ingenious and sometimes cruel. The automatic script would deteriorate, grow sentimental or confused, and when I pointed this out the communicator would say, "From such and such an hour, on such and such a day, all is frustration". I would spread out the script and he would cross all out back to the answer that began it, but had I not divined frustration he would have said nothing. Was he constrained by a drama which was part of conditions that made communication possible, was that drama itself part of the communication, had my question to be asked before his mind cleared? Only once did he break the rule and without waiting for a question declare some three or four days' work frustration. A predecessor of his had described the geometrical symbolism as created for my assistance and had seemed to dislike it, another had complained that I used it to make their thought mechanical, and a Frustrator doubtless played upon my weakness when he described a geometrical model of the soul's state after death which could be turned upon a lathe. The sudden indignant interruption suggested a mind under a dream constraint which it could throw off if desire were strong enough, as we can sometimes throw off a nightmare. It was part of their purpose to affirm that all the gains of man come from conflict with the opposite of his true being. Was communication itself such a conflict? One said, as though it rested with me to decide what part I should play in their dream, "Remember we will deceive you if we can". Upon the other hand they seem like living men, are interested in all that interests living men, as when at Oxford, where we spent our winters, one asked upon hearing an owl hoot in the garden, if he might be silent for a while. "Sounds like that", he said, "give us great pleasure."[32] But some frustrations found us helpless. Some six months before the communications came to an end, a communicator announced that he was about to explain a new branch of the philosophy and seemed to add, "But please do not write anything down, for when all is finished I will dictate a summary". He spoke almost nightly for I think three months, and at last I said, "Let me make notes, I cannot keep it all in my head". He was disturbed to find that I had written nothing down, and when I told him of the voice, said it was frustration and that he could not summarise.[33] I had already noticed that if their thought was interrupted they had to find some appropriate moment before they could take it up again, and that though they could sometimes foretell physical events they could not foretell those moments. Later still a frustration, if the communicator did not dream what he said, took, as will be seen, a more cruel form.

VII

The automatic writing and the speech during sleep were illustrated or accompanied by strange phenomena.[34] While we were staying at a village near Oxford we met two or three nights in succession what seemed a sudden warm breath coming up from the ground at the same corner of the road.[35] One night when I was about to tell my wife some story of a Russian mystic, without remembering that it might make her misunderstand an event in her own life, a sudden flash of light fell between us and a chair or table was violently struck. Then too there was much whistling, generally as a warning that some communicator would come when my wife was asleep.[36] At first I was inclined to think that these whistlings were made by my wife without her knowing it, and once, when I heard the whistle and she did not, she felt a breath passing through her lips as though she had whistled. I had to give up this explanation when servants at the other end of the house were disturbed by a "whistling ghost", and so much so that I asked the communicators to choose some other sign. Sweet smells were the most constant phenomena, now that of incense, now that of violets or roses or some other flower, and as perceptible to some half-dozen of our friends as to ourselves, though upon one occasion when my wife smelt hyacinth a friend smelt eau-de-cologne. A smell of roses filled the whole house when my son was born and was perceived there by the doctor and my wife and myself, and I have no doubt, though I did not question them, by the nurse and servants. Such smells came most often to my wife and myself when we passed through a door or were in some small enclosed place, but sometimes would form themselves in my pocket or even in the palms of my hands. When I took my hands out of my pocket on our way to Glastonbury they were strongly scented, and when I held them out for my wife to smell she said, "May-flower, the Glastonbury thorn perhaps".[37] I seldom knew why such smells came, nor why one sort rather than another, but sometimes they approved something said. When I spoke of a Chinese poem in which some old official described his coming retirement to a village inhabited by old men devoted to the classics,[38] the air filled suddenly with the smell of violets, and that night some communicator explained that in such a place a man could escape those "knots" of passion that prevent Unity of Being and must be expiated between lives or in another life.[39] (Have I not found just such a village here in Rapallo? for, though Ezra Pound is not old, we discuss Guido Cavalcanti and only quarrel a little.)[40]

Sometimes if I had been ill some astringent smell like that of resinous wood filled the room, and sometimes, though rarely, a bad smell. These were often warnings: a smell of cat's excrement announced some being that had to be expelled, the smell of an extinguished candle that the communicators were "starved". A little after my son's birth I came home to confront my wife with the statement "Michael is ill".[41] A smell of burnt feathers had announced what she and the doctor had hidden.[42] When regular communication was near its end and my work of study and arrangement begun, I was told that henceforth the Frustrators would attack my health and that of my children, and one afternoon, knowing from the smell of burnt feathers that one of my children would be ill within three hours, I felt before I could recover self-control the mediaeval helpless horror at witchcraft. I can discover no apparent difference between a natural and a supernatural smell, except that the natural smell comes and goes gradually while the other is suddenly there and then as suddenly gone. But there were other phenomena. Sometimes they commented on my thoughts by the ringing of a little bell heard by my wife alone, and once my wife and I heard at the same hour in the afternoon, she at Ballylee and I at Coole, the sound of a little pipe, three or four notes, and once I heard a burst of music in the middle of the night; and when regular communications through script and sleep had come to an end, the communicators occasionally spoke—sometimes a word, sometimes a whole sentence. I was dictating to my wife, perhaps, and a voice would object to a sentence, and I could no more say where the voice came from than I could of the whistling, though confident that it came through my wife's personality. Once a Japanese who had dined with my wife and myself talked of Tolstoy's philosophy, which fascinates so many educated Japanese, and I put my objections vehemently. "It is madness for the East", I said, "which must face the West in arms", and much more of the same sort, and was, after he had gone, accusing myself of exaggerated and fantastic speech when I heard these words in a loud clear voice: "You have said what we wanted to have said".[43] My wife, who was writing a letter at the other end of the room, had heard nothing, but found she had written those words in the letter, where they had no meaning. Sometimes my wife saw apparitions: before the birth of our son a great black bird, persons in clothes of the late sixteenth century and of the late seventeenth.[44] There were still stranger phenomena that I prefer to remain silent about for the present because they seemed so incredible that they need a long story and much discussion.

VIII

Exposition in sleep came to an end in 1920, and I began an exhaustive study of some fifty copy-books of automatic script, and of a much smaller number of books recording what had come in sleep. Probably as many words had been spoken in sleep as had been written, but I could only summarise and much had been lost through frustration. I had already a small concordance in a large manuscript book, but now made a much larger, arranged like a card index.[45] And then, though I had mastered nothing but the twenty-eight phases and the historical scheme, I was told that I must write, that I must seize the moment between ripe and rotten—there was a metaphor of apples about to fall and just fallen. They showed when I began that they assisted or approved, for they sent sign after sign. Sometimes if I stopped writing and drew one hand over another my hands smelt of violets or roses, sometimes the truth I sought would come to me in a dream, or I would feel myself stopped—but this has occurred to me since boyhood—when forming some sentence, whether in my mind or upon paper. When in 1926 the English translation of Spengler's book came out, some weeks after *A Vision*,* I found that not only were dates that I had been given the same as his but whole metaphors and symbols that had seemed my work alone.[46] Both he and I had symbolised a difference between Greek and Roman thought by comparing the blank or painted eyes of Greek statues with the pierced eyeballs of the Roman statues, both had described as an illustration of Roman character the naturalistic portrait heads screwed on to stock bodies, both had found the same meaning in the round bird-like eyes of Byzantine sculpture, though he or his translator had preferred "staring at infinity" to my "staring at miracle".[47] I knew of no common source, no link between him and me, unless through

> The elemental things that go
> About my table to and fro.[48]

*Published by Werner Laurie in 1925.

IX

The first version of this book, *A Vision*, except the section on the twenty-eight phases, and that called "Dove or Swan" which I repeat without change, fills me with shame.[49] I had misinterpreted the geometry, and in my ignorance of philosophy failed to understand distinctions upon which the coherence of the whole depended, and as my wife was unwilling that her share should be known, and I to seem sole author, I had invented an unnatural story of an Arabian traveller which I must amend and find a place for some day because I was fool enough to write half a dozen poems that are unintelligible without it.*[50]

X

When the proof sheets came I felt myself relieved from my promise not to read philosophy and began with Berkeley because a young revolutionary soldier who was living a very dangerous life said, "All the philosophy a man needs is in Berkeley", and because Lennox Robinson, hearing me quote that sentence, bought me an old copy of Berkeley's works upon the Dublin quays.[51] Then I took down from my wife a list of what she had read, two or three volumes of Wundt, part of Hegel's *Logic*, all Thomas Taylor's *Plotinus*, a Latin work of Pico della Mirandola, and a great deal of mediaeval mysticism.[52] I had to ignore Pico, for I had forgotten my school Latin and my wife had burnt her translation when she married me, "to reduce her luggage". I did not expect to find that the communicators echoed what she had read, for I had proof they were not dependent on her memory or mine, but did expect to find somewhere something from which their symbolic geometry had been elaborated, something used as they had used *Per Amica Silentia Lunae*. I read all MacKenna's incomparable translation of Plotinus, some of it several times, and went from Plotinus to his predecessors and successors whether upon her list or not.[53] And for four years now I have read nothing else except now and then some story of theft

**Michael Robartes and his Friends* is the amended version.

and murder to clear my head at night.[54] Although the more I read the better did I understand what I had been taught, I found neither the geometrical symbolism nor anything that could have inspired it except the vortex of Empedocles.[55]

XI

I might have gone on reading for some two or three years more but for something that happened at Cannes. I was ill after pneumonia and general nervous breakdown, had partly recovered but fallen ill again, and spent most of the days on my back considering a slowly narrowing circle.[56] Two months ago I had walked to the harbour at Algeciras, two miles; a month ago to the harbour at Cannes, a mile; and now thought two hundred yards enough. It had begun to widen again, and I had returned from my walk at a quarter to five one afternoon when I heard my wife locking her room door. Then walking in her sleep, as I could see by her fixed look, she came through the connecting door and lay down upon a sofa. The communicator had scarcely spoken before I heard somebody trying to get into her room and remembered that the nurse brought our daughter there every afternoon at five.[57] My wife heard and, being but half awakened, fell in trying to get on to her feet, and though able to hide her disturbance from the nurse and from our daughter, suffered from the shock. The communicator came next day, but later, and only to say over and over in different words, "It cannot happen again, for at this hour nobody comes", and then day after day to discuss what I had written. My wife's interests are musical, literary, practical, she seldom comments upon what I dictate except upon the turn of a phrase; she can no more correct it than she could her automatic script at a time when a slight error brought her new fatigue. But the communicator, as independent of her ignorance as of her knowledge, had no tolerance for error. He had no more than tolerated my philosophical study and was enraged by the intrusion, not so much into what I had written as into the questions I put, of a terminology not his. This led to one of those quarrels which I have noticed almost always precede the clearest statements, and seem to arise from an independence excited to injustice because kept with difficulty. "I am always afraid", he said in apology, "that when not at our best we may accept from you false reasoning." I had half forgotten—there had been no communication longer than a sentence or two for four years—how completely master they could be down to its least detail of what I could but know in outline, how confident and dominating. Sometimes they had seemed but messengers; they knew nothing but the thought that brought them; or they had forgotten and must refer to those that sent them. But now in a few minutes they drew that distinction between what their terminology calls the *Faculties* and what it calls the *Principles*, between experience and revelation, between understanding and reason, between the higher and lower mind, which has engaged the thought of saints and philosophers from the time of Buddha.

XII

I have heard my wife in the broken speech of some quite ordinary dream use tricks of speech characteristic of the philosophic voices. Sometimes the philosophic voices themselves have become vague and trivial or have in some other way reminded me of dreams. Furthermore their doctrine supports the resemblance, for one said in the first month of communication, "We are often but created forms", and another, that spirits do not tell a man what is true but create such conditions, such a crisis of fate, that the man is compelled to listen to his *Daimon*.[58] And again and again they have insisted that the whole system is the creation of my wife's *Daimon* and of mine, and that it is as startling to them as to us. Mere "spirits", my teachers say, are the "objective", a reflection and distortion; reality itself is found by the *Daimon* in what they call, in commemoration of the Third Person of the Trinity, the *Ghostly Self*. The blessed spirits must be sought within the self which is common to all.[59]

Much that has happened, much that has been said, suggests that the communicators are the personalities of a dream shared by my wife, by myself, occasionally by others—they have, as I must some day prove, spoken through others without change of knowledge or loss of power—a dream that can take objective form in sounds, in hallucinations, in scents, in flashes of light, in movements of external objects. In partly accepting and partly rejecting that explanation for reasons I cannot now discuss, in affirming a Communion of the

Living and the Dead, I remember that Swedenborg has described all those between the celestial state and death as plastic, fantastic and deceitful, the dramatis personae of our dreams; that Cornelius Agrippa attributes to Orpheus these words: "The Gates of Pluto must not be unlocked, within is a people of dreams".[60] What I have to say of them is in "The Soul in Judgment",* but because it came when my wife's growing fatigue made communication difficult and because of defects of my own, it is the most unfinished of my five books.[62]

XIII

Some, perhaps all, of those readers I most value, those who have read me many years, will be repelled by what must seem an arbitrary, harsh, difficult symbolism. Yet such has almost always accompanied expression that unites the sleeping and waking mind. One remembers the six wings of Daniel's angels, the Pythagorean numbers, a venerated book of the Cabbala where the beard of God winds in and out among the stars, its hairs all numbered, those complicated mathematical tables that Kelly saw in Dr. Dee's black scrying-stone, the diagrams in Law's *Boehme*, where one lifts a flap of paper to discover both the human entrails and the starry heavens.[63] William Blake thought those diagrams worthy of Michelangelo, but remains himself almost unintelligible because he never drew the like. We can (those hard symbolic bones under the skin) substitute for a treatise on logic the *Divine Comedy*, or some little song about a rose, or be content to live our thought.[64]

XIV

Some will associate the story I have just told with that popular spiritualism which has not dared to define itself, to go like all great spiritual movements through a tragedy of separation and rejection, which instead of asking whether it is not something almost incredible, because altogether new or forgotten, clings to all that is vague and obvious in popular Christianity; and hate me for that

*It is now finished, but less detailed than I once hoped.[61]

association. But Muses resemble women who creep out at night and give themselves to unknown sailors and return to talk of Chinese porcelain—porcelain is best made, a Japanese critic has said, where the conditions of life are hard—or of the Ninth Symphony—virginity renews itself like the moon—except that the Muses sometimes form in those low haunts their most lasting attachments.[65]

XV

Some will ask whether I believe in the actual existence of my circuits of sun and moon. Those that include, now all recorded time in one circuit, now what Blake called "the pulsation of an artery", are plainly symbolical, but what of those that fixed, like a butterfly upon a pin, to our central date, the first day of our Era, divide actual history into periods of equal length?[66] To such a question I can but answer that if sometimes, overwhelmed by miracle as all men must be when in the midst of it, I have taken such periods literally, my reason has soon recovered; and now that the system stands out clearly in my imagination I regard them as stylistic arrangements of experience comparable to the cubes in the drawing of Wyndham Lewis and to the ovoids in the sculpture of Brancusi.[67] They have helped me to hold in a single thought reality and justice.[68]

November 23rd 1928, and later

TO EZRA POUND

I

My dear Ezra,

Do not be elected to the Senate of your country. I think myself, after six years, well out of that of mine.[69] Neither you nor I, nor any other of our excitable profession, can match those old lawyers, old bankers, old business men, who, because all habit and memory, have begun to govern the world. They lean over the chair in front and talk as if to half a dozen of their kind at some board-meeting, and, whether they carry their point or not, retain moral ascendancy. When a politician follows, his thought shaped by newspaper and public meeting, it is as though somebody recited "Eugene Aram" as it used to be recited in my youth.[70] Once when I had called at a Dublin bank, rifle fire began all round the bank, and I was told that nobody could leave for an hour or two and invited to lunch with the Directors. We lunched in a room overlooking the courtyard, and from time to time I got up and looked out of the window at a young soldier who ran from the protection of a wall, fell upon one knee and fired through the gateway. The Republicans were attacking the next building, but was the bank well protected? How many such young soldiers stood or crouched about us? The bankers talked their ordinary affairs, not one went to the window or asked whether a particular shot was fired by the young soldier or at him; they had to raise their voices a little as we do when we have selected by accident a restaurant where there is an orchestra.

Should you permit yourself to enter the Senate, that irascible mind of yours will discover something of the utmost importance, and the group you belong to will invite you to one of those private meetings where the real work of legislation is done, and the ten minutes they can grant you, after discussing the next Bill upon the agenda for two hours with unperturbed lucidity, will outlast your self-confidence. No, Ezra, those generalities that make all men politicians and some few eloquent are not as true as they were. You and I, those impressive and convinced politicians, that young man reciting "Eugene Aram", are as much out of place as would be the first composers of sea-shanties in an age of steam. Whenever I stood up to speak, no matter how long I had pondered my words, unless I spoke of something that concerned the arts, or upon something that depended not upon precise knowledge but upon public opinion—we writers are public opinion's children though we defy our mother—I was ashamed until shame turned at last, even if I spoke but a few words—my body being somewhat battered by time—into physical pain.

II

I send you the introduction of a book which will, when finished, proclaim a new divinity. Oedipus lay upon the earth at the middle point between four sacred objects, was there washed as the dead are washed, and thereupon passed with Theseus to the wood's heart until amidst the sound of thunder earth opened, "riven by love", and he sank down soul and body into the earth.[71] I would have him balance Christ who, crucified standing up, went into the abstract sky soul and body, and I see him altogether separated from Plato's Athens, from all that talk of the Good and the One, from all that cabinet of perfection, an image from Homer's age. When it was already certain that he must bring himself under his own curse did he not still question, and when answered as the Sphinx had been answered, stricken with the horror that is in *Gulliver* and in the *Fleurs du Mal*, did he not tear out his own eyes?[72] He raged against his sons, and this rage was noble, not from some general idea, some sense of public law upheld, but because it seemed to contain all life, and the daughter who served him as did Cordelia Lear—he too a man of Homer's kind—seemed less attendant upon an old railing rambler than upon genius itself.[73] He knew nothing but his mind, and yet because he spoke that mind fate possessed it and kingdoms changed according to his blessing and his cursing. Delphi, that rock at earth's navel, spoke through him, and though men shuddered and drove him away they spoke of ancient poetry, praising the boughs overhead, the grass under foot, Colonus and its horses.[74] I think that he lacked compassion, seeing that it must be compassion for himself, and yet stood nearer to the poor than saint or apostle, and I mutter to myself stories of Cruachan, or of Cruchmaa, or of the road-side bush withered by Raftery's curse.*[75] What if Christ and Oedipus or, to shift the names, Saint Catherine of Genoa and Michelangelo, are the two scales of a balance, the two butt-ends of a seesaw?[77] What if every two thousand and odd years something happens in the world to make one sacred, the other secular; one

*Was Oedipus familiar to Theban "wren boys"? One of those Lives "collected out of good authors" at the end of North's *Plutarch* describes a meeting between Epaminondas and what I would like to consider some propitiation of his shade. "Even as they were marching away out of Thebes, divers of the souldiers thought they had had many unluckie signes. For as they were going out of the gates, Epaminondas met on his way a Herald, that following an auncient ceremonie and custome of theirs, brought an old blind man as if he had bene run away; and the Herald crying out aloud, Bring him not out of Thebes nor put him not to death, but carie him backe againe, and save his life." The accepted explanation is that he was a runaway slave welcomed back with some traditional ceremony because he returned of his own will; but imagination boggles at a runaway, old blind slave.[76]

wise, the other foolish; one fair, the other foul; one divine, the other devilish? What if there is an arithmetic or geometry that can exactly measure the slope of a balance, the dip of a scale, and so date the coming of that something?

You will hate these generalities, Ezra, which are themselves, it may be, of the past—the abstract sky—yet you have written "The Return", and though you but announce in it some change of style, perhaps, in book and picture it gives me better words than my own.

See, they return; ah, see the tentative
Movements, and the slow feet,
The trouble in the pace and the uncertain
Wavering!

See, they return, one, and by one,
With fear, as half-awakened;
As if the snow should hesitate
And murmur in the wind,
            and half turn back;
These were the "Wing'd-with-Awe",
        Inviolable.

Gods of the wingèd shoe!
With them the silver hounds
            sniffing the trace of air!

Haie! Haie!
        These were the swift to harry;
These the keen-scented;
These were the souls of blood.

Slow on the leash,
            pallid the leash-men![78]

STORIES OF MICHAEL ROBARTES AND HIS FRIENDS: AN EXTRACT FROM A RECORD MADE BY HIS PUPILS[1]

Huddon, Duddon and Daniel O'Leary*
Delighted me as a child;
But where that roaring, ranting crew
Danced, laughed, loved, fought through
Their brief lives I never knew.

Huddon, Duddon and Daniel O'Leary
Delighted me as a child.
I put three persons in their place
That despair and keep the pace
And love wench Wisdom's cruel face.

Huddon, Duddon and Daniel O'Leary
Delighted me as a child.
Hard-living men and men of thought
Burn their bodies up for nought,
I mock at all so burning out.[2]

I

Three of us, two young men and a young woman, sat round a fire at eleven o'clock at night on the ground floor of a house in Albert Road, Regent's Park.[3] Presently a third young man came in, drew a chair into the circle and said, "You do not recognise me, but I am

*As a child I pronounced the word as though it rhymed to "dairy".

the chauffeur: I always am on these occasions, it prevents gossip". Said I, "Where is Mr. Owen Aherne?"[4] "Owen", said he, "is with Michael Robartes making his report." Said I, "Why should there be a report?" Said he, "Oh, there is always a report. Meanwhile I am to tell you my story and to hear yours. There will be plenty of time, for as I left the study Michael Robartes called the universe a great egg that turns inside-out perpetually without breaking its shell, and a thing like that always sets Owen off.[5]

"My name is Daniel O'Leary, my great interest is the speaking of verse, and the establishment some day or other of a small theatre for plays in verse. You will remember that a few years before the Great War the realists drove the last remnants of rhythmical speech out of the theatre. I thought common sense might have returned while I was at war or in the starvation afterwards, and went to *Romeo and Juliet* to find out.[6] I caught those well-known persons Mr. . . . and Miss . . . at their kitchen gabble. Suddenly this thought came into my head: What would happen if I were to take off my boots and fling one at Mr. . . . and one at Miss . . . ? Could I give my future life such settled purpose that the act would take its place not among whims but among forms of intensity? I ran through my life from childhood and decided that I could. 'You have not the courage', said I, speaking aloud but in a low voice. 'I have', said I, and began unlacing my boots. 'You have not', said I, and after several such interchanges I stood up and flung the boots.

"Unfortunately, although I can do whatever I command myself to do, I lack the true courage, which is self-possession in an unforeseen situation. My aim was bad. Had I been throwing a cricket-ball at a wicket, which is a smaller object than an actor or an actress, I would not have failed; but as it was, one boot fell in the stalls and the other struck a musician or the brassy thing in his hand. Then I ran out of a side door and down the stairs. Just as I came to the street door I heard feet behind and thought it must be the orchestra, and that increased my panic. The realists turn our words into gravel, but the musicians and the singers turn them into honey and oil.[7] I have always had the idea that some day a musician would do me an injury. The street door opened on to a narrow lane, and down this lane I ran until I ran straight into the arms of an old gentleman standing at a street corner by the open door of a big covered motorcar. He pulled me into the car, for I was so out of breath that I could not resist, and the car drove off. 'Put on these boots', he said. 'I am afraid they are too large, but I thought it best to be on the safe side, and I have brought you a pair of clean socks.' I was in such a panic, and everything so like a dream, that I did what I was told. He dropped my muddy socks out of the window and said, 'You need not say what you have done, unless you care to tell Robartes. I was told to wait at the corner for a man without boots.' He brought me here. All I need add is that I have lived in this house since that night some six or seven months ago, and that it is a great relief to talk to people of my own generation. You at any rate cannot sympathise with a horrible generation that in childhood sucked Ibsen from Archer's hygienic bottle.[8] You can understand even better than Robartes why that protest must always seem the great event of my life."

"I find my parents detestable", said the young woman, "but I like my grandparents." "How could Mr. Aherne know", said I, "what was going to happen? You only thought of the protest when sitting in the theatre." "Robartes", said O'Leary, "sees what is going to happen, between sleeping and waking at night, or in the morning before they bring him his early cup of tea. Aherne is a pious Catholic, thinks it Pagan or something of the kind and hates it, but he has to do what Robartes tells him, always had to from childhood up. But Robartes says you must not ask me questions, but introduce yourselves and tell your story."

"My name is John Duddon," said I, "and this young woman insists on calling herself Denise de L'Isle Adam, and that tall fair young man is Peter Huddon.[9] He gets everything he wants and I hate him. We were friends until Denise began going about with him." At this point I was interrupted by Denise saying that I had starved until Huddon bought my pictures, that he had bought seven large landscapes, thirty sketches from life, nine portraits of herself, and that I had charged twice their value. Huddon stopped her, said that he would give more could he afford it, for my pictures were his greatest pleasure, and O'Leary begged me to continue my story. "This afternoon", I said, "Huddon came to my studio and I overheard an appointment for dinner at the Café Royal.[10] When I warned her that she would be sorry if she went, she declared that no such conversation had taken place. However, I bought a heavy stick and to-night stood outside the Café Royal waiting till they came out. Presently a man came out. I thought it was Huddon and brought my stick down on his head. He dropped on the pavement and I thought, 'I have knocked down my only patron, and that is a magnificent thing to have done', and I felt like dancing. Then I saw that the man on the pavement was a strange old gentleman. I found the café porter, said the old gentleman had fallen down in a fit, and we carried him a few doors up the street and into a chemist's shop. But I knew the truth would come out when he woke up, so I slipped into the café, found Huddon's table, told him what had happened and asked his advice. He said, 'The right thing is to get the old gentleman not to prosecute'. So we went to the chemist's shop where a small crowd had gathered. The old gentleman was sitting up in a little back room muttering, 'Just like my luck . . . bound to happen sooner or later'. Huddon said, 'It was an accident, sir; you cannot take offence at being knocked down in mistake for me'. 'In mistake for you?' said the old gentleman, staring steadily at Huddon. 'An upstanding man, a fine upstanding man—no offence.' And then as though he had suddenly thought of something, 'I will not say a word to the police on the condition that you and this young man and this young woman meet a friend of mine and drink a little wine'."

II

Presently Aherne came in with a big old man. Aherne, now that I saw him in a good light, was stout and sedentary-looking, bearded and dull of eye, but this other was lank, brown, muscular, clean-shaven, with an alert, ironical eye. "This is Michael Robartes", said Aherne, and took a plate of sandwiches, glasses and a bottle of champagne out of a cupboard and laid them upon a small table, and found chairs for himself and Robartes. Robartes asked which was which, for he already knew our names, and said, "I want the right sort of young men and women for pupils. Aherne acts as my messenger. What shall we talk about? Art?" Denise is shy with old men, and Huddon calls old men "sir" and makes them shy, so for the sake of saying something, I said, "No. That is my profession." "War?" said Robartes, and Huddon said, "That is my profession, sir, and I am tired of it". "Love?" said Robartes, and Denise, whose struggles with shyness always drive her into audacity, said, "Oh, no. That is my profession. Tell me the story of your life." "Aherne, the book", said Robartes. Aherne unlocked a bookcase and brought out a bit of goatskin and out of this an old battered book. "I have brought you here", said Robartes, "to tell you where I found that book, what followed from the finding of it, what is still to follow. I had founded a small Cabbalistic society in Ireland; but, finding time and place were against me, dissolved it and left the country.[11] I went to Rome and there fell violently in love with a ballet-dancer who had not an idea in her head. All might have been well had I been content to take what came; had I understood that her coldness and cruelty became in the transfiguration of the body an inhuman majesty; that I adored in body what I hated in will; that judgment is a Judith and drives the steel into what has stirred its flesh; that those my judgment approves seem to me, owing to an infliction of my moon, insipid.[12] The more I tried to change her character the more did I uncover mutual enmity. A quarrel, the last of many, parted us at Vienna where her troupe was dancing, and to make the quarrel as complete as possible I cohabited with an ignorant girl of the people and hired rooms ostentatious in their sordidness. One night I was thrown out of bed and saw when I lit my candle that the bed, which had fallen at one end, had been propped up by a broken chair and an old book with a pig-skin cover. In the morning I found that the book was called *Speculum Angelorum et Hominum*, had been written by a certain Giraldus, had been printed at Cracow in 1594, a good many years before the celebrated Cracow publications.[13] It was very dilapidated, all the middle pages had been torn out; but there still remained a series of allegorical pictures, a man torn in two by an eagle and some sort of wild beast, a man whipping his shadow, a man between a hunchback and a fool in cap and bells, and so on to the number of eight and twenty, a portrait of Giraldus, a unicorn several times repeated, a large diagram in the shape of a wheel where the phases of the moon were mixed up with an apple, an acorn, a cup, and what looked like a sceptre or wand.[14] My mistress had found it in a wall cupboard where it had been left by the last tenant, an unfrocked priest who had joined a troupe of gypsies and disappeared, and she had torn out the middle pages to light our fire. Though little

Portrait of Giraldus[15]
from the *Speculum Angelorum et Hominum*

remained of the Latin text, I spent a couple of weeks comparing one passage with another and all with the unintelligible diagrams. One day I returned from a library, where I had made a fruitless attempt to identify my Giraldus with Giraldus of Bologna, and found my mistress gone, whether in mere disgust at my preoccupation or, as I hope, to some more attentive man.[16] I had nothing now to distract my thoughts that ran through my past loves, neither numerous nor happy, back to the platonic love of boyhood, the most impassioned of all, and was plunged into hopeless misery. I have always known that love should be changeless and yet my loves drank their oil and died—there has been no ever-burning lamp."[17] He sank his head upon his breast and we sat in silence, until Denise said, "I do not think we should blame ourselves as long as we remain unmarried. I have always believed that neither Church nor State should grant divorce under any circumstances. It is necessary to keep in existence the symbol of eternal love." Robartes did not seem to have heard, for he took up his theme where he had left it. "Love contains all Kant's antinomies, but it is the first that poisons our lives.[18] Thesis, there is no beginning; antithesis, there is a beginning; or, as I prefer: thesis, there is an end; antithesis, there is no end.[19] Exhausted by the cry that it can never end, my love ends; without that cry it were not love but desire, desire does not end. The anguish of birth and that of death cry out in the same instant. Life is no series of emanations from divine reason such as the Cabbalists imagine, but an irrational bitterness, no orderly descent from level to level, no waterfall but a whirlpool, a gyre.

"One night, between three and four in the morning, as I lay sleepless, it came into my head to go pray at the Holy Sepulchre.[20] I went, prayed, grew somewhat calmer, until I said to myself, 'Jesus Christ does not understand my despair, He belongs to order and reason'. The day after, an old Arab walked unannounced into my room. He said that he had been sent, stood where the *Speculum* lay open at the wheel marked with the phases of the moon, described it as the doctrine of his tribe, drew two whorls working one against the other, the narrow end of one in the broad end of the other, showed that my single wheel and his two whorls had the same meaning. He belonged to a tribe of Arabs who called themselves Judwalis or Diagrammatists because their children are taught dances which leave upon the sand traces full of symbolical meaning.[21] I joined that tribe, accepted its dress, customs, morality, politics, that I might win its trust and its knowledge. I have fought in its wars and risen to authority. Your young Colonel Lawrence never suspected the nationality of the old Arab fighting at his side.[22] I have completed my life, balanced every pleasure with a danger lest my bones might soften."

III

Three months later, Huddon, Denise, O'Leary and I sat in silence round the same fire. For the last few days we had slept and eaten in the house that Robartes might teach us without interruption. Robartes came in carrying a little chest of carved ivory and sat down, the chest upon his knees. Denise, who had been in a state of suppressed excitement all day, said, "Nobody knows why I call myself Denise de L'Isle Adam, but I have decided to tell my story". "You told that story", said Huddon, "half a dozen times at the Café Royal and should be satisfied."[23]

At that moment, to my great relief, Aherne ushered in a pale slight woman of thirty-five and a spectacled man who seemed somewhat older. When Aherne had found them chairs, Robartes said: "This is John Bond and this is Mary Bell.[24] Aherne has brought John Bond from Ireland that you may hear what he has to say, and Mary Bell because I think her a suitable guardian for what I carry in this box. Before John Bond tells his story, I must insist upon Denise telling hers; from what I know of her, I feel certain that it will be a full and admirable introduction."

Denise began:[25] "I was reading *Axel* in bed. It was between twelve and one on the 2nd June last year. A date that I will never forget, because on that night I met the one man I shall always love. I was turning the pages of the Act where the lovers are in the vault under the castle. Axel and Sarah decide to die rather than possess one another. He talks of her hair as full of the odour of dead rose leaves—a pretty phrase—a phrase I would like somebody to say to me; and then comes the famous sentence: 'As for living, our servants will do that for us'.[26] I was wondering what made them do anything so absurd, when the candle went out. I said, 'Duddon, I heard you open the window, creep over the floor on your toes, but I never guessed that you would blow the candle out'. 'Denise,' he said, 'I am a great coward. I am afraid of unfamiliar women in pyjamas.' I said: 'No, my dear, you are not a coward, you were just shy, but why should you call me unfamiliar? I thought I had put everything right when I told you that I slept on the ground floor, that there was nobody else on that floor, and that I left the window open.' Five minutes later I said: 'Duddon, you are impotent, stop trembling; go over there and sit by the fire. I will give you some wine.' When he had drunk half a tumbler of claret, he said: 'No, I am not really impotent, I am a coward, that is all. When Huddon tires of a girl, I make love to her, and there is no difficulty at all. He has always talked about her, but if he had not, it would not make much difference. He is my greatest friend, and when she and he have been in the same bed, it is as though she belonged to the house. Twice I have found somebody on my own account, and been a failure, just as I have to-night. I had not indeed much hope when I climbed through the window but I had a little, because you had made it plain that I would be welcome.' I said: 'Oh, my dear, how delightful; now I know all about Axel. He was just shy. If he had not killed the Commander in the Second Act—and it would have been much more dramatic at the end of the play—he could have sent for him and all would have come right. The Commander was not a friend, of course; Axel hated him; but he was a relation, and afterwards Axel could have thought of Sarah as a member of the family. I love you because you would not be shy if you had not so great respect for me. You feel about me what I feel about a Bishop in a surplice. I would not give you up now for anything.' Duddon said, wringing his hands: 'Oh, what am I to do'. I said: 'Fetch the Commander'. He said, getting cheerful at once: 'I am to bring Huddon?'

"A fortnight later Duddon and I were in Florence. We had plenty of money, for Huddon had just bought a large picture, and were delighted with each other. I said: 'I am going to send Huddon this little cigarette-case'. It was one of those pretty malachite things they sell in Florence.[27] I had had it engraved with the words: 'In memory of the 2nd June'. He said: 'Why put into it only one cigarette?' I said: 'Oh, he will understand'.

"And now you know," said Denise, "why I have named myself

after the author of *Axel.*" I said: "You wish always to remember that upon that night I introduced you to Huddon". She said: "What a fool you are. It is you that I love, and shall always love." I said: "But you are Huddon's mistress?" She said: "When a man gives me a cigarette, and I like the brand, I want a hundred, but the box is almost empty".

"Now", said Robartes, "the time has come for John Bond." John Bond, after fixing a bewildered eye, first upon Denise and then upon me, began. He had evidently prepared his words beforehand. "Some fifteen years ago this lady married an excellent man, much older than herself, who lived in a large house on the more peaceable side of the Shannon. Her marriage was childless but happy and might have continued so had she not in its ninth year been told to winter abroad. She went alone to the South of France, for her husband had scientific and philanthropic work that he could not leave. I was resting at Cannes after completing the manuscript of a work on the migratory birds, and at Cannes we met and fell in love at first sight. Brought up in the strictest principles of the Church of Ireland, we were horror-struck and hid our feelings from one another. I fled from Cannes to find her at Monaco, from Monaco to find her at Antibes, from Antibes to find her at Cannes, until chancing upon the same hotel we so far accepted fate that we dined at the same table, and after parting for ever in the garden accepted fate completely. In a little while she was with child. She was the first woman that had come into my life, and had I not remembered an episode in the life of Voltaire I had been helpless.[28] We were penniless; for the child's sake and her own she must return to her husband at once.

"As Mary Bell left my letters unanswered I concluded that she meant me to drop out of her life. I read of our child's birth, heard nothing more for five years. I accepted a post in the Dublin Museum, specialised in the subject of the Irish migratory birds, and at four o'clock one afternoon an attendant brought her into my office.[29] I was greatly moved, but she spoke as if to a stranger. I was 'Mr. Bond', she was 'sorry to intrude upon my time' but I was 'the only person in Ireland who could give her certain information'. I took the hint and became the courteous Curator, I was there 'to help the student'. She wished to study the nests of certain migratory birds, thought the only exact method was to make their nests with her own hands. She had found and copied nests in her own neighbourhood, but as progress, entirely dependent on personal observation, was slow, wanted to know what had been published on the subject. Every species preferred some special materials, twigs, lichens, grasses, mosses, bunches of hair and so on, and had a special architecture. I told her what I knew, sent her books, proceedings of learned societies, and passages translated from foreign tongues. Some months later she brought me swift's, swallow's, corncrake's, and reed-warbler's nests made by her own hands and so well that, when I compared them with the natural nests in the cases of stuffed birds, I could see no difference. Her manner had changed; it was embarrassed, almost mysterious, as though she were keeping something back. She wanted to make a nest for a bird of a certain size and shape. She could not or would not name its species but named its genus. She wanted information about the nesting habits of that genus, borrowed a couple of books, and saying that she had a train to catch, went away. A month later a telegram called me to her country house. I found her waiting at the little station. Her husband was dying, and wished to consult with me about a scientific work he had carried on for many years; he did not know that we knew each other but was acquainted with my work. When I asked what his scientific work was, she said that he would explain, and began to speak of the house and its surroundings. The deplorable semi-gothic gate-way we had passed a moment before was the work of her husband's father, but I must notice the great sycamores and lucombe oaks and the clump of cedars, and there were great plantations behind the house. There had been a house there in the seventeenth century, but the present house was made in the eighteenth century, when most of the trees were planted. Arthur Young had described their planting and spoken of the great change it would make in the neighbourhood.[30] She thought a man who planted trees, knowing that no descendant nearer than his great-grandson could stand under their shade, had a noble and generous confidence. She thought there was something terrible about it, for it was terrible standing under great trees to say 'Am I worthy of that confidence?'

"The doors were opened by an elderly maid who met us with the smile of the country servant. As she brought me to my room and as I mounted the stairs I noticed walls covered with photographs and engravings, Grillion Club portraits, photographs signed by celebrities of the sixties and seventies of the last century.[31] I knew that Mr. Bell's father had been a man of considerable culture, that Mr. Bell himself had been in the Foreign Office as a young man, but here was evidence that one or other had known most of the famous writers, artists and politicians of his time.[32] I returned to the ground floor to find Mary Bell at the tea-table with a little boy. I had begun to discover in his face characteristics of my family when she said, 'Everybody thinks he is so like his great-uncle, the famous Chancery lawyer, the friend of Goldsmith and of Burke, but you can judge for yourself, that is his great-uncle's portrait by Gainsborough'.[33] Then she sent the little boy away but told him not to make a noise because of his father's illness. I stood at a window which opened on to the garden, noticed a number of square boxes much too large to be beehives, and asked their purpose. She said, 'They are connected with Mr. Bell's work', but seemed disinclined to say more. I wandered about the room studying family portraits; a Peter Lely; mezzotints, framed letters from Chatham and Horace Walpole, duelling swords and pistols arranged upon the walls by generations who did not care how incongruous the mixture that called up their own past history.[34] Presently an hospital nurse came to say, 'Mr. Bell has been asking for Mr. Bond. He is very weak; very near his end; but when he has spoken what is on his mind will die happier. He wants to see Mr. Bond alone.' I followed her upstairs and found the old man in a great four-poster, in a room hung with copies of paintings by Murillo and his contemporaries brought from Italy in the days of the Grand Tour, and one modern picture, a portrait of Mary in her early twenties, painted by Sargent."[35]

"The old man, who must have been animated and genial once, smiled and tried to rise from his pillow but fell back with a sigh. The nurse arranged the pillows, told me to call her when he had finished, and went into a dressing-room. He said: 'When I left the Foreign Office because I wanted to serve God I was a very young man. I wanted to make men better but not to leave this estate, and here nobody did wrong except as children do. Providence had surrounded me with such goodness that to think of altering it seemed blasphemy. I married, and it seemed wrong to give nothing in return for so much happiness. I thought a great deal and remembered that birds and beasts, dumb brutes of all kinds, were robbing and killing one another. There at any rate I could alter without blasphemy. I have never taken Genesis literally. The passions of Adam, torn out of his breast, became the birds and beasts of Eden. Partakers in original sin, they can be partakers in salvation.[36] I knew that the longest life could do but little, and wishing especially to benefit those who lacked what I possessed, I decided to devote my life to the cuckoos.[37] I put cuckoos in cages, and have now so many cages that they stand side by side along the whole southern wall of the garden. My great object was of course to persuade them to make nests; but for a long time they were so obstinate, so unteachable, that I almost despaired. But the birth of a son renewed my resolution and a year ago I persuaded some of the oldest and cleverest birds to make circles with matches, twigs and fragments of moss, but though the numbers who can do this are increasing, even the cleverest birds make no attempt to weave them into a structure. I am dying, but you have far greater knowledge than I and I ask you to continue my work.' At that moment I heard Mary Bell's voice behind me: 'It is unnecessary, a cuckoo has made a nest. Your long illness made the gardeners careless. I only found it by chance a moment ago, a beautiful nest, finished to the last layer of down.' She had crept unnoticed into the room and stood at my elbow holding out a large nest. The old man tried to take it but was too weak. 'Now let Thy servant depart in peace', he murmured.[38] She laid the nest upon the pillow and he turned over, closing his eyes. Calling the nurse we crept out, and shutting the door stood side by side. Neither of us spoke for almost a minute, then Mary flung herself into my arms and said amid her sobs, 'We have given him great happiness'.

"Next morning when I came down to breakfast I learnt that Mr. Bell had died in his sleep a little before daybreak. Mary did not come down, and when I saw her some hours later she spoke of nothing but the boy. 'We must devote our whole lives to him. You must think of his education. We must not think of ourselves.'

"At the funeral Mary noticed an old, unknown man among the neighbours and dependents, and when the funeral was over he introduced himself as Mr. Owen Aherne. He told us of scenes that had risen before Mr. Robartes' eyes on several successive mornings as he awaited his early tea. These scenes being part of our intimate lives, our first meeting in the South of France, our first meeting in the museum, the four-poster with the nest on the pillow, so startled us that we set out for London that very evening. All afternoon we have talked with Mr. Robartes, that inspired man, and Mary Bell has at his bidding undertaken a certain task. I return to Ireland to-morrow to take charge until her return of the estate and of her son."

IV

Said Robartes, "I have now two questions to ask, and four of you must answer. Mary Bell and John Bond need not, for I have taught them nothing. Their task in life is settled." Then he turned towards O'Leary, Denise, Huddon and myself, and said, "Have I proved by practical demonstrations that the soul survives the body?" He looked at me and I said, "Yes"; and after me the others, speaking in turn, said, "Yes". He went on: "We have read Swift's essay upon the dissensions of the Greeks and Romans; you have heard my comments, corrections, amplifications.[39] Have I proved that civilisations come to an end when they have given all their light like burned-out wicks, that ours is near its end?" "Or transformation", Aherne corrected. I said, speaking in the name of all, "You have proved that civilisations burn out and that ours is near its end". "Or transformation", Aherne corrected once more. "If you had answered differently", said Robartes, "I would have sent you away, for we are here to consider the terror that is to come."

Mary Bell then opened the ivory box and took from it an egg the size of a swan's egg, and standing between us and the dark window-curtains, lifted it up that we might all see its colour. "Hyacinthine blue, according to the Greek lyric poet", said Robartes.[40] "I bought it from an old man in a green turban at Teheran; it had come down from eldest son to eldest son for many generations."[41] "No", said Aherne, "you never were in Teheran." "Perhaps Aherne is right", said Robartes. "Sometimes my dreams discover facts, and sometimes lose them, but it does not matter. I bought this egg from an old man in a green turban in Arabia, or Persia, or India. He told me its history, partly handed down by word of mouth, partly as he had discovered it in ancient manuscripts. It was for a time in the treasury of Harun Al-Rashid and had come there from Byzantium, as ransom for a prince of the imperial house.[42] Its history before that is unimportant for some centuries. During the reign of the Antonines tourists saw it hanging by a golden chain from the roof of a Spartan temple.[43] Those of you who are learned in the classics will have recognised the lost egg of Leda, its miraculous life still unquenched.[44] I return to the desert in a few days with Owen Aherne and this lady chosen by divine wisdom for its guardian and bearer. When I have found the appointed place, Owen Aherne and I will dig a shallow hole where she must lay it and leave it to be hatched by the sun's heat." He then spoke of the two eggs already hatched, how Castor and Clytaemnestra broke the one shell, Helen and Pollux the other, of the tragedy that followed, wondered what would break the third shell.[45] Then came a long discourse founded upon the philosophy of the Judwalis and of Giraldus, sometimes eloquent, often obscure. I set down a few passages without attempting to recall their context or to arrange them in consecutive order.

"I found myself upon the third antinomy of Immanuel Kant, thesis: freedom; antithesis: necessity; but I restate it.[46] Every action of man declares the soul's ultimate, particular freedom, and the soul's disappearance in God; declares that reality is a congeries of beings and a single being; nor is this antinomy an appearance imposed upon us by the form of thought but life itself which turns, now here, now there, a whirling and a bitterness."[47]

"After an age of necessity, truth, goodness, mechanism, science, democracy, abstraction, peace, comes an age of freedom, fiction, evil, kindred, art, aristocracy, particularity, war. Has our age burned to the socket?"

"Death cannot solve the antinomy: death and life are its expression. We come at birth into a multitude and after death would perish into the One did not a witch of Endor call us back, nor would she repent did we shriek with Samuel: 'Why hast thou disquieted me?' instead of slumbering upon that breast."[48]

"The marriage bed is the symbol of the solved antinomy, and were more than symbol could a man there lose and keep his identity, but he falls asleep. That sleep is the same as the sleep of death."

"Dear predatory birds, prepare for war, prepare your children and all that you can reach, for how can a nation or a kindred without war become that 'bright particular star' of Shakespeare, that lit the roads in boyhood?[49] Test art, morality, custom, thought, by Thermopylae; make rich and poor act so to one another that they can stand together there.[50] Love war because of its horror, that belief may be changed, civilisation renewed. We desire belief and lack it. Belief comes from shock and is not desired. When a kindred discovers through apparition and horror that the perfect cannot perish nor even the imperfect long be interrupted, who can withstand that kindred? Belief is renewed continually in the ordeal of death."

Aherne said:

"Even if the next divine influx be to kindreds why should war be necessary? Cannot they develop their characteristics in some other way?"[51] He said something more which I did not hear, for I was watching Mary Bell standing motionless with ecstatic eyes. Denise whispered: "She has done very well, but Robartes should have asked me to hold it, for I am taller, and my training as a model would have helped".

Robartes put the egg in its box again, and said good-bye to us one after the other.

JOHN DUDDON

Dear Mr. Yeats,

I have access to records of Robartes' thought and action. There are diaries kept by my brother Owen during their tramps in Ireland in 1919, 1922 and 1923. Should I live, and my brother consent, I may publish some part of these, for they found themselves, as always, where life is at tension, and met, amidst Free State soldiers, irregulars, country gentlemen, tramps and robbers, events that suggest, set down as they are without context or explanation, recent paintings by Mr. Jack Yeats where one guesses at the forms from a few exciting blotches of colour.[52] There is a record made by Robartes' pupils in London that contains his diagrams and their explanations, and John Duddon's long narrative. You have sent me three poems founded upon "hearsay" as you put it, "The Phases of the Moon", "The Double Vision", and "The Gift of Harun Al-Rashid".[53] The first two compared with what I find in the diaries are sufficiently accurate. One has to allow of course for some condensation and heightening. "The Gift of Harun Al-Rashid" seems to have got the dates wrong, for according to the story Robartes told my brother, the Founder of the Judwali Sect, Kusta ben Luka, was a young or youngish man when Harun Al-Rashid died.[54] However, poetic licence may still exist.

I have compared what you sent of your unpublished book[55] with the diagrams and explanations recorded by his pupils, and find no essential difference. That you should have found what was lost in the *Speculum* or survives in the inaccessible encampments of the Judwalis, interests me but does not astonish. I recall what Plato said of memory, and suggest that your automatic script, or whatever it was, may well have been but a process of remembering.[56] I think that Plato symbolised by the word "memory" a relation to the timeless, but Duddon is more literal and discovers a resemblance between your face and that of Giraldus in the *Speculum*. I enclose a photograph of the woodcut.[57]

You ask if Robartes and my brother are as hot as ever about that old quarrel and exactly what is the quarrel. This is what I found after questioning various people. Some thirty years ago you made "Rosa Alchemica", "The Tables of the Law" and "The Adoration of the Magi", out of "a slight incident".[58] Robartes, then a young man, had founded a society, with the unwilling help of my brother Owen, for the study of the *Kabbala Denudata* and similar books, invented some kind of ritual and hired an old shed on Howth Pier for its meetings.[59] A foolish rumour got out among the herring or mackerel sorters, and some girls (from Glasgow, my brother says, for they come from all parts) broke the window. You hatched out of this the murder of Robartes and his friends, and though my brother incorporated Christ in the ritual, described a sort of orgy in honour of the pagan gods. My brother is very bitter about the pagan gods, but is so, according to Robartes, to prove himself an orthodox man. Robartes makes no complaint about your description of his death and says nobody would have thought the Aherne and Robartes of such fantastic stories real men but for Owen's outcry.[60] He is, however (and this I confirm from my own knowledge), bitter about your style in those stories and says that you substituted sound for sense and ornament for thought. What happened immediately before his separation from Europe must stand out with an unnatural distinction. I wrote once to remonstrate. I said that you wrote in those tales as many good writers wrote at the time over half Europe, that such prose was the equivalent of what somebody had called "absolute poetry" and somebody else "pure poetry"; that though it lacked speed and variety, it would have acquired both, as Elizabethan prose did after the *Arcadia*, but for the surrender everywhere to the sensational and the topical; that romance driven to its last ditch had a right to swagger.[61] He answered that when the candle was burnt out an honest man did not pretend that grease was flame.[62]

JOHN AHERNE[63]

THE PHASES OF THE MOON

THE PHASES OF THE MOON

An old man cocked his ear upon a bridge;
He and his friend, their faces to the South,
Had trod the uneven road. Their boots were soiled,
Their Connemara cloth worn out of shape;[1]
They had kept a steady pace as though their beds,
Despite a dwindling and late-risen moon,
Were distant still. An old man cocked his ear.

AHERNE

What made that sound?

ROBARTES

A rat or water-hen
Splashed, or an otter slid into the stream.
We are on the bridge; that shadow is the tower,
And the light proves that he is reading still.[2]
He has found, after the manner of his kind,
Mere images; chosen this place to live in
Because, it may be, of the candle-light
From the far tower where Milton's Platonist[3]
Sat late, or Shelley's visionary prince:[4]
The lonely light that Samuel Palmer engraved,[5]
An image of mysterious wisdom won by toil;
And now he seeks in book or manuscript
What he shall never find.

AHERNE

Why should not you
Who know it all ring at his door, and speak
Just truth enough to show that his whole life
Will scarcely find for him a broken crust
Of all those truths that are your daily bread;
And when you have spoken take the roads again?

ROBARTES

He wrote of me in that extravagant style
He had learned from Pater, and to round his tale
Said I was dead; and dead I choose to be.[6]

AHERNE

Sing me the changes of the moon once more;
True song, though speech: "mine author sung it me".[7]

ROBARTES

Twenty-and-eight the phases of the moon,
The full and the moon's dark and all the crescents,
Twenty-and-eight, and yet but six-and-twenty
The cradles that a man must needs be rocked in;
For there's no human life at the full or the dark.
From the first crescent to the half, the dream
But summons to adventure, and the man
Is always happy like a bird or a beast;
But while the moon is rounding towards the full
He follows whatever whim's most difficult
Among whims not impossible, and though scarred,
As with the cat-o'-nine-tails of the mind,
His body moulded from within his body
Grows comelier.[8] Eleven pass, and then
Athena takes Achilles by the hair,[9]

Hector is in the dust,[10] Nietzsche is born,[11]
Because the hero's crescent is the twelfth.
And yet, twice born, twice buried, grow he must,
Before the full moon, helpless as a worm.
The thirteenth moon but sets the soul at war
In its own being, and when that war's begun
There is no muscle in the arm; and after,
Under the frenzy of the fourteenth moon,
The soul begins to tremble into stillness,
To die into the labyrinth of itself!

AHERNE

Sing out the song; sing to the end, and sing
The strange reward of all that discipline.

ROBARTES

All thought becomes an image and the soul
Becomes a body: that body and that soul
Too perfect at the full to lie in a cradle,
Too lonely for the traffic of the world:
Body and soul cast out and cast away
Beyond the visible world.

AHERNE

All dreams of the soul
End in a beautiful man's or woman's body.

ROBARTES

Have you not always known it?

AHERNE

The song will have it
That those that we have loved got their long fingers

From death, and wounds, or on Sinai's top,
Or from some bloody whip in their own hands.[12]
They ran from cradle to cradle till at last
Their beauty dropped out of the loneliness
Of body and soul.

ROBARTES

The lover's heart knows that.

AHERNE

It must be that the terror in their eyes
Is memory or foreknowledge of the hour
When all is fed with light and heaven is bare.

ROBARTES

When the moon's full those creatures of the full
Are met on the waste hills by country men
Who shudder and hurry by: body and soul
Estranged amid the strangeness of themselves,
Caught up in contemplation, the mind's eye
Fixed upon images that once were thought,
For separate, perfect,[13] and immovable
Images can break the solitude
Of lovely, satisfied, indifferent eyes.

And thereupon with aged, high-pitched voice
Aherne laughed, thinking of the man within,
His sleepless candle and laborious pen.

ROBARTES

And after that the crumbling of the moon:
The soul remembering its loneliness
Shudders in many cradles; all is changed.
It would be the world's servant, and as it serves,

Choosing whatever task's most difficult
Among tasks not impossible, it takes
Upon the body and upon the soul
The coarseness of the drudge.[14]

AHERNE

Before the full
It sought itself and afterwards the world.

ROBARTES

Because you are forgotten, half out of life,
And never wrote a book, your thought is clear.[15]
Reformer, merchant, statesman, learned man,
Dutiful husband, honest wife by turn,
Cradle upon cradle, and all in flight and all
Deformed, because there is no deformity
But saves us from a dream.

AHERNE

And what of those
That the last servile crescent has set free?

ROBARTES

Because all dark, like those that are all light,
They are cast beyond the verge, and in a cloud,
Crying to one another like the bats;
But having no desire they cannot tell
What's good or bad, or what it is to triumph
At the perfection of one's own obedience;
And yet they speak what's blown into the mind;
Deformed beyond deformity, unformed,
Insipid as the dough before it is baked,
They change their bodies at a word.

AHERNE

And then?

ROBARTES

When all the dough has been so kneaded up
That it can take what form cook Nature fancies,
The first thin crescent is wheeled round once more.

AHERNE

But the escape; the song's not finished yet.

ROBARTES

Hunchback and Saint and Fool are the last crescents.[16]
The burning bow that once could shoot an arrow
Out of the up and down, the wagon-wheel
Of beauty's cruelty and wisdom's chatter—
Out of that raving tide—is drawn betwixt
Deformity of body and of mind.

AHERNE

Were not our beds far off I'd ring the bell,
Stand under the rough roof-timbers of the hall
Beside the castle door, where all is stark
Austerity, a place set out for wisdom
That he will never find; I'd play a part;
He would never know me after all these years
But take me for some drunken country man;
I'd stand and mutter there until he caught
"Hunchback and Saint and Fool", and that they came
Under the three last crescents of the moon,
And then I'd stagger out. He'd crack his wits
Day after day, yet never find the meaning.

And then he laughed to think that what seemed hard
Should be so simple—a bat rose from the hazels
And circled round him with its squeaky cry,
The light in the tower window was put out.[17]

The Great Wheel[1]
from the *Speculum Angelorum et Hominum*

THE GREAT WHEEL

BOOK I: THE GREAT WHEEL

PART I: THE PRINCIPAL SYMBOL

I

"When Discord", writes Empedocles, "has fallen into the lowest depths of the vortex"—the extreme bound, not the centre, Burnet points out—"Concord has reached the centre, into it do all things come together so as to be only one, not all at once but gradually from different quarters, and as they come Discord retires to the extreme boundary . . . in proportion as it runs out Concord in a soft immortal boundless stream runs in."[2] And again: "Never will boundless time be emptied of that pair; and they prevail in turn as that circle comes round, and pass away before one another and increase in their appointed turn". It was this Discord or War that Heraclitus called "God of all and Father of all, some it has made gods and some men, some bond and some free", and I recall that Love and War came from the eggs of Leda.[3]

II

According to Simplicius,* a late commentator upon Aristotle, the Concord of Empedocles fabricates all things into "an homogeneous sphere",[4] and then Discord separates the elements and so makes the world we inhabit, but even the sphere formed by Concord is not the

*Quoted by Pierre Duhem in *Le Système du monde*, vol. I, page 75.

changeless eternity, for Concord or Love but offers us the image of that which is changeless.[5]

If we think of the vortex attributed to Discord as formed by circles diminishing until they are nothing, and of the opposing sphere attributed to Concord as forming from itself an opposing vortex, the apex of each vortex in the middle of the other's base, we have the fundamental symbol of my instructors.

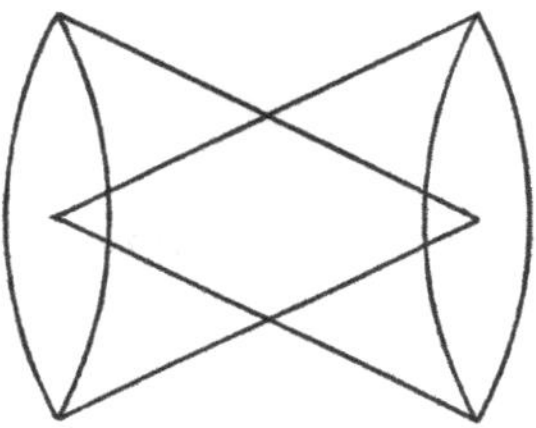

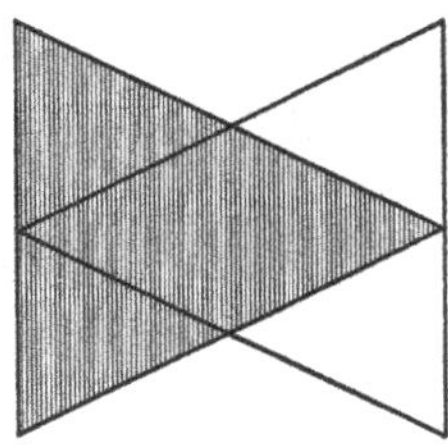

If I call the unshaded cone "Discord" and the other "Concord" and think of each as the bound of a gyre, I see that the gyre of "Concord" diminishes as that of "Discord" increases, and can imagine after that the gyre of "Concord" increasing while that of "Discord" diminishes, and so on, one gyre within the other always. Here the thought of Heraclitus dominates all: "Dying each other's life, living each other's death".[6]

The first gyres clearly described by philosophy are those described in the *Timaeus* which are made by the circuits of "the Other" (creators of all particular things), of the planets as they ascend or descend above or below the equator. They are opposite in nature to that circle of the fixed stars which constitutes "the Same" and confers upon us the knowledge of Universals.[7] Alcmaeon, a pupil of Pythagoras, thought that men die because they cannot join their beginning and their end.[8] Their serpent has not its tail in its mouth.[9] But my friend the poet and scholar Dr. Sturm sends me an account of gyres in St. Thomas Aquinas:[10] the circular movement of the angels which, though it imitates the circle of "the Same",[11] seems as little connected with the visible heavens as figures drawn by my instructors, his straight line of the human intellect and his gyre, the combination of both movements, made by the ascent and descent* of angels between God and man. He has also found me passages in Dr. Dee,[13] in Macrobius,[14] in an unknown mediaeval writer, which describe souls changing from gyre to sphere and from sphere to gyre.[15] Presently I shall have much to say of the sphere as the final place of rest.

Gyres are occasionally alluded to, but left unexplored, in Swedenborg's mystical writings. In the *Principia*, a vast scientific work written before his mystical life, he describes the double cone. All physical reality, the universe as a whole, every solar system, every atom, is a double cone; where there are "two poles one opposite to the other, these two poles have the form of cones".†[16] I am not concerned with his explanation of how these cones have evolved from the point and the sphere, nor with his arguments to prove that they govern all the movements of the planets, for I think, as did Swedenborg in his mystical writings, that the forms of geometry can have but a symbolic relation to spaceless reality, *Mundus Intelligibilis*.[17] Flaubert is the only writer known to me who has so used the double cone. He talked much of writing a story called "La Spirale". He died before he began it, but something of his talk about it has been collected and published.[18] It would have described a man whose dreams during sleep grew in magnificence as his life grew more and more unlucky, the wreck of some love affair coinciding with his marriage to a dream princess.

III

The double cone or vortex,[19] as used by my instructors, is more complicated than that of Flaubert. A line is a movement without extension, and so symbolical of time—subjectivity—Berkeley's stream of ideas—in Plotinus‡ it is apparently "sensation"—and a plane cutting it at right angles is symbolical of space or objectivity.[20] Line

*In an essay called "The Friends of the People of Faery" in my *Celtic Twilight* I describe such an ascent and descent. I found the same movement in some story I picked up at Kiltartan, and suspected a mediaeval symbolism unknown to me at the time.[12]

†Vol. ii, p. 555 of the Swedenborg Society's translation.

‡*Ennead*, vi. i. 8 (MacKenna's translation).

and plane are combined in a gyre which must expand or contract according to whether mind grows in objectivity or subjectivity.

The identification of time* with subjectivity is probably as old as philosophy; all that we can touch or handle, and for the moment I mean no other objectivity, has shape or magnitude, whereas our thoughts and emotions have duration and quality, a thought recurs or is habitual, a lecture or a musical composition is measured upon the clock. At the same time pure time

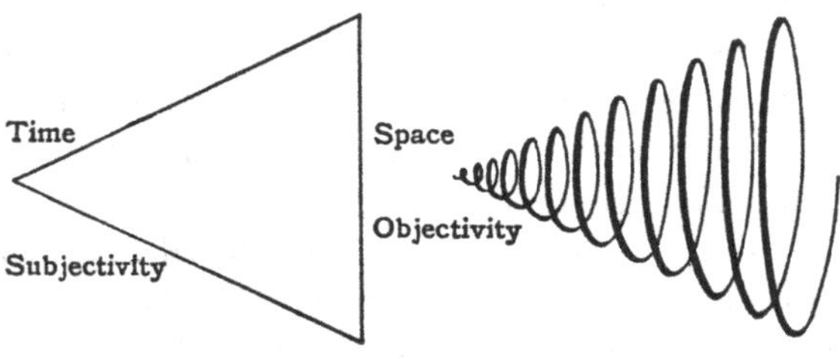

and pure space, pure subjectivity and pure objectivity—the plane at the bottom of the cone and the point at its apex—are abstractions or figments of the mind.

IV

My instructors used this single cone or vortex once or twice but soon changed it for a double cone or vortex, preferring to consider subjectivity and objectivity as intersecting states struggling one against the other. If the musical composition seek to suggest the howling of dogs or of the sea waves it is not altogether in time, it suggests bulk and weight. In what I call the cone of the *Four Facul-*

*Giovanni Gentile summarises Kant on time and space as follows: "Kant said that space is a form of external sense, time a form of internal sense. He meant that we represent nature, that is what we call the external world and think of as having been in existence before our knowledge and spiritual life began, in space, then we represent the multiplicity of the objects of our internal experience, or what we distinguish as diverse and manifold in the development of our spiritual life, not in space but in time" (*Theory of Mind as Pure Act*, chap. ix, H. Wildon Carr's translation). He thinks these definitions which seem to separate time and space from one another require re-statement. It will be seen, however, when I come to what I have called the *Four Principles*, that my symbols imply his description of time as a spatialising act.[21]

ties which are what man has made in a past or present life—I shall speak later of what makes man—the subjective cone is called that of the *antithetical tincture* because it is achieved and defended by continual conflict with its opposite; the objective cone is called that of the *primary tincture* because whereas subjectivity—in Empedocles "Discord" as I think—tends to separate man from man, objectivity brings us back to the mass where we begin. I had suggested the word *tincture*, a common word in Boehme,[22] and my instructors took the word *antithetical* from *Per Amica Silentia Lunae*.[23]

I had never read Hegel, but my mind had been full of Blake from boyhood up and I saw the world as a conflict—

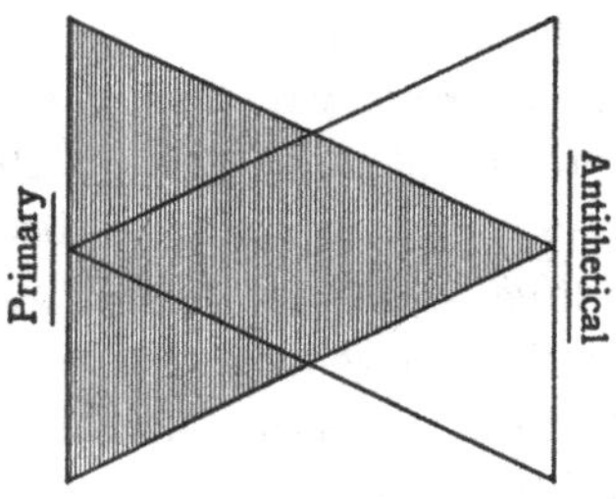

Spectre and Emanation—and could distinguish between a contrary and a negation. "Contraries are positive", wrote Blake, "a negation is not a contrary", "How great the gulph between simplicity and insipidity", and again, "There is a place at the bottom of the graves where contraries are equally true".[24]

I had never put the conflict in logical form,* never thought with Hegel that the two ends of the see-saw are one another's negation, nor that the spring vegetables were refuted when over.

The cones of the *tinctures* mirror reality but are in themselves pursuit and illusion. As will be presently seen, the sphere is reality. By the *antithetical* cone, which is left unshaded in my diagram, we express more and more, as it broadens, our inner world of desire and imagination, whereas by the *primary,* the shaded cone, we

*Though reality is not logical it becomes so in our minds if we discover logical refutations of the writer or movement that is going out of fashion. There is always error, which has nothing to do with "the conflict" which creates all life. Croce in his study of Hegel identifies error with negation.[25]

express more and more, as it broadens, that objectivity of mind which, in the words of Murray's Dictionary, lays "stress upon that which is external to the mind" or treats "of outward things and events rather than of inward thought" or seeks "to exhibit the actual facts, not coloured by the opinions or feelings".[26] The *antithetical tincture* is emotional and aesthetic whereas the *primary tincture* is reasonable and moral. Within these cones move what are called the *Four Faculties*: *Will* and *Mask*, *Creative Mind* and *Body of Fate*.

It will be enough until I have explained the geometrical diagrams in detail to describe *Will* and *Mask* as the will and its object, or the Is and the Ought (or that which should be), *Creative Mind* and *Body of Fate* as thought and its object, or the Knower and the Known, and to say that the first two are lunar or *antithetical* or natural, the second two solar or *primary* or reasonable. A particular man is classified according to the place of *Will*, or choice, in the diagram. At first sight there are only two *Faculties*, because only two of the four, *Will* and *Creative Mind*, are active, but it will be presently seen that the *Faculties* can be represented by two opposing cones so drawn that the *Will* of the one is the *Mask* of the other, the *Creative Mind* of the one the *Body of Fate* of the other. Everything that wills can be desired, resisted or accepted, every creative act can be seen as fact, every *Faculty* is alternately shield and sword.

V

These pairs of opposites whirl in contrary directions, *Will* and *Mask* from right to left, *Creative Mind* and *Body of Fate* like the hands of a clock, from left to right. I will confine myself for the moment to *Will* and *Creative Mind*, will and thought.[27] As *Will* approaches the utmost expansion of its *antithetical* cone it drags *Creative Mind* with it—thought is more and more dominated by will—

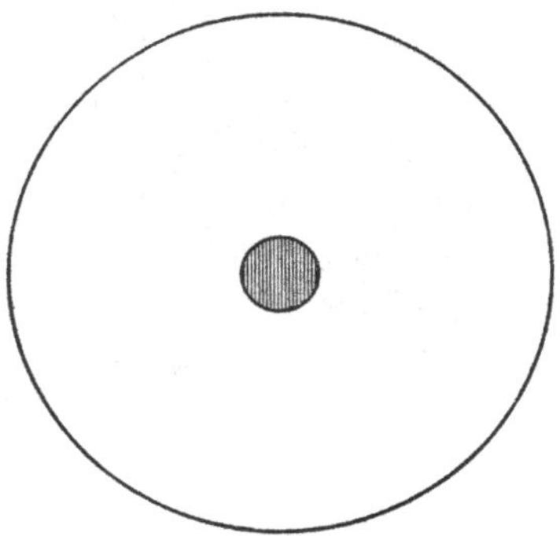

but *Creative Mind* remains at the same distance from its cone's narrow end that *Will* is from the broad end of the *antithetical* cone. Then, as though satiated by the extreme expansion of its cone, *Will* lets *Creative Mind* dominate, and is dragged by it until *Creative Mind* weakens once more. As *Creative Mind*, let us say, is dragged by *Will* towards the utmost expansion of its *antithetical* cone it is more and more contaminated by *Will*, while *Will* frees itself from contamination. We can, however, represent the two *Faculties* as they approach the full expansion of the *antithetical* cone by the same cross-sections of the cone.

The shaded, or *primary* part, is a contamination of *Will*; the unshaded, or *antithetical* part, a contamination of *Creative Mind*. We can substitute positions in the cones for either symbol: we can represent *Creative Mind* as approaching the extreme expansion of the *antithetical* cone and then as changing into the narrow end of the *primary* cone and expanding once more; the *Will* as approaching the narrow end of the *primary* cone and then, at the same instant when the *Creative Mind* changes cones, passing into the broad end of the *antithetical* cone, and contracting once more. The diagram is sometimes so used by my instructors and gives them a phrase which constantly occurs, "the interchange of the *tinctures*", but it is inconvenient.[28] For this reason they generally represent the *Faculties* as moving always along the outside of the diagram. Just before complete *antithetical* expression they are placed thus:

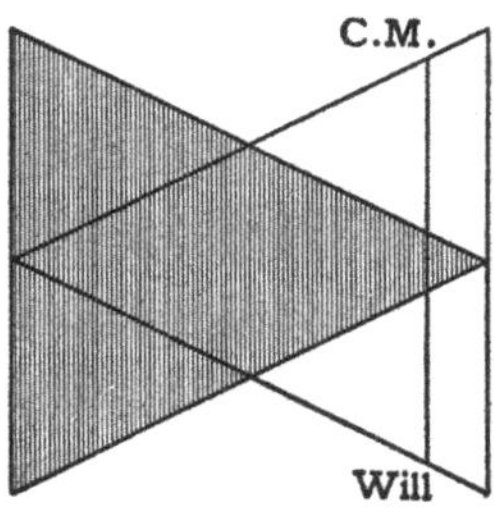

Just after it, thus:

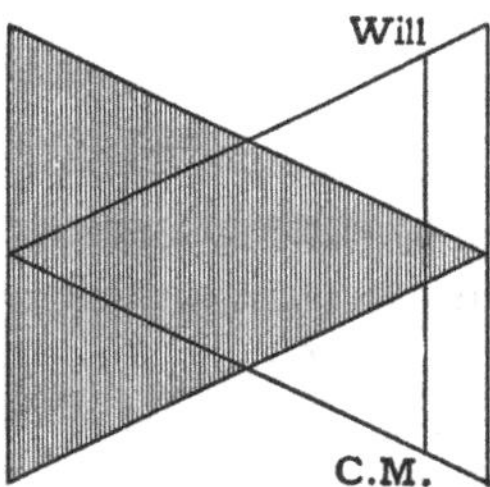

I think of the gyre of *Will* as approaching complete *antithetical* expansion—unshaded cone—along the lower side of the diagram or moving from right to left,[29] and the gyre of *Creative Mind* as approaching it along the upper side, left to right, and then of their passing one another at complete expansion, then of their receding from it, *Will* upon the upper side, *Creative Mind* upon the lower, and always on the outside of the diagram until they pass one another at complete *primary* expansion. These movements are but a convenient pictorial summary of what is more properly a double movement of two gyres. These gyres move not only forward to the *primary* and *antithetical* expansion, but have their own circular movement, the gyre of *Will* from right to left, that of *Creative Mind* from left to right. I shall consider presently the significance of these circlings.

VI

The *Mask* and *Body of Fate* occupy those positions which are most opposite in character to the positions of *Will* and *Creative Mind*. If

Will and *Creative Mind* are approaching complete *antithetical* expansion, *Mask* and *Body of Fate* are approaching complete *primary* expansion, and so on. In the following figure the man is almost completely *antithetical* in nature.

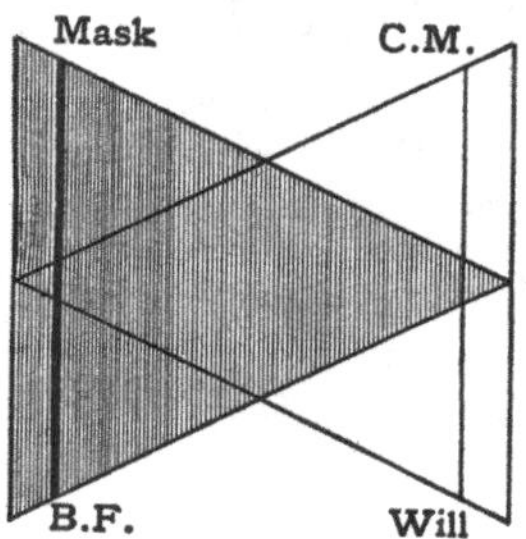

In the following almost completely *primary*.

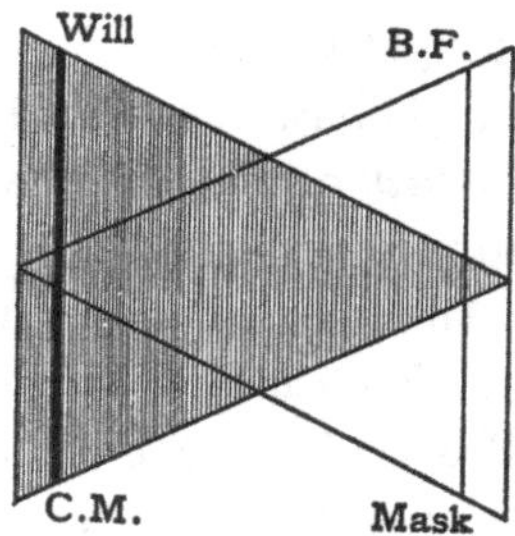

In the following he is completely *primary*, a state which is like the completely *antithetical* state, as I must show presently, only a supernatural or ideal existence.

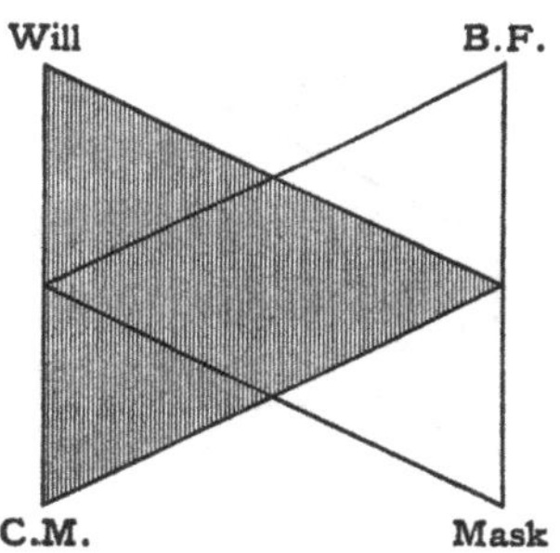

In the following he is midway between *primary* and *antithetical* and moving towards *antithetical* expansion. All four gyres are superimposed.

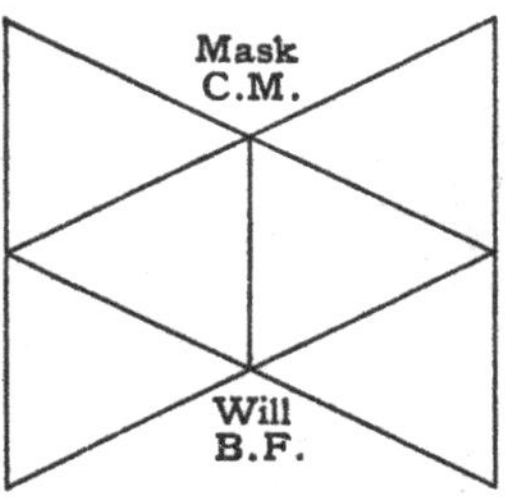

I have now only to set a row of numbers upon the sides to possess a classification, as I will show presently, of every possible movement of thought and of life, and I have been told to make these numbers correspond to the phases of the moon, including among them full moon and the moonless night when the moon is nearest to the sun. The moonless night is called Phase 1, and the full moon is Phase 15.[30] Phase 8 begins the *antithetical* phases, those where the bright part of the moon is greater than the dark, and Phase 22 begins the *primary* phases, where the dark part is greater than the bright. At Phases 15 and 1 respectively, the *antithetical* and *primary tinctures* come to a climax. A man of, say, Phase 13 is a man whose *Will* is at that phase, and the diagram which shows the position of the *Faculties* for a *Will* so placed, describes his character and destiny. The last phase is Phase 28, and the twenty-eight phases constitute a month of which each day and night constitute an incarnation and the discarnate

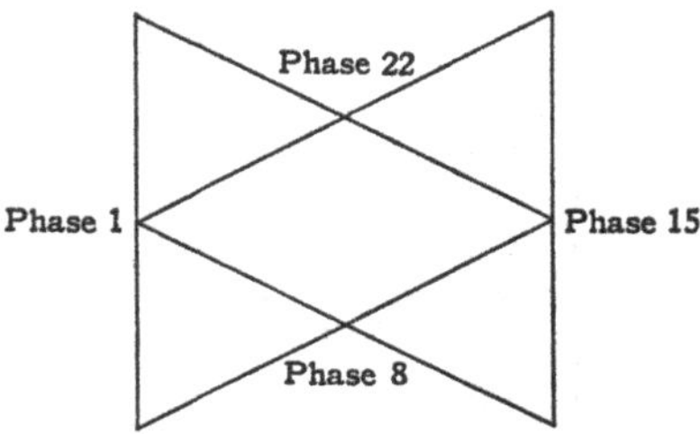

period which follows. I am for the moment only concerned with the incarnation, symbolised by the moon at night.

Phase 1 and Phase 15[31] are not human incarnations because human life is impossible without strife between the *tinctures*. They belong to an order of existence which we shall consider presently. The figure which I have used to represent *Will* at almost complete subjectivity represents the moon just before its round is complete, and instead of using a black disc with a white dot for *Will* at almost complete objectivity I think of the last crescent.

But it is more convenient to set these figures round a circle thus:[32]

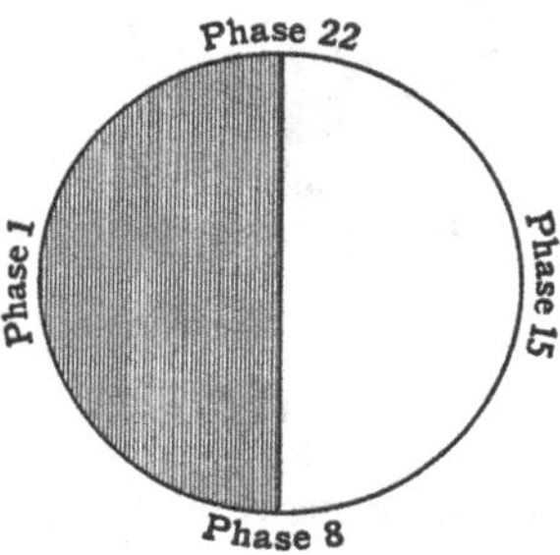

PART II: EXAMINATION OF THE WHEEL

I

During the first months of instruction I had the Great Wheel of the lunar phases as printed at the end of this paragraph, but knew nothing of the cones that explain it, and though I had abundant definitions and descriptions of the *Faculties* at their different stations, did not know why they passed one another at certain points, nor why two moved from left to right like the sun's daily course, two from right to left like the moon in the zodiac.[33] Even when I wrote the first edition of this book I thought the geometrical symbolism so difficult, I understood it so little, that I put it off to a later section; and as I had at that time, for a reason I have explained, to use a romantic setting, I described the Great Wheel as danced on the desert sands by mysterious dancers who left the traces of their feet to puzzle the Caliph of Bagdad and his learned men.[34] I tried to interest my readers in an unexplained rule of thumb that somehow explained the world.

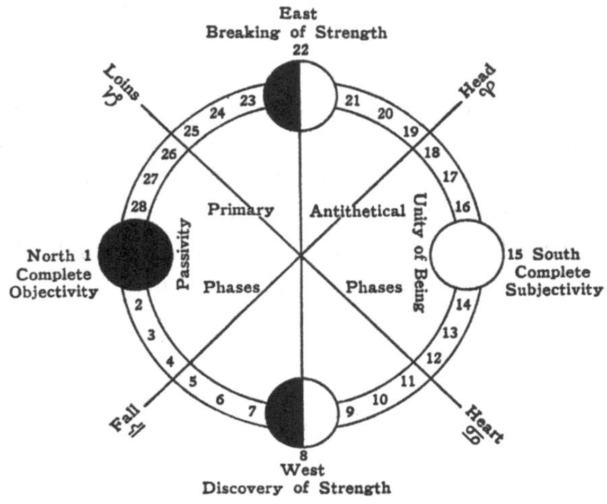

II

This wheel is every completed movement of thought or life, twenty-eight incarnations, a single incarnation, a single judgment or act of thought. Man seeks his opposite or the opposite of his condition, attains his object so far as it is attainable, at Phase 15 and returns* to Phase 1 again.

Phase 15 is called Sun in Moon because the solar or *primary tincture* is consumed by the lunar, but from another point of view it is *Mask* consumed in *Will*; all is beauty. The *Mask* as it were wills itself as beauty, but because, as Plotinus says, things that are of one kind are unconscious, it is an ideal or supernatural incarnation.[36] Phase 1 is called Moon in Sun because the lunar or *antithetical tincture* is consumed in the *primary* or solar, but from another point of

*A similar circular movement fundamental in the works of Giovanni Gentile is, I read somewhere, the half-conscious foundation of the political thought of modern Italy. Individuals and classes complete their personality and then sink back to enrich the mass. Government must, it is held, because all good things have been created by class war, recognise that class war though it may be regulated must never end. It is the old saying of Heraclitus, "War is God of all, and Father of all, some it has made Gods and some men, some bond and some free", and the converse of Marxian Socialism.[35]

view it is the *Body of Fate* consumed in *Creative Mind*; man is submissive and plastic: unless where supersensual power intervenes, the steel-like plasticity of water where the last ripple has been smoothed away. We shall presently have to consider the *Principles* where pure thought is possible, but in the *Faculties* the sole activity and the sole unity is natural or lunar, and in the *primary* phases that unity is moral. At Phase 1 morality is complete submission. All unity is from the *Mask*, and the *antithetical Mask* is described in the automatic script as a "form created by passion to unite us to ourselves", the self so sought is that Unity of Being compared by Dante in the *Convito* to that of "a perfectly proportioned human body".[37] The *Body of Fate* is the sum, not the unity, of fact, fact as it affects a particular man. Only in the Four *Principles* shall we discover the concord of Empedocles. The *Will* is very much the Will described by Croce.*[38] When not affected by the other *Faculties* it has neither emotion, morality nor intellectual interest, but knows how things are done, how windows open and shut, how roads are crossed, everything that we call utility. It seeks its own continuance. Only by the pursuit or acceptance of its direct opposite, that object of desire or moral ideal which is of all possible things the most difficult, and by forcing that form upon the *Body of Fate*, can it attain self-knowledge and expression. Phase 8 and Phase 22 are phases of struggle and tragedy, the first a struggle to find personality, the second to lose it. After Phase 22 and before Phase 1 there is a struggle to accept the fate-imposed unity, from Phase 1 to Phase 8 to escape it.

All such abstract statements are, however, misleading, for we are dealing always with a particular man, the man of Phase 13 or Phase 17 let us say. The *Four Faculties* are not the abstract categories of philosophy, being the result of the four memories of the *Daimon* or ultimate self of that man. His *Body of Fate*, the series of events forced upon him from without, is shaped out of the *Daimon's* memory of the events of his past incarnations; his *Mask* or object of desire or idea of the good, out of its memory of the moments of exaltation in his past lives; his *Will* or normal ego out of its memory of

*The *Four Faculties* somewhat resemble the four moments to which Croce has dedicated four books; that the resemblance is not closer is because Croce makes little use of antithesis and antinomy.

all the events of his present life, whether consciously remembered or not; his *Creative Mind* from its memory of ideas—or universals—displayed by actual men in past lives, or their spirits between lives.

III

When I wish for some general idea which will describe the Great Wheel as an individual life I go to the *Commedia dell' Arte* or improvised drama of Italy.[39] The stage-manager, or *Daimon*, offers his actor an inherited scenario, the *Body of Fate*, and a *Mask* or rôle as unlike as possible to his natural ego or *Will*, and leaves him to improvise through his *Creative Mind* the dialogue and details of the plot. He must discover or reveal a being which only exists with extreme effort, when his muscles are as it were all taut and all his energies active. But this is *antithetical* man. For *primary* man I go to the *Commedia dell' Arte* in its decline.[40] The *Will* is weak and cannot create a rôle, and so, if it transform itself, does so after an accepted pattern, some traditional clown or pantaloon. It has perhaps no object but to move the crowd, and if it "gags" it is that there may be plenty of topical allusions. In the *primary* phases man must cease to desire *Mask* and Image by ceasing from self-expression, and substitute a motive of service for that of self-expression. Instead of the created *Mask* he has an imitative *Mask*; and when he recognises this, his *Mask* may become the historical norm, or an image of mankind. The author of the *Imitation of Christ* was certainly a man of a late *primary* phase.[41] The *antithetical Mask* and *Will* are *free*, and the *primary Mask* and *Will enforced*; and the *free Mask* and *Will* are personality, while the *enforced Mask* and *Will* are code, those limitations which give strength precisely because they are *enforced*. Personality, no matter how habitual, is a constantly renewed choice, varying from an individual charm, in the more *antithetical* phases, to a hard objective dramatisation; but when the *primary* phases begin man is moulded more and more from without.

Antithetical men are, like Landor, violent in themselves because they hate all that impedes their personality,[42] but are in their intellect (*Creative Mind*) gentle, whereas *primary* men whose hatreds are impersonal are violent in their intellect but gentle in themselves, as doubtless Robespierre was gentle.[43]

The *Mask* before Phase 15 is described as a "revelation" because through it the being obtains knowledge of itself, sees itself in personality; while after Phase 15 it is a "concealment", for the being grows incoherent, vague and broken, as its intellect (*Creative Mind*) is more and more concerned with objects that have no relation to its unity but a relation to the unity of society or of material things known through the *Body of Fate*. It adopts a personality which it more and more casts outward, more and more dramatises. It is now a dissolving violent phantom which would grip itself and hold itself together. The being of *antithetical* man is described as full of rage before Phase 12, against all in the world that hinders its expression, after Phase 12, but before Phase 15, the rage is a knife turned against itself. After Phase 15, but before Phase 19, the being is full of phantasy, a continual escape from and yet acknowledgment of all that allures in the world, a continual playing with all that must engulf it. The *primary* is that which serves, the *antithetical* is that which creates.

At Phase 8 is the "Discovery of Strength", its embodiment in sensuality.[44] The imitation that held it to the enforced *Mask*, the norm of the race now a hated convention, has ceased and its own norm has not begun. *Primary* and *antithetical* are equal and fight for mastery; and when this fight is ended through the conviction of weakness and the preparation for rage, the *Mask* becomes once more voluntary. At Phase 22 is the "Breaking of Strength", for here the being makes its last attempt to impose its personality upon the world before the *Mask* becomes enforced once more, character substituted for personality. To these two phases, perhaps to all phases, the being may return up to four times, my instructors say, before it can pass on. It is claimed, however, that four times is the utmost possible. By being is understood that which divides into *Four Faculties*, by individuality the *Will* analysed in relation to itself, by personality the *Will* analysed in relation to the free *Mask*, by character *Will* analysed in relation to the enforced *Mask*. Personality is strongest near Phase 15, individuality near Phase 22 and Phase 8.

In the last phases, Phases 26, 27 and 28, the *Faculties* wear away, grow transparent, and man may see himself as it were arrayed against the supersensual; but of this I shall speak when I consider the *Principles*.

IV

The *Will* looks into a painted picture, the *Creative Mind* looks into a photograph, but both look into something that is the opposite of themselves. The *Creative Mind* contains all the universals in so far as its memory permits their employment, whereas the photograph is heterogeneous. The picture is chosen, the photograph is fated, because by Fate and Necessity—for I need both words—is understood that which comes from without, whereas the *Mask* is predestined, Destiny being that which comes to us from within. We can best explain the heterogeneity of the photograph when we call it the photograph of a crowded street, which the *Creative Mind* when not under the influence of the *Mask* contemplates coldly; while the picture contains but few objects and the contemplating *Will* is impassioned and solitary. When the *Will* predominates the *Mask* or Image is "sensuous"; when *Creative Mind* predominates it is "abstract", when *Mask* predominates it is "idealised", when *Body of Fate* predominates it is "concrete". The automatic script defines "sensuous" in an unexpected way. An object is sensuous if I relate it to myself, "my fire, my chair, my sensation", whereas "a fire, a chair, a sensation", are all concrete or appertain to the *Body of Fate*; while "the fire, the chair, the sensation", because they are looked upon as representative of their kind, are "abstract". To a miser his own money would be "sensuous", another's money "concrete", the money he lacked "idealised", the money economists speak of "abstract".

V

In the Table in section XII the characters of the *Faculties* at all the different phases are described, and the phasal characteristics of a man at any particular phase can be discovered by their means. The descriptions should not be considered as exhaustive but as suggestions to call into imagination the *Four Faculties* at any particular phase.

They were written in the automatic script sometimes two or three, sometimes eight or nine at a time. Even now after years of use I could not re-create them if the Table were lost. I should say they proved a use more prolonged than my own did I not remember that the creators of the script claim a rapidity of thought impossible to our minds. I think of the elaborate pictures one sees between sleeping and waking and often showing powers of design and invention that would have taken hours of an artist's time.

At Phases 11 and 12 occurs what is called the *opening of the tinctures*, at Phase 11 the *antithetical* opens, at Phase 12 the *primary*. A cone is for the moment substituted for the wheel, a gyre encircles the cone, ascending or descending, which completes its journey round the cone, while the larger movement completes a phase.[45] The opening means the reflection inward of the *Four Faculties*: all are as it were mirrored in personality, Unity of Being becomes possible. Hitherto we have been part of something else, but now discover everything within our own nature. Sexual love becomes the most important event in life, for the opposite sex is nature chosen and fated. Personality seeks personality. Every emotion begins to be related to every other as musical notes are related. It is as though we touched a musical string that set other strings vibrating. The *antithetical tincture* (*Will* and *Mask*) opens first because the phases signified by odd numbers are *antithetical*, the *primary tincture* at Phase 12 because those signified by even numbers are *primary*. Though all phases from Phase 8 to Phase 22 are *antithetical*, taken as a whole, and all phases from Phase 22 to Phase 8 *primary*; seen by different analysis the individual phases are alternately *antithetical* and *primary*.[46] At Phase 18 the *primary tincture* closes once more, and at Phase 19 the *antithetical*. At Phases 25 and 26 there is a new opening, and at Phases 4 and 5 a new closing, but this time the *tinctures* open not into personality but into its negation, the whole objectively perceived. One may regard the subjective phases as forming a separate wheel, its Phase 8 between Phases 11 and 12 of the larger wheel, its Phase 22 between Phases 19 and 20; the objective phases as another separate wheel, its Phase 8 between Phases 25 and 26, its Phase 22 between Phases 4 and 5. This wheel between its Phases 8 and 22 is not subjective, from the point of man, but a sharing of or submission to divine personality experienced as spiritual objectivity, whereas its three first and three last phases are physical objectivity. During this spiritual objectivity, or spiritual *primary*, the *Faculties* "wear thin", the *Principles*, which are, when evoked from the point of view of the

Faculties, a sphere, shine through.[47] At Phase 15 and Phase 1 occurs what is called the *interchange of the tinctures*, those thoughts, emotions, energies, which were *primary* before Phase 15 or Phase 1 are *antithetical* after, those that were *antithetical* are *primary*. I was told, for instance, that before the historical Phase 15 the *antithetical tincture* of the average European was dominated by reason and desire, the *primary* by race and emotion, and that after Phase 15 this was reversed, his subjective nature had been passionate and logical but was now enthusiastic and sentimental. I have made little use of this interchange in my account of the twenty-eight incarnations because when I wrote it I did not understand the relation between the change and Unity of Being. Every phase is in itself a wheel; the individual soul is awakened by a violent oscillation (one thinks of Verlaine oscillating between the church and the brothel) until it sinks in on that Whole where the contraries are united, the antinomies resolved.[48]

VI

Rules for discovering True and False Masks

When the Will is in antithetical phases the True Mask is the effect of Creative Mind of opposite phase upon that phase; and the False Mask is the effect of Body of Fate of opposite phase upon that phase.

The True *Mask* of Phase 17, for instance, is "Simplification through intensity", derived from Phase 3, modified by the *Creative Mind* of that phase, which is described as "Simplicity" and comes from Phase 27, which is that of the Saint.

The False *Mask* of Phase 17 is "Dispersal", derived from Phase 3, modified by the *Body of Fate* of the phase which comes from Phase 13 and is described as "Interest". It will be found that this word describes with great accuracy the kind of "Dispersal" which weakens men of Phase 17 when they try to live in the *primary tincture*.

When the Will is in primary phases the True Mask is the effect of Body of Fate of opposite phase upon that phase; and the False Mask is the effect of Creative Mind of opposite phase upon that phase.

The True *Mask* of Phase 3 is "Innocence", derived from Phase 17, modified by the *Body of Fate* of the phase which is described as "Loss" and comes from Phase 27, which is that of the Saint.

The False *Mask* of Phase 3 is "Folly" derived from Phase 17, modified by the *Creative Mind* of that phase which is described as "Creative imagination through *antithetical* emotion" and comes from Phase 13. The *primary* Phase 3, when it attempts to live *antithetically*, gives itself up to inconsequence because it cannot be creative in the *Mask*. On the other hand, when it lives according to the *primary*, and is true to phase, it takes from its opposite phase delight in passing things, sees "a world in a grain of sand, a Heaven in a wild flower" and becomes a child playing, knows nothing of consequence and purpose.[49] "Loss" affects Phase 17 itself as an enforced withdrawal of *primary* desire, for the *Body of Fate* is inimical to *antithetical* natures.

Only long familiarity with the system can make the whole Table of *Masks*, *Creative Minds*, etc.—see Section XII—intelligible; it should be studied by the help of these two following rules:

> *In an antithetical phase the being seeks by the help of the Creative Mind to deliver the Mask from Body of Fate.*
>
> *In a primary phase the being seeks by the help of the Body of Fate to deliver the Creative Mind from the Mask.*

VII

Rules for finding the True and False Creative Mind

When the Will is in antithetical phases the True Creative Mind is derived from the Creative Mind phase, modified by the Creative Mind of that phase; while the False Creative Mind is derived from the Creative Mind phase, modified by the Body of Fate of that phase.

For instance, the True *Creative Mind* of Phase 17, "Creative Imagination through *antithetical* Emotion", is derived from Phase 13 as that phase is modified by its *Creative Mind*, which is described as "Subjective truth" and comes from Phase 17.

The False *Creative Mind* of Phase 17, "Enforced self-realization", is derived from Phase 13 as that phase is modified by its *Body of Fate*, "Enforced love", "enforced love of another" derived from Phase 3.

When the Will is in primary phases the True Creative Mind is derived from Creative Mind phase, modified by the Body of Fate of that phase; while the False Creative Mind is derived from the Creative Mind phase modified by the False Creative Mind of that phase.

For instance, the True *Creative Mind* of Phase 27 is described as "Supersensual receptivity" and is derived from Phase 3 as that phase is modified by its *Body of Fate* derived from Phase 13, and described as "Interest"; while its False *Creative Mind* is described as "Pride" and is derived from Phase 3, modified by the False *Creative Mind* of that phase which is derived from Phase 27 and described as "Abstraction".

VIII

Rule for finding Body of Fate

The *Body of Fate* of any particular phase is the effect of the whole nature of its *Body of Fate* phase upon that particular phase. As, however, the *Body of Fate* is always *primary* it is in sympathy with the *primary* phase while it opposes the *antithetical* phase; in this it is the reverse of the *Mask*, which is sympathetic to an *antithetical* phase but opposes a *primary*.

IX

Subdivisions of the Wheel

Excluding the four phases of crisis (Phases 8, 22, 15, 1), each quarter consists of six phases, or of two sets of three. In every case the first phase of each set can be described as a manifestation of power, the second of a code or arrangement of powers, and the third of a belief, the belief being an appreciation of, or submission to some quality which becomes power in the next phase. The reason of this is that each set of three is itself a wheel, and has the same character as the Great Wheel. The Phases 1 to 8 are associated with elemental *earth*, being phases of germination and sprouting; those between Phase 8 and Phase 15 with elemental *water*, because there the image-making power is at its height; those between Phase 15 and Phase 22 with elemental *air*, because through *air*, or space, things are divided from one another, and here intellect is at its height; those between Phase 22 and Phase 1 with elemental *fire*, because here all things are made simple. The *Will* is strongest in the first quarter, *Mask* in second, *Creative Mind* in third, and the *Body of Fate* in fourth.

There are other divisions and attributions to be considered later.

X

Discords, Oppositions and Contrasts

The being becomes conscious of itself as a separate being, because of certain facts of Opposition and Discord, the emotional Opposition of *Will* and *Mask*, the intellectual Opposition of *Creative Mind* and *Body of Fate*, Discords between *Will* and *Creative Mind*, *Creative Mind* and *Mask*, *Mask* and *Body of Fate*, *Body of Fate* and *Will*. A Discord is always the enforced understanding of the unlikeness of *Will* and *Mask* or of *Creative Mind* and *Body of Fate*. There is an enforced attraction between Opposites, for the *Will* has a natural desire for the *Mask* and the *Creative Mind* a natural perception of the *Body of Fate*; in one the dog bays the Moon,[50] in the other the eagle stares on the Sun by natural right.[51] When, however, the *Creative Mind* deceives the *Will* in an *antithetical* phase, by offering it some *primary* image of the *Mask*, or when the *Will* offers to the *Creative Mind* an emotion that should be turned towards the *Mask* alone, the Discord emerges again in its simplicity because of the jarring of the emotion, the grinding out of the Image. On the other hand, it may be the *Mask* that slips on to the *Body of Fate* till we confuse what we would be with what we must be. As the Discords through the circling of the *Four Faculties* become Oppositions, when as at Phase 15 (say) the *Creative Mind* comes to be opposite the *Mask*, they share the qualities of Opposition. As the *Faculties* approach to one another, on the other hand, Discord gradually becomes identity, and one or other, according to whether it takes place at Phase 1 or Phase 15, is weakened and finally absorbed, *Creative Mind* in *Will* at Phase 15, *Will* in *Creative Mind* at Phase 1 and so on; while if it be at Phase 8 or Phase 22, first one predominates and then the other and there is instability.

Without this continual Discord through Deception there would be no conscience, no activity; Deception is a technical term of my teachers and may be substituted for "desire". Life is an endeavour, made vain by the four sails of its mill, to come to a double contemplation, that of the chosen Image, that of the fated Image.

There are also Harmonies, but these which are connected with the whole figure can be best considered in relation to another part of the System.

XI

The Four Perfections and the Four Automatonisms

The Four Perfections can only be understood when their phases are studied in detail; it will be obvious for instance that self-sacrifice must be the typical virtue of phases where instinct or race is predominant, and especially in those three phases that come before reflection. Automatonism in *antithetical* phases arises from the *Mask* and *Creative Mind,* when separated from the *Body of Fate* and *Will*, through refusal of, or rest from conflict; and in *primary* phases from the *Body of Fate* and *Will*, when weary of the struggle for complete *primary* existence or when they refuse that struggle. It does not necessarily mean that the man is not true to phase or, as it is said, out of phase; the most powerful natures are precisely those who most often need Automatonism as a rest. It is perhaps an element in our enjoyment of art and literature, being awakened in our minds by rhythm and by pattern. He is, however, out of phase, if he refuse for anything but need of rest the conflict with the *Body of Fate* which is the source of *antithetical* energy and so falls under imitative or creative Automatonism, or if in *primary* phases he refuse conflict with the *Mask* and so falls under obedient or instinctive Automatonism.

XII

Table of the Four Faculties

Each *Faculty* is placed after the number of the phase where it is formed, not after the phase which it affects.

TABLE OF THE FOUR FACULTIES

WILL	MASK	CREATIVE MIND	BODY OF FATE
1. No	description except	Complete plasticity.	
2. Beginning of energy.	*True*. Illusion. *False*. Delusion.	*True*. Physical activity. *False*. Cunning.	Enforced love of the world.
3. Beginning of ambition.	*True*. Simplification through intensity. *False*. Dispersal.	*True*. Supersensual receptivity. *False*. Pride.	Enforced love of another.
4. Desire for *primary* objects.	*True*. Intensity through emotions. *False*. Curiosity.	*True*. Beginning of the abstract supersensual. *False*. Fascination of sin.	Enforced intellectual action.
5. Separation from innocence.	*True*. Conviction. *False*. Domination.	*True*. Rhetoric. *False*. Spiritual arrogance.	Enforced belief.
6. Artificial individuality.	*True*. Fatalism. *False*. Superstition.	*True*. Constructive emotion. *False*. Authority.	Enforced emotion.
7. Assertion of individuality.	*True*. Self-analysis. *False*. Self-adaptation.	*True*. Creation through pity. *False*. Self-driven desire.	Enforced sensuality.
8. War between individuality and race.	*True*. Self-immolation. *False*. Self-assurance.	*True*. Amalgamation. *False*. Despair.	The beginning of strength.
9. Belief takes place of individuality.	*True*. Wisdom. *False*. Self-pity.	*True*. Domination of the intellect. *False*. Distortion.	Adventure that excites the individuality.
10. The image-breaker.	*True*. Self-reliance. *False*. Isolation.	*True*. Dramatisation of *Mask*. *False*. Self-desecration.	Humanity.

TABLE OF THE FOUR FACULTIES—*Continued*

WILL	MASK	CREATIVE MIND	BODY OF FATE
11. The consumer. The pyre-builder.	*True*. Consciousness of self. *False*. Self-consciousness.	*True*. Emotional intellect. *False*. The Unfaithful.	Natural law.
12. The Forerunner.	*True*. Self-realization. *False*. Self-abandonment.	*True*. Emotional philosophy. *False*. Enforced lure.	Search.
13. The sensuous man.	*True*. Renunciation. *False*. Emulation.	*True*. Creative imagination through *antithetical* emotion. *False*. Enforced self-realization.	Interest.
14. The obsessed man.	*True*. Oblivion. *False*. Malignity.	*True*. Vehemence. *False*. Opinionated will.	None except monotony.
15. No	description except	Complete beauty.	
16. The positive man.	*True*. Player on Pan's Pipes. *False*. Fury.	*True*. Emotional will. *False*. Terror.	The Fool is his own Body of Fate.
17. The *Daimonic* man.	*True*. Innocence. *False*. Folly.	*True*. Subjective truth. *False*. Morbidity.	None except impersonal action.
18. The emotional man.	*True*. Passion. *False*. Will.	*True*. Subjective philosophy. *False*. War between two forms of expression.	The Hunchback is his own Body of Fate.
19. The assertive man.	*True*. Excess. *False*. Limitation.	*True*. Moral iconoclasm. *False*. Self-assertion.	Persecution.

TABLE OF THE FOUR FACULTIES—*Continued*

WILL	MASK	CREATIVE MIND	BODY OF FATE
20. The concrete man.	*True*. Justice. *False*. Tyranny.	*True*. Domination through emotional construction. *False*. Reformation.	Objective action.
21. The acquisitive man.	*True*. Altruism. *False*. Efficiency.	*True*. Self-dramatisation. *False*. Anarchy.	Success.
22. Balance between ambition and contemplation.	*True*. Courage. *False*. Fear.	*True*. Versatility. *False*. Impotence.	Temptation through strength.[52]
23. The receptive man.	*True*. Facility. *False*. Obscurity.	*True*. Heroic sentiment. *False*. Dogmatic sentimentality.	Enforced triumph of achievement.
24. The end of ambition.	*True*. Organisation. *False*. Inertia.	*True*. Ideality. *False*. Derision.	Enforced success of action.
25. The conditional man.	*True*. Rejection. *False*. Moral indifference.	*True*. Social intellect. *False*. Limitation.	Enforced failure of action.
26. The multiple man also called The Hunchback.	*True*. Self-exaggeration. *False*. Self-abandonment.	*True*. First perception of character. *False*. Mutilation.	Enforced disillusionment.
27. The Saint.	*True*. Self-expression. *False*. Self-absorption.	*True*. Simplicity. *False*. Abstraction.	Enforced loss.
28. The Fool.	*True*. Serenity. *False*. Self-distrust.	*True*. Hope. *False*. Moroseness.	Enforced illusion.

XIII

Characters of Certain Phases

Four Perfections

At P. 2, P. 3, P. 4 .	Self-sacrifice
At P. 13 . .	Self-knowledge
At P. 16, P. 17, P. 18 .	Unity of Being
At P. 27 . .	Sanctity

Four Types of Wisdom*

At P. 4 . .	Wisdom of Desire
At P. 18 . .	Wisdom of Heart
At P. 12 . .	Wisdom of Intellect
At P. 26 . .	Wisdom of Knowledge

Four Contests

At P. 1 . .	Moral
At P. 8 . .	Emotional
At P. 15 . .	Physical
At P. 22 . .	Spiritual or supersensual

Rage, Fantasy, etc.

From P. 8 to P. 12 .	Rage
From P. 12 to P. 15 .	Spiritual or supersensual Rage
From P. 15 to P. 19 .	Fantasy
From P. 19 to P. 22 .	Power

*I give the Four Types of Wisdom as they were given. I have more than once transposed Heart and Intellect, suspecting a mistake; but have come to the conclusion that my instructors placed them correctly, the nature of the wisdom depending upon the position of the *Creative Mind*.

XIV

General Character of Creative Mind*

(1)	Affecting	28, 1, 2 from 2, 1, 28. Controlled.
(2)	"	3, 4, 5, 6 from 27, 26, 25, 24. Transformatory.
(3)	"	7, 8, 9 from 23, 22, 21. Mathematical.
(4)	"	10, 11, 12 from 20, 19, 18. Intellectually passionate.
(5)	"	13 from 17. Stillness.
(6)	"	14, 15, 16 from 16, 15, 14. Emotional.
(7)	"	17, 18, 19, 20 from 13, 12, 11, 10. Emotionally passionate.
(8)	"	21, 22, 23 from 9, 8, 7. Rational.
(9)	"	24 from 6. Obedient.
(10)	"	25, 26, 27 from 3, 4, 5. Serenity.

XV

General Character of Body of Fate affecting Certain Phases

(1)	Affecting	28, 1, 2 from 16, 15, 14. Joy.
(2)	"	3, 4, 5, 6 from 13, 12, 11, 10. Breathing.
(3)	"	7, 8, 9 from 9, 8, 7. Tumult.
(4)	"	10, 11, 12 from 6, 5, 4. Tension.
(5)	"	13 from 3. Disease.
(6)	"	14, 15, 16 from 2, 1, 28. The world.
(7)	"	17, 18, 19, 20 from 27, 26, 25, 24. Sorrow.
(8)	"	21, 22, 23 from 23, 22, 21. Ambition.
(9)	"	24 from 20. Success.
(10)	"	25, 26, 27 from 19, 18, 17. Absorption.

*This and the following Table are divided into ten divisions because they were given me in this form, and I have not sufficient confidence in my knowledge to turn them into the more convenient twelvefold divisions. At first my instructors divided the Great Year also into ten divisions.[53]

XVI

Table of the Quarters

The Four Contests
of the antithetical within itself

First quarter.	With body.	In the first quarter body should win, in second heart, etc.
Second "	With heart.	
Third "	With mind.	
Fourth "	With soul.	

Four automatonisms

First quarter.	Instinctive.
Second "	Imitative.
Third "	Creative.
Fourth "	Obedient.

Four Conditions of the Will

First quarter.	Instinctive.
Second "	Emotional.
Third "	Intellectual.
Fourth "	Moral.

Four Conditions of the Mask

First quarter.	Intensity (affecting third quarter).
Second "	Tolerance (affecting fourth quarter).
Third "	Convention or systematization (affecting first quarter).
Fourth "	Self-analysis (affecting second quarter).

Defects of False Creative Mind which bring the False Mask

First quarter.	Sentimentality.
Second "	Brutality (desire for root facts of life).
Third "	Hatred.
Fourth "	Insensitiveness.

Note.—In *primary* phases these defects separate *Mask* from *Body of Fate*, in *antithetical*, *Creative Mind* from *Body of Fate*.

Elemental Attributions

Earth . . .	First quarter
Water . . .	Second quarter
Air . . .	Third quarter
Fire . . .	Fourth quarter

XVII

Unclassified Attributes

Mask worn—moral and emotional.
Mask carried—emotional.

Abstraction

Strong at 6, 7, 8.
Strongest at 22, 23, 24, 25.
Begins at 19, less at 20, increases again at 21.

Three Energies

Images from self give emotion.
Images from world give passion.
Images from the supersensual give will.

Enforced and Free Faculties

In *primary* phases the *Mask* and *Will* are enforced, the *Creative Mind* and *Body of Fate* free.
In *antithetical* phases the *Creative Mind* and *Body of Fate* are enforced and the *Mask* and *Will* free.

The Two Conditions

Primary means democratic.
Antithetical means aristocratic.

The Two Directions

Phase 1 to Phase 15 is towards Nature.
Phase 15 to Phase 1 is towards God.

Relations

Those between *Will* and *Mask*, *Creative Mind* and *Body of Fate* are oppositions, or contrasts.
Those between *Will* and *Creative Mind*, *Mask* and *Body of Fate* discords.

Objectivities

From Phase 23 to Phase 25 is Physical Objectivity.
From Phase 26 to Phase 28 is Spiritual Objectivity.

Consciousness

From Phase 8 to Phase 22 is *Will*.
From Phase 28 to Phase 8 is *Creative Mind*.[54]

Part III: THE TWENTY-EIGHT INCARNATIONS[55]

Phase One and the Interchange of the Tinctures

As will be seen, when late phases are described, every achievement of a being, after Phase 22, is an elimination of the individual intellect and a discovery of the moral life. When the individual intellect lingers on, it is arrogance, self-assertion, a sterile abstraction, for the being is forced by the growing *primary tincture* to accept first the service of, and later on absorption in, the *primary* Whole, a sensual or supersensual objectivity.

When the old *antithetical* becomes the new *primary*, moral feeling is changed into an organisation of experience which must in its turn seek a unity, the whole of experience. When the old *primary* becomes the new *antithetical*, the old realisation of an objective moral law is changed into a subconscious turbulent instinct. The world of rigid custom and law is broken up by "the uncontrollable mystery upon the bestial floor".[56]

Phase 1 not being human can better be described after Phase 28. None of those phases where the *tinctures* open into the Whole, except Phase 27, produce character of sufficient distinctiveness to become historical.

Phase Two

Will—Beginning of Energy.
Mask (from Phase 16). *True*—Player on Pan's Pipes.[57]
False—Fury.
Creative Mind (from Phase 28). *True*—Hope. *False*—Moroseness.
Body of Fate (from Phase 14)—"None except monotony".

When the man lives out of phase and desires the *Mask*, and so permits it to dominate the *Creative Mind*, he copies the emotional explosion of Phase 16 in so far as difference of phase permits. He gives himself to a violent animal assertion and can only destroy;

strike right and left. Incapable of sharing the spiritual absorption of Phase 28, his *Creative Mind* fills him with ignorance and gloom.

> But when they find the frowning Babe,
> Terror strikes through the region wide:
> They cry "The babe! the babe is born!"
> And flee away on every side.[58]

But if he live according to phase, he uses the *Body of Fate* to clear the intellect of the influence of the *Mask*. He frees himself from emotion; and the *Body of Fate*, derived from Phase 14, pushes back the mind into its own supersensual impulse, until it grows obedient to all that recurs, and the *Mask*, now entirely *enforced*, is a rhythmical impulse. He gives himself up to Nature as the Fool (Phase 28) gave himself to God. He is neither immoral nor violent but innocent; is as it were the breath stirring on the face of the deep;[59] the smile on the face of a but half-awakened child. Nobody of our age has, it may be, met him, certainly no record of such meeting exists, but, were such meeting possible, he would be remembered as a form of joy, for he would seem more entirely living than all other men, a personification or summing up of all natural life. He would decide on this or that by no balance of the reason but by an infallible joy, and if born amid a rigid mechanical order, he would make for himself a place, as a dog will scratch a hole for itself in loose earth.

Here, as at Phase 16, the ordinary condition is sometimes reversed, and instead of ugliness, otherwise characteristic of this as of all *primary* phases, there is beauty. The new *antithetical tincture* (the old *primary* reborn) is violent. A new birth, when the product of an extreme contrast in the past life of the individual, is sometimes so violent that lacking foreign admixture it forestalls its ultimate physical destiny. It forces upon the *primary* and upon itself a beautiful form. It has the muscular balance and force of an animal good-humour with all appropriate comeliness as in the Dancing Faun.[60] If this rare accident does not occur, the body is coarse, not deformed, but coarse from lack of sensitiveness, and is most fitted for rough physical labour.

Seen by those lyrical poets who draw their *Masks* from early phases, the man of Phase 2 is transfigured. Weary of an energy that defines and judges, weary of intellectual self-expression, they desire some "concealment", some transcendent intoxication. The bodily instincts, subjectively perceived, become the cup wreathed with ivy.[61] Perhaps even a *Body of Fate* from any early phase may suffice to create this Image, but when it affects Phase 13 and Phase 14 the Image will be more sensuous, more like immediate experience. The Image is a myth, a woman, a landscape, or anything whatsoever that is an external expression of the *Mask*.

> The Kings of Inde their jewelled sceptres vail,
> And from their treasures scatter pearlèd hail;
> Great Brama from his mystic heaven groans
> And all his priesthood moans;
> Before young Bacchus' eye-wink turning pale.[62]

Phase Three

Will—Beginning of Ambition.
Mask (from Phase 17). *True*—Innocence. *False*—Folly.
Creative Mind (from Phase 27). *True*—Simplicity. *False*—Abstraction.
Body of Fate (from Phase 13)—Interest.

Out of phase and copying the opposite phase he gives himself up to a kind of clodhopper folly, that keeps his intellect moving among conventional ideas with a sort of make-believe. Incapable of consecutive thought and of moral purpose, he lives miserably seeking to hold together some consistent plan of life, patching rags upon rags because that is expected of him, or out of egotism. If on the other hand he uses his *Body of Fate* to purify his *Creative Mind* of the *Mask*, if he is content to permit his senses and his subconscious nature to dominate his intellect, he takes delight in all that passes; but because he claims nothing of his own, chooses nothing, thinks that no one thing is better than another, he will not endure a pang because all passes. Almost without intellect, it is a phase of perfect bodily sanity, for, though the body is still in close contact with supersensual rhythm, it is no longer absorbed in that rhythm; eyes and ears are open; one instinct balances another; every season brings its delight.

He who bends to himself a joy
Does the wingèd life destroy,
But he who kisses the joy as it flies
Lives in eternity's sunrise.[63]

Seen by lyrical poets, of whom so many have belonged to the fantastic Phase 17, the man of this phase becomes an Image where simplicity and intensity are united, he seems to move among yellowing corn or under overhanging grapes. He gave to Landor his shepherds and hamadryads,[64] to Morris his *Water of the Wondrous Isles*,[65] to Shelley his wandering lovers and sages,[66] and to Theocritus all his flocks and pastures;[67] and of what else did Bembo think when he cried, "Would that I were a shepherd that I might look daily down upon Urbino"?[68] Imagined in some *antithetical* mind, seasonal change and bodily sanity seem images of lasting passion and the body's beauty.

Phase Four

Will—Desire for Exterior World.
Mask (from Phase 18). *True*—Passion. *False*—Will.
Creative Mind (from Phase 26). *True*—First Perception of Character. *False*—Mutilation.
Body of Fate (from Phase 12)—Search.

When out of phase he attempts *antithetical* wisdom (for reflection has begun), separates himself from instinct (hence "mutilation"), and tries to enforce upon himself and others all kinds of abstract or conventional ideas which are for him, being outside his experience, mere make-believe. Lacking *antithetical* capacity, and *primary* observation, he is aimless and blundering, possesses nothing except the knowledge that there is something known to others that is not mere instinct. True to phase, his interest in everything that happens, in all that excites his instinct ("search"), is so keen that he has no desire to claim anything for his own will; nature still dominates his thought as passion; yet instinct grows reflective. He is full of practical wisdom, a wisdom of saws and proverbs, or founded upon concrete examples.[69] He can see nothing beyond sense, but sense expands and contracts to meet his needs, and the needs of those who trust him. It is as though he woke suddenly out of sleep and thereupon saw more and remembered more than others. He has "the wisdom of instinct", a wisdom perpetually excited by all those hopes and needs which concern his well-being or that of the race (*Creative Mind* from Phase 12 and so acting from whatever in race corresponds to personality unified in thought). The men of the opposite phase, or of the phases nearly opposite, worn out by a wisdom held with labour and uncertainty, see persons of this phase as images of peace. Two passages of Browning come to mind:

> An old hunter, talking with gods
> Or sailing with troops of friends to Tenedos.[70]

> A King lived long ago,
> In the morning of the world,
> When Earth was nigher Heaven than now:
> And the King's locks curled,
> Disparting o'er a forehead full
> As the milk-white space 'twixt horn and horn
> Of some sacrificial bull—
> Only calm as a babe new-born:
> For he was got to a sleepy mood,
> So safe from all decrepitude,
> From age with its bane, so sure gone by,
> (The Gods so loved him while he dreamed)
> That, having lived thus long, there seemed
> No need the King should ever die.[71]

The Opening and Closing of the Tinctures

Since Phase 26 the *primary tincture* has so predominated, man is so sunk in Fate, in life, that there is no reflection, no experience, because that which reflects, that which acquires experience, has been drowned. Man cannot think of himself as separate from that which he sees with the bodily eye or in the mind's eye. He neither loves nor hates though he may be in hatred or in love. Birdalone in *The Water of the Wondrous Isles* (a woman of Phase 3 reflected in an *antitheti-*

cal mind) falls in love with her friend's lover and he with her. There is great sorrow but no struggle, her decision to disappear is sudden as if compelled by some power over which she has no control. Has she not perhaps but decided as her unknown fathers and mothers compelled, but conformed to the lineaments of her race? Is she not a child of "Weird", are not all in the most *primary* phases children of "Weird" exercising an unconscious discrimination towards all that before Phase 1 defines their Fate, and after Phase 1 their race?[72] Every achievement of their souls, Phase 1 being passed, springs up out of the body, and their work is to substitute for a life where all is Fate frozen into rule and custom, a life where all is fused by instinct; with them to hunger, to taste, to desire, is to grow wise.

Between Phase 4 and Phase 5 the *tinctures* ceased to be drowned in the One, and reflection begins. Between Phases 25, 26 and Phases 4, 5, there is an approach to absolute surrender of the *Will*, first to God, then, as Phase 1 passes away, to Nature, and the surrender is the most complete form of the freedom of the *Body of Fate* which has been increasing since Phase 22. When Man identifies himself with his Fate, when he is able to say "Thy Will is our freedom" or when he is perfectly natural, that is to say, perfectly a portion of his surroundings, he is free even though all his actions can be foreseen, even though every action is a logical deduction from all that went before it.[73] He is all Fate but has no Destiny.

Phase Five

Will—Separation from Innocence.
Mask (from Phase 19). *True*—Excess. *False*—Limitation.
Creative Mind (from Phase 25). *True*—Social Intellect.
False—Limitation.
Body of Fate (from Phase 11)—Natural Law.

Out of phase, and seeking *antithetical* emotion, he is sterile, passing from one insincere attitude to another, moving through a round of moral images torn from their context and so without meaning. He is so proud of each separation from experience that he becomes a sort of angry or smiling Punch with a lath between his wooden arms striking here and there.[74] His *Body of Fate* is *enforced*, for he has reversed the condition of his phase and finds himself at conflict with a world which offers him nothing but temptation and affront. True to phase, he is the direct opposite of all this. Abstraction has indeed begun, but it comes to him as a portion of experience cut off from everything but itself and therefore fitted to be the object of reflection. He no longer touches, eats, drinks, thinks and feels Nature, but sees her as something from which he is separating himself, something that he may dominate, though only for a moment and by some fragmentary violence of sensation or of thought. Nature may seem half gone, but the laws of Nature have appeared and he can change her rhythms and her seasons by his knowledge. He lives in the moment but with an intensity Phases 2, 3 and 4 have never known, the *Will* approaches its climax, he is no longer like a man but half-awakened. He is a corrupter, disturber, wanderer, a founder of sects and peoples, and works with extravagant energy, and his reward is but to live in its glare.

Seen by a poet of the opposite phase, by a man hiding fading emotion under broken emphasis, he is Byron's Don Juan or his Giaour.[75]

PHASE SIX

Will—Artificial Individuality.
Mask (from Phase 20). *True*—Justice. *False*—Tyranny.
Creative Mind (from Phase 24). *True*—Ideality. *False*—Derision.
Body of Fate (from Phase 10)—Humanity.
Example: Walt Whitman.[76]

Had Walt Whitman lived out of phase, desire to prove that all his emotions were healthy and intelligible, to set his practical sanity above all not made in his fashion, to cry "Thirty years old and in perfect health!" would have turned him into some kind of jibing demagogue;[77] and to think of him would be to remember that Thoreau, picking up the jaw-bone of a pig with no tooth missing, recorded that there also was perfect health.[78] He would, that he might believe in himself, have compelled others to believe. Not being out of phase, he used his *Body of Fate* (his interest in crowds, in casual loves and affections, in all summary human experience) to clear intellect of *antithetical* emotion (always insincere from Phase 1 to Phase 8), and haunted and hunted by the now involuntary *Mask*, created an Image of vague, half-civilised man, all his thought and impulse a product of democratic bonhomie, of schools, of colleges, of public discussion. Abstraction had been born, but it remained the abstraction of a community, of a tradition, a synthesis starting, not as with Phases 19, 20 and 21 with logical deduction from an observed fact, but from the whole experience or from some experience of the individual or of the community: "I have such and such a feeling. I have such and such a belief. What follows from feeling, what from belief?" While Thomas Aquinas, whose historical epoch was nearly of this phase, summed up in abstract categories all possible experience, not that he might know but that he might feel, Walt Whitman makes catalogues of all that has moved him, or amused his eye, that he may grow more poetical. Experience is all-absorbing, subordinating observed fact, drowning even truth itself, if truth is conceived of as something apart from impulse and instinct and from the *Will*. Impulse or instinct begins to be all in all. In a little while, though not yet, it must, sweeping away catalogue and category, fill the mind with terror.

Phase Seven

Will—Assertion of Individuality.[79]
Mask (from Phase 21). *True*—Altruism. *False*—Efficiency.
Creative Mind (from Phase 23). *True*—Heroic sentiment. *False*—Dogmatic sentimentality.
Body of Fate (from Phase 9)—Adventure that excites the individuality.
Examples: George Borrow, Alexandre Dumas, Thomas Carlyle, James Macpherson.[80]

At Phases 2, 3 and 4 the man moved within tradition or seasonable limits, but since Phase 5 limits have grown indefinite; public codes, all that depend upon habit, are all but dissolved, even the catalogues and categories of Phase 6 are no longer sufficient. If out of phase the man desires to be the man of Phase 21; an impossible desire, for that man is all but the climax of intellectual complexity, and all men, from Phase 2 to Phase 7 inclusive, are intellectually simple. His instincts are all but at their apex of complexity, and he is bewildered and must soon be helpless. The dissolving character, out of phase, desires the breaking personality, and though it cannot possess or even conceive of personality, seeing that its thoughts and emotions are common to all, it can create a grandiloquent phantom and by deceiving others deceive itself; and presently we shall discover Phase 21, out of phase, bragging of an imaginary naïveté.

Phase 7 when true to phase surrenders to the *Body of Fate* which, being derived from the phase where personality first shows itself, is excited into forms of character so dissolved in *Will*, in instinct, that they are hardly distinguishable from personality. These forms of character, not being self-dependent like personality, are, however, inseparable from circumstance: a gesture or a pose born of a situation and forgotten when the situation has passed; a last act of courage, a defiance of the dogs that must soon tear the man into pieces. Such men have a passion for history, for the scene, for the adventure. They delight in actions, which they cannot consider apart from setting sun or a storm at sea or some great battle, and that are inspired by emotions that move all hearers because such that all understand.

Alexandre Dumas was the phase in its perfection, George Borrow when it halts a little, for Borrow was at moments sufficiently out of phase to know that he was naïve and to brag of imaginary intellectual subjectivity, as when he paraded an unbelievable fit of the horrors, or his mastery of many tongues. Carlyle like Macpherson showed the phase at its worst. He neither could nor should have cared for anything but the personalities of history, but he used them as so many metaphors in a vast popular rhetoric, for the expression of thoughts that seeming his own were the work of preachers and angry ignorant congregations. So noisy, so threatening that rhetoric, so great his own energy, that two generations passed before men noticed that he had written no sentence not of coarse humour that clings to the memory. Sexual impotence had doubtless weakened the *Body of Fate* and so strengthened the False *Mask*, yet one doubts if any mere plaster of ant's eggs could have helped where there was so great insincerity.[81]

Phase Eight

Will—War between Individuality and Race.
Mask (from Phase 22). *True*—Courage. *False*—Fear.
Creative Mind (from Phase 22). *True*—Versatility. *False*—Impotence.
Body of Fate (from Phase 8)—The beginning of strength.
Example: The Idiot of Dostoyevsky perhaps.[82]
Out of phase, a condition of terror; when true to phase, of courage unbroken through defeat.

From Phase 1 to Phase 7, there has been a gradual weakening of all that is *primary*. Character (the *Will* analysed in relation to the *enforced Mask*) has become individuality (the *Will* analysed in relation to itself), but now, though individuality persists through another phase, personality (the *Will* analysed in relation to the free *Mask*) must predominate. So long as the *primary tincture* predominated, the *antithetical tincture* accepted its manner of perception; character and individuality were enlarged by those vegetative and sensitive faculties excited by the *Body of Fate*, the nearest a *primary* nature can come to *antithetical* emotion. But now the bottle must be burst. The struggle of idealised or habitual theologised thought with instinct, mind with body, of the waning *primary* with the growing *antithetical*, must be decided, and the vegetative and sensitive faculties must for a while take the sway.[83] Only then can the *Will* be forced to recognise the weakness of the *Creative Mind* when unaided by the *Mask*, and so to permit the *enforced Mask* to change into the free. Every new modification or codification of morality has been its attempt, acting through the *Creative Mind*, to set order upon the instinctive and vegetative faculties, and it must now feel that it can create order no longer. It is the very nature of a struggle, where the soul must lose all form received from the objectively accepted conscience of the world, that it denies us an historical example. One thinks of possible examples only to decide that Hartley Coleridge is not amongst them,[84] that the brother of the Brontës may only seem to be because we know so little about him,[85] but that Dostoyevsky's Idiot is almost certainly an example. But Dostoyevsky's Idiot was too matured a type, he had passed too many times through the twenty-eight phases to help our understanding. Here for the most part are those obscure wastrels who seem powerless to free themselves from some sensual temptation—drink, women, drugs—and who cannot in a life of continual crisis create any lasting thing. The being is often born up to four times at this one phase, it is said, before the *antithetical tincture* attains its mastery. The being clings like a drowning man to every straw, and it is precisely this clinging, this seemingly vain reaching forth for strength, amidst the collapse of all those public thoughts and habits that are the support of *primary* man, that enables it to enter at last upon Phase 9. It has to find its strength by a transformation of that very instinct which has hitherto been its weakness and so to gather up the strewn and broken members. The union of *Creative Mind* and *Mask* in opposition to *Body of Fate* and *Will*, intensifies this struggle by dividing the nature into halves which have no interchange of qualities. The man is inseparable from his fate, he cannot see himself apart, nor can he distinguish between emotion and intellect. He is will-less, dragged hither and thither, and his unemotionalised intellect, gathered up into the mathematical Phase 22, shows him perpetually for object of desire, an emotion that is like a mechanical energy, a thought that is like wheel and piston. He is suspended; he is without bias, and until bias comes, till he has begun groping for strength within his own being, his thought and his emotion bring him to judgment but they cannot help. As those at Phase 22 must dissolve the dramatising *Mask* in abstract mind that they may discover the concrete world, he must dissolve thought into mere impersonal instinct, into mere race, that he may discover the dramatising *Mask*: he chooses himself and not his Fate. Courage is his True *Mask*, and diversity, that has no habitual purpose, his True *Creative Mind*, because these are all that the phase of the greatest possible weakness can take into itself from the phase of the greatest possible strength. When his fingers close upon a straw, that is courage, and his versatility is that any wave may float a straw. At Phase 7, he had tried out of ambition to change his nature, as though a man should make love who had no heart, but now shock can give him back his heart. Only a shock resulting from the greatest possible conflict can make the greatest possible change, that from *primary* to *antithetical* or from *antithetical* to *primary* again. Nor can anything intervene. He must be aware of nothing but the conflict, his despair is necessary, he is of all men the most tempted—"Eloi, Eloi, why hast thou forsaken me?"[86]

Phase Nine

Will—Belief instead of Individuality.
Mask (from Phase 23). *True*—Facility. *False*—Obscurity.
Creative Mind (from Phase 21). *True*—Self-dramatisation. *False*—Anarchy.
Body of Fate (from Phase 7)—Enforced Sensuality.
Example: An unnamed artist.[87]

Out of phase, blundering and ignorant, the man becomes when in phase powerful and accomplished; all that strength as of metallic rod and wheel discovered within himself. He should seek to liberate the *Mask* by the help of the *Creative Mind* from the *Body of Fate*—that is to say, to carve out and wear the now free *Mask* and so to protect and to deliver the Image. In so far as he does so, there is immense confidence in self-expression, a vehement self, working through mathematical calculation, a delight in straight line and right angle; but if he seek to live according to the *primary tincture*, to use the *Body of Fate* to rid the *Creative Mind* of its *Mask*, to live with objective ambition and curiosity, all is confused, the *Will* asserts itself with a savage, terrified violence. All these phases of incipient personality when out of phase are brutal, but after Phase 12, when true personality begins, brutality gives place to an evasive capricious coldness—"false, fleeting, perjured Clarence"—a lack of good faith in their *primary* relation, often accompanied in their *antithetical* relation by the most self-torturing scruples.[88] When an *antithetical* man is out of phase, he reproduces the *primary* condition, but with an emotional inversion, love for Image or *Mask* becomes dread, or after Phase 15, hatred, and the *Mask* clings to the man or pursues him in the Image. It may even be that he is haunted by a delusive hope, cherished in secret, or bragged of aloud, that he may inherit the *Body of Fate* and *Mask* of a phase opposed to his own. He seeks to avoid *antithetical* conflict by accepting what opposes him, and his *antithetical* life is invaded. At Phase 9, the *Body of Fate* that could purify from an unreal unity the mind of a Carlyle, or of a Whitman, breaks with sensuality (the rising flood of instinct from Phase 7), a new real unity, and the man instead of mastering this sensuality, through his dramatisation of himself as a form of passionate self-mastery, instead of seeking some like form as Image, becomes stupid and blundering. Hence one finds at this phase, more often than at any other, men who dread, despise and persecute the women whom they love. Yet behind all that muddy, flooded, brutal self, there is perhaps a vague timid soul knowing itself caught in an antithesis, an alternation it cannot control. It is said of it, "The soul having found its weakness at Phase 8 begins the inward discipline of the soul in the fury of Phase 9". And again, "Phase 9 has the most sincere belief any man has ever had in his own desire".

There is a certain artist who said to a student of these symbols, speaking of a notable man, and his mistress and their children, "She no longer cares for his work, no longer gives him the sympathy he needs, why does he not leave her, what does he owe to her or to her children?"[89] The student discovered this artist to be a Cubist of powerful imagination and noticed that his head suggested a sullen obstinacy, but that his manner and his speech were generally sympathetic and gentle.

PHASE TEN

Will—The Image-Breaker.
Mask (from Phase 24). *True*—Organisation. *False*—Inertia.
Creative Mind (from Phase 20). *True*—Domination through emotional construction. *False*—Reformation.
Body of Fate (from Phase 6)—Enforced emotion.
Example: Parnell.[90]

If he live like the opposite phase, conceived as *primary* condition—the phase where ambition dies—he lacks all emotional power (False *Mask*: "Inertia"), and gives himself up to rudderless change, reform without a vision of form. He accepts what form (*Mask* and Image) those about him admire and, on discovering that it is alien, casts it away with brutal violence, to choose some other form as alien. He disturbs his own life, and he disturbs all who come near him more than does Phase 9, for Phase 9 has no interest in others except in relation to itself. If, on the other hand, he be true to phase, and use his intellect to liberate from mere race (*Body of Fate* at Phase 6 where race is codified), and so create some code of personal conduct, which implies always "divine right", he becomes proud, masterful and practical. He cannot wholly escape the influence of his *Body of Fate*, but he will be subject to its most personal form; instead of gregarious sympathies, to some woman's tragic love almost certainly.[91] Though the *Body of Fate* must seek to destroy his *Mask*, it may now impose upon him a struggle which leaves victory still possible. As *Body of Fate* phase and *Mask* phase approach one another they share somewhat of each other's nature; the effect of mutual hate grows more diffused, less harsh and obvious. The effect of the *Body of Fate* of Phase 10, for instance, is slightly less harsh and obvious than that of the "enforced sensuality" of Phase 9. It is now "enforced emotion". Phase 9 was without restraint, but now restraint has come and with it pride; there is less need to insist on the brutality of facts of life that he may escape from their charm; the subjective fury is less uncalculating, and the opposition of *Will* and *Mask* no longer produces a delight in an impersonal precision and power like that of machinery (machinery that is emotion and thought) but rather a kind of burning restraint, a something that suggests a savage statue to which one offers sacrifice. This sacrifice is code, personality no longer perceived as power only. He seeks by its help to free the creative power from mass emotion, but never wholly succeeds, and so the life remains troubled, a conflict between pride and race, and passes from crisis to crisis. At Phase 9 there was little sexual discrimination, and now there is emotion created by circumstance rather than by any unique beauty of body or of character. One remembers Faust, who will find every wench a Helen, now that he has drunk the witches' dram, and yet loves his Gretchen with all his being.[92] Perhaps one thinks of that man who gave a lifetime of love because a young woman in capricious idleness had written his name with her umbrella upon the snow.[93] Here is rage, desire to escape but not now by mere destruction of the opposing fate; for a vague abstract sense of some world, some image, some circumstance, harmonious to emotion, has begun, or of something harmonious to emotion that may be set upon the empty pedestal, once visible world, image, or circumstance has been destroyed. With less desire of expression than at Phase 9, and with more desire of action and of command, the man (*Creative Mind* from Phase 20, phase of greatest dramatic power) sees all his life as a stage play where there is only one good acting part; yet no one will accuse him of being a stage player, for he will wear always that stony *Mask* (Phase 24, "The end of ambition", *antithetically* perceived). He, too, if he triumph, may end ambition through the command of multitudes, for he is like that god of Norse mythology who hung from the cliff's side for three days, a sacrifice to himself.[94] Perhaps Moses when he descended the mountain-side had a like stony *Mask*, and had cut Tables and *Mask* out of the one rock.[95]

John Morley says of Parnell, whose life proves him of the phase, that he had the least discursive mind he had ever known, and that is always characteristic of a phase where all practical curiosity has been lost wherever some personal aim is not involved, while philosophical and artistic curiosity are still undiscovered.[96] He made upon his contemporaries an impression of impassivity, and yet a follower has recorded that, after a speech that seemed brutal and callous, his hands were full of blood because he had torn them with his nails.[97] One of his followers was shocked during the impassioned discussion in Committee Room No. 15 that led to his abandonment,[98] by this most reticent man's lack of reticence in allusion to the operations of sex, an indifference as of a mathematician dealing with some arithmetical quantity, and yet Mrs. Parnell tells how upon a night of storm on Brighton pier, and at the height of his power, he held her out over the waters and she lay still, stretched upon his two hands, knowing that if she moved, he would drown himself and her.[99]

PHASE ELEVEN

Will—The Consumer, Pyre-builder.
Mask (from Phase 25). *True*—Rejection. *False*—Moral indifference.
Creative Mind (from Phase 19). *True*—Moral iconoclasm. *False*—Self-assertion.
Body of Fate (from Phase 5)—Enforced belief.
Examples: Spinoza, Savonarola.[100]

While Phase 9 was kept from its subjectivity by personal relations, by sensuality, by various kinds of grossness; and Phase 10 by associations of men for practical purposes, and by the emotions that arise out of such associations, or by some tragic love where there is an element of common interest; Phase 11 is impeded by the excitement of conviction, by the contagion of organised belief, or by its interest in organisation for its own sake. The man of the phase is a half-solitary, one who defends a solitude he cannot or will not inhabit, his *Mask* being from a phase of abstract belief, which offers him always some bundle of mathematical formulae, or its like, opposed to his nature. It will presently be seen that the man of Phase 25, where the *Mask* is, creates a system of belief, just as Phase 24 creates a code, to exclude all that is too difficult for dolt or knave; but the man of Phase 11 systematises, runs to some frenzy of conviction, to make intellect, intellect for its own sake, possible, and perhaps, in his rage against rough-and-ready customary thought, to make all but intellect impossible. He will be the antithesis of all this, should he be conquered by his *Body of Fate* (from Phase 5, where the common instinct first unites itself to reflection), being carried off by some contagion of belief, some general interest, and compelled to substitute for intellectual rage some form of personal pride and so to become the proud prelate of tradition.

In Spinoza one finds the phase in its most pure and powerful shape. He saw the divine energy in whatever was the most individual expression of the soul, and spent his life in showing that such expression was for the world's welfare and not, as might seem, a form of anarchy. His *Mask*, under the influence of his *Body of Fate*, would force him to seek happiness in submission to something hard and exterior; but the *Mask*, set free by a *Creative Mind* that would destroy exterior popular sanction, makes possible for the first time the solitary conception of God. One imagines him among the theologians of his time, who sought always some formula perhaps, some sheep-dog for common minds, turning himself into pure wolf, and making for the wilderness. Certainly his pantheism, however pleasing to his own bare bench of scholars, was little likely to help the oratory of any bench of judges or of bishops. Through all his cold definitions, on whose mathematical form he prided himself, one divines a quarrel with the thought of his fathers and his kin, forced upon him perhaps almost to the breaking of his heart: no nature without the stroke of fate divides itself in two.

Phase Twelve

Will—The Forerunner.
Mask (from Phase 26). *True*—Self-exaggeration. *False*—Self-abandonment.
Creative Mind (from Phase 18). *True*—Subjective philosophy. *False*—War between two forms of expression.
Body of Fate (from Phase 4)—Enforced intellectual action.
Example: Nietzsche.[101]

The man of this phase, out of phase, is always in reaction, is driven from one self-conscious pose to another, is full of hesitation; true to phase, he is a cup that remembers but its own fullness. His phase is called the "Forerunner" because fragmentary and violent. The phases of action where the man mainly defines himself by his practical relations are finished, or finishing, and the phases where he defines himself mainly through an image of the mind begun or beginning; phases of hatred for some external fate are giving way to phases of self-hatred. It is a phase of immense energy because the *Four Faculties* are equidistant. The *oppositions* (*Will* and *Mask*, *Creative Mind* and *Body of Fate*) are balanced by the *discords*, and these, being equidistant between *identity* and *opposition*, are at their utmost intensity. The nature is conscious of the most extreme degree of *deception*, and is wrought to a frenzy of desire for truth of self. If Phase 9 had the greatest possible "belief in its own desire", there is now the greatest possible belief in all values created by personality. It is therefore before all else the phase of the hero, of the man who overcomes himself, and so no longer needs, like Phase 10, the submission of others, or, like Phase 11, conviction of others to prove his victory. Solitude has been born at last, though solitude invaded, and hard to defend. Nor is there need any longer of the bare anatomy of Phase 11; every thought comes with sound and metaphor, and the sanity of the being is no longer from its relation to facts, but from its approximation to its own unity, and from this on we shall meet with men and women to whom facts are a dangerous narcotic or intoxicant. Facts are from the *Body of Fate*, and the *Body of Fate* is from the phase where instinct, before the complications of reflection, reached its most persuasive strength. The man is pursued by a series of accidents, which, unless he meet them *antithetically*, drive him into all sorts of temporary ambitions, opposed to his nature, unite him perhaps to some small protesting sect (the family or neighbourhood of Phase 4 intellectualised); and these ambitions he defends by some kind of superficial intellectual action, the pamphlet, the violent speech, the sword of the swashbuckler. He spends his life in oscillation between the violent assertion of some commonplace pose, and a dogmatism which means nothing apart from the circumstance that created it.

If, however, he meets these accidents by the awakening of his *antithetical* being, there is a noble extravagance, an overflowing fountain of personal life. He turns towards the True *Mask* and having by philosophic intellect (*Creative Mind*) delivered it from all that is topical and temporary, announces a philosophy which is the logical expression of a mind alone with the object of its desire. The True *Mask*, derived from the terrible Phase 26, called the phase of the Hunchback, is the reverse of all that is emotional, being emotionally cold; not mathematical, for intellectual abstraction ceased at Phase 11, but marble pure. In the presence of the *Mask*, the *Creative Mind* has the isolation of a fountain under moonlight; yet one must always distinguish between the emotional *Will*—now approaching the greatest subtlety of sensitiveness, and more and more conscious of its frailty—and that which it would be, the lonely, imperturbable, proud *Mask*, as between the *Will* and its *discord* in the *Creative Mind* where is no shrinking from life. The man follows an Image, created or chosen by the *Creative Mind* from what Fate offers; would persecute and dominate it; and this Image wavers between the concrete and sensuous Image. It has become personal; there is now, though not so decisively as later, but one form of chosen beauty, and the sexual Image is drawn as with a diamond, and tinted those pale colours sculptors sometimes put upon a statue. Like all before Phase 15 the man is overwhelmed with the thought of his own weakness and knows of no strength but that of Image and *Mask*.

PHASE THIRTEEN

Will—The Sensuous Man.
Mask (from Phase 27). *True*—Self-expression. *False*—Self-absorption.

Creative Mind (from Phase 17). *True*—Subjective truth.
False—Morbidity.
Body of Fate (from Phase 3)—Enforced love of another.
Examples: Baudelaire, Beardsley, Ernest Dowson.[102]

This is said to be the only phase where entire sensuality is possible, that is to say, sensuality without the intermixture of any other element. There is now a possible complete intellectual unity, Unity of Being apprehended through the images of the mind; and this is opposed by the Fate (Phase 3 where body becomes deliberate and whole) which offers an equal roundness and wholeness of sensation. The *Will* is now a mirror of emotional experience, or sensation, according to whether it is swayed by *Mask* or Fate. Though wax to every impression of emotion, or of sense, it would yet through its passion for truth (*Creative Mind*) become its opposite and receive from the *Mask* (Phase 27), which is at the phase of the Saint, a virginal purity of emotion. If it live objectively, that is to say, surrender itself to sensation, it becomes morbid, it sees every sensation separate from every other under the light of its perpetual analysis (*Creative Mind* at a phase of dispersal). Phase 13 is a phase of great importance, because the most intellectually subjective phase, and because only here can be achieved in perfection that in the *antithetical* life which corresponds to sanctity in the *primary*: not self-denial but expression for expression's sake. Its influence indeed upon certain writers has caused them in their literary criticism to exalt intellectual sincerity to the place in literature which is held by sanctity in theology. At this phase the self discovers, within itself, while struggling with the *Body of Fate*, forms of emotional morbidity which others recognise as their own; as the Saint may take upon himself the physical diseases of others. There is almost always a preoccupation with those metaphors and symbols and mythological images through which we define whatever seems most strange or most morbid. Self-hatred now reaches its height, and through this hatred comes the slow liberation of intellectual love. There are moments of triumph and moments of defeat, each in its extreme form, for the subjective intellect knows nothing of moderation. As the *primary tincture* has weakened, the sense of quantity has weakened, for the *antithetical tincture* is preoccupied with quality.

From now, if not from Phase 12, and until Phase 17 or Phase 18 has passed, happy love is rare, for seeing that the man must find a woman whose *Mask* falls within or but just outside his *Body of Fate* and *Mask*, if he is to find strong sexual attraction, the range of choice grows smaller, and all life grows more tragic. As the woman grows harder to find, so does every beloved object. Lacking suitable objects of desire, the relation between man and *Daimon* becomes more clearly a struggle or even a relation of enmity.

Phase Fourteen

Will—The Obsessed Man.
Mask (from Phase 28). *True*—Serenity. *False*—Self-distrust.
Creative Mind (from Phase 16). *True*—Emotional will.
False—Terror.
Body of Fate (from Phase 2)—Enforced love of the world.
Examples: Keats, Giorgione, many beautiful women.[103]

As we approach Phase 15 personal beauty increases and at Phase 14 and Phase 16 the greatest human beauty becomes possible. The aim of the being should be to disengage those objects which are images of desire from the excitement and disorder of the *Body of Fate,* and under certain circumstances to impress upon these the full character of the *Mask* which, being from Phase 28, is a folding up, or fading into themselves. It is this act of the intellect, begun at conception, which has given the body its beauty. The *Body of Fate*, derived from the phase of the utmost possible physical energy, but of an energy without aim, like that of a child, works against this folding up, yet offers little more of objects than their excitement, their essential honey. The images of desire, disengaged and subject to the *Mask*, are separate and still (*Creative Mind* from a phase of violent scattering). The images of Phase 13 and even of Phase 12 have in a lesser degree this character. When we compare these images with those of any subsequent phase, each seems studied for its own sake; they float as in serene air, or lie hidden in some valley, and if they move it is to music that returns always to the same note, or in a dance that so returns into itself that they seem immortal.

When the being is out of phase, when it is allured by *primary* curiosity, it is aware of its *primary* feebleness and its intellect becomes but a passion of apprehension, or a shrinking from solitude; it may even become mad; or it may use its conscious feebleness and its consequent terror as a magnet for the sympathy of others, as a means of domination. At Phase 16 will be discovered a desire to accept every possible responsibility; but now responsibility is renounced and this renunciation becomes an instrument of power, dropped burdens being taken up by others. Here are born those women who are most touching in their beauty. Helen was of the phase; and she comes before the mind's eye elaborating a delicate personal discipline, as though she would make her whole life an image of a unified *antithetical* energy. While seeming an image of softness and of quiet, she draws perpetually upon glass with a diamond.[104] Yet she will not number among her sins anything that does not break that personal discipline, no matter what it may seem according to others' discipline; but if she fail in her own discipline she will not deceive herself, and for all the languor of her movements, and her indifference to the acts of others, her mind is never at peace. She will wander much alone as though she consciously meditated her masterpiece that shall be at the full moon, yet unseen by human eyes, and when she returns to her house she will look upon her household with timid eyes, as though she knew that all powers of self-protection had been taken away, that of her once violent *primary tincture* nothing remained but a strange irresponsible innocence. Her early life has perhaps been perilous because of that nobility, that excess of *antithetical* energies, which may have so constrained the fading *primary* that, instead of its becoming the expression of those energies, it is but a vague beating of the wings, or their folding up into a melancholy stillness. The greater the peril the nearer has she approached to the final union of *primary* and *antithetical*, where she will desire nothing; already perhaps, through weakness of desire, she understands nothing yet seems to understand everything; already serves nothing, while alone seeming of service. Is it not because she desires so little, gives so little that men will die and murder in her service? One thinks of the *Eternal Idol* of Rodin: that kneeling man with hands clasped behind his back in humble adoration, kissing a young girl a little below the breast, while she gazes down, without comprehending, under her half-closed eyelids.[105] Perhaps, could we see her a little later, with flushed cheeks casting her money upon some gaming-table, we would wonder that action and form could so belie each other, not understanding that the Fool's *Mask* is her chosen motley, nor her terror before death and stillness. One thinks too of the women of Burne-Jones, but not of Botticelli's women, who have too much curiosity, nor Rossetti's women, who have too much passion;[106] and as we see before the mind's eye those pure faces gathered about the "Sleep of Arthur," or crowded upon the "Golden Stair," we wonder if they too would not have filled us with surprise, or dismay, because of some craze, some passion for mere excitement, or slavery to a drug.[107]

In the poets too, who are of the phase, one finds the impression of the *Body of Fate* as intoxication or narcotic. Wordsworth, shuddering at his solitude, has filled his art in all but a few pages with common opinion, common sentiment;[108] while in the poetry of Keats there is, though little sexual passion, an exaggerated sensuousness that compels us to remember the pepper on the tongue as though that were his symbol. Thought is disappearing into image; and in Keats, in some ways a perfect type, intellectual curiosity is at its weakest; there is scarcely an image, where his poetry is at its best, whose subjectivity has not been heightened by its use in many great poets, painters, sculptors, artificers.[109] The being has almost reached the end of that elaboration of itself which has for its climax an absorption in time, where space can be but symbols or images in the mind. There is little observation even in detail of expression, all is reverie, while in Wordsworth the soul's deepening solitude has reduced mankind, when seen objectively, to a few slight figures outlined for a moment amid mountain and lake. The corresponding genius in painting is that of Monticelli, after 1870, and perhaps that of Conder, though in Conder there are elements suggesting the preceding phase.[110]

All born at *antithetical* phases before Phase 15 are subject to violence, because of the indeterminate energy of the *Body of Fate*; this violence seems accidental, unforeseen and cruel—and here are women carried off by robbers and ravished by clowns.[111]

Phase Fifteen

Will. *Mask* (from Phase 1). *Creative Mind* (from Phase 15). *Body of Fate* (from Phase 1).	No description except that this is a phase of complete beauty.[112]

Body of Fate and *Mask* are now identical; and *Will* and *Creative Mind* identical; or rather the *Creative Mind* is dissolved in the *Will* and the *Body of Fate* in the *Mask*. Thought and will are indistinguishable, effort and attainment are indistinguishable; and this is the consummation of a slow process; nothing is apparent but dreaming *Will* and the Image that it dreams. Since Phase 12 all images, and cadences of the mind, have been satisfying to that mind just in so far as they have expressed this converging of will and thought, effort and attainment. The words "musical", "sensuous", are but descriptions of that converging process. Thought has been pursued, not as a means but as an end—the poem, the painting, the reverie has been sufficient of itself. It is not possible, however, to separate in the understanding this running into one of *Will* and *Creative Mind* from the running into one of *Mask* and *Body of Fate*. Without *Mask* and *Body of Fate* the *Will* would have nothing to desire, the *Creative Mind* nothing to apprehend. Since Phase 12 the *Creative Mind* has been so interfused by the *antithetical tincture* that it has more and more confined its contemplation of actual things to those that resemble images of the mind desired by the *Will*. The being has selected, moulded and remoulded, narrowed its circle of living, been more and more the artist, grown more and more "distinguished" in all preference. Now contemplation and desire, united into one, inhabit a world where every beloved image has bodily form, and every bodily form is loved. This love knows nothing of desire, for desire implies effort, and though there is still separation from the loved object, love accepts the separation as necessary to its own existence. *Fate* is known for the boundary that gives our *Destiny* its form, and—as we can desire nothing outside that form—as an expression of our freedom. Chance and Choice have become interchangeable without losing their identity.[113] As all effort has ceased, all thought has become image, because no thought could exist if it were not carried towards its own extinction, amid fear or in contemplation; and every image is separate from every other, for if image were linked to image, the soul would awake from its immovable trance. All that the being has experienced as thought is visible to its eyes as a whole, and in this way it perceives, not as they are to others, but according to its own perception, all orders of existence. Its own body possesses the greatest possible beauty, being indeed that body which the soul will permanently inhabit, when all its phases have been repeated according to the number allotted: that which we call the clarified or *Celestial Body*. Where the being has lived out of phase, seeking to live through *antithetical* phases as though they had been *primary*, there is now terror of solitude, its forced, painful and slow acceptance, and a life haunted by terrible dreams. Even for the most perfect, there is a time of pain, a passage through a vision, where evil reveals itself in its final meaning. In this passage Christ, it is said, mourned over the length of time and the unworthiness of man's lot to man, whereas his forerunner mourned and his successor will mourn over the shortness of time and the unworthiness of man to his lot; but this cannot yet be understood.[114]

PHASE SIXTEEN

Will—The Positive Man.
Mask (from Phase 2). *True*—Illusion. *False*—Delusion.
Creative Mind (from Phase 14). *True*—Vehemence. *False*—Opinionated will.
Body of Fate (from Phase 28)—Enforced Illusion.
Examples: William Blake, Rabelais, Aretino, Paracelsus, some beautiful women.[115]

Phase 16 is in contrast to Phase 14, in spite of their resemblance of extreme subjectivity, in that it has a *Body of Fate* from the phase of the Fool, a phase of absorption, and its *Mask* from what might have been called the phase of the Child, a phase of aimless energy, of physical life for its own sake; whereas Phase 14 had its *Body of Fate* from the phase of the Child and its *Mask* from that of the Fool.

Fate thrusts an aimless excitement upon Phase 14. Phase 14 finds within itself an *antithetical* self-absorbing dream. Phase 16 has a like dream thrust upon it and finds within itself an aimless excitement. This excitement, and this dream, are both illusions, so that the *Will*, which is itself a violent scattering energy, has to use its intellect (*Creative Mind*) to discriminate between illusions. They are both illusions, because, so small is the *primary* nature, sense of fact is an impossibility. If it use its intellect, which is the most narrow, the most unflinching, even the most cruel possible to man, to disengage the aimless child (*i.e.* to find *Mask* and Image in the child's toy), it finds the soul's most radiant expression and surrounds itself with some fairyland, some mythology of wisdom or laughter. Its own mere scattering, its mere rushing out into the disordered and unbounded, after the still trance of Phase 15, has found its antithesis, and therefore self-knowledge and self-mastery.

If, however, it subordinate its intellect to the *Body of Fate*, all the cruelty and narrowness of that intellect are displayed in service of preposterous purpose after purpose till there is nothing left but the fixed idea and some hysterical hatred. By these purposes, derived from a phase of absorption, the *Body of Fate* drives the *Will* back upon its subjectivity, deforming the *Mask* until the *Will* can only see the object of its desire in these purposes. It does not hate opposing desire, as do the phases of increasing *antithetical* emotion, but hates that which opposes desire. Capable of nothing but an incapable idealism (for it has no thought but in myth, or in defence of myth), it must, because it sees one side as all white, see the other side all black; what but a dragon could dream of thwarting a St. George?[116] In men of the phase there will commonly be both natures, for to be true to phase is a ceaseless struggle. At one moment they are full of hate—Blake writes of "Flemish and Venetian demons"[117] and of some picture of his own destroyed "by some vile spell of Stoddart's"[118]—and their hate is always close to madness; and at the next they produce the comedy of Aretino and of Rabelais or the mythology of Blake, and discover symbolism to express the overflowing and bursting of the mind. There is always an element of frenzy, and almost always a delight in certain glowing or shining images of concentrated force: in the smith's forge; in the heart; in the human form in its most vigorous development; in the solar disc;

in some symbolical representation of the sexual organs; for the being must brag of its triumph over its own incoherence.

Since Phase 8 the man has more and more judged what is right in relation to time: a right action, or a right motive, has been one that he thought possible or desirable to think or do eternally; his soul would "come into possession of itself for ever in one single moment"; but now he begins once more to judge an action or motive in relation to space.[119] A right action or motive must soon be right for any other man in similar circumstance. Hitherto an action, or motive, has been right precisely because it is exactly right for one person only, though for that person always. After the change, the belief in the soul's immortality declines, though the decline is slow, and it may only be recovered when Phase 1 is passed.

Among those who are of this phase may be great satirists, great caricaturists, but they pity the beautiful, for that is their *Mask*, and hate the ugly, for that is their *Body of Fate*, and so are unlike those of the *primary* phases, Rembrandt for instance, who pity the ugly, and sentimentalise the beautiful, or call it insipid, and turn away or secretly despise and hate it.[120] Here too are beautiful women, whose bodies have taken upon themselves the image of the True *Mask*, and in these there is a radiant intensity, something of "The Burning Babe" of the Elizabethan lyric.[121] They walk like queens, and seem to carry upon their backs a quiver of arrows, but they are gentle only to those whom they have chosen or subdued, or to the dogs that follow at their heels.[122] Boundless in generosity, and in illusion, they will give themselves to a beggar because he resembles a religious picture and be faithful all their lives, or if they take another turn and choose a dozen lovers, die convinced that none but the first or last has ever touched their lips, for they are of those whose "virginity renews itself like the moon".[123] Out of phase they turn termagant, if their lover take a wrong step in a quadrille where all the figures are of their own composition and changed without notice when the fancy takes them. Indeed, perhaps if the body have great perfection, there is always something imperfect in the mind, some rejection of or inadequacy of *Mask*: Venus out of phase chose lame Vulcan.[124] Here also are several very ugly persons, their bodies torn and twisted by the violence of the new *primary*, but where the body has this ugliness great beauty of mind is possible. This is indeed the only *antithetical* phase where ugliness is possible, it being complementary to Phase 2, the only *primary* phase where beauty is possible.

From this phase on we meet with those who do violence, instead of those who suffer it; and prepare for those who love some living person, and not an image of the mind, but as yet this love is hardly more than the "fixed idea" of faithfulness. As the new love grows the sense of beauty will fade.

PHASE SEVENTEEN

Will—The *Daimonic* Man.
Mask (from Phase 3). *True*—Simplification through intensity. *False*—Dispersal.
Creative Mind (from Phase 13). *True*—Creative imagination through *antithetical* emotion. *False*—Enforced self-realization.
Body of Fate (from Phase 27)—Loss.[125]
Examples: Dante, Shelley, Landor.[126]

He is called the *Daimonic* man because Unity of Being, and consequent expression of *Daimonic* thought, is now more easy than at any other phase. As contrasted with Phase 13 and Phase 14, where mental images were separated from one another that they might be subject to knowledge, all now flow, change, flutter, cry out, or mix into something else; but without, as at Phase 16, breaking and bruising one another, for Phase 17, the central phase of its triad, is without frenzy. The *Will* is falling asunder, but without explosion and noise. The separated fragments seek images rather than ideas, and these the intellect, seated in Phase 13, must synthesise in vain, drawing with its compass-point a line that shall but represent the outline of a bursting pod. The being has for its supreme aim, as it had at Phase 16 (and as all subsequent *antithetical* phases shall have), to hide from itself and others this separation and disorder, and it conceals them under the emotional Image of Phase 3; as Phase 16 concealed its greater violence under that of Phase 2. When true to phase the intellect must turn all its synthetic power to this task. It finds, not the impassioned myth that Phase 16 found, but a *Mask* of simplicity that is also intensity. This *Mask* may represent intellectual or sexual passion; seem some Ahasuerus or Athanase;[127] be the gaunt Dante of the *Divine Comedy*;[128] its corresponding Image may be Shelley's Venus Urania,[129] Dante's Beatrice, or even the Great Yellow Rose of the *Paradiso*.[130] The *Will*, when true to phase, assumes, in assuming the *Mask*, an intensity which is never dramatic but always lyrical and personal, and this intensity, though always a deliberate assumption, is to others but the charm of the being; and yet the *Will* is always aware of the *Body of Fate*, which perpetually destroys this intensity, thereby leaving the *Will* to its own "dispersal".

At Phase 3, not as *Mask* but as phase, there should be perfect physical well-being or balance, though not beauty or emotional intensity, but at Phase 27 are those who turn away from all that Phase 3 represents and seek all those things it is blind to. The *Body of Fate*, therefore, derived from a phase of renunciation, is "loss", and works to make impossible "simplification by intensity". The being, through the intellect, selects some object of desire for a representation of the *Mask* as Image, some woman perhaps, and the *Body of Fate* snatches away the object. Then the intellect (*Creative Mind*), which in the most *antithetical* phases were better described as imagination, must substitute some new image of desire; and in the degree of its power and of its attainment of unity, relate that which is lost, that which has snatched it away, to the new image of desire, that which threatens the new image to the being's unity. If its unity be already past, or if unity be still to come, it may for all that be true to phase. It will then use its intellect merely to isolate *Mask* and Image, as chosen forms or as conceptions of the mind.

If it be out of phase it will avoid the subjective conflict, acquiesce, hope that the *Body of Fate* may die away; and then the *Mask* will cling to it and the Image lure it. It will feel itself betrayed, and persecuted till, entangled in *primary* conflict, it rages against all that destroys *Mask* and Image. It will be subject to nightmare, for its *Creative Mind* (deflected from the Image and *Mask* to the *Body of Fate*) gives an isolated mythological or abstract form to all that excites its hatred. It may even dream of escaping from ill-luck by possessing the impersonal *Body of Fate* of its opposite phase and of exchanging passion for desk and ledger. Because of the habit of synthesis, and of the growing complexity of the energy, which gives many interests, and the still faint perception of things in their weight and mass, men of this phase are almost always partisans, propagandists and gregarious; yet because of the *Mask* of simplification, which holds up before them the solitary life of hunters and of fishers and "the groves pale passion loves", they hate parties, crowds, propaganda.[131] Shelley out of phase writes pamphlets, and dreams of converting the world, or of turning man of affairs and upsetting governments,[132] and yet returns again and again to these two images of solitude, a young man whose hair has grown white from the burden of his thoughts,[133] an old man in some shell-strewn cave whom it is possible to call, when speaking to the Sultan, "as inaccessible as God or thou".[134] On the other hand, how subject he is to nightmare! He sees the devil leaning against a tree, is attacked by imaginary assassins,[135] and, in obedience to what he considers a supernatural voice, creates *The Cenci* that he may give to Beatrice Cenci her incredible father.[136] His political enemies are monstrous, meaningless images. And unlike Byron, who is two phases later, he can never see anything that opposes him as it really is. Dante, who lamented his exile as of all possible things the worst for such as he, and sighed for his lost solitude, and yet could never keep from politics, was, according to a contemporary, such a partisan, that if a child, or a woman, spoke against his party he would pelt this child or woman with stones.[137] Yet Dante, having attained, as poet, to Unity of Being, as poet saw all things set in order, had an intellect that served the *Mask* alone, that compelled even those things that opposed it to serve, and was content to see both good and evil. Shelley, upon the other hand, in whom even as poet unity was but in part attained, found compensation for his "loss", for the taking away of his children, for his quarrel with his first wife, for later sexual disappointment, for his exile, for his obloquy—there were but some three or four persons, he said, who did not consider him a monster of iniquity—in his hopes for the future of mankind.[138] He lacked the Vision of Evil, could not conceive of the world as a continual conflict, so, though great poet he certainly was, he was not of the greatest kind.[139] Dante suffering injustice and the loss of Beatrice, found divine justice and the heavenly Beatrice, but the justice of *Prometheus Unbound* is a vague propagandist emotion and the women that await its coming are but clouds.[140] This is in part because the age in which Shelley lived was in itself so broken that true Unity of Being was almost impossible, but partly because, being out of phase so far as his practical reason was concerned, he was subject to an *automatonism* which he mistook for poetical invention, especially in his longer poems. *Antithetical* men (Phase 15 once passed) use this *automatonism* to evade hatred, or rather to hide it from their own eyes; perhaps all at some time or other, in moments of fatigue, give themselves up to fantastic, constructed images, or to an almost mechanical laughter.

Landor has been examined in *Per Amica Silentia Lunae*.[141] The most violent of men, he uses his intellect to disengage a visionary image of perfect sanity (*Mask* at Phase 3) seen always in the most serene and classic art imaginable. He had perhaps as much Unity of Being as his age permitted, and possessed, though not in any full measure, the Vision of Evil.

Phase Eighteen

Will—The Emotional Man.
Mask (from Phase 4). *True*—Intensity through emotion.
False—Curiosity.
Creative Mind (from Phase 12). *True*—Emotional philosophy. *False*—Enforced lure.
Body of Fate (from Phase 26)—Enforced disillusionment.
Examples: Goethe, Matthew Arnold.[142]

The *antithetical tincture* closes during this phase, the being is losing direct knowledge of its old *antithetical* life. The conflict between that portion of the life of feeling which appertains to his unity, and that portion he has in common with others, coming to an end, has begun to destroy that knowledge. "A Lover's Nocturne" or "Ode to the West Wind" are probably no more possible, certainly no more characteristic.[143] He can hardly, if action and the intellect that concerns action are taken from him, recreate his dream life; and when he says "Who am I?", he finds it difficult to examine his thoughts in relation to one another, his emotions in relation to one another, but begins to find it easy to examine them in relation to action. He can examine those actions themselves with a new clearness. Now for the first time since Phase 12, Goethe's saying is almost true: "Man knows himself by action only, by thought never".[144] Meanwhile the *antithetical tincture* begins to attain, without previous struggle or self-analysis, its active form which is love—love being the union of emotion and instinct—or when out of phase, sentimentality. The *Will* seeks by some form of emotional philosophy to free a form of emotional beauty (*Mask*) from a "disillusionment" differing from the "illusions" of Phase 16, which are continuous, in that it permits intermittent awakening. The *Will*, with its closing *antithetical*, is turning away from the life of images to that of ideas, it is vacillating and curious, and it seeks in this *Mask* (from a phase where all the functions can be perfect), what becomes, when considered *antithetically*, a wisdom of the emotions.

At its next phase it will have fallen asunder; already it can only preserve its unity by a deliberate balancing of experiences (*Creative Mind* at Phase 12, *Body of Fate* at Phase 26), and so it must desire that phase (though that transformed into the emotional life), where wisdom seems a physical accident. Its object of desire is no longer a single image of passion, for it must relate all to social life; the man seeks to become not a sage, not Ahasuerus, but a wise king, and seeks a woman who looks the wise mother of children.[145] Perhaps now, and for the first time, the love of a living woman ("disillusionment" once accepted) as apart from beauty or function, is an admitted aim, though not yet wholly achieved. The *Body of Fate* is from the phase where the "wisdom of knowledge" has compelled *Mask* and Image to become not objects of desire but objects of knowledge. Goethe did not, as Beddoes said, marry his cook, but he certainly did not marry the woman he had desired, and his grief at her death showed that, unlike Phase 16 or Phase 17, which forget their broken toys, he could love what disillusionment gave.[146] When he seeks to live objectively, he will substitute curiosity for emotional wisdom, he will invent objects of desire artificially, he will say perhaps, though this was said by a man who was probably still later in phase, "I was never in love with a serpent-charmer before";[147] the False *Mask* will press upon him, pursue him, and, refusing conflict, he will fly from the True *Mask* at each artificial choice. The nightingale will refuse the thorn and so remain among images instead of passing to ideas.[148] He is still disillusioned, but he can no longer through philosophy substitute for the desire that life has taken away, love for what life has brought. The *Will* is near the place marked *Head* upon the great chart, which enables it to choose its *Mask* even when true to phase almost coldly and always deliberately, whereas the *Creative Mind* is derived from the place marked *Heart*, and is therefore more impassioned and less subtle and delicate than if Phase 16 or Phase 17 were the place of the *Will*, though not yet argumentative or heated. The *Will* at *Head* uses the heart with perfect mastery and, because of the growing *primary*, begins to be aware of an audience, though as yet it will not dramatise the *Mask* deliberately for the sake of effect as will Phase 19.

Phase Nineteen

Will—The Assertive Man.
Mask (from Phase 5). *True*—Conviction. *False*—Domination.
Creative Mind (from Phase 11). *True*—Emotional intellect. *False*—The Unfaithful.
Body of Fate (from Phase 25)—Enforced failure of action.
Examples: Gabriele d'Annunzio (perhaps), Oscar Wilde, Byron, a certain actress.[149]

This phase is the beginning of the artificial, the abstract, the fragmentary, and the dramatic. Unity of Being is no longer possible, for the being is compelled to live in a fragment of itself and to dramatise that fragment. The *primary tincture* is closing, direct knowledge of self in relation to action is ceasing to be possible. The being only completely knows that portion of itself which judges fact for the sake of action. When the man lives according to phase, he is now governed by conviction, instead of by a ruling mood, and is effective only in so far as he can find this conviction. His aim is so to use an intellect which turns easily to declamation, emotional emphasis, that it serves conviction in a life where effort, just in so far as its object is passionately desired, comes to nothing. He desires to be strong and stable, but as Unity of Being and self-knowledge are both gone, and it is too soon to grasp at another unity through *primary* mind, he passes from emphasis to emphasis. The strength from conviction, derived from a *Mask* of the first quarter *antithetically* transformed, is not founded upon social duty, though that may seem so to others, but is temperamentally formed to fit some crisis of personal life. His thought is immensely effective and dramatic, arising always from some immediate situation, a situation found or created by himself, and may have great permanent value as the expression of an exciting personality. This thought is always an open attack; or a sudden emphasis, an extravagance, or an impassioned declamation of some general idea, which is a more veiled attack. The *Creative Mind* being derived from Phase 11, he is doomed to attempt the destruction of all that breaks or encumbers personality, but this personality is conceived of as a fragmentary, momentary intensity. The mastery of images, threatened or lost at Phase 18, may, however, be completely recovered, but there is less symbol, more fact. Vitality from dreams has died out, and a vitality from fact has begun which has for its ultimate aim the mastery of the real world. The watercourse after an abrupt fall continues upon a lower level; ice turns to water, or water to vapour: there is a new chemical phase.

When lived out of phase there is a hatred or contempt of others, and instead of seeking conviction for its own sake, the man takes up opinions that he may impose himself upon others. He is tyrannical and capricious, and his intellect is called "The Unfaithful", because, being used for victory alone, it will change its ground in a moment and delight in some new emphasis, not caring whether old or new have consistency. The *Mask* is derived from that phase where perversity begins, where artifice begins, and has its *discord* from Phase 25, the last phase where the artificial is possible; the *Body of Fate* is therefore enforced failure of action, and many at this phase desire action above all things as a means of expression. Whether the man be in or out of phase, there is the desire to escape from Unity of Being or any approximation towards it, for Unity can be but a simulacrum now. And in so far as the soul keeps its memory of that potential Unity there is conscious *antithetical* weakness. He must now dramatise the *Mask* through the *Will* and dreads the Image, deep within, of the old *antithetical tincture* at its strongest, and yet this Image may seem infinitely desirable if he could but find the desire. When so torn into two, escape when it comes may be so violent that it brings him under the False *Mask* and the False *Creative Mind*. A certain actress is typical, for she surrounds herself with drawings by

Burne-Jones in his latest period, and reveres them as they were holy pictures, while her manners are boisterous, dominating and egotistical.[150] They are faces of silent women, and she is not silent for a moment; yet these faces are not, as I once thought, the True *Mask* but a part of that incoherence the True *Mask* must conceal. Were she to surrender to their influence she would become insincere in her art and exploit an emotion that is no longer hers. I find in Wilde, too, something pretty, feminine, and insincere, derived from his admiration for writers of the 17th and earlier phases, and much that is violent, arbitrary and insolent, derived from his desire to escape.

The *antithetical Mask* comes to men of Phase 17 and Phase 18 as a form of strength, and when they are tempted to dramatise it, the dramatisation is fitful, and brings no conviction of strength, for they dislike emphasis; but now the weakness of the *antithetical* has begun, for though still the stronger it cannot ignore the growing *primary*. It is no longer an absolute monarch, and it permits power to pass to statesman or demagogue, whom, however, it will constantly change.

Here one finds men and women who love those who rob them or beat them, as though the soul were intoxicated by its discovery of human nature, or found even a secret delight in the shattering of the image of its desire. It is as though it cried, "I would be possessed by" or "I would possess that which is Human. What do I care if it is good or bad?" There is no "disillusionment", for they have found that which they have sought, but that which they have sought and found in a fragment.

Phase Twenty

Will—The Concrete Man.
Mask (from Phase 6). *True*—Fatalism. *False*—Superstition.
Creative Mind (from Phase 10). *True*—Dramatisation of *Mask*. *False*—Self-desecration.
Body of Fate (from Phase 24)—Enforced success of action.
Examples: Shakespeare, Balzac, Napoleon.[151]

Like the phase before it, and those that follow it immediately, a phase of the breaking up and subdivision of the being. The energy is always seeking those facts which being separable can be seen more clearly, or expressed more clearly, but when there is truth to the phase there is a similitude of the old unity, or rather a new unity, which is not a Unity of Being but a unity of the creative act. He no longer seeks to unify what is broken through conviction, by imposing those very convictions upon himself and others, but by projecting a dramatisation or many dramatisations. He can create, just in that degree in which he can see these dramatisations as separate from himself, and yet as an epitome of his whole nature. His *Mask* is derived from Phase 6, where man first becomes a generalised form, according to the *primary tincture*, as in the poetry of Walt Whitman, but this *Mask* he must by dramatisation rescue from a *Body of Fate* derived from Phase 24, where moral domination dies out before that of the exterior world conceived as a whole. The *Body of Fate* is called "enforced success", a success that rolls out and smooths away, that dissolves through creation, that seems to delight in all outward flowing, that drenches all with grease and oil; that turns dramatisation into desecration: "I have made myself a motley to the view".[152] Owing to the need of seeing the dramatic image, or images, as individuals, that is to say as set amongst concrete or fixed surroundings, he seeks some field of action, some mirror not of his own creation. Unlike Phase 19 he fails in situations wholly created by himself, or in works of art where character or story has gained nothing from history. His phase is called "The Concrete Man", because the isolation of parts that began at Phase 19 is overcome at the second phase of the triad; subordination of parts is achieved by the discovery of concrete relations. His abstraction too, affected by these relations, may be no more than an emotional interest in such generalisations as "God", "Man", a Napoleon may but point to the starry heavens and say that they prove the existence of God.[153] There is a delight in concrete images that, unlike the impassioned images of Phase 17 and Phase 18, or the declamatory images of Phase 19, reveal through complex suffering the general destiny of man. He must, however, to express this suffering, personify rather than characterise, create not observe that multitude, which is but his *Mask* as in a multiplying mirror, for the *primary* is not yet strong enough to substitute for the lost Unity of Being that of the external world perceived as fact. In a man of action this multiplicity gives the greatest possible richness of resource where he is not thwarted by his horoscope, great ductability, a gift for adopting any rôle that stirs imagination, a philosophy of impulse and audacity; but in the man of action a part of the nature must be crushed, one main dramatisation or group of images preferred to all others.

Napoleon sees himself as Alexander moving to the conquest of the East, *Mask* and Image must take an historical and not a mythological or dream form, a form found but not created; he is crowned in the dress of a Roman Emperor.[154] Shakespeare, the other supreme figure of the phase, was—if we may judge by the few biographical facts, and by such adjectives as "sweet" and "gentle" applied to him by his contemporaries—a man whose actual personality seemed faint and passionless.[155] Unlike Ben Jonson he fought no duels;[156] he kept out of quarrels in a quarrelsome age; not even complaining when somebody pirated his sonnets;[157] he dominated no Mermaid Tavern,[158] but—through *Mask* and Image, reflected in a multiplying mirror—he created the most passionate art that exists. He was the greatest of modern poets, partly because entirely true to phase, creating always from *Mask* and *Creative Mind*, never from situation alone, never from *Body of Fate* alone; and if we knew all we would find that success came to him, as to others of this phase, as something hostile and unforeseen; something that sought to impose an intuition of Fate (the condition of Phase 6) as from without and therefore as a form of superstition. Both Shakespeare and Balzac used the False *Mask* imaginatively, explored it to impose the True, and what Thomas Lake Harris,* the half-charlatan American visionary, said of Shakespeare might be said of both: "Often the hair of his head stood up and all life became the echoing chambers of the tomb".[159]

At Phase 19 we create through the externalised *Mask* an imaginary world, in whose real existence we believe, while remaining separate from it; at Phase 20 we enter that world and become a portion of it; we study it, we amass historical evidence, and, that we may dominate it the more, drive out myth and symbol, and compel it to seem the real world where our lives are lived.

*I quote from a book circulated privately among his followers. I saw it years ago but seem to remember it as now vague, now vulgar, and now magnificent in style.

A phase of ambition; in Napoleon the dramatist's own ambition; in Shakespeare that of the persons of his art; and this ambition is not that of the solitary lawgiver, that of Phase 10 (where the *Creative Mind* is placed) which rejects, resists and narrows, but a creative energy.

Phase Twenty-one

Will—The Acquisitive Man.
Mask (from Phase 7). *True*—Self-analysis. *False*—Self-adaptation.
Creative Mind (from Phase 9). *True*—Domination of the intellect. *False*—Distortion.
Body of Fate (from Phase 23)—Enforced triumph of achievement.
Examples: Lamarck, Mr. Bernard Shaw, Mr. Wells, George Moore.[160]

The *antithetical tincture* has a predominance so slight that the *Creative Mind* and *Body of Fate* almost equal it in control of desire. The *Will* can scarcely conceive of a *Mask* separate from or predominant over *Creative Mind* and *Body of Fate*, yet because it can do so there is personality not character. It is better, however, to use a different word, and therefore Phases 21, 22 and 23 are described as, like the phases opposite, phases of individuality where the *Will* is studied less in relation to the *Mask* than in relation to itself. At Phase 23 the new relation to the *Mask*, as something to escape from, will have grown clear.

The *antithetical tincture* is noble, and, judged by the standards of the *primary*, evil, whereas the *primary* is good and banal; and this phase, the last before the *antithetical* surrenders its control, would be almost wholly good did it not hate its own banality. Personality has almost the rigidity, almost the permanence of character, but it is not character, for it is still always assumed. When we contemplate Napoleon we can see ourselves, perhaps even think of ourselves as Napoleons, but a man of Phase 21 has a personality that seems a creation of his circumstance and his faults, a manner peculiar to himself and impossible to others. We say at once, "How individual he is". In theory whatever one has chosen must be within the choice of others, at some moment or for some purpose, but we find in practice that nobody of this phase has personal imitators, or has given his name to a form of manners. The *Will* has driven intellectual complexity into its final entanglement, an entanglement created by the continual adaptation to new circumstances of a logical sequence; and the aim of the individual, when true to phase, is to realise, by his own complete domination over all circumstance, a self-analysing, self-conscious simplicity. Phase 7 shuddered at its intellectual simplicity, whereas he must shudder at his complexity.

Out of phase, instead of seeking this simplicity through his own dominating constructive will, he will parade an imaginary naïveté, even blunder in his work, encourage in himself stupidities of spite or sentiment, or commit calculated indiscretions simulating impulse. He is under the False *Mask* (emotional self-adaptation) and the False *Creative Mind* (distortion: the furious Phase 9 acted upon by "enforced sensuality"). He sees the *antithetical* as evil, and desires the evil, for he is subject to a sort of possession by the devil, which is in reality but a theatrical scene. Precisely because his adaptability can be turned in any direction, when lived according to the *primary*, he is driven into all that is freakish or grotesque, mind-created passions, simulated emotions; he adopts all that can suggest the burning heart he longs for in vain; he turns braggart or buffoon. Like somebody in Dostoyevsky's *Idiot*, he will invite others to tell their worst deeds that he may himself confess that he stole a half-crown and left a servant-girl to bear the blame.[161] When all turn upon him he will be full of wonder, for he knows that the confession is not true, or if true, that the deed itself was but a trick, or a pose, and that all the time he is full of a goodness that fills him with shame. Whether he live according to phase and regard life without emotion, or live out of phase and simulate emotion, his *Body of Fate* drags him away from intellectual unity; but in so far as he lives out of phase he weakens conflict, refuses to resist, floats upon the stream. In phase he strengthens conflict to the utmost by refusing all activity that is not *antithetical*: he becomes intellectually dominating, intellectually unique. He apprehends the simplicity of his opposite phase as some vast systematisation, in which the will imposes itself upon the multiplicity of living images, or events, upon all in Shakespeare, in Napoleon even, that delighted in its independent life; for he is a tyrant and must kill his adversary. If he is a novelist, his characters must go his road, and not theirs, and perpetually demonstrate his thesis; he will love construction better than the flow of life, and as a dramatist he will create character and situation without passion, and without liking, and yet he is a master of surprise, for one can never be sure where even a charge of shot will fall. Style exists now but as a sign of work well done, a certain energy and precision of movement; in the artistic sense it is no longer possible, for the tension of the will is too great to allow of suggestion. Writers of the phase are great public men and they exist after death as historical monuments, for they are without meaning apart from time and circumstance.

Phase Twenty-two

Will—Balance between ambition and contemplation.
Mask (from Phase 8). *True*—Self-immolation. *False*—Self-assurance.
Creative Mind (from Phase 8). *True*—Amalgamation. *False*—Despair.
Body of Fate (from Phase 22)—Temptation through Strength.
Examples: Flaubert, Herbert Spencer, Swedenborg, Dostoyevsky, Darwin.[162]

The aim of the being, until the point of balance has been reached, will be that of Phase 21 except that synthesis will be more complete, and the sense of identity between the individual and his thought, between his desire and his synthesis will be closer; but the character of the phase is precisely that here balance is reached and passed, though it is stated that the individual may have to return to this phase more than once, though not more than four times, before it is passed. Once balance has been reached, the aim must be to use the *Body of Fate* to deliver the *Creative Mind* from the *Mask*, and not to use the *Creative Mind* to deliver the *Mask* from the *Body of Fate*. The being does this by so using the intellect upon the facts of the world that the last vestige of personality disappears. The *Will*, engaged in its last struggle with external fact (*Body of Fate*), must submit, until it sees itself as inseparable from nature perceived as fact, and it must see itself as merged into that nature through the *Mask*, either as a conqueror lost in what he conquers, or dying at the moment of conquest, or as renouncing conquest, whether it come by might of logic, or might of drama, or might of hand. The *Will* since Phase 8 has more and more seen itself as a *Mask*, as a form of personal power, but now it must see that power broken. From Phase 12 to Phase 18 it was or should have been a power wielded by the whole nature; but since Phase 19 it has been wielded by a fragment only, as something more and more professional, temperamental or technical.

It has become abstract, and the more it has sought the whole of natural fact, the more abstract it has become. One thinks of some spilt liquid which grows thinner the wider it spreads till at last it is but a film. That which at Phase 21 was a longing for self-conscious simplicity, as an escape from logical complication and subdivision, is now (through the *Mask* from Phase 8) a desire for the death of the intellect. At Phase 21 it still sought to change the world, could still be a Shaw, a Wells, but now it will seek to change nothing, it needs nothing but what it may call "reality", "truth", "God's Will": confused and weary, through trying to grasp too much, the hand must loosen.

Here takes place an interchange between portions of the mind which resembles the interchange between the old and new *primary*, the old and new *antithetical* at Phase 1 and Phase 15. It is reflected, however, from the Wheel of the *Principles* I shall describe in Book II. The mind that has shown a predominantly emotional character, called that of the *Victim*, through the *antithetical* phases, now shows a predominantly intellectual character, called that of the *Sage* (though until Phase 1 has been passed it can but use intellect when true to phase to eliminate intellect); whereas the mind that has been predominantly that of the *Sage* puts on *Victimage*.[163] An element in the nature is exhausted at the point of balance, and the opposite element controls the mind. One thinks of the gusts of sentimentality that overtake violent men, the gusts of cruelty that overtake the sentimental. At Phase 8, a blinded and throttled phase, there is not a similar interchange. I will return to this omission in Book II.[164] A man of Phase 22 will commonly not only systematise, to the exhaustion of his will, but discover this exhaustion of will in all that he studies. If Lamarck, as is probable, was of Phase 21, Darwin was probably a man of Phase 22, for his theory of development by the survival of fortunate accidental varieties seems to express this exhaustion. The man himself is never weak, never vague or fluctuating in his thought, for if he brings all to silence, it is a silence that results from tension, and till the moment of balance, nothing interests him that is not wrought up to the greatest effort of which it is capable. Flaubert is the supreme literary genius of the phase, and his *Temptation of St. Anthony* and his *Bouvard and Pécuchet* are the sacred books of the phase, one describing its effect upon a mind where all is concrete and sensuous, the other upon the more logical, matter-of-fact, curious, modern mind.[165] In both the mind exhausts all knowledge within its reach and sinks exhausted to a conscious futility. But the matter is not more of the phase than is the method. One never doubts for a moment that Flaubert was of the phase; all must be impersonal;[166] he must neither like nor dislike character or event; he is "the mirror dawdling down a road" of Stendhal, with a clear brightness that is not Stendhal's; and when we make his mind our own, we seem to have renounced our own ambition under the influence of some strange, far-reaching, impartial gaze.[167]

We feel too that this man who systematised by but linking one emotional association to another has become strangely hard, cold and invulnerable, that this mirror is not brittle but of unbreakable steel. "Systematised" is the only word that comes to mind, but it implies too much deliberation, for association has ranged itself by association as little bits of paper and little chips of wood cling to one another upon the water in a bowl. In Dostoyevsky the "amalgamation" is less intellectual, less orderly, he, one feels, has reached the point of balance through life, not through the deliberate process of his art; his Whole will, not merely his intellectual will, has been shaken. His characters, in whom is reflected this broken will, are aware, unlike those of *Bouvard and Pécuchet*, those of the *Temptation* even, of some ungraspable Whole to which they have given the name of God. For a moment that fragment, that relation, which is our very being, is broken; they are at Udan Adan "wailing upon the edge of nonentity, wailing for Jerusalem, with weak voices almost inarticulate"; yet full submission has not come.[168]

Swedenborg passes through his balance after fifty, a mind incredibly dry and arid, hard, tangible and cold, like the minerals he assayed for the Swedish government, studies a new branch of science: the economics, the natural history of Heaven; notes that there nothing but emotion, nothing but the ruling love exists.[169] The desire to dominate has so completely vanished, "amalgamation" has pushed its way so far into the subconscious, into that which is dark, that we call it a vision. Had he been out of phase, had he attempted to arrange his life according to the personal *Mask*, he would have been pedantic and arrogant, a Bouvard, or a Pécuchet, passing from absurdity to absurdity, hopeless and insatiable.

In the world of action such absurdity may become terrible, for men will die and murder for an abstract synthesis, and the more abstract it is the further it carries them from compunction and compromise; and as obstacles to that synthesis increase, the violence of their will increases. It is a phase as tragic as its opposite, and more terrible, for the man of this phase may, before the point of balance has been reached, become a destroyer and persecutor, a figure of tumult and of violence; or as is more probable—for the violence of such a man must be checked by moments of resignation or despair, premonitions of balance—his system will become an instrument of destruction and of persecution in the hands of others.

The seeking of Unity of Fact by a single faculty, instead of Unity of Being by the use of all, has separated a man from his genius. This is symbolised in the Wheel by the gradual separation (as we recede from Phase 15) of *Will* and *Creative Mind*, *Mask* and *Body of Fate*. During the supernatural incarnation of Phase 15, we were compelled to assume an absolute identity of the *Will*, or self, with its creative power, of beauty with body; but for some time self and creative power, though separating, have been neighbours and kin. A Landor, or a Morris, however violent, however much of a child he seem, is always a remarkable man; in Phases 19, 20 and 21 genius grows professional, something taken up when work is taken up, it begins to be possible to record the stupidities of men of genius in a scrapbook; Bouvard and Pécuchet have that refuge for their old age. Someone has said that Balzac at noonday was a very ignorant man, but at midnight over a cup of coffee knew everything in the world.[170] In the man of action, in a Napoleon, let us say, the stupidities lie hidden, for action is a form of abstraction that crushes everything it cannot express. At Phase 22 stupidity is obvious, one finds it in the correspondence of Karl Marx,[171] in his banal abusiveness, while to Goncourt, Flaubert, as man, seemed full of unconsidered thought.[172] Flaubert, says Anatole France, was not intelligent.[173] Dostoyevsky, to those who first acclaimed his genius, seemed when he laid down his pen an hysterical fool. One remembers Herbert Spencer dabbing the grapes upon a lodging-house carpet with an inky cork that he might tint them to his favourite colour, "impure purple".[174] On the other hand, as the *Will* moves further from the *Creative Mind*, it approaches the *Body of Fate*, and with this comes an increasing delight in impersonal energy and in inanimate objects, and as the *Mask* separates from the *Body of Fate* and approaches the *Creative Mind* we delight more and more in all that is artificial, all that is deliberately invented. Symbols may become hateful to us, the ugly and the arbitrary delightful, that we may the more quickly kill all memory of Unity of Being. We identify ourselves in our surroundings—in our surroundings perceived as fact—while at the same time the intellect so slips from our grasp, as it were, that we contemplate its energies as something we can no longer control, and give to each of those energies an appropriate name as though it were an animate being. Now that *Will* and *Body of Fate* are one, *Creative Mind* and *Mask* one also, we are no longer four but two; and life, the balance reached, becomes an act of contemplation. There is no longer a desired object, as distinct from thought itself, no longer a *Will*, as distinct from the process of nature seen as fact; and so thought itself, seeing that it can neither begin nor end, is stationary. Intellect knows itself as its own object of desire; and the *Will* knows itself to be the world; there is neither change nor desire of change. For the moment the desire for reform has ceased and an absolute realism becomes possible.

Phase Twenty-three

Will—The Receptive Man.
Mask (from Phase 9). *True*—Wisdom. *False*—Self-pity.
Creative Mind (from Phase 7). *True*—Creation through pity. *False*—Self-driven desire.

Body of Fate (from Phase 21)—Success.
Examples: Rembrandt, Synge.[175]

When out of phase, for reasons that will appear later, he is tyrannical, gloomy and self-absorbed. In phase his energy has a character analogous to the longing of Phase 16 to escape from complete subjectivity: it escapes in a condition of explosive joy from systematisation and abstraction. The clock has run down and must be wound up again. The *primary tincture* is now greater than the *antithetical*, and the man must free the intellect from all motives founded upon personal desire, by the help of the external world, now for the first time studied and mastered for its own sake. He must kill all thought that would systematise the world, by doing a thing, not because he wants to, or because he should, but because he can; that is to say, he sees all things from the point of view of his own technique, touches and tastes and investigates technically. He is, however, because of the nature of his energy, violent, anarchic, like all who are of the first phase of a quarter. Because he is without systematisation he is without a master, and only by his technical mastery can he escape from the sense of being thwarted and opposed by other men; and his technical mastery must exist, not for its own sake, though for its own sake it has been done, but for that which it reveals, for its laying bare—to hand and eye, as distinguished from thought and emotion—general humanity. Yet this laying bare is a perpetual surprise, is an unforeseen reward of skill. And unlike *antithetical* man he must use his *Body of Fate* (now always his "success") to liberate his intellect from personality, and only when he has done this, only when he escapes the voluntary *Mask*, does he find his true intellect, is he found by his True *Mask*.

The True *Mask* is from the frenzied Phase 9 where personal life is made visible for the first time, but from that phase mastered by its *Body of Fate*, "enforced sensuality", derived from Phase 7 where the instinctive flood is almost above the lips. It is called "wisdom" and this wisdom (personality reflected in a *primary* mirror) is general humanity experienced as a form of involuntary emotion and involuntary delight in the "minute particulars" of life.[176] The man wipes his breath from the window-pane, and laughs in his delight at all the varied scene. Because his *Creative Mind* is at Phase 7, where instinctive life, all but reaching utmost complexity, suffers an external abstract synthesis, his *Body of Fate* which drives him to intellectual life, at Phase 21; his *Will* at a phase of revolt from every intellectual summary, from all intellectual abstraction, this delight is not mere delight, he would construct a whole, but that whole must seem all event, all picture. That whole must not be instinctive, bodily, natural, however, though it may seem so, for in reality he cares only for what is human, individual and moral. To others he may seem to care for the immoral and inhuman only, for he will be hostile, or indifferent to moral as to intellectual summaries; if he is Rembrandt he discovers his Christ through anatomical curiosity, or through curiosity as to light and shade,[177] and if he is Synge he takes a malicious pleasure in the contrast between his hero, whom he discovers through his instinct for comedy, and any hero in men's minds.[178] Indeed, whether he be Synge or Rembrandt, he is ready to sacrifice every convention, perhaps all that men have agreed to reverence, for a startling theme, or a model one delights in painting; and yet all the while, because of the nature of his *Mask*, there is another summary working through bone and nerve. He is never the mere technician that he seems, though when you ask his meaning he will have nothing to say, or will say something irrelevant or childish.

Artists and writers of Phase 21 and Phase 22 have eliminated all that is personal from their style, seeking cold metal and pure water, but he will delight in colour and idiosyncrasy, though these he must find rather than create. Synge must find rhythm and syntax in the Aran Islands,[179] Rembrandt delight in all accidents of the visible world; yet neither, no matter what his delight in reality, shows it without exaggeration, for both delight in all that is wilful, in all that flouts intellectual coherence, and conceive of the world as if it were an overflowing cauldron. Both will work in toil and in pain, finding what they do not seek, for, after Phase 22, desire creates no longer, will has taken its place; but that which they reveal is joyous. Whereas Shakespeare showed, through a style full of joy, a melancholy vision sought from afar; a style at play, a mind that served; Synge must fill many notebooks, clap his ear to that hole in the ceiling;[180] and what patience Rembrandt must have spent in the painting of a lace collar though to find his subject he had but to open his eyes.[181] When out of phase, when the man seeks to choose his *Mask*, he is gloomy with the gloom of others, and tyrannical with the tyranny of others, because he cannot create. Phase 9 was dominated by desire, was described as having the greatest belief in its own desire possible to man, yet from it Phase 23 receives not desire but pity, and not belief but wisdom. Pity needs wisdom as desire needs belief, for pity is *primary*, whereas desire is *antithetical*. When pity is separated from wisdom we have the False *Mask*, a pity like that of a drunken man, self-pity, whether offered in seeming to another or only to oneself: pity corrupted by desire. Who does not feel the pity in Rembrandt, in Synge, and know that it is inseparable from wisdom? In the works of Synge there is much self-pity, ennobled to a pity for all that lived; and once an actress, playing his Deirdre, put all into a gesture. Concubar, who had murdered Deirdre's husband and her friends, was in altercation with Fergus, who had demanded vengeance; "Move a little further off", she cried, "with the babbling of fools"; and a moment later, moving like a somnambulist, she touched Concubar upon the arm, a gesture full of gentleness and compassion, as though she had said, "You also live".[182] In Synge's early unpublished work, written before he found the dialects of Aran and of Wicklow, there is brooding melancholy and morbid self-pity.[183] He had to undergo an aesthetic transformation, analogous to religious conversion, before he became the audacious, joyous, ironical man we know. The emotional life in so far as it was deliberate had to be transferred from Phase 9 to Phase 23, from a condition of self-regarding melancholy to its direct opposite. This transformation must have seemed to him a discovery of his true self, of his true moral being; whereas Shelley's came at the moment when he first created a passionate image which made him forgetful of himself. It came perhaps when he had passed from the litigious rhetoric of *Queen Mab* to the lonely reveries of *Alastor*.[184] *Primary* art values above all things sincerity to the self or *Will* but to the self active, transforming, perceiving.

The quarter of Intellect was a quarter of dispersal and generalisation, a play of shuttlecock with the first quarter of animal burgeoning, but the fourth quarter is a quarter of withdrawal and concentration, in which active moral man should receive into himself, and transform into *primary* sympathy the emotional self-realisation of the second quarter. If he does not so receive and transform he sinks into stupidity and stagnation, perceives nothing but his own interests, or becomes a tool in the hands of others; and at Phase 23, because there must be delight in the unforeseen, he may be brutal and outrageous. He does not, however, hate, like a man of the third quarter, being but ignorant of or indifferent to the feelings of others. Rembrandt pitied ugliness, for what we call ugliness was to him an escape from all that is summarised and known, but had he painted a beautiful face, as *antithetical* man understands beauty, it would have remained a convention, he would have seen it through a mirage of boredom.

When one compares the work of Rembrandt with that of David,[185] whose phase was Phase 21; the work of Synge with that of Mr. Wells;[186] one compares men whose *antithetical tincture* is breaking up and dissolving, with men in whom it is, as for a last resistance, tightening, concentrating, levelling, transforming, tabulating. Rembrandt and Synge but look on and clap their hands. There is indeed as much selection among the events in one case as in the other, but at Phase 23 events seem startling because they elude intellect.

All phases after Phase 15 and before Phase 22 unweave that which is woven by the equivalent phases before Phase 15 and after Phase 8.

The man of Phase 23 has in the *Mask*, at Phase 9, a contrary that seems his very self until he use the discord of that contrary, his *Body of Fate* at Phase 21, to drive away the *Mask* and free the intellect and rid pity of desire and turn belief into wisdom. The *Creative Mind*, a discord to the *Will*, is from a phase of instinctive dispersal, and must turn the violent objectivity of the self or *Will* into a delight in all that breathes and moves: "The gay fishes on the wave when the moon sucks up the dew".[187]

PHASE TWENTY-FOUR

Will—The end of ambition.
Mask (from Phase 10). *True*—Self-reliance. *False*—Isolation.
Creative Mind (from Phase 6). *True*—Humanitarianism.
through constructive emotion.[188] *False*—Authority.
Body of Fate (from Phase 20)—Objective action.
Examples: Queen Victoria, Galsworthy, Lady Gregory.[189]

As the *Mask* now seems the natural self, which he must escape, the man labours to turn all within him that is from Phase 10 into some quality of Phase 24. At Phase 23, when in what seemed the natural self, the man was full of gloomy self-absorption and its appropriate abstractions, but now the abstractions are those that feed self-righteousness and scorn of others, the nearest the natural self can come to the self-expressing mastery of Phase 10. Morality, grown passive and pompous, dwindles to unmeaning forms and formulae. Under the influence of the *Body of Fate*, the unweaver and *discord* of Phase 10, the man frees the intellect from the *Mask* by unflagging impersonal activity. Instead of burning, as did Phase 23, intellectual abstraction in a technical fire, it grinds moral abstraction in a mill. This mill, created by the freed intellect, is a code of personal conduct, which, being formed from social and historical tradition, remains always concrete in the mind. All is sacrificed to this code; moral strength reaches its climax; the rage of Phase 10 to destroy all that trammels the being from without is now all self-surrender. There is great humility—"she died every day she lived"[190]—and pride as great, pride in the code's acceptance, an impersonal pride, as though one were to sign "servant of servants".[191] There is no philosophic capacity, no intellectual curiosity, but there is no dislike for either philosophy or science; they are a part of the world and that world is accepted. There may be great intolerance for all who break or resist the code, and great tolerance for all the evil of the world that is clearly beyond it whether above it or below. The code must rule, and because that code cannot be an intellectual choice, it is always a tradition bound up with family, or office, or trade, always a part of history. It is always seemingly fated, for its subconscious purpose is to compel surrender of every personal ambition; and though it is obeyed in pain—can there be mercy in a rigid code?—the man is flooded with the joy of self-surrender; and flooded with mercy—what else can there be in self-surrender?—for those over whom the code can have no rights, children and the nameless multitude. Unmerciful to those who serve and to himself, merciful in contemplating those who are served, he never wearies of forgiveness.

Men and women of the phase create an art where individuals only exist to express some historical code, or some historical tradition of action and of feeling, things written in what Raftery called the Book of the People, or settled by social or official station, even as set forth in Directory or Peerage.[192] The judge upon the bench is but a judge, the prisoner in the dock is but the eternal offender, whom we may study in legend or in Blue Book.[193] They despise the Bohemian above all men till he turns gypsy, tinker, convict, or the like, and so finds historical sanction, attains as it were to some inherited code or recognised relation to such code.[194] They submit all their actions to the most unflinching examination, and yet are without psychology, or self-knowledge, or self-created standard of any kind, for they but ask without ceasing, "Have I done my duty as well as So-and-so?"[195] "Am I as unflinching as my fathers before me?" and though they can stand utterly alone, indifferent though all the world condemn, it is not that they have found themselves, but that they have been found faithful. The very Bohemians are not wholly individual men in their eyes, and but fulfil the curse, laid upon them before they were born, by God or social necessity.

Out of phase, seeking emotion instead of impersonal action, there is—desire being impossible—self-pity, and therefore discontent with people and with circumstance, and an overwhelming sense of loneliness, of being abandoned. All criticism is resented, and small personal rights and predilections, especially if supported by habit or position, are asserted with violence; there is great indifference to others' rights and predilections; we have the bureaucrat or the ecclesiastic of satire, a tyrant who is incapable of insight or of hesitation.

Their intellect being from Phase 6, but their energy, or will, or bias, from Phase 24, they must, if in phase, see their code expressed in multiform human life, the mind of Victoria at its best, as distinguished from that of Walt Whitman. Their emotional life is a reversal of Phase 10, as what was autocratic in Victoria reversed the personal autocracy of Parnell.[196] They fly the *Mask*, that it may become, when enforced, that form of pride and of humility that holds together a professional or social order.

When out of phase they take from Phase 10 isolation, which is good for that phase but destructive to a phase that should live for others and from others; and they take from Phase 6 a bundle of race instincts, and turn them to abstract moral or social convention, and so contrast with Phase 6, as the mind of Victoria at its worst contrasts with that of Walt Whitman. When in phase they turn these instincts to a concrete code, founded upon dead or living example.

That which characterises all phases of the last quarter, with an increasing intensity, begins now to be plain: persecution of instinct—race is transformed into a moral conception—whereas the intellectual phases, with increasing intensity as they approached Phase 22, persecuted emotion. Morality and intellect persecute instinct and emotion respectively, which seek their protection.

Phase Twenty-five

Will—The Conditional Man.
Mask (from Phase 11). *True*—Consciousness of self. *False*—Self-consciousness.
Creative Mind (from Phase 5). *True*—Rhetoric. *False*—Spiritual arrogance.
Body of Fate (from Phase 19)—Persecution.
Examples: Cardinal Newman, Luther, Calvin, George Herbert, George Russell (A. E.).[197]

Born as it seems to the arrogance of belief, as Phase 24 was born to moral arrogance, the man of the phase must reverse himself, must change from Phase 11 to Phase 25; use the *Body of Fate* to purify the intellect from the *Mask*, till this intellect accepts some social order, some condition of life, some organised belief: the convictions of Christendom perhaps. He must eliminate all that is personal from belief; eliminate the necessity for intellect by the contagion of some common agreement, as did Phase 23 by its technique, Phase 24 by its code. With a *Will* of subsidence, an intellect of loosening and separating, he must, like Phase 23 or Phase 24, find himself in such a situation that he is compelled to concrete synthesis (*Body of Fate* at Phase 19 the *discord* of Phase 11), but this situation compels the *Will*, if it pursue the False *Mask*, to the persecution of others, if found by the True *Mask*, to suffer persecution. Phase 19, phase of the *Body of Fate*, is a phase of breaking, and when the *Will* is at Phase 25, of breaking by belief or by condition. In this it finds impulse and joy. It is called the *Conditional Man*, perhaps because all the man's thought arises out of some particular condition of actual life, or is an attempt to change that condition through social conscience. He is strong, full of initiative, full of social intellect; absorption has scarce begun; but his object is to limit and bind, to make men better, by making it impossible that they should be otherwise, to so arrange prohibitions and habits that men may be naturally good, as they are naturally black, or white, or yellow. There may be great eloquence, a mastery of all concrete imagery that is not personal expression, because though as yet there is no sinking into the world but much distinctness, clear identity, there is an overflowing social conscience. No man of any other phase can produce the same instant effect upon great crowds; for codes have passed, the universal conscience takes their place. He should not appeal to a personal interest, should make little use of argument which requires a long train of reasons, or many technical terms, for his power rests in certain simplifying convictions which have grown with his character; he needs intellect for their expression, not for proof, and taken away from these convictions is without emotion and momentum. He has but one overwhelming passion, to make all men good, and this good is something at once concrete and impersonal; and though he has hitherto given it the name of some church, or state, he is ready at any moment to give it a new name, for, unlike Phase 24, he has no pride to nourish upon the past. Moved by all that is impersonal, he becomes powerful as, in a community tired of elaborate meals, that man might become powerful who had the strongest appetite for bread and water.

When out of phase he may, because Phase 11 is a phase of diffused personality and pantheistic dreaming, grow sentimental and vague, drift into some emotional abstract, his head full of images long separated from life, and ideas long separated from experience, turn tactless and tasteless, affirm his position with the greatest arrogance possible to man. Even when nearly wholly good he can scarce escape from arrogance; what old friend did Cardinal Newman cut because of some shade of theological difference?[198]

Living in the False *Creative Mind* produces, in all *primary* phases, insensitiveness, as living in the False *Mask* produces emotional conventionality and banality, because that False *Creative Mind*, having received no influence from the *Body of Fate*, no mould from individuals and interests, is as it were self-suspended. At Phase 25 this insensitiveness may be that of a judge who orders a man to the torture, that of a statesman who accepts massacre as an historical necessity. One thinks of Luther's apparent indifference to atrocities committed, now by the peasants, now against them, according to the way his incitements veered.[199]

The genius of Synge and Rembrandt has been described as typical of Phase 23. The first phase of a triad is an expression of unrelated power. They surprised the multitude, they did not seek to master it; while those chosen for examples of Phase 24 turn the multitude into a moral norm. At Phase 25 men seek to master the multitude, not through expressing it, nor through surprising it, but by imposing upon it a spiritual norm. Synge, reborn at Phase 25, might interest himself, not in the *primary* vigour and tragedy or his Aran Island countrymen, but in their conditions, their beliefs, and through some eccentricity (not of phase but horoscope), not in those shared with fellow Catholics, as Newman would, but in those shared with Japanese peasants, or in their belief as a part of all folk belief considered as religion and philosophy. He would use this religion and philosophy to kill within himself the last trace of individual abstract speculation, yet this religion and this philosophy, as present before his mind, would be artificial and selected, though always concrete. Subsidence upon, or absorption in, the spiritual *primary* is not yet possible or even conceivable.

Poets of this phase are always stirred to an imaginative intensity by some form of propaganda. George Herbert was doubtless of this phase; and George Russell (A. E.), though the signs are obscured by the influence upon his early years of poets and painters of middle *antithetical* phases. Neither Russell's visionary painting nor his visions of "nature spirits" are, upon this supposition, true to phase. Every poem, where he is moved to write by some form of philosophical propaganda, is precise, delicate and original, while in his visionary painting one discovers the influence of other men, Gustave Moreau, for instance.[200] This painting is like many of his "visions", an attempt to live in the *Mask*, caused by critical ideas founded upon *antithetical* art. What dialect was to Synge, his practical work as a cooperative organiser was to him, and he found precise ideas and sincere emotion in the expression of conviction. He learned practically, but not theoretically, that he must fly the *Mask*. His work should neither be consciously aesthetic nor consciously speculative but imitative of a central Being—the *Mask* as his pursuer—consciously apprehended as something distinct, as something never imminent though eternally united to the soul.

His False *Mask* showed him what purport to be "nature spirits" because all phases before Phase 15 are in nature, as distinguished from God, and at Phase 11 that nature becomes intellectually conscious of its relations to all created things. When he desires the *Mask*, instead of flying that it may follow, it gives, instead of the intuition of God, a simulated intuition of nature. That simulated intuition is arrayed in ideal conventional images of sense, instead of in some form of abstract opinion, because of the character of his horoscope.

Phase Twenty-six

Will—The Multiple Man, also called "The Hunchback".[201]
Mask (from Phase 12). *True*—Self-realisation. *False*—Self-abandonment.
Creative Mind (from Phase 4). *True*—Beginning of abstract supersensual thought. *False*—Fascination of sin.
Body of Fate (from Phase 18)—The Hunchback is his own *Body of Fate*.

The most difficult of the phases, and the first of those phases for which one can find few or no examples from personal experience. I think that in Asia it might not be difficult to discover examples at least of Phases 26, 27 and 28, final phases of a cycle. If such embodiments occur in our present European civilisation they remain obscure, through lacking the instruments for self-expression. One must create the type from its symbols without the help of experience.

All the old abstraction, whether of morality or of belief, has now been exhausted; but in the seemingly natural man, in Phase 26 out of phase, there is an attempt to substitute a new abstraction, a simulacrum of self-expression. Desiring emotion the man becomes the most completely solitary of all possible men, for all normal communion with his kind, that of a common study, that of an interest in work done, that of a condition of life, a code, a belief shared, has passed; and without personality he is forced to create its artificial semblance. It is perhaps a slander of history that makes us see Nero so, for he lacked the physical deformity which is, we are told, first among this phase's inhibitions of personality.[202] The deformity may be of any kind, great or little, for it is but symbolised in the hump that thwarts what seems the ambition of a Caesar or of an Achilles.[203] He commits crimes, not because he wants to, or like Phase 23 out of phase because he can, but because he wants to feel certain that he can; and he is full of malice because, finding no impulse but in his own ambition, he is made jealous by the impulse of others. He is all emphasis, and the greater that emphasis the more does he show himself incapable of emotion, the more does he display his sterility. If he live amid a theologically minded people, his greatest temptation may be to defy God, to become a Judas, who betrays, not for thirty pieces of silver, but that he may call himself creator.[204]

In examining how he becomes true to phase, one is perplexed by the obscure description of the *Body of Fate*, "The Hunchback is his own *Body of Fate*". This *Body of Fate* is derived from Phase 18, and (being reflected in the physical being of Phase 26) can only be such a separation of function—deformity—as breaks the self-regarding False *Mask* (Phase 18 being the breaking of Phase 12). All phases from Phase 26 to Phase 11 inclusive should be gregarious; and from Phase 26 to Phase 28 there is, when the phase is truly lived, contact with supersensual life, or a sinking-in of the body upon its supersensual source, or desire for that contact and sinking. At Phase 26 has come a subconscious exhaustion of the moral life, whether in belief or in conduct, and of the life of imitation, the life of judgment and approval. The *Will* must find a substitute, and as always in the first phase of a triad energy is violent and fragmentary. The moral abstract being no longer possible, the *Will* may seek this substitute through the knowledge of the lives of men and beasts, plucked up, as it were, by the roots, lacking in all mutual relations; there may be hatred of solitude, perpetual forced bonhomie; yet that which it seeks is without social morality, something radical and incredible. When Ezekiel lay upon his "right and left side" and ate dung, to raise "other men to a perception of the infinite",[205] he may so have sought, and so did perhaps the Indian sage or saint who coupled with the roe.[206]

If the man of this phase seeks, not life, but knowledge of each separated life in relation to supersensual unity; and above all of each separated physical life, or action,—that alone is entirely concrete—he will, because he can see lives and actions in relation to their source and not in their relations to one another, see their deformities and incapacities with extraordinary acuteness.[207] His own past actions also he must judge as isolated and each in relation to its source; and this source, experienced not as love but as knowledge, will be present in his mind as a terrible unflinching judgment. Hitherto he could say to *primary* man, "Am I as good as So-and-so?" and when still *antithetical* he could say, "After all I have not failed in my good intentions taken as a whole"; he could pardon himself; but how pardon where every action is judged alone and no good action can turn judgment from the evil action by its side? He stands in the presence of a terrible blinding light, and would, were that possible, be born as worm or mole.[208]

From Phase 22 to Phase 25, man is in contact with what is called the physical *primary*, or physical objective; from Phase 26 and Phase 4, the *primary* is spiritual; then for three phases, the physical *primary* returns. Spiritual, in this connection, may be understood as a reality known by analogy alone. How can we know what depends only on the self? In the first and in the last crescents lunar nature is but a thin veil; the eye is fixed upon the sun and dazzles.

Phase Twenty-seven

Will—The Saint.
Mask (from Phase 13). *True*—Renunciation. *False*—Emulation.
Creative Mind (from Phase 3). *True*—Supersensual receptivity. *False*—Pride.
Body of Fate (from Phase 17)—None except impersonal action.
Examples: Socrates, Pascal.[209]

In his seemingly natural man, derived from *Mask*, there is an extreme desire for spiritual authority; and thought and action have for their object display of zeal or some claim of authority. Emulation is all the greater because not based on argument but on psychological or physiological difference. At Phase 27, the central phase of the soul, of a triad that is occupied with the relations of the soul, the man asserts when out of phase his claim to faculty or to supersensitive privilege beyond that of other men; he has a secret that makes him better than other men.

True to phase, he substitutes for emulation an emotion of renunciation, and for the old toil of judgment and discovery of sin, a beating upon his breast and an ecstatical crying out that he must do penance, that he is even the worst of men. He does not, like Phase 26, perceive separated lives and actions more clearly than the total life, for the total life has suddenly displayed its source. If he possess intellect he will use it but to serve perception and renunciation. His joy is to be nothing, to do nothing, to think nothing; but to permit the total life, expressed in its humanity, to flow in upon him and to express itself through his acts and thoughts. He is not identical with it, he is not absorbed in it, for if he were he would not know that he is nothing, that he no longer even possesses his own body, that he must renounce even his desire for his own salvation, and that this total life is in love with his nothingness.

Before the self passes from Phase 22 it is said to attain what is called the "Emotion of Sanctity", and this emotion is described as a contact with life beyond death. It comes at the instant when synthesis is abandoned, when fate is accepted. At Phases 23, 24 and 25 we are said to use this emotion, but not to pass from Phase 25 till we have intellectually realised the nature of sanctity itself, and sanctity is described as the renunciation of personal salvation. The "Emotion of Sanctity" is the reverse of that realisation of incipient personality at Phase 8, which the *Will* related to collective action till Phase 11 had passed.[210] After Phase 22 the man becomes aware of something which the intellect cannot grasp, and this something is a supersensual environment of the soul. At Phases 23, 24 and 25 he subdues all attempts at its intellectual comprehension, while relating it to his bodily senses and faculties, through technical achievement, through morality, through belief. At Phases 26, 27 and 28 he permits those senses and those faculties to sink in upon their environment. He will, if it be possible, not even touch or taste or see: "Man does not perceive the truth; God perceives the truth in man".[211]

Phase Twenty-eight

Will—The Fool.[212]
Mask (from Phase 14). *True*—Oblivion. *False*—Malignity.
Creative Mind (from Phase 2). *True*—Physical activity. *False*—Cunning.
Body of Fate (from Phase 16)—The Fool is his own *Body of Fate*.

The natural man, the Fool desiring his *Mask*, grows malignant, not as the Hunchback, who is jealous of those that can still feel, but through terror and out of jealousy of all that can act with intelligence and effect. It is his true business to become his own opposite, to pass from a semblance of Phase 14 to the reality of Phase 28, and this he does under the influence of his own mind and body—he is his own *Body of Fate*—for having no active intelligence he owns nothing of the exterior world but his mind and body. He is but a straw blown by the wind, with no mind but the wind and no act but a nameless drifting and turning, and is sometimes called "The Child of God".[213] At his worst his hands and feet and eyes, his will and his feelings, obey obscure subconscious fantasies, while at his best he would know all wisdom if he could know anything. The physical world suggests to his mind pictures and events that have no relation to his needs or even to his desires; his thoughts are an aimless reverie; his acts are aimless like his thoughts; and it is in this aimlessness that he finds his joy. His importance will become clear as the system elaborates itself, yet for the moment no more need be said but that one finds his many shapes on passing from the village fool to the Fool of Shakespeare.

Out of the pool,
Where love the slain with love the slayer lies,
Bubbles the wan mirth of the mirthless fool.[214]

PHASE ONE

Will. *Mask* (from Phase 15). *Creative Mind* (from Phase 1). *Body of Fate* (from Phase 15).	No description except complete plasticity.

This is a supernatural incarnation, like Phase 15, because there is complete objectivity, and human life cannot be completely objective. At Phase 15 mind was completely absorbed by being, but now body is completely absorbed in its supernatural environment. The images of mind are no longer irrelevant even, for there is no longer anything to which they can be relevant, and acts can no longer be immoral or stupid, for there is no one there that can be judged. Thought and inclination, fact and object of desire, are indistinguishable (*Mask* is submerged in *Body of Fate*, *Will* in *Creative Mind*), that is to say, there is complete passivity, complete plasticity. Mind has become indifferent to good and evil, to truth and falsehood; body has become undifferentiated, dough-like; the more perfect be the soul, the more indifferent the mind, the more dough-like the body; and mind and body take whatever shape, accept whatever image is imprinted upon them, transact whatever purpose is imposed upon them, are indeed the instruments of supernatural manifestation, the final link between the living and more powerful beings.[215] There may be great joy; but it is the joy of a conscious plasticity; and it is this plasticity, this liquefaction, or pounding up, whereby all that has been knowledge becomes instinct and faculty. All plasticities do not obey all masters, and when we have considered cycle and horoscope it will be seen how those that are the instruments of subtle supernatural will differ from the instruments of cruder energy; but all, highest and lowest, are alike in being automatic.

Finished at Thoor Ballylee, 1922,
in a time of Civil War.[216]

THE COMPLETED SYMBOL

BOOK II: THE COMPLETED SYMBOL

I

I knew nothing of the *Four Principles* when I wrote the last Book: a script had been lost through frustration, or through my own carelessness.[1] The *Faculties* are man's voluntary and acquired powers and their objects; the *Principles* are the innate ground of the *Faculties*, and must act upon one another in the same way, though my instructors, to avoid confusion, have given them a different geometry. The whole system is founded upon the belief that the ultimate reality, symbolised as the Sphere, falls in human consciousness, as Nicholas of Cusa was the first to demonstrate, into a series of antinomies.[2] The *Principles* are the *Faculties* transferred, as it were, from a concave to a convex mirror, or vice versa. They are *Husk*, *Passionate Body*, *Spirit* and *Celestial Body*. *Spirit* and *Celestial Body* are mind and its object (the Divine Ideas in their unity),*

*In the following passage from *The Friend* Coleridge writes "reason" where I write "mind". "I shall have no objection to define reason with Jacobi, with my friend Helvetius, as an organ bearing the same relation to its spiritual object, the universal, the eternal, the necessary, as the eye bears to material and contingent phenomena. But then it must be added that it is an organ identical with its appropriate objects. Thus God, the soul, eternal truth etc. are the objects of reason; but they are themselves reason . . . whatever is conscious self-knowledge is reason." Later on he distinguishes between "the outward sense and the mind's eye which is reason"; on the next page between mind and its object, or as we put it *Spirit* and *Celestial Body*, "reasoning (or reason in this its secondary sense) does not consist in the ideas or in their clearness but simply, when they are in the mind, in seeing whether they coincide with each other or no".[3]

while *Husk* and *Passionate Body*, which correspond to *Will* and *Mask*, are sense* (impulse, images; hearing, seeing, etc., images that we associate with ourselves—the ear, the eye, etc.) and the objects of sense. *Husk* is symbolically the human body. The *Principles* through their conflict reveal reality but create nothing. They find their unity in the *Celestial Body*. The *Faculties* find theirs in the *Mask*.

The wheel or cone of the *Faculties* may be considered to complete its movement between birth and death, that of the *Principles* to include the period between lives as well. In the period between lives, the *Spirit* and the *Celestial Body* prevail, whereas *Husk* and *Passionate Body* prevail during life.[5] Once again, solar day, lunar night. If, however, we were to consider both wheels or cones as moving at the same speed and to place, for purposes of comparison, the *Principles* in a double cone, drawn and numbered like that of the *Faculties*, and superimpose it upon that of the *Faculties*, a line drawn between Phase 1 and Phase 15 on the first would be at right angles to a line drawn between the same phases upon the other. Phase 22 in the cone of the *Principles* would coincide with Phase 1 in the cone of the *Faculties*. "Lunar South in Solar East."[6] In practice, however, we do not divide the wheel of the *Principles* into the days of the month, but into the months of the year.

At death consciousness passes from *Husk* to *Spirit*; *Husk* and *Passionate Body* are said to *disappear*, which corresponds to the *enforcing* of *Will* and *Mask* after Phase 22,[7] and *Spirit* turns from *Passionate Body* and clings to *Celestial Body* until they are one and there is only *Spirit*; pure mind, containing within itself pure truth, that which depends only upon itself: as in the *primary* phases, *Creative Mind* clings to *Body of Fate* until mind deprived of its obstacle can create no more and nothing is left but "the *spirits* at one", unrelated facts and aimless mind, the burning out that awaits all voluntary effort.

Behind the *Husk* (or sense) is the *Daimon's* hunger to make apparent to itself certain *Daimons*, and the organs of sense are that

*Indian Philosophy has active and passive senses. Seeing is passive, walking active.[4]

hunger made visible. The *Passionate Body* is the sum of those *Daimons*. The *Spirit*, upon the other hand, is the *Daimon's* knowledge, for in the *Spirit* it knows all other *Daimons* as the Divine Ideas in their unity. They are one in the *Celestial Body*. The *Celestial Body* is identified with necessity; when we perceive the *Daimons* as *Passionate Body*, they are subject to time and space, cause and effect; when they are known to the *Spirit*, they are known as intellectual necessity, because what the *Spirit* knows becomes a part of itself. The *Spirit* cannot know the *Daimons* in their unity until it has first perceived them as the objects of sense, the *Passionate Body* exists that it may "save the *Celestial Body* from solitude". In the symbolism the *Celestial Body* is said to age as the *Passionate Body* grows young, sometimes the *Celestial Body* is a prisoner in a tower rescued by the *Spirit*.[8] Sometimes, grown old, it becomes the personification of evil. It pursues, persecutes and imprisons the *Daimons*.*

II

And because the *Daimon* seeks through the *Husk* that in *Passionate Body* which it needs, when *Passionate Body* predominates all is *Destiny*; the man dominated by his *Daimon* acts in spite of reason; whereas the man finds through reason or through the direct vision of the *Spirit* Fate or Necessity, which lies outside himself in *Body of Fate* or *Celestial Body*.†

*See Blake's *Mental Traveller*. Neither Edwin Ellis nor I, nor any commentator has explained the poem, though one or another has explained certain passages. The student of *A Vision* will understand it at once. Did Blake and my instructors draw upon some unknown historical source, some explanation perhaps of the lunar circuit?[9]

†The Hermetic Fragments draw somewhat the same distinction. Necessity comes, they say, upon us through the events of life and must be obeyed. Destiny sows the seeds of those events and impels evil men. One fragment adds "Order" connecting "Necessity" and "Destiny" and identifies it with the Cosmos. The three seem to constitute a Hegelian triad. I am summarising from Scott's *Hermetics* Exc. vii. Exc. viii. and Asclepius iii. Section 39. The difference between their point of view and mine is that I cannot consider that Destiny inspires only evil men. The Hermetic Fragments are full of Platonic Intellectualism. Destiny becomes evil when the *Passionate Body* is subject to Necessity.[10]

The *Passionate Body* is in another of its aspects identical with physical light; not the series of separated images we call by that name, but physical light, as it was understood by mediaeval philosophers, by Berkeley in *Siris*, by Balzac in *Louis Lambert*, the creator of all that is sensible.[11]

It is because of the identification of light with nature that my instructors make the *antithetical* or lunar cone of the *Faculties* light and leave the solar dark. In the cone of the *Principles*, the solar cone is light and the other dark, but their light is thought not nature.*

III

Spirit is the future, *Passionate Body* the present, *Husk* the past, deriving its name from the husk that is abandoned by the sprouting seed.[13] The *Passionate Body* is the present, creation, light, the objects of sense.[14] *Husk* is the past not merely because the objects are passed before we can know their images, but because those images fall in patterns and recurrences shaped by a past life or lives. At moments it is identified with race or instinct. It is the involuntary self as *Will* the voluntary. I am not, however, certain that I understand the statement that *Spirit* is the future.[15] I would have understood had my instructors said that *Celestial Body* was the future,

*Collyns Simon in his index to *The Principles of Human Knowledge* calls Light a "Sensation, not the condition or cause of one, as some physicists endeavour to teach". Berkeley, according to Hone and Rossi, meant by Light not "Sensation" but that which "brings out Sensation . . . a semi-material agent" discoverable by mind alone; but Simon is right, for Berkeley speaks of Light as discoverable by animals, where all to us seems dark, and uses this argument to prove that Light is all-pervading. In the *Commonplace Book* he warned himself to avoid the theologically dangerous theme of personality. Did he in his private thoughts come to regard Light as the creative act of a universal self dwelling in all selves? Grosseteste, Bishop of Lincoln, described Light as corporeality itself, and thought that in conjunction with the first matter, it engendered all bodies. Pierre Duhem analyses his philosophy in *Le Système du Monde*, vol. v, pp. 356, 357, 358. Plotinus describes the Light seen with our eyes open and that seen when we rub our closed eyes, as a light coming from the soul itself. The modern term "Astral Light" implies this source and is probably derived from some seventeenth-century Platonist, who symbolised the soul as a star, but the popular writers who employ it seem to think that the Light seen in Spiritual Vision alone is from that star.[12]

for the ideal forms are only apparent through hope; perhaps they mean that we do not in reality seek these forms, that while separate from us they are illusionary, but that we do seek *Spirit* as complete self-realisation, and do not spirits sometimes say, "We have no present,* we are the future", meaning that they are reality as we perceive it under the category of the future? From another point of view, the spirits can have neither past nor present, because *Husk* and *Passionate Body* have *disappeared.* My teachers do not characterise the *Celestial Body*, but it is doubtless the timeless. There seems to be a reversed attribution in the *Faculties*. In the *Faculties*, *Mask* (the forms "created by passion to unite us to ourselves",[17] in the *antithetical* phases beauty) is apparently the timeless, *Will* the future, *Body of Fate*, or Fact, the present, *Creative Mind* the past. The past of the *Faculties* is abstract, a series of judgments. "When did Julius Caesar die?" "What are the chemical constituents of water?" Memory is a series of judgments and such judgments imply a reference to something that is not memory, that something is the *Daimon*, which contains within it, co-existing in its eternal moment, all the events of our life, all that we have known of other lives, or that it can discover within itself of other *Daimons*. Seeing that object and judgment imply space, we may call *Husk* and *Creative Mind* by that name, for in both Time spatialises.

In the wheel of the *Faculties*, *Will* predominates during the first quarter, *Mask* during the second, *Creative Mind* during the third, *Body of Fate* during the fourth. In the wheel of the *Principles*, *Husk* (the new still unopened *Husk*) predominates during the first quarter, *Passionate Body* during the second, *Spirit* during the third, and *Celestial Body* during the fourth. If we put future, present, past and the timeless in the four quarters of each wheel according to their attribution to *Faculty* or *Principle*, we find that the present and the timeless, past and future, are opposite.

*Dante describes the spirits in the *Inferno* as having no present, as they approach the present all grows dim. Their future is not, however, the future of spiritual freedom.[16]

IV

The ultimate reality because neither one nor many, concord nor discord, is symbolised as a phaseless sphere, but as all things fall into a series of antinomies in human experience it becomes, the moment it is thought of, what I shall presently describe as the thirteenth cone.[18] All things are present as an eternal instant to our *Daimon* (or *Ghostly Self* as it is called, when it inhabits the sphere), but that instant is of necessity unintelligible to all bound to the antinomies. My instructors have therefore followed tradition by substituting for it a *Record* where the images of all past events remain for ever "thinking the thought and doing the deed".[19] They are in popular mysticism called "the pictures in the astral light", a term that became current in the middle of the nineteenth century, and what Blake called "the bright sculptures of Los's Hall".[20] We may describe them as the *Passionate Body* lifted out of time.[21]

V

My instructors, keeping as far as possible to the phenomenal world, have spent little time upon the sphere, which can be symbolised but cannot be known, though certain chance phrases show that they have all the necessary symbols.[22] When I try to imagine the *Four Principles* in the sphere, with some hesitation I identify the *Celestial Body* with the First Authentic Existant of Plotinus, *Spirit* with his Second Authentic Existant, which holds the First in its moveless circle; the discarnate *Daimons*, or *Ghostly Selves*, with his Third Authentic Existant or soul of the world (the Holy Ghost of Christianity), which holds the Second in its moving circle. Plotinus has a fourth condition which is the Third Authentic Existant reflected first as sensation and its object (our *Husk* and *Passionate Body*), then as discursive reason (almost our *Faculties*).[23] The *Husk* as part of the sphere merges in *The Ghostly Self*.

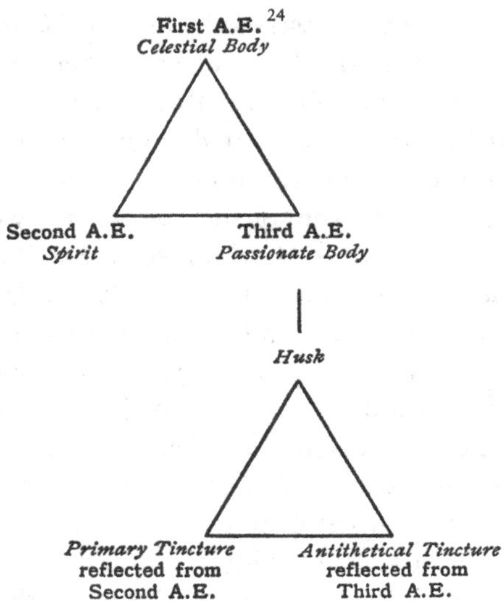

But this diagram implies a descent from *Principle* to *Principle*, a fall of water from ledge to ledge, whereas a system symbolising the phenomenal world as irrational because a series of unresolved antinomies, must find its representation in a perpetual return to the starting-point. The resolved antinomy appears not in a lofty source but in the whirlpool's motionless centre, or beyond its edge.*

I must now enumerate certain interactions of *Faculties* and *Principles* which are not defined by diagrams.

The emotions are formed by *Will*, acted upon by *Mask* and *Celestial Body*, or by *Mask* and *Passionate Body*. When *Will*, *Passionate Body* and *Mask* act together there is pleasure and pain in the act itself, but when *Will* acts alone all is abstract utility, economics, a mechanism to prolong existence. When *Passionate Body* and *Celestial Body* give way to *Mask* we dwell in aesthetic process, so much skill in bronze or paint, or on some symbol that rouses emotion for emotion's sake. When *Mask* and *Passionate Body* are in unison we desire emotion that excites the senses.[26] When *Mask* and *Celestial*

*The whirlpool is an *antithetical* symbol, the descending water a *primary*.[25]

Body are in unison we are possessed by love *antithetical* to our normal self. When *Creative Mind* is added to either combination love or desire is unified or objectified whether in action or in a work of art. When *Creative Mind* is separated from *Spirit* there is abstract thought, classification, syllogism, number, everything whereby the fact is established, and the sum of such facts is the world of science and common sense. *Creative Mind* united to *Spirit* brings not fact but truth, not science but philosophy. The *Principles* alone cannot distinguish between fact and hallucination. Ruskin, according to Frank Harris, saw a phantom cat at the end of the room and stooped to fling it out of the window.[27] That cat may have had more significant form than the house cat; displayed all cat nature as if it were the work of some great artist; symbolised with every movement *Spirit* and *Celestial Body*; been visible to others—there are houses haunted by animals—but it was never littered, could not overset the jug, had no settled place in that continuity of images, that sum of facts that has yet no value in itself. Spurious art is the conquest of *Mask* by *Husk* and *Passionate Body*, and commercial art its conquest by *Will*. Common realism is conquest by *Body of Fate*, and so on.

VI

I am told to give Phases 1, 8, 15, 22 a month apiece, the other phases the third of a month, and begin the year like the early Roman year in the lunar month corresponding to March, when days begin to grow longer than nights:[28]

March . . .	Phase 15
April . . .	Phases 16, 17, 18
May . . .	Phases 19, 20, 21
June . . .	Phase 22

and so on.[29] There is no reason why March, June, etc., should have one phase, all others three; it is classification not symbolism. The relation between the wheel of twenty-eight phases and that of twelve months has turned out as insoluble to the symbolist as was that between the solar and lunar year to the ancient astronomers. I must keep myself at liberty to consider any period, whether between signs or enclosed in a lunar phase, as a simple microcosm containing days, months, years.[30] At the Ides of March, at the full moon in March, is the Vernal Equinox, symbolical of the first degree of Aries, the first day of our symbolical or ideal year, and at the middle of each month the sign changes. Aries changes to Taurus at the middle of the second month, the middle of Phase 17, and so on. The *Will* marks its course by the lunar months, the *Creative Mind* by the signs. When the Great Wheel is a month the symbolism seems simpler, for the lunar periods are the natural phases of such a month, each solar period beginning and ending in the middle of a phase.

A solar period is a day from sunrise to sunrise, or a year from March to March, a month from full moon to full moon. On the other hand a lunar period is a day from sunset to sunset, a year from September to September, a month from moonless night to moonless night. In other words every month or phase when we take it as a whole is a double vortex moving from Phase 1 to Phase 28, or two periods, one solar and one lunar, which in the words of Heraclitus "live each other's death, die each other's life".[31]

If we consider East as symbolical of the head, as in Astrology, a diagonal line drawn from East in a solar wheel will cross at right angles a similar line drawn from East in a lunar. My instructors fixed this upon my mind by saying that the man of a solar wheel stood upright whereas the man of a lunar lay horizontal like a sleeping man. That the small wheels and vortexes that run from birth to birth may be part of the symbolism of the wheel of the twenty-eight incarnations without confusing it in the mind's eye, my instructors have preferred to give to the *Principles* of these small wheels cones that cannot be confused with that of the *Faculties*. The dominant thought is to show *Husk* starting on its journey from the centre of the wheel, the incarnate *Daimon*, and *Spirit* from the circumference as though it received its impulse from beyond the *Daimon*. These cones are drawn across the centre of the wheel from *Faculty* to *Faculty*, two with bases joined between *Creative Mind* and *Body of Fate*, and two with apexes joined between *Will* and *Mask*.

Within these figures move the *Principles*; *Spirit* and *Celestial Body* in the figure shaped like an ace of diamonds, *Husk* and *Passionate Body* in that shaped like an hour-glass. The first figure is divided according to the signs of the Zodiac, though it can be divided as readily according to the points of the compass, the East or sunrise taking the place of the Vernal Equinox, the second divided into the twenty-eight lunar phases. In the cones of the *Spirit* and the *Celestial Body* there is only one gyre, that of *Spirit*, *Celestial Body* being represented by the whole diamond. The union of *Spirit* and *Celestial Body* has a long approach and is complete when the gyre reaches its widest expansion. There is only one gyre because, whereas *Husk* faces an object alien to itself, *Spirit's* object is of like nature to itself. The gyre of the *Husk* starts at the centre (its Phase 1), reaches its Phase 8, where the circumference can be marked *Mask*, and returns to its centre for Phase 15, passes from its centre to its Phase 22, where the circumference can be marked *Will*, and finishes at the centre. One records these movements upon the edges of the figures, phases for *Husk*, Zodiacal signs for *Spirit*,* *Husk* and *Passionate Body* moving from right to left and the single gyre of *Spirit* from left to right. *Husk* and *Passionate Body* remain always opposite, *Passionate Body* at Phase 15 when *Husk* is at Phase 1 and so on. When *Husk* is at Phase 15, *Spirit* sets out from Aries. It reaches Cancer when *Husk* is at Phase 22 and Libra when *Husk* is at Phase 1. When *Spirit* is at edge of Wheel *Husk* is at centre.

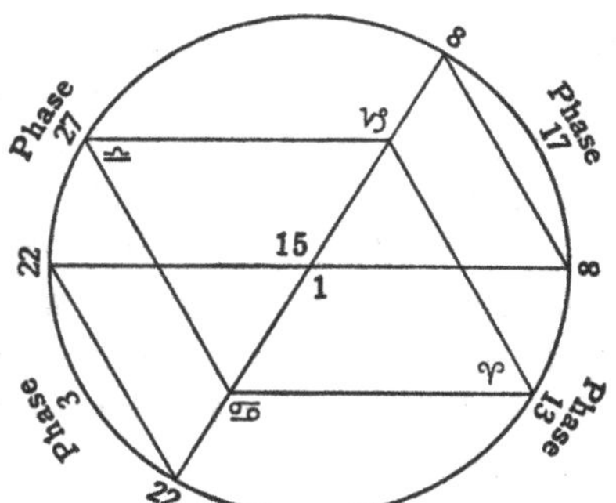

*My instructors sometimes give *Husk* and *Will* Zodiacs of their own; these lunar Zodiacs are counted from right to left, a line joining Cancer and Capricorn in a lunar Zodiac cuts a line joining Cancer and Capricorn in a solar Zodiac at right angles. "Lunar South is Solar East." I have left them out for the sake of simplicity, but will return to them later.[32]

When cone and diamond are superimposed (diagram below)[33] we get a simple figure corresponding to the double cone (p. 58[34] and elsewhere). Diamond and hour-glass revolve on one another like the sails of a windmill. As the diamond represents a sphere, at its gyre's greatest expansion *Spirit* contains the whole Wheel. Though for convenience we make the diamond narrow, like the diamond of a playing-card, its widest expansion must be considered to touch the circumference of the wheel where the wheel meets the gyre of the *Thirteenth Cone*. Indeed, its gyre touches that circumference throughout. The diamond is a convenient substitute for a sphere, the hour-glass for two meeting spheres. Taken in relation to the wheel, the diamond and the hour-glass are two pulsations, one expanding, one contracting. I can see them like jelly fish in clear water.

The foregoing figure shows the position of diamond and hour-glass when *Will* on the wheel is passing Phase 17. The following diagram shows such cones when *Will* on the wheel of the twenty-eight phases is at Phase 15.

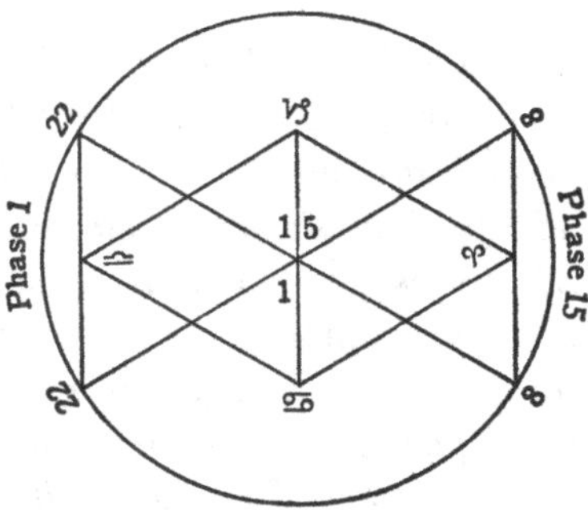

At Phases 15, 22, 1 and 8 of the wheel of the incarnations the cones are superimposed. These gyres complete their movement, whether of twelve months or twenty-eight days, while *Will* as marked upon the circumference completes its phase, their *Husk* starting at the centre when the phase begins and returning there at its end. Sometimes the automatic script substitutes this figure for the wheel itself, the revolving cones drawn without any containing circle, roughly indicating the phase by their position in relation to one another. The Communicators often scribbled it on margins, or on scraps of paper, without relation to the text as if to remind themselves of some phase they would speak of later.[35]

VII

The *Four Faculties* have a movement also within the cones of the *Principles.* Their double vortex is superimposed upon the half of the cone of *Husk* and *Passionate Body* which lies between *Will* (the *Will* on the circumference of the wheel) and the centre of the wheel.

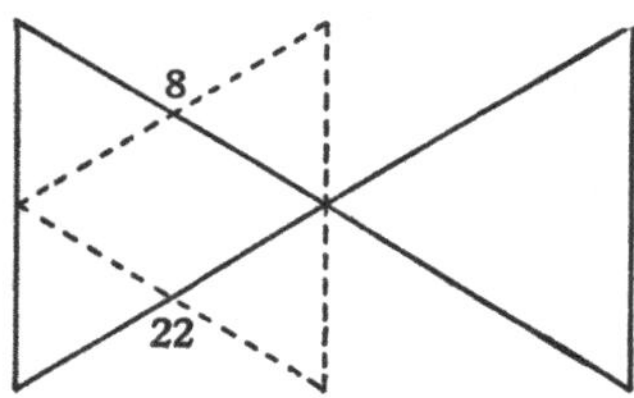

When *Husk* has reached Phase 8 they are at Phase 15; when *Husk* has reached its Phase 15 they are at Phase 1.[36] While *Will* (*Will* on circumference) is passing through half a phase, *Husk* passing from Phase 1 to Phase 15, the *Faculties* complete their full movement, Phase 1 to Phase 28, and when their movement represents an incarnation disappear at its completion. The *Principles* thereupon take their place defining the state between death and birth.[37] Death which comes when the *Spirit* gyre is at Aries is symbolised as spring or dawn; and birth which comes when the *Spirit* gyre is at Libra, as autumn or sunset. Incarnate life is night or winter, discarnate life is day or summer.

VIII

A Great Wheel of twenty-eight incarnations is considered to take, if no failure compels repetition of a phase, some two thousand odd years, and twelve such wheels or gyres constitute a single great cone or year of some twenty-six thousand years. But these twenty-six thousand years* are but a norm, a convenient measure, much may shorten or lengthen the whole or some part of the whole. All men, it is assumed, once passed through their year at the same pace; all were at the same moment, at the same phase, but gradually some fell behind, and some ran ahead, and now there is a year that ends when the life-period of the individual winds itself up, and a Great Year which is a norm or average struck among the individual years. I shall, when I come to write upon the Great Year of antiquity, refer to the fact that Proclus had the same conception and gave to the smallest living creature its individual year.[39]

IX

Hegel identifies Asia with Nature; he sees the whole process of civilisation as an escape from Nature; partly achieved by Greece, fully achieved by Christianity. Oedipus—Greece—solved the riddle of the Sphinx—Nature—compelled her to plunge from the precipice, though man himself remained ignorant and blundering. I accept his definition.[40] When my great diagram of the wheel was first drawn for me, all from Phase 1 to Phase 15 had the word "Nature" written beside it; all from Phase 15 to Phase 1 the word "God". I reject, however, his description of Nature in the *Philosophy of History*, a description that seems applicable to the first eight phases alone. Nor do I see Asia as he sees it. Asia is *primary*, *solar*, and only becomes Nature at Phase 1.[41] A wheel of the Great Year must be thought of as the marriage of symbolic Europe and symbolic Asia, the one begetting upon the other.† When it commenced at its sym-

*My instructors are playing with the period necessary to complete the precession of the Equinox from Aries to Aries. It has been a part of literary tradition since Edmund Spenser described it in *The Faerie Queene*, Book V, Introd. stanzas i–ii. They have, however, adopted the twenty-six thousand years of modern astronomy instead of the thirty-six thousand years Spenser took from the Platonic Year.[38]

†Flinders Petrie in *The Revolutions of Civilisation* says that the Eastern phase is five hundred years ahead of Europe, and draws attention to the coincidence between the rise of Arabian civilisation and the fall of that of Europe. My system seems to imply that the rise of Arabian civilisation and that of Christianity are the same phenomena. European art did not cast off the influence

bolic full moon in March—Christ or Christendom was begotten by the West upon the East. This begetting has been followed by a spiritual predominance of Asia.[43] After it must come an age begotten by the East upon the West that will take after its Mother in turn. The Lunar Months of 2200 years apiece, in a year of 26,000 years, are years of civilisation, while the Solar Months of a similar symbolical length* correspond to periods of religion.

Each solar month may be called a revolution of *Creative Mind* and *Body of Fate* beginning and ending with *Creative Mind* in Aries, each lunar month a revolution of *Will* and *Mask* beginning and ending with *Will* at Phase 1. When, however, one wants to show, as the automatic script generally does, that each civilisation and religious dispensation is the opposite of its predecessor, a single revolution constitutes two solar or lunar months. For instance, classical civilisation—1000 B.C. to A.D. 1000 let us say—is represented by the movement of *Will* from Phase 1, the place of birth, to Phase 15, the place of death, and our own civilisation is now almost midway in the movement of the *Will* from Phase 15 to Phase 1. The student of ancient symbolism discovers the darkening and brightening fortnights of Brahminical symbolism, the fortnight during which the moon increases in light and represents an *antithetical* civilisation, and that during which it decreases and represents a *primary* civilisation.[45] At or near the central point of a lunar month of classical civilisation—the first degree of Aries on the Great Wheel—came the Christian *primary* dispensation, the child born in the Cavern. At or near the central point of our civilisation must come *antithetical* revelation, the turbulent[46] child of the Altar.† The antithesis between

of Eastern art, as the Japanese interpreter of Botticelli has shown, until the establishment of "tonal values" after the Renaissance as a principal vehicle of expression. They have been accompanied by the decline of Christianity. It is not, however, easy to say how far I should interpret my symbols according to the letter.[42]

*We may compare these equal periods to the incarnations of equal length attributed by Plato to his man of Ur, his ideal man, whose individual year of 36,000 years or of 360 incarnations later generations identified with the Platonic Year. The Platonic Year is an average or norm fixed by many individual years, but the year of an ideal man would conform to it.[44]

†I am thinking of the two symbols discovered by Frobenius in Africa, the Cavern, symbol of the nations moving westward, the Altar at the centre of radiating roads, symbol of the nations moving eastward.[47]

lunar and solar is emphasised by the correspondence of summer to the darkening fortnight and of winter to the brightening.

X

When I relate this symbol to reality various fancies pass before the mind. The Great Wheel revolved innumerable times before the beast changed into man and many times before the man learned to till the ground. Perhaps the hunting age gave way to agriculture when our present revolution brought round Phase 4 or 5. At Phase 4 or 5 or perhaps a little later may have emerged the Sacred Legend of the sun's annual journey, symbol of all history and of individual life, foundation of all the earliest civilisations; and at the phases where Unity of Being became possible began perhaps those civilisations, Egypt or Sumer, which had made a progressive, conscious, intellectual life possible by the discovery of writing.[48]

Is that marriage of Europe and Asia a geographical reality? Perhaps, yet the symbolic wheel is timeless and spaceless.

When I look in history for the conflict or union of *antithetical* and *primary* I seem to discover that conflict or union of races stated by Petrie and Schneider as universal law.[49] A people who have lived apart and so acquired unity of custom and purity of breed unite with some other people through migration, immigration or conquest. A race (the new *antithetical*) emerges that is neither the one nor the other, after somewhere about 500 years it produces, or so it seems, its particular culture or civilisation. This culture lives only in certain victorious classes; then comes a period of revolution (Phase 22) terminated by a civilisation of policemen, schoolmasters, manufacturers, philanthropists, a second soon exhausted blossoming of the race. Schneider* finds three such race cultures, each with its double blossoming, in China and India, four in Egypt, though doubtful whether the final imitative period can be called a distinct culture, two among the Greeks, one and part of another among the Romans, and I forget how many in Persia, Babylon, Judea. All these cultures, as I am directed to see them, having attained some Achilles

***The History of World Civilisation*, by Hermann Schneider, translated by Margaret M. Green.

in the first blossoming, find pious Aeneas in their second, and that second is preceded by Utopian dreams that come to little because no civilisation can spend what it has not earned.[50] The Saint suffers a like impediment; the love he brings to God at his twenty-seventh phase was found in some past life upon a woman's breast, his loyalty and wisdom were prepared perhaps a thousand years before in serving a bad master, and that is why the Indian minstrel sings God as woman, husband, lover and child.[51]

The historian thinks of Greece as an advance on Persia, of Rome as in something or other an advance of Greece, and thinks it impossible that any man could prefer the hunter's age to the agricultural. I, upon the other hand, must think all civilisations equal at their best; every phase returns, therefore in some sense every civilisation. I think of the hunter's age and that which followed immediately as a time when man's waking consciousness had not reached its present complexity and stability. There was little fear of death, sometimes men lay down and died at will, the world of the gods could be explored easily whether through some orgiastic ceremony or in the trance of the ascetic. Apparitions came and went, bringing comfort in the midst of tragedy.

XI

I shall write little of the *Principles* except when writing of the life after death. They inform the *Faculties* and it is the *Faculties* alone that are apparent and conscious in human history. Vico said that we know history because we create it, but as nature was created by God only God can know it.[52]

I must now explain a detail of the symbolism which has come into my poetry and, in ways I am not yet ready to discuss, into my life. When *Will* is passing through Phases 16, 17 and 18 the *Creative Mind* is passing through the Phases 14, 13 and 12, or from the sign Aries to the sign Taurus, that is to say, it is under the conjunction of Mars and Venus.* When *Will* upon the other hand is

*I set down what follows less for present use than because at some later date I may return to the theme and wake these dry astrological bones into breathing life.

passing through Phases 12, 13 and 14 the *Creative Mind* is passing through the Phases 18, 17 and 16, or from the sign Pisces to the sign Aquarius, it is, as it were, under the conjunction of Jupiter and Saturn. These two conjunctions which express so many things are certainly, upon occasion, the outward-looking mind, love and its lure, contrasted with introspective knowledge of the mind's self-begotten unity, an intellectual excitement.[53] They stand, so to speak, like heraldic supporters guarding the mystery of the fifteenth phase.[54] In certain lines written years ago in the first excitement of discovery I compared one to the Sphinx and one to Buddha. I should have put Christ instead of Buddha, for according to my instructors Buddha was a Jupiter-Saturn influence.

Although I saw it all in the mind's eye
There can be nothing solider till I die;
I saw by the moon's light
Now at its fifteenth night.

One lashed her tail; her eyes lit by the moon
Gazed upon all things known, all things unknown,
In triumph of intellect
With motionless head erect.

The other's moonlit eyeballs never moved,
Being fixed on all things loved, all things unloved,
Yet little peace he had,
For those that love are sad.[55]

XII

As a religious dispensation begins and ends at Phase 15, a Mars-Venus conjunction presides over its beginning and a Saturn-Jupiter over its close. The group of phases so dominated are those where Unity of Being is possible. The influx that dominates a *primary* dispensation comes a little after the start of the dispensation itself, at its Phase 16 perhaps, and that which dominates an *antithetical* dispensation a considerable time before the close of the preceding *primary* dispensation, its Phase 26 let us say; it is, as it were, not so much a breaking out of new life as the vivification of old intellect. A *primary* revelation begins therefore under Mars-Venus, an *antithetical* under Saturn-Jupiter.

XIII

Nations, cultures, schools of thought may have their *Daimons*. These *Daimons* may move through the Great Year like individual men and women and are said to use men and women as their bodies, to gather and disperse those bodies at will. Leibniz, whose logical monads resemble somewhat my perceptive *Daimons*, thought there must be many monads much greater than those of individual men and women.[56] Lionel Johnson was fond of quoting from Dionysius the Areopagite, "He has set the borders of his nations according to his angels", but Swedenborg thought that all angels had once been men.[57]

XIV

The twelve months or twelve cycles can be considered not as a wheel but as an expanding cone, and to this is opposed another cone which may also be considered as divided into twelve cycles or months. As the base of each cone has at its centre the apex of the other cone the double vortex is once more established. The twelve cycles or months of the second cone are so numbered that its first month is the last of the first cone, the summer of the one the winter of the other. It resembles exactly every other double cone in the system. The passage from Phase 1 to Phase 15 is always, whether we call it a month or six months or twelve months, or an individual life, set over against a passage from Phase 15 to Phase 1; and whether we consider the cone that of incarnate or that of discarnate life, the gyre of *Husk* or *Will* cuts the gyre of *Spirit* or *Creative Mind* with the same conflict of seasons,* a being racing into the fu-

*I thought I discovered this antithesis of the seasons when some countryman told me that he heard the lambs of Faery bleating in November, and, read in some heroic tale of supernatural flowers in midwinter. I may have deceived myself, but if I did I got out of the deception the opening passage in my play *The Hour-Glass*: "Where is the passage I am to explain to my pupils to-day? Here

ture passes a being racing into the past, two footprints perpetually obliterating one another, toe to heel, heel to toe.

I shall consider the gyre in the present expanding cone for the sake of simplicity as the whole of human life, without waiting to portion out the *Faculties* and *Principles*, and the contrasting cone as the other half of the antinomy, the "spiritual objective". Although when we are in the first month of this expanding cone we are in the twelfth of the other, when we are in the second in the eleventh of the other, and so on, that month of the other cone which corresponds to ours is always called by my instructors the Thirteenth Cycle or *Thirteenth Cone*, for every month is a cone. It is that cycle which may deliver us from the twelve cycles of time and space. The cone which intersects ours is a cone in so far as we think of it as the antithesis to our thesis, but if the time has come for our deliverance it is the phaseless sphere, sometimes called the Thirteenth Sphere, for every lesser cycle contains within itself a sphere that is, as it were, the reflection or messenger of the final deliverance. Within it live all souls that have been set free and every *Daimon* and *Ghostly Self*; our expanding cone seems to cut through its gyre; spiritual influx is from its circumference, animate life from its centre. "Eternity also", says Hermes in the Asclepius dialogue, "though motionless itself, appears to be in motion."[59] When Shelley's Demogorgon—eternity—comes from the centre of the earth it may so come because Shelley substituted the earth for such a sphere.*[60]

XV

All these symbols can be thought of as the symbols of the relations of men and women and of the birth of children. We can think of the *antithetical* and *primary* cones, or wheels, as the domination,

it is, and the book says that it was written by a beggar on the walls of Babylon: 'There are two living countries, the one visible and the other invisible; and when it is winter with us it is summer in that country, and when the November winds are up among us it is lambing-time there'."[58]

*Shelley, who had more philosophy than men thought when I was young, probably knew that Parmenides represented reality as a motionless sphere. Mrs. Shelley speaks of the "mystic meanings" of *Prometheus Unbound* as only intelligible to a "mind as subtle as his own".[61]

now by the man, now by the woman, and of a child born at Phase 15 or East as acquiring a *primary* character from its father who is at Phase 1 or West and of a child born at Phase 1 or West as acquiring an *antithetical* character from its father at Phase 15, or East, and so on, man and woman being alternately Western and Eastern. Such symbolical children, sealed as it were by Saturn and Jupiter or Mars and Venus, cast off the mother and display their true characters as their cycle enters its last quarter. We may think of the wheel as an expression of alternations of passion, and think of the power of the woman beginning at symbolical East or Aries and seated in *Creative Mind*, and of the power of the man as seated in *Will* and beginning at symbolical West when *Creative Mind* is in Libra, or half-way through its course, and *Will* at Phase 1 (Blake's *Mental Traveller*), or think of the wheel as an expression of the birth of symbolical children bound together by a single fate.[62] When we so think of it we recreate the lives of Christ and St. John as they are symbolised in the Christian year, Christ begotten in spring and brought forth in midwinter, begotten in joy and brought forth in sorrow, and St. John begotten in autumn and brought forth in midsummer, begotten in sorrow and brought forth in joy.[63] Coventry Patmore claimed the Church's authority for calling Christ supernatural love and St. John natural love, and took pleasure in noticing that Leonardo painted a Dionysus like a St. John, a St. John like a Dionysus.[64] But I need not go further, for all the symbolism of this book applies to begetting and birth, for all things are a single form which has divided and multiplied in time and space.

There are certain numbers, certain obscure calculations in Plato's *Republic* meant to suggest and hide the methods adopted by the ruling philosophers to secure that the right parents shall beget the right children, and it is foretold that when these numbers and calculations are forgotten the Republic must decay.[65] The latest authoritative work, Taylor's *Plato*, thinks it probable that the "Golden Number", on which these calculations are based, is 36,000 years or a lunar year of 360 days, each day 100 years.[66] If I may think of those days or incarnations as periods wherein symbolic man grows old and young alternately, as he does in certain other Platonic periods, I have, but for a different length and enumeration, my Great Wheel of twelve cycles. Plato may have brought such an ideal year into the story, its periods all of exactly the same length, to remind us that he dealt in myth. My instructors, however, insist that a man of, let us say, the seventh cycle married to a woman of, let us say, the sixth cycle will have a certain type of child, that this type is further modified by the phases and by the child's position in time and place at birth, a position which is itself but an expression of the interaction of cycles and phases. Will some mathematician some day question and understand, as I cannot, and confirm all, or have I also dealt in myth?

XVI

When my instructors see woman as man's goal and limit, rather than as mother, they symbolise her as *Mask* and *Body of Fate*, object of desire and object of thought, the one a perpetual rediscovery of what the other destroys; the seventh house of the horoscope where one finds friend and enemy; and they set this double opposite in perpetual opposition to *Will* and *Creative Mind*.[67] In Book III I shall return to this symbolism, which perhaps explains, better than any I have used, Blake's *Mental Traveller*.[68]

XVII

I have now described many symbols which seem mechanical because united in a single structure, and of which the greater number, precisely because they tell always the same story, may seem unnecessary. Yet every symbol, except where it lies in vast periods of time and so beyond our experience, has evoked for me some form of human destiny, and that form, once evoked, has appeared everywhere, as if there were but one destiny, as my own form might appear in a room full of mirrors. When one discovers, as will be seen presently, at a certain moment between life and death, what ancient legends have called the Shape-Changers, one illustrates a moment of European history, of every mind that passes from premise to judgment, of every love that runs its whole course.[69] The present Pope has said in his last Encyclical that the natural union of man and woman has a kind of sacredness.[70] He thought doubtless of the marriage of Christ and the Church, whereas I see in it a symbol of that eternal instant where the antinomy is resolved. It is not the resolution itself. There is a passage in Lucretius translated by Dryden, to the great scandal of his enemy Collier, which is quite conclusive.[71]

XVIII

My instructors identify consciousness with conflict, not with knowledge, substitute for subject and object and their attendant logic a struggle towards harmony, towards Unity of Being. Logical and emotional conflict alike lead towards a reality which is concrete, sensuous, bodily. My imagination was for a time haunted by figures that, muttering "The great systems", held out to me the sun-dried skeletons of birds, and it seemed to me that this image was meant to turn my thoughts to the living bird. That bird signifies truth when it eats, evacuates, builds its nest, engenders, feeds its young; do not all intelligible truths lie in its passage from egg to dust? Passages written by Japanese monks on attaining Nirvana, and one by an Indian, run in my head. "I sit upon the side of the mountain and look at a little farm. I say to the old farmer, 'How many times have you mortgaged your farm and paid off the mortgage?' I take pleasure in the sound of the rushes." "No more does the young man come from behind the embroidered curtain amid the sweet clouds of incense; he goes among his friends, he goes among the flute-players; something very nice has happened to the young man, but he can only tell it to his sweetheart." "You ask me what is my religion and I hit you upon the mouth." "Ah! Ah! The lightning crosses the heavens, it passes from end to end of the heavens. Ah! Ah!"*

*I have compared these memories with their source in Suzuki's *Zen Buddhism*, an admirable and exciting book, and find that they are accurate except that I have substituted here and there better sounding words.[72]

THE SOUL IN JUDGMENT

BOOK III: THE SOUL IN JUDGMENT[1]

I

Paul Valéry in the "Cimetière Marin" describes a seaside cemetery, a recollection, some commentator explains, of a spot known in childhood.[2] The midday light is the changeless absolute and its reflection in the sea "les œuvres purs d'une cause éternelle".[3] The sea breaks into the ephemeral foam of life; the monuments of the dead take sides as it were with the light and would with their inscriptions and their sculptured angels persuade the poet that he is the light, but he is not persuaded. The worm devours not only the dead, but as self-love, self-hate, or whatever one calls it, devours the living also. Then after certain poignant stanzas and just when I am deeply moved he chills me. This metropolitan, who has met so many reformers, who has learnt as a part of good manners to deny what has no remedy, cries out "Cruel Zénon! Zénon d'Elée!", condemning that problem of a tortoise and Achilles because it suggested that all things only seemed to pass; and in a passage of great eloquence rejoices that human life must pass.*[4] I was about to put his poem among my sacred books, but I cannot now, for I do not believe him. My imagination goes some years backward, and I remember a beautiful young girl singing at the edge of the sea in Normandy words and music of her own composition. She thought herself alone, stood barefooted between sea and sand; sang with

*Professor Bradley believed also that he could stand by the death-bed of wife or mistress and not long for an immortality of body and soul. He found it difficult to reconcile personal immortality with his form of Absolute idealism, and besides he hated the common heart; an arrogant, sapless man.[5]

lifted head of the civilisations that there had come and gone, ending every verse with the cry: "O Lord, let something remain".[6]

II

I cannot imagine an age without metropolitan poet and singing girl, though I am convinced that the Upanishads—somebody had already given her the Pyramids—were addressed to the girl.

Certain Upanishads describe three states of the soul, that of waking, that of dreaming, that of dreamless sleep, and say man passes from waking through dreaming to dreamless sleep every night and when he dies.[7] Dreamless sleep is a state of pure light, or of utter darkness according to our liking, and in dreams "the spirit serves as light for itself". "There are no carts, horses, roads, but he makes them for himself."[8]

III

The *Spirit* is not those changing images—sometimes in ancient thought as in the "Cimetière Marin" symbolised by the sea*—but the light,† and at last draws backward into itself, into its own changeless purity, all it has felt or known. I am convinced that this ancient generalisation, in so far as it saw analogy between a "separated spirit", or phantom and a dream of the night, once was a universal belief, for I find it, or some practice founded upon it, everywhere. Certainly I find it in old Irish literature, in modern Irish folk-lore, in Japanese plays, in Swedenborg, in the phenomena of spiritualism, accompanied as often as not by the belief that the living can assist the imaginations of the dead.[10] A farmer near Doneraile once told me that an aunt of his own appeared stark naked after her death and complained that she could not go about with the other spirits unless somebody cut a dress to her measure and gave it to a poor woman in her name.[11] This done she appeared wearing the dress

*I think it was Porphyry who wrote that the generation of images in the mind is from water.[9]

†In my symbolism solar light, intellectual light; not the lunar light, perception.

and gave thanks for it. Once an old woman came to Coole Park, when I was there, to tell Lady Gregory that Sir William Gregory's ghost had a tattered sleeve and that a coat must be given to some beggar in his name.[12] A man, returned after many years spent in the West Indies, once told me and others of the apparition of a woman he had known in a dress that he had not known, copied, he discovered, from her portrait made after he had left England.[13] May I not use such tales to interpret all those model houses, boats, weapons, slaves, all those portraits and statues buried in ancient tombs?[14]

Certain London spiritualists for some years past have decked out a Christmas tree with presents that have each the names of some dead child upon it, and sitting in the dark on Christmas night they hear the voice of some grown-up person, who seems to take the presents from the tree, and the clamorous voices of the children as they are distributed.[15] Yet the presents still hang there and are given next day to an hospital. Could anything be more Egyptian, more Assyrian? It was essential that the clothes should be given in the name of the dead, that the portrait should be the ghost's own portrait, that the presents for the children should be dedicated or given, not merely hung there; in dreams we finish what we began awake or what the waking suggest. I think of two ghost lovers in a Japanese play asking a wandering Buddhist priest to marry them, of two that appeared to a Catholic priest in Aran, according to an Aran tale, with a like object,[16] of a young spirit medium who promised that she would marry a certain old man after death but was compelled by her controls to withdraw the promise because, though she had not meant it, she might have had to fulfil it, of an Indian who told Florence Farr[17] that he hated acting, for if a man died playing Hamlet he would be Hamlet after death.[18] Upon the other hand a spirit may meet some spirit in the séance-room to ask forgiveness for something done in life, a forgiveness not always granted, and once at the request of a certain dead Sister of Mercy I discovered where the Mother Superior she had served under in the Crimea lived and died, and she came again to thank me.[19] Because I had connected their lives here she had found her there, though not to share her state, being less holy. I had suggested away the nightmare as though sitting by the bedside of a somnambulist.

IV

The *Mandookya Upanishad* describes a fourth state, which is reached not in dreamless sleep but in contemplation and in wakefulness.[20] This fourth state, pure light to those that reach it, is that state wherein the soul, as much ancient symbolism testifies, is united to the blessed dead.

Because we no longer discover the still unpurified dead through our own and others' dreams, and those in freedom through contemplation, religion cannot answer the atheist, and philosophy talks about a first cause or a final purpose, when we would know what we were a little before conception, what we shall be a little after burial.

V[21]

The period between death and birth is divided into states analogous to the six solar months between Aries and Libra.*[22] The first state is called *The Vision of the Blood Kindred*, a vision of all those bound to us through *Husk* and *Passionate Body*.[23] Apparitions seen at the moment of death are part of the vision, a synthesis, before *disappearance*, of all the impulses and images which constitute the *Husk*. It is followed by the *Meditation*, which corresponds to what is called the "emotion of sanctity" on the Great Wheel; the *Spirit* and *Celestial Body appear*.[24] The *Spirit* has its first vision and understanding of the *Celestial Body*, but that it may do so, it requires the help of the incarnate, for without them it is without language and without will. During the *Meditation*† *Husk* and *Passionate*

*They correspond roughly to Phase 22, Phases 23, 24, 25, Phases 26, 27, 28, etc., upon the wheel of the *Faculties* which is at right angles to that of the *Principles*.

†An automatic script describes this *Meditation* as lasting until burial and as strengthened by the burial service and by the thoughts of friends and mourners. I left this statement out of the text because it did not so much seem a necessary deduction from the symbol as an unverifiable statement of experience. The meaning is doubtless that the ceremonial obliteration of the body symbolises the *Spirit's* separation from the *Husk*. Another automatic script describes the *Spirit* as rising from the head at death, *Celestial Body* from the feet, the *Passionate Body* from the genitals, while the *Husk* remains prone in the body (the *Husk*

Body disappear, but may persist in some simulacrum of themselves as do the *Mask* and *Will* in *primary* phases. If the *Husk* so persist, the *Spirit* still continues to feel pleasure and pain, remains a fading distortion of living man, perhaps a dangerous succuba or incubus, living through the senses and nerves of others. If there has been great animal egotism, heightened by some moment of tragedy, the *Husk* may persist for centuries, recalled into a sort of life, and united to its *Spirit*, at some anniversary, or by some unusually susceptible person or persons connected with its past life.

In the third discarnate state, a state I shall presently describe, it may renounce the form of a man and take some shape from the social or religious tradition of its past life, symbolical of its condition. Leap Castle, though burnt down during our Civil War and still a ruin, is haunted by what is called an evil spirit which appears as a sheep with short legs and decaying human head.[26] I suggest that some man with the *Husk* exaggerated and familiar with religious symbolism, torn at the moment of death between two passions, terror of the body's decay with which he identified himself, and an abject religious humility, projected himself in this image.[27] If the *Passionate Body* does not *disappear*, the *Spirit* finds the *Celestial Body*, only after long and perhaps painful dreams of the past, and it is because of such dreams that the second state is sometimes called the *Dreaming Back*.[28] If death has been violent or tragic the *Spirit* may cling to the *Passionate Body* for generations. A gambler killed in a brawl may demand his money,* a man who has believed that death ends all may see himself as a decaying corpse,[†30] nor is there any reason why some living man might not see reflected in a mirror or otherwise some beloved ghost, thinking herself unobserved, powdering her face as in Mr. Davies' poem.[31‡]

itself seen objectively) and shares its form. The *Spirit* is described as awakened from its sleep in the dead body.[25]

*The late Dr. Abraham Wallace told me that he brought a medium to a haunted house and had a conversation with just such a ghost. He afterwards found, in an *Annual Register* for somewhere about 1770, a record of just such a brawl at that very house.[29]

†I came on this example years ago; it seemed well authenticated.

‡This would be one of the most poignant poems in the language had not Mr. Davies in a verse I have not quoted made an inexplicable transition from "thou" to "you".[32]

The first night she was in her grave,
As I looked in the glass
I saw her sit upright in bed;
Without a sound it was;
I saw her hand feel in the cloth
To fetch a box of powder forth.

She sat and watched me all the while
For fear I looked her way;
I saw her powder cheek and chin,
Her fast corrupting clay.
Then down my lady lay and smiled,
She thought her beauty saved, poor child.

VI

The true name of the second state,* that of Taurus, is the *Return* and it has for its object the *Spirit's* separation from the *Passionate Body*, considered as nature, and from the *Husk* considered as pleasure and pain.[33] In the *Dreaming Back*, the *Spirit* is compelled to live over and over again the events that had most moved it; there can be nothing new, but the old events stand forth in a light which is dim or bright according to the intensity of the passion that accompanied them. They occur in the order of their intensity or luminosity, the more intense first, and the painful are commonly the more intense, and repeat themselves again and again. In the *Return*, upon the other hand, the *Spirit* must live through past events in the order of their occurrence, because it is compelled by the *Celestial Body* to trace every passionate event to its cause until all are related and understood, turned into knowledge, made a part of itself.[34] All that keeps the *Spirit* from its freedom may be compared to a knot that has to be untied or to an oscillation or a violence that must end in a return to equilibrium.[35] I think of the Homeric contrast between Heracles passing through the night, bow in hand, and Heracles, the freed spirit, a happy god among the gods. I think of it in William Morris' translation:

*Roughly Phases 23, 24, 25 on the wheel of the *Faculties*.

And Heracles the mighty I saw when these went by;
His image indeed: for himself mid the gods that never die
Sits glad at the feast, and Hebe fair-ankled there doth hold,
The daughter of Zeus the mighty and Hera shod with gold.[36]

After its imprisonment by some event in the *Dreaming Back*, the *Spirit* relives that event in the *Return* and turns it into knowledge, and then falls into the *Dreaming Back* once more. The *Spirit* finds the concrete events in the *Passionate Body*, but the names and words of the drama it must obtain, the *Faculties* having gone when the *Husk* and *Passionate Body disappeared*, from some incarnate Mind, and this it is able to do because all spirits inhabit our unconsciousness or, as Swedenborg said, are the Dramatis Personae of our dreams.*[37] One thinks of those apparitions haunting the places where they have lived that fill the literature† of all countries and are the theme of the Japanese Nō drama. Though only visible to the seer when *Spirit* and *Passionate Body* are joined, they are constantly repeated until, at last forgotten by the *Spirit*, they fade into the *Thirteenth Cone*.[39] The more complete the *Dreaming Back* the more complete the *Return* and the more happy or fortunate the next incarnation.‡ After each event of the *Dreaming Back* the

*My instructors said once that under certain circumstances a *Spirit* can draw knowledge of such things as language from the *Husks* of the other dead, but only if those *Husks* are separated from their *Spirits*. It seems that a mind must, as it were, release a thought before it becomes general property. Somebody years ago, at, I think, a meeting of the Society of Psychical Research, suggested that we transferred thought at some moment when we ceased to think of it.

†See *An Adventure* (Faber & Faber). This anonymous book was the work of two women, one the Head of St. Hugh's College, Oxford, the other her predecessor. It describes with minute detail a vision of Marie Antoinette and her Court, and of the gardens of the Petit Trianon as they were before the Revolution, and the research that proved the vision's accuracy. The two ladies walking in the garden of the Petit Trianon shared the same vision. I have confirmed, as far as the meagre records permitted, a similar vision in my own family, and Sligo pilots and Galway farmers have told me of visions that seem to reproduce the costumes of past times.[38]

‡Compare the account of the *Dreaming Back* in Swedenborg's *Heaven and Hell*. My account differs from his mainly because he denied or ignored rebirth. Somebody has suggested that he kept silent deliberately, that it was amongst those subjects that he thought forbidden. It is more likely that his instructors were silent. They spoke to the Christian Churches, explaining the "linen clothes

Spirit explores not merely the causes but the consequences of that event.

Where the soul has great intensity and where those consequences affected great numbers, the *Dreaming Back* and the *Return* may last with diminishing pain and joy for centuries.[41] The *Spirit*,* that it may make the *Passionate Body* intelligible, can not only tap the minds of the living but examine letters and books, once they come before the eyes of the living, although it can see nothing that does not concern the dream, for it is without reflection or the knowledge that it is dead.[43] If the event was shared by many, those many may seem present and yet be but the figures of the dream. Each must dream the event alone. Sometimes the *Spirit* under the influence of the *Celestial Body* and what are called *Teaching Spirits—Spirits* of the *Thirteenth Cone*—may not merely dream through the consequences of its acts but amend them, bringing this or that to the attention of the living.[44] I have found a belief among Irish country people that the death of father or mother may sometimes bring good luck to child or family. Upon the other hand our actions affect the dead. Some years ago there were various small inexplicable noises and movements in my house, and I was told that a certain *Spirit* wanted to discover certain facts necessary to her *Dreaming Back* by creating discussion, or that *Teaching Spirits* wished to assist her by creating that discussion. It is from the *Dreaming Back* of the dead, though not from that of persons associated with our past, that we get the imagery of ordinary sleep. Much of a dream's confusion comes from the fact that the image belongs to some unknown person, whereas emotion, names, language, belong to us alone. Having kept a steady watch upon my dreams for years I know that so long as I dream in words I know that my father, let us say, was tall and bearded. If, on the other hand, I dream in images

folded up", and even what they said or sought to say was half-transformed into an opium dream by the faith of those Churches in the literal inspiration of the Bible.[40]

*A Robinson Crusoe who died upon his island and had not even a Man Friday for witness could, I am told, get the necessary information from his own *Husk*, but his *Dreaming Back* would be imperfect. He would lack not only physical but spiritual burial. The contents of his *Husk* being, as I suppose, too much himself, he would continue to look through a window-pane upon which he had breathed.[42]

and examine the dream immediately upon waking I may discover him there represented by a stool or the eyepiece of a telescope, but never in his natural shape, for we cast off the concrete memory (lose contact with the *Record* as it affects ourselves) but not the abstract memory when we sleep.[45]

Teaching Spirits are *Spirits* of the *Thirteenth Cone*, or their representatives who may be chosen from any state, and are those who substitute for *Husk* and *Passionate Body* supersensual emotion and imagery; the "unconscious" or unapparent for that which has *disappeared*; the *Spirit* itself being capable of knowledge only. They conduct the *Spirit* through its past acts; should the code that *Spirit* accepted during life permit, they may conduct it through those in past lives, especially those that fell where the *Four Faculties** of its phase fall upon the wheel of the cycle, seeking always the source of its action. We must, however, avoid attributing to them the pure benevolence our exhausted Platonism and Christianity attribute to an angelical being. Our actions, lived in life, or remembered in death, are the food and drink of the *Spirits* of the *Thirteenth Cone*, that which gives them separation and solidity.

But knowledge of the past is not sufficient. The second stage contains in addition to the *Dreaming Back* and the *Return* what is called the *Phantasmagoria*, which exists to exhaust, not nature, not pain and pleasure, but emotion, and is the work of *Teaching Spirits*.[47] The physical and moral life is completed, without the addition of any new element that the objects of hope may be completed, for only that which is completed can be known and dismissed. Houses appear built by thought in a moment, the spirit seems to eat, drink and smoke, the child appears to grow to maturity, or

*The past incarnations corresponding to his *Four Faculties* seem to accompany a living man. Once when a child was born in the house, the doctor, the mother and I smelt roses everywhere. Years afterwards I read in a book called *Nursery Life Three Hundred Years Ago* (I forget the author's name) of a custom that lasted into the seventeenth century of washing new-born children in a bath "made wholesome . . . with red roses", of rolling them in salt and roses, and of sprinkling them, when the parents could afford it, with oil of roses. If I assume that the *Thirteenth Cone* can send the forms from any incarnation which correspond to the place of *Faculty* or *Principle*, whether in the present or an earlier cycle, I have an explanation of that emergence during vision of an old Cretan myth described in my book *Autobiographies*.[46]

perhaps with the help of *Teaching Spirits* a Christmas Tree is created, Christ or some saint or angel descends, dressed as in statue or picture; if the life was evil, then the *Phantasmagoria* is evil, the criminal completes his crime. It is indeed a necessary act of the human soul that has cut off the incarnate and discarnate from one another, plunging the discarnate into our "unconsciousness". The *Phantasmagoria* completes not only life but imagination. Cornelius Agrippa speaks of those among the dead who imagine themselves "surrounded by flames and persecuted by demons" and, according to his seventeenth-century translator, confers upon them the name "Hobgoblin".[48] The various legends of spirits that appear under the impulse of moral and emotional suffering must be attributed to this state and not to the *Dreaming Back*, where the constraint is physical. I think of a girl in a Japanese play whose ghost tells a priest of a slight sin, if indeed it was sin, which seems great because of her exaggerated conscience. She is surrounded by flames, and though the priest explains that if she but ceased to believe in those flames they would cease to exist, believe she must, and the play ends in an elaborate dance, the dance of her agony.[49] I think of those stories which I have already summarised where some ghost seeks not to perfect an event that concerns the living, but its own emotional or moral peace.

VII

At the end of the second state, the events of the past life are a whole and can be dismissed; the emotional and moral life, however, is but a whole according to the code accepted during life. The *Spirit* is still unsatisfied, until after the third state, which corresponds to Gemini,* called the *Shiftings*, where the *Spirit* is purified of good and evil.[50] In so far as the man did good without knowing evil, or evil without knowing good, his nature is reversed until that knowledge is obtained. The *Spirit* lives—I quote the automatic script—"The best possible life in the worst possible surroundings" or the contrary of this; yet there is no suffering: "For in a state of equilibrium

*My instructors do not seem to use the astrological character of this, or indeed of any sign except Taurus, Pisces and the Cardinal signs.

there is neither emotion nor sensation".[51] In the limits of the good and evil of the previous life . . . the soul is brought to a contemplation of good and evil; "neither its utmost good nor its utmost evil can force sensation or emotion". I remember MacKenna's translation of the most beautiful of the *Enneads*, "The Impassivity of the Dis-Embodied".[52] This state is described as a true life, as distinguished from the preceding states; the soul is free in the sense that it is subject to necessary truth alone, the *Celestial Body* is described as present in person instead of through "Messengers".[53]

It is followed by a state corresponding to Cancer which is said to pass in unconsciousness, or in a moment of consciousness called the *Marriage* or the *Beatitude*.[54] It is complete equilibrium after the conflict of the *Shiftings*; good and evil vanish into the whole. It is followed by an oscillation, a reversal of the old life; this lasts until birth and death bring the *Shiftings* and the *Marriage* once more, a reversal not in knowledge but in life, or until the *Spirit* is free from good and evil.* My instructors have described the *Marriage* as follows: "The *Celestial Body* is the Divine Cloak lent to all, it falls away at the consummation and Christ is revealed", words which seem to echo Bardesan's "Hymn of the Soul", where a King's son asleep in Egypt (physical life) is sent a cloak which is also an image of his body.† He sets out to his father's kingdom wrapped in the cloak.

VIII

In the *Purification* (corresponding to the sign Leo) a new *Husk* and *Passionate Body* take the place of the old; made from the old, yet, as it were, pure. All memory has vanished, the *Spirit* no lon-

*The reversals of *The Shiftings* and the *Purification* are reflected in the alternation between *Sage* and *Victim*. Solar South (Cancer) is Lunar East. Lunar East is Phase 22. The interchange of Sage and Victim is comparable to the exchange of the *Tinctures*, but there is no reversal at the opposite point because the wheel of the *Faculties* completes itself while that of the *Principles* goes but half its distance (Book II, section VII).

†A living man sees the *Celestial Body* through the *Mask*. I awoke one night when a young man to find my body rigid and to hear a voice that came from my lips and yet did not seem my voice saying, "We make an image of him who sleeps and it is not he who sleeps and we call it Emmanuel".[55]

ger knows what its name has been, it is at last free and in relation to *Spirits* free like itself. Though the new *Husk* and *Mask*[56] have been born, they do not *appear*, they are subordinate to the *Celestial Body*. The *Spirit* must substitute for the *Celestial Body*, seen as a Whole, its own particular aim. Having substituted this aim it becomes self-shaping, self-moving, plastic to itself, as that self has been shaped by past lives. If its nature is unique it must find circumstances not less unique before rebirth is possible. It may stay in the *Purification* for centuries—become, if it died amidst some primitive community, the guardian of well or temple or be called by the *Thirteenth Cone* to the care of the newly dead. I think of those phantoms in ancient costumes seen by some peasant seers exercising such authority. "We have no power", said an inhabitant of the state, "except to purify our intention", and when I asked of what, replied: "Of complexity".[57] But that *Purification* may require the completion of some syntheses left unfinished in its past life. Because only the living create it may seek the assistance of those living men into whose "unconsciousness" or incarnate *Daimon*, some affinity of aim, or the command of the *Thirteenth Cone*, permits it to enter. Those who taught me this system did so, not for my sake, but their own.*[58] The *Spirit's* aim, however, appears before it as a form of perfection, for during the *Purification* those forms copied in the Arts and Sciences are present as the *Celestial Body*. In piecing together detached statements, I remember that some spirit once said to me: "We do nothing singly, every act is done by a number at the same instant."[59] Their perfection is a shared purpose or idea. I connect them in my imagination with an early conviction of mine, that the creative power of the lyric poet depends upon his accepting some one of a few traditional attitudes, lover, sage, hero, scorner of life. They bring us back to the spiritual norm. They may, however, if permitted by the *Thirteenth Cone*, so act upon the events of our lives as to compel us to attend to that perfection which, though it seems theirs, is the work of our own *Daimon*.

*They say that only the words spoken in trance or written in the automatic script assist them. They belong to the "unconscious" and what comes from them alone serves. My interpretations do not concern them. In the mediumistic condition it sometimes seems as if dreams awoke and yet remained dreams.

IX

The sixth and final state (corresponding to Scorpio[60]) called the *Foreknowledge* must substitute the next incarnation, as fate has decreed it, for that form of perfection. The *Spirit* cannot be reborn until the vision of that life is completed and accepted. The *Spirit*, now almost united to *Husk* and *Passionate Body*, may know the most violent love and hatred possible, for it can see the remote consequences of the most trivial acts of the living, provided those consequences are part of its future life. In trying to prevent them it may become one of those frustrators dreaded by certain spirit mediums. It cannot, however, without the assistance of the *Thirteenth Cone* affect life in any way except to delay its own rebirth. With that assistance it can so shape circumstances as to make possible the rebirth of a unique nature. One must suppose such spirits gathered into bands—for as yet they are without individuality—and with the consent of the *Thirteenth Cone* playing a part resembling that of the "censor" in modern psychology.[61] During its sleep in the womb the *Spirit* accepts its future life, declares it just.

X

The *Spirits* before the *Marriage* are spoken of as the dead. After that they are spirits, using that word as it is used in common speech. During the *Dreaming Back* the *Spirit* is alone with its dream; during the *Return* in the presence of those who had a part in the events explored in the *Dreaming Back*; in the *Phantasmagoria* and in the *Shiftings* of those summoned by the *Thirteenth Cone* and the *Celestial Body* respectively; in the *Purification*, of those chosen by itself.

In the *Meditation* it wears the form it had immediately before death; in the *Dreaming Back* and the *Phantasmagoria*, should it appear to the living, it has the form of the dream, in the *Return* the form worn during the event explored, in the *Shiftings* whatever form was most familiar to others during its life; in the *Purification* whatever form it fancies, for it is now the Shape-changer of legend:

'Twas said that she all shapes could wear;
And oftentimes before him stood,
Amid the trees of some thick wood,
In semblance of a lady fair;
And taught him signs, and showed him sights
In Craven's dens, on Cumbrian heights.[62]

The *Dreaming Back* is represented upon the cone or wheel by a periodical stoppage of movement.

Indian Buddhists cease to offer sacrifice for a particular dead person after three generations, for after that time he must, they believe, have found a new body. A typical series of lives described by my instructors suggest that as an average limit, but in some cases rebirth comes very soon.[63] If a *Spirit* cannot escape from its *Dreaming Back* to complete its expiation, a new life may come soon and be, as it were, a part of its *Dreaming Back* and so repeat the incidents of the past life. There are stories Asiatic and European of those who die in childhood being reborn almost at once.

The more complete the expiation, or the less the need for it, the more fortunate the succeeding life. The more fully a life is lived, the less the need for—or the more complete is—the expiation. Neither the *Phantasmagoria*, nor the *Purification*, nor any other state between death and birth should be considered as a reward or paradise. Neither between death and birth nor between birth and death can the soul find more than momentary happiness; its object is to pass rapidly round its circle and find freedom from that circle.

Those who inhabit the "unconscious mind" are the complement or opposite of that mind's consciousness and are there, unless as messengers of the *Thirteenth Cone*, because of spiritual affinity or bonds created during past lives.

XI

All the involuntary acts and facts of life are the effect of the whirring and interlocking of the gyres; but gyres may be interrupted or twisted by greater gyres, divide into two lesser gyres or multiply into four and so on. The uniformity of nature depends upon the constant return of gyres to the same point. Sometimes individuals are *primary* and *antithetical* to one another and joined by a bond so powerful that they form a common gyre or series of gyres. This gyre or these gyres no greater gyre may be able to break till exhaustion comes. We all to some extent meet again and again the same people and certainly in some cases form a kind of family of two or three or more persons who come together life after life until all passionate relations are exhausted, the child of one life the husband, wife, brother or sister of the next. Sometimes, however, a single relationship will repeat itself, turning its revolving wheel again and again, especially, my instructors say, where there has been strong sexual passion. All such passions, they say, contain "cruelty and deceit"[64]—I think of similar statements in D. H. Lawrence's *Rainbow* and in his *Women in Love*[65]—and this *antithetical* cruelty and deceit must be expiated in *primary* suffering and submission, or the old tragedy will be repeated.

They are expiated between birth and death because they are actions, but their victim must expiate between death and birth the ignorance that made them possible. The victim must, in the *Shiftings*, live the act of cruelty, not as victim but as tyrant; whereas the tyrant must by a necessity of his or her nature become the victim. But if one is dead and the other living they find each other in thought and symbol, the one that has been passive and is now active may from within control the other, once tyrant now victim. If the act is associated with the *Return* or the *Purification* the one that controls from within, reliving as a form of knowledge what once was tyranny, gives not pain but ecstasy. The one whose expiation is an act needs for the act some surrogate* or symbol of the other and offers to some other man or woman submission or service, but because the unconscious mind knows that this act is fated no new gyre is started. The expiation, because offered to the living for the dead, is called "expiation for the dead" but is in reality expiation for the *Daimon*, for passionate love is from the *Daimon* which seeks by union with some other *Daimon* to reconstruct above the antinomies its own true nature.[67] The souls of victim and tyrant are bound

*A Bombay friend of mine once saw an Indian peasant standing by the road with many flowers beside her. She gave a flower to each passer-by with the words "I give this to my Lord". Her Lord was the god Krishna, but the passionate may offer to their own dead a similar worship.[66]

together and, unless there is a redemption through the intercommunication of the living and the dead, that bond may continue life after life, and this is just, for there had been no need of expiation had they seen in one another that other and not something else. The expiation is completed and the oscillation brought to an end for each at the same moment. There are other bonds, master and servant, benefactor and beneficiary, any relation that is deeper than the intellect may become such a bond. We get happiness, my instructors say, from those we have served, ecstasy from those we have wronged.

XII

Sometimes the bond is between an incarnate *Daimon* and a *Spirit of the Thirteenth Cone*. This bond created by the fixed attention of the *Daimon* will pass through the same stages as if it were between man and some ordinary discarnate spirit. *Victimage for the Dead* arises through such act as prevents the union of two incarnate *Daimons* and is therefore the prevention or refusal of a particular experience, but *Victimage* for a *Spirit of the Thirteenth Cone* results from the prevention or refusal of experience itself. This refusal may arise from pride, from the fear of injuring another or oneself, from something which we call asceticism; it may have any cause, but the *Spirit of the Thirteenth Cone* is starved. Such *Spirit* may itself create the events that incited the man to refuse experience, St. Simeon may be driven to his pillar.[68] In the whirling of the gyres the incarnate *Daimon* is starved in its turn, but starved not of natural experience, but of supernatural; for, compelled to take the place of the *Spirit*, it transforms its natural craving—*Eli! Eli! Lama Sabacthani!*?[69]—and this state is called *Victimage for the Ghostly Self*, and is described as the sole means for acquiring a supernatural guide. So closely do all the bonds resemble each other that in the most ascetic schools of India the novice tortured by his passion will pray to the God to come to him as a woman and have with him sexual intercourse; nor is the symbol subjective, for in the morning his pillow will be saturated with temple incense, his breast yellow with the saffron dust of some temple offering. Such experience is said, however, to wear itself out swiftly giving place to the supernatural union.[70]

Sometimes the God may select some living symbol of himself. If the ascetic is a woman, some wandering priest perhaps, if a man, some wandering priestess, but such loves are brief. Sometimes, however, *Victimage for the Ghostly Self* and *Victimage for the Dead* coincide and produce lives tortured throughout by spirituality and passion. Cruelty and ignorance, which echo the *Sage* and *Victim* of Book I, constitute evil as my instructors see it, and are that which makes possible the conscious union of the *Daimons* of Man and Woman or that of the *Daimon* of the Living and a *Spirit of the Thirteenth Cone*, which is the deliverance from birth and death.

The *Thirteenth Cone* is a sphere because sufficient to itself; but as seen by Man it is a cone. It becomes even conscious of itself as so seen, like some great dancer, the perfect flower of modern culture, dancing some primitive dance and conscious of his or her own life and of the dance. There is a mediaeval story of a man persecuted by his Guardian Angel because it was jealous of his sweetheart, and such stories seem closer to reality than our abstract theology.[71] All imaginable relations may arise between a man and his God. I only speak of the *Thirteenth Cone* as a sphere and yet I might say that the gyre or cone of the *Principles* is in reality a sphere, though to Man, bound to birth and death, it can never seem so, and that it is the antinomies that force us to find it a cone. Only one symbol exists, though the reflecting mirrors make many appear and all different.

THE GREAT YEAR OF THE ANCIENTS

BOOK IV: THE GREAT YEAR OF THE ANCIENTS[1]

I

When a religious-minded Roman of the first century before Christ thought of the first month of a new Great Year, did he think of some ideal king such as Virgil foretold, or think of Attis who died and rose again at the beginning of their old lunar year?[2] Which did he prefer of those incompatible ideas, Triumph or Sacrifice, Sage or Victim? When did he expect the one or the other?

To the time when Marius sat at home planning a sedition that began the Roman civil wars, popular imagination attributed many prodigies; the wooden support of the eagles burst into flames; three ravens brought their young into the open field, picked their bones and carried the bones back into the nest; a mouse gnawed the consecrated corn in the temple and when caught brought forth five young and devoured them; and, greatest marvel of all, out of the calm and clear sky came the sound of a trumpet. The Etruscans declared that this trumpet meant "the mutation of the age and a general revolution of the world".[3] A generation later Virgil sang his song: "the latest age of the Cumaean song is at hand; the cycles in their vast array begin anew; Virgin Astraea comes, the reign of Saturn comes, and from the heights of Heaven a new generation of mankind descends. . . . Apollo now is king and in your Consulship, in yours, Pollio, the age of glory shall commence and the mighty months begin their course."[4]

II[5]

Caesar and Christ always stand face to face in our imagination. Did not Dante put Judas and Brutus into the mouth of Satan?[6] Some nine months before the assassination of Caesar his image was carried among the images of the gods in a procession at the Ludi Circenses, and a rumour, afterwards disproved, reached Cicero that Cotta, the official exponent of the Oracles, proposed announcing to the Senate "That he whom we really had as King should be given the title of King if we desired to remain safe". If this was really in the Sibylline Books, to what man and to what time did it refer?* Cicero thought such books were so written that they could fit any time or man, and adds: "Let us ask their Priests to produce anything out of those books rather than a King". He was writing after the assassination. Had what Cicero calls elsewhere "the religious party of the Sibyl" found that prophecy Virgil was to sing in the next generation?[7] Did they expect a mystic king to restore justice, "the girl Astraea"? What did the Roman slums hope for when their half-oriental population under the influence of a fanatical cow-doctor, horse-doctor or eye-doctor, for scholars differ as to his occupation—the Clare and Galway of my youth had such men—burnt the body of Caesar on the Capitol, and with, it may be, some traditional ceremony of apotheosis set up his statue and worshipped him?[8] They drove the tyrannicides from Rome, and when Dolabella, Cicero's son-in-law, dispersed and punished them Cicero thanked him for a deed equal in courage and importance to the assassination of Caesar.[9] Did the Julian House inherit from that apotheosis and those prayers the Cumaean song? Caesar was killed on the 15th day of March, the month of victims and of saviours. Two years before he had instituted our solar Julian Year, and in a few generations the discovery of the body of Attis among the reeds would be commemorated upon that day, though, before "Ides" lost its first meaning, the ceremony needed a full moon or the fifteenth day of a lunar March.[10] Even Easter, which the rest of Christendom commemorated on the first full moon after the Vernal Equinox,

*See Cicero's letter to Atticus, XIII. 44, and his *De Divinatione*.

would sometimes be commemorated by Christians living under the influence of the Julian Year upon the day before the fifteenth day of the solar March.* It seemed as if the magical character of the full moon was transferred to a day and night where the moon had as it were a merely legal or official existence. One thinks of Mommsen's conviction that though Caesar chose the lesser of two evils the Roman State was from his day to the end a dead thing, a mere mechanism.[12]

III

"By common consent men measure the year", wrote Cicero, "by the return of the sun, or in other words by the revolution of one star. But when the whole of the constellations shall return to the positions from which they once set forth, thus after a long interval re-making the first map of the heavens, that may indeed be called the Great Year wherein I scarce dare say how many are the generations of men."[13] But that Great or Greatest Year was sometimes divided into lesser periods by the return of the sun and moon to some original position,[14] by the return of a planet or of all the planets to some original position, or by their making an astrological aspect with that position; and sometimes it was dissociated from the actual position of the stars and divided into twelve months, each month a brightening and a darkening fortnight, and at the same time perhaps a year with its four seasons. I do not remember the brightening and darkening fortnights in any classical author, but they are in the Upanishads and in the Laws of Manu for the Great Year and its Months pervaded the ancient world.[15] Perhaps at the start a mere magnification of the natural year, it grew more complicated with the spread of Greek astronomy, but it is always the simpler, more symbolic form, with its conflict of light and dark, heat and cold, that concerns me most.

*The sacrifice of the Passover took place upon the fourteenth lunar day and night which were counted full moon.[11]

IV*

Anaximander, a pre-Socratic philosopher, thought there were two infinities, one of co-existence where nothing ages, the other of succession and mortality, world coming after world and lasting always the same number of years.[17] Empedocles and Heraclitus thought that the universe had first one form and then its opposite in perpetual alternation, meaning, as it seems, that all things were consumed with fire when all the planets so stood in the sign Cancer that a line could be drawn through all their centres and the centre of the earth, destroyed by water when all stood in Capricorn; a fire that is not what we call fire but "the fire of heaven", "the fire where all the universe returns to its seed", a water that is not what we call water but a "lunar water" that is nature.[18] Love and Discord, Fire and Water, dominate in turn, Love making all things One, Discord separating all, but Love no more than Discord the changeless eternity. Here originated perhaps the symbol expounded in this book of a phaseless sphere that becomes phasal in our thought, Nicholas of Cusa's undivided reality which human experience divides into opposites, and here too, as Pierre Duhem points out, we discover for the first time the Platonic doctrine of imitation—the opposing states copy eternity.[19]

But when the age of Fire or that of Water returns, did the same man return, or a new man who resembled him, and if the same man, must he have the old wart upon his nose? Some thought one thing and some another. Was the world completely destroyed at the solstice or did it but acquire a new shape? Philolaus thought the fire and water but destroyed the old shape and nourished the new. Did one world follow another without a break? Empedocles thought there must be an intermediate state of rest.[20]

So far the Ideas had been everything, the individual nothing; beauty and truth alone had mattered to Plato and Socrates,[21] but Plotinus thought that every individual had his Idea, his eternal counterpart; the Greatest Year and the Great Years that were

*Most of the quotations and summaries in this section are from Pierre Duhem's *Le Système du monde*, vol. i, chap. v, sections VI and VII.[16]

its Months became a stream of souls.[22] To the next generation it seemed plain that the Eternal Return,[23] though it remained for the stream as a whole, had ceased for the wise man, for the wise man could withdraw from the circuit. Proclus discovered in the Golden Number of the *Republic* a Greatest Year, that is "the least common number of all revolutions visible and invisible", and in the *Timaeus* a much smaller year, "which is the least common multiple" of the revolutions of the eight spheres, and thought this smaller year alone calculable by reason.[24]

Yet Plato's statements are there that scholars may solve the Golden Number, and they have found fourteen different solutions.[25] To Taylor they suggest 36,000 years, 360 incarnations of Plato's Man of Ur.[26] Proclus thought the duration of the world is found "when we bring into contemplation the numerical unity, the one self-unfolding power, the sole creation that completes its work, that which fills all things with universal life. One must see all things wind up their careers and come round again to the beginning; one must see everything return to itself and so complete by itself the circle allotted to that number; or that unity which encloses an infinity of numbers, contains within itself the instability of the Duad and yet determines the whole movement, its end and its beginning, and is for that reason called the Number and the Perfect Number."[27] It is as though innumerable dials, some that recorded minutes alone, some seconds alone, some hours alone, some months alone, some years alone, were all to complete their circles when Big Ben struck twelve upon the last night of the century. My instructors offer for a symbol the lesser unities that combine into a work of art and leave no remainder, but we may substitute if we will the lesser movements which combine into the circle that in Hegel's *Logic* unites not summer solstice to summer solstice but absolute to absolute.[28] "The Months and Years are also numbered, but they are not perfect numbers but parts of other numbers. The time of the development of the universe is perfect, for it is a part of nothing, it is a whole and for that reason resembles eternity. It is before all else an integrity, but only eternity confers upon existence that complete integrity which remains in itself; that of time develops, development is indeed a temporal image of that which remains in itself."[29]

V

A doctrine which showed all things returning to the seed of Fire at the midsummer of the Great Year may have sounded the more natural to a Greek because Athenian years began at midsummer.[30] But from somewhere in Asia Minor, Persia perhaps, spread a doctrine which transferred attention from Cancer and Capricorn to Aries, from the extremes where the world was destroyed to the midway point where it was restored, where Love began to prevail over Discord, Day over Night.[31] The destroying flood rose in Capricorn but lasted through the two succeeding signs, only disappearing when the World-restorer appeared; the creation itself had been but a restoration. To many Christians and Jews, though the doctrine soon ceased to be orthodox, not the Messiah alone but the Spirit that moved upon the Waters, and Noah on Mount Ararat, seemed such world-restorers. "Certain Christians", wrote Nemesius, Bishop of Emessa, "would have us consider the Resurrection linked to the restoration of the world, but they deceive themselves strangely, for it is proved by the words of Christ that the Resurrection could not happen more than once, that it came not from a periodical revolution but from the Will of God."*[32] The doctrine, however, reappears in various forms as a recognised heresy until the thirteenth century, though that learned scholar, great poet and devout man, Francis Thompson, did not recognise it as such when he wrote:

Not only of cyclic Man
Thou here discern'st the plan,
Not only of cyclic Man, but of the cyclic Me,
Not solely of Mortalities great years
  The reflex just appears,
But thine own bosom's year, still circling round
In ample and in ampler gyre

*Quoted by Pierre Duhem, *Le Système du monde*, vol. ii, part 2, chap. i, section VIII. The section shows the attitude of the Fathers of the Church to the Great Year and is of great interest. Defending the freedom of the will they seem to know the Eternal Return in its most mechanical form. Their argument does not affect the position of Proclus.

Towards the far completion, wherewith crowned,
Love unconsumed shall chant in his own funeral pyre.[33]

VI

Christ rose from the dead at a full moon in the first month of the year, the month that we have named from Mars the ruler of the first of the twelve signs.[34]

I do not know if my instructors were the first to make a new lunar circuit equal in importance with the solar out of that archetypal month. To this month, to touch upon a symbolism I have hitherto avoided for the sake of clarity, they gave a separate zodiac where the full moon falls at Capricorn. The two abstract zodiacs are so imposed the one upon the other that a line drawn between Cancer and Capricorn in the one is at right angles to a similar line in the other. As Capricorn is the most southerly sign—"lunar south is solar east"—a line drawn between east and west in the one is at right angles to a line drawn between east and west in the other. As every period of time is both a month and a year the circles can be superimposed, the signs in the lunar circle running from right to left, those in the solar from left to right. They have much the same character, being respectively particular and universal, as the circles of the Other and the Same in the *Timaeus*.[35] In the first *Will* moves and its opposite, in the second *Creative Mind* and its opposite, or we may consider the first the wheel of the *Faculties*, the second that of the *Principles*.

VII

There was little agreement as to the length of the Great Year, every philosopher had a different calculation, but the majority divided it into 360 days or 365 days according to the prevailing view as to the number of days in the year. The Stoics of Cicero's time thought it was divided into 365 days of 15,000 years apiece.[36] Cicero thought it began with an eclipse at the time of Romulus, or wished men to think so to confound the local Mother Shipton who had gone over to his enemies; and why did Virgil make that prophecy accepted all through the Middle Ages as prophesying Christ?[37] There were similar prophecies elsewhere, for the world felt itself at the beginning of a great change, but I know no book that has studied them and traced them to their origin.

VIII

In the second century before Christ, Hipparchus discovered* that the Zodiacal constellations were moving, that in a certain number of years the sun would no longer rise at the Vernal Equinox in the constellation Aries, but his discovery seems to have been little noticed until the third century after Christ when Ptolemy fixed the rate of movement at 100 years† for each degree, that Aries might return to its original position every 36,000[38] years, the 360 incarnations of a man of Ur.[39] He named these 36,000 years the Platonic Year and by that name they were known henceforth. But if the eighth sphere, the sphere of the fixed stars, moved, it was necessary to transfer the diurnal movement to a ninth sphere or abstract zodiac divided into twelve equal parts; the first month of the year must, no matter where the constellations went, retain its martial energy of the Ram, midwinter its goatish cold and wet even if the constellations of Goat had strayed.[40] So too must each individual life retain to the end the seal set upon it at birth.[41]

Ptolemy must have added new weight to the conviction of Plotinus that the stars did not themselves affect human destiny but were pointers which enabled us to calculate the condition of the universe at any particular moment and therefore its effect on the individual life.[42]‡ "It is impossible that any single form", said Hermes in a

*If we judge by written evidence alone we must say that Hipparchus discovered precession, but there are scholars who think that he but introduced into the Graeco-Roman world a very ancient Asiatic discovery.

†The rate is about one-third less, and the whole precession takes some 26,000 years.

‡This doctrine must have spread widely during the Middle Ages. Lady Gregory was told in County Clare that there was a "woman in the sky" and whatever she did at any particular moment a child born at that moment did throughout life. Mr. Robin Flower found a like story in the Blasket Islands; and has not Mr. Wyndham Lewis accused Mr. Bertrand Russell of turning Mr. Smith into Mr. Four-thirty-in-the-afternoon by his exposition of space-time?[43]

passage from which I have already quoted a few words, "should come into being which is exactly like a second, if they originate at different points and at times differently situated; the forms change at every moment in each hour of the revolution of that celestial circuit . . . thus the type persists unchanged but generates at successive moments copies of itself as numerous and different as the revolutions of the sphere of heaven; for the sphere of heaven changes as it revolves, but the type neither changes nor revolves."[44] But nations also were sealed at birth with a character derived from the whole, and had, like individuals, their periods of increase and decrease. When the trumpet sounded in the sky in Sulla's time the Etruscan sages, according to Plutarch, declared the Etruscan cycle of 11,000 years at an end, and that "another sort of men were coming into the world."[45]

IX

Syncellus said that a new epoch began when the constellation Aries returned to its original position, and that this was the doctrine of "Greeks and Egyptians . . . as stated in the *Genetica* of Hermes and in the Cyrannic books".* Was Ptolemy the first to give a date to that return? The inventor of the ninth sphere, whether Ptolemy or another, was bound to make that calculation.[47] What was the date? I have not read his *Almagest*, nor am I likely to, and no historian or commentator on his discoveries known to me has given it. It would depend on the day he selected for the equinox (at Rome March 25th), and upon what star seemed to mark the end of Aries and the beginning of Pisces. It was certainly near enough to the assassination of Caesar to make the Roman Empire seem miraculous, near enough to the Crucifixion to confer upon the early Church, had it not been committed to its war with Grecian fatalism, the greatest of its miracles:

> Then did all the Muses sing
> Of Magnus Annus at the spring.[48]

*Quoted in E. M. Plunkett's *Ancient Calendars.*[46]

X[49]

On the map of Twenty-eight Incarnations—Book I, part ii, sec. I—there is the sign of Aries between Phases 18 and 19.[50] Some years passed before I understood the meaning of this sign or of the other cardinal signs in the original automatic map. It is the position that will be occupied by the vernal equinox at the central moment of the next religious era, or at the beginning of the succeeding *antithetical* civilisation, for the position of the equinox marks the phase of *Will* in the wheel of 26,000 years. It is the Aries or solar east of the double cone of its particular era set within the circuit of the Great Year. At present it approaches the central point of Phase 17 where the next influx must take place. It passed into Phase 16 at the end of the eleventh century when our civilisation began. That position between Phases 18 and 19 is said to define the greatest possible intellectual power because it is the centre of that quarter of the Wheel symbolical of the logical intellect, and because it is one of the four moments where the *Faculties* are at equal distance from one another: conflict, and therefore intensity of consciousness, apportioned out through the whole being.[51]

The corresponding moment in the lesser wheel of our Gothic civilisation came near the close of the seventeenth century just before that first decade of the eighteenth where Oliver thinks the European intellect reached its climax in power and authority.[52] It is a moment of supreme abstraction; nor do I think of Spinoza, Leibniz, Newton alone, I think of those monks at Port Royal who cut up live dogs to study the circulation of the blood, believing the lower animals but automata constructed to simulate by bellows and whistle the scream of agony.[53] That such a moment echoed the greater period to come gave it importance, a special shaping power. It does not, however, help us to judge what form abstraction may take in a religious era which must move towards an *antithetical* civilisation and the concrete and sensuous unity of Phase 15. An historical symbolism which covers too great a period of time for imagination to grasp or experience to explain may seem too theoretical, too arbitrary, to serve any practical purpose; it is, however, necessary to the myth if we are not to suggest, as Vico did, civilisation perpetually returning to the same point.[54]

XI

At the opening of Book V is a diagram where every date was fixed by my instructors.[55] They have adopted a system of cones not used elsewhere in this exposition. If one ignores the black numbers it is simple enough. It shows the gyre of religion expanding as that of secular life contracts, until at the eleventh century the movements are reversed. *Mask* and *Body of Fate* are religion, *Will* and *Creative Mind* secular life. My instructors have inserted the black numbers because it enables them to bring into a straight line four periods corresponding to the *Four Faculties* that are in Flinders Petrie's sense of the word "contemporaneous".[56] If we push this line of *Faculties* down from its starting-point at the birth of Christ (Year 1, and Phase 1 in the red letters), to the eleventh century, with *Will* on the left red line, *Body of Fate* on the left black line, *Mask* on the next and so on; then push it upward, changing the order of the *Faculties* to that on the diagram, every moment of the era reveals itself as constituted by four interacting periods. If we keep the straight line passing through the *Four Faculties* of the same length as the bases of the triangles we can mark upon it the twenty-eight phases, putting Phase 1 at the left hand, and the line will show what the position of the *Faculties* would be upon an ordinary double cone which completed its movement in the two thousand years of the era. My instructors scrawled a figure with a line so marked once or twice upon the margin of the automatic script while writing of something else, and left me to guess its relevance. When one examines the line so divided one discovers that at the present moment, although we are passing into Phase 23 on the cone of civilisation, we are between Phases 25 and 26 on the cone of the era. I consider that a conflict between religious and secular thought, because it governs all that is most interior and spiritual in myself, must be the projector of the era, and I find it upon this slow-moving cone. Its *Four Faculties* so found are four periods of time eternally co-existent, four co-existent acts; as seen in time we explain their effect by saying that the spirits of the three periods that seem to us past are present among us, though unseen.

When our historical era approaches Phase 1, or the beginning of a new era, the *antithetical* East will beget upon the *primary* West and the child or era so born will be *antithetical*. The *primary* child or era is predominantly western, but because begotten upon the East, eastern in body, and if I am right in thinking that my instructors imply not only the symbolical but the geographical East, Asiatic. Only when that body begins to wither can the Western Church predominate visibly.

XII[57]

That most philosophical of archaeologists Josef Strzygowski haunts my imagination.[58] To him the East, as certainly to my instructors, is not India or China, but the East that has affected European civilisation, Asia Minor, Mesopotamia, Egypt. From the Semitic East he derives all art which associates Christ with the attributes of royalty. It substitutes Christ Pantokrator for the bearded mild Hellenic Christ, makes the Church hierarchical and powerful. The East, in my symbolism, whether in the circle of the *Principles* or the *Faculties*, is always human power, whether *Will* or *Spirit*, stretched to its utmost. In the decorative diagram from the *Stories of Michael Robartes and his Friends*, printed at the opening of Book I, the East is marked by a sceptre. From the South, whether India or Egypt, he derives all representation of naturalistic human form, and has not Dante compared Unity of Being, the unity of man not of God, and therefore of the *antithetical tincture*, to a perfectly proportioned human body? I am not, however, so certain, though more than half convinced, that his geographical North and my symbolical North are the same. He finds amid the nomad Aryans of northern Europe and Asia the source of all geometrical ornament, of all non-representative art. It is only when he comes to describe such art as a subordination of all detail to the decoration of some given surface, and to associate it with domed and arched buildings where nothing interferes with the effect of the building as a whole, and with a theology which so exalts the Deity that every human trait disappears, that I begin to wonder whether the non-representative art of our own time may not be but a first symptom of our return to the *primary tincture*. He does not characterise the West except to describe it as a mirror where all movements are reflected. It is symbolised in the diagram in the Robartes stories as a cup, for it is an emotional or natural intoxication. If I translate his geographical symbolism into the language of the system I say that South and East are human form and intellectual authority, whereas North and West are superhuman form and emotional freedom.

XIII

The German traveller Frobenius discovered among the African natives two symbolical forms, one founded upon the symbol of the Cavern, one upon that of a central Altar and sixteen roads radiating outward; and the races of the Cavern seemed of eastern origin while the races of the roads had moved eastward from the Atlantic seaboard.[59] These races and their forms had passed everywhere. He found methods of divination based upon the symbolism of the roads in the furthest East, and the symbolism of the Cavern in the West. One thinks of them as existing side by side as does fair Northern hair with the dark hair of the South. I do not know how far he has been supported by other ethnologists, but certainly Spengler's vast speculation was founded in part upon his discovery, and I think that my instructors,* who seemed to know so much of Spengler, knew something of Frobenius. Spengler continually refers to the symbol of the Cavern and gives Frobenius as his authority, but, as I think, inverts his meaning; he never refers to the Altar and the radiating roads but shows in all his interpretations of the Faustian or modern mind that he is thinking of them. The Cavern is identified in the Hermetic Fragments with the Heavens, and it is so identified by Spengler, but to the Hermetic writer the Heavens were the orbit of the stars and planets, the source of all calendars, the symbol of the soul's birth and rebirth. The Cavern is Time, and to call it Space, as Spengler does, is to suffer the modern conception of a finite space always returning to itself to obsess one's thought; and nothing but a like obsession with what somebody has called the "Time philosophy" of our day can have made Spengler identify the Faustian soul, which, as he points out, has created the great windows of the cathe-

*I am amused to notice, though I do not give it great significance, that the Etruscans, who, according to Frobenius, had a mythology of the central Altar, turned like the *Creative Mind* from East to West when they prayed, whereas the races of the Cavern turned like the *Will* from West to East.[60]

drals and is always moving outwards, always seeking the unlimited, with Time.[61] The radiating roads and that mind, which I too consider essentially Western, could never suggest anything to ancient man but Space. Though Spengler inverted the meaning of his symbols, he has so constantly described them as if he had not, that I find, putting aside his great learning, and my lack of any, that our thoughts run together. He probably kept silent about the Altar and the radiating roads through the scholar's dread that a too simplifying metaphor might cast doubt upon the sincerity of his research.

XIV

Only the later Upanishads, according to certain scholars, were aware of the soul's rebirth. They substituted the doctrine of Karma for sacrifice and ritual purgation. At first the sacrifice was almost the sole source of symbol, its smoke had such and such a meaning, its ascending flame such another, and by it stood the Brahmin and the priest; then came the new doctrine "which no Brahmin ever knew".* Instead of a levelling pantheism came innumerable souls, no two souls alike, a belief that nothing else exists or that nothing exists, a doctrine first taught not by priest but by king, a discipline that seemed always aristocratic, solitary and *antithetical*. I do not know what Frobenius has written in German, for I have not that language, but it seems possible that he found in ancient India also his Altar and Cavern where I have found the first distinction between *primary* and *antithetical* civilisations.

XV

When the automatic script began, neither I nor my wife knew, or knew that we knew, that any man had tried to explain history philosophically.[63] I, at any rate, would have said that all written upon the subject was a paragraph in my own *Per Amica Silentia Lunae*, so ignorant a man is a poet and artist.[64] When I came to summarise

*When I wrote this sentence I had not met Shree Purhoit Swami, who considers that the Sanskrit words do not mean that the doctrine is not known, but that it is not innate even in a Brahmin (*Ten Principal Upanishads*, p. 157).[62]

on paper or in speech what the scripts contained no other theme made me so timid. Then Mr. Gerald Heard, who has since made his own philosophy of history, told me of Henry Adams' two essays, where I found some of the dates I had been given and much of the same interpretation, of Petrie's *Revolutions of Civilisation*, where I found more, and then a few months after the publication of the first edition of *A Vision* a translation of Spengler's *Decline of the West* was published, and I found there a correspondence too great for coincidence between most of his essential dates and those I had received before the publication of his first German edition.[65] After that I discovered for myself Spengler's main source in Vico, and that half the revolutionary thoughts of Europe are a perversion of Vico's philosophy. Marx and Sorel have taken from Vico's cycle, writes Croce, his "idea of the struggle of classes and the regeneration of society by a return to a primitive state of mind and a new barbarism".[66]* Certainly my instructors have chosen a theme that has deeply stirred men's minds though the newspapers are silent about it; the newspapers have the happy counter-myth of progress; a theme as important perhaps as Henry Adams thought when he told the Boston Historical Association that were it turned into a science powerful interests would prevent its publication.[68]

XVI

My instructors certainly expect neither a "primitive state" nor a return to barbarism as primitivism and barbarism are ordinarily understood; *antithetical* revelation is an intellectual influx neither from beyond mankind nor born of a virgin, but begotten from our spirit and history.

XVII

At the birth of Christ took place, and at the coming *antithetical* influx will take place, a change equivalent to the *interchange of the tinctures*. The cone shaped like an ace of diamonds—in the histor-

*I have read in an essay of Squire's that Lenin studied *The Philosophy of History* at the British Museum.[67]

ical diagram the cone is folded upon itself—is Solar, religious and vital; those shaped like an hour-glass Lunar, political and secular; but *Body of Fate* and *Mask* are in the Solar cones during a *primary* dispensation, and in the Lunar during an *antithetical*, while *Will* and *Creative Mind* occupy the opposing cones. *Mask* and *Body of Fate* are symbolic woman, *Will* and *Creative Mind* symbolic man; the man and woman of Blake's *Mental Traveller*.[69] Before the birth of Christ religion and vitality were polytheistic, *antithetical*, and to this the philosophers opposed their *primary*, secular thought. Plato thinks all things into Unity and is the "First Christian".[70] At the birth of Christ religious life becomes *primary*, secular life *antithetical*—man gives to Caesar the things that are Caesar's.[71] A *primary* dispensation looking beyond itself towards a transcendent power is dogmatic, levelling, unifying, feminine, humane, peace its means and end; an *antithetical* dispensation obeys imminent power, is expressive, hierarchical, multiple, masculine, harsh, surgical. The approaching *antithetical* influx and that particular *antithetical* dispensation for which the intellectual preparation has begun will reach its complete systematisation at that moment when, as I have already shown, the Great Year comes to its intellectual climax. Something of what I have said it must be, the myth declares, for it must reverse our era and resume past eras in itself; what else it must be no man can say, for always at the critical moment the *Thirteenth Cone*, the sphere, the unique intervenes.

Somewhere in sands of the desert
A shape with lion body and the head of a man,
A gaze blank and pitiless as the sun,
Is moving its slow thighs, while all about it
Reel shadows of the indignant desert birds.[72]

XVIII[73]

The wheel of the *Four Principles* completes its movement in four thousand years. The life of Christ corresponds to the mid-period between birth and death; A.D. 1050 to death; the approaching influx to the mid-point between death and birth.[74]

DOVE OR SWAN

THE HISTORICAL CONES[1]

The numbers in brackets refer to phases, and the other numbers to dates A.D. The line cutting the cones a little below 250, 900, 1180 and 1927 shows four historical *Faculties* related to the present moment. May 1925.

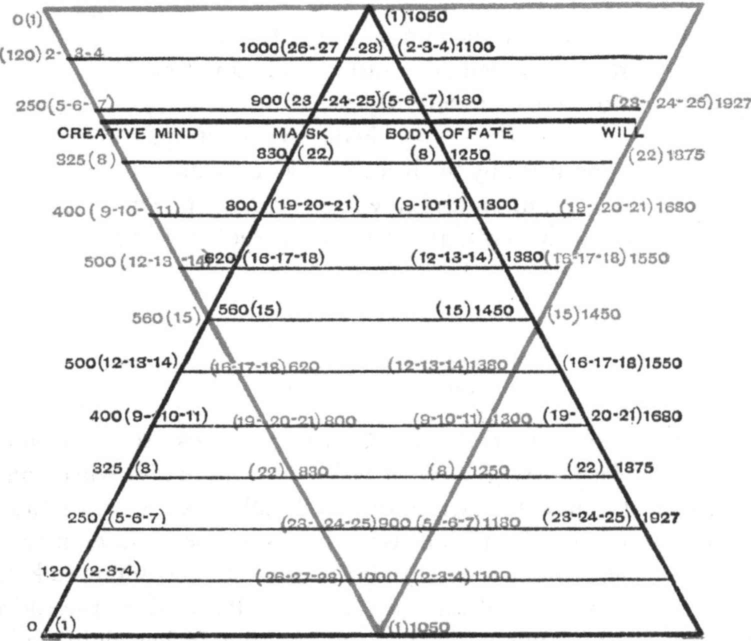

BOOK V: DOVE OR SWAN

I

LEDA[2]

A sudden blow: the great wings beating still
Above the staggering girl, her thighs caressed
By the dark webs, her nape caught in his bill,
He holds her helpless breast upon his breast.

How can those terrified vague fingers push
The feathered glory from her loosening thighs,
And how can body, laid in that white rush,
But feel the strange heart beating where it lies?

A shudder in the loins engenders there
The broken wall, the burning roof and tower
And Agamemnon dead.[3]
Being so caught up,
So mastered by the brute blood of the air,
Did she put on his knowledge with his power
Before the indifferent beak could let her drop?

II

Stray Thoughts

One must bear in mind that the Christian Era, like the two thousand years, let us say, that went before it, is an entire wheel, and each half of it an entire wheel, that each half when it comes to its 28th Phase reaches the 15th Phase or the 1st Phase of the entire era. It follows therefore that the 15th Phase of each millennium, to keep the symbolic measure of time, is Phase 8 or Phase 22 of the entire era, that Aphrodite rises from a stormy sea, that Helen could not be Helen but for beleaguered Troy.[4] The era itself is but half of a greater era and its Phase 15 comes also at a period of war or trouble. The greater number is always more *primary* than the lesser and precisely because it contains it. A millennium is the symbolic measure of a being that attains its flexible maturity and then sinks into rigid age.

A civilisation is a struggle to keep self-control, and in this it is like some great tragic person, some Niobe who must display an almost superhuman will or the cry will not touch our sympathy.[5] The loss of control over thought comes towards the end; first a sinking in upon the moral being, then the last surrender, the irrational cry, revelation—the scream of Juno's peacock.[6]

III

2000 B.C. to A.D. 1[7]

I imagine the annunciation that founded Greece as made to Leda, remembering that they showed in a Spartan temple, strung up to the roof as a holy relic, an unhatched egg of hers; and that from one of her eggs came Love and from the other War.[8] But all things are from antithesis, and when in my ignorance I try to imagine what older civilisation that annunciation rejected I can but see bird and woman blotting out some corner of the Babylonian mathematical starlight.*

Was it because the older civilisation like the Jewish thought a long life a proof of Heavenly favour that the Greek races thought those whom the Gods love must die young, hurling upon some age of crowded comedy their tragic sense?[10] Certainly their tribes, after a first multitudinous revelation—dominated each by its *Daimon* and oracle-driven—broke up a great Empire and established in its stead an intellectual anarchy.[11] At some 1000 years before Christ I imagine their religious system complete and they themselves grown barbaric and Asiatic.[12] Then came Homer, civil life, a desire for civil order dependent doubtless on some oracle, and then (Phase 10 of the new millennium) for independent civil life and thought. At, let me say, the sixth century B.C. (Phase 12) personality begins, but there is as yet no intellectual solitude. A man may rule his tribe or

*Toynbee considers Greece the heir of Crete, and that Greek religion inherits from the Minoan monotheistic mother goddess its more mythical conceptions (*A Study of History*, vol. i, p. 92). "Mathematic Starlight" Babylonian astrology is, however, present in the friendships and antipathies of the Olympic gods.[9]

town but he cannot separate himself from the general mass. With the first discovery of solitude (Phases 13 and 14) comes, as I think, the visible art that interests us most to-day, for Phidian art, like the art of Raphael, has for the moment exhausted our attention.[13] I recall a Nike at the Ashmolean Museum with a natural unsystematised beauty like that before Raphael, and above all certain pots with strange half-supernatural horses dark on a light ground.[14] Self-realisation attained will bring desire of power—systematisation for its instrument—but as yet clarity, meaning, elegance, all things separated from one another in luminous space, seem to exceed all other virtues. One compares this art with the thought of Greek philosophers before Anaxagoras, where one discovers the same phases, always more concerned with the truth than with its moral or political effects. One longs for the lost dramatists, the plays that were enacted before Aeschylus and Sophocles arose, both Phidian men.[15]

But one must consider not the movement only from the beginning to the end of the ascending cone, but the gyres that touch its sides, the horizontal dance.[16]

> Hands gripped in hands, toes close together,
> Hair spread on the wind they made;
> That lady and that golden king
> Could like a brace of blackbirds sing.[17]

Side by side with Ionic elegance there comes after the Persian wars a Doric vigour, and the light-limbed dandy of the potters, the Parisian-looking young woman of the sculptors, her hair elaborately curled, give place to the athlete.[18] One suspects a deliberate turning away from all that is Eastern, or a moral propaganda like that which turned the poets out of Plato's Republic, and yet it may be that the preparation for the final systematisation had for its apparent cause the destruction, let us say, of Ionic studios by the Persian invaders, and that all came from the resistance of the *Body of Fate* to the growing solitude of the soul.[19] Then in Phidias Ionic and Doric influence unite—one remembers Titian—and all is transformed by the full moon, and all abounds and flows.[20] With Callimachus pure Ionic revives again, as Furtwängler has proved, and upon the only example of his work known to us, a marble chair, a Persian is represented, and may one not discover a Persian symbol in that bronze lamp, shaped like a palm, known to us by a description in Pausanias?[21] But he was an archaistic workman, and those who set him to work brought back public life to an older form.[22] One may see in masters and man a momentary dip into ebbing Asia.

Each age unwinds the thread another age had wound, and it amuses one to remember that before Phidias, and his westward-moving art, Persia fell, and that when full moon came round again, amid eastward-moving thought, and brought Byzantine glory, Rome fell; and that at the outset of our westward-moving Renaissance Byzantium fell; all things dying each other's life, living each other's death.[23]

After Phidias the life of Greece, which being *antithetical* had moved slowly and richly through the *antithetical* phases, comes rapidly to an end. Some Greek or Roman writer whose name I forget will soon speak of the declining comeliness of the people, and in the arts all is systematised more and more, and the antagonist recedes.[24] Aristophanes' passion-clouded eye falls before what one must believe, from Roman stage copies, an idler glance.[25] (Phases 19, 20, 21.) Aristotle and Plato end creative system—to die into the truth is still to die—and formula begins.[26] Yet even the truth into which Plato dies is a form of death, for when he separates the Eternal Ideas from Nature and shows them self-sustained he prepares the Christian desert and the Stoic suicide.[27]

I identify the conquest of Alexander and the break-up of his kingdom, when Greek civilisation, formalised and codified, loses itself in Asia, with the beginning and end of the 22nd Phase, and his intention recorded by some historian to turn his arms westward shows that he is but a part of the impulse that creates Hellenised Rome and Asia.[28] There are everywhere statues where every muscle has been measured, every position debated, and these statues represent man with nothing more to achieve, physical man finished and complacent, the women slightly tinted, but the men, it may be, who exercise naked in the open air, the colour of mahogany. Every discovery after the epoch of victory and defeat (Phase 22) which substitutes mechanics for power is an elimination of intellect by delight in technical skill (Phase 23), by a sense of the past (Phase 24), by some dominant belief (Phase 25). After Plato and Aristotle, the mind is as exhausted as were the armies of Alexander at his death, but the Stoics can discover morals and turn philosophy into a rule of life. Among them doubtless—the first beneficiaries of Plato's hatred of imitation—we may discover the first benefactors of our modern individuality, sincerity of the trivial face, the mask torn away. Then, a Greece that Rome has conquered, and a Rome conquered by Greece, must, in the last three phases of the wheel, adore, desire being dead, physical or spiritual force.[29]

This adoration which begins in the second century before Christ creates a world-wide religious movement as the world was then known, which, being swallowed up in what came after, has left no adequate record. One knows not into how great extravagance Asia, accustomed to abase itself, may have carried what soon sent Greeks and Romans to stand naked in a Mithraic pit, moving their bodies as under a shower-bath that those bodies might receive the blood of the bull even to the last drop.[30] The adored image took everywhere the only form possible as the *antithetical* age died into its last violence—a human or animal form. Even before Plato that collective image of man dear to Stoic and Epicurean alike, the moral double of bronze or marble athlete, had been invoked by Anaxagoras when he declared that thought and not the warring opposites created the world.[31] At that sentence the heroic life, passionate fragmentary man, all that had been imagined by great poets and sculptors began to pass away, and instead of seeking noble antagonists, imagination moved towards divine man and the ridiculous devil. Now must sages lure men away from the arms of women because in those arms man becomes a fragment; and all is ready for revelation.

When revelation comes athlete and sage are merged; the earliest sculptured image of Christ is copied from that of the Apotheosis of Alexander the Great;[32] the tradition is founded which declares even to our own day that Christ alone was exactly six feet high, perfect physical man.[33] Yet as perfect physical man He must die, for only so can *primary* power reach *antithetical* mankind shut within the circle of its senses, touching outward things alone in that which seems most personal and physical. When I think of the moment before revelation I think of Salome—she, too, delicately tinted or maybe mahogany dark—dancing before Herod and receiving the Prophet's head in her indifferent hands, and wonder if what seems to us decadence was not in reality the exaltation of the muscular flesh and of civilisation perfectly achieved.[34] Seeking images, I see her anoint her bare limbs according to a medical prescription of that time, with lion's fat, for lack of the sun's ray, that she may gain the favour of a king, and remember that the same impulse will create the Galilean revelation and deify Roman Emperors whose sculptured heads will be surrounded by the solar disk.[35] Upon the throne and upon the cross alike the myth becomes a biography.[36]

IV

A.D. 1 to A.D. 1050[37]

God is now conceived of as something outside man and man's handiwork, and it follows that it must be idolatry to worship that which Phidias and Scopas made, and seeing that He is a Father in Heaven, that Heaven will be found presently in the Thebaid, where the world is changed into a featureless dust and can be run through the fingers;[38] and these things are testified to from books that are outside human genius, being miraculous, and by a miraculous Church, and this Church, as the gyre sweeps wider, will make man also featureless as clay or dust. Night will fall upon man's wisdom now that man has been taught that he is nothing.[39] He had discovered, or half-discovered, that the world is round and one of many like it,[40] but now he must believe that the sky is but a tent spread above a level floor, and that he may be stirred into a frenzy of anxiety and so to moral transformation, blot out the knowledge or half-knowledge that he has lived many times, and think that all eternity depends upon a moment's decision. Heaven itself, transformation finished, must appear so vague and motionless that it seems but a concession to human weakness.[41] It is even essential to this faith to declare that God's messengers, those beings who show His will in dreams or announce it in visionary speech, were never men. The Greeks thought them great men of the past, but now that concession to mankind is forbidden.[42] All must be narrowed into the sun's image cast out of a burning-glass and man be ignorant of all but the image.

The mind that brought the change, if considered as man only, is a climax of whatever Greek and Roman thought was most a contradiction to its age; but considered as more than man He controlled what Neo-Pythagorean and Stoic could not—irrational force. He could announce the new age, all that had not been thought of, or touched, or seen, because He could substitute for reason, miracle.

We say of Him because His sacrifice was voluntary that He was love itself, and yet that part of Him which made Christendom was not love but pity, and not pity for intellectual despair, though the man in Him, being *antithetical* like His age, knew it in the Garden, but *primary* pity, that for the common lot, man's death, seeing that He raised Lazarus, sickness, seeing that He healed many, sin, seeing that He died.[43]

Love is created and preserved by intellectual analysis, for we love only that which is unique, and it belongs to contemplation, not to action, for we would not change that which we love. A lover will admit a greater beauty than that of his mistress but not its like, and surrenders his days to a delighted laborious study of all her ways and looks, and he pities only if something threatens that which has never been before and can never be again. Fragment delights in fragment and seeks possession, not service; whereas the Good Samaritan discovers himself in the likeness of another, covered with sores and abandoned by thieves upon the roadside, and in that other serves himself.[44] The opposites are gone; he does not need his Lazarus; they do not each die the other's life, live the other's death.

It is impossible to do more than select an arbitrary general date for the beginning of Roman decay (Phases 2 to 7, A.D. 1 to A.D. 250).[45] Roman sculpture—sculpture made under Roman influence whatever the sculptor's blood—did not, for instance, reach its full vigour, if we consider what it had of Roman as distinct from Greek, until the Christian Era.[46] It even made a discovery which affected all sculpture to come. The Greeks painted the eyes of marble statues and made out of enamel or glass or precious stones those of their bronze statues, but the Roman was the first to drill a round hole to represent the pupil, and because, as I think, of a preoccupation with the glance characteristic of a civilisation in its final phase.[47] The colours must have already faded from the marbles of the great period, and a shadow and a spot of light, especially where there is much sunlight, are more vivid than paint, enamel, coloured glass or precious stone. They could now express in stone a perfect composure.

The administrative mind, alert attention had driven out rhythm, exaltation of the body, uncommitted energy. May it not have been precisely a talent for this alert attention that had enabled Rome and not Greece to express those final *primary* phases? One sees on the pediments troops of marble Senators, officials serene and watchful as befits men who know that all the power of the world moves before their eyes, and needs, that it may not dash itself to pieces, their unhurried, unanxious, never-ceasing care. Those riders upon the Parthenon had all the world's power in their moving bodies, and in a movement that seemed, so were the hearts of man and beast set upon it, that of a dance; but presently all would change and measurement succeed to pleasure, the dancing-master outlive the dance.[48] What need had those young lads for careful eyes? But in Rome of the first and second centuries, where the dancing-master himself has died, the delineation of character as shown in face and head, as with us of recent years, is all in all, and sculptors, seeking the custom of occupied officials, stock in their workshops toga'd marble bodies upon which can be screwed with the least possible delay heads modelled from the sitters with the most scrupulous realism.[49] When I think of Rome I see always those heads with their world-considering eyes, and those bodies as conventional as the metaphors in a leading article, and compare in my imagination vague Grecian eyes gazing at nothing, Byzantine eyes of drilled ivory staring upon a vision, and those eyelids of China and of India, those veiled or half-veiled eyes weary of world and vision alike.[50]

Meanwhile the irrational force that would create confusion and uproar as with the cry "The Babe, the Babe is born"[51]—the women speaking unknown tongues, the barbers and weavers expounding Divine revelation with all the vulgarity of their servitude, the tables that move or resound with raps—but creates a negligible sect.[52]

All about it is an *antithetical* aristocratic civilisation in its completed form, every detail of life hierarchical, every great man's door crowded at dawn by petitioners, great wealth everywhere in few men's hands, all dependent upon a few, up to the Emperor himself who is a God dependent upon a greater God, and everywhere in court, in the family, an inequality made law, and floating over all the Romanised Gods of Greece in their physical superiority.[53] All is rigid and stationary, men fight for centuries with the same sword and spear, and though in naval warfare there is some change of tactics to avoid those single combats of ship with ship that needed the seamanship of a more skilful age, the speed of a sailing ship remains unchanged from the time of Pericles to that of Constantine.[54] Though sculpture grows more and more realistic and so renews its vigour, this realism is without curiosity. The athlete becomes the boxer that he may show lips and nose beaten out of shape, the individual hairs show at the navel of the bronze centaur, but the theme has not changed. Philosophy alone, where in contact with irrational force—holding to Egyptian thaumaturgy and the Judean miracle but at arm's length—can startle and create.[55] Yet Plotinus is as *primary*, as much a contradiction of all that created Roman civilisation, as St. Peter, and his thought has its roots almost as deep among the *primary* masses. The founder of his school was Ammonius Sacca, an Alexandrine porter.[56] His thought and that of Origen, which I skimmed in my youth,[57] seem to me to express the abstract synthesis of a quality like that of race, and so to display a character which must always precede Phase 8.[58] Origen, because the Judean miracle has a stronger hold upon the masses than Alexandrian thaumaturgy, triumphs when Constantine (Phase 8) puts the Cross upon the shields of his soldiers and makes the bit of his war-horse from a nail of the True Cross, an act equivalent to man's cry for strength amid the animal chaos at the close of the first lunar quarter. Seeing that Constantine was not converted till upon his deathbed, I see him as half statesman, half thaumaturgist, accepting in blind obedience to a dream the new fashionable talisman, two sticks nailed together.[59] The Christians were but six millions of the sixty or seventy of the Roman Empire, but, spending nothing upon pleasure, exceedingly rich like some Nonconformist sect of the eighteenth century. The world became Christian, "that fabulous formless darkness" as it seemed to a philosopher of the fourth century, blotted out "every beautiful thing", not through the conversion of crowds or general change of opinion, or through any pressure from below, for civilization was *antithetical* still, but by an act of power.[60]

I have not the knowledge (it may be that no man has the knowledge) to trace the rise of the Byzantine State through Phases 9, 10 and 11.[61] My diagram tells me that a hundred and sixty years brought that State to its 15th Phase, but I that know nothing but the arts and of these little, cannot revise the series of dates "approximately correct" but given, it may be, for suggestion only.[62] With a desire for simplicity of statement I would have preferred to find in the middle, not at the end, of the fifth century Phase 12, for that was, so far as the known evidence carries us, the moment when Byzantium became Byzantine and substituted for formal Roman magnificence, with its glorification of physical power, an architecture that suggests the Sacred City in the Apocalypse of St. John.[63] I think if I could be given a month of Antiquity and leave to spend it where I chose, I would spend it in Byzantium a little before Justinian opened St. Sophia and closed the Academy of Plato.[64] I think I could find in some little wine-shop some philosophical worker in mosaic who could answer all my questions, the supernatural descending nearer to him than to Plotinus even, for the pride of his delicate skill would make what was an instrument of power to princes and clerics, a murderous madness in the mob, show as a lovely flexible presence like that of a perfect human body.[65]

I think that in early Byzantium, maybe never before or since in recorded history, religious, aesthetic and practical life were one, that architect and artificers—though not, it may be, poets, for language had been the instrument of controversy and must have grown abstract—spoke to the multitude and the few alike.[66] The painter, the mosaic worker, the worker in gold and silver, the illuminator of sacred books, were almost impersonal, almost perhaps without the consciousness of individual design, absorbed in their subject-matter and that the vision of a whole people. They could copy out of old Gospel books those pictures that seemed as sacred as the text, and yet weave all into a vast design, the work of many that seemed the work of one, that made building, picture, pattern, metal-work of rail and lamp, seem but a single image; and this vision, this proclamation of their invisible master, had the Greek nobility, Satan always the still half-divine Serpent, never the horned scarecrow of the didactic Middle Ages.[67]

The ascetic, called in Alexandria "God's Athlete", has taken the place of those Greek athletes whose statues have been melted or broken up or stand deserted in the midst of cornfields, but all about him is an incredible splendour like that which we see pass under our closed eyelids as we lie between sleep and waking, no representation of a living world but the dream of a somnambulist.[68] Even the drilled pupil of the eye, when the drill is in the hand of some Byzantine worker in ivory, undergoes a somnambulistic change, for its deep shadow among the faint lines of the tablet, its mechanical circle, where all else is rhythmical and flowing, give to Saint or Angel a look of some great bird staring at miracle.[69] Could any visionary of those days, passing through the Church named with so un-theological a grace "The Holy Wisdom",[70] can even a visionary of to-day wandering among the mosaics at Ravenna or in Sicily, fail to recognise some one image seen under his closed eyelids?[71] To me it seems that He, who among the first Christian communities was little but a ghostly exorcist, had in His assent to a full Divinity made possible this sinking-in upon a supernatural splendour, these walls with their little glimmering cubes of blue and green and gold.

I think that I might discover an oscillation, a revolution of the horizontal gyre like that between Doric and Ionic art, between the two principal characters of Byzantine art. Recent criticism distinguishes between Greco-Roman figures, their stern faces suggesting Greek wall-painting at Palmyra, Greco-Egyptian painting upon the cases of mummies, where character delineations are exaggerated as in much work of our time, and that decoration which seems to undermine our self-control, and is, it seems, of Persian origin, and has for its appropriate symbol a vine whose tendrils climb everywhere and display among their leaves all those strange images of bird and beast, those forms that represent no creature eye has ever seen, yet are begotten one upon the other as if they were themselves living creatures.[72] May I consider the domination of the first *antithetical* and that of the second *primary*, and see in their alternation the work of the horizontal gyre? Strzygowski thinks that the church decorations where there are visible representations of holy persons were especially dear to those who believed in Christ's double nature, and that wherever Christ is represented by a bare Cross and all the rest is bird and beast and tree, we may discover an Asiatic art dear to those who thought Christ contained nothing human.[73]

If I were left to myself I would make Phase 15 coincide with Justinian's reign, that great age of building in which one may conclude Byzantine art was perfected; but the meaning of the diagram may be that a building like St. Sophia, where all, to judge by the contemporary description, pictured ecstasy, must unlike the declamatory St. Peter's precede the moment of climax.[74] Of the moment of climax itself I can say nothing, and of what followed from Phase 17 to Phase 21 almost nothing, for I have no knowledge of the time; and no analogy from the age after Phidias, or after our own Renaissance, can help.[75] We and the Greeks moved towards intellect, but Byzantium and the Western Europe of that day moved from it. If Strzygowski is right we may see in the destruction of images but a destruction of what was Greek in decoration accompanied perhaps by a renewed splendour in all that came down from the ancient Persian Paradise, an episode in some attempt to make theology more ascetic, spiritual and abstract. Destruction was apparently suggested to the first iconoclastic Emperor by followers of a Monophysite Bishop, Xenaias, who had his see in that part of the Empire where Persian influence had been strongest.[76] The return of the images may, as I see things, have been the failure of synthesis (Phase 22) and the first sinking-in and dying-down of Christendom into the heterogeneous loam. Did Europe grow animal and literal? Did the strength of the victorious party come from zealots as ready as their opponents to destroy an image if permitted to grind it into powder, mix it with some liquid and swallow it as a medicine?[77] Did mankind for a season do, not what it would, or should, but what it could, accept the past and the current belief because they prevented thought? In Western Europe I think I may see in Johannes Scotus Erigena the last intellectual synthesis before the death of philosophy, but I know little of him except that he is founded upon a Greek book of the sixth century, put into circulation by a last iconoclastic Emperor, though its Angelic Orders gave a theme to the image-makers.[78] I notice too that my diagram makes Phase 22 coincide with the break-up of Charlemagne's Empire and so clearly likens him to Alexander, but I do not want to concern myself, except where I must, with political events.[79]

Then follows, as always must in the last quarter,[80] heterogeneous art; hesitation amid architectural forms, some book tells me; an interest in Greek and Roman literature; much copying out and gathering together; yet outside a few courts and monasteries another book tells me an Asiatic and anarchic Europe.[81] The intellectual cone has so narrowed that secular intellect has gone, and the strong man rules with the aid of local custom; everywhere the supernatural is sudden, violent, and as dark to the intellect as a stroke or St. Vitus' dance.[82] Men under the Caesars, my own documents tell me, were physically one but intellectually many, but that is now reversed, for there is one common thought or doctrine, town is shut off from town, village from village, clan from clan. The spiritual life is alone overflowing, its cone expanded, and yet this life—secular intellect extinguished—has little effect upon men's conduct, is perhaps a dream which passes beyond the reach of conscious mind but for some rare miracle or vision. I think of it as like that profound reverie of the somnambulist which may be accompanied by a sensuous dream—a Romanesque stream perhaps of bird and beast images—and yet neither affect the dream nor be affected by it.[83]

It is indeed precisely because this double mind is created at full moon that the *antithetical* phases are but, at the best, phases of a momentary illumination like that of a lightning flash. But the full moon that now concerns us is not only Phase 15 of its greater era, but the final phase, Phase 28, of its millennium, and in its physical form, human life grown once more automatic. I knew a man once who, seeking for an image of the Absolute, saw one persistent image, a slug, as though it were suggested to him that Being which is beyond human comprehension is mirrored in the least organised forms of life. Intellectual creation has ceased, but men have come to terms with the supernatural and are agreed that, if you make the usual offerings, it will remember to live and let live; even Saint or Angel does not seem very different from themselves: a man thinks his guardian Angel jealous of his mistress;[84] a King, dragging a Saint's body to a new church, meets some difficulty upon the road, assumes a miracle, and denounces the Saint as a churl. Three Roman courtesans who have one after another got their favourite lovers chosen Pope have, it pleases one's mockery to think, confessed their sins, with full belief in the supernatural efficacy of the act, to ears that have heard their cries of love, or received the Body of God from hands that have played with their own bodies.[85] Interest has narrowed to what is near and personal and, seeing that all abstract secular thought has faded, those interests have taken the most physical forms. In monasteries and in hermit cells men freed from the intellect at last can seek their God upon all fours like beasts or children. Ecclesiastical Law, in so far as that law is concerned not with government, Church or State, but with the individual soul, is complete; all that is necessary to salvation is known, yet there is apathy everywhere. Man awaits death and judgment with nothing to occupy the worldly faculties and helpless before the world's disorder, drags out of the subconscious the conviction that the world is about to end. Hidden, except at rare moments of excitement or revelation, even then shown but in symbol, the stream set in motion by the Galilean Symbol has filled its basin, and seems motionless for an instant before it falls over the rim. In the midst of the basin stands, in motionless contemplation, blood that is not His blood upon His Hands and Feet, One that feels but for the common lot, and mourns over the length of years and the inadequacy of man's fate to man. Two thousand years before, His predecessor, careful of heroic men alone, had so stood and mourned over the shortness of time, and man's inadequacy to his fate.

Full moon over, that last Embodiment shall grow more like ourselves, putting off that stern majesty, borrowed, it may be, from the Phidian Zeus—if we can trust Cefalù and Monreale; and His Mother—putting off her harsh Byzantine image—stand at His side.[86]

V

A.D. 1050 to the Present Day

When the tide changed and faith no longer sufficed, something must have happened in the courts and castles of which history has perhaps no record, for with the first vague dawn of the ultimate *antithetical* revelation man, under the eyes of the Virgin, or upon the breast of his mistress, became but a fragment. Instead of that old alternation, brute or ascetic, came something obscure or uncertain that could not find its full explanation for a thousand years. A certain Byzantine Bishop had said upon seeing a singer of Antioch, "I looked long upon her beauty, knowing that I would behold it upon the day of judgment, and I wept to remember that I had taken less care of my soul than she of her body",[87] but when in the *Arabian Nights* Harun Al-Rashid looked at the singer Heart's Miracle, and on the instant loved her, he covered her head with a little silk veil to show that her beauty "had already retreated into the mystery of our faith".[88] The Bishop saw a beauty that would be sanctified, but the Caliph that which was its own sanctity, and it was this latter sanctity, come back from the first Crusade or up from Arabian Spain or half Asiatic Provence and Sicily, that created romance. What forgotten reverie, what initiation, it may be, separated wisdom from the monastery and, creating Merlin, joined it to passion? When Merlin in Chrestien de Troyes loved Ninian he showed her a cavern adorned with gold mosaics and made by a prince for his beloved, and told her that those lovers died upon the same day and were laid "in the chamber where they found delight". He thereupon lifted a slab of red marble that his art alone could lift and showed them wrapped in winding-sheets of white samite. The tomb remained open, for Ninian asked that she and Merlin might return to the cavern and spend their night near those dead lovers, but before night came Merlin grew sad and fell asleep, and she and her attendants took him "by head and foot" and laid him "in the tomb and replaced the stone", for Merlin had taught her the magic words, and "from that hour none beheld Merlin dead or alive".[89] Throughout the German *Parsifal* there is no ceremony of the Church, neither Marriage nor Mass nor Baptism, but instead we discover that strangest creation of romance or of life, "the love trance". Parsifal in such a trance, seeing nothing before his eyes but the image of his absent love, overcame knight after knight, and awakening at last looked amazed upon his dinted sword and shield; and it is to his lady and not to God or the Virgin that Parsifal prayed upon the day of battle, and it was his lady's soul, separated from her entranced or sleeping body, that went beside him and gave him victory.[90]

The period from 1050 to 1180 is attributed in the diagram to the first two gyres of our millennium, and what interests me in this period, which corresponds to the Homeric period some two thousand years before, is the creation of the Arthurian Tales and Romanesque architecture. I see in Romanesque the first movement to a secular Europe, but a movement so instinctive that as yet there is no antagonism to the old condition. Every architect, every man who lifts a chisel, may be a cleric of some kind, yet in the overflowing ornament where the human form has all but disappeared and where no bird or beast is copied from nature, where all is more Asiatic than Byzantium itself, one discovers the same impulse that created Merlin and his jugglery.

I do not see in Gothic architecture, which is a character of the next gyre, that of Phases 5, 6 and 7, as did the nineteenth-century historians, ever looking for the image of their own age, the creation of a new communal freedom, but a creation of authority, a suppression of that freedom though with its consent, and certainly St. Bernard when he denounced the extravagance of Romanesque saw it in that light.[91] I think of that curious sketchbook of Villard de Honnecourt with its insistence upon mathematical form, and I see that form in Mont St. Michel—Church, Abbey, Fort and town, all that dark geometry that makes Byzantium seem a sunlit cloud—and it seems to me that the Church grows secular that it may fight a new-born secular world.[92] Its avowed appeal is to religion alone: nobles and great ladies join the crowds that drag the Cathedral stones, not out of love for beauty but because the stones as they are trundled down the road cure the halt and the blind; yet the stones once set up traffic with the enemy. The mosaic pictures grown transparent[93] fill the windows, quarrel one with the other like pretty women, and draw all eyes, and upon the faces of the statues flits once more the smile that disappeared with archaic Greece. That smile is physical, *primary* joy, the escape from supernatural terror, a moment of irresponsible common life before *antithetical* sadness begins. It is as though the pretty worshippers, while the Dominican was preaching with a new and perhaps incredible sternness, let their imaginations stray, as though the observant sculptor, or worker in ivory, in modelling his holy women has remembered their smiling lips.[94]

Are not the cathedrals and the philosophy of St. Thomas the product of the abstraction that comes before Phase 8 as before Phase 22, and of the moral synthesis that at the end of the first quarter seeks to control the general anarchy?[95] That anarchy must have been exceedingly great, or man must have found a hitherto unknown sensitiveness, for it was the shock that created modern civilisation. The diagram makes the period from 1250 to 1300 correspond to Phase 8, certainly because in or near that period, chivalry and Christendom having proved insufficient, the King mastered the one, the Church the other, reversing the achievement of Constantine, for it was now the mitre and the crown that protected the

Cross.[96] I prefer, however, to find my example of the first victory of personality where I have more knowledge. Dante in the *Convito* mourns for solitude, lost through poverty, and writes the first sentence of modern autobiography, and in the *Divina Commedia* imposes his own personality upon a system and a phantasmagoria hitherto impersonal; the King everywhere has found his kingdom.[97]

The period from 1300 to 1380 is attributed to the fourth gyre, that of Phases 9, 10 and 11, which finds its character in painting from Giotto to Fra Angelico, in the Chronicles of Froissart and in the elaborate canopy upon the stained glass of the windows.[98] Every old tale is alive, Christendom still unbroken; painter and poet alike find new ornament for the tale, they feel the charm of everything but the more poignantly because that charm is archaistic; they smell a pot of dried roses. The practical men, face to face with rebellion and heresy, are violent as they have not been for generations, but the artists separated from life by the tradition of Byzantium can even exaggerate their gentleness, and gentleness and violence alike express the gyre's hesitation. The public certainty that sufficed for Dante and St. Thomas has disappeared, and there is yet no private certainty. Is it that the human mind now longs for solitude, for escape from all that hereditary splendour, and does not know what ails it; or is it that the Image itself encouraged by the new technical method, the flexible brush-stroke instead of the unchanging cube of glass, and wearied of its part in a crowded ghostly dance, longs for a solitary human body? That body comes in the period from 1380 to 1450 and is discovered by Masaccio, and by Chaucer who is partly of the old gyre, and by Villon who is wholly of the new.[99]

Masaccio, a precocious and abundant man, dying like Aubrey Beardsley in his six-and-twentieth year, cannot move us, as he did his immediate successors, for he discovered a naturalism that begins to weary us a little;[100] making the naked young man awaiting baptism shiver with the cold, St. Peter grow red with the exertion of dragging the money out of the miraculous fish's mouth, while Adam and Eve, flying before the sword of the Angel, show faces disfigured by their suffering.[101] It is very likely because I am a poet and not a painter that I feel so much more keenly that suffering of Villon—of the 13th Phase as man, and of it or near it in epoch—in whom the human soul for the first time stands alone before a death ever present to imagination, without help from a Church that is fading away; or is it that I remember Aubrey Beardsley, a man of like phase though so different epoch, and so read into Villon's suffering our modern conscience which gathers intensity as we approach the close of an era?[102] Intensity that has seemed to me pitiless self-judgment may have been but heroic gaiety. With the approach of solitude bringing with it an ever-increasing struggle with that which opposes solitude—sensuality, greed, ambition, physical curiosity in all its species—philosophy has returned driving dogma out. Even amongst the most pious the worshipper is preoccupied with himself, and when I look for the drilled eyeball, which reveals so much, I notice that its edge is no longer so mechanically perfect, nor, if I can judge by casts at the Victoria and Albert Museum, is the hollow so deep.[103] Angel and Florentine noble must look upward with an eye that seems dim and abashed as though to recognise duties to Heaven, an example to be set before men, and finding both difficult seem a little giddy. There are no miracles to stare at, for man descends the hill he once climbed with so great toil, and all grows but natural again.

As we approach the 15th Phase, as the general movement grows more and more westward in character, we notice the oscillation of the horizontal gyres, as though what no Unity of Being, yet possible, can completely fuse displays itself in triumph.

Donatello, as later Michelangelo, reflects the hardness and astringency of Myron, and foretells what must follow the Renaissance; while Jacopo della Quercia and most of the painters seem by contrast, as Raphael later on, Ionic and Asiatic.[104] The period from 1450 to 1550 is allotted to the gyre of Phase 15, and these dates are no doubt intended to mark somewhat vaguely a period that begins in one country earlier and in another later. I do not myself find it possible to make more than the first half coincide with the central moment, Phase 15 of the Italian Renaissance—Phase 22 of the cone of the entire era—the breaking of the Christian synthesis as the corresponding period before Christ, the age of Phidias, was the breaking of Greek traditional faith. The first half covers the principal activity of the Academy of Florence which formulated the reconciliation of Paganism and Christianity.[105] This reconciliation, which to Pope Julius meant that Greek and Roman Antiquity were as sacred as that of Judea, and like it "a vestibule of Christianity", meant to the mind of Dürer—a visitor to Venice during the movement of the gyre—that the human norm, discovered from the measurement of ancient statues, was God's first handiwork, that "perfectly proportioned human body" which had seemed to Dante Unity of Being symbolised.[106] The ascetic, who had a thousand years before attained his transfiguration upon the golden ground of Byzantine mosaic, had turned not into an athlete but into that unlabouring form the athlete dreamed of: the second Adam had become the first.[107]

Because the 15th Phase can never find direct human expression, being a supernatural incarnation, it impressed upon work and thought an element of strain and artifice, a desire to combine elements which may be incompatible, or which suggest by their combination something supernatural. Had some Florentine Platonist read to Botticelli Porphyry upon the Cave of the Nymphs? for I seem to recognise it in that curious cave, with a thatched roof over the nearer entrance to make it resemble the conventional manger, in his "Nativity"* in the National Gallery.[108] Certainly the glimpse of forest trees, dim in the evening light, through the far entrance, and the deliberate strangeness everywhere, gives one an emotion of mystery which is new to painting.

Botticelli, Crivelli, Mantegna, Da Vinci,[109] who fall within the period, make Masaccio and his school seem heavy and common by something we may call intellectual beauty or compare perhaps to that kind of bodily beauty which Castiglione called "the spoil or monument of the victory of the soul".[110] Intellect and emotion,

*There is a Greek inscription at the top of the picture which says that Botticelli's world is in the "second woe" of the Apocalypse, and that after certain other Apocalyptic events the Christ of the picture will appear. He had probably found in some utterance of Savonarola's promise of an ultimate Marriage of Heaven and Earth, sacred and profane, and pictures it by the Angels and shepherds embracing, and as I suggest by Cave and Manger. When I saw the Cave of Mithra at Capri I wondered if that were Porphyry's Cave. The two entrances are there, one reached by a stair of a hundred feet or so from the sea and once trodden by devout sailors, and one reached from above by some hundred and fifty steps and used, my guide-book tells me, by Priests. If he knew that cave, which may have had its recognised symbolism, he would have been the more ready to discover symbols in the cave where Odysseus landed in Ithaca.

primary curiosity and the *antithetical* dream, are for the moment one. Since the rebirth of the secular intellect in the eleventh century, faculty has been separating from faculty, poetry from music, the worshipper from the worshipped, but all have remained within a common fading circle—Christendom—and so within the human soul. Image has been separated from image but always as an exploration of the soul itself; forms have been displayed in an always clear light, have been perfected by separation from one another till their link with one another and with common associations has been broken; but, Phase 15 past, these forms begin to jostle and fall into confusion, there is as it were a sudden rush and storm.[111] In the mind of the artist a desire for power succeeds to that for knowledge, and this desire is communicated to the forms and to the onlooker.

The eighth gyre, which corresponds to Phases 16, 17 and 18 and completes itself say between 1550 and 1650, begins with Raphael, Michelangelo and Titian, and the forms, as in Titian, awaken sexual desire[112]—we had not desired to touch the forms of Botticelli or even of Da Vinci—or they threaten us like those of Michelangelo, and the painter himself handles his brush with a conscious facility or exultation. The subject-matter may arise out of some propaganda as when Raphael in the Camera della Segnatura, and Michelangelo in the Sistine Chapel, put, by direction of the Pope, Greek Sages and Doctors of the Church, Roman Sibyls and Hebrew Prophets, opposite one another in apparent equality.[113] From this on, all is changed, and where the Mother of God sat enthroned, now that the Soul's unity has been found and lost, Nature seats herself, and the painter can paint only what he desires in the flesh, and soon, asking less and less for himself, will make it a matter of pride to paint what he does not at all desire. I think Raphael almost of the earlier gyre—perhaps a transitional figure—but Michelangelo, Rabelais, Aretino, Shakespeare, Titian—Titian is so markedly of the 14th Phase as a man that he seems less characteristic—I associate with the mythopoeic and ungovernable beginning of the eighth gyre. I see in Shakespeare a man in whom human personality, hitherto restrained by its dependence upon Christendom or by its own need for self-control, burst like a shell. Perhaps secular intellect, setting itself free after five hundred years of struggle, has made him the greatest of dramatists, and yet because an *antithetical* age alone could confer upon an art like his the unity of a painting or of a temple pediment, we might, had the total works of Sophocles survived—they too born of a like struggle though with a different enemy—not think him greatest. Do we not feel an unrest like that of travel itself when we watch those personages, more living than ourselves, amid so much that is irrelevant and heterogeneous, amid so much *primary* curiosity, when we are carried from Rome to Venice, from Egypt to Saxon England, or in the one play from Roman to Christian mythology?

Were he not himself of a later phase, were he of the 16th Phase like his age and so drunk with his own wine, he had not written plays at all, but as it is he finds his opportunity among a crowd of men and women who are still shaken by thought that passes from man to man in psychological contagion. I see in Milton, who is characteristic of the moment when the first violence of the gyre has begun to sink, an attempted return to the synthesis of the Camera della Segnatura and the Sistine Chapel. It is this attempt made too late that, amid all the music and magnificence of the still violent gyre, gives him his unreality and his cold rhetoric. The two elements have fallen apart in the hymn "On the Morning of Christ's Nativity", the one is sacred, the other profane; his classical mythology is an artificial ornament;[114] whereas no great Italian artist from 1450 to the sack of Rome saw any difference between them, and when difference came, as it did with Titian, it was God and the Angels that seemed artificial.

The gyre ebbs out in order and reason, the Jacobean poets succeed the Elizabethan, Cowley and Dryden the Jacobean as belief dies out.[115] Elsewhere Christendom keeps a kind of spectral unity for a while, now with one, now with the other element of the synthesis dominant; a declamatory holiness defaces old churches, innumerable Tritons and Neptunes pour water from their mouths. What had been a beauty like the burning sun fades out in Vandyke's noble ineffectual faces, and the Low Countries, which have reached the new gyre long before the rest of Europe, convert the world to a still limited curiosity, to certain recognised forms of the picturesque constantly repeated, chance travellers at an inn door, men about a fire, men skating, the same pose or grouping, where the subject is different, passing from picture to picture.[116] The world begins to long for the arbitrary and accidental, for the grotesque, the repulsive and the terrible, that it may be cured of desire. The moment has come for the ninth gyre, Phases 19, 20 and 21, for the period that begins for the greater part of Europe with 1650 and lasts, it may be, to 1875.

The beginning of the gyre like that of its forerunner is violent, a breaking of the soul and world into fragments, and has for a chief character the materialistic movement at the end of the seventeenth century, all that comes out of Bacon perhaps, the foundation of our modern inductive reasoning, the declamatory religious sects and controversies that first in England and then in France destroy the sense of form, all that has its very image and idol in Bernini's big Altar in St. Peter's with its figures contorted and convulsed by religion as though by the devil.[117] Men change rapidly from deduction to deduction, opinion to opinion, have but one impression at a time and utter it always, no matter how often they change, with the same emphasis. Then the gyre develops a new coherence in the external scene; and violent men, each master of some generalisation, arise one after another: Napoleon, a man of the 20th Phase in the historical 21st—personality in its hard final generalisation—typical of all. The artistic life, where most characteristic of the general movement, shows the effect of the closing of the *tinctures*. It is external, sentimental and logical—the poetry of Pope and Gray, the philosophy of Johnson and of Rousseau—equally simple in emotion or in thought, the old oscillation in a new form.[118] Personality is everywhere spreading out its fingers in vain, or grasping with an always more convulsive grasp a world where the predominance of physical science, of finance and economics in all their forms, of democratic politics, of vast populations, of architecture where styles jostle one another, of newspapers where all is heterogeneous, show that mechanical force will in a moment become supreme.

That art discovered by Dante of marshalling into a vast *antithetical* structure *antithetical* material became through Milton Latinised and artificial—the Shades, as Sir Thomas Browne said, "steal or contrive a body"[119]—and now it changes that it may marshal into a still *antithetical* structure *primary* material, and the modern novel is created, but even before the gyre is drawn to its end the happy ending, the admired hero, the preoccupation with desirable things, all that is undisguisedly *antithetical* disappears.

All the art of the gyre that is not derived from the external scene is a Renaissance echo growing always more conventional or more shadowy, but since the Renaissance—Phase 22 of the cone of the era—the "Emotion of Sanctity", that first relation to the *spiritual primary*, has been possible in those things that are most intimate and personal, though not until Phase 22 of the millennium cone will general thought be ready for its expression.[120] A mysterious contact is perceptible first in painting and then in poetry and last in prose. In painting it comes where the influence of the Low Countries and that of Italy mingle, but always rarely and faintly. I do not find it in Watteau, but there is a preparation for it, a sense of exhaustion of old interests—"they do not believe even in their own happiness", Verlaine said—and then suddenly it is present in the faces of Gainsborough's women as it has been in no face since the Egyptian sculptor buried in a tomb that image of a princess carved in wood.[121] Reynolds had nothing of it, an ostentatious fashionable man fresh from Rome, he stayed content with fading Renaissance emotion and modern curiosity.[122] In frail women's faces the soul awakes—all its prepossessions, the accumulated learning of centuries swept away—and looks out upon us wise and foolish like the dawn. Then it is everywhere, it finds the village Providence of the eighteenth century and turns him into Goethe, who for all that comes to no conclusion, his Faust after his hundred years but reclaiming land like some Sir Charles Grandison or Voltaire in his old age.[123] It makes the heroines of Jane Austen seek, not as their grandfathers and grandmothers would have done, theological or political truth, but simply good breeding, as though to increase it were more than any practical accomplishment.[124] In poetry alone it finds its full expression, for it is a quality of the emotional nature (*Celestial Body* acting through *Mask*); and creates all that is most beautiful in modern English poetry from Blake to Arnold, all that is not a fading echo. One discovers it in those symbolist writers who like Verhaeren substitute an entirely personal wisdom for the physical beauty or passionate emotion of the fifteenth and sixteenth centuries.[125] In painting it shows most often where the aim has been archaistic, as though it were an accompaniment of what the popular writers call decadence, as though old emotions had first to be exhausted. I think of the French portrait-painter Ricard, to whom it was more a vision of the mind than a research, for he would say to his sitter, "You are so fortunate as to resemble your picture", and of Charles Ricketts, my education in so many things.[126] How often his imagination moves stiffly as though in fancy dress, and then there is something—Sphinx, Danaides—that makes me remember Callimachus' return to Ionic elaboration and shudder as though I stared into an abyss full of eagles. Everywhere this vision, or rather this contact, is faint or intermittent and it is always fragile; Dickens was able with a single book, *Pickwick*, to substitute for Jane Austen's privileged and perilous research the camaraderie of the inn parlour, qualities that every man might hope to possess, and it did not return till Henry James began to write.[127]

Certain men have sought to express the new emotion through the *Creative Mind*, though fit instruments of expression do not yet exist, and so to establish, in the midst of our ever more abundant *primary* information, *antithetical* wisdom; but such men, Blake, Coventry Patmore at moments, Nietzsche, are full of morbid excitement and few in number, unlike those who, from Richardson to Tolstoy, from Hobbes down to Spencer, have grown in number and serenity.[128] They were begotten in the Sistine Chapel and still dream that all can be transformed if they be but emphatic; yet Nietzsche, when the doctrine of the Eternal Recurrence drifts before his eyes, knows for an instant that nothing can be so transformed and is almost of the next gyre.[129]

The period from 1875 to 1927 (Phase 22—in some countries and in some forms of thought the phase runs from 1815 to 1927) is like that from 1250 to 1300 (Phase 8) a period of abstraction, and like it also in that it is preceded and followed by abstraction. Phase 8 was preceded by the Schoolmen and followed by legalists and inquisitors, and Phase 22 was preceded by the great popularisers of physical science and economic science, and will be followed by social movements and applied science. Abstraction which began at Phase 19 will end at Phase 25, for these movements and this science will have for their object or result the elimination of intellect. Our generation has witnessed a first weariness, has stood at the climax, at what in *The Trembling of the Veil* I call *Hodos Chameliontos*, and when the climax passes will recognise that there common secular thought began to break and disperse.[130] Tolstoy in *War and Peace* had still preference, could argue about this thing or that other, had a belief in Providence and a disbelief in Napoleon, but Flaubert in his *St. Anthony* had neither belief nor preference, and so it is that, even before the general surrender of the will, there came synthesis for its own sake, organisation where there is no masterful director, books where the author has disappeared, painting where some accomplished brush paints with an equal pleasure, or with a bored impartiality, the human form or an old bottle, dirty weather and clean sunshine.[131] I too think of famous works where synthesis has been carried to the utmost limit possible, where there are elements of inconsequence or discovery of hitherto ignored ugliness, and I notice that when the limit is approached or past, when the moment of surrender is reached, when the new gyre begins to stir, I am filled with excitement. I think of recent mathematical research; even the ignorant can compare it with that of Newton—so plainly of the 19th Phase—with its objective world intelligible to intellect; I can recognise that the limit itself has become a new dimension, that this ever-hidden thing which makes us fold our hands has begun to press down upon multitudes.[132] Having bruised their hands upon that limit, men, for the first time since the seventeenth century, see the world as an object of contemplation, not as something to be remade, and some few, meeting the limit in their special study, even doubt if there is any common experience, doubt the possibility of science.[133]

. . . . .

Written at Capri, February 1925

THE END OF THE CYCLE[134]

I

Day after day I have sat in my chair turning a symbol over in my mind, exploring all its details, defining and again defining its elements, testing my convictions and those of others by its unity, attempting to substitute particulars for an abstraction like that of algebra. I have felt the convictions of a lifetime melt though at an age when the mind should be rigid, and others take their place, and these in turn give way to others. How far can I accept socialistic or communistic prophecies? I remember the decadence Balzac foretold to the Duchess de Castries.[135] I remember debates in the little coach-house at Hammersmith or at Morris' supper-table afterwards.[136] I remember the Apocalyptic dreams of the Japanese Saint and labour leader Kagawa, whose books were lent me by a Galway clergyman.[137] I remember a Communist described by Captain White in his memoirs ploughing on the Cotswold Hills, nothing on his great hairy body but sandals and a pair of drawers, nothing in his head but Hegel's *Logic.*[138] Then I draw myself up into the symbol and it seems as if I should know all if I could but banish such memories and find everything in the symbol.

II

But nothing comes—though this moment was to reward me for all my toil. Perhaps I am too old. Surely something would have come when I meditated under the direction of the Cabbalists. What discords will drive Europe to that artificial unity—only dry or drying sticks can be tied into a bundle—which is the decadence of every civilisation?[139] How work out upon the phases the gradual coming and increase of the counter movement, the *antithetical* multiform influx:

> Should Jupiter and Saturn meet,
> O what a crop of mummy wheat![140]

Then I understand. I have already said all that can be said. The particulars are the work of the *Thirteenth Cone* or cycle which is in every man and called by every man his freedom. Doubtless, for it can do all things and knows all things, it knows what it will do with its own freedom but it has kept the secret.

III

Shall we follow the image of Heracles that walks through the darkness bow in hand, or mount to that other Heracles, man, not image, he that has for his bride Hebe, "The daughter of Zeus, the mighty, and Hera, shod with gold"?[141]

1934–1936

ALL SOULS' NIGHT[1]

AN EPILOGUE

Midnight has come and the great Christ Church bell
And many a lesser bell sound through the room;
And it is All Souls' Night.
And two long glasses brimmed with muscatel
Bubble upon the table. A ghost may come;
For it is a ghost's right,
His element is so fine
Being sharpened by his death,
To drink from the wine-breath
While our gross palates drink from the whole wine.

I need some mind that, if the cannon sound
From every quarter of the world, can stay
Wound in mind's pondering,
As mummies in the mummy-cloth are wound;
Because I have a marvellous thing to say,
A certain marvellous thing
None but the living mock,
Though not for sober ear;
It may be all that hear
Should laugh and weep an hour upon the clock.

Horton's the first I call.[2] He loved strange thought
And knew that sweet extremity of pride
That's called platonic love,
And that to such a pitch of passion wrought
Nothing could bring him, when his lady died,

Anodyne for his love.
Words were but wasted breath;
One dear hope had he:
The inclemency
Of that or the next winter would be death.

Two thoughts were so mixed up I could not tell
Whether of her or God he thought the most,
But think that his mind's eye,
When upward turned, on one sole image fell;
And that a slight companionable ghost,
Wild with divinity,
Had so lit up the whole
Immense miraculous house
The Bible promised us,
It seemed a gold-fish swimming in a bowl.

On Florence Emery I call the next,
Who finding the first wrinkles on a face
Admired and beautiful,
And by foreknowledge of the future vexed;
Diminished beauty, multiplied commonplace;
Preferred to teach a school
Away from neighbour or friend,
Among dark skins, and there
Permit foul years to wear
Hidden from eyesight to the unnoticed end.[3]

Before that end much had she ravelled out
From a discourse in figurative speech
By some learned Indian
On the soul's journey. How it is whirled about
Wherever the orbit of the moon can reach,
Until it plunge into the sun;
And there, free and yet fast,
Being both Chance and Choice,
Forget its broken toys
And sink into its own delight at last.[4]

I call MacGregor Mathers from his grave,
For in my first hard spring-time we were friends,
Although of late estranged.
I thought him half a lunatic, half knave,
And told him so, but friendship never ends;
And what if mind seem changed,
And it seem changed with the mind,
When thoughts rise up unbid
On generous things that he did
And I grow half contented to be blind![5]

He had much industry at setting out,
Much boisterous courage, before loneliness
Had driven him crazed;
For meditations upon unknown thought
Make human intercourse grow less and less;
They are neither paid nor praised.
But he'd object to the host,
The glass because my glass;
A ghost-lover he was
And may have grown more arrogant being a ghost.

But names are nothing. What matter who it be,
So that his elements have grown so fine
The fume of muscatel
Can give his sharpened palate ecstasy
No living man can drink from the whole wine.
I have mummy truths to tell
Whereat the living mock,
Though not for sober ear,
For maybe all that hear
Should laugh and weep an hour upon the clock.

Such thought—such thought have I that hold it tight
Till meditation master all its parts,
Nothing can stay my glance
Until that glance run in the world's despite
To where the damned have howled away their hearts,

And where the blessed dance;
Such thought, that in it bound
I need no other thing,
Wound in mind's wandering
As mummies in the mummy-cloth are wound.

Oxford, Autumn 1920

Textual Matters and Notes

APPENDIX I

PROOFS, VERSIONS, EMENDATIONS, AND HYPHENATIONS

Corrections to the Yeatses' Copies of *A Vision* (1937) and *A Vision* (1938)

The Yeatses kept copies of the 1937 and 1938 printings of *A Vision* in their library, and corrections have been marked in each. The two tables that follow present the changes made to these copies with indications of the changes and who made them (when it is possible to distinguish whether the marking was made by WBY or GY). Page numbers are given for the original book (in parentheses) and this edition. The final column indicates whether the correction also appears in the copy sent to Macmillan of New York to set the 1956 edition. This copy, held in the Russell K. Alspach Yeats Collection at the University of Massachusetts, Amherst, is inscribed "George Yeats, 46 Palmerston Road, Dublin," and marked as "Partially corrected copy."

Table 1. *A Vision* (1937), W. B. Yeats, YL 2434.

Page.Line	Change	By	Alspach?
Flyleaf	Inscription in ink: "George Yeats' own copy not to be taken by me WB Yeats December, 1937"	WBY	
	Inscription in pencil: "Partially corrected copy. July 1939"	GY	
	Inscription in ink: "Pages 260 | 245 | 79 | WBY."	GY	
(12.18) 10.11	"Cabalistic" changed in gray pencil to "Cabbalistic"	GY	✓
(12.19) 10.13	"Cabala" changed in gray pencil to "Cabbala"	GY	✓

Page.Line	Change	By	Alspach?
(18.8) 14.11	In "the twenty-eight phases," capitalization added in gray pencil: "Phases"	GY	✓
(19.7) 15.3	In "the twenty-eight phases," capitalization added in blue pencil: "Phases"	GY?	✓
(27.13) 20.24	"Sea-shanties" changed in gray pencil to "sea-shanties"	GY	✓
(27.14) 20.24	"of Steam." changed in gray pencil to "of steam."	GY	✓
(28.8) 21.9	"his own eyes." changed in gray pencil to "his own eyes?"	GY	✓
(28.24) 21.22	"Crickmaa," changed in gray pencil to "Cruchmaa,"	GY	
(59.7) 41.8	"*late risen moon,*" changed in gray pencil to "*late-risen moon,*"	GY	✓
(62.8) 44.19	"For perfected, completed," changed to "For separate, perfect"	GY	✓
(79.14) 59.3	"Phase 1 and Phase 28" changed in black ink to "Phase 1 and Phase 15"	WBY	✓
(88.30) 65.28	"negation. The whole" changed in gray pencil to "negation, the whole"	GY	
(91.11) 67.13	"Sec. XII" changed in gray pencil to "Section XII"	GY	
(97.r12.c3) 72.r12.c3	"Enforced law." changed in gray pencil, and then again in black ink, to "Enforced lure."	GY	✓
(99.r24.c4) 73.r24.c4	"Enforced success in action." changed in gray pencil to "Enforced success of action."	GY	✓
(104.21) 78.19	"Phase 29" changed in gray pencil and then in black ink to "Phase 28"	GY	✓
(104.23) 78.21	"Well." changed in gray pencil and then in black ink to "Will."	GY	✓
(108.7) 81.20	"copying the opposite phase, he" changed in gray pencil and then in black ink to "copying the opposite phase he"	GY	✓
(111.22) 84.10	"life, where" changed in gray pencil and then in black ink to "life where"	GY	✓

Page.Line	Change	By	Alspach?
(112.3) 84.20	"perfectly, a" changed in gray pencil and then in black ink to "perfectly a"	GY	✓
(114.6) 86.2	"*Image* of a vague," changed in gray pencil to "Image of a vague,"	GY	✓
(119.31) 90.8	"Enforced sensuality." changed in gray pencil and then in black ink to "Enforced Sensuality."	GY	✓
(124.3) 93.9	"had cut table" changed in gray pencil and then in black ink to "had cut Tables"	GY	✓
(124.26) 93.27	"The Image-Burner" is struck through in gray pencil and in same pencil, written beside it: "See table"	GY	✓[1]
(129.11) 96.34	"Sensuous Ego" is struck through in gray pencil and in same pencil, written beside it: "See table"	GY	✓[2]
(153.30) 114.26	"Luke" is changed in gray pencil to "Lake"	GY	✓
(154.19) 115.8	"Self-adaption." is changed in gray pencil to "Self-adaptation."	GY	✓
(155.26) 116.6	"adaption" is changed in gray pencil to "adaptation"	GY	✓
(156.5) 116.15	"self-adaption)" is changed in gray pencil to "self-adaptation)"	GY	✓
(157.23) 117.20	"The 'breaking of strength'." is changed in gray pencil to "Temptation through Strength."	GY	✓
(219.3) 159.4	"PAUL VALERY in the *Cimitière Marine*" is changed in gray pencil and then in black ink to "PAUL VALÉRY in the *Cimitière Marin*"	GY	✓
(220.23) 160.16	"*Cimitière Marine*" is changed in black ink to "*Cimitièr Marine*"	GY	✓[3]
(222.28) 162.2	"*Mandooka*" is changed in black ink to "*Mandookya*"	GY	✓

Page.Line	Change	By	Alspach?
(226.2) 164.16	"considered as Nature," is changed in gray pencil and black ink to "considered as nature,"	GY	✓
(232.8) 169.5	"*Aeneids*," is changed in gray pencil to "*Enneads*,"	GY	✓
(232.26) 169.20	"'Hymn of the Soul'," is changed in gray pencil and black ink to "*Hymn of the Soul*,"	GY	✓
(233.30) 169.37	"sleeps, that is not him" is changed in gray pencil and black ink to "sleeps, and it is not he"	GY	✓
(245.17) 179.2	"before, the fifteenth" is changed in black ink to "before the fifteenth"	WBY?	✓
(250.13) 182.27	"Immortalities" is changed in black ink to "Mortalities"	GY	✓
(260.29) 190.31	"Shru Purhoit" is changed in black ink to "Shree Purohit"	WBY?	✓

Table 2. *A Vision* (1938), W. B. Yeats, YL 2435.
All markings in pencil.

Page.Line	Change	By	Alspach?
Front board	Inscription: "George Yeats"	GY	
(24.48) 19.10	"'the pulsaters of an artery'" changed to "'the pulsation of an artery'"	GY	
(44.4) 31.34	Beside "It was one of those pretty malachite things they sell in Florence," underlining added, is written "Masefield's gift to WBY!"	GY	
(59.7) 41.8	"*late risen moon,*" changed to "*late-risen moon,*"	GY	✓
(62.8) 44.19	"For perfected, completed," changed to "For separate, perfect,"	GY	✓
(79.14) 59.3	"Phase 28" changed to "Phase 15"	GY	✓
(99.r24.c4) 73.r24.c4	"Enforced success in action." changed to "Enforced success of action."	GY	✓
(104.21) 78.19	"Phase 29" changed to "Phase 28"	GY	✓

Page.Line	Change	By	Alspach?
(104.23) 78.21	"*Well.*" changed to "*Will.*"	GY	✓
(111.22) 84.10	"substitute for a life, where" changed to "substitute for a life where"	GY	✓
(153.30) 114.26	"Luke" changed to "Lake"	GY	✓
(157.23) 117.20	"The 'breaking of strength'." changed to "Temptation through strength."	GY	✓
(222.28) 162.2	"*Mandooka*" changed to "*Mandookya*"	GY	✓
(243.23) 177.20	Beside "A generation later Virgil sang his song" is written "IVth Ecologue" [*sic*]	GY	
(245.17) 179.2	"before, the fifteenth" is changed to "upon the day before the fifteenth"	GY	✓
(261.6) 190.26	Beside "When the automatic script began, neither I nor my wife knew, or knew that we knew, that any man had tried to explain history philosophically." is written "X untrue. GY had read Hegel's Philosophy of History."	GY	
(273.20) 199.1	Beside "Seeking images, I see her anoint" is written "Diary 1930"	GY	
(278.9) 202.15	Beside "His thought and that of Origen, which I skimmed in my youth," underlining added, is written, "+ re-read in Sept. 1913 at the Prelude, Coleman's Hatch GY"	GY	
(280.30) 204.9	"Ravenne" changed to "Ravenna"	GY	
(288.8) 209.18	Beside "The mosaic pictures grown transparent fill the windows," underlining added, is written "Justinian & Theodora"	GY	

Comparison of *A Vision* (1937) with the Coole proofs, Thomas Mark's Notebook, and *A Vision* (1962)

This table compares the 1937 printing of *A Vision* with the first- and second-pull Coole proofs (BL Add. 55893 and 55886) and the 1962 printing of *A Vision*. In the first column, page numbers are given for the 1937 text (in parentheses) and this edition. Pagination is the same in the 1937 and 1962 texts. The next three columns give the location of the text in the Coole proofs, the reading as printed, and the corrected reading. The next two columns present the printed reading in the Coole proofs and any corrections. The second-pull Coole proofs have the same pagination as the first-pull, but this second set lacks pages 1–58; see Editors' Introduction, xlvii. For the second-pull proofs, the table does not include changes made to move commas or periods outside quotation marks. In most cases where the second-pull Coole proofs reverse a change made in the first pull, it is on the authority of the New York edition. The Coole proofs have a different signature P (209–24) than the bound copies of unmarked proofs in the British Library. Endnotes to this table note variants between these two versions of signature P. The penultimate column notes whether the correction appears in Thomas Mark's notebook (see Editors' Introduction, xlviii). The final column gives the reading as it appears in the 1962 Macmillan edition.

Table 3. Comparison of *A Vision* (1937) with the Coole proofs, Thomas Mark's Notebook, and *A Vision* (1962)

Page.Line	Reading: 1937 ed.	Loc. Coole proofs	As printed: 1st Coole proofs	1st Coole correction	As printed: 2nd Coole proofs	2nd Coole correction	TM nb?	Reading: 1962 ed.
		[1]	[no date after title]	1929				[no date after title]
			[stamped on first page:] FIRST PROOF ‖ Please return this | MARKED PROOF ‖ 15 JUL 1939	[written on first page:] This is Vol IX Sig. P. for revise to Mr. Mark (Type should be same as in Autobiographies Vol. II Dram. Personae, Estrangement, etc.) A VISION 269, 270 to follow				
		4.header	*A Vision*	Or should heading be A PACKET FOR E.P. I think book title is better[4]				*A Vision*
(4.2) 3.26	roof which	4.2	roof which	roof, which				roof which
(4.3) 4.1	seven and twenty	4.3	seven and twenty	seven-and-twenty				seven and twenty
(4.31) 4.35	Matter as wise logi-cians say	4.n2	Matter as wise logicians say	Matter, as wise logi-cians say,			✓	Matter, as wise logi-cians say,

Page.Line	Reading: 1937 ed.	Loc. Coole proofs	As printed: 1st Coole proofs	1st Coole correction	As printed: 2nd Coole proofs	2nd Coole correction	TM nb?	Reading: 1962 ed.
(5.23) 5.8	all Hodos Chamelion-tos,	5.24	all Hodos Chamelion-tos,	all *Hodos Chame-liontos,*			✓	all *Hodos Chamelion-tos,*
(6.5) 5.21	four-storied	6.9	four-storied	four-storeyed				four-storied
(6.25) 6.1	Romantic Movement,	6.28	Romantic Movement,	romantic movement, [note: "lc on pp. 46–76 of Vol. VI, cap p. 187"]				Romantic Movement,
(7.12) 6.16	then God Save the King,	7.14	then God Save the King,	then *God Save the King,*				then God Save the King,
(7.12) 6.17	and He's a Jolly Good Fellow.	7.14–15	and He's a Jolly Good Fellow.	and *He's a Jolly Good Fellow.*				and He's a Jolly Good Fellow.
(12.15) 10.9	Prophetic Books	13.21	Prophetic Books	'Prophetic Books'				Prophetic Books
(12.18) 10.11	Cabalistic	13.23–24	Cabalistic	Cabbalistic				Cabalistic
(12.19) 10.13	Cabala	13.25	Cabala	Cabbala				Cabala
(13.8) 10.28	such and such an	14.13–14	such and such an	such-and-such an				such and such an

(13.8) 10.28	such and such a	14.14	such and such a	such-and-such a				such and such a
(17.11) 13.27	Tolstoi's	18.24	Tolstoi's	Tolstoy's [note: "as Vol VI p. 193"]				Tolstoi's
(18.8) 14.11	twenty-eight phases	19.20	twenty-eight phases	twenty-eight Phases				twenty-eight phases
(19.7) 15.3	twenty-eight phases	20.22	twenty-eight phases	twenty-eight Phases				twenty-eight phases
(19.19) 15.13	proof sheets	21.6	proof sheets	proof-sheets				proof sheets
(23.26) 18.16	Cabala	25.18	Cabala	Cabbala				Cabala
(24.28) 19.10	pulsaters	26.23	pulsaters	pulsation			✓	pulsation
(26.14) 19.33	"Eugene Aram"	28.14	'Eugene Aram'	*Eugene Aram*				"Eugene Aram"
(27.12) 20.23	"Eugene Aram",	29.12	'Eugene Aram,'	*Eugene Aram*,				"Eugene Aram",
(27.13) 20.24	Sea-shanties	29.13	Sea-shanties	sea-shanties			✓	sea-shanties
(27.14) 20.24	Steam	29.14	Steam	steam			✓	steam
(28.8) 21.9	eyes.	30.10	eyes.	eyes?			✓	eyes?

Page.Line	Reading: 1937 ed.	Loc. Coole proofs	As printed: 1st Coole proofs	1st Coole correction	As printed: 2nd Coole proofs	2nd Coole correction	TM nb?	Reading: 1962 ed.
(28.24) 21.22	Crickmaa,	30.26	Crickmaa,	Cruachmaa,			✓	Cruach-maa,
(29.12) 22.6	"The Re-turn",	31.13	'The Return,'	*The Return*				"The Re-turn",
(29.25) 22.19	Inviolable. [stanza break]	32.2–3	Inviolable. [stanza break]	Inviolable, [no stanza break]			✓	Inviolable. [no stanza break]
(29.27) 22.21	hounds	32.4	hounds,	hounds			✓	hounds,
(29.28) 22.22	[page break after "air!"]	32.5–6	[no line break after "air!"]	[inserts line break after "air!" and note: "space here as in Pound's Selected Poems?"]			✓	[page break after "air!"]
([31]) 23.3	[no date after title]	[33]	[no date after title]	1931				[no date after title]
(33.10) 24.4	"Oh,	35.10	'Oh,	'O,				"Oh,
(35.22) 25.26	Denise de L'Isle Adam,	37.23	Denise de L'Isle Adam,	Denise de l'Isle-Adam,				Denise de L'Isle Adam,
(36.12) 26.7	café	38.15	café	Café				café

(36.16) 26.10	café	38.19	café	Café				café
(37.20) 27.2	"Oh,	39.23	'Oh,	'O,				"Oh,
(37.27) 27.8	Cabalistic	39.29	Cabalistic	Cabbalistic				Cabalistic
(38.25) 27.32	eight and twenty	40.28–29	eight and twenty	eight-and-twenty				eight and twenty
(38.30) 27.35	wand.	42.2	wand.	wand.[1] [then adds note below: "[1] See page 70: The Great Wheel."]			✓	wand.[1] [then be-low: [1] See p. 66.]
(40.30) 29.24	Cabalists	43.4	Cabalists	Cabbalists				Cabalists
(42.1) 30.15	Denise de L'Isle Adam	44.8	Denise de L'Isle Adam	Denise de l'Isle-Adam				Denise de L'Isle Adam
(42.16) 30.25	*Axel*	44.23	*Axel*	*Axël* [and note: "as in other vols"]				*Axel*
(42.21) 30.29	Axel	44.28	Axel	Axël				Axel
(42.32) 31.4	said:	45.9	said:	said, [and note: "Commas in other vols usually except for long speeches"]				said:
(43.4) 31.8	said:	45.15	said:	said,				said:

Page.Line	Reading: 1937 ed.	Loc. Coole proofs	As printed: 1st Coole proofs	1st Coole correction	As printed: 2nd Coole proofs	2nd Coole correction	TM nb?	Reading: 1962 ed.
(43.7) 31.10	said:	45.18	said:	said,				said:
(43.18) 31.19	said: 'Oh,	45.28	said: "Oh,	said, "O,				said: 'Oh,
(43.19) 31.20	Axel	45.29	Axel	Axël				Axel
(43.23) 31.24	Axel	46.3	Axel	Axël				Axel
(43.24) 31.25	Axel	46.4	Axel	Axël				Axel
(43.29) 31.29	hands: 'Oh	46.9	hands: "Oh	hands, "O				hands: 'Oh
(43.30) 31.29	do'. I said:	46.10	do." I said:	do?" I said,			✓	do?' I said:
(44.3) 31.33	said:	46.15	said:	said,				said:
(44.6) 31.36	said:	46.18	said:	said,				said:
(44.7) 31.37	said: 'Oh	46.19	said: "Oh,	said, "O,				said: 'Oh
(44.10) 32.1	*Axel*." I said:	46.21	*Axel*.' I said:	*Axël*.' I said,				*Axel*." I said:
(44.12) 32.2	said: "What a fool you are.	46.23	said: 'What a fool you are.	said, 'What a fool you are!				said: "What a fool you are.

(44.14) 32.3	said:	46.24	said:	said,				said:
(44.14) 32.4	said:	46.25	said:	said,				said:
(46.18) 33.24	semi-gothic	49.2	semi-gothic	semi-Gothic				semi-gothic
(47.5) 34.1	Grillion	49.21–22	Grillion	Grillion's			✓	Grillion's
(53.7) 38.10	said: [line break] "Even	56.3–4	said: [line break] 'Even	said: [no line break] 'Even				said: [line break] "Even
(54.2) 38.33	"The Phases of the Moon", "The Dou-ble Vision", and "The Gift of Harun Al-Rashid".	56.30–57.1	'The Phases of the Moon,' 'The Double Vision,' and 'The Gift of Harun Al-Rashid.'	*The Phases of the Moon*, *The Double Vision*, and *The Gift of Harun Al-Rashid*.				"The Phases of the Moon", "The Dou-ble Vision", and "The Gift of Harun Al-Rashid".
(54.6) 38.37	"The Gift of Harun Al-Rashid"	57.4–5	'The Gift of Harun Al-Rashid'	*The Gift of Harun Al-Rashid*				"The Gift of Harun Al-Rashid"
(54.9) 39.2	Sect,	57.7	Sect,	sect,				Sect,

Page.Line	Reading: 1937 ed.	Loc. Coole proofs	As printed: 1st Coole proofs	1st Coole correction	As printed: 2nd Coole proofs	2nd Coole correction	TM nb?	Reading: 1962 ed.
(54.28) 39.19	"Rosa Alchemica", "The Tables of the Law" and "The Adoration of the Magi",	57.26–29	'Rosa Alchemica,' 'The Tables of the Law' and 'The Adoration of the Magi,'	*Rosa Alchemica, The Tables of the Law* and *The Adoration of the Magi,*				"Rosa Alchemica", "The Tables of the Law" and "The Adoration of the Magi",
		[59]	THE PHASES OF THE MOON		THE PHASES OF THE MOON	[written on page: Last revise ‖ 1–58 removed | to send to | Mrs Yeats | Aug 1960]		
(59.7) 41.8	*late risen*	61.7	*late risen*	*late-risen*	*late-risen*		✓	*late-risen*
(60.23) 42.30	Athena	62.27	Athena	Athene	Athene		✓	Athene
(62.3) 44.14	country men	64.14	country men	countrymen	countrymen		✓	country-men
(62.8) 44.19	perfected, completed,	64.19	perfected, completed,	separate, perfect,	separate, perfect		✓	separate, perfect,
(63.21) 46.5	fancies,	66.8	fancies,	fancy,	fancies,			fancies,

(64.11) 46.23	country man	66.26	country man	countryman	countryman		✓	country-man
(69.3) 50.24	St.	73.5	St.	Saint	Saint			St.
(69.29) 51.30	"The Friends of the People of Faery"	73.n1	'The Friends of the People of Faery'	*The Friends of the People of Faery*	*The Friends of the People of Faery*			"The Friends of the People of Faery"
(70.3) 51.18	"La Spirale".	74.4–5	'La Spirale.'	*La Spirale.* [and note: "This is mentioned in another vol. where I think the title of the story is distorted. I can probably check it on the sectioned proofs"]	*La Spirale.*			"La Spi-rale".
(79.14) 59.3	Phase 28	83.10	Phase 28	Phase 15	Phase 15		✓	Phase 15
(80.12) 59.19	zodiac.	84.10	zodiac.	Zodiac.	zodiac.		✓	Zodiac.
(83.16) 61.28	Phase 17	87.1	Phase 17	Phase 17,	Phase 17,			Phase 17
(85.21) 63.14	phantasy,	89.9	phantasy,	fantasy, [and note: "see p. 104?"]	phantasy,		✓	fantasy,
(85.25) 63.18	"Discov-ery of Strength",	89.13	'Discovery of Strength,'	-	'Discovery of Strength,'		✓	"Begin-ning of Strength",

Page.Line	Reading: 1937 ed.	Loc. Coole proofs	As printed: 1st Coole proofs	1st Coole correction	As printed: 2nd Coole proofs	2nd Coole correction	TM nb?	Reading: 1962 ed.
(85.32) 63.24	"Breaking of Strength",	89.20–21	'Breaking of Strength,'	-	'Breaking of Strength,'		✓	"Temp-tation through Strength",
(87.17) 64.27	section XII	91.9	section XII	Section XII	Section XII			section XII
(88.30) 65.28	negation. The whole	92.24	negation. The whole	negation, the Whole	negation, the Whole		✓	negation, the Whole
(90.27) 67.1	"Folly"	94.20	'Folly'	'Folly',	'Folly',		✓	"Folly",
(91.5) 67.8	sand, a Heaven	94.29	sand, a Heaven	sand, and a heaven	sand, and a heaven		✓	sand, and a heaven
(91.11) 67.13	Sec. XII	95.5–6	Sec. XII	Section XII [note: "? 'section' as on p. 91"]	Sec. XII			Sec. XII
(92.5) 67.34	*from Creative*	95.30	*from Creative*	*from the Creative*	*from the Creative*		✓	*from the Creative*
(93.4) 68.25	to	97.1	to	to,	to,		✓	to,
(93.8) 68.29	*earth,*	97.5	*earth*	*earth,*	*earth,*			*earth,*
(93.18) 69.4	and the *Body*	97.15	and the *Body*	and *Body*	and *Body*		✓	and *Body*
(94.10) 69.24	grinding out	98.9	grinding out	grinding-out	grinding-out			grinding out

(95.4) 70.23	obvious for instance that	99.5–6	obvious for instance that	obvious, for instance, that	obvious, for instance, that			obvious for instance that
(97.r12.c3) 72.r12.c3	law.	101.r12.c3	law.	lure.	lure.		✓	lure.
(97.r13.c3) 72.r13.c3	antithetical	101.r13.c3	antithetical	-	antithetical		✓	*antithetical*
(99.r22.c4) 73.r22.c4	versus	103.r22.c4	versus	through	through	versus [note: "versus in U.S."]	✓	through
(99.r24.c4) 73.r24.c4	in	103.r24.c4	in	of	of		✓	of
(99.r26.c1) 73.r26.c1	man	103.r26.c1	man	man,	man,		✓	man,
(104.21) 78.19	Phase 29	108.21	Phase 29	Phase 28 [and note: "Do these go beyond 28?"]	Phase 28		✓	Phase 28
(104.23) 78.21	*Well.*	108.23	*Well.*	*Will.*	*Will.*			*Well.*
(107.13) 80.31	Dancing Faun.		111.17	Dancing Faun.		*Dancing Faun.*		*Dancing Faun.*
(107.31) 81.11	Brama	112.5	Brama	Brahma	Brahma		✓	Brahma
(108.26) 82.1	joy	113.5	joy	Joy	Joy			joy

Page.Line	Reading: 1937 ed.	Loc. Coole proofs	As printed: 1st Coole proofs	1st Coole correction	As printed: 2nd Coole proofs	2nd Coole correction	TM nb?	Reading: 1962 ed.
(108.27) 82.2	Does	113.6	Does	Doth	Doth		✓	Doth
(108.27) 82.2	destroy,	113.6	destroy,	destroy;	destroy;			destroy,
(108.28) 82.3	joy	113.7	joy	Joy	Joy			joy
(108.29) 82.4	eternity's	113.8	eternity's	Eternity's	Eternity's			eternity's
(110.17) 83.10	mind:	114.26	mind:	mind:—	mind:—			mind:
(110.31) 83.24	dreamed)	115.10	dreamed)	dreamed,)	dreamed,)			dreamed)
(111.22) 84.10	life, where	116.4	life, where	life where	life where		✓	life where
(112.3) 84.20	perfectly, a portion	116.17	perfectly, a portion	perfectly a portion	perfectly a portion		✓	perfectly a portion
(114.6) 86.2	*Image*	118.24	*Image*	Image [note: "Rom. as on p. 125?"]	Image		✓	Image
(114.8) 86.5	had	118.26	has	had	had			had

(114.14) 86.9	such and such a feeling. I have such and such	119.3	such and such a feeling. I have such and such	such-and-such a feeling. I have such-and-such	such-and-such a feeling. I have such-and-such			such and such a feeling. I have such and such
(115.1) 86.23	*True*—Heroic sentiment. *False*—Dogmatic sentimen-tality.	119.20–21	*True*—Heroic sentiment. *False*—Dogmatic sentimental-ity.	*True*—Heroic Sentiment. *False*—Dogmatic Sentimentality.	*True*—Heroic Sentiment. *False*—Dogmatic Sentimental-ity.			*True*—Heroic sentiment. *False*—Dogmatic sentimen-tality.
(117.1) 88.5	beginning of strength.	121.24–25	beginning of strength.	Beginning of Strength.	Beginning of Strength.		✓	Beginning of Strength.
(119.31) 90.8	Enforced sensuality.	124.28–29	Enforced sensuality.	Enforced Sensuality.	Enforced Sensuality.			Enforced sensuality.
(121.28) 91.24	emotional construc-tion.	127.2	emotional construction.	Emotional Construc-tion.	Emotional Construction.			emotional construc-tion.
(121.30) 91.25	Enforced emotion.	127.3	Enforced emotion.	Enforced Emotion.	Enforced Emotion.			Enforced emotion.
(124.3) 93.9	table	129.13	table	Tables [note: "of the Law"]	Tables		✓	Tables
(124.26) 93.27	The Image-Burner.	130.4	The Image-Burner.	The Consumer, Pyre-builder. [note: "as in Table?"]	The Consumer, Pyre-builder.		✓	The Con-sumer, Pyre-builder.

Page.Line	Reading: 1937 ed.	Loc. Coole proofs	As printed: 1st Coole proofs	1st Coole correction	As printed: 2nd Coole proofs	2nd Coole correction	TM nb?	Reading: 1962 ed.
(124.29) 93.30	iconoclasm.	130.7–8	iconoclasm.	Iconoclasm.	Iconoclasm.			iconoclasm.
(125.1) 93.32	belief.	130.9	belief.	Belief.	Belief.			belief.
(126.26) 95.5	philosophy.	132.6	philosophy.	Philosophy.	Philosophy.			philosophy.
(126.28) 95.6	intellectual action.	132.8–9	intellectual action.	Intellectual Action.	Intellectual Action.			intellectual action.
(127.16) 95.20	degree of	132.26	degree or [or partial printing?]	degree of	degree of			degree of
(129.4) 96.29	*Image*	134.21	*Image*	Image	Image		✓	Image
(129.6) 96.30	Phase	134.23	Phrase	Phase	Phase			Phase
(129.11) 96.34	Sensuous Ego.	134.27	Sensuous Ego.	The Sensuous Man. [note: "Table p. 103"]	The Sensuous Man.		✓	The Sensu-ous Man.
(129.15) 97.1	truth.	135.2	truth.	Truth.	Truth.			truth.
(129.16) 97.3	love of another.	135.3–4	love of anoth-er.	Love of Another.	Love of An-other.			love of another.

(131.8) 98.12	will.	137.2	will.	Will.	Will.			will.
(131.10) 98.14	love of the world.	137.3–4	love of the world.	Love of the World.	Love of the World.			love of the world.
(133.16) 99.37	"Eternal Idol"	139.12	'Eternal Idol'	*Eternal Idol*	*Eternal Idol*			"Eternal Idol"
(133.29) 100.10	"Sleep of Arthur,"	139.26	'Sleep of Arthur,'	*Sleep of Arthur*,	*Sleep of Arthur*,			"Sleep of Arthur,"
(133.30) 100.10	"Golden Stair,"	139.26	'Golden Stair,'	*Golden Stair*,	*Golden Stair*,			"Golden Stair,"
(137.8) 102.26	will.	143.13	will.	Will.	Will.			will.
(138.21) 103.28	St.	144.29	St.	Saint	Saint			St.
(140.8) 104.33	perhaps if	146.21–22	perhaps if	perhaps, if	perhaps, if			perhaps if
(140.28) 105.11	intensity.	147.10	intensity.	Intensity.	Intensity.			intensity.
(140.30) 105.13	*antithetical* emotion.	147.12	*antithetical* emotion.	*Antithetical* Emotion.	*Antithetical* Emotion.			*antithetical* emotion.
(140.31) 105.13	self-realization.	147.13	self-realisation.	Self-realisation.	Self-realisation.			self-realization.
(141.1) 105.15	—Loss.	147.14	—Loss.	—Enforced Loss.	—Enforced Loss.		✓	—Enforced Loss.

Page.Line	Reading: 1937 ed.	Loc. Coole proofs	As printed: 1st Coole proofs	1st Coole correction	As printed: 2nd Coole proofs	2nd Coole correction	TM nb?	Reading: 1962 ed.
(141.20) 105.31	*Image*	148.5	*Image*	Image	Image		✓	Image
(142.12) 106.15	by	148.29	by	through	by		✓	through
(142.33) 106.31	*Image*	149.19	*Image*	Image	Image		✓	Image
(143.22) 107.12	devil	150.10	devil	Devil	Devil			devil
(143.32) 107.20	partisan,	150.20	partisan,	partisan	partisan		✓	partisan
(144.30) 108.9	*Lunae.*	151.22–23	*Lunae.*	-	*Lunae.*	*Lunae.*[1] / [1] See <u>Essays</u>?		*Lunae.*
(145.8) 108.17	emotion.	152.4	emotion.	Emotions.	Emotions.		✓	emotions.
(145.10) 108.20	philosophy.	152.6	philosophy.	Philosophy.	Philosophy.			philosophy.
(145.11) 108.21	disillusion-ment.	152.7–8	disillusion-ment.	Disillusionment.	Disillusion-ment.			disillusion-ment.
(145.19) 108.27	"A Lover's Nocturne" or "An Ode to the West Wind"	152.15–16	'A Lover's Nocturne' or 'An Ode to the West Wind'	A *Love's Nocturn* or an *Ode to the West Wind*	*A Lover's Nocturne* or an *Ode to the West Wind*	*A Lover's Nocturne* or *An Ode to the West Wind*	✓	A "Love's Nocturn" or an "Ode to the West Wind"

(147.31) 110.15	intellect.	154.28–29	intellect.	Intellect.	Intellect.			intellect.
(148.1) 110.17	failure of action.	155.1–2	failure of action.	Failure of Action.	Failure of Action.			failure of action.
(150.1) 111.35	*Image*	157.6	*Image*	Image	Image		✓	Image
(151.12) 112.32	action.	158.19	action.	Action.	Action.			action.
(153.30) 114.26	Luke	161.11	Luke	Lake	Lake		✓	Lake
(154.19) 115.8	Self-adaption.	162.4	Self-adaption.	Self-adaptation.	Self-adaptation.		✓	Self-adaptation.
(154.22) 115.11	intellect.	162.6	intellect.	-	intellect.	Intellect.		intellect.
(154.23) 115.12	triumph of achieve-ment.	162.7–8	triumph of achievement.	Triumph of Achieve-ment.	Triumph of Achievement.			triumph of achieve-ment.
(155.26) 116.6	adaption	163.12	adaption	adaptation	adaptation		✓	adaptation
(156.5) 116.15	self-adaption)	163.24	self-adaption)	self-adaptation)	self-adaptation)		✓	self-adaptation)
(156.9) 116.18	devil,	163.28	devil,	Devil,	devil,	Devil,		devil,
(156.16) 116.24	Dostoieff-sky's	164.4	Dostoieffsky's	Dostoievsky's [note: "Dostoievsky Mythol 475 vi 244"]	Dostoievsky's			Dostoieff-sky's

Page.Line	Reading: 1937 ed.	Loc. Coole proofs	As printed: 1st Coole proofs	1st Coole correction	As printed: 2nd Coole proofs	2nd Coole correction	TM nb?	Reading: 1962 ed.
(157.23) 117.20	The "breaking of strength".	165.13–14	The 'breaking of strength.'	Temptation through Strength	Temptation through Strength		✓	Temptation through strength
(157.26) 117.23	Dostoieff-sky,	165.16	Dostoieffsky,	Dostoievsky	Y			Dostoieff-sky,
(158.1) 117.27	synthesis will	165.21	synthesis will	synthesis, will	synthesis, will			???
(160.3) 119.10	*St.*	167.30	*St.*	*Saint*	*Saint*			*St.*
(160.27) 119.28	Dostoieff-sky	168.22	Dostoieffsky	Dostoievsky	Dostoievsky			Dostoieff-sky
(160.30) 119.31	Whole	168.25	Whole	whole	whole	[note: "cap. in N.Y."]	✓	whole
(161.24) 120.14	carries	169.20	carried	carries	carries			carries
(162.26) 121.6	Dostoieff-sky,	170.26	Dostoieffsky,	Dostoievsky,	Dostoievsky,			Dostoieff-sky,
(163.18) 121.26	nature	171.20	nature	-	nature	Nature		nature
(165.12) 123.2	synthesis,	173.19	synthesis,	synthesis;	synthesis;		✓	synthesis;
(167.6) 124.13	Concubar,	175.17	Concubar,	Conchubar, [note: "Conchubar elsewhere"]	Conchubar,		✓	Conchubar,

(167.9) 124.15	"Move a little further off", she cried, "with the babbling of fools";	175.20–21	'Move a little further off,' she cried, 'with the babbling of fools';	'Draw a little back,' she cried, 'with the squabbling of fools'; [note: "see Death of Synge Autobiogra-phies"]	'Draw a little back,' she cried, 'with the squabbling of fools';		✓	"Draw a little back", she cried, "with the squabbling of fools";
(167.11) 124.17	Concubar	175.22	Concubar	Conchubar	Conchubar		✓	Conchubar
(167.29) 124.31	*Will*	176.9	*Will*	*Will*,	*Will*,		✓	*Will*,
(168.3) 124.37	sympathy	176.16	sympathy	sympathy,	sympathy,		✓	sympathy,
(169.8) 125.31	end of ambition.	177.23	end of ambi-tion.	sympathy,	sympathy,			end of ambition.
(169.11) 125.33	Humani-tarianism. through constructive emotion.	177.26–27	Humani-tarianism through constructive emotion.	Constructive Emo-tion.	Constructive Emotion.		✓	Con-structive emotion.
(169.13) 125.35	action.	177.28	action.	Action.	Action.			action.
(170.3) 126.16	climax;	178.19	climax	climax;	climax;			climax;
(171.2) 127.5	Blue Book.	179.20	Blue Book.	blue-book.	blue-book	Blue Book [note: "Blue Book N.Y."]		Blue Book.

Page.Line	Reading: 1937 ed.	Loc. Coole proofs	As printed: 1st Coole proofs	1st Coole correction	As printed: 2nd Coole proofs	2nd Coole correction	TM nb?	Reading: 1962 ed.
(172.26) 128.15	arrogance.	181.17	arrogance.	Arrogance.	Arrogance.			arrogance.
(174.30) 129.37	banality,	183.26	banality	banality,	banality,			banality,
(175.15) 130.13	Synge,	184.13	Syne,	Synge,	Synge,			Synge,
(175.19) 130.17	fellow Catholics,	184.17	fellow Cath- olics,	fellow-Catholics,	fellow- Catholics,			fellow Catholics,
(176.18) 131.4	imminent	185.18	imminent	immanent	imminent	immanent	✓	immanent
(177.3) 131.19	of abstract supersensu- al thought. *False*— Fascination of sin.	186.6–7	of abstract supersensual thought. *False*— Fascination of sin.	of the abstract supersensual. *False*— Fascination of Sin.	of the abstract supersensual. *False*— Fascination of Sin.	of abstract supersensu- al thought. *False*— Fascination of Sin. [note: "abstract supersensual thought in N.Y."]	✓	of the abstract supersensu- al. *False*— Fascination of sin.
(180.5) 133.29	receptivity.	189.18	receptivity.	Receptivity.	Receptivity.			receptivity.
(180.7) 133.30	impersonal action.	189.19– 20	impersonal action.	Impersonal Action.	Impersonal Action.			impersonal action.

(180.10) 133.33	*Mask*, [but comma raised]	189.22	*Mask*,	-	*Mask*,		✓	*Mask*,
(181.23) 134.34	achieve- ment,	191.8–9	achievement;	achievement,	achievement,			achieve- ment,
(183.4) 136.3	complete plasticity.	192.23–24	complete plasticity.	Complete Plasticity.	Complete Plasticity.			complete plasticity.
(184.5) 136.31	Finished at Thoor Ballylee, 1922, | in a time of Civil War.	193.28–29	Finished at THOOR BALLYLEE, 1922 | in a time of Civil War	*Finished at* THOOR BALLYLEE, 1922 | *in a time of Civil War*	*Finished at* THOOR BALLYLEE, 1922 | *in a time of Civil War*			Finished at Thoor Ballylee, 1922, | in a time of Civil War.
(189.2) 138.28	*Primary*	199.8	*Primary*	*primary*	*primary*		✓	*primary*
(190.11) 140.3	light,	200.13	light,	-	light,	light		light,
(190.26) 139.34	Exc. vii. Exc. viii.	200.n2	Exc. vii. Exc. viii.	-	Exc. vii. Exc. viii.	Exc. vii, Exc. viii,		Exc. vii. Exc. viii.
(192.8) 141.10	*Faculties'*	202.19	*Faculties*',	*Faculties,*	*Faculties*',	*Faculties*,	✓	*Faculties,*
(192.13) 141.14	*Faculties*	202.23	Faculties	-	Faculties	*Faculties*		*Faculties*
(192.17) 141.17	memory,	202.27	memory,	memory;	memory;		✓	memory;
(192.31) 141.32	*The Inferno*	202.n1	*The Inferno*	the *Inferno*	*the Inferno*	the *Inferno*	✓	the *Inferno*

Page.Line	Reading: 1937 ed.	Loc. Coole proofs	As printed: 1st Coole proofs	1st Coole correction	As printed: 2nd Coole proofs	2nd Coole correction	TM nb?	Reading: 1962 ed.
(193.6) 142.2	reality	203.18	reality	reality,	reality,		✓	reality,
(194.12) 143.1	diagram implies	204.24	diagram implies	diagram (p. 205) implies	diagram (p. 203) implies	diagram (p. 205) implies		diagram implies
(194.diag) 143.diag	First A.E.	205. diag	First A.E.	First Authentic Ex-istant	Anthentic Existant	First Authen-tic Existant	✓	First Authentic Existant
(195.12) 143.14	in	205.11	in	on	on		✓	on
(198.9) 145.37	figure is	208.28	figure is	figure (p. 209) is	figure (p. 209) is			figure is
(199.8) 146.20	Wheel	210.7	wheel[5]	-	wheel		✓	wheel
(199.9) 147.1	superim-posed (see p. 200) we	210.8–9	superimposed (see p. 210) we	superimposed (see below) we	superimposed (see below we	superimposed (see below) we		superim-posed (see p. 200) we
(199.14) 147.5	Wheel	210.13	wheel[6]		wheel		✓	wheel
(200.4) 147.13	jelly fish	211.2	jelly-fish[7]		jelly-fish		✓	jelly-fish
(200.5) 147.14	The forego-ing figure shows	211.3	The foregoing figure shows	The figure on p. 209 shows	The figure on p. 209 shows			The foregoing figure shows

(200.7) 147.15	The follow-ing diagram shows	211.6	The follow-ing diagram shows	The diagram on p. 210 shows	The diagram on p. 210 shows			The following diagram shows
(200.diag) 147.diag		211. diag		[note suggests moving diag down 4 lines]	[moved to indicated location]			[same position as 1937]
(203.34) 150.34	man of Ur	214.n1	man of Ur	Man of Ur	man of Ur		✓	Man of Ur
(209.6) 154.8	Leibnitz,	220.2	Leibnitz,	Leibniz,	Leibnitz,		✓	Leibniz,
(210.26) 154.31	November, and,	220.n1	November, and[8]		November, and		✓	November, and
(211.17) 156.3	1 or West	222.15	1, or West,[9]		1, or West,		✓	1, or West,
(211.23) 156.14	wheel	222.21	Wheel[10]		Wheel	wheel	✓	Wheel
(214.7) 157.31	The present Pope has said in his last Encyclical that	225.11	The present Pope has said in his last Encyclical that	Pope Pius XI said in an Encyclical that [note: "Correct at time book was written. We could alter to Pope Pius XI has said"]	Pope Pius XI. said in an Encyclical that		✓	Pope Pius XI said in an Encyclical that
(219.3) 159.4	VALERY in the *Cimitière Marine*	229.1	VALERY in the *Cimitière Marine*	VALÉRY in the *Cim-itière Marin*	VALÉRY in the *Cimitière Marin*		✓	VALÉRY in the *Cimitière Marin*

Page.Line	Reading: 1937 ed.	Loc. Coole proofs	As printed: 1st Coole proofs	1st Coole correction	As printed: 2nd Coole proofs	2nd Coole correction	TM nb?	Reading: 1962 ed.
(219.6) 159.7	sea "les œuvres purs d'une cause éternelle".	229.5	sea 'les œuvres purs d'une cause éternelle.'	sea the 'ouvrages purs d'une éternelle cause.'	sea 'les œuvres purs d'une cause éternelle.'		✓	sea the "ouvrages purs d'une éternelle cause".
(220.18) 160.10	light, or of utter darkness	230.17	light, or of utter dark- ness	light or of utter darkness,	light or of utter darkness,		✓	light or of utter darkness,
(220.23) 160.16	*Marine*	230.22	*Marine*	*Marin*	*Marin*		✓	*Marin*
(221.2) 160.20	spirit",	231.3	spirit,'	spirit'	spirit'		✓	spirit"
(221.28) 161.12	it,	231.29	it,	them,	them,		✓	them,
(222.28) 162.2	*Mandooka*	233.2	*Mandooka*	*Mandukya* [note: "as in later essays"]	*Mandukya*		✓	*Mandukya*
(224.30) 162.34	feet,	234.n1	feet	feet,	feet,			feet,
(226.2) 164.16	Nature,	236.10	Nature,	nature, [note: "Is it 'nature'—character, etc—or Nature?"]	nature,		✓	nature,
(226.15) 164.27	understood,	236.23	understood	-	understood	understood,		understood,

(226.23) 164.33	translation:	237.2	translation:	translation:—	translation:—			translation:
(231.30) 168.35	Cardinal	242.n1	Cardinal	cardinal	cardinal	Cardinal	✓	cardinal
(232.8) 169.5	*Aeneids,*	242.24	*Aeneids,*	*Enneads,*	*Enneads,*		✓	*Enneads,*
(232.26) 169.20	"Hymn of the Soul",	243.17	'Hymn of the Soul,'	*Hymn of the Soul,*	*Hymn of the Soul,*			"Hymn of the Soul",
(232.28) 169.28	*The Shift-ings*	243.n1	*The Shiftings*	the *Shiftings*	the *Shiftings*			*The Shiftings*
(232.34) 169.33	(Book II, section VII).	243.n1	(Book II, section VII).	(Book II, Section VII).	(Book II, Section VII).			(Book II, section VII).
(233.12) 170.5	Whole,	244.9	Whole,	whole,	whole,		✓	whole,
(233.30) 169.37	sleeps that is not him who sleeps and	243.n2	sleeps that is not him who sleeps and	sleeps, that is not he who sleeps, and [note: "Vol vii p. 379"]	sleeps, and it is not he who sleeps, and		✓	sleeps, and it is not he who sleeps, and
(234.8) 170.23	Arts and Sciences	245.3	Arts and Sciences	arts and sciences	arts and sciences	Arts and Sciences	✓	arts and sciences
(234.25) 171.3	fate	245.20	fate	Fate	Fate		✓	Fate
(235.24) 171.25	*Shiftings*	246.20	*Shiftings*	*Shiftings,*	*Shiftings,*		✓	*Shiftings,*
(239.8) 174.13	*of the*	250.9	*of the*	of the [note: "rom on pp. 239, 240"]	of the		✓	of the

Page.Line	Reading: 1937 ed.	Loc. Coole proofs	As printed: 1st Coole proofs	1st Coole correction	As printed: 2nd Coole proofs	2nd Coole correction	TM nb?	Reading: 1962 ed.
(239.14) 174.18	*of the*	250.15	*of the*	of the	of the		✓	of the
(239.18) 174.22	*of the*	250.20	*of the*	of the	of the		✓	of the
(239.21) 174.23	St.	250.22	St.	Saint	Saint			St.
(240.3) 174.36	swiftly	251.7	swiftly	swiftly,	swiftly,		✓	swiftly,
(240.14) 175.7	Man and Woman	251.17–18	Man and Woman	man and woman	man and woman		✓	man and woman
(240.15) 175.8	*of the*	251.19	*of the*	of the	of the		✓	of the
(240.18) 175.11	Man	251.22	Man	man	man	Man	✓	man
(240.29) 175.20	Man,	252.2	Man,	man,	man,	Man,	✓	man,
(243.4) 177.5	When a religious-minded Roman	255.3	WHEN A RELIGIOUS-MINDED Roman	-	WHEN A RELIGIOUS-MINDED Roman	WHEN A RELIGIOUS-MINDED ROMAN		When a religious-minded Roman
(243.14) 177.13	prodigies;	255.11	prodigies;	prodigies:	prodigies:		✓	prodigies:
(244.24) 178.18	half-oriental	256.21	half-oriental	half-Oriental	half-Oriental	half-oriental		half-oriental

(244.31) 178.35	*De Divina-tione.*	256.n1	*De Divinati-one.*	-	*De Divinati-one*[11]	*De Divinati-one.*		*De Divina-tione.*
(245.7) 178.29	before	257.6	before	before,	before,		✓	before,
(245.17) 179.2	before,	257.15	before,	before	before		✓	before
(246.15) 179.25	Manu	258.15	Manu	Manu,	Manu,		✓	Manu,
(246.30) 180.35	vol. i, chap. v,	258.n1	vol. i. chap. v.	-	vol. i. chap. v.	vol. i, chap. v,		vol. i, chap. v,
(247.8) 180.13	nature.	259.10	nature.	Nature.	Nature.	nature.	✓	Nature.
(248.12) 181.11	Golden	260.16	Golen	Golden	Golden			Golden
(249.29) 182.14	Waters,	262.5	Waters,	waters,	waters,		✓	waters,
(250.9) 182.23	wrote:	262.17	wrote:	wrote:—	wrote:—			wrote:
(250.13) 182.27	Immortal-ities	262.21	Immortalities	Mortality's	Immortality's		✓	Mortality's
(250.18) 183.2	funeral pyre	262.26	funeral pyre	furnace pyre	funeral pyre		✓	furnace-pyre
(252.14) 184.12	man of Ur	264.23	man of Ur	Man of Ur	Man of Ur		✓	Man of Ur
(252.22) 184.19	of Goat	265.7	of Goat	of the Goat	of the Goat	of Goat	✓	of the Goat

Page.Line	Reading: 1937 ed.	Loc. Coole proofs	As printed: 1st Coole proofs	1st Coole correction	As printed: 2nd Coole proofs	2nd Coole correction	TM nb?	Reading: 1962 ed.
(252.32) 184.30	26,000	264.n2	260,000	26,000	260,000	26,000		26,000
(254.16) 185.31	Then	266.27	Then	And then	And then		✓	And then
(254.20) 186.2	sec.	267.3	sec.	Section	sec.			sec.
(254.24) 186.6	vernal equinox	267.7	vernal equinox	Vernal Equinox	Vernal Equinox	vernal equinox	✓	Vernal Equinox
(255.18) 186.24	Leibnitz,	267.30	Leibnitz,	Leibniz,	Leibniz,		✓	Leibniz
(256.22) 187.18	triangles	269.9	triangles	triangles,	triangles,		✓	triangles,
(257.32) 188.17	*Stories of Michael Robartes and his Friends,*	270.20	*Stories of Michael Robartes and his Friends,*	*Speculum Angelorum et Hominum,* [Query: "Is it from the Stories or should it be from the Speculum Angelorum etc?" Answer: "It is mentioned in the Stories, but the source is Speculum"	*Speculum Angelorum et Hominum,*	*Stories of Michael Robartes and his Friends,*	✓	*Speculum Angelorum et Hominum,*

(258.22) 188.36	in the Robartes stories	271.14	in the Robar-tes stories	of 'The Great Wheel'	of 'The Great Wheel'	in the Robartes stories	✓	of the "Great Wheel"
(260.20) 190.14	such and such	273.14	such and such	such-and-such	such-and-such			such and such
(260.29) 190.31	Shru Purhoit	273.n1	Shru Purhoit	Shri Purohit	Shri Purohit		✓	Shri Purohit
(268.12) 195.7	sinking in	280.17	sinking in	sinking-in	sinking-in			sinking in
(268.30) 195.34	'Mathematic Starlight' Babylonian astrology is,	281.n1	'Mathematic Starlight' Babylonian astrology is,	'Mathematical Starlight', Babylonian astrology, is, [note: "al as in line 2?"]	'Mathematical Starlight', Babylonian astrology, is,		✓	"Mathematical Starlight", Babylonian astrology, is,
(273.2) 198.24	devil	285.19	devil	Devil	Devil			devil
(277.21) 201.36	court,	290.16	court,	Court,	court,		✓	Court,
(277.21) 201.36	and	290.16	and	and,	and		✓	and,
(277.22) 201.36	all	290.17	all	all,	all		✓	all,
(278.6) 202.13	St.	291.3	St.	Saint	Saint			St.
(278.28) 202.30	darkness"	291.25	darkness'	darkness',	darkness',		✓	darkness",

Page.Line	Reading: 1937 ed.	Loc. Coole proofs	As printed: 1st Coole proofs	1st Coole correction	As printed: 2nd Coole proofs	2nd Coole correction	TM nb?	Reading: 1962 ed.
(279.15) 203.8	St.	292.14	St.	Saint	Saint			St.
(279.18) 203.11	St.	292.17	St.	Santa	Saint			St.
(280.28) 204.7	Church	293.27	Church	church	church		✓	church
(280.30) 204.9	Ravenne	293.30	Ravenne	Ravenna	Ravenna		✓	Ravenna
(281.9) 204.18	Greco-Roman	294.10	Greco-Roman	Graeco-Roman [note: "As VI p. 245 ix p. 264"]	Graeco-Roman		✓	Græco-Roman
(281.10) 204.19	Greco-Egyptian	294.11	Greco-Egyptian	Graeco-Egyptian	Graeco-Egyptian		✓	Græco-Egyptian
(282.1) 204.38	St.	295.4	St.	Santa	Santa			St.
(282.3) 205.2	St.	295.6	St.	Saint	Saint			St.
(283.12) 205.36	courts and monasteries another book tells me	296.17–18	courts and monasteries another book tells me	courts and monasteries, another book tells me,	courts and monasteries, another book tells me,		✓	Courts and monaster-ies, another book tells me,
(283.17) 206.3	St.	296.22	St.	Saint	Saint			St.

(285.1) 207.5	faculties and	298.9	faculties and	faculties, and,	faculties, and,		✓	faculties, and,
(285.24) 207.24	courts	299.4	courts	Courts	Courts		✓	Courts
(286.12) 208.5	half Asiatic	299.23–24	half Asiatic	half-Asiatic	half-Asiatic		✓	half-Asiatic
(287.6) 208.27	was	300.19	is	was	is	was	✓	was
(287.28) 209.7	St.	301.11	St.	Saint	Saint			St.
(287.32) 209.11	St.	301.16	St.	Saint	Saint			St.
(288.7) 209.17	yet the stones once set up	301.24	yet the stones once set up	yet, the stones once set up,	yet, the stones once set up,		✓	yet, the stones once set up,
(288.21) 209.28	St.	302.6	St.	Saint	Saint			St.
(289.22) 210.19	St.	303.10	St.	Saint	Saint			St.
(289.26) 210.22	itself	303.14	itself	itself,	itself,		✓	itself,
(290.5) 210.32	St.	303.27	St.	Saint	Saint			St.
(292.10) 212.16	Porphyry upon the Cave of the Nymphs?	306.6–7	Porphyry upon the Cave of the Nymphs?	Porphyry's *On the Cave of the Nymphs*?	Porphyry's *On the Cave of the Nymphs*?		✓	Porphyry's *On the Cave of the Nymphs*?

Page.Line	Reading: 1937 ed.	Loc. Coole proofs	As printed: 1st Coole proofs	1st Coole correction	As printed: 2nd Coole proofs	2nd Coole correction	TM nb?	Reading: 1962 ed.
(293.20) 213.15	itself say	307.17	itself say	itself, say,	itself, say,		✓	itself, say,
(293.33) 213.25	Soul's	307.30	Soul's	soul's	soul's		✓	soul's
(295.6) 214.19	"On the Morning of Christ's Nativity",	309.7–8	'On the Morning of Christ's Nativity,'	*On the Morning of Christ's Nativity*,	*On the Morning of Christ's Nativity*,			"On the Morning of Christ's Nativity",
(296.9) 215.12	St.	310.12	St.	Saint	Saint			St.
(296.11) 215.13	devil.	310.14	devil.	Devil.	Devil.			devil.
(299.12) 217.19	Tolstoi,	313.20	Tolstoi,	Tolstoy,	Tolstoy,	Tolstoi,		Tolstoi,
(300.2) 217.38	Tolstoi	314.12	Tolstoi	Tolstoy	Tolstoy	Tolstoi		Tolstoi
(300.17) 218.12	past,	314.27	past,	-	past,	passed,		past,
(301.12) 219.10	Duchess	316.13	Duchess	Duchesse	Duchess	Duchesse	✓	Duchesse
(301.15) 219.13	Saint and labour leader	316.16	Saint and labour leader	saint and labour-leader	saint and labour-leader			saint and labour leader

(301.29) 219.23	Cabalists.	317.2	Cabalists.	Cabbalists.	Cabbalists.	Cabalists.		Cabalists.
(302.5) 219.27	counter movement,	317.6–7	counter movement,	counter-movement,	counter-movement,		✓	counter-movement
(302.9) 219.31	*thirteenth sphere*	317.11–12	*thirteenth sphere*	*Thirteenth Cone*	*Thirteenth Cone*		✓	*Thirteenth Cone*
(302.18) 220.7	Zeus, the mighty, and Hera, shod with gold"?	317.20–21	Zeus, the mighty, and Hera, shod with gold'?	Zeus the mighty and Hera shod with gold'? [note: "as p. 237"]	Zeus, the mighty, and Hera, shod with gold'?		✓	Zeus the mighty and Hera shod with gold"?
(303.3) 221.3	come	321.3	COME	COME,	COME,		✓	come,
(303.5) 221.5	Night.	321.6	Night.	Night,	Night,		✓	Night,
(304.14) 222.19	And by foreknowl-edge of the future vexed;	322.20	And by fore-knowledge of the future vexed;	And knowing that the future would be vexed	And by knowing that the future would be vexed	[note: "N.Y. And by fore-knowledge of the future vexed;"]	✓	And knowing that the future would be vexed
(304.15) 222.20	Diminished beauty, multiplied common-place;	322.21	Diminished beauty, mul-tiplied com-monplace;	With 'minished beauty, multiplied commonplace,	With 'min-ished beauty, multiplied commonplace,	[note: "Diminished beauty, multiplied common-place;"]	✓	With 'minished beauty, multiplied common-place,

Page.Line	Reading: 1937 ed.	Loc. Coole proofs	As printed: 1st Coole proofs	1st Coole correction	As printed: 2nd Coole proofs	2nd Coole correction	TM nb?	Reading: 1962 ed.
(304.24) 222.29	about	323.2	about	about,	about,		✓	about,
(304.31) 223.1	I call MacGregor Mathers	323.9	I call MacGregor Mathers	And I call up Mac-Gregor	And I call up MacGregor	[note: "N.Y. has I call MacGregor Mathers"	✓	And I call up MacGregor
(304.32) 223.2	spring-time	323.10	spring-time	springtime	springtime			spring-time

Table 4. Emendations to the Copy Text

Page.Line	As Printed	As Corrected	Authority
(3.10) 3.10	*Ode on a Grecian Urn*	"Ode on a Grecian Urn"	title
(5.23) 5.8	Hodos Chame-liontos	*Hodos Chame-liontos*	terminology
(7.4) 6.10	Sant' Ambrogio	Sant'Ambrogio	proper name
(7.12) 6.16	God Save the King	'God Save the King'	title
(7.12) 6.17	He's a Jolly Good Fellow	'He's a Jolly Good Fellow'	title
(12.18) 10.11	Cabalistic	Cabbalistic	GY in YL 2434
(12.19) 10.13	Cabala	Cabbala	GY in YL 2434
(17.11) 13.27	Tolstoi's	Tolstoy's	standard Anglicization
(22.21) 17.23	Daimon.	*Daimon.*	terminology
(22.22) 17.24	Daimon	*Daimon*	terminology
(22.26) 17.27	Daimon	*Daimon*	terminology
(22.27) 17.28	Ghostly Self	*Ghostly Self*	terminology
(23.26) 18.16	Cabala	Cabbala	see above 10.13
(24.3) 18.21	Michael Angelo	Michelangelo	proper name
(24.48) 19.10	pulsaters	pulsation	GY in YL 2435
(27.13) 20.24	Sea-shanties	sea-shanties	GY in YL 2434
(27.14) 20.24	Steam	steam	GY in YL 2434
(28.8) 21.9	eyes.	eyes?	GY in YL 2434
(28.24) 21.22	Crickmaa,	Cruchmaa,	GY in YL 2434
(29.2) 21.25	Michael Angelo	Michelangelo	proper name

Page.Line	As Printed	As Corrected	Authority
(29.26) 22.20	wingéd	wingèd	standard diacritical mark
(37.27) 27.8	Cabalistic	Cabbalistic	see above 10.11
(40.30) 29.24	Cabal-/ists	Cabbalists	see above 10.11
(59.7) 41.8	*late risen moon,*	*late-risen moon,*	GY in YL 2434, GY in YL 2435
(62.8) 44.19	perfected, completed,	separate, perfect,	GY in YL 2434, GY in YL 2435
(68.23) 50.20	Alcemon	Alcmaeon	proper name
(70.29) 52.25	*Theory of Mind as Pure Art*	*Theory of Mind as Pure Act*	correct title
(79.14) 59.3	Phase 28	Phase 15	WBY in YL 2434, GY in YL 2435
(88.30) 65.28	negation. The whole	negation, the whole	GY in YL 2434
(89.11) 66.1	Faculties	*Faculties*	terminology
(90.14) 66.26	Phase	phase	terminology
(90.24) 66.34	Phase	phase	terminology
(91.11) 67.13	Sec. XII	Section XII	GY in YL 2434
(97.r10.c3) 71.r10.c3	Mask	*Mask*	terminology
(97.r12.c3) 72.r12.c3	Enforced law	Enforced lure	GY in YL 2434
(97.r13.c3) 72.r13.c3	antithetical	*antithetical*	terminology
(98.r17.c1) 72.r17.c1	Daimon-/ic	*Daimon-/ic*	terminology
(98.r20.c3) 73.r20.c3	constriction	construction	correct on 91.24
(99.r22.c4) 73.r22.c4	Temptation versus strength	Temptation through strength	GY in YL 2433a
(99.r24.c4) 73.r24.c4	Enforced success in action	Enforced success of action	GY in YL 2434, GY in YL 2435
(102.1) 75.22	Affecting	[nothing]	repetition because of pagination

Page.Line	**As Printed**	**As Corrected**	**Authority**
(103.1) 76.22	quarter	[nothing]	repetition because of pagination
(103.20) 77.16	Mask	*Mask*	terminology
(103.21) 77.17	Mask	*Mask*	terminology
(104.19) 78.17	OBJECTIVTIES	OBJECTIVITIES	missing letter
(104.21) 78.19	Phase 29	Phase 28	GY in YL 2434, GY in YL 2435
(104.23) 78.21	*Well.*	*Will.*	GY in YL 2434, GY in YL 2435
(108.7) 81.20	phase, he	phase he	GY in YL 2434
(111.22) 84.10	life, where	life where	GY in YL 2434, GY in YL 2435
(112.3) 84.20	perfectly, a	perfectly a	GY in YL 2434
(114.6) 86.2	*Image*	Image	GY in YL 2434
(117.3) 88.7	Dostieffsky	Dostoyevsky	standard Anglicization
(118.5) 88.34	Dostoieffsky's	Dostoyevsky's	standard Anglicization
(118.6) 88.35	Dostoieffsky's	Dostoyevsky's	standard Anglicization
(119.8) 89.28	true	True	terminology
(119.10) 89.29	true	True	terminology
(119.31) 90.8	sensuality	Sensuality	GY in YL 2434
(124.3) 93.9	table	Tables	GY in YL 2434
(124.26) 93.27	The Image-Burner	The Consumer, Pyre-builder	GY in YL 2434
(129.4) 96.29	*Image*	Image	see above 86.2
(129.11) 96.34	Sensuous Ego	The Sensuous Man	GY in YL 2434

Page.Line	As Printed	As Corrected	Authority
(133.16) 99.37	"Eternal Idol"	*Eternal Idol*	title
(136.24) 102.12	Celestial Body	*Celestial Body*	terminology
(141.20) 105.31	*Image*	Image	see above 86.2
(142.33) 106.31	*Image*	Image	see above 86.2
(145.15) 108.24	antithetical	*antithetical*	terminology
(145.20) 108.27	"An Ode to the West Wind"	"Ode to the West Wind"	title
(147.15) 110.2	Head	*Head*	terminology
(147.19) 110.5	Heart	*Heart*	terminology
(147.22) 110.7	Head	*Head*	terminology
(150.1) 111.35	*Image*	Image	see above 86.2
(151.3) 112.26	i	in	missing letter
(153.30) 114.26	Luke	Lake	GY in YL 2434, GY in YL 2435
(154.19) 115.8	Self-adaption	Self-adaptation	GY in YL 2434
(155.26) 116.6	adaption	adaptation	GY in YL 2434
(156.5) 116.15	self-adaption	self-adaptation	GY in YL 2434
(156.16) 116.24	Dostoieffsky's	Dostoyevsky's	standard Anglicization
(157.23) 117.20	The "breaking of strength"	Temptation through Strength	GY in YL 2434, GY in YL 2435
(157.26) 117.23	Dostieffsky	Dostoyevsky	standard Anglicization
(160.27) 119.28	Dostieffsky	Dostoyevsky	standard Anglicization
(162.26) 121.6	Dostieffsky	Dostoyevsky	standard Anglicization

Page.Line	As Printed	As Corrected	Authority
(163.23) 121.30	desire for a form	desire for reform	"Version B" (*YVP* 4:216).
(189.2) 138.28	*Primary*	*primary*	terminology
(190.26) 139.34	Aeslepius	Asclepius	proper name
(192.8) 141.10	*Faculties' Mask*	*Faculties, Mask*	raised comma
(192.31) 141.32	*The Inferno*	the *Inferno*	title
(196.21) 144.30	Phase,	phase,	terminology
(196.23) 144.32	Phases	phases	terminology
(196.28) 145.1	Phase	phase	terminology
(199.9) 147.1	see p. 200	diagram below	pagination of edition
(199.11) 147.2	p. 79	p. 58	pagination of edition
(201.2) 148.2	Phase	phase	terminology
(203.5) 149.18	Nature	"Nature"	word used as word
(203.6) 149.19	God	"God"	word used as word
(209.6) 154.8	Leibnitz	Leibniz	proper name
(211.4) 155.21	Aeslepius	Asclepius	proper name
(212.14) 156.23	Dionysius	Dionysus	proper name
(212.15) 156.24	Dionysius	Dionysus	proper name
(215.11) 158.26	Zazuki's	Suzuki's	proper name
(219.3) 159.4	PAUL VALERY in the *Cimitière Marine*	Paul Valéry in the "Cimitière Marin"	GY in YL 2434, title

Page.Line	As Printed	As Corrected	Authority
(220.23) 160.16	*Cimitière Marine*	"Cimitière Marin"	Alspach 1938, title
(222.28) 162.2	*Mandooka*	*Mandookya*	GY in YL 2434, GY in YL 2435
(226.2) 164.16	Nature	nature	GY in YL 2434
(229.27) 167.14)	Phase	phase	terminology
(232.8) 169.5	*Aeneids*	*Enneads*	GY in YL 2434
(233.30) 169.37	that is not him	and it is not he	GY in YL 2434
(239.20) 174.23	Simon	Simeon	proper name
(245.17) 179.2	before, the	before the	WBY? in YL 2434, GY in YL 2435
(247.23) 180.26	Philaus	Philolaus	proper name
(250.13) 182.27	Immortalities	Mortalities	GY in YL 2434
(255.18) 186.24	Leibnitz	Leibniz	proper name
(260.29) 190.31	Shru Purhoit	Shree Purohit	WBY? in YL 2434
(280.30) 204.9	Ravenne	Ravenna	GY in YL 2435
(287.9) 208.29	1005	1050	correct in The Historical Cones, p. 193
(287.31) 209.9	Villars de Honecourt	Villard de Honnecourt	proper name
(291.8) 211.24	Michael Angelo	Michelangelo	proper name
(291.10) 211.26	Guercia	Quercia	proper name
(293.21) 213.16	Michael Angelo	Michelangelo	proper name
(293.24) 213.18	Michael Angelo	Michelangelo	proper name

(293.28) 213.21	Michael Angelo	Michelangelo	proper name
(294.6) 213.30	Michael Angelo	Michelangelo	proper name
(299.12) 217.19	Tolstoi	Tolstoy	standard Anglicization
(300.2) 217.38	Tolstoi	Tolstoy	standard Anglicization
(301.29) 219.23	Cabalists.	Cabbalists.	see above 10.11
(302.9) 219.31	*thirteenth sphere*	*Thirteenth Cone*	Coole proofs

Table 5. End-of-Line Word Division in the Copy Text

Page. Line this edition	**Reading in this edition]**	**Reading in copy text**	**Page.Line in copy text**
5.21	four-storied]	four-/ storied	6.5
16.8	breakdown]	break-/ down	20.23
19.14	overwhelmed]	over-/ whelmed	25.3
26.18	upstanding]	up-/ standing	36.25
29.26	whirlpool]	whirl-/ pool	40.32
31.34	cigarette-case]	cigarette-/ case	44.3
32.19	horror-struck]	horror-/ struck	44.31
38.18	good-bye]	good-/ bye	53.16
58.17	twenty-eight]	twenty-/ eight	79.8
61.3	steel-like]	steel-/ like	82.11
62.7	stage-manager]	stage-/ manager	84.1
62.19	self-expression]	self-/ expression	84.16
67.30	self-realization]	self-/ realization	91.30
72.r18.c4	Hunchback]	Hunch-/ back	98.r18.c4
89.1	twenty-eight]	twenty-/ eight	118.7
95.17	self-hatred]	self-/ hatred	127.10
106.31	nightmare]	night-/ mare	142.32
107.9	shell-strewn]	shell-/ strewn	143.18
107.14	supernatural]	super-/ natural	143.23

Page. Line this edition	Reading in this edition]	Reading in copy text	Page.Line in copy text
110.32	self-knowledge]	self-/ knowledge	148.20
115.3	lawgiver]	law-/ giver	154.13
115.8	Self-/ adaptation]	Self-/ adaption	154.19
116.9	self-analysing]	self-/ analysing	155.29
116.15	self-adaptation]	self-/ adaption	156.5
120.7	subconscious]	sub-/ conscious	161.14
126.29	subconscious]	sub-/ conscious	170.18
131.28	self-expression]	self-/ expression	177.13
132.21	self-regarding]	self-/ regarding	178.17
147.11	hour-glass]	hour-/ glass	200.2
147.19	twenty-eight]	twenty-/ eight	200.11
148.5	superimposed]	super-/ imposed	201.6
148.24	twenty-six]	twenty-/ six	202.6
153.12	Jupiter-Saturn]	Jupiter-/ Saturn	208.2
156.21	supernat-/ ural]	super-/ natural	212.12
159.12	self-hate]	self-/ hate	219.12
161.30	séance-room]	séance-/ room	222.17
168.10	seventeenth-century]	seventeenth-/ century	231.2
172.12	re-/ birth]	re-/ birth	236.16
177.24	mankind]	man-/ kind	243.27
178.19	eye-doctor]	eye-/ doctor	244.25
178.24	son-in-law]	son-/ in-law	245.1
187.31	slow-moving]	slow-/ moving	257.5
191.18	counter-myth]	counter-/ myth	262.3
197.24	break-up]	break-/ up	271.21
200.2	Neo-Pythagorean]	Neo-/ Pythagorean	274.31
201.12	dancing-master]	dancing-/ master	276.27
204.9	to-day]	to-/ day	280.29
209.9	sketchbook]	sketch-/ book	287.30
209.22	supernatural]	super-/ natural	288.13
210.4	autobiography]	auto-/ biography	289.4

APPENDIX II

EARLIER VERSIONS

This appendix compiles lengthy sections of text where the last document approved by WBY differs significantly from the text as printed in 1937. In the absence of the setting copy, and of all galleys and proofs, these texts gesture to WBY's processes of revision between his preparation of the setting typescript and the publication of *A Vision*. See Editors' Introduction, xxxix–l.

Excised Section of "Rapallo" (*Packet*, 7–9)

In *A Packet for Ezra Pound* (Dublin: The Cuala Press, 1929), "Rapallo" includes a sixth section, struck through on the setting copy for *A Vision* and so excised from the 1937 printing.

VI

Four weeks ago I read poetry again after four years philosophical study; at first it was faint like an old faded letter, and then an excitement that I had not felt for years. I read contemporary poets in various pamphlets of verse, in a couple of anthologies, finding a great deal I had forgotten or had never known, and then came Ezra Pound's 'Personæ'. One is a harder judge of a friend's work than of a stranger's because one knows his powers so well that his faults seem perversity, or we do not know his powers and think he should go our way and not his, and then all in a moment we see his work as a whole and judge as with the eyes of a stranger. In this book just published in America are all his poems except those Twenty-seven Cantos which keep me procrastinating, and though I had read it all in the little books I had never understood until now that the translations from Chinese, from Latin, from Provencal, are as much a part of his original work, as much chosen as to theme, as much characterised as to style, as the vituperation, the railing, which I had hated but which now seem a necessary balance. He is not trying to create forms because he believes, like so many of his contemporaries, that old forms are dead, so much as a new style, a new man. Again and again he breaks the metrical form which the work seemed to require, or which, where he is translating, it once had, or interjects some anachronism, as when he makes Propertius talk of an old Wordsworthian, that he may pull it back not into himself but into this hard, shining, fastidious modern man, who has no existence, who can never have existence, except to the readers of his poetry. I remember the devil's imps & their nightly drop of blood from the witch's head, some German story of the devil's name that sounded Greek and noble but no man could remember it, and I try to remember a passage from Plotinus 'On the Titular Genius.' Yes, a Titular Genius, that from which a man obtains his special quality and honour, but having, unlike his character, universality, detachability; a being therefore to be introduced to our sons and daughters![1] Synge once said to me 'All our modern poetry is the poetry of the lyrical boy',[2] but here, in spite of all faults and flaws,—sometimes that exasperation is but nerves—is the grown man, in 'Cathay' his passion and self-possession, in 'Homage to Sextus Propertius' his self-abandonment that recovers itself in mockery, everywhere his masterful curiosity.[3]

> 'Go, my songs, seek your praise from the young
> and from the intolerant,
> Move among the lovers of perfection alone.
> Seek ever to stand in the hard Sophoclean light' . . .[4]

March and October, 1928 (7–9).

Book II Typescript (NLI 36,272/6/1b, leaves 2–5)

As rendered in the carbon of the setting TS, the ending of Section I of Book II (138–39) differs substantially from the printed text, even in being separated into two sections.

At death consciousness passes from Husk to Spirit Husk and Passionate Body are said to "disappear", which corresponds to Creative Mind and Body of Fate ceasing to be "enforced" at their phase 22, and from that on to birth Spirit turns from Passionate Body and clings to Celestial Body, as Creative Mind in the primary phases turns from Mask and clings to Body of Fate.

II

The Husk is more than kind or race, and Passionate Body is more than what is sensible or perceivable. Through the Husk is expressed the needs of a particular daimon: it draws to itself and turns into pleasure and pain those objects of sense that symbolise those daimons that are its natural associates. Through the Body of Fate we touch the Creative Minds of all other beings; through the Passionate Body their Husks, for every daimon is a centre that has all other daimons for circumference. The Spirit knows by an act of pure consciousness; what the Spirit knows becomes a part of itself and is accepted as intellectual necessity, and for this reason my instructors have called the Celestial Body "fate" although I have preferred to keep the word for the Faculties where it describes the sum of fact. The Husk is not only the natural senses but what Blake called the enlarged and numerous senses, it knows the ultimate reality through its Passionate Body as multitude, but the Spirit knows it in the Celestial Body as one, and I must not attempt to solve the impossible. "In aeternitatis opposita coincidunt".[5] It must not be thought that spirit is reality and sense illusionary, both are illusionary because abstracted from that reality symbolised as the sphere.

The Spirit cannot find those others in their unity unless unless [*sic*] it first seeks them in the objects of sense separate from it and from one another (the Passionate Body exists "to save the Celestial Body from solitude") and only because it so seeks as it were in hunger and thirst can it receive the Celestial Body in marriage. In the symbolism of my instructors the Celestial Body is a captive, sometimes in a lonely tower, and is said to age as the Passionate Body grows young.

The Spirit begets the next life, the stream of images and events, and then from birth "disappears" but continues to act through the

Huskk spearating [*sic*] from one another those forms which now constitute the Passionate Body but were once through past unions with the Celestial Body a part of itself; but the Celestial Body, now evil because separate, pursues the forms and encloses them in time and space.[6] The Passionate Body, which somewhat resembles Aristotle's matter, cannot be known to sense or Husk except through Spirit which alone can make one Principle known to another, nor can it be known to intellect until the Faculties which are a derivation from Husk find names and attributes. Some srtists [*sic*] seek to undo the work of the Faculties and to reach through associations of excitement pure Passionate Body—perhaps some philosophers have attempted an equal impossibility—the discovery of pure Celestial Body.

Book II Typescript (NLI 36,272/6/1b, leaves 14–18)

From the paragraph that in the printed text begins "If we consider East . . ." on 145, and continuing to "The foregoing figure shows the position . . ." on 147, the TS carbon differs significantly from the printed text, and so is reproduced here.

The pole of the Principles, if we place it in that of the year, is at right angles to that of the Faculties. My instructors fixed this upon my mind by saying that the man of the Principles stood upright whereas the man of the Faculties lay horizontal like a sleeping man. That the small Wheels and Vortexes that run from birth to birth may be part of the symbolism of the Wheel of the 28 incarnations without confusing it in the minds [*sic*] eye, my instructors have preferred to give to the Principles of these small Wheels a cone that cannot be confused with that of the Faculties. The dominant thought is to show Husk starting on its journey from the centre of the Wheel as if from the incarnate daimon, and Spirit from the circumference as though it received its impulse from beyond the daimon. These cones are drawn across the centre of the Wheel from Faculty to Faculty, two with bases joined between Creative Mind and Body of Fate, and two with apexes joined between Will and Mask. Within these figures move the Principles, Spirit and Celestial Body in the figure shaped like an ace of diamonds, Husk and Passionate Body in that shaped like an hour glass. The first figure I shall for convenience think of as divided according to the signs of the Zodiac, though it can be divided as readily according to the points of the compass, the East or sunrise taking the place of the Vernal Equinox, and the second figure I shall divide into the 28 lunar phases. In the cones of the Spirit and the Celestial Body there is only one gyre, that of Spirit, Celestial Body being represented by the whole diamond. The union of Spirit and Celestial Body has a long approach and is complete when the gyre reaches its widest expansion. There is only one gyre because whereas Husk faces an object alien to itself, S pirit's [*sic*] object is of like nature to itself. The gyre of the Husk starts at the centre (its phase 1) reaches its phase 8 at the circumference where the Mask is and returns to its centre for phase 15, passes from its centre to its phase 22 (at the circumference) where the Will is and finishes at the centre. One records these movements, phases for Husk, zodiacal signs for Spirit,[7] upon the edges of the figures, Husk and Passionate Body moving from right to left and the single gyre of Spirit from left to right. Husk and Passionate Body remain always opposite, Passionate Body at phase 15 when Husk is at phase 1 and so on. When the gyres of Husk and Passionate Body are at the centre of their figure Spirit is at the widest expansion of the Diamond.

The converging and diverging lines of this figure should be first considered. When Spirit is at either end of the diamond it is upon the pole, upon the antithetical or lunar centre of its movement; and when at the widest expansion is where that movement is primary or solar. When Husk is at the greatest contraction of the hourglass it is upon the pole, upon the antithetical or lunar centre of its movement, which is also the centre of the Wheel of 28 incarnations. Though for convenience we make the diamond narrow like the diamond on a playing card, its widest expansion must be considered to touch the circumference of the Wheel where it meets the gyre of the 13th cone. When Spirit is at Cancer, its symbolical summer, Spirit and Celestial Body in union predominate though Husk and Passionate Body are at their centre. When Husk is at phase 15 Husk and Passionate Body in union predominate. Taken in relation to the Wheel of the diamond and the hourglass are two pulsations, one moving outward, one moving inward. Owing to the fact that the diamond touches the circumference of the Wheel with its narrow ends this is the least satisfactory of the diagrams pictorially. The figure shows the position of the diamond and hourglass when Will on the Wheel is passing phase 17, the arrows show Husk and Spirit as they are placed just after the beginning of the phase.

The following diagram shows such cones when Will on the Wheel of the 28 phases is at phase 15.

Book II Typescript (NLI 36,272/6/1b, leaves 30–32)

The TS carbon includes an additional section, appearing between the current sections XVI and XVII (157).

XVII

As the Will moves through the 28 phases, the three other Faculties awaken their phases in regular order, but there is a seemingly disorderly movement which my instructors have named the "Lightning Flash". The flash starts at Will and moves with seeming irregularity from phase to phase until it ends at the phase that gives its character to the next incarnation. We can mark this flash upon the Wheel when we consider the Wheel as all instantaneously present, but when we consider the W heel [*sic*] in time the flas[h] becomes but an image in the eye. The phases it has touched are more important than the others and are called "Initiatory Moments" and differentiate certain points among others touched by the gyres at one or other side of its cone, whereas the ends of the cones are called "Critical Moments". The "Initiatory Moments" change the symbol, a new love or the transformation of an old love, a new historical purpose, whereas the "Critical Moments" liberate from all symbol. The "Lightning Flash" is what makes two men at the same phase and as near to the same moment and the same place as may be, two men who are twins let us say, differ from one another. It is a conscious act as distinguished from the circular course of nature; its origin never explained, unexplainable, lies in the past and the future and yet lies fully in the present, and though the "flash" may seem to occupy many years it is but an instant of the last initiation.

When its Initiatory and Critical Moments are moments of activity or change in sexual life my instructors can without difficulty—I have tested this—date them in the "Ephemeris" by their association with certain planets. These irregularly placed moments determine the phasal character of the sexual lure and explain why a woman, of, let us say, phase 25 does not always follow a woman of an earlier phase. She is as it were uprooted, planted elsewhere in the temporal or natural order. Sometimes my instructors have constructed a s igil [*sic*] like those in old books of magic, and only when re-drawn ypon [*sic*] the Wheel, only when one has noticed where its first point, its last point, and its angles fall, does one discover in this zig-zag sigil or "Flash" a series of initiatory moments, the essential character of an action or a man. Certain mystics have indeed drawn similar lines between the petals of a symbolic Rose, where every petal has its separate meaning, marking the beginning and end with a minute circle.

Book III Typescript (NLI 36,272/6/2a, leaves 5–8)

The TS carbon contains a lengthy section of text that in the printed version is replaced by the first five sentences of section V (162). This text is heavily corrected in ink in WBY's hand, and text rendered *in italics* was added in manuscript.

V

Should one say, Like Swedenborg, that the spirits enter into our dreams and thoughts, into our unconscious life whether we wake or sleep, or that their daimons (<u>Principles</u>) are present to our daimons (our <u>Principles</u>) and that it is our daimon that compels us to dream and think. The second seems most compatible with the system I am expounding. All ghosts controls, communicators, materialisations, poltergeists, apparitions, instructors, are personnifications [*sic*], dramatisations of what would otherwise remain unknown, but these dramatisations conveyed from one man to another as daimon becomes aware of daimon, or if you prefer by "suggestion", "thought transference" take their forms from general experience, forms that can be studied as we study dreams in the old dream books or in those of the psycho-analysts. The true spirits, the discarnate daimons, the objective principles, are served by these subjective fabrications, relieved of certain burdens, but are of another nature, for all that speaks, reasons, dramatises, wills, belongs to the Faculties and the Faculties are cast off at death. Whenever I speak of spirits having form or voice it must be understood that such dramatisations are implied.

I have explained the symbolism of the state between birth and death in book II, section *1*. At death (phase 15 on the Wheel of the Faculties) Husk and Passionate Body "disappear"[,] Spirit and Celestial Body "appear"; at birth (phase ~~8~~ *1* on the Wheel of the Faculties) Husk and Passionate Body "appear", Spirit and Celestial Body "disappear". These words take the place of 'enforced' and 'unenforced' which are appropriate to the acquired or voluntary Faculties.

Discarnate life corresponds to the months from mid-March to mid-September, and the si~~s~~*x* states described in the book are the "Vision of the Blood Kindred" (March), the "Return" or "Dreaming Back" (April), the ~~"Shiftings"~~ *"First Purification"* (May), ~~t~~*T*he ~~"Beatitude"~~ *"Marriage"* (June), the "*Second* Purification" (July), the ~~"Preparation"~~ *"Foreknowledge"* (August). The six states are states of learning that climax in ~~t~~*T*he ~~"Beatitude"~~ *"Marriage"* whereas the primary phases in the Wheel of the Faculties are states of obedience that climax in phase 1.

VI

~~The~~ *In "the* Vision of the Blood Kindred" ~~I do not fully understand, but it is too picturesque to ignore.~~ , ~~T~~*t*he blood kindred appear to the dying man, the more recent the more vivid~~ly~~, from amongst them come those visions of husband or wife seen by the dying. The Husk ~~as an expression of Passionate Body~~ [text added in ink and then struck through], now separated from the acquired Faculties (the particular man as a part of nature) is about to "disappear" and can only do so by completing itself in a moment of perception *comparable to the act of synthesis that accompanies the breaking of the Will at phase 22.* ~~It~~ *This Vision* is followed by the "Meditation"[8] *corresponding to the acceptance, fate or "emotion of Sanctity" at* *these[?] phases;* ~~where~~ the Spirit discovers its relation to the Celestial Body. During this "Meditation" the Husk [. . .]

Book III Typescript (NLI 36,272/6/2a, leaves 14–26)

Beginning on 167 ("*Teaching Spirits* are *Spirits* of the *Thirteenth Cone* . . ."), and continuing to the end of Book III, the text of the TS carbon differs radically from that of the printed text. Text rendered *in italics* was added in manuscript.

The Spirit oscillates between the *D*reaming *B*ack and the Celestial Body, and these two states are compared to sleeping and The dreaming back may be supplemented by what is called the phantasmagoria. The spirit has itself no creative power, but the spirits of the thirteenth cone may create an illusionary life which exhausts emotion. Houses appear to satisfy hope or habit, the child seems to grow to maturity, or with the help of some medium a christmas tree is created.* The spirit oscillates between the Dreaming Back or Phantasmagoria and the celestial body. The first two states are compared to sleep and are represented upon the gyre by a stoppage of movement. The celestial body is made apparent by the spirits of the 13th cone during what my instructors have called the teaching. They may make the man aware not merely of the events of his past life in the order of their occurrence but of the events of their earlier lives especially those which occurred where celestial body, husk and passionate body fall upon the wheel of a cycle. The act of teaching is by its very nature a recession through time, a disappearance of the present moment.

~~Book III. Chap. 8~~

*The past incarnations corresponding to his Four Faculties seem to accompany a living man. Once when a child was born in the house I smelt roses everywhere, though none were visible, nor were they in my head alone for the doctor and the child's mother smelt them. Years afterwards I read in a book called "Nursery Life Three Hundred Years Ago" of a custom that lasted into the Seventeenth Century of washing new-born children in a bath "made wholesome . . . . . . with red roses", of rolling them in salt and roses, and of sprinkling them, when the parents could afford it,with [*sic*] oil of roses. If I assume that the Thirteenth Cone can sendthe [*sic*] forms from any incarnation which correspond to the place of Faculty or Principle, whether in the present or an earlier cycle, I have an explanation of that emergence during vision of an old Cretan myth described in my autobiography.

VIII

The passage from event to event with the periodical falling back into Passionate Body when some event seems to complete itself shows to the Spirit the course and effect of all the passionate events of life. This showing is not the work of Spirit itself because Spirit separated from the Faculties cannot choose, can but attend or withold attention, nor that even without the collaboration of some living man. It has been purified of pleasure and pain and must now be purified of good and evil, and in this the Celestial Body is present as it were in person and not through its messengers. Events are no longer seen and explained but are lived, and the Spirit is now saidto [*sic*] live a true life. The past life seen as cause and effect is almost identical with the timeless Celestial Body, almost apprehended as a single simultaneous act. It is not completely identical with the Celestial Body nor with Spirit because it has been judged in relation to the code accepted during life. But nowthe [*sic*] Code itself must be judged and transcended; as Spirit and Celestial Body approach each other events losetheir [*sic*] separate identity, reveal themselves as an abstraction from Divine Wisdom or Reality.

The change from the Return to the First Purification is analogous to that after phase II. The unity that had hitherto been sought in external events and some accepted code is revealed through the One, but the One is not now within the human personality but in Celestial Body, present to the Spirit as its Other. In the Dreaming Back associated with this state concrete acts that studied by the Spirit in relation to the code accepted during life have disturbed the conscience are relieved in the order of their intensity. Their pain, when they are painful, is moral suffering and cannot be cast off until the code itself is merged in reality. Cornelius Agrippa speaks of those who among the dead imagine themselves "surrounded by flames and persecuted by demons" and confers upon them the name "Hobgoblin". There is a girl in a Japanese play whose ghost tells a Priest of a slight sin, if indeed it was sin, which seems great because of her exaggerated conscience. She is surrounded by flames, and though the Priest explains that if she but ceased to believe in those flames they would cease to exist, believe she must, and the play ends with an elaborate dance, the dance of her agony. Here too, it seems plain, the Spirit may eke out its knowledge with that of the living, or be helped as that Priest might have helped, be released from Purgatory as we say; that it has still its part among those whose beliefs it shared, or shared in some measure while living.

The Third State called the Marriage, Celestial Body is completely absorbed in Spirit (as Mask is in Will at phase 15) or in a timeless moment of pure consciousness or unconsciousness that must not be called the present because the present divides past and future and implies their existence. This moment has been compared to two mirrors which are empty because face to face. My instructors have described it as follows, "the Celestial Body is the Divine Cloak lent to all, it falls away at the consummation and Christ is revealed", words which seem to echo Bardesan's "Hymn of the Soul" where a King's son asleep in Egypt (physical life) is sent a cloak which is also an image of his body.* He sets out to his father's kingdom wrapped in the cloak. This state must not be confused with the Beatitude a state analagous [*sic*] to Unity of Being which may occur either in the first or second Purification according to the nature of the soul. Antithetical man has a Primary daimon, or Primary Principles, and will enter the Beatitude if at all during the Second Purification. Primary man has an antithetical daimon and will enter the Beatitude in the First Purification. It is a state symbolical of ultimate reality, or of the final solution of the antinomies. All is not lost in Spirit but the Spirit finds itself in all.

IX.

Before and after the Marriage occurs an experience called the Shiftingswhich [*sic*] corresponds to the Interchange of the Tinctures in the Wheel of the Faculties. The Solar and Lunar Principles exchange their contents. What was motive may become environment and vice-versa. This may last until the mid-point between birth and death when the Shiftings recur once more. A life may however have

*A living man sees the Celestial Body through the Mask. I awoke one night when a young man to find my body rigid and to hear a voice that came from my lips and yet did not seem my voice saying "We make an image of him who sleeps that is not him who sleeps and we call it Emmanuel".

to be re-lived before the exchange is either complete or unnecessary. I will quote the actual words of the automatic script which were made perhaps harsh and paradoxical to startle me into attention. I am compelled to remember that my instructors once defined the Antithetical Tincture as evil, the Primary as good.

During the Purifications when the Spirit no longer knows the particular events of its past or future lives every experience is universalised, made absolute, keyed to the utmost intensity. The Spirit lives either "the best possible life in the worst possible surroundings" or the contrary of this. The Beatitude and the Shiftings can be described as contrary states for in the first the Spirit returns to the Whole in the second to its opposite. Yet there is no suffering "for in a state of equilibrium there is neither emotion nor sensation", and seeing thatfor [*sic*] all "in the limits of the good and evil of the previous life——————————the soul is brought to a comprehension of good and evil, neither its utmost good not [*sic*] its utmost evil can force sensation or emotion". One remenbers [*sic*] the most beautiful of the Enneads that upon "The Impassivity of the Disembodied".

X

My instructors speak of those in the states before the Beatitude as the dead and confine the word spirit (as distinct from Spirit) to those in the Beatitude or later states. The dead, if they approach the living during the Meditation, appear as they were a little before death, if during the Return as they appeared during the moment of life just lived through in the Dreaming Back, if during the First Purification in whatever form they most impressed themselves upon the living. If a spirit appear during the Beatitude it wears a form symbolical of the Divine Intellect. In the state I am about to describe the spirit appears as the shape-changer of tradition.

> "'Twas said that she all shapes could wear;
> And often times before him stood
> Amid the trees of some thick wood,
> In semblance of a lady fair;
> And taught him signs, and showed him sights
> In Craven's dens, or Cumbrian heights".

XI

The dead meet one another under the constraint of necessity. In the Dreaming Back each is alone in his dream though many may compose a single event; during the Return they are not alone but meet only as some past event permits. During the Phantasmagoria they may meet at the permission of the 13th Cone; during the First Purification as that of the Celestial Body. During the Second Purification spirits are drawn like to like. "We have no freedom" said an inhabitant of this state "but to purify our intention", meaning, as I found afterward, to purify it of "complication" or of all that is not compatible with its ideal aim or ruling love of its group. It is a state not of thought but of contemplation. These aims unseal the soul's ultimate rest whereas the First Purification unsealed its source by turning necessity into thought. It is in the presence of those forms copied in the Fine Arts, the forms and acts of those liberated Daimons that await the cycles' end and their final absorption in God. But Spirits must draw upon the Faculties of the living whose daimonic or unconscious words or actions they control that they may turn their vision into knowledge. Those who taught me this system claim to have done so not for my sake but for the sake of their own "purification".* We say Spirit has no present moment but only after the Marriage is a spirit truly Spirit. When truly Spirit it is identical with the life it perceives or knows. The forms and voices that seem to display it and in so doing to possess a present moment are created by the daimons of the living. For that reason my instructors have said "we never give thoughts, we create such a situation as compels you to listen to your daimon . . . . . . we are objectivity". Under the directions of the 13th cone they display, that they may achieve their own purification, the ruling love or hate of their group.

*They insist however that only the actual words spoken or written in a super-normal way assist them. My interpretation of those words does not concern them.

XII

The *"Foreknowledge"* is a vision of the next incarnation in its concrete detailin [*sic*] its alliances and groups, if the spirit is not in phase it may seek to act upon the living so as to influence its own future life but it cannot affect that life unless at the bidding of the 13th cone. It may be full of a partizan [*sic*] intensity unknown to living men because it foresees the remote consequence of some perhaps trivial act and this emotion and the action it inspires constitutes the frustration dreaded by mediums. This frustration this partizan [*sic*] intensity have however no consequencef or [*sic*] the spirit, for the discarnate spirit cannot create, except that it may delay its birth which cannot take place until all it has foreseen is admitted to be just. In the sleep of the womb it recognises its future life as its own choice.

XIII

All the involuntary acts and facts of life are the effect of the whirring and interlocking of the gyres, but gyres may be broken or twisted by greater gyres. Sometimes individuals are *primary* and *antithetical* to one another and joined by a bond so powerful that they form a common gyre or series of gyres. This gyre or these gyres no greater gyre may be able to break till exhaustion comes. Doubtless we all to some extent meet again and again the same people and certainly in some cases form a kind of family of two or three or more persons who come together life after life until all passionate relations are exhausted, the child of one life the husband, wife, brother or sister of the next. Sometimes however a single relationship will repeat itself, turning its revolving wheel again and again, especially, my instructors say, where there has been strong sexual passion. All such passions they say, with an unexpected austerity, contain "cruelty and deceit", and this *antithetical* cruelty and deceit must be expiated in *primary* suffering and submission, or the old tragedy will be repeated. They are expiated between birth and death life because they are actions, but their victim must expiate between death and birth the ignorance that made them possible.

The victim must life in a state analagous [*sic*] to the Interchange of the Tinctures or to The Shiftings, the act of cruelty, not as victim but as tyrant; whereas the tyrant must by a necessity of his or her nature become the victim. But if one is dead and the other living they find each other in thought and symbol, the one that has been passive and is now active may from within control the other once tyrant now victim. If the act is associated with the Return or the Purification the one that controls from within, re-living as a form of, knowledge what once was tyranny,gives [*sic*] not pain but ecstasy. The one whose expiation is an act needs for the act some surrogate* or symbol of the other and offers to some other man or woman submission or service, but because the unconscious mind knows that this act isfated [*sic*] no new gyre is started. The expiation because offered to the living for the dead is called "expiation for the dead" but is in reality expiation for the daimon, for passionate love is from *the Daimon which seeks* by union with some other daimon to reconstruct above the antinomies its own true nature. The souls of victim and tyrant are bound together and unless there is a redemption, through the intercommunication of the living and the dead, that bond may continue life after life, and this is just for there had been no need of expiation had they seen in one another each other and not something else. The expiation is completed and the oscillation brought to an end for each at the same moment. There are other bonds besides those between tyrant and victim but of these I know nothing. We get happiness, my instructors say, from those we have served, ecstacy [*sic*] from those we have wronged.

XIV

When describing phase 22 Book I Part II I spoke of the alternation between Sage and Victim "Here takes place an interchange between portions of the mind which corresponds————to the interchange between the old and new Primary, the old and new

*A Bombay friend of mine once saw an Indian peasant standing by the road with many flowers beside her. She gave a flower to each passer-by with the words "I give this to my Lord". Her Lord was the god Krishna, but the passionate offer to no God but to their [own] dead a similar worship.

Antithetical at phase I and 15. The mind that has shown a predominately emotional character, called that of the victim, through the antithetical phases, now shows a predominately intellectual character, called that of the Sage . . . . whereas the mind that has been predominately that of the Sage puts on Victimage etc.". This symbolism becomes intelligible when we so superimpose the cones of the Principles upon those of the Faculties that they lie at right angles to one another. The interchange of Sage and Victim is the interchange upon the upon the [*sic*] Wheel of the Faculties at what corresponds to the mid-point between death and birth, birth and death. It seems strange that Sage and Victim should suggest Tyrant and Victim, but the Sage and Tyrant echo the Antithetical Tincture. The Sage is described as dependent for his strength upon a tradition or logical process independent of himself, a wing of the antinomy asserted against the whole; and both victims expiate ignorance. The Victim that is the opposite of the Sage is the One present in all things and he suffers because he shares the sufferings of all. I think of Ramakrishna and certain followers of his who if they saw a man or beast beaten in the street displayed the stripes upon their own bodies, and of Saint Lydwine of Schiedam who took the diseases of others upon herself.

XV

In Book II Section XV I described how the cone of the twelve cycles is cut by a cone to which we give the name of the 13th cone. The double cone so constituted is a cone of the Faculties and at its phase 22 and phase 8 comes an Interchange that has no technical name. It is that whereby a supernatural guide is brought into existence. The 13th cone contains the Ghostly Self, the self that does not incarnate, and there is a Victimage for the Ghostly Self corresponding to that which though it be for the incarnate daimon is called Victimage for the dead. The soul in Victimage for the Dead takes upon itself suffering because it has through some excess or particularity of living wounded that body which represents the body of the whole. Victimage for the Ghostly Self follows a refusal to live, whether from fear of injuring oneself or others or necessitated by conviction. Because the Ghostly Self hungers for nature and seeks it thro,ugh [*sic*] man and starves if the man refuse to live the man when the Interchange takes place becomes the Victim and is starved for the supernatural that is now the Sage—Eli! Eli! Lama Sabacthani.

In this double cone the human cycles run from phase 15 to phase I, and at phase 22 which corresponds with cycle 6 and 7 there is a state analogous to the ~~Beatitude Marriage~~ *Beatitude.*

Sometimes expiation for the Ghostly Self and Expiation for the dead coincide.

Book IV Typescript (NLI 36,272/26, leaves 10–12)

The latest surviving typescript of the latter parts of Book IV contains two short but interesting sections that were cut before the printed text. In that typescript, they appear between the material that would become sections XI and XIII in the printed text, possibly in lieu of the current section XII (188–89). Text rendered *in italics* was added in manuscript.

7

Upon the other hand we may regard the whole period of two thousand years as a dark fortnight, a movement through the Phases from Phase I5 to Phase I. When an historical Phase is Phase I5, the bierth of Christ, there is what is called when we speak of the individual life a Critical Moment. The primary west as I have explained in the completed symbol begets ~~the primary east~~ upon the antithetical east—Libra upon Aries in the solar symbolism—or seals it with its character, and the child so begotten is Christ or Christendom. When our historical era approaches Phase I, or the beginning of a new era the antithetical east will beget upon the primary west and the child or era so born will be antithetical. The primary child or era is predominately western, but because begotten upon the east, eastern in body, and if I am right in thinking that my Instructors imply not only the symbolical but the geographical east, Asiatic. Only when that body begins to wither can the western church predominate visibly.

8

Some years ago I repeated in Westminster Abbey a trick of the mind I had first practised in a baroque Italian church. ~~All~~ *I compared* those preposterous *crowded* marble figures *to Asiatic figures with half a dozen* ~~seemed at my bidding to thrust out three or four~~ arms apiece. I said to myself "I am somewhere in Thibet and in the Temple of some old decadent Asiatic faith", and now all that marble seemed so full of exciting history that I would not for the world have an inch of it away. I understood for the first time, though it sounds simple enough, that Christianity in its present form was an eastern religion that had spread through Europe as the Mahomet~~t~~an conquest spread into Sicily and Spain, that when the neo-Thomist bids us cling to what is western he is turning away from all that has made his Christianity a religion, *turning* to its inmost character indeed, but to something that is not religion, to something that declares itself at the moment when ~~faith sees its~~ the tomb shows at the turn of the road. The next era should have a harsh secular western body but gradually as that body dies reveal its Asiatic soul. It may even be as my Instructors have said that we shall seek through hate and science what we once sought through faith and love[.]

Book IV Typescript (NLI 36,272/30, leaf 28)

A folder of rejected odd pages of what would become Book IV contains two very brief sections that might initially have been intended to follow what is in the printed Macmillan text the final section (192). We here transcribe the text from the typescript. Text rendered *in italics* was added in manuscript.

XIX

The circuit of the four principles occupies four thousand years and a few years over, the life of Christ corresponding to the mid-point between birth and death, 1050 A.D. to death, the approaching influx to the mid-point between death and birth, a date some 1500 years later to birth and the place ~~of~~ Aries *marked in [of?] the [Sign?]* ~~on the wheel of the four thousand years.~~ *Aries in the diagram of the Great Wheel.*

XX

I have left unexpounded certain automatic scripts about the relations of man and woman as this book is sufficiently complicated, though I have touched upon their symbols. The more historically important of the phases marked upon the upper and lower sides of the figure correspond to loves or episodes in love that fix some new symbol or lure and constitute initiatory moments and the final influx to that liberation from all lures and symbols, that presence of a love which does not pass away being fated and accepted that my instructors have named a critical moment.

Book V Typescript (NLI 36,272/6/2c)

Preserved with the TS carbon are two draft stages, dated September 1932, of what would become "The End of the Cycle" (see 219–20). The first text, typed on different paper from the rest of the setting-copy carbon, comprises 9 leaves, and it is heavily marked with corrections. The second text, also 9 leaves and on the same paper as the rest of the carbon of the setting-copy typescript, is unmarked and incorporates the changes from the first version. We reproduce here the second text, with annotations representing the most substantial changes from the first text.

DOVE AND SWAN.

(Directions to printer)

After the words "possibility of science["] in "Dove or Swan"—"A Vision" page 210—put a row of dots and then the words "finished at Capri. February 1925."

Omit all from "possibility of science" to the end of page 215 and insert instead what follows, under the heading "1931 to the end of the cycle".

I.

The most honoured historians describe great public events as the result of inevitable social or economic forces but never announce those events beforehand; no government sends for them as did that of the commonwealth for Lilly the astrologer;[9] yet science is prophecy, the laboratory corroborates the text book, the stars the calendar. Karl Marx said that the opponents of Hegel, "that great mind" as he calls him, would see the dialectic at work and has foretold its work, but Karl Marx thought his words could shape that work.

Day after day I have sat in my chair turning a symbol over in my mind, exploring all its details, defining and again defining its elements, testing my convictions and those of others by its unity, attempting to substitute particulars for an abstraction like that of an algebra. I have felt the convictions of a life-time melt though at an age when the mind should be rigid, and others take their place, and these in turn give way to others. How far can I expect socialistic or communistic prophecies? I remember debates in the little coach-house at Hammersmith or at Morris' supper table afterwards. I remember the Apocalyptic dreams of the Japanese saint and labour leader Kagawa whose books were lent me by a Galway Clergyman; and a communist described by Captain White in his memoirs ploughing on the Cotswold Hills nothing on his great hairy body but sandals and a pair of drawers, nothing in his head but Hegel's Logic.[10] Then I draw myself up into the symbol and it seems as if I should know all if I could but banish such memories and questions and find everything in the symbol.

II

No, that is impossible, I must think of some other age like and yet unlike what the symbol seems to foretell. Perhaps certain pages of Schneider's analysis of Roman civilisation* give me what I need though my instructors spoke of Greek civilisation alone in their examination of the pre-Christian age. The Roman wheel was different-

*"The History of World Civilization" Vol. II.

ly timed. It began and finished its revolution some centuries later and could be ignored. "Dove or Swan" has a more important omission for which I am responsible. I knew nothing of the Principles when I wrote it. Perhaps my imagination in my own despite will some day force meto [*sic*] discover their effect upon the 12th and 14th centuries and upon the epoch that has just closed. For the present all I need say is that for a generation or so to come a state analagous to The Beatitude is possible in the daemonic life, but such a state can not act directly on more than a few trained or gifted minds. Schneider does not help me to separate the Roman 23rd phase from the general turbulence of the civil wars (phase 22), he sees however in Augustus Caesar and his poet Virgil the characters I attribute to an antithetical twentyfourth [*sic*] phase: tradition remained, Augustus ruled in its name, but the public welfare seemed the sole test of tradition and action alike, and every god a public god; personality returned within narrow limits in Ovid, Catullus, Propertius, only private [joys] and sorrows mattered and at last artificial and therefore violent personality (phase 26) created the counter Augustus in Nero. When order accompanied the philosophical identification of the individual and the One: Epicetus [*sic*] became emperor in Marcus Aurelius (phase 27).

III

Instead of the turbulence of some great person our phase 23 is a movement of unconscious forces and revolutionary ideas which affect the general mass. The European movement from 1680 yo [*sic*] 1927, an age of industrialism, individualism, capitalism,—Kagawa—insists that capitalism is the only possible cement between developed individuals—latterly democracy seems about to reverse itself. Something has happened which has affected literature and art and still more their criticism. I know young men, not all under the influence of Marxian Russia, who in criticising literature repudiate individual chracterisation and commend, let us say, the second act of Casey's "Silver Tassie" because man there is described in the mass.[11] Others with finer susceptibilities create sacred books, "Ulysses" or "The Waste Land", where character and detail however clearly seen summon thought to an undefined immensity.[12] I remember Pirandello whose dramatis personae find their own characters so plastic that they flow into any mould.[13] "You are happy", says somebody to some woman whose mind has gone, "because nobody can do anything to you now". She will never again be compelled to torture herself into some strange shape. I remember Wyndham Lewis, who seems to have found a stone where he can stand and watch stream by, those artists, idlers, rich men, low and high-born parasites, who create out of some carefully selected vice, crime or eccentricity, an artificial character. But these artificial characters protect themselves not against suggestibility which implies a suggesting mind but against imitativeness. They resist absorption in the mass of men, in public ideals, in a material external unity as the Hunchback will resist absorption in a spiritual unity; yet it is from their half accomplished absorption that they get their plasticity. The moment (phase 24) has all but come for the Comedia [*sic*] del arte, for a drama where all characters express the public conscience as it is shaped by history or necessity, or by some resistance to that conscience that soon must seem stupid or in bad taste. Personality, still possible in private, or as it were in a monk's cell, will lose all public significance. I can imagine much talk of physical health, a preoccupation with the most salubrious scenes and habits, but neither Georgics nor Eclogues, nor sculptured images of mahogany-dark athletes. As we are not in Rome or Greece where politics, always an expression of power, delayed and shaped the decadence, but in primary Europe, economics may create our values. Men see the future in Russia as a hundred and odd years ago they saw it in France, but the Russian revolution will be absorbed like the French revolution in the growing complexity of Europe. The historical conflict does not work itself out, as Marx believed, through a single preoccupation of the conscious mind, but is conterminous with the mind, conscious and unconscious. The Europe of Personality (phases 17, 18, 19) found its expression in Shakespeare, the Europe of Will (phases 19, 20, 21), as I think in Balzac; the moral Europe (phases 23, 24, 25) yet to come may form some man of genius as inferior to Balzac as Balzac is to Shakespeare. That moment too will create its appropriate reaction; many men will turn from what has destroyed their spontaneity and sincerity but find no sanctuary in themselves or in the external world, nor will their study of the next discover analogies of their need. The great nations of the past were in themselves antithetical or belonged to a world that was predominately antithetical. There will be no Ovid, no Catullus, no Marcus Aurelius, but I can imagine a public licence beyond anything we have known, followed by some sudden outbreak of psychic phenomena which, whether it sustain or undermine traditional religion, will cause as much excitement as did witchcraft in the sixteenth and seventeenth centuries. But all that is speculation; we cannot know the future in its particulars. What I hold certain is that the soul which has seemed since 1680 (end of phase 18 the counter of phase 26) a part of something else and little better than a process will recover its autonomy and after violent rebellion substitute in certain chosen minds, for man's slavery to an external unity submission to a unity that is itself.

IV

Every ancient civilisation in its last phase (harvest and decadence) has ceased to be intelligible to the mass of men and the mass of men have accepted in its place the horseman and the shepherd. How that change will come or under what disguise, eludes my imagination though I seek for it in my own mind. Our civilisation, from its birth in the 10th to the Exchange of the Tinctures in the 15th century faced a vivid, concrete, exciting life (Will and Body of Fate in the natural phases) with a desire growing clearer in the depth of the mind for an abstract external order (Creatice [*sic*] Mind and Mask in the intellectual and moral phases), but since the Exchange they have faced an abstract and external order with a desire in the depth of the mind (a secret committed to painters, poets and musicians alone), for all that is vivid, concrete and exciting. But this desire can no more bring the shepherd and the horseman than could the pastoral poetry of Rome and Alexandrian Greece bring the migrating hordes; the final change is not from desire but from fate acting through submission and exhaustion.

V.

The unity we move towards will not be that deduced by Graeco-Roman civilisation from Christ's "I and My Father are One", Historical Christianity turning in its greater wheel has awakened like the Civilisation, an opposition in the depth of the mind. After the predominance of a single ideal figure, or of a single interpretation, must come multiform influx, the One present in every form, but conscious alone in all that is perfect after its kind; and that is why I foretell the horseman, the ruler, not the shepherd who breaks up and settles.

September 1932.

NOTES

Editors' Introduction

1 Harold Macmillan to H[ansard] Watt, December 31, 1934, BL Add. 55761 f. 462.

2 "The Visionary Yeats," *The New Statesman* (March 27, 1926), 750; [Ernest de Selincourt], "Mr. Yeats's Occultism," *Times Literary Supplement* 25:1266 (April 22, 1926), 296; and Edmund Wilson, "Yeats's Guide to the Soul," *The New Republic* 57:737 (January 16, 1929), 249–51.

3 [G. R. S. Mead], "A Vision," *The Quest* 18:1 (October 1926), 96–98.

4 WBY to Olivia Shakespear, September 13 [postmark 1929], *L* 768; WBY to Olivia Shakespear, February [postmark February 9, 1931], *L* 781.

5 Drafted material in the NLI, containing over a thousand sheets, is contained in manuscripts 36,272/1–36,272/33.

6 NLI 13,576, Notebook begun April 7, 1921, containing *Vision* material and diary entries.

7 The "Introduction to the Great Wheel" in *Packet* became, with few changes, the "Introduction to 'A Vision'" in *AVB*.

8 See this edition, 10 and 15.

9 WBY marked in books he read, so a fairly reliable guide to which books and passages interested him may be found in books he owned. The Yeatses' personal library, now housed in the National Library of Ireland, is described in *The Library of William Butler Yeats: Guide for Readers* (http://www.nli.ie/pdfs/mss%20lists/Yeats%20Librarylistforpublic.pdf); O'Shea; Wayne C. Chapman: *The W. B. and George Yeats Library: A Short-Title Catalog* (Clemson: Clemson University Digital Press, 2006; http://www.clemson.edu/cedp/cudp/pubs/YeatsSTC/). See also Edward O'Shea, "The 1920s Catalogue of W. B. Yeats's Library," *YA* 4 (1986), ed. Warwick Gould, 279–90.

10 See for example *LWBY/GY* 162–63; *LTSM* 60–126 passim.

11 WBY wrote many letters about his reading of Lewis: see, for example, *CL InteLex* 5048, 5055, 5076, and 5097.

12 William David Soud notes that "Yeats's letters and other writings from the time offer an extensive list [of Hindu texts]: the Yoga Sūtras of Patañjali, the Bhakti Sūtras of Narada, the Bhagavad Gītā, the autobiography of Bahinabai, and, much later, the Avadhūta Gītā" ("Toward a Divinised Poetics: God, Self, and *Poiesis* in W. B. Yeats,

David Jones, and T. S. Eliot," PhD diss., University of Oxford, 2013, 59).

13 These essays are collected in *Wheels and Butterflies* (in WBY's terminology, the short plays are the "butterflies" and the deliberately provocative introductory essays the "wheels") and are reprinted as appendices in *Plays*; the quotations are from 721 and 725.

14 *Le système du monde, histoire des doctrines cosmologiques de Platon à Copernic* (10 vols.; Paris: Hermann, 1913–59).

15 *CL InteLex* 7117.

16 WBY to GY, October 22, 1931, and April 4, 1932, *LWBY/GY* 259 and 311.

17 See *LWBY/GY* 277, Foster 2:427, YL 881 and 2122.

18 *AVA* lv-lvi.

19 These are YL 2433, 2433a, 2433b, and 2433c. See *AVA* 339–52.

20 Frank Pearce Sturm to WBY, January 19, 1926, *FPS* 87. Sturm refers to Book II of *AVA*, "What the Caliph Refused to Learn"; see *AVA* 95–143. See 51 and note.

21 WBY to Frank Pearce Sturm, March 1, 1926, *FPS* 98.

22 NLI 13,576.

23 WBY to Ignatius McHugh, May 26 [1926], *CL InteLex* 4874.

24 See leaf 8 of the 1921 notebook, dated "Jun 8" and following an entry of May 28, 1926, on E. M. Plunkett to be added to *A Vision* (NLI 13,576).

25 Leaf 8v, referring to sections IX, "The Beatitude," and XII, "The Spirits at Fifteen and at One," of Book IV, "The Gates of Pluto." See *AVA* 193–94, 198–201.

26 See, for instance, leaf 3, Rapallo Notebook C (NLI 13,580).

27 NLI 13,576, leaf [24]. See *AVA* 128–30.

28 WBY to Olivia Shakespear, May 25 [1926], *CL InteLex* 4871.

29 NLI 13,576, leaves [11v] and [12] and following.

30 NLI 13,576, leaf 24v. See *AVA* 109–12.

31 NLI 13,576, leaves 31 and 31v. The issue seems concerned with WBY's attempt to integrate the start of the Great Year, when equinoxes and star markers coincided, with the system's other cycles (*AVA* 114–28 gives an earlier conception, and see this volume 184 and 186). He faced a variety of circles marked out either in phases, zodiac signs, or compass points, some offset from each other by ninety degrees and possibly running in opposite directions. As the comment that, in Dulac's woodcut, "the East is marked by a sceptre" (188) indicates, Phase 22 in the circle of the phases coincides with East and Aries, and South at Phase 15 with Capricorn (see *AVA* 114ff). This, however, is the lunar alignment, and WBY thought the Great Year should possibly be measured by the solar version in which East and the start of Aries coincide with the center of Phase 15 ("Lunar South is Solar East"; see 138, 146n, and 183). After publishing *AVA*, he had also

concluded that the solar zodiac ran in the opposite direction to the lunar one (causing alterations: see 344–45 n1, #4). The diary entry indicates that, at this point, WBY favored the lunar Aries coinciding with Phase 22 as the starting point.

32 WBY to Maud Gonne, October 7, 1927, *CL InteLex* 5036, and October 25, 1927, *CL InteLex* 5039. See 375–76 n163 of this edition. WBY to Lady Gregory, March 12 [1928], *CL InteLex* 5089. See also a later letter to Lady Gregory, April 1 [1928], *CL InteLex* 5097. WBY to Jack Lindsay, April 2 [1928], *CL InteLex* 5098. *LWBY/GY* 205. Dionertes is one of the Controls in the automatic experiments. WBY to Olivia Shakespear, September 13 [1929], *CL InteLex* 5285. WBY to Sturm, *FPS* 100.

33 WBY to Olivia Shakespear, February (postmark February 9, 1931), *L* 781. WBY refers to Allan Duncan; see *CL InteLex* 5455. WBY to GY, October 13 [1931], *LWBY/GY* 253. The Cicero passage appears on 178. This passage provided the subject for a good bit of the Yeatses' correspondence of October 1931: see *LWBY/GY* 253–58. For other, later claims of completion, see *L* 788, 812, 819; *LWBY/GY* 311.

34 See Hood, "Search" and "Remaking," esp. 48–52.

35 See NLI 36,272/8–33. On the (undated) version WBY titled "Michael Robartes Foretells," see Walter Kelly Hood, "Michael Robartes: Two Occult Manuscripts," *YO* 204–24.

36 WBY to Olivia Shakespear, January 27 [1934], *CL InteLex* 5998. WBY to Frank Pearce Sturm, January 7, 1935, *FPS* 105.

37 WBY to Lady Gregory, [February 24, 1928], *L* 738.

38 WBY to GY, [February 25, 1928] and February 27 [1928], *LWBY/GY* 190–91.

39 WBY to Lennox Robinson, March 10 [1928], *CL InteLex* 5088.

40 Rapallo Notebook B (NLI 13,579, leaf 1). For more extensive treatment of these drafts, WBY's treatment of Pound therein, and their relationship to *A Vision*, see Paul. WBY to Olivia Shakespear, August 2 [1928], *CL InteLex* 5142. See also *L* 739, 748.

41 WBY, Rapallo Notebook C (NLI 13,580, leaf [2]).

42 WBY, "Introduction," Rapallo Notebook B (NLI 13,579, leaf [83]).

43 See, for instance, NLI 30,757, NLI 30,758, NLI 36,272/7, NLI 30,308, and NLI 39,121/1. For the source of this line, see 312–13 n23.

44 WBY to Olivia Shakespear, November 23 [1928], *L* 748.

45 See Gallup C47 and A8.

46 See WBY to Oliver St John Gogarty, May 5 [1929], *CL InteLex* 5247.

47 The drafts of the first and second sections (see NLI 13,580, leaves 10–15), as in *Packet*, are dated February 4 and 9, 1929, respectively. In *Words for Music Perhaps and Other Poems*, the first poem was titled "A Meditation written during Sickness at Algeciras." See *Poems* 250–52. The copy of *Packet* sent to Macmillan as setting copy for *A Vision* suggests that WBY may not have initially intended to cut the

poem: its first page includes numerous manuscript revisions, suggesting that WBY originally planned to make changes in the poem before deciding to cut it altogether.

48 Wade 163. The book's colophon gives June 1929 as the month of completion.

49 G. W. Russell (Æ), "A Packet for Ezra Pound: AE Reviews W. B. Yeats's Latest Book," *The Living Age* 337:4347 (October 1, 1929), 187.

50 Seán Ó Faoláin, "Mr. Yeats's Trivia," *Commonweal* 10:30 (September 18, 1929), 513. Seán Ó Faoláin, "Mr. Yeats's Kubla Khan," *The Nation* (December 4, 1929), 681.

51 Manuscript Notebook for *Stories of Michael Robartes and His Friends* (1931) (NLI 13,577, leaves [1] and [29v]).

52 Wade 167.

53 See *AVA* lix–lx.

54 *Stories* 24.

55 WBY to Hansard Watt, December 14, 1930, *CL InteLex* 5419.

56 "Remaking," 44–48.

57 WBY to Dorothy Wellesley, July 26, 1936, *L* 859.

58 C[harles] P[owell], "Mr W. B. Yeats," *Manchester Guardian*, May 2, 1932, 5; and [Austin Clarke], *TLS*, March 24, 1932, 214.

59 The setting copy of *AVA-Laurie* is YL 2433c. Many of the changes in the setting copy of *A Packet* aim toward Macmillan house style, and more substantive changes have been noted in our annotations.

60 See Hood, "Remaking," 55–57.

61 Correspondence concerning the proof process for *A Vision* appears in the letter books of Macmillan (BL Add. 54902–54904, 55003, and 55764–55800).

62 GY to A. P. Watt, February 11, 1936, *CL InteLex* 6520.

63 See Wade 191 and 192.

64 WBY to Ethel Mannin, October 9 [?1938], *L* 916.

65 Charles Williams, "Staring at Miracle," *Time and Tide* (December 4, 1937), 1674.

66 G[eoffrey] E. G[rigson], "Thy Chase Had a Beast in View," *New Verse* 29 (March 1938), 20; Michael Roberts, "The Source of Poetry," *The Spectator* 159:5708 (November 19, 1937), Literary Supplement, 14; Kerker Quinn, "Through Frenzy to Truth," *The Yale Review* 27:4 (Summer 1938), 834; Mary M. Colum, "Life and Literature: The Individual vs. Society," *Forum and Century* 99:4 (April 1938), 214; Horace Reynolds, "W. B. Yeats Expounds His 'Heavenly Geometry,'" *The New York Times Book Review* [43] (March 13, 1938), 2.

67 Michael Williams, "Doom," *The Commonweal* 27:22 (March 25, 1938), 611; Reynolds, "W. B. Yeats Expounds," 2; Seán Ó Faoláin, "Mr. Yeats's Metaphysical Man," *The London Mercury* 37:217 (November 1937), 70.

68 William Rose Benét, "Speculations of a Poet," *The Saturday Review*

17:20 (March 12, 1938), 239; Stephen Spender, [Review], *The Criterion* 17:68 (April 1938), 536; M. L. Cazamian, [Review], *Études Anglaises* 2:3 (July–September 1938), 315. Cazamian's original reads: "Le lecteur non initié tournera donc avec curiosité ces pages où le poète trace l'historique de ses rapports avec le monde des esprits, grâce à la capacité d'écriture automatique soudain révélée chez sa jeune femme d'abord."

69 Edmund Wilson, "Yeats's Vision," *The New Republic* 94:1220 (April 20, 1938), 339; Roberts, "The Source of Poetry," 14, 16.

70 Roberts, "The Source of Poetry," 16; Wilson, "Yeats's Vision," 339; G[rigson], "Thy Chase Had a Beast in View," 20.

71 Wilson, "Yeats's Vision," 339; Babette Deutsch, "Bones of a Poet's Vision," *New York Herald Tribune Books* 14:36 (May 8, 1938), 16; Eda Lou Walton, "Lend a Myth to God," *The Nation* (July 9, 1938), 52; C. E. B., "Books of the Day," *The Illustrated London News* 192:5153 (January 22, 1938), 126.

72 Quinn, "Through Frenzy to Truth," 835; G[rigson], "Thy Chase Had a Beast in View," 21–22.

73 Roberts, "The Source of Poetry," 16; J. Bronowski, "Yeats's Mysticism," *The Cambridge Review* 59:1440 (November 19, 1937), 113; Stephen Spender, [Review], *The Criterion* 17:68 (April 1938), 537.

74 R. C. Bald, [Review], *Philosophical Review* 48:284 (March 1939), 239; Bronowski, "Yeats's Mysticism," 113; [Unsigned brief review], *The New Statesman and Nation* 15:361 (January 22, 1938), 140.

75 Benét, "Speculations of a Poet," 239; Spender, [Review], 537; H. T. Hunt Grubb, "A Poet's Dream," *Poetry Review* 29:2 (March–April 1938): 123-41; Ó Faoláin, "Mr. Yeats's Metaphysical Man," 70.

76 Watt to Macmillan, April 17, 1939 (Add. MS. 54904. Vol. CXIX, f. 171). In 1935, plans began for a separate deluxe edition from Charles Scribner, dubbed the "Dublin" Edition, and for which WBY wrote introductions to his poetry and plays. See Edward Callan (ed.), *Yeats on Yeats: The Last Introductions and the "Dublin" Edition* (Dublin: Dolmen Press, 1981).

77 See Warwick Gould, "The Definitive Edition: a History of the Final Arrangements of Yeats's Work," in A. Norman Jeffares' edition of *Yeats's Poems* (London: Palgrave, 1996), 706–49. Gould notes that the original Edition de Luxe, as contracted in 1916 and planned beginning in 1930, had only seven volumes (708).

78 Thomas Mark to GY, TLS carbon, June 26, 1939 (BL Add. 55826, f. 50). The bulk of BL Add. 55893 is the first-pull proof; the exception is signature P (pages 209–24 of the proofs, roughly 145–57 of the present edition), which is stamped "Second Proof" and dated "1 Sept 1939." Unmarked bound copies of the complete set of first-pull proofs are also housed in the British Library (shelfmarks Vx29/189, RF.2008a.43–45), and differences between the first and second pulls

of signature P have been noted in Table 3: these differences point to changes marked on the first pull of signature P, now lost.

79 Harold Macmillan [MHM/JGB] to Mrs. Yeats, October 17, 1939 (BL Add. 55830, f. 281).

80 T. Mark [TM/JVL] to Mrs. Yeats, October 19, 1939, BL Add. 55830, f. 334. On the relationships between *Poems* (1949) and the Coole Edition, see Gould, "The Definitive Edition."

81 Hood, "Search," 151. As Hood notes, this copy is now in the Russell K. Alspach Collection at the University of Massachusetts Library at Amherst. The corrections marked in this copy are enumerated on 151–54. Among the materials given to us by the Hoods is a copy of these markings, together with a photocopy of Alspach's own listing of his collection, which includes this note for this copy: "A Vision (N.Y.) George Yeats's signed copy, corrected by her for Macmillan of New York for the edition of 1956 (211M). The Title-page is torn out." A letter written to Connie K. Hood from John D. Kendall (of the University Library) on November 19, 1981, notes the presence in Alspach's list of three other items inscribed by GY (*A Speech and Two Poems* [1937], *Mosada* [1943], and *Collected Poems* [1950]), "which latter fact would seem to lend credence (if it were needed) to Alspach's statement that the New York 1938 Vision was indeed annotated by whom and for what purpose he says."

82 Wade 211M.

83 Richard J. Finneran suggests that the proofs for the first 58 pages were sent to GY in August 1960, when GY and Thomas Mark were considering incorporating these sections into *Explorations* ("On Editing Yeats: The Text of *A Vision* [1937]," *Texas Studies in Literature and Language* 19 [1977], 123–24). See also BL Add. 55896.

84 Hood, "Search," 155.

85 Hood, "Search," 164.

86 Hood, "Search," 170; see also Warwick Gould, "The Definitive Edition," 708–9.

A Packet for Ezra Pound

1 It took many years for WBY to use the etched portrait made in 1907 at Coole Park by the painter Augustus John (1878–1961), of which WBY wrote John Quinn at the time that John, "who has made a very fine thing of me has made me sheer tinker, drunken, unpleasant and disreputable, but full of wisdom, a melancholy English Bohemian, capable of everything, except of living joyously on the surface" (*CL InteLex* 751). WBY sat for John again in the summer of 1930, while working on *A Vision*. Remembering the first portrait at that time, WBY noted in his diary that he "shuddered" at first seeing it: "Always particular about my clothes, never dissipated, never unshaven except

during illness, I saw myself there an unshaven, drunken bar-tender, and then I began to feel John had found something that he liked in me, something closer than character, and by that very transformation made it visible. He had found Anglo-Irish solitude, a solitude I have made for myself, an outlawed solitude" (*Diary 1930* 308).

In September 1934, WBY suggested to Harold Macmillan that the 1930 image be used for *A Vision*: "when you come to print the next book I shall send you my philosophical book A Vision (it is ready) you use as a frontispiece Augustus John's portrait painted four or five years ago. It is in the Glasgow gallery" (*CL InteLex* 6096). The plan for "Etching by Augustus John to be used as frontispiece" was in place by March 1935 (*CL InteLex* 6193; see also 6199, 6299). The decision to use the portrait from 1907 (Manchester) rather than 1930 (Glasgow) may have involved permission: in October 1935, GY wrote R. A. Scott James, the editor of the *London Mercury*, that he could not use the 1930 image for this reason. Of the two portraits, GY wrote, "One has already been reproduced in the Macmillan COLLECTED POEMS, the other is in the City Art Gallery at Manchester. As regards the second of these two portraits, Dr Oliver Edwards, who is writing a life of WBY has been writing to John at intervals for five months or so asking for permission to reproduce the portrait. So far he has had no reply. The Curator of the Manchester Gallery says that John's permission is essential! So I am afraid there is nothing doing" [*CL InteLex* 6395]. See also D. J. Gordon and Ian Fletcher, "The Image of the Poet," in *W. B. Yeats: Images of a Poet: My permanent or impermanent images* (Manchester: Manchester University Press, 1961; rpt. 1970), 17–18, 22–24.

2 *A Packet for Ezra Pound* was first published by Cuala Press in 1929; see Editors' Introduction, xxxii–xxxvi.

3 The Yeatses came to this small Italian city on the Ligurian coast in the Genova province of Italy in February 1928. Although the town was not as glamorous as the French Riviera, it was not expensive to live there (see *FPS* 100) and therefore had a sizable if variable population of expatriates. While there, Pound connected Yeats with prominent members of contemporary artistic circles, including Basil Bunting, George Antheil, Gerhart Hauptmann, and Max Beerbohm. In a letter to the Japanese scholar Shotaro Oshima of March 24, 1929, WBY writes, "My wife and I have got a little flat here looking out over the sea and over mountains often wreathed in mist which continually remind me of the landscape painting of your country, even mist" (*CL InteLex* 5228).

4 The reference is to the fourth stanza of the ode (1819) by the Romantic poet John Keats (1795–1821):

> What little town by river or sea shore,
> Or mountain-built with peaceful citadel,
> Is emptied of this folk, this pious morn?

And, little town, thy streets for evermore
Will silent be: and not a soul to tell
Why thou art desolate, can e'er return.
(lines 35–40, *The Poems of John Keats*, ed. Sidney Colvin [2 vols.; London: Chatto & Windus, 1920; YL1055], 2.87)

5 The German dramatist is playwright and Nobel Prize winner Gerhard Hauptmann (1862–1946). As WBY wrote to Olivia Shakespear, March 2 [1929], "To-night we dine with Ezra—the first dinner-coated meal since I got here—to meet Hauptmann who does not know a word of English but is fine to look at—after the fashion of William Morris" (*L* 758). The next day, Pound wrote to his mother: "Ceremony of introducing Yeatsz and Hauptmanns passed off calmly last evening with sacrifice of two pheasants. No other bloodshed" (*Pound to his Parents* 682). The barber's brother, the retired skipper, and the specific tourists are unidentified. For the Italian prince: on February 25, 1928, WBY wrote to GY: "Tonight Ezra & Dorothy bring me to dine with a Mrs. Stein & her daughter & her son in law who is an Italian Prince of the Holy Roman Empire, & descended from Charlemagne. They have a villa out on a headland. Mrs. Stein is of course an American, the widow, I gather, of several millionaires" (*CL InteLex* 5083).

6 American poet Ezra Pound (1885–1972) moved to Rapallo in 1924, and by this time he had taken up residence at via Marsala 20, where the balcony of his top-floor apartment had a view over the Lungotevere to the Golfo del Tigullio. This is not Pound's first appearance in *A Vision* and its surrounding materials. In *AVA*, he appears as a subject of some of WBY's reflections on his contemporaries (*AVA* 174–75), and Pound was cut as an example for Phase 12 only in galleys. In January and February 1925, the Yeatses traveled in southern Italy with Ezra and Dorothy Pound, and it was during that trip that WBY finished writing many sections of *AVA*.

WBY offered a complicated assessment of Pound's character in his introduction to *OBMV*; see especially *LE* 193. On WBY's comments about Pound in drafts for *Packet*, see Paul.

7 By the time this material was compiled into *AVB*, Pound had published *A Draft of XXX Cantos* (1930) and *Eleven New Cantos, XXXI–XLI* (1934)—forty-one poems (see Gallup A31, A37). Pound also published these poems in periodicals, individually or in small groups; for instance, "Cantos XLII–XLIV" appeared in *The Criterion* in April 1937 (Gallup C1401). *The Fifth Decad of Cantos* (including Cantos 42–51) would be published in June 1937. "There are now forty-nine" suggests conversations with Pound about poems written and/or forthcoming.

8 In *Packet*, this sentence reads: "I have often found there some scene of distinguished beauty but have never discovered why all the suits could not be dealt out in some quite different order" (2).

9 A fugue is a musical composition written for two or more voices in which a theme is introduced in one voice and then recurs directly and in imitation in the other voice(s). Baroque composer Johann Sebastian Bach (1685–1750) wrote many fugues. On February 25, 1928, WBY wrote to GY concerning Pound's *Cantos*, which in its latest printed form includes 116 numbered cantos as well as additional fragments, "Ezra has spent several hours explaining the structure of his cantos, & all I know is that there is a structure & that it is founded on that of a Fugue—that word looks wrong" (*CL InteLex* 5083). Carroll F. Terrell notes, "Pound is on record as saying that Yeats's explanation did more harm than good because he had as little idea of a fugue as he had of a frog" (*A Companion to* The Cantos *of Ezra Pound* [Berkeley, Los Angeles, London: University of California Press, 1980], viii). Nevertheless, in a letter to his father of April 11, 1927, Pound describes the overarching scheme of *The Cantos* as "[r]ather like, or unlike subject and response and counter subject in fugue" (*The Selected Letters of Ezra Pound, 1907–1941*, ed. D. D. Paige [New York: New Directions, 1971], 210). WBY similarly describes *The Cantos* in his introduction to *OBMV* (*LE* 192–93).

10 The dates for the legendary Greek poet Homer, to whom the epic poems the *Iliad* and the *Odyssey* are ascribed, are not known. Herodotus dates him at about 850 BCE while other accounts position him as early as the tenth or eleventh centuries BCE; the best guesses seem to suggest between 750 and 650 BCE. Pound famously described epic as "a poem including history" (*ABC of Reading* [1934], [New York: New Directions, 1987], 46), and his *Cantos* are no exception. The *Cantos* opens with a translation of a passage from Homer's *Odyssey* 11, known as the *Nekuia*, or ritual calling-up of ghosts from the Underworld (*Cantos* 1:3–5). The *Metamorphoses* of Publius Ovidius Naso (43 BCE–17 CE) comprise fifteen books of more than 250 myths focused on changes of shape. Stories from the *Metamorphoses* permeate the *Cantos*, beginning in Canto 2 with references to books 3 and 10. Notable medieval characters include such troubadours and poets as Sordello (13th cent., known especially to Pound from Browning's poem of the same name), Guido Cavalcanti (c. 1250–1300), and Arnaut Daniel (12th cent.), as well as numerous Italian princes, most prominently Sigismondo Malatesta (1498–1553) of Rimini. Modern characters range from personal friends to celebrities, prominent practitioners and theorists in the arts, and political leaders.

11 In *Time and Western Man* (1927), the English writer and painter Percy Wyndham Lewis (1882–1957) condemns the art of his fellow

modernist writers Ezra Pound, James Joyce, and Gertrude Stein for having allowed their supposedly "revolutionary" writing to become a vehicle for ideologies contrary to real human creativity and progress. In the ninth chapter, called "Ezra Pound, Etc.," Lewis writes, "I could not reconcile the creative principles I have been developing with this sensationalist half-impresario, half-poet [Pound]; whose mind can be best arrived at, perhaps, by thinking of what would happen if you could mix in exactly equal proportions Bergson-Marinetti-Mr. Hueffer (with a few pre-Raphaelite 'christian names' thrown in), Edward Fitzgerald and Buffalo Bill" ([London: Chatto and Windus, 1927; Boston: Beacon Press, 1957], 38). For more of WBY's reaction to Lewis's book, see n17 below. WBY's note closes with a quatrain from "The Progress of Beauty" (1719) by Jonathan Swift (1667–1745), which contrasts an aging woman's appearance upon waking with the magic rendered by four hours of applying makeup.

12 *Le Chef-d'œuvre inconnu* (or "The Unknown Masterpiece," 1831) by Honoré de Balzac (1799–1850) tells the story of a series of encounters between the young and as yet unknown French painter Nicolas Poussin (1594–1665), the mature Flemish painter Porbus (not Porteous) (1569–1622), and the aging (fictional) artist Master Frenhofer. See YL 109. See Warwick Gould, "The Unknown Masterpiece: Yeats and the Design of the *Cantos*," in *Pound in Multiple Perspective: A Collection of Critical Essays*, ed. Andrew Gibson (London: Macmillan, 1993), 40–92.

Paul Cézanne (1839–1906) was a French post-impressionist painter regarded as a principal predecessor of Cubism. There is no historical basis for the suggestion that Cézanne draws specifically on Porbus' thinking, although Émile Bernard does seem to identify him with Balzac's visionary painter (*Souvenirs sur Paul Cézanne* [Paris: Société des Trente, 1925], 34–36).

Ulysses (1922) by James Joyce (1882–1941) takes place on a single day and entirely in the city of Dublin. WBY wrote to John Quinn on July 23, 1918, that *Ulysses* in serial form "looks like becoming the best work he has yet done. It is an entirely new thing—neither what the eye sees nor the ear hears, but what the rambling mind thinks and imagines from moment to moment. He has certainly surpassed in intensity any novelist of our time . . ." (*L* 651; see also *L* 679). On July 27, 1922, WBY wrote to Pound,

> I have read a great part of "Ulysses" and then gave myself a course of Trollope for a change and then just as I wanted to take up Ulysses again which I admire immensely, found my eyes out of sorts; this does not mean that I do not see the immense importance of the book, and it has been Trollope not it that destroyed my eyes. I read a few pages of Ulysses at a time as if

> he were a poem. Some passages have great beauty, lyric beauty, even in the fashion of my generation, and the whole book incites to philosophy.
>
> (*CL InteLex* 4152)

Writing to Olivia Shakespear in late June of 1923, WBY spoke of inviting Joyce to visit, but confessed that "[i]f he comes I shall have to use the utmost ingenuity to hide the fact that I have never finished *Ulysses*" (*L* 698). In *AVA*, in a passage not retained in *AVB*, WBY similarly joins Pound and Joyce in the description of the historical Phase 23, which he associated with many experimental writers of his time (174–75). See also *VPl* 569.

13 Cosimo (or Cosmè) Tura (1433–95), who worked regularly for the d'Este family, is considered a founder of the Ferrara school of art. Among the eighteen sections of the fresco decoration of the Salone dei Mesi (or Hall of the Months) in the Palazzo di Schifanoia, a former d'Este palace, six contain jousting scenes and cityscapes and twelve are devoted to the months of the year. The sections each have three horizontal bands. The top band of each panel illustrates the triumphal procession of the pagan god or goddess of the month. The middle band contains the zodiacal sign of each month surrounded by the three astrological "faces" or phases of the decans (36 divisions of the zodiac, dividing each sign in three and so called because they comprise 10° each). The bottom zone depicts scenes of daily life at the court of Borso d'Este. What WBY identifies as "The Triumph of Love" is April, whose upper zone contains a triumph of Venus. "The Triumph of Chastity" may be May, whose upper zone holds a Triumph of Apollo. Although art historians do not believe Cosimo Tura responsible for this hall and suggest Francesco del Cossa as more likely to have produced these frescos, Tura is one candidate for the creation of some of them. See *Cantos* 79:505 and Terrell, *A Companion to* The Cantos *of Ezra Pound*, viii.

14 "Hodos Chameliontos," a phrase meaning "the Path of the Chameleon," appears prominently in and as a title of a section of the autobiographical work *The Trembling of the Veil* to suggest the experience of being lost amid multivarious esoteric ideas and experiences. "But now image called up image in an endless procession, and I could not always choose among them with any confidence," WBY writes, describing himself as "lost in that region a cabbalistic manuscript, shown to me by MacGregor Mathers, had warned me of; astray upon the Path of the Chameleon, upon Hodos Chameliontos" (*Au* 215). *Hodos Chamelionis* is the title by which the Introducing Adept in the Adeptus Minor (5 = 6) Ritual of the Golden Dawn is known, and also the name given to the newly installed Aspirant to the rank. At the climax of the ceremony, the Chief greets the new Adeptus Minor

with the words, "And therefore do I greet thee with the Mystic Title of 'Hodos Chamelionis,' the Path of the Chamelion, the Path of Mixed Colours . . ." (Israel Regardie, *The Golden Dawn. A Complete Course in Practical Ceremonial Magic. Four Volumes in One. The Original Account of the Teachings, Rites and Ceremonies of the Hermetic Order of the Golden Dawn* [*Stella Matutina*], 6th ed. [Saint Paul, Minn.: Llewellyn Publications, 1992], 225, 242). The spelling is not standard; family friend and Trinity College don Louis C. Purser informed WBY that "the genitive is chameleontos" if used as a Greek word (*LWBY* 436), and WBY changed the spelling. Concerning the use of the manual in the Golden Dawn, see George Mills Harper, *Yeats's Golden Dawn* (London: Macmillan, 1974), 177. Elsewhere in *A Vision*, WBY uses the same phrase to explain the confusion facing those of his generation: "Our generation has witnessed a first weariness, has stood at the climax, at what in *The Trembling of the Veil* I call *Hodos Chameliontos*, and when the climax passes will recognize that there common secular thought began to break and disperse" (217; cf. *AVA* 173). See also "The Dedication to Vestigia" (*AVA* liv).

In *Le Chef-d'œuvre inconnu* (see n12), Frenhofer finds excellence of detail in the woman's shoulder and bosom but deems her throat (not foot, as WBY misremembers) "all false." In *Packet*, the current paragraph is followed by another, struck through on the setting copy:

> It is almost impossible to understand the art of a generation younger than one's own. I was wrong about "Ulysses" when I had read but some first fragments, and I do not want to be wrong again—above all in judging verse. Perhaps when the sudden Italian spring has come I may have discovered what will seem all the more, because the opposite of all I have attempted, unique and unforgettable. (4)

15 The street mentioned is now Via Gramsci, and the first of the hotels is Hotel Riviera on the current Piazza IV Novembre (Massimo Bacigalupo, "Tigullio Itineraries," *Quaderni di Palazzo Serra* 15 [2008]: 391).

In a letter to GY of February 27 [1928], WBY writes: "All well here—Ezra explains his cantos, & reads me Cavalcanti & we argue about it quite amicably. We have twice dined to get variety at another hotel—almost under our trees—where he purloins sraps [*sic*] that he may feed a black & two grey cats who wait for him about fifty yards from the hotel. He has been feeding them for quite a considerable time & brags of there [*sic*] fatness" (*LWBY/GY* 191). See also *YVP* 3:37.

16 In a letter to Olivia Shakespear of November 23, 1928, WBY credits T. S. Eliot with this observation (*L* 748).

17 This reference is to WBY's close friend the Irish revolutionary Maud

Gonne (MacBride) (1866–1953), with whom he was in love for many years. WBY frequently referred to Pound's feeding of cats in letters to his friends in Ireland. On April 1, 1928, he wrote to Lady Gregory, comparing Pound and Gonne:

> Have you read Wyndham Lewis? He attacked Ezra Pound and Joyce in *Time and Western Man,* and is on my side of things philosophically. My essay takes up the controversy and explains Ezra Pound sufficiently to keep him as a friendly neighbour, for I foresee that in the winter he must take Russell's place of a Monday evening. He has most of Maud Gonne's opinions (political and economic) about the world in general, being what Lewis calls "the revolutionary simpleton." The chief difference is that he hates Palgrave's *Golden Treasury* as she does the Free State Government, and thinks even worse of its editor than she does of President Cosgrave. He has even her passion for cats and large numbers wait him every night at a certain street corner knowing that his pocket is full of meat bones or chicken bones. They belong to the oppressed races. (*L* 739)

On Lewis's treatment of Pound in *Time and Western Man*, see also n11 above.

18 WBY refers to several churches. The first regular Anglican chaplaincy in Rapallo was established in 1875, and the first services were held in the Church of St. George in 1904. The chapel at All Souls College, Oxford (or The Warden and the College of the Souls of all Faithful People deceased in the University of Oxford), was built 1438–42. The Yeatses had lodgings in Oxford from late 1917 to 1922. The National Cathedral and Collegiate Church of St. Patrick in Dublin was founded in 1191 and is the larger of Dublin's two Church of Ireland cathedrals. Its building dates from 1220, and it was granted cathedral status in 1224. Jonathan Swift was Dean of the Cathedral and is buried there. The Basilica of Sant'Ambrogio in Milan was built by St. Ambrose in 379–386, and then rebuilt in the Romanesque style in the twelfth century.

19 René Descartes (1596–1650) is a foundational figure in modern philosophy and mathematics, famous for his seemingly skeptical questioning about the possibilites of knowledge. The Comune di Zoagli in Liguria is about five kilometers southeast of Rapallo, along the via Aurelia. The American violinist Olga Rudge, mother of Ezra Pound's daughter Mary, had a house in Sant'Ambrogio di Zoagli during the time that the Yeatses lived in Rapallo. Gerhard Hauptmann's villa was on the Zoagli Road. Nietzsche lived in Rapallo for a time, a fact that WBY knew, probably from Pound (see *L* 773). *Packet* included a sixth, concluding section of "Rapallo," struck through on the setting copy of *Packet* and so excluded in the 1937 text of *A Vision*: see Appendix II, 275–76.

20 The Anglo-Irish satirist, poet, and essayist Jonathan Swift (1667–1745) was Dean of St. Patrick's Cathedral in Dublin; in the 1920s and 1930s especially, as WBY writes in the introduction to *The Words upon the Window-Pane*, "Swift haunts me; he is always just round the next corner" (*Plays* 708). This quotation is the opening sentence of Swift's "A Preface to the Bishop of Sarum's Introduction to the Third Volume of the History of the Reformation of the Church of England by Gregory Misosarum," a pamphlet written, in the words of Dr. Johnson, "to warn the nation of the approach of popery" (*The Works of Jonathan Swift in Two Volumes* [London: Henry G. Bohn, 1850], 1:379). See YL 2043.

21 Isabella Augusta Persse, Lady Gregory (1852–1932), Irish nationalist, dramatist, folklorist, and theater manager, was an important mentor to WBY and one of his closest friends. WBY and Lady Gregory collaborated extensively, and he stayed often at her house Coole Park, near Gort in Co. Galway. In *A Vision*, she is an example for Phase 24; see 125. *The Tower* and *The Winding Stair* were first published in 1928 and 1929 respectively, with a larger edition of the latter published in September 1933. Together they contain many of WBY's best known poems, as well as a wealth of poetry influenced by the AS.

22 GY, born Bertha Georgie Hyde Lees (1892–1968), married WBY on October 20, 1917. See Saddlemyer for the authoritative account of the life of "a remarkably clever, creative, witty, energetic, and wily woman" (xx), and Margaret Mills Harper, *Wisdom of Two: The Spiritual and Literary Collaboration of George and W. B. Yeats* (Oxford: Oxford University Press, 2006), for a study of the automatic writing as a collaboration between the Yeatses.

23 On the first draft of this passage, see Editors' Introduction, xxxiii–xxxiv. As George Mills Harper notes, WBY's first direct reference to the AS occurs in a letter to Lady Gregory of October 29:

> The last two days Georgie and I have been very happy. . . . There has been something very like a miraculous intervention. Two days ago I was in great gloom, (of which I hope, and believe, George knew nothing). I was saying to myself "I have betrayed three people;" then I thought "I have lived all through this before." Then George spoke of the sensation of having lived through something before (she knew nothing of my thought). Then she said she felt that something was to be written through her. She got a piece of paper, and talking to me all the while so that her thoughts would not affect what she wrote, wrote these words (which she did not understand) "with the bird" (Iseult) "all is well at heart. Your action was right for both but in London you mistook its meaning." (*L* 633)

The dates in this letter seem to question WBY's assertion that the AS began on October 24, and the exact date is unclear (see *YVP* 3:349, *MYV* 1:3–5, Saddlemyer 105). As Margaret Mills Harper notes, although no such statement occurs in the extant AS, ten sheets of MS filed with drafts of this introduction contain very early script with this response to an unrecorded question: "I give you philosophy to give you new images you ought not to use it as philosophy and it is not only given for you—" (Harper, *Wisdom of Two*, 6, citing NLI 36,260/4).

24 Written in early 1917 and published by Macmillan in January 1918, *PASL* (translated by WBY in a letter to Lady Gregory as "through the friendly silences of the moon") lays out concepts important to *A Vision*, including *Daimons*, the antithetical or anti-self, and *Anima Mundi* as a source of common images (*LE* 1–33). WBY makes the distinction in *PASL* that "We make of the quarrel with others, rhetoric, but of the quarrel with ourselves, poetry" (*LE* 8). Noting differences between "the winding movement of nature and the straight line," he writes:

> I do not doubt those heaving circles, those winding arcs, whether in one man's life or in that of an age, are mathematical, and that some in the world, or beyond the world, have foreknown the event and pricked upon the calendar the life-span of a Christ, a Buddha, a Napoleon: that every movement, in feeling or in thought, prepares in the dark by its own increasing clarity and confidence its own executioner. (*LE* 14)

The French general and emperor Napoleon Bonaparte (1769–1821) is an example for Phase 20, and he appears in the description of Phase 21 (see 112–17). In the AS, Christ is placed at Phase 22.

25 The dramatic poem *Paracelsus* (1835) by Robert Browning (1812–89) accounts Paracelsus' attempts to attain complete knowledge of human nature and fate through intellectual discipline, but he gains this knowledge only through the acceptance of love, embodied in the "Byzantine teacher" Aprile. Browning's *Paracelsus* bears slight resemblance to the historical Paracelsus (1493–1541), a Swiss physician and alchemist. On August 22, 1923, WBY wrote that GY was guided by a spirit voice to pull Browning from the shelf and turn to a passage from "Paracelsus" (*YVP* 3:185). See also YL 297, 298. The bildungsroman *Wilhelm Meister's Apprenticeship*, by Johann Wolfgang von Goethe (1749–1832), traces its eponymous hero's apprenticeships in bourgeois business and the theater (1796; trans. Thomas Carlyle, 2 vols., 1895; Edward O'Shea, "The 1920s Catalogue of W. B. Yeats's Library," *YA* 4 [1986], ed. Warwick Gould, 283). At the close of the novel, Wilhelm is presented with an account of his apprenticeship, signaling his initiation.

26 WBY and GY honeymooned at the Ashdown Forest Hotel, in East Sussex, England. They were in England—in Oxford, London, and Sussex (to which they returned to escape zeppelin raids)—before arriving in Ireland on March 9, 1918. In Ireland, they spent time in Dublin, the ancient monastic center Glendalough, and the neighboring valley Glenmalure, the latter two in Co. Wicklow. They also spent time in Galway, Coole, and Ballinamantane House on the Coole estate, as well as making brief visits elsewhere in the west. They moved into the cottage next to the castle at Ballylee, near Coole, on September 12, 1918 (see John Kelly, *A W. B. Yeats Chronology* [Basingstoke: Palgrave Macmillan, 2003], 195–200). They did not travel to Rosses Point, the seaside village north of Sligo that meant much to WBY and his family.

27 The Yeatses arrived in New York on January 22, 1920, for a four-month tour including stops in Toronto; Utah; Waco, Texas; Chicago; Pasadena, California; Portland, Oregon; and then a lengthy stay in New York.

28 In the AS of March 29, 1920, Dionertes communicates, "I do not really want script here—I prefer to use other methods—sleeps" (*YVP* 2:539). In an entry in a notebook of "sleeps," dated "28(?) March 1920," and made in Pasadena, WBY notes a "New Method": "George speaks while asleap." He continues: "Sees herself dead. Sees many sleapers as if floating in air. All in dark except for a little light round flowers left by living. They by help of this light smell the flowers. They only hear & see, when living think of them, as dead. They are dreaming. She insists that these sleapers are not yet spirits" (*YVP* 3:9). On May 28 (from Montréal), GY writes (and Dionertes interrupts):

> There was to be a new method. We were to read over sleep accounts & Dionertes would then develop the subject day by day (no no no I said I would write *in once* the entire subjective after life state
> Yes
> Script)
> We were told that he would describe without questions the after death state of subjective man. We were then to go on to subjective. But first there was to be one more sleep to get meaning of colours. (*YVP* 3:21)

For a summary of sleeps and of the Sleep and Dream Notebooks, see *YVP* 3:1–7.

The record of the sleep of September 29, 1920, recounts: "While he [Dionertes] was talking he was interrupted by George making a lapping sound. He said 'She dreams herself a Cat, & that she is lapping up something from the floor'. I said 'what is to be done' He said 'Pretend you are a dog' I could think of nothing better than to say 'Bow Wow' as one does to a child. To my surprise the Interpreter sprang away from me in great terror & lay panting for a long time after. I had spoken in an ordinary voice but Dionertes said I had been merely too loud. I woke George soon after, & she had a series of nightmares the whole night after in connectin [*sic*] with a large wolf" (*YVP* 3:49–50). See also *YVP* 3:51, 55–56, 76, 92. Such dreams also feature in the Robartes-Aherne fiction in *AVA* 202.

29 *YVP* substantiates this chronology. The twenty-eight embodiments appear in the AS on the evening of November 23, 1917, in a diagram composed of a circle of numbers from 1 to 28, and a listing of a first draft of the characteristics of the *Will* for the Table of the Four Faculties (*YVP* 1:115–16; see 71–73). This list speaks to the significance of GY's collaboration. Although a number of the terms were changed, the meaning of the descriptive characteristics remained consistent through *AVA* and *AVB*. After about three weeks, the Yeatses had established the basis of their theory of human personality and history, though the twenty-eight phases—their characteristics and who might be associated with each—continued to be a preoccupation for months to come. See especially *YVP* 1:115–16, and *MYV* 1:53–54. On the soul's judgment after death, see *YVP* 1:148–52. The "first symbolical map" refers to the diagram in the AS of June 5 (*YVP* 1:477), an early incarnation of the historical cones. See also *YVP* 3:60–61, 172; *AVA* 147; and 193.

The first volume of *Der Untergang des Abendlandes* by Oswald Spengler (1880–1936) was published in 1918, with a revision in 1922; the second volume appeared that same year. WBY's copies of both volumes of *The Decline of the West*, trans. Charles Francis Atkinson (London: George Allen & Unwin, [1926–29]; YL 1975 and 1975a), are heavily marked. In a letter of July 2, 1926, WBY wrote to Olivia Shakespear:

> By the way do get Spengler's *Decline of the West* and compare his general scheme with mine in "Dove or Swan." While his first volume was going through the press in 1918 I was getting the outline—and I think all the main diagrams of mine. There is exact correspondence in date after date. He was not translated till after my book was published. Had he been I could not have written. (*L* 716)

30 The famous dialogues of the Athenian philosopher Plato (427–c. 347 BCE), foundational texts for Western philosophy, typically feature conversations between Socrates and a student or others. In *Examination of Sir William Hamilton's Philosophy* (1865), the English philos-

opher and political economist John Stuart Mill (1806–73) attacked "intuitionist" philosophy in favor of rational principles. Mystics, from many religious traditions including Judaism, Hinduism, Buddhism, Christianity, and Islam, emphasize direct experience of the divine; the term also applies to initiates of esoteric religious practices.

The prophetic books of the English poet, printmaker, and artist William Blake (1757–1827), for which Blake supplied both mythopoeia and engravings, include *Tiriel* (c. 1789), *The Book of Thel* (c. 1789), *America: A Prophecy* (1793), *Europe: A Prophecy* (1793), *The Book of Urizen* (1794), *The Book of Ahania* (1795), *The Book of Los* (1795), *Milton: A Poem* (1804–10), and *Jerusalem: The Emanation of the Giant Albion* (1804–20). WBY owned facsimile editions of a number of these, including *The Book of Ahania* (YL 199), *Milton* (YL 206, 215), and *Jerusalem* (YL 214, 220a).

The Yeatses owned many books by Emanuel Swedenborg (1688–1772), the Swedish scientist, mystic, philosopher, and theologian; see YL 2036–40 and Edward O'Shea, "The 1920s Catalogue of W. B. Yeats's Library," *YA* 4 (1986), ed. Warwick Gould, 289. See also WBY's essay "Swedenborg, Mediums, and the Desolate Places" (written 1914, pub. 1920; *LE* 47–73). The Yeatses also owned numerous volumes by the German Christian mystic and theologian Jacob Boehme (1575–1624); see YL 234–39, O'Shea, "The 1920s Catalogue of W. B. Yeats's Library," 281. The "Hermetic Students" of the Golden Dawn were a group of occultists founded in London around 1888. WBY's printed invitation to join the group is dated March 7, 1890 (George Mills Harper, "From Zelator to Theoricus: Yeats's 'Link with the Invisible Degrees,'" *Yeats Studies* 1 [1971], 80, n4).

Cabbala, or Kabbalah, is a Jewish theosophical system of mystical teachings aimed at explaining the relationships between an eternal creator and a finite universe. The term "Cabbala" (variantly spelled, sometimes beginning with "Q") is also used in Christian and hermetic traditions, including the underlying system of such magical societies as the Golden Dawn. See, for instance, *The Kabbalah Unveiled* (1887; YL1292a), translated and edited by S. L. MacGregor Mathers.

31 Frustrators, a group of spirits who seek to thwart the inquiry of the AS or sleeps, make many appearances in the records of the Yeatses' sessions. Leo, linked later to Leo Africanus, is the most ill-willed, and his presence is noted in the first preserved AS: Thomas of Dorlowicz (the Control) notes, "Better not act by Leo ever but may give good information," and he adds "Malignant sometimes—not to be trusted in—never believe his prophecy" (*YVP* 1:56). See also *YVP* 2:137–39, 3:99–101; *MYV* 2:180–85; and *AVA* 196.

32 In a notebook entry headed "Oxford—Sleep of August 30. night—11 pm," GY records: "After Dionertes had been speaking for some time there was a bird's cry which he said was an Owl, & he made me keep

silent that he might listen but it did not come again. A little later the clocks began to strike 12; and he asked what sound that was. I told him & he again asked me to keep silent. When the last strike was finished he said 'Sounds like that are sometimes a great pleasure to us'" (*YVP* 3:41).

33 On January 15 [1922], WBY notes, "After long interruption from influenza there have been many short sleeps which I am not yet to write out." On May 2, GY notes, "I found out that when we were told not to write out the results of Sleeps it was frustration. Many sleeps have been wasted for we are not now trusted to write them out without going over it again" (*YVP* 3:104).

34 Sensory phenomena of various kinds—smells pleasant and foul, knocks, voices, other sounds, etc.—are a common component of séances and other mediumistic practices. For instance, WBY's early encounters with Leo Africanus involve voices (presumed not to be that of the medium), "Lights," "Touches," and "Sounds apart from voices" (see "The Manuscript of 'Leo Africanus,'" ed. Steve L. Adams and George Mills Harper, *YA* 1 [1982]: 3–47).

35 Hone identifies this village as Shillingford, on the Oxfordshire/Berkshire border (*W. B. Yeats, 1865–1939*, 2nd ed. [London: Macmillan, 1962], 336). The Yeatses rented a cottage in Shillingford from April to June 1921, after which they moved to Thame, also in Oxfordshire, where they stayed until September. Michael Butler Yeats was born in Thame on August 22.

36 As an instance of flashes of light and table blows, WBY writes on September 12 [1921], "Before W. M. [William Michael—later changed to Michael Butler] was born Dionertes once drew Georges attention on something I said, which might have started some morbid suggestion, by two loud blows on the table as it seemed, & once by a flash of light which she saw" (*YVP* 3:95). On whistling, see, for example, the entry for sleeps of September 26–28, 1920 (*YVP* 3:48), and that of December 4 [1920] (*YVP* 3:58).

37 In Note 44 (w. 1914) to *Visions and Beliefs in the West of Ireland* by Lady Gregory (1920), WBY writes: "The sudden filling of the air by a sweet odour is a common event of the séance room" (*LE* 288). Descriptions of smells are common in the notebooks of sleeps: see *YVP* 3:35, 51–52, 99, 104–5, 107. The Yeatses devoted some inquiry to determining the significance of these fragrances; see *YVP* 3:96–97. For an instance of the smell of roses, see *YVP* 3:95–96; see also WBY's note to 167; see also Appendix II, 283; and *FPS* 119–20. For the smell of Glastonbury thorn, see *YVP* 3:84–85. The ancient English town of Glastonbury in Somerset has been linked through legend to the hiding place of the Holy Grail and the tomb of Arthur and Guinevere. The Glastonbury thorn blooms at Christmas; according to legend, when Joseph of Arimathea arrived in Glastonbury, he thrust his staff into

the ground, which then flowered into the Glastonbury thorn. Michael Butler Yeats was born August 22, 1921.

38 Sutherland suggests that this poem is likely "Moving House" by T'ao Ch'ien (365–427) (Sutherland 621). Arthur Waley's translation of the poem appears in *A Hundred and Seventy Chinese Poems* (London: Constable, 1920; YL 2216).

39 "Knots" are discussed at length in the AS from November 22, 1917. The Control Thomas defines a "complex" as "any knot of hidden thought lying in the subconscious that originates in some passion or violent emotion." He distinguishes knots from sequences, noting that knots "should be untied" and that they "are the root of inaction & inarticulateness and incapacity for expression" (*YVP* 1:105). WBY develops this idea more fully in Book III, 164. See also *LE* 25–29 and *AVA* 193.

40 Guido Cavalcanti was an Italian poet associated with Dante. See also xxxiii and nn10 and 15 above.

41 Michael Butler Yeats (1921–2007), Irish politician and diplomat, was the son of WBY and GY.

42 On November 18, 1920, WBY writes in a notebook, "There has been much minor phenomena. In the boat's cabin coming from Ireland for instance there was a very strong antiseptic smell & in a short 'sleap' we were told that I would be much better next day which I was. There have been sweet fragrances from time [to time] & once after our return here a smell of burnt feathers. This was to warn me that Anne—'feathers'—would have a night mare unless we prevented it. George too—we were told I think in script—would have one" (*YVP* 3:53–54).

43 In an entry in a sleep notebook dated "March 28(?) 1920," WBY writes: "The day the Japanese gave me the old Japanese sword, the Japanese dined with us & after dinner I spoke to him of certain [of] our philosophic ideas which are the reverse of all Tolstoy—who had influenced him—commends. After he went away & while George was getting out script book of script of March 21, a voice said in clear loud tones 'quite right that is what I wanted'. The script repeated this & said what I heard was by 'direct voice'" (*YVP* 3:9). See also *YVP* 2:534. WBY received this ceremonial sword from Junzo Sato on March 20, 1920.

While better known for his fiction, Leo Nikolayevich Tolstoy (1828–1910) wrote such works of political and religious philosophy as *A Confession* (1882), *The Kingdom of God Is Within You* (1894), "On Anarchy" (1900), and *A Letter to a Hindoo* (1908).

44 On November 25 [1920], WBY writes in a notebook of sleeps, "Walking back from Bridges yesterday by the light of the moon George saw a very large bird in the sky. She said 'I first thought it was an aeroplane'. Dorothy Pound and I saw nothing" (*YVP* 3:56). In a postscript to his entry of January 11 [1921], WBY writes, "PS.

George saw the Black Eagle again a couple of weeks ago. Shortly after wards she found that there has been conception. Black Eagle = fourth Daimon" (*YVP* 3:65). WBY dictated an entry to GY on September 5 [1921], saying, "*N.B.* Asked about apparitions seen by Interpreter during William Michael's illness 2 days after birth. 6 formed. a man & woman of early 16th century; 2 scholars in costume of middle of 17th & 2 undefined figures" (*YVP* 3:97).

45 The Yeatses preserved thirty-six notebooks or bundles of AS and four substantial notebooks recording sleeps, along with other loose sheets and partial collections of both methods. See *YVP* 1:11 and 3:1. The Card File, consisting of 782 three-by-five-inch cards, represents a late stage in the Yeatses' synthesis of the AS, sleeps, and other materials, assembled toward the drafting of *A Vision*. See *YVP* 3:222–430.

46 In *Packet*, the date is given as 1925 (24); WBY might have been thinking of Oswald Spengler's essay "The Downfall of Western Civilization," translated from German by Kenneth Burke, appearing in installments in the November 1924 (361–78), December 1924 (482–504), and January 1925 (9–26) issues of *The Dial*. On May 13, 1925, WBY wrote to Edmund Dulac, "A German called Oswald Spengler has lit on a number of the same ideas as those in my book. The American *Dial* has just published a long essay by him—the introduction to his book now being translated which might have been a chapter of 'A Vision'. He applies the fundamental thought to things outside my knowledge, but his thought & mine differ in nothing. It seems that the thought came to him suddenly & with great excitement" (*CL InteLex* 4728). On July 30, 1926, WBY wrote to William Force Stead that Spengler's book "has filled me with astonishment. [. . .] there are exact thoughts and dates that I recorded in Galway in 1918 when it was passing through the press in Germany. [. . .] I have reached it all from a different point of view but the result is the same. Coincidence is impossible" (*CL InteLex* 4904).

47 Spengler writes that "The Classical sculptor had fashioned the eyes as blind, but now the pupils are bored, the eye, unnaturally enlarged, looks into the space that in Attic art it had not acknowledged as existing" (1:329; see also 1:216 and 1:264). Compare with 200 and *AVA* 156. Concerning portrait heads on stock bodies, Spengler claims, "All the Roman portrait statues, male and female, go back for posture and mien to a very few Hellenic types; those copied more or less true to style, served for torsos, while the heads were executed as 'likenesses' by simple craftsmen who possessed the knack" (1:295). Compare with 201 and *AVA* 156–57. Spengler describes "the portraits of the Constantinian age, with their fixed stare into the infinite" (1:306; see also 1:329). Compare with 200, 204 and *AVA* 157, 159.

48 Taken from "To Ireland in the Coming Times" (*Poems* 46–47), which first appeared in *The Countess Kathleen and Various Legends and*

Lyrics (London, 1892; Boston and London, 1892); these lines were among several that were revised considerably over time.

49 On the setting copy of *Packet*, WBY had added direction to include a note specifying "The first edition published by Werner Laurie in 1925," but this note was not incorporated. While these sections received significantly less revision than other sections after their publication in *AVA-Laurie*, they are not reproduced "without change." Most notably, WBY eliminated several pages from *AVA* about his contemporary moment and the near future from the end of the text of "Dove or Swan" before publishing *AVB*, leaving in their place a row of dots (see 218) and adding a new section called "The End of the Cycle" (219–20). See *AVA* 174–78 and *AVA* 340–52.

50 WBY refers to the framing fiction of *AVA*, lvii–12.

51 WBY refers here to his copy of *The Works of George Berkeley* (1784; YL 160). The Anglo-Irish philosopher Berkeley (1685–1753) was of great importance to WBY as he worked on *AVB* (see especially 52 and 140n); see also "Bishop Berkeley" (*LE* 103–112). The playwright and poet Lennox Robinson (1886–1958) was one of WBY's collaborators at the Abbey Theatre and a close friend of both WBY and GY.

52 Saddlemyer notes that GY had studied *Principles of Physiological Psychology* by the German psychologist Wilhelm Wundt (1832–1920), "with his emphasis on introspection in investigating the immediate experiences of consciousness and his concept of the 'folk soul'" (44, and see 672 n7). GY's knowledge of the German philosopher Georg Wilhelm Friedrich Hegel (1770–1831) dates from at least 1913 (Saddlemyer 39); WBY wrote to Olivia Shakespear in 1927 that he had taken up reading Hegel only to find the system there already: "I write verse & read Hegel & the more I read I am but the more convinced that those invisible persons knew all" (June 23, 1927, *CL InteLex* 5008; see YL 1589–94). WBY had known the translations of the English Neoplatonist Thomas Taylor (1758–1835) for many years. Taylor produced the first complete translations of Plato and Aristotle, as well as translations of the Orphic fragments, Neoplatonic philosophers such as Porphyry and Proclus, and other philosophers; see *Thomas Taylor the Platonist: Selected Writings*, ed. Kathleen Raine and George Mills Harper (Princeton: Princeton University Press, 1969). GY purchased her first copy of Thomas Taylor's translation of Plotinus also in 1913 and bought another the following year (Saddlemyer 45; YL 1595, 1595A). On her study of Pico, whose eccentric defenses of Cabbalistic thought were very influential on Renaissance humanism, see Saddlemyer 60, 121, and *MYV* 1:41–42 and 273 n5; and see YL 1595, 1567.

53 On November 5, 1928, WBY wrote to Stephen MacKenna, "I have read all your translations from Plotinus, some of them several times

and want more," and asking for "translations from the Irish" for the Cuala Press.

54 WBY enjoyed crime fiction, westerns, and other light reading: see a letter to GY on February 25, 1928, mentioning a trip to the library for "more base fiction" (*LWBY/GY* 191).

55 The Greek Pre-Socratic philosopher Empedocles (495–435 BCE) is known for his identification of four elements in nature (earth, air, fire, and water), and his belief that existence is shaped by a continual struggle between Love and Strife. In *On Nature*, when Strife reaches the depths of the central point (the vortex) around which the cosmos turns, Love appears in the middle of the whirl. Love unites what Strife had divided, thereby creating mortal beings.

56 This illness began in October 1927. To escape the Irish winter, WBY and GY traveled to Spain—to Gibraltar, Algeciras, and Seville—and then by late November, to Cannes. Concerning WBY's illness and the Yeatses' ensuing travel, see Foster 2:353–56.

57 Anne Butler Yeats (1919–2001), daughter of WBY and GY, was a painter and set designer.

58 *Daimon* is one of the more confusing Yeatsian terms, whose meaning changed over time. In both versions of *A Vision*, *Daimon* refers basically to two concepts: that of an anti-self, i.e., a being opposite to its human counterpart (as in the poem "Ego Dominus Tuus" [*Poems* 161–63]); and that of a greater self, akin to the spirit intermediary between the gods and men of Plato as explained by Proclus (*The Six Books of Proclus, The Platonic Successor, on the Theology of Plato*, trans. Thomas Taylor [2 vols.; London: A. J. Valpy, 1816], Chap. 43, 260–65). Not only individual people but "Nations, cultures, schools of thought may have their *Daimons*" (209).

The *Daimon* derives from classical and occult texts and traditions as well as the AS. Plato discusses daimons as wise spirits in *Cratylus* (397e), in terms of the soul in *Phaedo*, and with reference to inspiration for art in *Ion* (cf. *UP* 1:399). Other influential Platonic ideas include the spirit intermediaries in *Symposium*, a third term of divinity within humanity in *Timaeus*, and the myth of souls and their chosen genii in *Republic* 10. See also the fourth tractate of the third *Ennead* of Plotinus; Plutarch's essay "On the Genius of Socrates" (*LE* 65–66, 269; YL 1598); Heraclitus's fragment 121 and Empedocles's *Purifications* v. 369 ff. (*LE* 11–12, 28–29; see also Burnet, *Early Greek Philosophy* 141, 233–34, 270); the work of various Neoplatonists (see *LE* 67–68); and such later figures as Cornelius Agrippa (*LE* 24), Blake (Blake 1), Henry More (*LE* 22), and Golden Dawn teachings. See also *AVA* 239 n62.

In *AVA*, first, the *Daimon* is opposite to her human counterpart (including in gender); see 24–25. Second, the *Daimon* is a sort of guardian spirit; see 182. The concept of the *Ghostly Self* is distinct from the *Daimon*; see 183. In *AVB*, however, as Neil Mann notes, WBY's thinking had altered: by 1937, "he generally came to see the *Ghostly Self* in terms of the 'discarnate *Daimon*'" ("The *Thirteenth Cone*," Mann et al., 189). To some degree, the confusing quality of this concept derives from the fact that, even when composing *AVB*, WBY was attempting to describe a system he did not fully understand.

59 This sentence and the sentence preceding it do not appear in *Packet*.

60 Rather than "partly accepting and partly rejecting," the text in *Packet* reads simply "rejecting"; WBY added this emendation in the setting copy. He repeats this reference to Swedenborg on 165. The quotation, attributed to Orpheus, the legendary Greek musician and poet, is taken from *Three Books of Occult Philosophy* (w. 1510; Book 3, Chap. 41, 479–80) by the German physician, theologian, and occultist Heinrich Cornelius Agrippa von Nettesheim (1486–1535). WBY also gives this quotation in "Swedenborg, Mediums, and Desolate Places" (*LE* 68), and uses it as the source of the title for Book IV of *AVA* (179). GY studied Agrippa seriously beginning in 1913; see YL 24; Saddlemyer 60 and 679 n11; NLI 40,568/2.

In *Packet*, this sentence includes further phrasing, struck through on the setting copy and so omitted: ". . . dreams'; that John Philoponus thinks that, if they show in recognisable form, that form is but as frozen water that keeps the shape after the jug is broken; and that they are much called in legend 'The Shape-changers'" (30).

61 WBY added this note on the setting copy, dating it "1931."

62 In *Packet*, the number given is "four" (31). As Connie K. Hood notes, much of the material that would become Book II originated in drafts of Book I, and WBY did not separate the books until after 1932 ("Remaking," 48–50).

63 WBY misattributes the six-winged angels to Daniel rather than Isaiah (6:1–2), possibly conflating it with the vision in Daniel 7:1–12.

The Greek philosopher, mathematician, and mystic Pythagoras of Samos (6th cent. BCE) is known through the writings of others, including Plato, Aristotle, Proclus, and Porphyry. Pythagoras came to be credited with the Pythagorean theorem; an understanding of relationships of musical notes and mathematical equations; and the mystical symbol of the "tetractys," a triangular figure of ten dots in four rows with one, two, three, and four dots in each row (symbolizing key mystical Pythagorean ideas, with the number ten showing unity of a higher order). Both Freemasonry and Rosicrucianism claim connections to the Pythagorean Brotherhood, the esoteric Order established by his followers. Cf. "The Statues" (*Poems* 344–45).

Chap. 11 of S. L. MacGregor Mathers's translation of *The Kabbalah Unveiled (Kabbala Denudata)* (London: George Redway, 1887), entitled "Concerning the Beard of Macroprosopus in General," describes the thirteen forms of "that most glorious supernal beard of the Holy Ancient One, the concealed of all" (134–42). GY owned a copy (YL 1292).

Dr. John Dee (1527–1608), a mathematician, geographer, and alchemist, as well as advisor to Queen Elizabeth, explored the world of magic and divination. In collaboration with Edward Kelley, Dee received angelic communications in the Enochian language that were used by later occultists, especially the Hermetic Order of the Golden Dawn. See also 51; *FPS* 95–99; and *AVA* lix.

In a letter of September 9, 1933, to an unidentified correspondent who had inquired about the 1925 version of *A Vision*, WBY explains "scrying": "The word 'scrying' is old English for such acts of clairvoyance as looking in a crystal" (*CL InteLex* 5938).

William Law (1686–1761) was a great promoter of the work of Jacob Boehme (see n30 above) in the English-speaking world. WBY refers to *The Works of Jacob Behmen, the Teutonic Theosopher . . . left by the Rev. William Law* (London: Joseph Richardson, 1763; YL 239). The "diagrams" are thirteen elaborate pen and ink drawings that appear at the back. According to the "Advertisement," "The Figures annexed to this Volume, were left by the Reverend Mr. *Law*, and by him intended for Publication. They contain an Illustration of the deep Principles of *Jacob Behmen*, in which the *Mysteries* of *Nature* and *Grace* are unfolded."

64 Concerning the Florentine architect, painter and sculptor Michelangelo di Lodovico Buonarroti Simoni (1475–1564), see also 21 and 211–13. Henry Crabb Robinson, a contemporary of William Blake, wrote about his visits to the poet in a diary, from which Yeats and Ellis quote the "entire reference to Blake" in *WWB* 1:142–50. Robinson notes Blake's opinions: "Jacob Boehmen was spoken of as a divinely inspired man. Blake praised, too, the figures in Law's translation as being very beautiful. Michael Angelo could not have done better" (*WWB* 1:144; *The Diary, Reminiscences, and Correspondence of Henry Crabb Robinson*, ed. Thomas Sadler, 2nd ed. [London: Macmillan, 1869], 2:305).

La Divina Commedia, by Florentine poet Dante Alighieri (1265–1321), traces a path through Hell and Purgatory into Heaven. For the first two parts of the journey, Dante is guided by Virgil, but as that classical Roman poet is unable to enter the Christian heaven, Dante's ideal beloved Beatrice Portinari (1266–90)—with whom Dante says he fell in love at first sight at age nine—guides him through the third section of the poem.

65 On May 22 [1936], WBY wrote to Dorothy Wellesley about a letter he sent to Laura Riding, noting "that poets were good liars who never forgot that the Muses were women who liked the embrace of gay warty lads" (*L* 857). Concerning the making of porcelain, Sutherland notes a correspondence with Mr. Hin-Cheung Lovell, Assistant Curator of Chinese Art at the Freer Gallery of Art of the

Smithsonian Institution, who writes that "this statement is blatantly untrue in the context of Chinese ceramics" (Letter of June 7, 1973, qtd. in Sutherland, 642). Ludwig van Beethoven's final complete symphony, Symphony No. 9 in D minor, Op. 125, was completed in 1824.

The source for virginity renewing itself like the moon is ultimately Giovanni Boccaccio's *Decameron* and the story of Alatiel, protagonist of the seventh story of the second day, who sleeps with nine men but is able on her wedding night to convince her husband of her virginity. The story concludes: "E per ciò si disse: 'Bocca basciata non perdre ventura, anzi rinnuova come fa la luna'" (ed. Vittore Branca [Torino: Einaudi, 1956], 164). In the not particularly literal translation of J. M. Rigg, "wherefore 'twas said: 'Mouth, for kisses, was never the worse: like as the moon reneweth her course" (London: A. H. Bullen, 1903; YL 231). The anecdote was used for the title of a painting by Dante Gabriel Rossetti, *Bocca Baciata* (1859), and is quoted by Shelley in *Peter Bell III* (lines 228–29) and by Verdi in *Falstaff*. See Robin Barrow, "An Identification in Yeats's *A Vision* (B)," *Notes and Queries* June 2004: 162–63; and Massimo Bacigalupo, "Yeats, Boccaccio, and Leopardi," *Notes and Queries* December 2005: 499–500. See also *AVA* 62 and 104 in this edition.

66 In *Milton* (1804), William Blake writes:

> Every Time less than a pulsation of the artery
> Is equal in its period & value to Six Thousand Years.
> For in this Period the Poets Work is Done: and all the Great
> Events of Time start forth & are conceivd in such a Period
> Within a Moment: a Pulsation of the Artery.
> (*Milton*, plates 28 & 29; Blake, 16–27)

67 The artistic style of geometric abstraction practiced by Wyndham Lewis was influenced by Cubism and by the philosophy of Friedrich Nietzsche and Henri Bergson. The works of the Romanian-born sculptor Constantin Brancusi (1876–1957) often have a curvilinear quality and smooth contours. Works that could be described as "ovoid" include *Prometheus* (1911) and *The Newborn* (1915), and various versions of *Sleeping Muse* (1909–10) and *Mademoiselle Pogany* (1912ff.).

In a passage from "Dove or Swan" in *AVA* that was eliminated in *AVB*, WBY describes the modern period in art and letters, similarly examining the works of Lewis and Brancusi together (174). Yeats's thinking about Brancusi here may draw from Ezra Pound's "Brancusi" (1921, *Literary Essays of Ezra Pound*, ed. T. S. Eliot [Norfolk, Conn.: New Directions, 1954]), esp. 442–43.

68 This passage is significantly reworked from its appearance in *Packet*:

> Some will ask if I believe all that this book contains, and I will not know how to answer. Does the word belief, used as they will use it, belong to our age, can I think of the world as there and I here judging it? I will never think any thoughts but these, or some modification or extension of these; when I write prose or verse they must be somewhere present though not it may be in the words; they must affect my judgment of friends and of events; but then there are many symbolisms and none exactly resembles mine. What Leopardi in Ezra Pound's translation calls that "concord" wherein "the arcane spirit of the whole mankind turns hardy pilot"—how much better it would be without that word "hardy" which slackens speed and adds nothing—persuades me that he has best imagined reality who has best imagined justice. (32–33)

This section was highly revised at various stages of composition.

69 WBY became a member of the Seanad Éireann, the upper house of the Oireachtas (the Senate and Houses of Parliament, respectively), in late 1922; he decided in late 1928 not to accept an offer to return after recuperation from illness. On July 30 [1928], WBY wrote to Lady Gregory, "Probably I have made my last Senate appearance. A little speech of three sentences, was followed by a minute of great pain & that comforts me for I find I could have been re-elected & that would have been 360 a year for nine years and I hate taking all that money from my family. Personally I gain greatly by the change. I have arranged two interviews & other things to fight the censor-ship so I am still in public life & shall be till I get to Rapallo. Glenavy stopped me coming out of the Senate the other day to say 'the Senate will re-elect you whenever you like'. He meant they would co-opt me if I wished when there was a vacancy. I doubt it, but am pleased that he should think so" (*CL InteLex* 5137).

By contrast, WBY wrote to Pound on July 29, 1923, "My work at the Senate does not interfear [*sic*] as it is mainly in the afternoon—& it is just sufficiently exciting to fill the afternoon pleasantly. We are beginning to develop a little oratory & oratory too of a structured eighteenth century kind. The kind being probably because dread of bombs & bullets has, till very lately, kept us from admitting to the strangers gallery 20th century impatience & ignorance" (*CL InteLex* 4352).

70 Thomas Hood's ballad "The Dream of Eugene Aram" (1831) tells the story of teacher and philologist Eugene Aram (1704–59) and his arrest for the murder of Daniel Clark. See also *IDM* 102.

71 The ancient Greek legend of Oedipus, son of Laius and Jocasta, king and queen of Thebes, who is fated to commit patricide and incest, is retold in Sophocles's three Theban plays: *Antigone*, *Oedipus Tyrannus*,

and *Oedipus at Colonus.* WBY translated the latter two in 1926 and 1927 (published 1928 and 1934); *Plays* 369–400, 401–441. The "four sacred things" are "the basin of brass, the hollow pear-tree, the marble tomb, the stone from Thoricus" (*Plays* 439). For earth "riven not by pain but by love," see *Plays* 440. On this passage, see Arkins 124–41.

72 The Sphinx is a mythological monster with a human (female) head and body of a lion. She terrorized the city of Thebes, posing riddles and then killing those who could not answer them; Oedipus answers the riddle, slays her, and rescues the city.

Jonathan Swift's prose satire *Gulliver's Travels into Several Remote Nations of the World* (1726, 1735) follows its titular character's voyage through fictional nations and eviction from the country of the Houyhnhnms, figures of ideal rationale and virtue. On returning to England, Gulliver is horrified at Britain's vice and lack of reason. WBY owned two separate editions of this work, one edited and inscribed by Harold Williams (London: First Edition Club, 1926; YL 2041), and another edited and inscribed by John Hayward (London: Nonesuch Press, 1934; YL 2042). He additionally owned the 17-volume *Works of the Rev. Dr. Jonathan Swift, Dean of St. Patrick's Dublin*, ed. Thomas Sheridan (London: Printed for W. Strahan, B. Collins and others, 1784; YL 2043).

Charles Baudelaire's *Les Fleurs du mal* (1855, 1857) ruminates on the limitations of modern culture. WBY owned this text in a French edition by Bibliotheca Mundi (Leipzig: Insel-Verlag, n.d.; YL 129).

73 According to *Oedipus Tyrannus*, when Oedipus blinds and exiles himself, his daughter Antigone accompanies him out of Thebes. William Shakespeare's *King Lear* (1604–5) opens with an aging Lear dividing his kingdom among his three daughters, according to their professed affection for him. Cordelia is disinherited for professing to love her father according to her duty, but later in the play she receives him when his other daughters have turned him out and he has gone mad.

74 Located on the southwestern spur of Mount Parnassus, Delphi housed the Delphic oracle and a major site of worship of the god Apollo. The *omphalos* at Delphi was said to be the navel, or center, of the world. Hippeios Colonus, or Colonus of the Horses, is where Oedipus is traditionally buried; it is a deme of Athens and associated with the god Poseidon, who created horses.

75 Cruachan, in Co. Roscommon, Ireland, is the traditional capital of the ancient dynasties of Connacht. A ringfort or *rath* there is identified as the seat of Medb (Maeve) and Ailill, queen and king of the Connachta. Medb features prominently in the Ulster Cycle of mythological stories.

Crickmaa (Cnoc Meadha or Knockmaa) is a hill near Tuam in Co. Galway. It is traditionally the home of King Finvarra of the Sidhe. In "The Galway Plains" (1903), WBY describes a visit there and the folk association of the place with the Sidhe (*EE* 156). Cnoc Meadha is also mentioned in the story "The Crucifixion of the Outcast," in *The Secret Rose* (*Myth1* 152, *Myth2* 102), there spelled Cruachmaa. In GY's copy of *A Vision* (1937; YL 2434), "Crickmaa" is changed to "Cruchmaa."

Anthony Raftery (Antoine Ó Raifteirí, c. 1748–1835) was an Irish-language oral poet who is often said to be the last of the Irish bards. He made a long poem called "Seanchus (nó Caisimirt) na Sgeiche" "The History of (or, Dispute with) the Bush," which includes a curse on a bush for not keeping him dry in a rainstorm; the bush answers back with an entire history of Ireland. See the version collected by Douglas Hyde (*Abhráin atá leagtha ar an Reachtúireor, Songs ascribed to Raftery: being the fifth chapter of the Songs of Connacht*, collected, edited and translated by Douglas Hyde [An Craoibhín Aoibhínn] [Baile Átha Cliath: Gill, 1903], 284–321).

76 WBY quotes from the English translation of "The Life of Epaminondas" in Plutarch's *Lives of the Noble Grecians and Romans.* The Yeatses owned a copy of Thomas North's elegant translation (8 vols.; Stratford-upon-Avon: Basil Blackwell for the Shakespeare Head Press, 1928; 8:19; YL 1597). "Wren boys" hunt a nonexistent wren on St. Stephen's Day (December 26) in a folk custom commonly practiced in Ireland and elsewhere. The footnote in *Packet* lacks this note's final sentence, which was added in WBY's hand on the setting copy (36).

77 St. Catherine of Genoa, Caterinetta Fieschi Adorno (1447–1510), became patron saint of Genoa for her charitable work, her intense experiences of the saving presence of God, and her penances. For Michelangelo, see n64 above.

78 Pound published "The Return" as one of "Two Poems" in *English Review* 11:3 (June 1912), 343–44; and in October of that same year in his poetic volume *Ripostes* (London: Stephen Swift, 1912). The poem also appears in *Personae* (74), which collection WBY described in November 1928 as "a great excitement to me" (*L* 748). In his introduction to *OBMV*, WBY quotes the poem through line 14 (*LE* 193–94). As printed in *A Vision* (1937), this poem includes small differences from the text of *Personae*; see Table 3.

Stories of Michael Robartes and His Friends

1 The magus Michael Robartes, invented for the stories "Rosa Alchemica" (1896), "The Tables of the Law" (1896), and "The Adoration of the Magi" (1897), was also used as a named speaker of three poems in *The Wind Among the Reeds* (1899). For historical sources for this character, see *Myth2* 367–68 n1. Robartes and his counterpart Owen Aherne were revived in 1917 and 1918 (with a brother, John, added for Aherne), and they appear in poems and notes to the volumes *The*

Wild Swans at Coole (1916, 1919) and *Michael Robartes and the Dancer* (1921). As WBY explains in the Preface to *The Wild Swans at Coole*, "Michael Robartes and John Aherne . . . are characters in some stories I wrote years ago, who have once again become a part of the phantasmagoria through which I can alone express my convictions about the world" (*VP* 852; see also *VP* 821). The two versions of *A Vision* adopt different fictions involving these characters to explain the provenance of the system (and indeed, the genetic materials include early attempts to write the book itself as a dialogue between Robartes and Aherne [see *YVP* 4]). See *AVA* 221–22 n31.

This section follows *Stories of Michael Robartes and his Friends: An Extract from a Record Made by his Pupils: And a Play in Prose by W. B. Yeats* (Dublin: Cuala, 1931), a copy of which was used as the setting copy. For details, see Editors' Introduction, xxxvi–xxxix. A complete list of changes appears in Hood, "Remaking," 47–48; we note here only the most significant.

2 The characters Huddon, Duddon, and Daniel O'Leary occur (as "Hudden and Dudden and Donald O'Nery") in the tale "Donald and his Neighbours," in *The Royal Hibernian Tales* (Dublin: C. M. Warren, n.d.), included in WBY's edition of *Fairy and Folk Tales of the Irish Peasantry* (London: Walter Scott, 1888). They are mentioned in "Tom The Lunatic" from the 1931 collection *Words For Music Perhaps* (*Poems* 273). In *Stories,* the last line reads "But how they mock us burning out" ([viii]).

3 Prince Albert Road in the Regent's Park area of London is an expensive and exclusive location. The London home of John B. Yeats, 23 Fitzroy Road, to which WBY's family moved when he was two years old, was several blocks from Albert Road. In 1887, WBY took lodgings at 6 Berkley Road, Regent's Park. Primrose Hill, a prominent landmark across Albert Road from Regent's Park, was prophesied by the Yorkshire soothsayer Mother Shipton to become the center of London one day (Augustus Hare, *Walks in London*, 6th rev. ed. [London: George Allen, 1896], 2:112). Primrose Hill is also the site of Blake's vision of the Spiritual Sun (*WWB* 1:144).

4 Owen Aherne, like his friend Michael Robartes, is a character returned to and refined over the course of years. See n1 above.

5 The world egg occurs in a number of religious and mythological traditions; see, for example, the summary by Madame Blavatsky in *The Secret Doctrine* 1:359–68. See *AVA* lxiv, 142, and 229 n65. See also Giorgio Melchiori, *The Whole Mystery of Art: Pattern into Poetry in the Work of W. B. Yeats* (London: Routledge and Kegan Paul, 1960), 164–99; and Raine, *Yeats the Initiate* (Montrath, Ireland: Dolmen Press; London: George Allen & Unwin, 1986), 111–48.

6 Shakespeare's *Romeo and Juliet* is frequently staged in London as elsewhere.

7 Realism as a theatrical movement involves the adoption of stylistic and dramatical conventions aimed at bringing a natural representation of real life to texts and performances. The movement, to which WBY was opposed, is associated with playwrights such as Henrik Ibsen (1828–1906) and Anton Chekhov (1860–1904), and practitioners such as Constantin Stanislavski (1863–1938).

8 The social-realist plays of the Norwegian dramatist Henrik Ibsen explore the emotional currents that lie behind the façades of everyday life. They are unrelenting in their exposition and were often scandalous. William Archer (1856–1924) was a Scottish drama critic and editor who translated Ibsen's plays into English. WBY refers to his translations in the introduction to *OBMV* (*LE* 185).

9 Denise has named herself after the writer of the play *Axël* (1890) by the French symbolist writer Jean-Marie-Mathias-Philippe-Auguste, comte de Villiers de l'Isle-Adam (1838–89). WBY was fond of this play; he often cited passages from it and wrote an introduction to a fine-press edition published in 1925, designed and decorated by his friend the poet T. Sturge Moore (1870–1944) (Wade 275; introduction *P&I* 156–58).

10 The Café Royal was a restaurant and meeting place on 68 Regent Street in London's Piccadilly. It was a place where the fashionable and the intellectual gathered, and famous patrons included Oscar Wilde and Aleister Crowley. It closed in 2008.

11 See the story "Rosa Alchemica" about this episode (*Myth1* 267–92; *Myth2* 177–91; and *The Secret Rose, Stories by W. B. Yeats: A Variorum Edition*, ed. Warwick Gould, Phillip L. Marcus, and Michael J. Sidnell, 2nd ed. [London: Macmillan, 1992], 126–50).

12 Judith, an apocryphal book present in the Septuagint and both Roman Catholic and Eastern Orthodox Old Testaments, tells the story of the widow Judith, who ingratiates herself with the enemy general Holofernes before finally beheading him, thus defeating the Assyrian forces and saving Israel from threat.

13 The fictions of the ballet-dancer, the "fiery handsome girl of the poorer classes" (*AVA* lix), and this book, embedded in an essay by Owen Aherne, form the introduction to *AVA* (lvii–lxiv). The title of the book, meaning "The Mirror of Angels and Men," was printed in incorrect Latin in *AVA* (l, lix). In correspondence, Frank Pearce Sturm pointed out to WBY that he could not get away with the egregious error, which was duly corrected for *AVB*. Giraldus has several possible historical antecedents, including Giraldus Cambrensis (Gerald de Barry), a Cambro-Norman historian who wrote about Ireland in the twelfth century; Gerard of Cremona (1114–87), a translator from Arabic into Latin and a scholar of Arabic science; and Lilio Gregorio Giraldus of Ferrara (1479–1552), a Latin poet, philosopher, and scholar, who was a friend of Pico della Mirandola and other prominent humanists

(see Kathleen Raine, *Yeats the Initiate*, 408–30). Cracow was a center of printing in the early sixteenth century. Dee and Kelley (see 322–23 n63 above) had traveled there in 1584 and again in 1585.

14 A correction in the Coole Proofs (BL Add. 55893) adds a note pointing the reader to the engraving of "The Great Wheel" (see 48); this note appears in the 1962 edition.

15 The French illustrator, composer, and writer Edmund Dulac (1882–1953) made the portrait of Giraldus as well as "The Great Wheel" diagram (48) and the small illustration of a unicorn (47). Dulac, one of the most well-known illustrators of the day, collaborated with WBY on various projects, including designing masks, costumes, makeup, and sets for theatrical productions, as well as composing music for the stage and radio.

On January 10, 1918, soon after deciding to publish the results of the AS using the fictions of Giraldus and the mysterious Judwali tribe, WBY wrote Dulac, "Every evening the Speculum of Gyraldus becomes more imposing. I am more and more astonished at the profundity of that learned author and at the neglect into which he has fallen, a neglect only comparable to that which has covered with the moss of oblivion the even more profound work of Kusta iben Luka of Bagdad, whose honour remains alone in the obscure sect of the Jadwalis" (*CL InteLex* 3388). In a letter dated February 15, 1918, Dulac sent WBY a sketch of the portrait, which WBY thought "a masterpiece" (*CL InteLex* 3411).

The portrait, like the book, took much longer than anticipated to complete. Although WBY had sent "remainder of Speculum" to Dulac in January 1919, other work (and many events) seem to have taken precedence for both artist and writer. On July 17, 1923, with the book nearly finished, WBY wrote to Sturge Moore that he was "very anxious to have a talk with you about the big design for the philosophy book" (*LTSM* 47–48). A week later, though, on July 24, Dulac wrote saying that he had "done a sketch in pencil of the portrait of Gyraldus by an unknown artist of the early sixteenth century" and asking whether the date was right and if there were "Any device to be incorporated?" (*LWBY* 439). WBY wrote back that "The date is nothing; if you want early sixteenth century let it be 1524 or any date you please. I have not thought of any particular device. He would certainly be an astrologer & a mathematician & this is about all I know" (*CL InteLex* 4602). On August 18, WBY had to withdraw his offer to Moore: "I find that Dulac has actually begun designs for my philosophy or rather practically finished a portrait of Giraldus as frontispiece. He offered some time ago but I had not taken him seriously as I know how busy he is. He says he wants to do also the big diagram to keep the two in harmony. If he does so I shall ask you to do something else for me instead" (*LTSM* 49). Dulac did send a sketch on September 30, 1923, writing, "Here is the best I can do with Gyraldus. It is a little 'early' in style, but I think it better suited to a book of that kind than the 'Durer' manner. One can argue that Mr Gyraldus did not go to a first class artist as otherwise the book would be known" (*LWBY* 439).

16 On October 24, 1924, Frank Pearce Sturm wrote to WBY, "I cannot trace Gyraldus. He is not Giraldus Cambrensis, but may be Gerard (or Gerald) of Cremona, who gave his life & great wealth to translation and had a go at everything from Aristotle to Kusta ben Luki. His passion was the Almagest, which he translated into what then passed for Latin in 1175" (*FPS* 86). Richard Taylor suggests that WBY's mention of "Bologna" may have been an erroneous substitution for "Cremona" (*FPS* 58). Alternately, WBY may refer to the Italian Carmelite theologian Gerardo di Bologna (d. 1317). See n13.

17 WBY may borrow this lamp from *Axël* by Villiers de l'Isle Adam. In the third act, Axël says "I know that lamp, it was burning before Solomon" (as quoted in *LE* 33). Other possible sources are accounts of finding the body of Father Christian Rosenkreuz, which, according to WBY in an early essay, describe his body being buried surrounded by "inextinguishable magical lamps" (*EE* 144).

18 In his *Critique of Pure Reason* (1781, 1787), one of the major works of modern Western philosophy, the German philosopher Immanuel Kant (1724–1804) asserts four antinomies of reason, or countering claims about the nature of reality that have equal validity.

19 *Stories* contains a variation here: ". . . or, as I prefer; thesis, there is no end. I cry out 'My love will never end'" (9).

20 The Church of the Holy Sepulcher, in the old walled city of Jerusalem, contains the place venerated as Jesus' tomb; it is located on the site of what many Christians believe to be Golgotha (or Calvary), the hill where Jesus was crucified.

21 Called Bacleones (or perhaps Badeones, i.e., Bedouins) in an early manuscript (*YVP* 4:122), this fictitious group may get its name from Sir Edward Denison Ross (1871–1940), an Orientalist and linguist. Ross may have invented the slightly incorrect Arabic term when WBY approached him for help with the "fable"; see S. B. Bushrui, "Yeats's Arabic Interests," in A. Norman Jeffares and K. G. W. Cross, eds., *In Excited Reverie: A Centenary Tribute to William Butler Yeats* (London: Macmillan, 1965), 295–97.

22 Thomas Edward Lawrence (1888–1955), also known as Lawrence of Arabia, was an archaeologist and British army officer renowned for his role during the Arab Revolt against the Ottoman Empire (1916–18). The Yeatses owned a copy of his autobiographical account, *Seven Pillars of Wisdom* (London: Jonathan Cape, 1935; YL 1094). In 1932, WBY nominated him for membership in the Irish Academy of Letters.

23 *Stories* lacks this interruption. Instead, after Denise declares her plan to tell her story, the text reads, "Her story was never told; for at that moment Aherne ushered in a pale slight woman . . ." (11).

24 *Stories* reads: "We will call them John Bond and Mary Bell from the characters in a doggerel of Blake's. For reasons which will become apparent when you have heard their story you must not know their true names" (11). As this variant indicates, the names of John Bond and Mary Bell are alterations from the names of characters in two poems in Blake's Pickering Manuscript, "Long John Brown & Little Mary Bell" and "William Bond" (whose beloved is Mary Green), Blake 496–98.

25 Denise's story, beginning here and continuing through 32, is not included in *Stories.* As Wayne K. Chapman notes, this episode was suppressed until WBY "was well into the correction of proof copy for *A Vision* and motivated by a desire to entertain and perhaps shock Dorothy Wellesley." He cites a letter written by WBY to Wellesley on July 26, 1936, "To-morrow I write a story to be added to the Michael Robartes series (a prelude to *A Vision* which I am now revising in proof). It is an almost exact transcript from fact. I have for years been creating a group of strange disorderly people on whom Michael Robartes confers the wisdom of the east" (*L* 859; "Denise's Story: W. B. Yeats, Dorothy Wellesley, and the Remaking of 'Stories of Michael Robartes and His Friends: An Extract from a Record Made by His Pupils,'" *New Hibernia Review / Iris Éireannach Nua* [Earrach/Spring 2013], 134–38; see also "Remaking," 47). Chapman provides transcription of these manuscript leaves (NLI 30,390 and 13,593) on 144–51. The last sentence of the previous paragraph was added to make a transition to Denise's story.

26 See n9 above. The final scene of *Axël* contains the famous line "Vivre? Les serviteurs feront cela pour nous."

27 In the Yeatses' copy of the 1938 printing (YL 2435), GY has underlined "malachite," and written in pencil beside this line, "Masefield's gift to WBY!"

28 The French writer and historian Francoise Marie Arouet de Voltaire (1694–1778), whose best-known pen name is Voltaire, had a longstanding relationship with the mathematician and physicist Gabrielle-Émilie Le Tonnelier de Breteuil, marquise du Châtelet, whose older husband tolerated their affair for many years.

29 The Natural History collection, part of the National Museum of Ireland, is known for its zoological holdings and antique, nineteenth-century-style organization. It is housed in the center of Dublin in a building opened in 1857, which was originally an extension of Leinster House (former home of the Royal Dublin Society, now housing the Dáil or Irish Parliament).

30 Arthur Young (1741–1820) was an English writer who published *A Tour in Ireland* in 1780. Three of Young's works (though not this

one) are recorded in the list of books in the library at Coole. Lady Gregory mentions Young twice in her diary, once in 1920 and once in 1921. In spring 1920, she wrote,

> I think of all the arguments—through so many storms, through 150 years or more, Coole has been a place of peace. We came through the Land League days and through the sale of the outlying property without war, without police protection or any application to the country for compensation—for there were no outrages. . . . Coole has been not only a place of peace during all that time, but a home of culture in more senses than one. Arthur Young found Mr. Gregory making a "noble nursery, the plantations for which would change the face of the district" and those woods still remain; my husband added rare trees to them and I have added acres and acres of young wood.
>
> (*Lady Gregory: The Journals*, ed. Daniel J. Murphy [2 vols.; Gerrards Cross: Colin Smythe, 1978], 1:148; this passage appears also in *Lady Gregory's Journals, 1916–1930*, ed. Lennox Robinson [London: Putnam & Company, 1946], 15)

On August 1, 1921, she mentions "old Robert Gregory's planting so as to 'change the character of the county' as Arthur Young says" (*Lady Gregory: The Journals*, 2:283). Neither phrase appears in Young's *Tour*; insofar as Gregory quotes it differently each time, her *Journals* suggest that she may have written this quotation without checking the source.

Lady Gregory, who believed strongly that "Ireland, more than other countries, ought to be a country of trees," planted many thousands of trees at Coole Park ("Tree Planting," *The Irish Homestead* 4 [February 12 and 19, 1898]: 141). The estate was taken over by the Forestry Commission in 1927, though she continued to live in the house for the remainder of her life. In early 1909, WBY commented in his journal, "Lady Gregory is planting trees; for a year they have taken up much of her time. Her grandson will be fifty years old before they can be cut. We artists, do not we also plant trees and it is only after some fifty years that we are of much value?" (*Mem* 155–56; *Au* 350).

31 In *Dramatis Personae*, WBY describes Coole House: "In the hall, or at one's right hand as one ascended the stairs, hung . . . portraits of the members of Grillion's Club, illuminated addresses presented in Ceylon or Galway, signed photographs or engravings of Tennyson, Mark Twain, Browning, Thackeray, at a later date paintings of Galway scenery by Sir Richard Burton, bequeathed at his death, and etchings by Augustus John" (*Au* 293).

Grillion's was a nonpartisan dining club in London founded in 1812 as a meeting place for men interested in contemporary discussions. It took its name from the Grillion's Hotel on Albemarle Street where the first meetings were held; illustrious members included several prime ministers. In 1826, a motion was passed to commission engraved portraits of members, 274 of which are housed in the National Portrait Gallery in London.

32 The Foreign Office was the British governmental department responsible for promoting and protecting the interests of the nation overseas.

33 The Chancery courts addressed complaints that could not be resolved in the common law courts. Oliver Goldsmith (1730–74) was a playwright, novelist, and poet, author of *The Vicar of Wakefield*, *She Stoops to Conquer*, and "The Deserted Village," among other works. Edmund Burke (1729–97) was a philosopher, political theorist, and statesman, author of *A Philosophical Enquiry into the Origin of Our Ideas of the Sublime And Beautiful*; his political theories have been widely influential in conservative political thought. Both Goldsmith and Burke were Anglo-Irish, and statues of both (by John Henry Foley) are in the yard by the front gates of Trinity College Dublin. WBY mentions them as his symbolic forebears in several late works: see, inter alia, "Blood and the Moon" and "The Seven Sages" (*Poems* 241–42, 245–46); and *The Senate Speeches of W. B. Yeats*, ed. Donald R. Pearce (Bloomington: Indiana University Press, 1960), 99, 172. Thomas Gainsborough (1727–88) was an English portrait and landscape painter known for meticulous detail and acute observation; he was a founding member of the Royal Academy along with his rival Joshua Reynolds, but his relationship with the Academy was uneasy.

34 Sir Peter Lely (1618–80) was a painter of Dutch origin, born Pieter van der Faes in Soest, Westphalia. He moved to London and became one of the more prominent portrait painters at court, holding the post of Principal Painter in Ordinary to Charles II. He was also one of the early proponents of the mezzotint, helping to bring this tonal method of printmaking to Britain. Sir William Pitt (1708–78), first Earl of Chatham, was a Whig statesman, wartime political leader, and brilliant orator, who led Britain in the Seven Years' War. He was known as Pitt the Elder or Chatham to distinguish him from his son, Pitt the Younger. The author Horace Walpole (1717–97), fourth Earl of Orford, was an antiquarian, art historian, Whig politician, and writer. He is best known for his home Strawberry Hill, a villa in Twickenham that anticipated the Gothic Revival, and for his popular gothic novel *The Castle of Otranto*.

35 Bartolomé Esteban Murillo (1617–82) is the most widely known painter in the Spanish Baroque style, known for religious paintings and idealized portraits. The Grand Tour was a traditional tour of Eu-

rope for young men from the upper classes in Europe and, eventually, the Americas, popular between the mid-seventeenth century until the advent of travel by steamship and rail in the mid-nineteenth century. John Singer Sargent (1856–1925) was the leading portrait painter of his time. He was born in the United States but lived most of his life in Europe, training in Paris and working for many years in London. His work is famous for large striking canvases of wealthy women and for depictions of Edwardian luxury. He made a charcoal portrait of WBY that was used as frontispiece to Vol. 1, *Poems Lyrical and Narrative*, of the 1908 collected edition (Wade 75) and several others (Wade 128, 139, 165, 177, 178, 209, and 211d).

36 Genesis, the first book of the Hebrew Bible and the Christian Old Testament, includes a tale of creation featuring the first man and woman (Adam and Eve) in the garden of Eden. If interpreted through the Christian doctrine of original sin, the story means that humans are separated from God at birth due to a fall from grace.

37 Cuckoos are a family of mostly arboreal birds common to many areas of the world. A distinguishing feature of many species, and one by which they are known in popular culture, is brood parasitism, whereby they lay their eggs in the nests of other birds.

38 See Luke 2:25–29.

39 Swift's *Discourse of the Contests and Dissensions between the Nobles and the Commons in Athens and Rome With the Consequences They Had upon Both These States* was published by John Nutt in 1701. It outlines Swift's views on national politics, likening contemporary England to the ancient world. In his diary, WBY claims that this essay "might be for us [the Irish] what Vico is to the Italians, had we a thinking nation" (*Diary 1930*, *Ex* 292) and that it "is more important to modern thought than Vico and certainly foreshadowed Flinders Petrie, Frobenius, Henry Adams, Spengler, and very exactly and closely Gerald Heard. . . . He [Swift] saw civilisations 'exploding'—to use Heard's term—just before the final state, and that final state as a tyranny, and he took from a Latin writer the conviction that every civilisation carried with it from the first what shall bring it to an end" (313–34).

40 One of the fragments of the Greek lyric poet Sappho (c. 610–c. 570 BCE) speaks of an egg of hyancinthine blue (Edgar Lobel and Denis Page, eds., *Poetarum Lesbiorum Fragmenta* [Oxford: Oxford University Press, 1955], 166).

41 Teheran, also Tehran, is the capital city of Persia (Iran).

42 Under the reign of the Abbasid caliph Harun al-Rashid (c. 763–809 CE), the fifth and most famous Abbasid caliph, Baghdad became the world's preeminent center of trade, learning, and culture. WBY read of Harun in *The Arabian Nights* (YL 251 and 676) and in Gibbon (YL 746).

The ancient trading city Byzantium, located on the Bosphorus, was rebuilt and established as the capital of the Roman Empire by Constantine in 330 CE. Renamed Constantinople, it was the capital of the Roman and Byzantine Empires. After its conquest by Ottoman Turks in 1453, it became the capital of the Ottoman Empire. The city has been known by its Turkish name, Istanbul, since the formation of the modern Turkish state in 1923. Byzantium is of great importance in the system and the works that use it (such as the poems "Sailing to Byzantium" and "Byzantium," *Poems* 197–98, 252–53; for an overview of sources and criticism, see Liebregts 298–307). In the historical overview in Book V, the midpoint between the primary and the antithetical poles in the cycle of about 1,000 years (half of the larger 2,000-year gyre), is expressed by the reign of Justinian, representing the full flowering of Byzantine culture and power. See 202–5.

43 The Antonines were Roman emperors who ruled from roughly 138–92 CE: Antoninus Pius (138–61 CE), Marcus Aurelius (161–80), with Commodus (180–92) sometimes added under the appellation. They ruled the empire at the height of its power and influence, from which point Gibbon begins his narrative of decline and fall. Sparta was a prominent city state in ancient Greece, situated in the Peloponnesian region of Laconia or Lacedaemonia. The second-century traveler Pausanias, who wrote guide-books for ancient tourists, describes a temple of Hilaeira and Phoebe, daughters of Apollo, in which "has been hung from the roof an egg tied to ribands, and they say that it is the famous egg that legend says Leda brought forth," *Description of Greece* 3.16.1 (Books 3–5, trans. W. H. S. Jones and H. A. Ormerod [Loeb, 1918], 96–97). The Yeatses' library contains a copy of Books 1 and 2 of Pausanias (YL 1545); cf. 197. Other translations of Pausanias include those of Thomas Taylor (1784) and Sir James G. Frazer (1898), both of whom were admired by WBY. An "unhatched egg of Leda's" is discussed also in the 1927 version of *The Resurrection* (*VPl* 918).

44 In ancient Greek legend, Leda was the daughter of the Aetolian king Thestius, the wife of King Tyndareus of Sparta, and the mother of Helen, Clytemnestra, Castor, and Pollux. Zeus raped Leda in the guise of a swan, impregnating her after she had just conceived with her husband. Two eggs were hatched containing Helen, Clytemnestra, Castor, and Pollux, although ancient sources differ on the question of which progeny were mortal and which were immortal, and which came from which egg. The story that most closely matches the pairing here is told by Apollodorus in the *Library* 3.10.7, trans. J. G. Frazer (2 vols.; Loeb, 1921), 2:23; this is the first source mentioned in the entry on "Leda" in the *Encyclopaedia Brittanica* (16:358). See Arkins (100) and Liebregts (280–81) for discussion.

45 As told in numerous versions, notably the *Oresteia* by Aeschylus, Clytemnestra was the wife of Agamemnon, who murdered him and the prophetess Cassandra. Helen was the wife of Menelaus; her ab-

duction by Paris brought about the Trojan War. Castor and Pollux (or Polydeuces) were called the Dioscuri (sons of Zeus) or Tyndaridae (sons of Tyndareus), who, after the death of the mortal twin, were transformed by Zeus into the constellation Gemini. In ancient Greek, Roman, and early Christian cultures, they were revered as patrons of sailors and athletes in particular.

46 See n18 above. The third of Kant's four antinomies has to do with the question of freedom. It states:

> *Thesis.*
> There are in the World Causes [acting] through *Freedom* [Liberty].
> *Antithesis.*
> There is no Liberty, but all is *Nature.*

WBY marked this quotation in his copy of J. P. Mahaffey and J. H. Bernard, *Kant's Critical Philosophy for English Readers*, 3rd ed., Vol. 2: The Prolegomena (London: Macmillan, 1915), 103; YL 1052.

47 On October 9 [1929], WBY sent Frank Pearce Sturm six propositions, including this first: "Reality is a timeless & spaceless community of spirits which perceive each other & perceive nothing else . . . Each spirit is determined by, and determines those it perceives. Each spirit is unique" (*FPS* 101). In *Diary 1930*, WBY writes, "I think that two conceptions, that of reality as a congeries of beings, that of reality as a single being, alternate in our emotion and in history, and must always remain something that human reason, because subject always to one or the other, cannot reconcile" (*Ex* 305).

48 In the Hebrew Bible, the witch of Endor is a woman commanded by King Saul to summon up the spirit of the prophet Samuel in order to ask for his advice about the warring Philistines (1 Samuel 28).

49 From *All's Well That Ends Well* 1.1.86 by English playwright and poet William Shakespeare (1564–1616).

50 Thermopylae is a pass on the east coast of Greece where a battle was joined in 480 BCE, during the second Persian invasion of Greece, between a small Greek force led by King Leonidas of Sparta and the Persian army led by Xerxes. The battle, in which the Greeks held off the Persians long enough to accomplish their larger strategic purpose before dying to the last man, is often invoked as a symbol of dauntless courage against great odds.

51 In *Stories*, Aherne adds another line to this statement: "You are not sane when you talk like that" (22).

52 The Irish Civil War (1922–23) was fought between supporters (the Free State or National Army) and opponents (anti-treaty forces or Irregulars) of the Anglo-Irish Treaty, which was signed in 1921 at the end of the War of Independence. The artist, playwright, and novelist

Jack B. Yeats (1871–1957) was the brother of WBY. From the 1920s, he became interested in Expressionism, and later paintings characteristically display vigorous and experimental uses of paint.

53 "The Phases of the Moon" and "The Double Vision of Michael Robartes" (*Poems* 164–68, 172–74) were two of the poems added to the Macmillan edition of *The Wild Swans at Coole* (1919; Wade 124, 125), expanded from its original fine press edition (Cuala Press, 1917; Wade 118). "The Gift of Harun Al-Rashid," written in 1923, was first published in *English Life and The Illustrated Review* and *The Dial* (1924), then in the volumes *The Cat and the Moon and Certain Poems* (Cuala, 1924; Wade 145). It appears at the beginning of Book II of *AVA* 97–102. It is a thinly disguised biographical parallel to the occultistic aspects of the marriage between WBY and GY: Harun al-Rashid gives Kusta ben Luka a bride who unexpectedly speaks and writes words of otherworldly wisdom while asleep, shortly after their wedding. The poem was included in *The Tower* (1928, Wade 158).

54 Kusta ben Luka (Qusta ibn Luqa, 820–912 CE) was a doctor and translator of Greek and Syrian texts into Arabic; a letter from Frank Pearce Sturm to WBY suggests that WBY's source for the name was Sir Edward Denison Ross (*FPS* 86).

In a letter of October 11, 1924, Sturm pointed out to WBY the difficulty of these characters' dates:

> Fifty seven years after the death of Harun-al-Rashid the *Mechanica* of Hero of Alexandria was translated into Arabic by Costa ibn Luca, whom you call Kusta ben Luka. He therefore could not have been an old man when the Caliph made him a present of the sleep-walking girl, unless he lived to a very great age indeed. I know you hate pedantry, & so do I, but if "A Vision" is to be founded on supposedly existing *MS*, the dates will have to be right. The Caliph died in 809. Kusta was still hard at work with his pen in 866. (*FPS* 83)

55 Leaf 27 of NLI 13,577 includes a footnote, pointing to this spot in the text: "* I published in 1925 ~~a book~~ inaccurate confused obscure incomplete ["incomplete" inserted above the line] work called "A Vision" ~~I have worked~~. It has beside me now corrected, clarified & completed after ~~four years~~ four years almost continuous labour." The note is retained in *Stories*.

56 In the *Meno* dialogue, Socrates proposes that "all enquiry and all learning is but recollection" (81), *The Dialogues*, trans. B. Jowett (5 vols.; Oxford: Clarendon Press, 1875), 1:282, YL 1586.

57 See n15 above.

58 "Rosa Alchemica" and "The Tables of the Law" were published in 1896, and "The Adoration of the Magi" in 1897.

59 My brother Owen: the three stories from the 1890s featured only one Aherne, i.e., Owen. By 1918, however, possibly due to misremembering his old character's given name, WBY had added John. The preface to *The Wild Swans at Coole* explains that

> I have the fancy that I read the name John Aherne among those of men prosecuted for making a disturbance at the first production of "The Play Boy," which may account for his animosity to myself. (*VP* 852)

"The Play Boy" is *The Playboy of the Western World* by J. M. Synge. *Kabbala Denudata*, by Christian Knorr von Rosenroth (1636–89), was translated into English as *The Kabbalah Unveiled* by WBY's old friend and fellow magician S. L. MacGregor Mathers in 1887. Howth is a suburb of Dublin located on a peninsula in the north of the city, where WBY lived with his family between 1881 and 1884. The pier is on the northern side of the peninsula.

60 In his "Introduction" to *AVA*, Owen Aherne reports that he "felt a slight chill" when Robartes mentioned trying to find Yeats,

> for we had both quarrelled with Mr Yeats on what I considered good grounds. Mr Yeats had given the name of Michael Robartes and that of Owen Aherne to fictitious characters, and made those characters live through events that were a travesty of real events. "Remember," I said, "that he not only described your death but represented it as taking place amid associations which must, I should have thought, have been highly disagreeable to an honourable man." "I was fool enough to mind once," he said, "but I soon found that he had done me a service. His story started a rumour of my death that became more and more circumstantial as it grew. One by one my correspondents ceased to write. My name had become known to a large number of fellow-students, and but for that rumour I could not have lived in peace even in the desert[."] . . . "What have you to say to Yeats?" I said, and instead of answering he began to describe his own life since our last meeting. "You will remember the village riot which Yeats exaggerated in 'Rosa Alchemica.' A couple of old friends died of their injuries, and that, and certain evil results of another kind, turned me for a long time from my favourite studies[."] (lvii–lix)

61 "Absolute poetry" and "pure poetry" gesture toward late nineteenth-century movements such as French Symbolism and English Aestheticism with their emphases on aesthetic or immaterial effects rather than a physical world. *The Countess of Pembroke's Arcadia* by Sir Philip Sidney (1554–86) is a pastoral and romantic prose work in a

highly ornate style; it was extremely popular in its day but eclipsed by the rise of the novel.

62 Leaf 29v of NLI 13,577 contains this postscript to John Aherne's letter, struck through: "PS. I enclose some photographs Duddon took from of Wood Cuts in Speculum. He says that Gyraldus is in portrait so like you that he may [have] been one of your incarnations. I cannot myself see the resemblance."

63 *Stories* here turns to *The Resurrection* (*Plays* 481–92).

The Phases of the Moon

1 Connemara is a region in the west of Ireland (Co. Galway), known for its rugged yet beautiful landscape. Historically, it was a very poor part of Ireland and many of its inhabitants suffered terribly during the Famine. "Connemara cloth" is presumably homespun, of the sort worn by Synge's Aran islanders and men and women of the west in Jack B. Yeats's paintings. The imagined figure in "The Fisherman" wears "grey Connemara clothes" (*Poems* 148), but WBY notes in *The Trembling of the Veil* the ironies of this symbol of Irish nationalism: "'Public opinion', said an anonymous postcard sent to a friend of mine, 'will compel you to learn Irish', and it certainly did compel many persons of settled habits to change tailor and cloth. I believed myself dressed according to public opinion, until a letter of apology from my tailor informed me that 'It takes such a long time getting Connemara cloth as it has to come all the way from Scotland'" (*Au* 272).

2 The setting of the poem is Ballylee, the Yeatses' tower near Gort and Coole Park.

3 "Milton's Platonist" refers to the title character of "Il Penseroso" (1632), an ode to melancholy by English poet John Milton (1608–74). This passage refers to lines 85–92:

> Or let my lamp at midnight hour,
> Be seen in some high lonely tower,
> Where I may oft outwatch the Bear,
> With thrice great Hermes, or unsphere
> The spirit of Plato to unfold
> What Worlds, or what vast regions hold
> The immortal mind that hath forsook
> Her mansion in this fleshly nook . . .
>
> (*The Poems of John Milton*, ed. John Carey and Alastair Fowler [London and Harlow: Longmans, Green, 1968], 143)

The references to the constellation Ursa Major (the Great Bear), which never sets if seen from the Northern Hemisphere; Hermes Trismegistus; and the summoning of the spirit of Plato from his celestial sphere offer parallels between "Milton's Platonist" and the figure (presumably WBY) in this tower. See Wayne K. Chapman on the Miltonic and Platonic scaffolding of the poem ("'Metaphors for Poetry': Concerning the Poems of *A Vision* and Certain Plays for Dancers," Mann et al., 261–64).

4 The "visionary prince" is the title character of "Prince Athanase" (1817) by the English Romantic poet Percy Bysshe Shelley (1792–1822), whose work was greatly important to WBY. Shelley echoes the lines from Milton above:

> The Balearic fisher, driven from shore,
> Hanging upon the peakèd wave afar,
> Then saw their lamp from Laian's turret gleam,
> Piercing the stormy darkness, like a star. . . .
> (Shelley 1:182)

5 The English printmaker and landscape painter Samuel Palmer (1805–81) was known especially for works inspired by the style of Blake, often produced in Shoreham, Kent; a group of fellow artists and he were known as the Ancients or Shoreham Ancients. WBY refers here to the engraving entitled *The Lonely Tower* illustrating "Il Penseroso" in *The Shorter Poems of John Milton* (London: Seeley, 1889). See Chapman, "'Metaphors for Poetry,'" 246 n14.

6 The English essayist and critic Walter Pater (1839–94) was known for the richness and depth of his language, and for such works as *The Renaissance* (1878), a collection of essays about Renaissance humanists and artists. His *Marius the Epicurean* (1885) displays Pater's ideal of the aesthetic life, his cult of beauty as opposed to bare asceticism, and his theory of the pursuit of beauty as an ideal of its own. The Yeatses' library contains a copy as printed in 2 volumes (London: Macmillan, 1902; YL 1537).

Robartes's death is alluded to in "The Adoration of the Magi" (*Myth1* 310, *Myth2* 202) and mentioned in notes to *Michael Robartes and the Dancer* (*VP* 821) and in Owen Aherne's "Introduction" to *AVA* (lviii–lix); see also 327 n1 and 339 n60.

7 This phrase, slightly misquoted, is from the second edition of John Milton's *The Doctrine and Discipline of Divorce* (London, 1644); WBY also used it in his essay "J. M. Synge and the Ireland of his Time," published in *The Cutting of an Agate* (1912, *EE* 245). Wayne Chapman notes that "mine author" is Plato ("The Miltonic Crux of 'The Phases of the Moon,'" *YA* 8 [1991]: 65–66 and 76 n23) and that WBY probably found the phrase in his copy of *Prose of Milton*, ed. Richard Garnett (London: Scott, [1911]), 238 (see Edward O'Shea, "The 1920s Catalogue of W. B. Yeats's Library," *YA* 4 [1986], ed.

Warwick Gould, 286). Chapman suggests that WBY might have noted the passage by reading the preface to the five-volume edition by J. A. St John (1848–54).

8 See Book I, Part III: "The Twenty-eight Incarnations" (79–136). "The full" refers to Phase 15; "the moon's dark" is Phase 1; "all the crescents" include Phases 2–27; "but six-and-twenty" indicates that Phase 1 and Phase 15 are not phases of human life; "the first crescent to the half" embraces Phases 2–8; "the moon is rounding" refers to Phases 9–14.

9 In *Iliad* 1:197, Athena grabs Achilles by the hair and then urges him to curb his passion rather than battle Agamemnon.

10 After Hector kills Achilles's friend Patroclus, Achilles, overly enraged, kills Hector and desecrates his body, dragging it before the walls of Troy and refusing it funeral rites. See *Iliad* 22.330.

11 The German philosopher Friedrich Nietzsche (1844–1900) is listed as an example for Phase 12 (see 95), perhaps because of the Nietzschean idea of the *Übermensch*, which establishes a natural hierarchy of the strong over the weak, or because of his concept of "will to power," a process of expansion and venting of creative energy that he believed was the basic driving force of nature.

12 According to Exodus 19:1–25, Sinai is the mountain where God gave the Ten Commandments to Moses. Whether this place is the same as the modern Jabal Musa ("Moses' Mountain") on the Sinai Peninsula is a matter of contention. See also Exodus 34 and 35.

13 In the 1937 printing, the beginning of this line reads "For perfected, completed. . . ." In the Yeatses' copies of the 1937 printing (YL 2434) and the 1938 printing (YL 2435), the line is corrected to "For separate, perfect. . . ." This change is also made on the first-pull Coole proofs, noted in Thomas Mark's notebook, and implemented in the 1962 edition.

14 Cf. an early typescript, in which Michael Robartes says that WBY in *PASL* "contends that a man of genius works at whatever task—among those not impossible—is hardest to him, for in that way he finds his direct opposite, that which most stirs his desire, and so the greater the opposition the greater the genius." "Yes," says Owen Aherne, "I remember thinking that the one original thing in the book" (*YVP* 4:14). See also *LE* 8–9.

15 Hugh Kenner has suggested ("A Possible Source in Coleridge for 'The Phases of the Moon,'" *YAACTS* 3 [1985]: 173–74) that WBY may here be remembering a passage in the *Biographia Literaria* (ed. James Engell and Walter Jackson Bate, *The Collected Works of Samuel Taylor Coleridge* 7 [London: Routledge & Kegan Paul; Princeton: Princeton University Press, 1973], pt. 1, 231) where Coleridge translates a passage from Herder's *Briefe, das Studium der Theologie betreffend* (1790):

> With the greatest possible solicitude avoid authorship. Too early or immoderately employed, it makes the head *waste* and

> the heart empty; even were there no other worse consequences. A person, who reads only to print, in all probability reads amiss; and he, who sends away through the pen and press every thought, the moment it occurs to him, will in a short time have sent all away, and will be a mere journeyman of the printing-office, a *compositor*.

WBY owned a copy of the *Biographia Literaria* (London: George Bell, 1876; YL 401).

16 The reference is to Phases 26–28; see 131–35.

17 Like the portrait of Giraldus and the image of the Great Wheel, the illustration of a unicorn was made by Edmund Dulac. Its placement, pasted into the book at this point (in *AVA* as well as *AVB*), remedied a small confusion. As Dulac explained to WBY in a letter of April 30, 1925, accompanying his finished diagram of the Great Wheel,

> When it [the diagram] was done I remembered that in your description of it you mention that the square in the center is occupied by a design of a unicorn. Thence the accompanying design of the Animal in question. If it is not absolutely necessary that the Diagram should incorporate it leave it as it is, but if its presence in the Diagram is of vital importance, the engraver can make the two blocks and fit that of the Unicorn in its proper place for purposes of printing. Otherwise it may be used as a tail piece somewhere else in the book. (*LWBY* 462)

There was confusion at the printer about the placement of this image. Macmillan wrote to WBY on March 17, 1937, "The printers are asking us for the block which should apparently come at the end of the 'The Phases of the Moon' in 'A Vision'. They have been unable to obtain a copy of the earlier edition of that work, and we accordingly write to ask if you could once more lend us the marked copy from which the text was set up, in order that we may see what block it is they require" (BL Add. 55792, f. 175). WBY responded with confusion, thinking they were unclear about placement of one of the diagrams, but nevertheless asked GY to send the copy (*CL InteLex* 6867). In *Stories*, this illustration appears on the title page.

The image recalls Monoceros de Astris, the title given an aspirant in the Practicus grade of the Order of the Golden Dawn. In 1920, WBY explained in a letter to his sister Elizabeth Corbet (Lolly) that "Unicorn from the Stars . . . is a private symbol belonging to my mystical order & nobody knows what it comes from. It is the soul" (*CL InteLex* 3787). Cf. WBY's plays *Where There Is Nothing* (1902), *The Unicorn from the Stars* (1908), and *The Player Queen* (1922).

Book I: The Great Wheel

1 The diagram of the Great Wheel was designed and executed by Edmund Dulac for *AVA* (see 330 n15). On October 14, 1923, WBY wrote thanking Dulac for the portrait of Giraldus and giving suggestions for the Great Wheel: "I enclose the sketch for the diagram. The pencilled words will have to be in Latin & I will get the Latin I hope tomorrow. The man I count on for it was out yesterday. You can use any symbolism you like for the elements—nymphs, salamanders, air spirits, or Roman gods or more natural objects. . . . The round objects in the enclosed diagram are of course the lunar phases 1. 8. 15. 22 making new moon, half moon, full moon & half moon respectively" (*CL InteLex* 4381). A week later, WBY wrote to supply the Latin phrases: "Put Pulcritudo at 15, Sapientia at 1, Tentatio at 8 and Dominatio (or Potestas) at 22. I enclose Pursers letter as his spelling may correct mine" (*CL InteLex* 4384; for Purser's help, see 419 n7). The completed diagram, which pleased WBY greatly (his comment to Dulac was that it "would take in the whole British Museum" [*CL InteLex* 4536]), contains six elements:

1. Four symbols are arranged in a central square, described in "Stories" as "an apple, an acorn, a cup, and what looked like a sceptre or wand" (27). These four symbols, unique to *A Vision*, suggest the four suits in playing cards or Tarot cards. The woodcut actually includes only three of the four symbolic objects described in the text.
2. Latin terms correspond to the symbols: Pulchritudo (a flower), Sapientia (a fruit, possibly an apple, perhaps alluding to the fruit of the tree of the knowledge of good and evil in the Garden of Eden myth), Temptatio (an overturned cup), and Violentia (a staff or sceptre held aloft in a clenched hand).
3. A wheel surrounding the central images is placed so that the four objects and terms are adjacent to the lunar phases at 1, 8, 15, and 22 (new, first quarter, full, last quarter moons) they presumably describe. These phases, as WBY described to Dulac, are indicated by four circles, one with a full human face, two half faces that are partially darkened, and one fully dark.
4. The quadrants of the circle between the four key phases are labeled with the four cardinal signs of the zodiac, so called (from L. *cardo*, "hinge") because their starts mark the astronomical turning points of the seasons: Aries [♈] the spring equinox, Cancer [♋] the summer solstice, Libra [♎] the autumn equinox, and Capricorn [♑] the winter solstice. Cf. WBY's admission that "Some years passed before I understood the meaning of this sign or of the other cardinal signs in the original automatic map" (186). The positions of Cancer and Capricorn are interchanged from the original version

of the woodcut in *AVA*, and the same change is made to fig. 17 (60) with respect to the equivalent diagram in *AVA* (14, fig. 6). As the zodiac follows a set order, this interchange means that instead of moving counterclockwise like the phases (*AVA*), the zodiac moves clockwise in the opposite direction to the phases (*AVB*).

5. The circle is also described by a band of Arabic numbers from two to twenty-eight (except 1, 8, 15, and 22), representing the other lunar phases.
6. Alchemical symbols of the four elements, Fire [△], Air [🜁], Earth [🜃], and Water [▽], are placed in the outside corners of the diagram, adjacent to quarters of the wheel (see the list of Elemental Attributions in the Table of the Quarters, 76). There are three slightly different versions of this woodcut, in *AVA* (*lviii*), *Stories* (between 8 and 9), and *AVB*. The version in *Stories* reverses two signs of the zodiac from *AVA* (see #4 above) as well as reversing the signs for Fire and Water; *AVB* restores the elements to their position in *AVA* while keeping the change to the signs (see also *AVA* 341). Cf. a chart of "Elements" in a notebook (*YVP* 3:172) and the associations of astrological signs with quarters of the wheel in *AVA* 14 (fig. 6). The semi-Blakean terms *Head*, *Heart*, *Loins*, and *Fall*, terms discussed at some length in the AS and used in *AVA* but discarded in *AVB*, were part of personal discussions that were also structural elements of the play *The Only Jealousy of Emer*. The only remnant of these terms in *AVB* is the equivalent diagram (fig. 17) and the mention of *Head* and *Heart* in the phasal essay for Phase 18 (GY's phase), 110.

2 WBY misquotes slightly from Empedocles's *On Nature* as translated by Burnet 226 ("When Strife was fallen to the lowest depth of the vortex . . .") and 223 ("nor ever, methinks, will boundless time be emptied of that pair"). WBY also quotes these passages in *AVA*, where he misattributes them to Heraclitus, but there he follows Burnet's version more closely (see *AVA* 106). WBY's substitution of "Discord" for Burnet's "Strife" may derive from Duhem's "Discorde" in his summary of Simplicius's use of Empedocles (1:75). In the TS carbon WBY misquotes Burnet, "Love has reached the centre . . ." (see NLI 36,272/6/1a, leaf 1).

3 Heraclitus (fl. 500 BCE), a Pre-Socratic philosopher, is identified with the ideas of universal change, the interplay of opposites, and that fire is the fundamental element in the world. The quotation, slightly altered, is from Burnet 136.

4 Simplicius (c. 490–c. 560 CE) was a late Platonist whose commentary on the work of Aristotle (384–322 BCE) is marked by an endeavor to identify areas of concord between Platonic and Aristotelian philosophies. As WBY notes, his source is Duhem, who gives quotations from Heraclitus and Empedocles by Simplicius including discussion of

"une sphère homogène" and the alteration between Love and Discord (1:75).

5 At this point, the TS carbon contains a paragraph deleted from the final draft:

> I have seen somewhere a series of illustrations showing first a coin with a horse, then later coins where the horse breaks up into meaningless blobs until at last a designer turns the four blobs that were once legs into the spokes of a wheel. The passage I have quoted from Empedocles had probably some relation to the diurnal movement of the heavens, or to planetary movements, but one cannot guess what that relation was, so little of his system has survived. Such a system is the horse upon the first coin, and the system I am about to describe the wheel that takes its place.
>
> (NLI 36,272/6/1a, leaf 2)

6 The translation of Heraclitus frag. 67 is taken from Burnet 138. Cf. *AVA* 105 and 270 n21. WBY first referred to this fragment (in a slightly different form) in his journal in 1909 (*Mem* 216). See also *The Resurrection* (*Plays* 492, *VPl* 931), 145 and 197 in this edition, and *On the Boiler* (*LE* 227, 234, and 236).

7 Plato's late dialogue *Timaeus* (360 BCE) explores theories relating to the creation of the universe, including the description of the circles of Same and Other: see *Timaeus* 38–39 (*The Dialogues*, trans. B. Jowett [5 vols.; Oxford: Clarendon Press, 1875], 3:621). This dialogue was one of the first items on WBY's philosophical reading list after the completion of *AVA* on April 22, 1925. On May 22, after the finished book went to press, WBY wrote to GY, "I have read the Timaeus very slowly & carefully. It seems the root of most mystical thought & Flinders Petrie thinks that it is Egyptian in oregen apparently" (*LWBY/GY* 162).

8 Alcmaeon of Croton (fl. 500–450 BCE) was a philosopher and scientist. His dates and relationship to other Pre-Socratic philosophers, including Pythagoras (570–490 BCE), are subjects of debate. He was the first thinker to locate the brain as the seat of thought and to separate the activities of the senses from the understanding. WBY cites Fragment 2 of his book (later titled *On Nature*), which is quoted by Duhem (1:78). Duhem also identifies Alcmaeon as a disciple of Pythagoras, a claim that was first advanced by Diogenes Laertius (fl. 3rd cent. BCE) in his influential history of Greek philosophy. Cf. Diogenes, *The Lives and Opinions of Eminent Philosophers*, trans. C. D. Yonge (London: George Bell, 1909; YL 523), 371.

9 The preceding three sentences (beginning with "They are opposite in nature . . .") were added in ink in WBY's hand on the Basingstoke setting-copy TS.

10 Frank Pearce Sturm (1879–1942), a medical doctor, poet, and mystic, corresponded with WBY during the composition of *AVA*, suggesting corrections and revisions to draft versions of the text, especially details involving Macrobius, Latin, the figure of Giraldus, and the astronomical/astrological movements of lunar circuits. WBY refers to Sturm several times in correspondence as the ideal reader of *A Vision*, "a very learned doctor in the north of England who sends me profound and curious extracts from ancient philosophies on the subjects of gyres" and one of "a few very devoted readers" for whom WBY wrote the book (*L* 712, 781, 899). In a note to the Macmillan edition of *The Winding Stair*, WBY acknowledges Sturm, "that too little known poet and mystic," for help with Macrobius (*Poems* 607). See *FPS*.

St. Thomas Aquinas (1225–74), an Italian Dominican priest, was one of the most influential philosophers and theologians in the Scholastic tradition of the Roman Catholic Church. The school of thought he founded was the primary philosophical approach of the Roman Catholic Church for much of its subsequent history, and exerted considerable influence over Western philosophy generally. In a lengthy postscript to a letter to WBY in January 1926, Sturm wrote that "St Thomas Aquinas was very interested in gyres, and his opinions would make a very apposite footnote when *A Vision* is reprinted in your collected works." For Aquinas, according to Sturm, the "Spiral motion" that characterizes the "intellectual relations" between the minds of angels (who contemplate God in a circle) and "the mind of man" (who thinks in a straight line) is "exactly a gyre." WBY replied that he was "most grateful to you for that quotation from St. Thomas. It is the exact thought of my work for at harmonization the soul is in a sphere not in a gyre. The sphere is his circle. I believe that I have been given a simplification of ancient thought" (*FPS* 87–89). The passage in Aquinas, as Sturm notes, is from his Commentary on Pseudo-Dionysius the Areopagite (*In librum beati Dionysii De divinis nominibus exposito*, ed. Ceslas Pera [Taurini and Rome: Marietti, 1950], 4.7.371 and 373, 120–22).

11 The phrase "which, though it imitates the circle of 'the Same'," was added in manuscript (in WBY's hand) on the Basingstoke TS.

12 *The Celtic Twilight* was first published in 1893, with a second revised edition published in 1902. See the story and WBY's note (dated 1924 and first added to *Early Poems and Stories* [London: Macmillan, 1925, Wade 147]): "A countryman near Coole told me of a spirit so ascending. Swedenborg, in his *Spiritual Diary*, speaks of gyres of spirits, and Blake painted Jacob's Ladder as an ascending gyre" (*Myth1* 123, *Myth2* 81).

13 Sturm did indeed find passages about gyres and other matters in Dr. Dee, "the crystal gazer, who so interested Queen Elizabeth," remark-

ing that he had himself translated some of Dee's *Monas Hieroglyphica*, "an amazing Latin Treatise," but "gave up in despair at its obscurity." Sturm informed WBY that the Latin is "crabbed & cob-webby, like the mind of Dee, & needs a key which is lost if it ever existed. . . . I don't pretend to understand a word of Dee's book" (*FPS* 96).

14 Macrobius Ambrosius Theodosius (fl. 400 CE) was a late Roman philosopher who wrote a commentary on the *Somnium Scipionis*, which concludes the book *De re publica* by Cicero. Macrobius was one of the important sources for information about Platonic philosophy in medieval Europe. On January 22, 1926, Sturm quoted Macrobius in a postscript to a letter to WBY (*FPS* 92; see also 93). Cf. *AVA* 122–23 and 279–80 nn65 and 69.

15 Also Macrobius; see *FPS* 102.

16 On the last flyleaf of Vol. 2 of Swedenborg's *Principia Rerum Naturalium* (1734; *The Principia or the First Principles of Natural Things*, trans. James R. Rendell and Isaiah Tansley [2 vols.; London: Swedenborg Society, 1912]; YL 2039A), WBY drew diagrams of double cones with the note "See page 555."; on that page, he drew another diagram of a spiral (i.e., a gyre seen from its broad end). At this point in the text, Swedenborg, advancing his broad claim that mathematics and philosophy/theology are identical, writes in a chapter entitled "The first or simple finite" that the result of the two most primary entities in the universe, the point and motion, "is a spiral reciprocating from the centre to the periphery and from the periphery to the centre. If the continual motion is spiral it must be reciprocal, that is from the centre to the periphery and contrariwise. From the motion of the points arises the fixed arrangement of all, consequently, in a finite as a result of motion and position there arise two poles, one opposite to the other; these two poles have the form of cones" (2:555).

17 Swedenborg uses the terms *Mundus Intelligibilis*, referring to the world of intelligible realities, where things exist in ideal form, in contrast with the notion of a *Mundus Sensibilis,* where things are perceived imperfectly through the filter of human senses. The terms are famously used also in Leibniz and Kant.

The TS carbon contains a significantly longer passage here, following the reference to Swedenborg's mystical writings and in place of the rest of this sentence:

> So far I know of no scholar who has collected these passages or expounded a geometrical symbolism which so many mediaeval writers thought important, for scholars, like other men, prefer such matters of fact or abstract doctrines as may be important to themselves. We still await the historian who will re-create the past out of itself as an actor who creates a character upon the stage.
>
> (NLI 36,272/6/1a, leaf 4)

18 The French novelist Gustave Flaubert (1821–80) mentioned this unwritten novel in correspondence during 1852 and 1853, and a description of it was published by E. W. Fischer ("La Spirale, plan inédit de Gustave Flaubert," trans. François D'Aignuy, *Études sur Flaubert inédit* [Lepzig: Zeitler, 1908]). Flaubert mentions the writing of the story in two letters to Louise Colet, one from 1852 and the other from 1853: see *The Letters of Gustave Flaubert*, ed. and trans. Francis Steegmuller (2 vols.; Cambridge, Mass.: Harvard University Press), 1:243–44, 251–52. WBY mentions the story in his introduction to *Selections from the Poems of Dorothy Wellesley* (1936), *P&I* 185. William O'Donnell suggests that WBY knew of the story from either Arthur Symons or Sturge Moore (*P&I* 306 n13). See also A. Norman Jeffares, *The Circus Animals: Essays on W. B. Yeats* (London: Macmillan, 1970, 103), for another suggestion that WBY knew of Flaubert's project through Moore's *Art and Life* (London: Methuen, 1910; YL 1361). Cf. *AVA* 103. Flaubert appears as an example for Phase 22; see 117–21.

19 The phrase "cone or" was added in manuscript on the Basingstoke setting-copy TS.

20 Early in the *Commonplace Book*, Berkeley notes, "Time train of ideas succeeding each other" (*Berkeley's Commonplace Book*, ed. G. A. Johnston [London: Faber, 1930; YL 159], 2). The thought that "We perceive a continual succession of ideas" is foundational for Berkeley (*Principles of Human Knowledge* 1:26, in *Berkeley: Essay, Principles, Dialogues, with Selections from Other Writings*, ed. Mary Whiton Calkins [New York: Charles Scribner's Sons, 1929], 138; *The Works of George Berkeley* [2 vols.; London: Exshaw, 1784, YL 160], 1:35). G. A. Johnston, whose book *The Development of Berkeley's Philosophy* WBY owned and read carefully, begins his discussion of time according to Berkeley reiterating that "If we consider . . . Berkeley's attitude to time, we find that he reduces time to an experienced succession of ideas" ([London: Macmillan, 1923; YL 1025] 239).

Ennead 6.1.8 does not have to do with "sensation" or time. The TS carbon has the reference as "Ennead V.I.8." (NLI 36,272/6/1a, leaf 4), which does mention (in MacKenna's translation) that "Earlier, Parmenides made some approach to the doctrine of identifying Being with Intellectual-Principle while separating Real Being from the realm of sense" (Plotinus 4:12). More appropriately, see *Ennead* 5.1.7, where Plotinus describes the "Intellectual-Principle" as engendered by the One:

> Yet the One is not an Intellectual-Principle; how then does it engender an Intellectual-Principle?
>
> Simply by the fact that in its self-quest it has vision: this very seeing is the Intellectual-Principle. Any perception of the exter-

nal indicates either sensation or intellection, sensation symbolized by line, intellection by a circle. (Plotinus 4:9–10)

21 Giovanni Gentile (1875–1944), a neo-Hegelian, was closely linked to Benito Mussolini, in whose government he served as minister for education from 1922–24, and whose *A Doctrine of Fascism* he co-wrote in 1932. The copy in the Yeatses' library of Gentile's *The Theory of Mind as Pure Act*, trans. from the third edition by H. Wildon Carr (London: Macmillan, 1922; YL 742), is marked with various underscorings and marginal markings, including the passage on 126 from which this quotation is taken. Astrological symbols for water and fire are drawn in the margins. Foster notes that WBY first encountered the ideas of Gentile during the Yeatses' Italian travel with the Pounds in January 1925 (2:279). See also n34 below.

22 See *AVA* 14 and 235 n33. For the term *tincture* in Boehme, see for example the *Clavis, or Key*, section 195: "The power and virtue of fire and light is called tincture; and the motion of this virtue is called the holy and pure element"; or sections 124–25, on the seventh of the seven properties of nature: "124. And though they work in different kinds and manners, yet here there is but one only substance, whose power and virtue is called tincture; that is, a holy penetrating, growing or springing bud. 125. Not that the seventh property is the tincture, but it is the body of it; the power and virtue of the fire and light is the tincture in the substantial body: but the seventh property is the substance which the tincture penetrateth and sanctifieth; we mean, that it is thus according to the power and virtue of the divine manifestation; but as it is a property of nature, it is the substance of the attracted desire of all properties" (Jacob Boehme, *The Forty Questions of the Soul and the Clavis*, trans. John Sparrow [London: John Watkins, 1911; YL 236], 47, 30).

23 In *PASL*, WBY introduces the concept of the antithetical in his discussion of differences between poetry and rhetoric. He writes: "Nor has any poet I have read or heard of or met with been a sentimentalist. The other self, the anti-self or the antithetical self, as one may choose to name it, comes but to those who are no longer deceived, whose passion is reality" (*LE* 8).

24 The first three phrases are derived from the mirror writing in the decorative heading of Plate 30 [33] of Blake's *Milton,* Book the Second (Blake 129; the plate is reproduced in *WWB* 1). The final quotation is adapted from *Jerusalem*, Chap. 2 (Plate 48): "Beneath the bottoms of the Graves, which is Earths central joint, / There is a place where Contrarieties are equally true" (Blake 196; *WWB* 1).

25 A slightly different version of this note was added by WBY in manuscript on the Basingstoke setting-copy TS: "Though not so in reality it may become so in our minds. If we discover logical refutations of the

writer or movement that is going out of fashion. Then there is always error, which has nothing to do with 'the conflict', 'the dialectic.'" Presumably the references to Croce and Hegel were added later.

Benedetto Croce (1866–1952) was an Italian Idealist philosopher who is best known for his theory of aesthetics and his opposition to Fascist ideologies. WBY owned a copy of Croce's widely read work on Hegel, *What is Living and What is Dead of the Philosophy of Hegel* (trans. Douglas Ainslie; London: Macmillan, 1915; YL 448). See especially Chap. 5, 100–119, on error and non-being as outside the Hegelian intellectual triangle. According to Croce, error "is the incentive to progress: it is the not-being, the necessary moment of development; without contradiction and doubt, without perplexity and dissatisfaction, we should make no advance" (106). WBY may also be remembering Croce, *Logic as the Science of the Pure Concept*, trans. Douglas Ainslie, a book he owned and read carefully. Part 3, Chap. 1, begins, "Error has sometimes been called privation or *negativity*" (London: Macmillan, 1917, YL 444, 391). The Translator's Preface to this work draws attention also to the concept (vii).

26 "Murray's Dictionary" refers to the *Oxford English Dictionary*. The Scottish lexicographer Sir James Augustus Henry Murray (1837–1915) was the first editor of the Dictionary. See definition 3a of "objective": "Of a person, a writing, work of art, etc.: Dealing with, or laying stress upon, that which is external to the mind; treating as outward things or events, rather than inward thoughts or feelings; regarding or representing things from an objective standpoint. (Occas., after mod. Ger. *objektiv*: Treating a subject so as to exhibit the actual facts, not coloured by the feelings or opinions of the writer.)" (Vol. 7, O, P. [Oxford: Clarendon Press, 1909]). Cf. the parallel passage in *AVA*, where WBY mentions that "[t]he volume of Murray's dictionary containing letter S is not yet published"; that volume was published in 1919.

27 The TS carbon includes at the end of this sentence, "Empedocles' Discord and Love as I think" (NLI 36,272/6/1a, leaf 8), and this phrase is struck through on the Basingstoke setting-copy TS.

28 See, for example, the session of November 22, 1917 (*YVP* 1:99–110), and WBY's summary of the general concept on a card in his file, *YVP* 3:418–19.

29 "[R]ight to left" should be "left to right": the point of the diagrams of the cones is that *Will* and *Creative Mind* both move together, from left to right in the upper diagram and from right to left in the lower diagram. In the diagram of the wheel, however, the *Faculties* have "their own circular movement" in opposite directions, *Will* always moving counterclockwise—"right to left" in WBY's formulation—and *Creative Mind* always moving clockwise—"left to right," as later in the paragraph. The error here seems to arise from confusion of the two situations.

30 The TS carbon contains a different version of this sentence: "The moonless night, though not a phase at all, is for convenience called phase 1, and the full moon which is not strictly a phase is called phase 15" (NLI 36,272/6/1a, leaf 12). Revisions to the current text were made in manuscript on the Basingstoke setting-copy TS.

31 In GY's copy of *AVB* (1937; YL 2434; also emended in the 1938 edition; YL 2435), WBY has corrected this text from "Phase 1 and Phase 28" to "Phase 1 and Phase 15"; the correction is also noted in GY's copy of the 1938 edition (YL 2435). While the Coole proofs also read "Phase 28," they have been corrected to read "Phase 15," with a circled note in pencil emphasizing "Author's correction" (BL Add. 55893, 83). This correction also appears in Thomas Mark's notebook and in the 1962 edition.

32 On July 24, 1935, WBY wrote to Harold Macmillan with a concern that seems to pertain to this diagram: "I have numbered each diagram with a blue pencil + put similar numbers where the diagrams occur in the text. One diagram was forgotten—No. 12. All the explanatory words are in pencil [only?] ought to be printed as in the other diagrams" (*CL InteLex* 6299).

33 WBY and Sturm discussed these movements in correspondence just after the publication of *AVA*. Sturm suggested the diagrams were "incomprehensible simply because of inaccuracies in the text." WBY replied that "You will get all mixed up if you think of my symbolism as astrological or even astronomical in any literal way" and that he feared "book II would be almost unintelligible but I could do no better. I have no gift for explanation & am the least mathematical of men. I made myself ill over it. It took me months to understand the simplest things." Sturm wrote back that his Daimon "says that I was wrong to think that you had made a mistake in giving opposite movements to your lunar & solar circles. He says that you also are wrong in supposing your symbolism to be arbitrary, for in spite of what you say or think *it is astronomical in a literal way*." The rest of his letter contains diagrams along with detailed explanations showing that although actual movements of earth and moon are from west to east, "the apparent motion of the Sun is from east to west" and therefore "the statement that Solar & Lunar circles move in opposite directions will be as reasonable as it is literally true" (*FPS* 88–92).

34 See *AVA* 10–12.

35 In *The Reform of Education* (trans. Dino Bigongiari, London: Macmillan, 1922; YL 741), Gentile proposes education of the individual as an aspect of the whole: "the State, considered as Universal Will, is one with our concrete and actual ethical personality. . . . our whole life which concretely flows into that Will which is the State and which thus makes itself felt in the world" (14). For "I read somewhere": Paul Stanfield cites transcriptions by Curtis Bradford of notes WBY made in 1933 identifying

this concept with the thinking of Croce rather than Gentile ("W. B. Yeats and Politics in the 1930s," PhD dissertation, Northwestern University, 1984, 147). For the "old saying," see Burnet 136 and 49 in this edition.

36 In the fifth *Ennead*, Plotinus posits that the One is by necessity indivisible ("the source of all things is not all things. . . . It is precisely because there is nothing within the One that all things are from it" (5.2.1, Plotinus 5:16). Consciousness, however, requires plurality: "a knowing principle must handle distinct items: its object must, at the moment of cognition, contain diversity; otherwise the thing remains unknown" (5.3.1, Plotinus 5:32–33). Thus, "the utterly simplex . . . must, then, transcend the Intellectual Principle" (5.3.11, Plotinus 5:34): i.e., "things that are of one kind are unconscious."

37 This is one of WBY's more frequent allusions. Dante Alighieri's *Il Convito* (1304–7), also known as the *Convivio* (or *The Banquet*), is one of two prose works written immediately following his exile from Florence. The work is a synthesis of philosophical readings presented as a series of commentaries on previously composed canzoni. Although WBY's exact reference to Dante has not been identified, two passages are illuminating (trans. Philip H. Wicksteed [London: J. M. Dent, 1903]):

(1) Amongst the effects of divine wisdom man is the most marvellous, seeing how the divine power has united three natures in one form, and how subtly harmonized his body must be harmonized for such a form, having organs for almost all its powers. Wherefore, because of the complex harmony amongst so many organs which is required to make them perfectly answer to each other, few of all the great number of men are perfect. (3.8, 178)

(2) And when it [the body] is well ordained and disposed, then it is beauteous as a whole and in its parts; for the due order of our members conveys the pleasure of a certain wondrous harmony. . . . And so, to say that the noble nature beautifies its body, and makes it comely and alert, is to say not less than that it adjusts it to the perfection of order. (4.25, 358)

GY owned a copy of this translation in the widely read Temple Classics edition of Dante and was very familiar with it. Unlike WBY's copies of Dante's works, whose pages are for the most part unmarked and some of which are even uncut, hers, including the *Convito*, contain marginalia, including corrections of the translation (YL 466–77). On October 13, 1919, the Control Ameritus informed WBY and GY, "I want you both to read the whole of Dante's Convito—only a little every day—she can read it to you" (*YVP* 2:445). That they took the advice is evident in *AVA* 18 and 167, as well as the essay "A People's Theatre," which appeared the following month (*IDM* 128). The AS contains numerous discussions of Unity of Being. It "is a harmony," GY wrote in a notebook on June 30, 1920: "All the being vibrates to the note, it is like striking a chord. It is like sounding on the piano certain harmonic notes which are responded to by others in their sequence" (*YVP* 3:27). Later, she recorded that it is "a co-equality of Primary & Antithetical" (October 7, 1921, *YVP* 3:99). On September 3, 1918, WBY asked, "What is unity of being?" to which the Control Thomas replied, "Complete harmony between physical body intellect & spiritual desire—*all may be imperfect* but if harmony is perfect it is unity" (*YVP* 2:41). See also *Au* 164, 200, and 227; *Plays* 714; *LE* 162 and 179.

38 The TS carbon does not include the sentence mentioning Empedocles (NLI 36,272/6/1a, leaf 15). The philosophy of Croce, under the general title *Filosofia della Spirito* (Philosophy of Mind or Spirit), is set out in four volumes: *Estetica come scienza dell'espressione e linguistica generale*, 1902; *Logica come scienza del concetto puro*, 1909; *Filosofia della pratica. Economica ed etica*, 1909; and *Teoria e storia della storiografia*, 1916. All were translated into English by Douglas Ainslie, and WBY owned and read his copies of the first three (YL 440, 444, 446). The four "moments" are described by H. Wildon Carr, in a book WBY also owned and read: "There are therefore four moments . . . in the unfolding of mind. . . . [:] the first, the intuition . . . ; the second the concept . . . ; the third, the individual end or the utility . . . ; the fourth, the ethical end. . . ." The moments are also distinct and universal concepts: "These four distinct concepts are the beautiful, the true, the useful, and the good" (*The Philosophy of Benedetto Croce: The Problem of Art and History* [London: Macmillan, 1917; YL 348], 137). Carr distinguishes the Crocean distinct concept from Hegelian logic: "The distinct concept, then, is a synthesis, or unity, or identity in difference, of opposites. It is not itself in its turn an opposite, a thesis or antithesis within a new synthesis. . . . [it] cannot itself be an opposite, just because in it reality is fully determined" (151).

39 Italian *commedia dell'arte* is a form of improvisational theatre still performed today but popular from the sixteenth through eighteenth centuries. Performances include juggling, acrobatics, and humorous plays based on a repertoire of established characters. In the AS for January 17, 1918, in response to the statement of the Control Thomas (assisted by the guide Fish), "The Ego in his part chooses the part he plays & writes the words," WBY commented, "You have described Commedia Dell Arte." Thomas replied, "That is like the Nō partially a dramatisation of the soul—it is all great art" (*YVP* 1:270).

40 This art form began to decline in the mid-seventeenth century, and improvisation and new creation became less frequent, with performers instead relying on booklets of stock speeches.

41 Thomas à Kempis (1380–1471), a German monk, is widely accepted to be the author of *The Imitation of Christ* (c. 1418). He was a follower of Geert Groote and Florentius Radewijns, founders of the Brethren of the Common Life.

42 Walter Savage Landor (1775–1864), poet, prose writer, and intellec-

tual, is the author of *Imaginary Conversations* (1824–46; YL 1080, 1081). Ezra Pound wrote to Iris Barry on July 27, 1916, "Yeats and I spent our last winter's months on Landor. . . . he [Landor] isn't very good as a poet save in a few places, where he is fine, damn fine" (*The Selected Letters of Ezra Pound, 1907–1941*, ed. D. D. Paige [New York: New Directions, 1971], 89). See also *PASL* (*LE* 6, 15).

43 Maximilien François Marie Isidore de Robespierre (1758–94) was one of the best-known leaders of the French Revolution, an influential member of the Committee of Public Safety during the period known as the Reign of Terror.

44 In the 1962 printing of *AVB*, "Discovery of Strength" was changed to "Beginning of Strength," and "Breaking of Strength" to "Temptation through Strength." These corrections also appear in pencil in Thomas Mark's notebook.

45 This sentence does not appear on the TS carbon (NLI 36,272/6/1a, leaf 21).

46 This sentence does not appear on the TS carbon (NLI 36,272/6/1a, leaf 22).

47 The preceding four sentences were added after the production of the TS carbon, where they do not appear (NLI 36,272/6/1a, leaf 22).

In *AVA*, WBY described the "opening" and "closing" of the *Tinctures* on 17, probably with an unnoted error:

> Between Phase 12 and Phase 13, and between Phase 4 and Phase 5 in diagram 1 occurs what is called "the *opening* of the *Tinctures*," and between Phase 18 and Phase 19, and between Phase 4 [should read: 26] and Phase 5 [should read: 27] what is called "the *closing*." This means that between Phase 12 and Phase 13 each *Tincture* divides into two, and closes up again between Phase 18 and Phase 19. Between Phase 26 and Phase 27 the *Tinctures* become one *Tincture*, and between Phase 4 and Phase 5 become two again.

In *AVB* at this point, WBY explains a more complicated understanding of the idea from the earlier book: the "closing" has here become "a new opening" and into not "personality" but "its negation," the *Faculties* wearing thin and the *Principles* able to "shine through."

48 At this point, the TS carbon includes the note: "NOTE FOR PRINTER. Quote 'Vision' from page 17, section IV, to page 117 inclusive, omitting section II – the section headed The Daimon, the sexes, Unity of Being etc. Omit Section XIII (pages 59 and first half of page 61)" (NLI 36,272/6/1a, leaf 23). WBY points Macmillan to sections from *AVA*, used as a setting copy for the following sections. See *AVA* 17–94. In fact, section V from *AVA*, "Drama of the Faculties and of the Tinctures, etc." (*AVA* 17–19), is not retained *verbatim* in *AVB*, although a

revised version of it appears in section III above (62–63). The reference to omitting "section II" should refer to section XI, "The Daimon, the Sexes, Unity of Being, Natural and Supernatural Unity" (*AVA* 24–27). For section XIII, "Characters of Certain Phases," see *AVA* 30–31.

The private life of French Symbolist poet Paul Verlaine (1844–96) caused public scandal, in particular his sexual relationship with the poet Arthur Rimbaud, which ended in Verlaine's imprisonment for shooting Rimbaud in 1873. WBY had met Verlaine: see *Au* 261–62, *EE* 197, and *UP* 1:397–99.

49 Quotation slightly modified from the first two lines of "Auguries of Innocence" (1803) by William Blake (Blake 490; *WWB* 3:76).

50 This line echoes Brutus's remark in Shakespeare's *Julius Caesar* that "I had rather be a dog and bay the moon / Than such a Roman" (4.3.27–28). A dog barking at the moon is a proverbial expression of futility and indifference, as in the expression "the moon does not heed the barking of dogs" (David Pickering, *Cassell's Dictionary of Proverbs* [London: Cassell, 2001], 242). Cf. the Tarot card "The Moon," in which a dog and a wolf howl at the moon. According to A. E. Waite, "The card represents life of the imagination apart from life of the spirit. The path between the towers is the issue into the unknown. The dog and wolf are the fears of the natural mind in the presence of that place of exit, when there is only reflected light to guide it" (*The Pictorial Key to the Tarot* [London: Rider, 1911]; http://www.sacred-texts.com/tarot/pkt/pktar18.htm).

51 Cf. Edmund Spenser's "Hymne of Heavenly Beautie," lines 134–40:

> Thence gathering plumes of perfect speculation,
> To impe the wings of thy high-flying mynd,
> Mount up aloft through heavenly contemplation,
> From this darke world, whose damps the soule do blynd,
> And like the native brood of Eagles kynd,
> On that bright Sunne of glorie fixe thine eyes,
> Cleared from grosse mists of fraile infirmities.

Wayne K. Chapman notes WBY's gloss to this passage in his edition of *Poems of Spenser*, mentioning the "common tradition in mediæval natural history that the eagle strengthened its eyesight by gazing at the noonday sun" (Edinburgh: T. C. & E. C. Jack, [1906], Wade 235, YL 1977), 265; Chapman, *Yeats and English Renaissance Literature* (London: Macmillan, 1991), 129–30.

52 After the publication of *AVA*, in one of the copies the Yeatses kept in their library (YL 2433a; see *AVA* 341), GY changed the Body of Fate of Phase 22 in the Table of the Four Faculties, "Temptation versus strength," to "Temptation through strength," creating consistency with the phasal essay for Phase 22 (117). An attempt was made at some point, perhaps by Thomas Mark, to make consistent also

the description in section III above. On the second-pull set of Coole proofs, a correction changes this back again, with a note recording the fact that the word remains "versus in U.S."

53 See *YVP* 1:476–77 and 3:170–72, cf. *MYV* 2:45–48.

54 "Phase 28" here should probably read "Phase 22"; we are uncertain when this error was introduced.

55 The phasal essays that comprise this section were some of the earliest parts of *A Vision* to be composed, after WBY had abandoned the dialogue form of the earliest drafts. The essays were for a time intended to be the majority of the book and remain rhetorically central. They also remained more textually stable than many other sections after 1926 as WBY revised *A Vision*; in fact, one of the Yeatses' copies of the 1926 printing (YL 2433c) was used as setting copy for this section; see *AVA* 19–74. For an early version, see *YVP* 4:139–237.

56 This is line 8 of WBY's "The Magi," with one small alteration: "upon" is replaced by "on" (*Poems* 125).

57 In Greek mythology, Pan is god of shepherds and flocks, of nature, music, and the wild, with hindquarters, legs, and horns of a goat, and upper body of a man. He is usually depicted with his pipes. The figure of Pan became popular in the late nineteenth and early twentieth centuries, associated with the Decadent movement as well as Symbolism, neopaganism, esotericism, and Celticism. The cult of Pan included *The Great God Pan* (1894), by the Welsh writer Arthur Machen; Machen's notorious book was published in John Lane's Keynote series with a cover illustration by Aubrey Beardsley. Pan is the "Piper at the Gates of Dawn" in Kenneth Grahame's *The Wind in the Willows* (1908) and the old god whose worship is revived in Lord Dunsany's *The Blessing of Pan* (1927). WBY knew Machen (through the Order of the Golden Dawn, of which they were both members) and the Irish writer Lord Dunsany (Edward Plunkett). Pan's pipes are played in Mallarmé's famous poem "L'après-midi d'un faune," which inspired the tone poem by Debussy and controversial ballet by Nijinsky.

In a TS entitled "Book II Introduction," WBY recalls that this image was his own, not that of the Instructors:

> The list of attributes in the "Table of the Four Faculties" or in "Characters of Certain Phases" is not my work, nor could I replace it if it were lost. It was dictated nine or ten attributes at a time, and all I have done is to change two or three words for reasons of style and to fill, after I had asked permission, a blank space with the somewhat vague inscription "Player on Pan's Pipes."
> (NLI 36,272/18/4, leaf 6)

58 This passage is taken from Blake's "The Mental Traveller," lines 93–96 (Blake 486; *WWB* 2:33).

59 See Genesis 1:2: "And the earth was without form, and void; and darkness was upon the face of the deep. And the Spirit of God moved upon the face of the waters" (Authorized Version).

60 The *Drunken Faun* of the Capitoline Museums in Rome is made of *rosso antico* marble, the faun accompanied by a goat and smiling, holding up in his right hand a bunch of grapes and in his left a cane and more fruit. It has been displayed in the eponymous Hall of the Faun of the Palazzo Nuovo since 1817. The piece has long aroused admiration of travelers and cataloguers alike: it appears in Chap. 2 of Nathaniel Hawthorne's *The Marble Faun* (1859, 1860) and in Blake's "A Descriptive Catalog of Pictures, Poetical and Historical Inventions" (Blake 544; *WWB* 2:375). In Roman mythology, fauns were place-spirits (*genii*) of untamed woodland; like the Greek satyrs, they were wild and orgiastic drunken followers of Dionysus/Bacchus, with the result that they have come to represent physical strength and beauty unguided by intelligence.

61 This image of the cup of Bacchus also appears in Matthew Arnold's "Strayed Reveller" (lines 84–85). Note that the passage from John Keats's *Endymion* from which WBY quotes below also mentions Dionysus's ivy.

62 These lines are from John Keats's *Endymion* (4.263–67).

63 See Blake's "Eternity" (lines 1–4) and his "Several Questions Answered" (lines 1–4), Blake 470, 474; *WWB* 1:72 (as "Opportunity").

64 "The Hamadryad" (meaning "tree-nymph") is one of the best-known poems of Walter Savage Landor's *Hellenics* (1847).

65 WBY knew the English designer, artist, writer, and socialist thinker William Morris (1834–96) and admired such medieval romances as *The Water of the Wondrous Isles* (1897). For WBY's view of Morris's work, see "The Happiest of the Poets" (*EE* 42–50).

66 The allusion may be to various characters from poems by Shelley, including the poet of *Alastor; or the Spirit of Solitude* (1816) and Ahasuerus, the Wandering Jew of *Hellas* (1821). In an earlier version of the Dedication to *AVA*, WBY quotes two lines (155–56) about Ahasuerus from *Hellas* (NLI 36,264/3) and Alastor is the name of one of the Controls in the sleeps of 1920, arriving on October 6 (*YVP* 3:50).

67 Theocritus of Syracuse (fl. 3rd cent. BCE) is the founding figure associated with bucolic or pastoral poetry, which has played an important role in the Western poetic tradition. His poetry has traditionally been assumed to be gathered in a collection of *Idylls*, or country songs and hymns, often a competition between a shepherd and goatherd over love or skill at music and verse.

68 Pietro Bembo (1470–1547) was a native of Venice but a proponent of the Florentine language as a literary norm. His great facility in Latin, Greek, and Tuscan made him successful as a literary pundit, poet, and courtier. The city-state of Urbino, in the Marche region of Italy,

was a cultural center during the fifteenth and sixteenth centuries, although it endured a volatile political history during this time. Both Bembo and Urbino figure symbolically in WBY's work, as Urbino stood as an example of a well-run cultural center; see, for example, "To a Wealthy Man who promised a Second Subscription to the Dublin Municipal Gallery if it were proved the People wanted Pictures" (*Poems*, 106–7). WBY knew of both Bembo and Urbino from L. E. Opdycke's translation of Baldassare Castiglione's *The Book of the Courtier* (written 1508–18, published 1528; trans. Sir Thomas Toby [London: Peter Nutt, 1900]; YL 351). Castiglione's book presents a series of conversations among courtiers, including Bembo, who were guests at the Palace of Urbino in March 1507. WBY repeated this untraced exclamation in "The Bounty of Sweden" (*Au* 400).

69 In the famous "seven ages of man" speech from Shakespeare's *As You Like It* (2.7.139–66), Jacques describes the fifth age as a justice, "In fair round belly with good capon lined, / With eyes severe and beard of formal cut, / Full of wise saws and modern instances" (153–56).

70 This passage is slightly misquoted from Robert Browning's "Pauline" (lines 323–25); WBY uses the same passage in "Bishop Berkeley" (*LE* 111) and *P&I* 127.

71 This passage reproduces a song from Robert Browning's *Pippa Passes* (3:164–77).

72 *Weird* here has the old meaning of "fate," based on the Old English *wyrd*. In *The Water of the Wondrous Isles*, the heroine Birdalone laments, "I am led away by Weird into the waste and wilderness of love" (Morris, *Collected Works* 20:256). Other references to "Weird" in that work appear on 203, 211, 313, and 314.

73 This quotation adapts Dante's "*In la sua volontade è nostra pace*" (*Paradiso* 3.85), which WBY quotes in "Edmund Spenser" (*EE* 266) and "Prometheus Unbound" (*LE* 120), substituting "freedom" for "peace."

74 The Punch-and-Judy show was a popular British glove puppet show originating in the seventeenth century, featuring stock characters and a storyline derived from Italian *commedia dell'arte*. Punch wears a jester's motley, is hunchbacked, and his hooked nose almost meets his curved, jutting chin. He carries a stick as large as himself, which he freely uses upon all the other characters in the show.

75 The figures are the title characters of two poems by Byron: *Don Juan* (1821), about the legendary libertine, and *The Giaour* (1813), an orientalizing romance.

76 The American Romantic poet Walt Whitman (1819–92) is best known for his *Leaves of Grass*. The simplicity of the phase accords with WBY's description of Whitman and Emerson in "Ireland after Parnell" as "writers who have begun to seem superficial precisely because they lack the Vision of Evil" (*Au* 200). It should be noted that the phase of the moon at the time of birth bears no relation to the

phase attributed by the system of *A Vision*. The latter is, rather, a symbolic notation for the relative strengths of the primary and antithetical *Tinctures*. It is also noteworthy that human examples begin with this phase; in a sleep of July 6, 1920, recorded by GY, the Yeatses were informed that "Till five, or was it till after 5? no eminent famous personality is possible" (*YVP* 3:29).

A list of people who are examples of the phases, with identification also by astrological sign indicating placement into one of the twelve cycles (Taurus for the first cycle of twenty-eight phases, then Gemini for the second, and so on), was compiled by GY and filed with the AS for June 2, 1918 (*YVP* 1:549). Over three days, from June 2 through 4, the Yeatses received many of the examples retained in these phasal essays (*YVP* 1:187–97).

77 This line is slightly misquoted from line 8 of Whitman's "Song of Myself," where the speaker notes his age as thirty-seven.

78 See paragraph 11 of "Higher Laws" in *Walden* (1854) by American writer Henry David Thoreau (1817–62), a work that was an influence on "The Lake Isle of Innisfree" (*Au* 139). WBY owned a copy (YL 2133).

79 In the early draft labelled "Version B," the description for Self (not yet changed to be called *Will*) makes clear why human examples begin to multiply beginning with Phase 7: here occurs the "First realization of Self (?Premonition of personality)" (*YVP* 4:177).

80 George Borrow (1803–81) primarily wrote novels and travelogues about his journeys around Europe. In the DMR-TS, WBY noted Borrow's "insistence in Lavengro upon his recurring attack of the horrors" (*YVP* 4:30), referring to Chap. 84 of Borrow's largely autobiographical novel. It may be that WBY was reading or rereading *Lavengro* while composing *AVA*, as he refers to the novel in a letter to Olivia Shakespear dated June 28, 1923, calling some of its events "a little heightened" (*L* 699).

The reference seems to be to French novelist Alexandre Dumas (1802–70), who wrote such tales of high adventure as *The Three Musketeers* (1844) and *The Count of Monte Cristo* (1845–46), among many others, rather than to Dumas's son (1824–95), the author of a number of commercially successful novels, including *The Lady of the Camellias* (1848), which famously served as the basis of Verdi's opera *La Traviata*.

Thomas Carlyle (1795–1881) was an influential Scottish essayist and historian, best known as the author of *Sartor Resartus* (1831).

The Scottish poet James Macpherson (1736–96) is best known as the "translator" of Ossianic poems about Finn mac Cumhail, including *Fingal, an Ancient Epic Poem in Six Books, together with Several Other Poems composed by Ossian, the Son of Fingal, translated from the Gaelic Language* (1761), *Temora* (1763), and a collected edition,

The Works of Ossian (1765). The authenticity of the translated documents was challenged by Samuel Johnson, and although Macpherson insisted on their genuineness, he never published his originals.

81 This assertion might be rooted in J. A. Froude's posthumous *My Relations with Carlyle* (London: Longmans Green; New York: Scribner, 1903, 21ff.) or Frank Harris's "Talks with Carlyle" (*English Review*, 1911; reproduced in *Contemporary Portraits* [London: Methuen, New York: Mitchell Kennerley, 1915, 1–33, esp. 25–33]). WBY's assessment of Carlyle's work as abstraction and empty rhetoric occurs also in a letter of March 14, 1916, which also presents a comparison with Macpherson's *Ossian* (*L* 608). On "plaster of ant's eggs," Sutherland reports, "Mr. Per Guldbeck of Parks Canada, Cornwall, Ontario, advises me that a 'plaster of ant's eggs' was an old remedy for impotence. He directs my attention to R. Dunglison, *A Dictionary of Medical Science* (Philadelphia: Lea & Blanchard, 1845), where Formica, or the ant, is described as containing 'an acid juice and gross oil which were formerly extolled as aphrodisiacs . . .' (p. 320)" (759).

82 Prince Lyov Nikolaievich Myshkin, the protagonist of *The Idiot* (1869) by the Russian novelist Fyodor Dostoyevsky (1821–81), is a character whose mental condition is unclear: when younger he had blackouts and learning difficulties, but what his society views as idiocy may simply be honesty and trustfulness. WBY seems to have read *The Possessed* and *The Idiot* by 1922 (*Au* 176, 199), but Gabriel Fallon recalls Lady Gregory responding to WBY's mention of Dostoyevsky by saying "You know, Willie, you never read a novel by Dostoievsky" and promising to send him a copy of *The Idiot* (*Sean O'Casey: The Man I Knew* [London: Routledge, 1965], 21–22).

83 In a common way of understanding humanity's relationship to nature and God in the early modern West, a human being was a microcosm of all creation, in possession of three souls: with plants and animals were shared the "vegetative" and "sensitive" souls, but the possession of a rational soul made a human godlike, distinguished from the lower orders of creation.

84 The eldest son of the English Romantic poet and philosopher Samuel Taylor Coleridge (1772–1834), Hartley Coleridge (1796–1849) wrote poetry, biographies, and literary criticism, as well as the unfinished lyric drama *Prometheus*. He is less known for his slight literary reputation than for his intemperate life and early death.

85 Patrick Branwell Brontë (1817–48), the only brother of writers Charlotte, Emily, and Anne Brontë, was an artist but also an alcoholic and perhaps a drug addict, and his early death is blamed on these addictions.

86 From one of the Seven Last Words, phrases the gospels report to have been uttered by Jesus on the cross. See Mark 15:34: "And at the ninth hour Jesus cried with a loud voice, saying, Eloi, Eloi, lama sabachthani? which is, being interpreted, My God, my God, why hast thou

forsaken me?" A similar passage occurs in Matthew 27:46. Psalm 22, a prayer for deliverance from a mortal illness, begins, "My God, my God, why hast thou forsaken me? / Why art thou so far from helping me, from the words of my groaning?" (Authorized Version). WBY quotes this phrase also in *PASL* (*LE* 13). Cf. 174.

87 An early draft had no example; the "unnamed artist" is likely Wyndham Lewis. See n89 below.

88 In William Shakespeare's *Richard III*, George, Duke of Clarence, tells of a dream in which he visits the underworld, encountering, among others, the shade of Prince Edward, son of Henry VI. As Clarence describes the dream to the Keeper in the Tower, "Then came wand'ring by / A shadow like an angel, with bright hair / Dabbled in blood, and he shriek'd out aloud, / 'Clarence is come—false, fleeting, perjur'd Clarence, / That stabb'd me in the field by Tewksbury: / Seize on him, Furies, take him unto torment!'" (1.4.52–57).

89 The "certain artist" is the British painter and writer Wyndham Lewis (1882–1957), the "notable man" Augustus John, and the "mistress" Dorothy (Dorelia) McNeill, with whom John had four children. In the DMR-TS, Robartes says, "I wonder too if I should not place at ten or eleven the genius of Augustus John the images of whose art unlike those of Rembrandt or Valasquez, men of late phases whose intellectual egos have separated themselves from the images of their art, seem accidental and instinctive as though their creator saw from within the race, his soul unfixed and floating" (*YVP* 4:31). In the discussion of Phase 9 in "Version B," WBY writes, "Last night after I wrote these words I was sitting in the Cafe Royal when I got into conversation with a bullet headed young man, who had that short neck which I associate with passion." Lewis spoke to WBY (not to a "student of these symbols") of "a certain notable man" and his mistress. WBY noted that this young man was "a cubist artist of powerful imagination," adding, "There I thought is my example" for Phase 9 (*YVP* 4:183). See also other mentions of Lewis in *A Vision*: WBY's note about him on 4, the final section of "Introduction to 'A Vision'" (19), and the mention of Lewis in a passage from *AVA* not retained in *AVB* (*AVA* 174–76). Robartes says that "in Gyraldus' allegorical woodcut that phase is symbolised by an eagle tearing out a man's eyes" (DMR-TS, *YVP* 4:30).

90 Charles Stewart Parnell (1846–91) was an Irish nationalist leader whose Irish Parliamentary Party fought in the 1880s for Home Rule for Ireland and Irish land reform in the British House of Commons. He was mythologized by many as a national hero, but his career was ruined by a combination of forces, the most dramatic of which was the revelation of his long-standing affair with Katherine O'Shea. By the time that WBY and GY were generating the system, Parnell's reputation had been largely resurrected, a process that began with his

death and intensified especially after the Irish party reunited in 1900 under John Redmond. WBY's poetic treatments of Parnell include the early "Mourn—And Then Onward!" and three later poems, "Parnell's Funeral," "Come Gather Round Me Parnellites," and "Parnell," *Poems* 537–38, 285–86, 315–16, and 318.

91 The reference is to Mrs. Katherine O'Shea (better known as "Kitty O'Shea," a name given her by Parnell's enemies using a slang term for a prostitute), Parnell's mistress and later wife, whose shocking divorce trial was the catalyst for Parnell's fall from power. She gives her account in *Charles Stewart Parnell: His Love Story and Political Life* (2 vols.; London: Cassell, 1914).

92 Gretchen appears in *Faust* by the German novelist, dramatist, philosopher, and humanist Johann Wolfgang von Goethe (1749–1832). In his reference to Helen of Troy, WBY draws on lines 2603–4, where Mephistopheles says that after drinking a diabolical drink, Faust will see Helen in every woman (*The First Part of the Tragedy of Faust*, trans. Thomas E. Webb [2nd ed., with "The Death of Faust" from the second part, London: Longmans Green, 1898; YL 753], 124).

93 In Victor Hugo's *The Toilers of the Sea* (1866), Déruchette writes Gilliatt's name in the snow, albeit with her finger rather than a parasol (Book 1, Chap. 1). This incident serves as an example in Walter Pater's essay "Romanticism" (revised as "Postscript" in *Appreciations* [London and New York: Macmillan, 1889], 260). WBY wrote that he "read all Victor Hugo's romances" in his youth (*Au* 95).

94 Odin, according to the *Hávamál* in the *Elder Edda*, committed a self-sacrifice by wounding himself and then hanging himself from the branches of the ash tree Yggdrasil, the world tree. After nine days and nights, Odin saw some runes below him, and in lifting them was set free by their magical power, soon discovering himself filled with new youth and vigor. WBY refers to this same incident in *Mem* 146, *Plays* 704, and *EE* 233 ("the sacrifice of a man to himself"). WBY may have encountered the story in various contexts: by 1917, GY had read the *Eddas* (*L* 635), and MacGregor Mathers mentioned the passage in the Golden Dawn Flying Roll No. 10 (in Francis King [ed.], *Astral Projection: Ritual Magic and Alchemy by S. L. MacGregor Mathers and Others, Being Hitherto Unpublished Golden Dawn Material* [New York: Samuel Weiser, 1971], 121): "Recall to your mind that passage in one of the Eddas 'I hung on the Tree three days and three nights, wounded with a spear, myself a sacrifice offered to my (highest) Self,—Odin unto Odin.'" The passage also appears in Sir James George Frazer's *The Golden Bough* (3rd ed., 12 vols.; 1907–15; rpt. New York: Macmillan, 1951; YL 700), 5:290. Frazer's source seems less immediate, because unlike the Golden Dawn source it retains the original nine days and nights, but the Yeatses discussed *The Golden Bough* in the automatic experiments on several occasions.

95 Moses brings down the Ten Commandments from Mount Sinai in Exodus 34:39. A similar comparison of Moses and Parnell is made in the last couplet of WBY's poem "Mourn—And Then Onward!" (*Poems* 537).

96 Viscount John Morley writes of Parnell in *Recollections* (2 vols.; New York: Macmillan, 1917) that "In ordinary conversation he was pleasant, without much play of mind; temperament made him the least discursive of the human race" (1:238).

97 See Katherine O'Shea, *Charles Stewart Parnell* 1:176–77; cf. *Poems* 674–75, *Au* 191.

98 In the months following Parnell's trial for adultery, his rejection by William Gladstone's Liberal party, and his loss of popular Catholic Irish support, Parnell fought to retain his hold on parliamentary power. From December 1–6, 1890, the Irish party famously met in Committee Room 15 of the House of Commons to consider whether to retain him as leader. After several days of angry discussion, during which Parnell used his position as chair to prevent the issue from coming to a vote, a majority of members left the room and declared his deposition. A minority remained in the room with Parnell, splitting the party and ensuring Parnell's political downfall.

99 This description follows Katherine O'Shea's account, as given in *Charles Stewart Parnell* 2:153; see also *Au* 191.

100 Although WBY thought of the pantheistic philosopher Baruch de Spinoza (1632–77) as a mystic, he was less fond of his rationalism (*L* 650). According to George Mills Harper and Walter Kelly Hood, an early manuscript seems to describe Spinoza as one who embraces "some abstract system of belief, some bundle of almost mathematical principles and convictions" (*A Critical Edition of Yeats's "A Vision" (1925)*, ed. Harper and Hood [London: Macmillan 1978], Note 18). Robartes is more concrete in the DMR-TS: "at eleven one discovers now a Pantheistic image of man little more precise than my own legs when I study them through the water where I am bathing and now the reason[ed] conviction of Spinoza" (*YVP* 4:31).

The Dominican friar Girolamo Savonarola (1452–98) rose to power in Florence after the exile of Piero de' Medici in 1494, becoming a spokesman for a moral crusade damning the ruling families for such vices and frivolity as theater and the fine arts. He sponsored infamous "bonfires of the vanities," in which books, works of art, musical instruments, and other objects deemed occasions of sin were burned. For WBY's sense of Savanarola, see *EE* 167. On the list filed with the AS of June 2, 1918, Schopenhauer also appears in Phase 11 (*YVP* 1:549).

101 The list filed with the AS for June 2, 1918, lists Nietzsche, Pound, and Virgil as examples for this phase, with the names Keats and Tennyson crossed out (*YVP* 1:549). The DMR-TS includes a passage about

Pound that WBY omitted, although he kept Pound as an example until the galleys of *AVA*. In that TS, Robartes says, "His enemy is that which opposes isolation some form of collective thought & many among whom I would be sorry to include your enemy Ezra Pound, by the frenzy of their attack increase more & more the power of the vehicle, & so bring the creative power to its death & remain themselves not transfigured but transfixed" (*YVP* 4:31–32, and see also the references to Pound in the DMR-MS, *YVP* 4:86–88). WBY asked on May 23, 1918, "Ezra of violence, Nietzsche violence?" although the Control Thomas did not respond (*YVP* 1:454).

102 The examples listed are the French poet Charles Baudelaire (1821–67), the English illustrator and poet Aubrey Beardsley (1872–98), and the English poet and member of the Rhymers' Club Ernest Dowson (1867–1900). Baudelaire and Verlaine were the two examples given in the list filed with the AS for June 2, 1918 (*YVP* 1:549), and the DMR-TS (*YVP* 4:32). In this list, Beardsley accompanied Blake and others at Phase 16 (*YVP* 1:549, 4:35). Dowson was added at some point in revision. WBY recounts numerous stories of Dowson in *The Trembling of the Veil*, including one (*Au* 252) frequently repeated by Pound (see James Longenbach, *Stone Cottage: Pound, Yeats & Modernism* [New York and Oxford: Oxford University Press, 1988], 165–66). In that text, WBY says of Beardsley, "He was in my Lunar metaphor a man of the thirteenth Phase, his nature on the edge of Unity of Being, the understanding of that Unity by the intellect his one overmastering purpose" (*Au* 254).

103 The English Romantic poet John Keats (1795–1821) plays a role from before the arrival of the AS in topics that would be developed there and in *A Vision*, and he is also discussed in many automatic sessions. See his appearances in "Ego Dominus Tuus" from 1915 (*Poems* 161) and *PASL* (*LE* 7). In 1918, WBY set up a contrast between Keats and Shelley that is borne out in their placement on the wheel in Phases 14 and 17, respectively: "If you accept metempsychosis, Keats was moving to greater subjectivity of being, and to unity of that being, and Shelley to greater objectivity and to consequent break-up of unity of being" (*L* 653). In the AS of December 6 and 21, 1917, Keats appears in Phase 12 (*YVP* 1:146, 169), although on June 2, 1918, he is first in Phase 12 then moved to Phase 14 with Wordsworth, Iseult Gonne, and Tennyson because they all loved the world or nature (*YVP* 1:549). WBY frequently cites "Ode to a Nightingale" as an example of the daimonic influence on an artwork already in the *Anima Mundi*. "Thoughts & images received by Keats . . . still remain & can be transfered to us" (Card File, *YVP* 3:413).

The Venetian painter Giorgione (Giorgio Barbarelli da Castelfranco, c. 1477–1510) was one of the most important figures of the High Renaissance, founder with his close associate Titian of "the Venetian school." Cf. Walter Pater's famous essay "The School of Giorgione," *The Renaissance: Studies in Art and Literature* (1873; London: Macmillan, 1935, YL 1539, 120–43). The unspecified "many beautiful women" include Iseult Gonne and Helen of Troy.

104 WBY's *The Words Upon the Window-Pane* (1930) takes place in a house that belonged to friends of Jonathan Swift and features lines of poetry written by his friend Stella (Esther Johnson) cut into a windowpane, perhaps by Stella herself (*Plays* 465–79).

105 This statue by French sculptor Auguste Rodin (1840–1917) resides in the Musée Rodin in Paris. For a reproduction, see *YVP* 4:93.

106 The references are to portraits of women painted by the English Pre-Raphaelite painter Sir Edward Burne-Jones (1833–98), the Florentine painter Sandro Botticelli (Alessandro Filipepi [di Mariano di Vanni], c. 1445–1510), and the English painter and poet Dante Gabriel (Gabriel Charles Dante) Rossetti (1828–82). In the list filed with the AS of June 2, 1918, Rossetti appears first in Phase 14 and then is moved to Phase 17 (*YVP* 1:549).

107 Sir Edward Burne-Jones painted *The Golden Stair* (in the Tate Britain) and the late work *The Sleep of King Arthur in Avalon* (begun 1881; in the Museo de Arte de Ponce, Puerto Rico). The DMR-TS mentions *Briar Rose* (1870–90, exhibited 1890), Burne-Jones's popular series of four large paintings, instead of *The Golden Stair* (*YVP* 4:35).

108 The description of the "soul's deepening solitude" in Wordsworth is repeated almost verbatim from the DMR-TS, in which Wordsworth was still placed in Phase 14 (*YVP* 4:35). In January 1915, WBY and Pound proposed "to read through the whole seven vols of Wordsworth in Dowden's edition" (*L* 590). Longenbach notes, "In January 1915 the local vicar paid Pound and Yeats a visit, which Pound told his companion they had brought on themselves by reading too much Wordsworth" (*Stone Cottage: Pound, Yeats & Modernism* [New York and Oxford: Oxford University Press, 1988], 4; see also 142–43). In February 1917, in "Anima Hominis," WBY depicted "Wordsworth withering into eighty years, honoured and empty-witted" (*LE* 16).

109 On Keats's sensualism, see *Early Articles and Reviews*, ed. John P. Frayne and Madeleine Marchaterre, *The Collected Works of W. B. Yeats*, Vol. 9, gen. eds. Richard J. Finneran and George Mills Harper (New York: Scribner, 2004), 387; *Poems* 163, *LE* 6–7. For "the pepper on the tongue," see a sensationalized anecdote in *The Autobiography and Journals of Benjamin Robert Haydon*, ed. Malcolm Elwin (1853; London: MacDonald, 1950), that Keats "—to show what a man does to gratify his appetites when once they get the better of him—once covered his tongue and throat as far as he could reach with cayenne pepper in order to appreciate the 'delicious coldness of

claret in all its glory'" (352–53; see also Walter Jackson Bate, *John Keats* [Cambridge, Mass.: Harvard University Press, 1963], 463).

110 Adolphe Joseph Thomas Monticelli (1824–86), French painter of the Barbizon school, returned to his native Marseilles after the outbreak of the Franco-Prussian War (1870) and there developed his mature style, often painting with Paul Cézanne. English painter Charles Conder (1868–1909) was an acquaintance of WBY and a member of the Decadent movement (see *L* 508–9 and *Au* 250, 266).

111 Sutherland connects Helen of Troy's abduction by Paris to Maud Gonne's marriage to John MacBride; see lines from WBY's unpublished poem from 1909, "My dear is angry that of late / I cry all base blood down / As though she had not taught me hate / By ~~kindness~~ / kisses to a clown" (*Mem* 145) and Iseult Gonne's marriage to Francis Stuart—in "Why should not Old Men be Mad?" he writes "A girl that knew all Dante once / Live to bear children to a dunce" (*Poems* 592).

112 Phase 15 is that of complete beauty, so it can contain no human life. The phase description stresses the connection between physical and spiritual beauty. In the DMR-TS, Robartes emphasizes that "all beauty has been, would be or will be physical and that is why those creatures at the Fifteenth phase—though invisible to our eyes—are ponderable and plant their feet upon this earth and why, no longer limited by thought their eyes have such an eagle gaze." A bit later WBY inserted a note by John Aherne: "It is one of the doctrines of Kusta ben Luka that the retina of the eye has an incalculable range and that it is limited by our expectations alone. He explained many miraculous phenomena in this way." Touch and hearing have "a like range" (*YVP* 4:37–38). Cf. 356 n51.

113 For this recurring set of polarities, see, for example, "Solomon and the Witch" (*Poems* 179–80).

114 A primary man and *Teacher*, Christ desired the other world, while his "forerunner," an antithetical man and *Victim*, connected the physical beauty of this world with the spiritual. Another avatar, of which there can be only one "to each cycle," is Krishna, according to the AS of June 2, 1918 (*YVP* 1:468, summarized on *YVP* 3:339). "This cannot yet be understood" until the "successor" (also called "New Messiah," "Initiate," or "Avatar" in the AS) appears at the end of the present cycle of 2,000 years. This concept was often discussed in the AS, beginning as early as November 21, 1917 (*YVP* 1:94–95); see, for example, the AS for May 26, 1918 (*YVP* 1:458–62), and the notebook entry for December 12, 1920 (*YVP* 3:62). For the terms *Teacher* (or *Sage*) and *Victim*, see 375–76 n163.

115 Besides WBY's favorite Blake, the examples are François Rabelais (c. 1493–1553), the French author of *Gargantua* and *Pantagruel*; the Italian author, poet, playwright, and satirist Pietro Aretino (1492–

1556); and the alchemist, physician, astrologer, and general occultist Paracelsus (1493–1541, born Theophrastus Bombastus von Hohenheim). The names on this list varied at different stages: the sheet accompanying the automatic script of June 2, 1918, names Blake, Beardsley, Stephens, Madame Gonne, Cervantes (*YVP* 1:549), while the DMR-TS includes "Blake and Beardsley and perhaps Boehme" (*YVP* 4:35), and "Version B" gives only Blake and Rabelais (*YVP* 4:193). The relationships among these examples may be explained by the explanation in DMR-TS that the list should include (1) satirists "who hate the ugly and pity the beautiful" (thus Blake and Rabelais); (2) "certain rare sages who are permitted to pity intellectual despair that pity Christ never knew" (thus Paracelsus or the rejected Boehme and Cervantes); and (3) "the termagants those women who are the most beautiful of all escaping distortion of feature by distortion of mind enraged by all that is hostile to the loneliness of the Self" (thus Maud Gonne). Robartes says, "if a man has not loved a woman of the fourteenth or of the Sixteenth phase he has not known the greatest earthly beauty" (*YVP* 4:36–37).

116 St. George (c. 275–303), according to tradition a Roman soldier and Christian martyr, is one of Christianity's most venerated saints. The story of him slaying a dragon in order to end its demands for regular human sacrifice is usually interpreted as the triumph of good over evil.

117 Blake so speaks of schools of art in "A Descriptive Catalogue" (Number IX): "These Pictures . . . were the result of temptations and perturbations, labouring to destroy Imaginative power, by means of that infernal machine, called Chiaro Oscuro, in the hands of Venetian and Flemish Demons . . ." (Blake 547; *WWB* 2:377). See also *EE* 89.

118 For a narration of this incident, see Alexander Gilchrist, *Life of William Blake*, ed. Ruthven Todd (London: J. M. Dent, 1942), 241; and G. E. Bentley, *Blake Records* (Oxford: Clarendon, 1969), 180–81. WBY misspells the name of English illustrator, painter, and engraver Thomas Stothard (1775–1834).

119 In "Swedenborg, Mediums, and the Desolate Places," WBY quotes Villiers de l'Isle Adam quoting Aquinas as saying, "Eternity is the possession of one's self, as in a single moment" (*LE* 52); see also *PASL* (*LE* 19, 26) and *On the Boiler* (*LE* 247). The passage in the first English translation of *Axël* (1890), published in 1925 with WBY's preface, reads, "For eternity, as Saint Thomas well remarks, is merely the full and entire possession of oneself in one and the same instant" (trans. H. P. R. Finberg [London: Jarrolds, 1925], 60; YL 2201). In the *Summa theologica*, Aquinas tests the Boethian position that eternity is "interminabilis vitae tota simul et perfecta possessio" (part 1, *quaestio* 10, referring to *De consolatione philosophiae* 5:6).

120 The work of Dutch painter Rembrandt Harmenszoon van Rijn

(1606–69), one of the greatest European painters, shows great empathy with his subjects and humanity.

121 "The Burning Babe" is a poem by the Elizabethan Jesuit martyr and poet Robert Southwell (1561–95).

122 See the DMR-TS:

> One marble shape rises before me a French Diana of the 16th Century her exquisite head alert she lies half sitting amid the wild deer that in a moment she will destroy, dogs and deer alike gathered about her in fascinated affection: A king's mistress, a quiver of arrows to symbolise that bitter wit that kept ministers in dread, whom the artist solitary it may be as herself saw transfigured as the goddess lingering amid her woodland court after all Olympus elfs had vanished, Was she in truth Diana of Poitiers, was a King of France great enough to love such a beauty and did he turn away at last from that never empty quiver? (*YVP* 4:36–37)

This sculpture of Diana known as *The Fountain of Diana* and *Diana of Anet* (mid-sixteenth cent.), is in the Louvre. It was long incorrectly attributed to Jean Goujon, but because it was heavily restored in the eighteenth century its original artist is unknown. It is often seen as praising Diane de Poitiers, mistress of Henry II of France. It appeared reproduced in plate 2 between pages 496–97 of the *Encyclopaedia Britannica*, 11th ed. (YL 629–30). For a reproduction, see *YVP* 4:36. WBY almost certainly intended Maud Gonne to be the archetypal woman who walks like a queen (an allusion to *Cathleen Ní Houlihan* by WBY and Lady Gregory, *Plays* 93); she is the only woman named in Phase 16 in the AS and in early versions of *AVA*.

123 This quotation appears twice in *AVB*; see 19.

124 Hephaestus, the Greek analogue of the Roman god of fire and volcanoes, is often depicted as lame from birth, ill-made in both legs, with twisted feet and stumbling gait. The early Roman god Vulcan later took on qualities from the Greek god, including his marriage to Venus/ Aphrodite.

125 Although the 1937 edition as here reads simply "Loss," "Enforced" is added as a descriptor in manuscript on the first-pull Coole proofs (BL Add. 55893); the change is noted in Thomas Mark's notebook and retained in the 1962 edition.

126 While this printed list includes Dante, Shelley, and Landor, Landor's name was omitted, perhaps accidentally, from this list in *AVA*. The earliest list of examples (AS June 2, 1918) names WBY, Shelley, Landor, Dante, Homer, Botticelli, Burne-Jones, Rossetti (*YVP* 1:549). Elsewhere in the AS and Card File, WBY appears here. A sleep dated July 6, 1920, notes "M[aud]G[onne], 16, my self 17" (*YVP* 3:128),

and a detailed diagram in the Card File shows "individual horoscope 'WBY' being placed to show ascendant at 17" (*YVP* 3:296). WBY does not use his own name in the description of Phase 17 in the DMR-TS or other early drafts, although numerous passages show him thinking of himself.

127 These are both characters from Shelley's work. Ahasuerus appears in *Hellas* and *Queen Mab; A Philosophical Poem* (1813) and Athanase in "Prince Athanase."

128 If Dante's Mask is "gaunt," then his Will is the opposite, as WBY had suggested in the poem "Ego Dominus Tuus." One voice in the dialogue of the poem, "Hic," notes that Dante's *Commedia* has made "that hollow face of his / More plain to the mind's eye than any face / But that of Christ"; but the voice of "Ille" counters, "is that spectral image / The man that Lapo and that Guido knew?" "Ille" continues,

> Being mocked by Guido for his lecherous life,
> Derided and deriding, driven out
> To climb that stair and eat that bitter bread,
> He found the unpersuadable justice, he found
> The most exalted lady loved by a man.
> (*Poems* 162)

The AS contains further discussion of the idea that Dante created an opposite for the self-named subject of his work; see, for example, a passage from a notebook entry by GY: "We took Dante as an example" of the movement of the soul through the *Faculties*, thus discovering that a True *Mask* "accepts its doom, is 'Doom-eager' Dante sees himself in his exile as the tragic Dante of the Poems. He sees him self as he is fated & desires that self" (*YVP* 3:27).

129 Mary Shelley's note to Percy Bysshe Shelley's "Prince Athanase" suggests that the poem traces a development from material to transcendent love, "Pandemos, or the earthly and unworthy Venus." The distinction between earthly (Aphrodite Pandemos) and heavenly love (Aphrodite Urania) comes from Plato's *Symposium* (Mary Wollstonecraft Shelley, ed., *Poetical Works of Percy Bysshe Shelley* [3 vols.; London: Edward Moxon, 1847, YL 1907]), 2:242. See *EE* 67 and George Bornstein, *Yeats and Shelley* (Chicago: University of Chicago Press, 1970), 72–73.

130 Beatrice Portinari (1266–90), with whom Dante claims to have fallen in love at first sight, was the basis for his *Vita nuova* as well as his ultimate spiritual guide and symbol of salvation in the *Commedia*. The Great Yellow Rose appears in canto 30 of *Paradiso* (line 113) and served as standard Rosicrucian background in such works as A. E. Waite's *The Brotherhood of the Rosy Cross* (London: W. Rider, 1924), 94.

131 WBY used the phrase "pale passion loves" several times (see *EE* 171, 271). The line "Fountaine heads, and pathlesse Groves, / Places which pale passion loves" is from the song "Hence all you vaine Delights," praising "sweetest melancholy," from the play *The Nice Valour* by John Fletcher and possibly Thomas Middleton, 3.3.46–47 (*The Dramatic Works in the Beaumont and Fletcher Canon*, gen. ed. Fredson Bowers [10 vols.; Cambridge: Cambridge University Press, 1966–96], 7:468).

132 The reference might be to Shelley's "Address to the Irish People" (1812), "Declaration of Rights" (1812), "Letter to Lord Ellenborough" (1812), and "Vindication of Natural Diet" (1813).

133 See Shelley's *Alastor*, lines 248–50, 413, 471, 534–35 (Shelley 1:8, 11, 13, 14).

134 See Shelley's *Hellas*, lines 164–65: "less accessible / Than thou or God!" (Shelley 2:54). This section of *Hellas* is also quoted at length in *Au* 152–53.

135 See Edward Dowden's *The Life of Percy Bysshe Shelley* (1886; rpt. New York: Barnes and Noble, 1966; see *Au* 95). Although some did not believe him, Shelley in 1813 claimed to have been attacked, and in a letter he used the word "assassination" (Dowden 184). The wife of one witness said that Shelley, who thought he had been fired upon through a window, "bounced out on the grass, and there he saw leaning against a tree the ghost, or, as he said, the devil . . ." (Dowden 188).

136 *The Cenci* (1819), Shelley's verse drama about incest and revenge, relates the tale of Beatrice Cenci (1577–99), executed with the rest of her family for murdering her abusive and violent father, the Roman patriarch Francesco Cenci.

137 The contemporary here is Giovanni Boccaccio (1313–75), the scholar, poet, and author of *The Decameron*: see *Life of Dante*, trans. Philip Henry Wicksteed (San Francisco: Printed by John Henry Nash for his friends, 1922; YL 232), 38. WBY owned one of the 250 copies of this fine limited edition of Boccaccio's biography, which presented Dante as a poet of the people rather than a man of classical learning. The biography experienced a surge of popularity in English-speaking countries around the turn of the century, after no less than four new translations appeared between 1898 and 1904. See also a reference in *PASL* (*LE* 7) and *AVA* lv.

138 Shelley wrote to Thomas Love Peacock in a letter dated April 6, 1819, "I am regarded by all who know or hear of me, except, I think, on the whole five individuals as a rare prodigy of crime & pollution whose look even might infect" (*Letters of Percy Bysshe Shelley*, ed. Frederick L. Jones [Oxford: Clarendon, 1964], 2:94).

139 Emerson and Whitman are similarly described in *Au* 200. The AS of June 10, 1918, lays out the necessity of oppositions and the nature of evil: "In so far as knowledge of evil is attained," the Control Thomas

said, "one becomes good but in as far as one is good the visible world becomes evil because it is no virtue to be good knowing no evil—& it is no sin to be evil knowing no good" (*YVP* 1:492).

140 In Shelley's play *Prometheus Unbound* (1820), the great triumph of the Good that ends the play is awaited and witnessed by the personified Earth and Moon, and by the Oceanides Ione and Panthea. George Bornstein notes that WBY's version of Shelley is self-reflective rather than representative of the earlier poet (*Yeats and Shelley* 207–8).

141 Landor appears twice in *PASL* (*LE* 6, 15).

142 Besides Goethe and the Victorian poet and cultural critic Matthew Arnold (1822–88), the list of examples for this phase on the sheet filed with the AS of June 2, 1918, was longer: Zarathustra, GY, Goethe, Dulac, George Frederic Watts, Villon, Plutarch, Montaigne, Dürer, Titian, and two indecipherable names (*YVP* 1:549). As with WBY himself and Phase 17, numerous aspects of the following essay suggest that WBY had GY, the philosophically minded receiver, interpreter, and organizer of the material and its uses, in mind as he wrote.

143 WBY slightly misquotes the titles of Rossetti's "Love's Nocturne" (see *EE* 213 and *Au* 234) and Shelley's "Ode to the West Wind."

144 Paraphrased from Goethe's *Wilhelm Meisters Wanderjahre*: "Wie kann man sich selbst kennen lernen? Durch Betrachten niemals, wohl aber durch Handeln" (*Werke,* ed. Enrich Trunz et al. [Hamburg: Christian Webner Verlag, 1964–67], 8:283).

145 Ahasuerus is the mythical Wandering Jew, appearing in Shelley's poems *The Wandering Jew* (1810), *Queen Mab; A Philosophical Poem* (1813), and the verse drama *Hellas* (1921). This "old man, master of all human knowledge, hidden from human sight in some shell-strewn cavern on the Mediterranean shore" (*Au* 151) was important to WBY from a young age. See *Au* 150–59.

146 Thomas Lovell Beddoes notes, "Goethe married his maid servant & drinks brandy" (*Works*, ed. H. W. Donner [London: Oxford, 1935], 626), but the letter in Edmund Gosse's edition of *The Letters of Thomas Lovell Beddoes* (1894; [rpt. New York: Benjamin Blom, 1971], 119–25) does not include the passage, so WBY would not have known of it directly. Goethe loved Charlotte von Stein, but she was married to the Master of the Horse of the Duke of Saxe-Weimar.

147 These words were spoken by Arthur Symons (*Au* 257 and *Mem* 97, and see *L* 298). In "Version B," WBY wrote that "The one man of this phase I have known intimately, the serpent charming lover, was a connosseur in several arts, a man of great tecnical mastery who saw art, life, literature as tecnical problems, & his life had lacked all momentum but for his bodily lusts" (*YVP* 4:200).

148 This passage may refer to the proverb "To sit (or sing) like a nightingale with a thorn against one's breast" or to that proverb's appear-

ance in *The Spanish Tragedy* by Thomas Kyd, *The Rape of Lucrece* by William Shakespeare, and elsewhere.

149 The Italian poet, novelist, and nationalist politician Gabriele d'Annunzio (1863–1938) led a seizure of the city of Fiume (Rijeka in Croatia) in 1919, maintaining control of the "independent state" until December 1920; his approach foreshadowed many aspects of Italian fascism. The Irish playwright, critic, and novelist Oscar Wilde (1854–1900) was one of the most successful writers of his day, but he was also infamous for his involvement in the Queensberry Scandal and his trial in 1895. For WBY's assessment of Wilde, see *Au* 124–30.

The examples also include the English Romantic poet George Gordon, Lord Byron (1788–1824), of whose life WBY knew partly from Ralph Milbank, Earl of Lovelace's *Astarte: A Fragment of Truth concerning George Gordon Byron, Sixth Lord Byron* (London: Chiswick Press, 1905), which WBY read in 1906 (*L* 468). WBY may have been aware of the second edition in 1921. WBY knew that Byron had a sexual relationship with his half-sister, Augusta Leigh.

"A certain actress" is the English actress Mrs. Patrick Campbell (née Beatrice Stella Tanner, 1865–1940), whom WBY saw in Maeterlinck's *Blue Bird* (*L* 544) and who performed the part of Mélisande in *Pelléas and Mélisande* (in 1898 and July 1904). In the AS of November 21, 1917, the Control Thomas describes her as one in whom the antithetical is "losing" to the primary. WBY asked, "Am I right in supposing that Mrs C violent egotism is aroused by the intensity of her consciousness of Materlinck emotion," to which Thomas responded, "The egotism in its endeavour to anihilate the meterlinc emotion becomes more violent until it has achieved its purpose when it becomes more normal" (*YVP* 1:93; see also *YVP* 2:17). This information is transferred to "Tinctures" in the Card File (*YVP* 3:419), and a rejected section of "Version B" addresses George Bernard Shaw and Mrs. Campbell (*YVP* 4:200–202). In *PASL*, WBY enforced the distinction between Mrs. Campbell's selfless presence as a Maeterlinck queen and her personal egotism (*LE* 5).

The examples for this phase in the list filed with the AS of June 2, 1918, differed significantly, naming Browning, Velázquez, and Cromwell (*YVP* 1:549).

150 Mrs. Campbell's collection of Burne-Jones engravings drew attention from many. See *LE* 217 (quoting from "Yeux Glauques" from Ezra Pound's "Hugh Selwyn Mauberley") and Penelope Fitzgerald, *Edward Burne-Jones: A Biography* (London: Michael Joseph, 1975), 244.

151 William Shakespeare, the French novelist Honoré de Balzac (1799–1850), and Napoleon replace the longer list of examples in the AS of June 2, 1918: Dickens, Shakespeare, Chaucer, Plato, Fielding, Meredith, Anatole France (*YVP* 1:549). WBY struck through Fielding

in "Version B," replacing him with 'Balzac. Perhaps Ben Johnson' (*YVP* 4:203). WBY spent much time in the 1930s rereading Balzac's *Comédie Humaine*; he wrote to Joseph Hone in 1932 that "I was educated upon Balzac & Shakespeare & cannot go beyond them" (*CL InteLex* 5598).

152 See Shakespeare, Sonnet 110.

153 This episode derives from the *Mémoires* of Napoleon's secretary Bourrienne, but WBY may have encountered it in the sixth lecture of Carlyle's *On Heroes, Hero-Worship, and the Heroic in History*; see also Emil Ludwig, *Napoleon*, trans. Eden and Cedar Paul (Garden City, N.J.: Garden City Publishing Company, 1926), 120. In the DMR-TS, Robartes comments that "Balzac said of Napoleon that he was always the second lieutenant meaning that he was coarse and crude whom he admired extravagantly" (*YVP* 4:39).

154 Napoleon admired and emulated Alexander the Great, mounting a campaign to conquer Egypt and intending to move from there to India, and often looked to the trappings of the Roman Empire for symbols of his regime. WBY wrote in "Four Years" (1921):

> Napoleon was never of his own time, as the naturalistic writers and painters bid all men be, but had some Roman emperor's image in his head and some condottiere's blood in his heart; and when he crowned that head at Rome with his own hands he had covered, as may be seen from David's painting, his hesitation with that emperor's old suit. (*Au* 139)

155 Both words appear in Ben Jonson's eulogy attached to the First Folio of Shakespeare's plays (1623).

156 The English playwright, poet, and classical scholar Ben Jonson (1572–1637) had a famously explosive temper. While a member of the theatrical company the Admiral's Men, managed by Philip Henslowe, in 1598, he killed his fellow actor Gabriel Spenser in a duel. He was tried for murder and was for a short time imprisoned as a result.

157 The sonnets of Shakespeare were first published by Thomas Thorpe in the 1609 Quarto, a publication that was probably not authorized by the author.

158 Shakespeare, Jonson, and others gathered at this tavern in Cheapside, in London.

159 Thomas Lake Harris, slightly misquoted, thus writes in *The Wisdom of the Adepts: Esoteric science in human history* (privately printed, Fountain Grove, 1882), 442. WBY repeats this quotation in *Au* 217 (see also *Au* 193–94, *LE* 49, 70, 111). W. T. Horton introduced WBY to Harris's religious writing, much of which was automatic, including epic poems. After a brief time with the Golden Dawn, Horton joined an occult religious order called the Brotherhood of the New

Life, founded by Harris. In 1896, Horton tried to convince WBY to follow suit and loaned him books by Harris.

160 The figures are the French naturalist Jean-Baptiste Lamarck (1744–1829); the Irish playwright George Bernard Shaw (1856–1950); the British novelist and science fiction writer Herbert George Wells (1866–1946); and the Irish novelist, poet, and critic George A. Moore (1852–1933). For the connection between "distortion" (the description of the False *Creative Mind* for this phase) and "the mischievous malicious pranks of George Moore," see the sleep of September 10, 1920 (*YVP* 3:43). The sheet filed with the AS for June 2, 1918, lists Milton, Horace, Dr Johnson, Flaubert, Napoleon, Richelieu. Dickens is marked through (*YVP* 1:549). Writing in 1934, WBY called Shaw, Wilde, and Moore "the most complete individualists in the history of literature, abstract, isolated minds, without a memory or a landscape" (*Poems* 673–74).

161 In *Au* 320–21, WBY also refers to this passage, which mentions the character Ferdyshchenko and an incident occurring in part 1, chaps. 13 and 14, of Dostoyevsky's *The Idiot.*

162 The figures listed are Gustave Flaubert; the English philosopher, biologist, and sociologist Herbert Spencer (1820–1903); Emanuel Swedenborg; Fyodor Dostoyevsky; and the naturalist Charles Darwin (1809–82). The list filed with the AS of June 2, 1918, includes F. [W. H.] Myers, founder and early president of the Society for Psychical Research, and an authority on automatic writing. Darwin was added after the publication of *AVA*.

163 In the AS and in *AVA*, the terms *Victim* and *Sage* are given considerable discussion. The *Sage* or *Teacher* is a *primary* embodiment, the *Victim* an *antithetical* one (see especially *AVA* 76, 91, 137); they exchange places on the wheels both of individual life and history. *Victimage* also occurs as part of the complex mechanisms of expiation in the after life states; see especially *AVA* 185 and 173–74 in this edition. On October 7, 1927, in a letter to Maud Gonne, WBY explains that he has "taken advantage of having a typist for the day & dictate what may I think interest you—an abstract impersonal statement of what I believe to be the ancient doctrine—which must soon be modern doctrine also—of the effects of hate & love. The whole of mystical philosophy seems to me a deduction from this single thought." A typed enclosure reads:

> As things only exist in being perceived (or as Bergson puts it, echoing Plotinus, "The universe is itself consciousness") when we forget a thought or an emotion, which we will recall perhaps years later, it does not pass out of existence. It is still somewhere, still a part of some mind. I will add to that commonplace of philosophy this further thought that when

we forget something for ever, or die, that thing—thought or emotion—still remains in some other mind, all the bad passions so remain and only come to an end through those minds, who are in the mystic sense of the word Victims. A Victim is a person so placed in life that he would be excited into the most violent hatred or into some other bad passion, if he did not dissolve that passion into the totality of mind, or to use the common language into God. Until that act of Victimage takes place, an act not of simple renunciation, but of sanctification, the passion remains passing from mind to mind from being to being among the living and the dead. In so passing it arouses everywhere its like just as do the good passions, those who hate receiving the influx of hate, subjecting themselves as old writers believe to streams of disaster, those who love receiving the influx of love, human and divine. (*CL InteLex* 5036)

164 See WBY's note, 169.

165 *La Tentation de Saint Antoine* (1874), written in the form of a play script, focuses on one night in which St. Anthony the Great (c. 250–351), the Egyptian founder of Christian monasticism, is faced with great temptations; *Bouvard et Pécuchet* (published posthumously 1881), although incomplete, follows two narrow-minded Parisian copy-clerks in their search for a suitable intellectual pursuit, parodying their findings along the way. The Yeatses owned copies of both these novels by Flaubert (YL 679, 682).

166 In *Art and Life* (London: Methuen, 1910; YL 1361), T. Sturge Moore writes about Flaubert and "Impersonal Art," beginning the essay with an epistolary quotation from Flaubert: "I believe that great art is scientific and impersonal" (79).

167 The phrase is from the epigraph of Part 1, Chap. 13, of *Le Rouge et le Noir* by Stendhal (see also Part 2, Chap. 14). John Butler Yeats brought this passage to WBY's attention (see *Passages from the Letters of John Butler Yeats*, ed. Ezra Pound [Dublin: Cuala Press, 1917], 46), and WBY repeated it several times (*Au* 270, *LE* 194, *Ex* 333, and *Plays* 703). "Version B" has "sauntering" instead of "dawdling" (*YVP* 4:213).

168 The first part of this inexact quotation is in Blake's *Visions of the Daughters of Albion*, plate 7, line 15 (Blake 50; the plate is reproduced in *WWB* 3). The Lake of Udan-Adan is featured in Blake's *Jerusalem.*

169 WBY refers to Swedenborg's entry into a new phase of his spiritual life, characterized by dreams, visions, and direct divine revelation; this occurred in 1744, when he was 56. See *LE* 49.

170 Balzac usually worked at night, sleeping during the day. He wrote about his use of specially prepared coffee in "Traité des excitants modernes" (1838; *Études analytiques* [Paris: Les Bibliophiles de l'Originale, 1968]), 260–65. See also *LE* 40.

171 The German economist, philosopher, and revolutionary Karl Marx (1818–83) wrote about government, economy, history, and class structure in work that founded Marxist political thought. Marx's correspondence with his friend and collaborator Friedrich Engels was published in England in 1936 as *Selected Correspondence 1846–1895 with Commentary and Notes: Marx and Engels* by the radical press Lawrence & Wishart.

172 WBY may be drawing on T. Sturge Moore's *Art and Life*, where remarks by Edmond and Jules Goncourt are quoted on 133 and 280. WBY may have been confusing the brothers with Rémy de Gourmont, from whose *Problem of Style* Moore also quotes: "Far from its being his [Flaubert's] work which is impersonal, the roles are here reversed: it is the man who is vague and a tissue of incoherences; it is the work which lives, breathes, suffers, and smiles nobly" (301).

173 In *Art and Life*, Moore writes: "Artists cannot be rigidly intellectual, since logic to become practical must yield something to the sensuous illusion in which life is immersed. Anatole France was perhaps feeling after this fact when he made the clumsy assertion that Flaubert was unintelligent" (134–35).

174 WBY conflates two incidents related in *Home Life with Herbert Spencer* by Two [M. & D. Baker], ed. A. G. L. Rogers (1906), 39–41, 208–10.

175 Rembrandt joins WBY's friend the Irish playwright and poet John Millington Synge (1871–1909) as an example. In "The Bounty of Sweden" (1923–24), WBY wrote: "Synge has described, through an exaggerated symbolism, a reality which he loved precisely because he loved all reality" (*Au* 417). The sheet accompanying the AS of June 2, 1918, also lists as examples Michelangelo, Balzac (marked through), and Daniel O'Connell (*YVP* 1:549).

176 WBY frequently quoted or paraphrased this line from Blake's *Jerusalem*: "You shall want all the Minute Particulars of Life" (plate 88, line 43; Blake 247; the plate is reproduced in *WWB* 3). In addition to the appearance here, see the poem "The Double Vision of Michael Robartes": "the minute particulars of mankind" (*Poems* 173, *VPl* 384). The poem originated in the AS of January 7, 1919 (*YVP* 2:162–64).

177 This passage might refer to the anatomically represented image of Christ in Rembrandt's *Descent from the Cross* (there is one in Munich and one in Leningrad) or of the more literal representation of anatomical discovery in *The Anatomy Lesson of Dr. Nicholas Tulp*. Rembrandt's dramatic use of light and shade, or chiaroscuro, is a highly regarded characteristic of his work.

178 Synge's play *The Playboy of the Western World* contrasts its hero Christy Mahon with a traditional hero.

179 WBY was proud to have urged Synge, in late 1896, to "Go to the Aran Islands. Live there as if you were one of the people themselves; express a life that has never found expression" (see Synge 3:63 and

EE 216–17; see also *Au* 262). Beginning in 1898, Synge spent six summers in the Aran Islands collecting stories and folklore and strengthening his skills in the Irish language.

180 Synge writes in the preface to *The Playboy of the Western World*, "I got more aid than any learning could have given me, from a chink in the floor of the old Wicklow house where I was staying, that let me hear what was being said by the servant girls in the kitchen" (Synge 4:53). Concerning his notebooks kept while on the Aran Islands, see David Herbert Greene and Edward M. Stephens, *J. M. Synge, 1871–1909*, rev. ed. (New York and London: New York University Press, 1989), 84–96 and passim.

181 Many of Rembrandt's portraits show minute details of bourgeois clothing.

182 These characters are in Synge's play *Deirdre of the Sorrows* (1910); WBY slightly misquotes the line, "Draw a little back with the squabbling of fools when I am broken up with misery" (Synge 4:267). The actress may be Maire O'Neill, who was successful with Dublin audiences, if not with WBY (see *Au* 386–87).

183 See also *Au* 262 and *EE* 216.

184 *Queen Mab* is Shelley's earliest long poetic work, laying out his theory of revolution. *Alastor*, on the other hand, is an early expression of Shelley's doctrine of love, expressing a conflict between a desire for an ideal vision of love and an actual human (and imperfect) lover.

185 Jacques-Louis David (1748–1825) was a French Neoclassical painter.

186 The English writer Herbert George Wells is best known for novels like *The Time Machine* (1895) and *The War of the Worlds* (1898).

187 This slightly misquoted line from Blake's *Europe* (plate 14, line 3; Blake 65; the plate is reproduced in *WWB* 3) is also quoted in *Myth1* 282, *Myth2* 185.

188 On the first-pull Coole proofs (BL Add. 55893), the text is changed in manuscript to "Constructive emotion," and the change is noted in Thomas Mark's notebook and retained in the 1962 edition.

189 Alexandrina Victoria (1819–1901), Queen of Great Britain and Ireland from 1837 until her death, joins English novelist and playwright John Galsworthy (1867–1933) and Lady Gregory. In *AVA*, WBY refers to Gregory as "A certain friend," in keeping with his avoidance of the names of living people; she died in 1932. The list filed with the AS of June 2, 1918, lists Mazarin and Lady Gregory, dubbed "Placens uxor" (or "pleasing wife") (*YVP* 1:549). In the AS on January 2, 1918, WBY asked, without naming, "Where does Placens uxor come" and received the answer "24" (*YVP* 1:190). The Latin comes from Horace's *Odes* (2.14.20–21), about the inevitability of death. "Version B" lists Queen Victoria and "a certain personal friend," "personal" later crossed out (*YVP* 4:223). This phase was extensively revised, but its original opening seems to be an indirect tribute to

Lady Gregory: "The most obviously impressive of all the phases when true to phase" (*YVP* 4:223).

190 WBY used this line from *Macbeth* (4.3.111) to describe Lady Gregory in *Mem* 162 and *Au* 336 (see also *Myth1* 116, *Myth2* 77).

191 Pope St Gregory I (pope 590–604) first used the Latin moniker *servus servorum Dei*, or "Servant of the servants of God" to refer to himself as pope.

192 In her essay about Antoine Ó Raifteirí, Lady Gregory writes of "The truths of God that he strove in his last years . . . 'to have written in the book of the people'" ("Raftery," *Poets and Dreamers: Studies and Translations from the Irish* [Dublin: Hodges, Figgis, 1903], 21–22; YL 807). WBY also uses the phrase in *IDM* 103 and line 44 of "Coole Park and Ballylee, 1931" (*Poems* 249).

193 Named for the color of its covers, a blue book is an official report of Parliament or the Privy Council.

194 According to the *Oxford English Dictionary*, the term Bohemian, which originally referred to a native of Bohemia, and later became a synonym for Gypsy, came to be used in the mid-nineteenth century for a person (especially an artist, writer, or actor) who leads a free or irregular life, without being particular as to the society he or she frequents.

195 WBY uses similar phrasing in his characterization of George Russell in *The Trembling of the Veil* (*Au* 201).

196 Katherine O'Shea wrote that Parnell's "will was autocratic, and once he had made up his mind to any course he would brook no interference, nor suffer anything to stand in the way" (*Charles Stewart Parnell* 2:243).

197 The figures listed are the Anglican priest, leader of the Oxford Movement, and convert to Roman Catholicism John Henry Newman (Cardinal Newman, 1801–90); the German theologian and ecclesiastical reformer Martin Luther (1483–1546); the French Protestant theologian John Calvin (1509–64); the English metaphysical poet George Herbert (1593–1633); and the Irish nationalist, critic, poet, and mystical writer George William Russell (known as Æ, 1867–1935). The sheet accompanying the AS of June 2, 1918, lists as examples "Luther. Calvin. Ignatius Loyola. George Herbert. G. Russell" (*YVP* 1:549), although "Version B" includes only Newman and Luther (*YVP* 4:229).

198 Newman wrote *A Letter Addressed to the Rev. E. B. Pusey, D. D., on Occasion of His Eirenicon* (1866) to one of several possible people WBY may have had in mind. Prior to Newman's conversion, Pusey was one of Newman's fellows in the Oxford Movement, which sought a renewal of Roman Catholic practice in the Church of England. Pusey tried to bring the two churches closer together, but Newman resented Pusey's representation of the Catholic doctrine of the

Blessed Virgin. WBY got some of his knowledge of Newman from Lionel Johnson, but WBY later discovered that Johnson had imagined some of the meetings he described (*Au* 236–37).

199 In the Peasants' War of 1524–26, the lower classes in Germany revolted against repressive measures against them. Although many viewed Luther as a revolutionary, he opposed the peasants.

200 See similar ideas and wording in *Au* 197–98. Æ was a talented amateur painter whose paintings reflect a sense of the insubstantiality of the visible world. Gustave Moreau (1826–98) was a French Symbolist painter.

201 In the AS (January 3, 1918), WBY asked, "Can there [be] nobody of note at 26 & 28," but no answer was recorded (*YVP* 1:194). The Yeatses concluded, as WBY states in "Version B," that "I must create from imagination, with some help from legend & from literature" (*YVP* 4:234). His source for the hunchback is not entirely clear. Melchiori (*The Whole Mystery of Art*, 277–79) suggests WBY drew from Byron's play *The Deformed Transformed.* Other sources might be Shakespeare's *Richard III*, Victor Hugo's Quasimodo (see *Au* 95), and "an old hunchback" painted by WBY's father, John B. Yeats (*Au* 91).

202 Nero Claudius Caesar Augustus Germanicus (54–68 CE), the fifth Roman emperor: Nero replaced his stepfather Claudius in 54 CE at the latter's murder, probably by Claudius's wife and Nero's mother, Agrippina Minor. Nero became infamous for widely believed stories of his debauched life, his persecution of Christians, and his burning of Rome.

203 As examples of ambitious men, WBY offers the Roman military and political leader Gaius Julius Caesar (c. 100–44 BCE), who was instrumental in transforming the Roman republic into an empire, and Achilles, the legendary Greek hero of the Trojan War.

204 In the New Testament, Judas Iscariot, one of Jesus' friends and disciples, betrays Jesus for thirty pieces of silver (Matthew 26:14–15). Judas is featured often in the AS and the system-related plays *Calvary* (1920) and *The Resurrection* (1931), as well as *A Vision.*

205 More than to the biblical allusion to Ezekiel 4:4 and 13, this passage refers to Blake's *The Marriage of Heaven and Hell* (plates 12–14; Blake 39; the plate is reproduced in *WWB* 3); see *LNI* 102.

206 In the great Sanskrit epic the *Mahabharata*, the Pandava princes (Yudhishtira, Bhima, Arjuna, Nakula, and Sahadeva), the five acknowledged sons of the king Pandu (by his two wives Kunti and Madri) are not his biological offspring but the sons of various gods. One day, while on a hunt, Pandu saw a deer coupling with its mate. He killed it and then discovered that the buck was in fact a *rishi* (a sage) in the form of a deer. The deer, changing its form, delivered a curse: that the king too would die in the act of lovemaking. The king then refrained

from intercourse with his wives, but the gods granted them the boon of having sons through other means. The ancient practice of *niyoga*, or the begetting of children by proxy when a husband is unable to father them, derived from the story of this family.

207 At this point in *AVA*, the sentence continues after a comma: "and we shall *discover, when we come to consider the nature of victimage, that their images beset him in states analogous to hypnagogic vision." The note reads: "*This topic belongs to the psychology of the system, which I have not yet mastered. I have yet to put together and study many obscure scattered passages in the documents.—W.B.Y., July, 1925" (*AVA* 91).

208 This point in *AVA* is the end of the essay on Phase 26; the paragraph that follows was added in revision. The spiritual *primary* occurs as "the *Faculties* 'wear thin'" around the New Moon (65) and is linked to the closing and opening of the *tinctures*, when the Will is between Phase 26 and Phase 4 and "Unity with God is possible" (*AVA* 27; see also *YVP* 2:134 and *YVP* 3:415). Since the *Faculties* are "lunar nature," particularly *Will* and *Mask*, these phases show the preponderance of the solar *Creative Mind* and *Body of Fate*, but the spiritual and physical *primary* are here described in terms of solar *Principles*, which "shine through" (66). We are indebted to Neil Mann for assistance with this section.

209 The examples are the Greek philosopher Socrates (c. 470–399 BCE), a prominent figure in the dialogues of his student Plato; and the French mathematician and physicist Blaise Pascal (1623–62). In the AS (January 3, 1918), both Socrates and Pascal appeared in Phase 27 (*YVP* 1:193–94).

210 See *YYP* 2:147; 3:366, 372, 403; and 4:233 on the "emotion of sanctity," which enables a "link with the after life state" in Phases 22 and following. Cf. 162 and 216 in this edition.

211 Arthur Symons uses this phrase in "Maeterlinck as a Mystic": "Jacob Boehme has said, very subtly, 'that man does not perceive the truth, but God perceives the truth in man'; that is, that whatever we perceive or do is not perceived or done consciously by us, but unconsciously through us" (*The Symbolist Movement in Literature* [London: William Heinemann, 1899, YL 2068], 162–63). WBY uses it in the *North-American Review* version of *The Hour-Glass* (*VPl* 634). As Neil Mann points out, WBY may have introduced the idea to Symons, given how extensive WBY's reading in and about Boehme was by 1897, when Symons's essay first appeared in *The Contemporary Review* (Mann, "*A Vision* [1925]: A Review Essay," *YA* 18 [2013], 280–81). See Franz Hartmann's *Personal Christianity: A Science; The Life and Doctrines of Jacob Boehme, the God-Taught Philosopher*, a book WBY used when editing Blake and which contains extensive marginalia. The epigraph to Chap. 1 quotes Boehme's *Apology to*

Balthazar Tylken: "Not I, the I that I am, know these things, but God knows them in me" (New York: Macoy Publishing, 1919; YL 853), 46; http://jacobboehmeonline.com/yahoo_site_admin/assets/docs/Tylcken_part_12.359131920.pdf).

212 Sources for this figure probably include the Tarot card The Fool (which Waite describes as "the spirit in search of experience," *Pictorial Key to the Tarot* (http://www.sacred-texts.com/tarot/pkt/pktar00.htm); the fool of the East (*Au* 196); "the pure fool of European tradition" such as Parsifal (see *LE* 150); the jester or licensed fool, as exemplified in Shakespeare's *King Lear*; and the *Amadán-na-Breena*, "a fool of the forth" (see *Myth1* 112, *Myth2* 75; see also *Myth2* 460 and Lady Gregory, *Visions and Beliefs in the West of Ireland* [1920; Gerrards Cross: Colin Smythe, 1970], 250–54), in Irish *amadán na briona*, "the fool who loves fighting."

213 Fools are widely connected with innocence and goodness. In the New Testament, followers of Christ are sometimes referred to as "children of God," and the Gospel is often referred to as seeming folly: see, for example, 1 Corinthians 1:20: "Hath not God made foolish the wisdom of this world?" (Authorized Version). The phrase can also be a euphemism for "idiot" or "simpleton"; Neil Mann points to such a definition in R. W. Holder, *A Dictionary of American and British Euphemisms* (Bath: Bath University Press, [1987], 95) and to usage in a contemporary reference *Education through the Imagination*, by Margaret McMillan: "the 'simple' or 'idiot' as distinguished from the poor lunatic seems to have always had kinder treatment and was even called 'God's fool,' and 'God's child' by his neighbours" (New York: Appleton, 1924, 96; Mann, "*A Vision* [1925]: A Review Essay," 283). In the AS, the Yeatses were informed that the state of the *Will* (ego) at 28 was "the mystical child of God" (*YVP* 2:28), that the "parentage of the spiritual child at 28" is "the child of God" (*YVP* 2:122), and that the fool of Phase 28 is "mentally transparent" and "absorbed in the contemplation of god" (*YVP* 1:297–98). Cf. a sleep from August 20, 1920 (*YVP* 3:37).

214 Misquoted from Sir William Watson's epigram on "The Play of *King Lear*" from *Wordsworth's Grave and Other Poems* (London: T. Fisher Unwin, 1890), 72. It is quoted correctly by WBY in *LNI* 105.

215 See "The Phases of the Moon": "And yet they speak what's blown into the mind; / Deformed beyond deformity, unformed, / Insipid as the dough before it is baked, / They change their bodies at a word" (45).

216 WBY probably finished a draft of Book I of *AVA* (reprinted with very few changes for *AVB*) between October and December 1922, having left Ballylee for Dublin with his family in September. The Irish civil war, which began in June 1922, was a conflict between two republican factions over whether to accept the Anglo-Irish Treaty of 1921.

The anti-treaty forces, including a large section of Sinn Féin and the majority of the Irish Republican Army (IRA), called the Irregulars, fought the pro-treaty forces of the Provisional Government of the Free State under Michael Collins. The pro-treaty side eventually prevailed and hostilities had ceased by the spring of 1923, but there was no negotiated peace and consequently no official end to the war.

Book II: The Completed Symbol

1 By "Book," WBY refers to Book I above, not the complete 1925 *A Vision*, whose fourth Book "The Gates of Pluto" treats the *Principles*. A manuscript fragment contains more description: "a loss, that left a great part of the system in confusion for years. I have no doubt that my present knowledge of the fundamental system is sufficient, helped by sentences here & there in other scripts to restore the loss" (NLI 36,272/5/1).

2 Cardinal Nicolaus Cusanus (Nicholas of Cusa, 1401–64) was a philosopher, theologian, church reformer, and mathematician, whose thinking owes much to Christian Neoplatonism but is highly original in its mystical syntheses. WBY was engaged with his thinking in 1931; see the letter thanking Mario M. Rossi for "your long and valuable quotations from Nicolas of Cusa, which I hope to understand better in a few days" (*L* 783–84). Nicholas is listed at the head of WBY's manuscript entitled "Genealogical Tree of Revolution" (NLI 30,280, rpt. in Jeffares, *W. B. Yeats, Man and Poet* [New York: Barnes and Noble, 1966], 351–52). See also Mann, "The *Thirteenth Cone*" (Mann et al. 185 n24).

3 WBY is misquoting slightly from *The Friend* by Coleridge (London: George Bell and Sons, 1906; YL 402A), 102–4, the most important alteration being the substitution of "Helvetius" for Coleridge's "Hemsterhuis." Coleridge refers to the German philosopher Friedrich Heinrich Jacobi (1743–1819). Jacobi quotes from correspondence with the Dutch aesthetician Franciscus Hemsterhuis (1721–90); Yeats's misquotation suggests his greater familiarity with the Dutch physician and alchemist Johann Friedrich Schweitzer, also known as John Frederick Helvetius (1625–1709); see A. E. Waite, *Lives of the Alchemystical Philosophers* (London: Redway, 1888; YL 2210), 201–8.

4 Several of the orthodox schools of Indian philosophy (including Sāṅkhya, Yoga, Mīmāṁsā, and Vedānta) distinguish between *Karmendriyas* and *Gyanendriyas* (*Jñānendriyas*). According to John Grimes, *Karmendriyas* are "the five conative sense organs" (speech, prehension, movement, excretion, and generation); *Jñānendriyas* are "organs of knowledge" or "internal senses" (hearing, touch, sight, taste, and smell), *A Concise Dictionary of Indian Philosophy*, rev. ed.

(Varanasi, India: Indica Books, 2009), 199, 188. Patañjali belongs to the Sāṅkhya school, and the yoga sutras he compiled are based on this philosophy. WBY supplied an introduction to Shri Purohit Swāmi's translation of Patañjali's *Aphorisms of Yoga* (London: Faber, 1938). WBY marked his copy of James Haughton Woods's edition of *The Yoga-System of Patanjali* (Cambridge: Harvard University Press, 1927; YL 1536) describing senses and supernatural senses (72–75); cf. the discussion of senses in WBY's introduction to *The Holy Mountain* by Bhagwān Shri Hamsa, trans. Shri Purohit Swāmi, *E&I* 461–62, *LE* 148. Characterizing *Jñānendriyas* as "passive" is not strictly correct: these sense-activities are usually considered to be of greater implication for human life than *Karmendriyas*.

WBY's interest in Indian philosophy was growing stronger in the 1930s, when many of the notes to *AVB* were added to the text. The Yeatses' friend Dermott MacManus told Kathleen Raine in an interview that "when Yeats at last made his full discovery of the tradition of Indian thought, he no longer concerned himself with spiritualism, mediumship, magic, or any of his former interests in such matters" and that both the Yeatses gave up spiritualist practice as "incompatible with the . . . teachings of Hinduism," *Yeats the Initiate* (Montrath, Ireland: Dolmen Press; London: George Allen & Unwin, 1986), 334.

5 In the TS carbon, both occurrences of "prevail" in this sentence are followed by the phrase "and attain their union" (NLI 36,272/6/1b, leaf 2).

6 This sentence and the final sentence of the paragraph were added after the TS carbon (see NLI 36, 272/6/1b, leaf 2).

7 Beginning here and continuing to the end of Section I, the TS carbon differs significantly from the final text. See Appendix II, 276–78.

8 The "Tower Story" or "Tower Myth," in which the *Celestial Body* was "prisoned in tower till rescued from solitude [by PB]," is discussed in the AS in conjunction with a mysterious figure called "The Black Eagle" (*YVP* 3:53, 247).

9 "The Mental Traveller" (*WWB* 2:31–33; Blake 483–86) is mentioned often in the genetic materials for *A Vision*; see *YVP* 2:240; 3:50–51. In one draft, WBY notes that "we symbolise the conflict between man['s] discarnate & his incarnate life, each dying the others life, living the others death": "Blakes 'Mental Traveller' is the only expression in literature of those circular movements and is probably the key to his philosophy" (NLI 36,272/2/1). For the attempted explanation, see *WWB* 2:34–36.

10 WBY's copy of the Hermetic Fragments contains marginal notations pertaining to this idea (*Hermetica. The Ancient Greek and Latin writings which contain religious or philosophic teaching ascribed to Hermes Trismegistus*, ed. and trans. Walter Scott [3 vols.; Oxford: Clarendon Press, 1924–36]; YL 881). WBY wrote "Destiny defined"

in the margin by Asclepius 3.39, on Destiny, Necessity, and Order (1:363). Excerpts 7 and 8 from the *Anthologium* of Stobaeus concern Necessity, "Penal Justice" (Gr. *diké*), and Destiny; and "Providence, Necessity, and Destiny" (1:423), respectively (1:419–23).

11 WBY discusses the notion that light is not "the child but . . . the parent or grandparent of the physical senses" (*LE* 124), allied with medieval philosophers such as St. Bonaventure (1221–74) and Robert Grosseteste, and also links Berkeley's *Siris* with Balzac's *Louis Lambert*, in WBY's introduction to *Louis Lambert* (*LE* 123–25, *E&I* 438–41) and in his introduction to *OBMV* (*LE* 197). *Siris: A Chain of Philosophical Reflections and Inquiries concerning the Virtues of Tar Water* (1744), the last work by Berkeley, extols the medicinal properties of tar-water as well as advancing a range of philosophical and theological topics. WBY marked his copy of *Siris* at the section describing the "element of aetherial fire or light" and its importance to philosophers from Heraclitus to Plato (*The Works of George Berkeley* [2 vols.; Dublin: John Exshaw, 1784; YL 160], 2:538–39). Similarly, the propositions of the doomed young philosopher Louis Lambert in Balzac's 1832 novella assert the primacy of light to the human will and senses (*Seraphita & Other Stories*, trans. Clara Bell; Vol. 34 of the Temple Edition of the *Comédie Humaine*, ed. George Saintsbury [New York: Macmillan, 1901; YL 106], 270–71). WBY owned this forty-volume edition of the writer he told Ethel Mannin inspired his "perpetual re-reading" (February [15, 1935], *CL InteLex* 6188). See WBY's introductions to J. M. Hone and M. M. Rossi, *Bishop Berkeley: His Life, Writings, and Philosophy* (*E&I* 396–411, *LE* 103–12), and to *Louis Lambert* (*E&I* 438–47, *LE* 123–29). See also sections of *Diary 1930* (*Ex* 304–5, 320, 322–25). At an early stage of his thinking, WBY planned to call an essay that would become "Rapallo" in *A Packet* "Siris." See Paul.

12 The General Index "with Metaphysical Definitions and Supplementary Remarks" to Thomas Collyns Simon's edition of Berkeley's *Principles of Human Knowledge* (London: George Routledge and Sons, 1893) contains this description of Light (215). WBY may be misquoting Hone and Rossi; we have not discovered an exact source for WBY's quotation about Sensation as a "semi-material agent." Hone and Rossi do discuss Berkeley in *Siris* advancing the idea that "Fire is now the instrument of the Pure Intelligence of the Supreme Spirit" (215). They continue, "But fire, being active, cannot be known 'after the manner of ideas' but only as we know spirits—by reason. Although fire is a natural element, it is also an intellectual element, the real medium between spirit and idea, between God and the world. . . . Nature is no longer a pure appearance, for this intellectual fire which brings out sensations is a reality in itself" (215). In aphorism 725 of his *Commonplace Book*, Berkeley notes, "The concrete of the will

& understanding I must call mind; not person, lest offence be given, there being but one volition acknowledged to be God. *Mem.* Carefully to omit Defining of Person, or making much mention of it" (*Berkeley's Commonplace Book*, ed. G. A. Johnston [London: Faber, 1930], 87; YL 159).

Robert Grosseteste (c. 1168–1253), Bishop of Lincoln from 1235 to 1253, was a philosopher, translator of Aristotle and Greek patristic thinkers, theologian, writer on science, and bishop who campaigned against abuses of pastoral duties. One of his most important works is *De luce*, an analysis of the physical and metaphysical role of light. Pierre Duhem discusses Grosseteste's Neoplatonism as well as his place among the early European Aristotelians in *Le système du monde* 5:341–58. The discussion of light in Plotinus is from *Enneads* 5.5.7: "At night in the darkness a gleam leaps from within the eye: or again we make no effort to see anything; the eyelids close; yet a light flashes before us; or we rub the eye and it sees the light it contains. This is sight without the act, but it is the truest seeing, for it sees light whereas its other objects were the lit, not the light" (4:55–56).

The term "astral light" is protean and its origins complicated; WBY confuses matters further in his own comments. The term "astral *spirit*" probably originates with Paracelsus (1493–1541). This term was used in translations of Jacob Boehme; in writings on witchcraft in the seventeenth century, especially by John Webster (1610–82) and Joseph Glanvill (1636–80); and by Glanvill's friend the Cambridge Platonist Henry More (1614–87). More connects the astral spirit with "the *Universal Soul of the World* or *Spirit of Nature*" (*The Immortality of the Soul*, Book 3, Chap. 12, in *A Collection of Several Philosophical Writings* [London: William Morden, 1662; YL 1377], 195), and in *PASL* WBY writes at some length about More's Soul of the World, *Anima Mundi* (*LE* 20–23). It is likely, therefore, that the "seventeenth-century Platonist" to whom WBY refers is More, even though More never uses the term "astral light."

In the notes to Lady Gregory's *Visions and Beliefs in the West of Ireland*, WBY observes that what More refers to as "*Spiritus Mundi*" was given the "name 'Astral Light'" by Éliphas Lévi (*Visions and Beliefs* [New York and London: G. P. Putnam's Sons, 1920], 278, *LE* 271). Indeed, in the sense that WBY understood it, the Astral Light was formulated by Éliphas Lévi (1810–75): "the great magical agent, by us termed the astral light, by others the soul of the earth," the "primordial light, which is the vehicle of all ideas, is the mother of all forms" (*Dogme et Rituel de la Haute Magie* [1855], as *Transcendental Magic: Its Doctrine and Ritual*, translated by A. E. Waite [London: George Redway, 1896; YL 1109], 97 and 62). Madame Blavatsky remarked on its kinship to the "animal magnetism" of Mesmer (1734–1815), the "odic" force of von Reichenbach (1788–1869), and the Indian concept of "akasa." Her Theosophical Society played a major part in popularizing the idea, publishing works such as that of "Nizida" (Louise A. Off), *The Astral Light: an attempted exposition of certain occult principles in nature: with some remarks upon modern spiritism* (1889) and C. W. Leadbeater, *The Astral Plane: its scenery, inhabitants and phenomena* (1895), probably among the "popular writers" to whom WBY refers. By this period, WBY's enthusiasm for the Theosophical Society had waned. He referred in 1935 to "the vulgarization of mystical philosophy by the theosophists" (*CL InteLex* 6304; see also 5609).

The idea of "the soul as a star" may derive from the *augoeides* or *astroeides*, the luminous or star-like body, a Neoplatonic idea that WBY could have found in the translations of Thomas Taylor, for example in Taylor's *A History of the Restoration of the Platonic Theology by the Later Platonists,* in *The Philosophical and Mathematical Commentaries of Proclus, on the First Book of Euclid's Elements* (2 vols.; London, 1789), 2:291n. It was popularized in the nineteenth century by Edward Bulwer Lytton: "Soul of mine, the luminous, the Augoeides" (*Zanoni* [London: Saunders & Otley, 1842], 1:156). Blavatsky uses the term extensively in *Isis Unveiled*, distinguishing a "perishable . . . Astral Soul" from an "incorruptible and immortal . . . *Augoeides*" (*Isis Unveiled* [New York: Bouton, 1877], 1:12), and the Theosophist G. R. S. Mead wrote several times on the subject, including an essay that Yeats had "clipped out of his magazine, *The Quest*" (*LE* 67), "The Augoeides or Radiant Body" (*The Quest*, July 1910, 1:705–26; see *LE* 330n and YL 1299), incorporated with little change into *The Doctrine of the Subtle Body in the Western Tradition* (London: J. M. Watkins, 1919). We are indebted to Neil Mann for much of this information.

13 The setting typescript adds: "My instructors identify Spirit with the future for the same reason that McTaggart puts all wholes into the future and therefore everything that we love for we love only that which is whole. The Spirit is that which sees unity or Celestial Body whether in the daimons—the archetypal forms—or in nature as a whole. Sometimes the Spirits have said 'We have no present . . . , we are in the future' meaning that they are perfect" (NLI 36,272/6/1b). The reference is to the British idealist philosopher John McTaggart Ellis McTaggart (1866–1925). See *YVP* 2:258 and 3:308 for the origin of the ideas in the AS.

14 The earlier stage typescript reads, "The passionate body is the present because it is sensation and it is also time because time, as Berkeley has shown, is a stream of sensation. I feel loath to continue the argument, which is too abstract for me and brings me into competition with a beautiful difficult chapter in Gentile's 'Mind as Pure Act', and They identify the Husk with the past and with space. I remind my reader that but for the mind nature would be, Berkeley thought, a flat surface

pressed down upon our eyes." The passage ends with another canceled section: "I am dissatisfied with this section: the script where it touched upon this theme became difficult, one or two errors remained uncorrected. I would have omitted this theme but for the necessity of accounting for the word husk" (NLI 36,272/4/1). The references are to Giovanni Gentile, *The Theory of Mind as Pure Act*, and Berkeley's famous insistence that *esse est percipi* (*Principles of Human Knowledge* 14).

15 See Card F25 (*YVP* 3:308) for structural relations between *Faculties*, *Principles*, and *Daimons* and past, present, and future.

16 "'Like one who has imperfect vision, we see the things,' he said, 'which are remote from us; so much light the Supreme Ruler still gives to us; when they draw nigh, or are, our intellect is altogether void; and except what others bring us, we know nothing of your human state. Therefore thou mayest understand that all our knowledge shall be dead, from that moment when the portal of the Future shall be closed'" (Dante, *Inferno*, 10.100–105, trans. John Aitken Carlyle [Temple Classics, London: J. M. Dent, 1912, YL 470], 107).

17 See *YVP* 1:262, 3:164, and 4:15; and *AVA* 18.

18 The "phaseless sphere" or thirteenth cone (also called Thirteenth Sphere or Thirteenth Cycle, as WBY explains on 155 below) is a complex concept in *AVB*, which nonetheless insofar as it hints at an Absolute has been the source of much commentary and criticism. It is the closest concept to that of a deity in the system. As WBY noted in *Diary 1930*,

> Berkeley in the *Commonplace Book* thought that "we perceive" and are passive whereas God creates in perceiving. He creates what we perceive. I substitute for God the Thirteenth Cone, the Thirteenth Cone therefore creates our perceptions—all the visible world—as held in common by our wheel. (*Ex* 320)

The thirteenth cone (there usually called Cycle) appears in the AS, as for example in the session from August 26, 1918 (*YVP* 2:26–27). It is not a major concept either there or in *AVA*, where it occurs (as it does in the AS) sometimes in conjunction with a fourteenth and fifteenth cycle (see 138, 143, 182, 189, 191, 194). It receives considerably greater emphasis in *AVB*.

As WBY explains, the Sphere and Cone are the same concept, though human perspective cannot conceive of the Sphere. When imagined as the "antithesis to our thesis," it is a cone opposite to the cones of the system, but "if the time has come for our deliverance it is the phaseless sphere" (155). The thirteenth cone/sphere has some qualities that suggest "it" to be "them," i.e., multiple rather than single (so that, as WBY puts it in this section, it is "neither one nor many, concord nor discord"), especially insofar as it is the realm of "all souls that have been set free and every *Daimon* and *Ghostly Self*" (155).

The thirteenth cone is both like and unlike a deity. It is, as WBY states, like a place or time, where and when "[a]ll things are present," both still and moving like eternity (142), and describable in terms that suggest a Great Memory or *Record*. The thirteenth cone is also like a person. At the end of Book III, it is described as "conscious of itself" and compared to a modern dancer. See Neil Mann, "The *Thirteenth Cone*," Mann et al., 159–93.

19 WBY quotes this phrase in "The Philosophy of Shelley's Poetry" (1900), and again in his essay "Magic" (1901), *EE* 37, 57.

20 For "pictures in the astral light," see *YVP* 1:304, and cf. n12 above. In notes to Lady Gregory's *Visions and Beliefs in the West of Ireland*, WBY explains a vision of coaches, horses, and a drawbridge seen by Mrs. Sheridan, a local woman: "A 'theosophist' or 'occultist' of almost any modern school explains such visions by saying they are 'pictures in the astral light' and that all objects and events leave their images in the astral light as upon a photographic plate, and that we must distinguish between spirits and these unintelligent pictures" (*LE* 270). The "bright sculptures" are from *Jerusalem*, Chap. 1: "All things acted on Earth are seen in the bright Sculptures of / Los's Halls & every Age renew its powers from these Works / With every pathetic story possible to happen from Hate or / Wayward Love & every sorrow & distress is carved here . . ." (*Jerusalem*, plate 16, lines 61–64, Blake 161; reproduced in *WWB* 3). See *Diary 1930*: "Blake did not use the word 'picture' but spoke of the bright sculptures of Los's Halls from which all love stories renew themselves, and that remain on, one does not see the picture as it appeared to the living actor but the action itself, and that we feel as if we could walk round it as if there was no fixed point of view" (*Ex* 331).

21 This sentence was added after the setting typescript (NLI 36,272 /6/1b, leaf 9).

22 The setting typescript includes the word "unknowable" before "sphere," but lacks the phrase "which can be symbolised but cannot be known" (NLI 36,272/6/1b, leaf 10).

23 Plotinus's three Hypostases (which correlate roughly to the One or the Good, Intellect, and Soul) are described in Stephen MacKenna's Explanatory Matter to his translation of the *Enneads* (London: Medici Society, 1917; YL 1589), 1:118–20. "Authentic Existents" ([*sic*], MacKenna's term, explained in his Explanatory Matter under "Minor Points of Terminology," 124) are associated with the second and third Hypostases. See Rosemary Puglia Ritvo, "*A Vision B*: The Plotinian Metaphysical Basis," *Review of English Studies* 26 (1975):

34–46; and the discussion of Plotinus in Matthew Gibson, "Classical Philosophy," *W. B. Yeats in Context*, ed. David Holdeman and Ben Levitas (Cambridge: Cambridge University Press, 2010), 280–84.

24 In the Coole proofs, "First A.E." is expanded to "First Authentic Existant" (BL Add. 55893).

25 This note was added after the setting typescript (NLI 36,272/6/1b, leaf 11).

26 The setting typescript reads ". . . we desire some practical success or victory" (NLI 36,272/6/1b, leaf 12).

27 WBY refers to novelist and memoirist Frank Harris (1856–1931), whose sensational multivolume *My Life and Loves* (1922–27) tells the story of Ruskin's phantom cat, which in turn anchors a philosophical argument of several years' duration between WBY and Sturge Moore; see *LTSM* 63–68 and passim.

28 The earliest Roman calendars are thought to have been lunar; the first calendar, attributed to Romulus, was believed to begin the year on the Ides of March, the full moon closest to the vernal equinox. See 421–23 nn10 and 11.

In the TS carbon, this sentence (slightly modified) is preceded by the following paragraph:

> I must now relate what I have written of symbolic years and months, and unroll a symbolism—for I must return to my task of verse—but partly warm into life. I regard every month or year as a unity of consciousness, a conflict begun and ended, the greater conflicts containing the lesser and are for the most part unaware of their existence, as I am for the most part of the conflict of the muscles in my leg against road or floor.
>
> (NLI 36,272/6/1b, leaf 13)

29 See *AVA* 113–20; cf. *YVP* 4:19, 44.

30 These most recent three sentences (following "and so on") do not appear in the TS carbon (NLI 36,272/6/1b, leaf 13).

31 See 50 above and note. In the description of this geometry, the TS carbon diverges greatly from the printed text, from this point up to "The foregoing figure shows the position . . ." on 147. See Appendix II, 278–80.

32 See *YVP* 2:187–88.

33 The diagram is fig. 20 in this edition.

34 The diagram is fig. 15 in this edition.

35 Cf. a number of such cones drawn by WBY in a MS fragment treating "thought & life gyres," *YVP* 4:238–46. This sentence was added after the setting typescript (NLI 36,272/6/1b).

36 This sentence was added after the TS carbon (NLI 36,272/6/1b, leaf 19).

37 In the TS carbon, this sentence reads, "The Principles thereupon take their place in a state analagous [*sic*] to contemplation" (NLI 36,272 /6/1b, leaf 19).

38 On precession of the equinox, see 184–85 and 414–15 n1. The instructors' "play" is with the three different but related notions of the sidereal Great Year, equinoctial precession (the slow change in the rotational axis of the earth), and the number of years it takes a human soul to move through the 28 lunar phases of the Yeatses' system. The stylistic and thematic influence of the English poet Edmund Spenser (c. 1552–99) on WBY was profound as well as conflicted (see especially *EE* 257–76). *The Faerie Queene* (1590–96) is Spenser's major work, a long allegorical and mythological epic. WBY may be referring more to stanzas 5–8 of the Proem of Book 5, where Spenser invokes more astronomical, astrological, and temporal details. WBY owned a five-volume edition of *The Works of Edmund Spenser*, ed. J. Payne Collier (London: Bell and Daldy, 1862; YL 1978). The "Proem" to Book V appears in volume 3 (YL 1978B) and that section of the book is heavily marked. WBY included the entirety of the Proem as "The Wandering of the Stars" in *Poems of Spenser: Selected and with an Introduction by W. B. Yeats* (Edinburgh: T. C. and E. C. Jack, [1906], Wade 235, YL 1977), 179–82. In his introduction to that volume, WBY writes, "I have put into this book only those passages of Spenser that I want to remember and carry about with me" (xliv, *EE* 274).

39 The Greek philosopher Proclus ([412]–485 CE) explained Neoplatonic thought in a largely Christian environment. He is a pivotal figure for the transmission of Neoplatonism from classical Hellenistic to medieval Christian and Islamic philosophy. WBY's source here is Duhem 1:289–93.

40 *Lectures on the Philosophy of History* is a text compiled from notes of lectures Hegel presented at the University of Berlin from 1821 through 1831, the year of his death, compiled and published in 1837. See *The Philosophy of History*, trans. J. Sibree (1858), rev. ed. (New York and London: Colonial Press, 1889). For ideas WBY summarizes here, see discussions of nature on 25 and 80, the Sphinx on 199, and Oedipus on 220–21, as well as sections on "The course of the World's History" (54–79) and "Classification of Historic Data" (103–15). See the parallel discussion in WBY's introduction to *The Holy Mountain* by Bhagwān Shri Hamsa, trans. Shri Purohit Swāmi, *E&I* 466–67, *LE* 151–52.

41 All text from the beginning of section IX to this point was added after the TS carbon (NLI 36,272/6/1b, leaf 20).

42 In *The Revolutions of Civilisation*, a small book that WBY found congenial for his revisions of *A Vision*, the English Egyptologist Sir William Matthew Flinders Petrie (1853–1942) theorizes the compar-

ative rising and falling, through eight distinct periods, of different civilizations, based on an Egyptian model. Petrie finds that "the Eastern phase on the whole, keeps about 3½ centuries in advance of the Mediterranean, varying from 2 to 5½ centuries" and "The Mediterranean was almost an Arab lake at the time of El Mamun; Persia dominated all the civilised Mediterranean in the sixth century B.C." (London and New York: Harper & Brothers, 1911), 108–9. WBY had in his possession two copies of the third (1922) edition (YL 1559 and 1559a). Cf. *Diary 1930*, *Ex* 313, 316.

Yukio Yashiro (1890–1975) was an art historian and art critic who graduated from Tokyo University and studied in Europe from 1921 to 1925. In February 1926, just after the publication of *AVA*, GY gave WBY a copy of Yashiro's three-volume study *Sandro Botticelli* (London and Boston: The Medici Society, 1925). See Chap. 1, "Linear and Tonal Values," in which Yashiro argues that a theory of art history relying on ideas of the archaic and realistic is unsatisfactory: "It is better to think there are two kinds of artistic attitudes toward Nature, one linear and the other tonal. . . . One artist conceives the visual world as architecture of rhythmic line; another as a bas-relief of changing tone. . . . theoretically, the tonal view of Nature must be said to be truer to reality than the linear. In the Art of the Renaissance, where the main motive was to advance deeper and deeper towards Nature, the progress of Art was, roughly speaking, along the way from the linear to the tonal" (6).

43 This passage is quite different in the TS carbon:

> When it commenced at its symbolic full moon in March—the moon of the Faculties not of the Principles—Christ or Christendom was begotten by the West or phase 1 upon the East or full moon, and this Christ or Christendom cast off the mother's influence in our own time, or at phase 22. This begetting of symbolic West upon symbolic East was accompanied by a bodily[x] predominance of the geographical East.
>
> (NLI 36,272/6/1b, leaf 20)

The "x" above refers to the note concerning Flinders Petrie on 149: the note is unchanged, although its location has shifted.

44 The myth of Er concludes Plato's *Republic* (10.614–21). WBY here confounds, as he regularly does, Plato's Er, son of Armenios, with the "Man of Ur," probably deriving from the Bible's description of Abraham as coming "from Ur of the Chaldees" (Gen. 11:31), possibly conflated with Job "a man of the land of Uz" (Job 1:1). For example, in Rapallo Notebook D, which contains numerous jottings about the Great Year and ages of the world in various ancient astronomical and mythological systems, WBY remarks to himself about Indian calcula-

tions "(note resemblance to Platos perfect number 36.00—360 x 100 the year of the Man of Ur)" (NLI 13,581, leaf 23). WBY's characteristic inattention to spelling may be a factor here, though this note also conflates the "man of Ur" (*Republic*) with the Perfect Year (*Timaeus*). Cf. 181 below.

WBY mentions the myth of Er as well as the ideal length of 36,000 years for the "Greatest Year" in his introduction to his play *The Resurrection* (*Ex* 394, *Plays* 722). Book IV below is an extended discussion of the Great Year.

45 For the "darkening and brightening fortnights," see 179 below.

46 On the TS carbon, "blasphemous" is struck through and replaced by "turbulent" (NLI 36,272/6/1b, leaf 21).

47 See 189.

48 The ancient Sumerians (also known as proto-Euphrateans or Ubaidians) lived around 4500–4000 BCE on the flood plains of the Tigris and Euphrates rivers. They flourished as farmers, sailors, traders, and musicians, and are thought to have invented the first form of writing, "cuneiform," meaning wedge-shaped. The Egyptians also developed a system of writing, involving hieroglyphics.

49 Hermann Schneider (1872–1939), professor of philosophy at Leipzig University, developed a comparative survey, based on an idea of cultural evolution, aiming to trace the rise and development of humanity from the monuments left by various civilizations. WBY marked moments of first, second, and third "Cultures" in sections on Egyptian civilizations in his copy of *The History of World Civilization from Prehistoric Times to the Middle Ages* (trans. Margaret M. Green [London: George Routledge and Sons, 1931]; YL 1853), 41–44.

50 Aeneas, a character from Roman mythology, is the hero of *The Aeneid* by Virgil (Publius Vergilius Maro, 70–19 BCE). His epithet *pius* (dutiful) describes one of his main qualities and the moral emphasis on *pietas* (respect for the gods and acceptance of their workings) in the epic. Utopian Dreams: *Utopia*, from the Greek words for "no place," is an idealized state created by Sir Thomas More in his book by this title (1516) and has come to refer to any real or imagined place considered in terms of perfection or the ideal. WBY owned a copy (*Utopia*, ed. Robert Steele, trans. Ralph Robinson [London: Chatto and Windus, 1908]; YL 1381).

51 The Baul are groups of ecstatic religious minstrels in Bengal, whose musical and mystical traditions often celebrate a mystic love of God in concrete terms. The Baul were strong influences on Rabindranath Tagore (1861–1941), a prolific poet (as well as painter, educator, musician, and writer of fiction, nonfiction, plays, and songs) who was the first non-European to be awarded the Nobel Prize for Literature in 1913 and whom WBY much admired. In his 1912 introduction to

Tagore's collection *Gitanjali (Song Offerings)*, WBY wrote of Tagore's poems, "The traveller in the red-brown clothes that he wears that dust may not show upon him, the girl searching in her bed for the petals fallen from the wreath of her royal lover, the servant or the bride awaiting the master's home-coming in the empty house, are images of the heart turning to God. Flowers and rivers, the blowing of conch shells, the heavy rain of the Indian July, or the parching heat, are images of the moods of that heart in union or in separation; and a man sitting in a boat upon a river playing upon a lute, like one of those figures full of mysterious meaning in a Chinese picture, is God Himself" (*E&I* 391–92, *LE* 168; cf. *LE* 202).

52 Giambattista Vico (1668–1744) was an Italian philosopher, whose best-known work is *Scienza Nuova.* As WBY wrote to Mario Rossi in 1931, "Vico is known to me through Croce's book which has been translated" (*L* 784), referring to Benedetto Croce's *The Philosophy of Giambattista Vico*, trans. R. C. Collingwood (London: Howard Latimer, 1913; YL 445). See Croce's description of Vico's discovery of "the 'convertibility of the true with the created.' The reason why man could have perfect knowledge of man's world was simply that he had himself made that world. 'When it happens that he who creates things also describes them, then the history is certain in the highest degree'" (23). See also WBY's introduction to *The Words Upon the Window-Pane*, which mentions "that *Scienza Nuova* which Mr. James Joyce is expounding or symbolising in the strange fragments of his *Work in Progress*" and that "Vico's thought is current through its influence upon Croce and Gentile" (*Plays* 712–13).

53 The TS carbon has "desire" instead of "love" and "the magnificence of dreams" instead of "an intellectual excitement" (NLI 36,272/6/1b, leaf 23).

54 In heraldry, supporters are figures placed usually on either side of a shield, holding it up. They usually take the form of animals (real or imaginary) or human figures. WBY here uses astrological terminology, including signs of the zodiac (Aries, Taurus, Pisces, Aquarius) and planetary influences (Mars, Venus, Jupiter, Saturn), as well as symbolic figures (Sphinx, Buddha, Christ) to distinguish religious dispensations or "revelations."

55 This excerpt is from "The Double Visions of Michael Robartes" from *The Wild Swans at Coole* (*Poems* 173).

56 Gottfried Wilhelm Leibniz (1646–1716) was a philosopher and mathematician who co-invented infinitesimal calculus. His monads (from the Greek word for unity) are mind-like substantial forms of being, each with their own internal principle of being. Cf. WBY's Commentary on *Words Upon the Window-Pane*, as published in the *Dublin Magazine* Jan–Mar 1932: "There is something within a man or enclosing him that Liebnitz called a monad, and that I prefer to call a daimon" (*VPl* 975).

57 Lionel Pigot Johnson (1867–1902), English poet, essayist, and critic, member of the Rhymers' Club with WBY, was also the cousin of Olivia Shakespear and of Lord Alfred Douglas. WBY dedicated the section of *Poems* entitled *The Rose* (1893) to him and edited a selection of his poems (Dun Emer Press, 1904). Pseudo-Dionysius the Areopagite was a Christian theologian and philosopher from the late fifth to early sixth century, author of the *Corpus Areopagiticum*; his work was one major route through which Neoplatonism influenced medieval thought (especially in terms of negative theology). During the medieval period, he and Saint Denis of Paris were thought to be the same Dionysius of Athens converted to Christianity by Saint Paul. The quotation is from *The Celestial Hierarchy* Chap. 9, Section 2 (John Parker, trans., *The Celestial and Ecclesiastical Hierarchy of Dionysius the Areopagite* [London: Skeffington & Son, 1894], 35). Yeats uses the phrase in *Beltaine*, February 1900 (*IDM* 161). In their editorial notes, Mary Fitzgerald and Richard J. Finneran point out that Yeats heard this phrase from Charles Johnston (1867–1931), an old school friend and fellow Theosophist in Dublin (*IDM* 276 n3). Swedenborg reports, "They [angels] wish . . . that I should declare from their lips that there is not one angel in the whole heaven who was so created from the beginning, nor any devil in hell who was created an angel of light and was cast down thither; but that all, both in heaven and in hell, are from the human race," *Heaven and its Wonders, and Hell: From Things Heard & Seen* (London: J. M. Dent & Sons; New York: E. P. Dutton, 1909), 146. See also *LE* 49.

58 The opening passage of *The Hour-Glass* has a wise man sitting at a desk wondering how to explain to his pupils the coexistence of another world, where it is summer when we have winter (*Plays* 95, 277).

59 The quotation is from the Latin, Asclepius 3.31, *Hermetica* (YL 881) 1:351–53.

60 The Demogorgon in Shelley's four-act lyrical drama *Prometheus Unbound* is the offspring of Jupiter and Thetis and is seen as a dark, genderless spirit. See WBY's essay "Prometheus Unbound," written in 1932: "What does Shelley mean by Demogorgon? It lives in the centre of the earth, the sphere of Parmenides perhaps, in a darkness that sends forth 'rays of gloom' as 'light from the meridian sun'; it names itself 'eternity'. . . . Demogorgon made his [Shelley's] plot incoherent, its interpretation impossible, it was thrust there by that something which again and again forced him to balance the object of desire conceived as miraculous and superhuman, with nightmare" (*LE* 118–19).

61 Parmenides of Elea (5th century BCE) is one of the most important of the Pre-Socratic philosophers. His description of reality as a sphere may be found in John Burnet, *Early Greek Philosophy* (London: Adam and Charles Black, 1892; YL 308), 187. WBY used this book in writ-

ing Book II, "What the Caliph Refused to Learn," of *AVA* (106–7). The quotation from "Mrs. Shelley" comes from Mary Shelley's edition of *The Poetical Works of Percy Bysshe Shelley* (3 vols.; London: Edward Moxon, 1847; YL 1907), specifically her *Preface to the Poetical Works* and *Note on the Prometheus Unbound*. In the *Preface*, she praises Shelley's translations of Plato; in the *Note*, she writes:

> Shelley develops, more particularly in the lyrics of this drama, his abstruse and imaginative theories with regard the Creation. It requires a mind as subtle and penetrating as his own to understand the mystic meanings scattered throughout the poem. They elude the ordinary reader by their abstraction and delicacy of distinction, but they are far from vague. (1:372)

Cf. WBY's essay "The Philosophy of Shelley's Poetry" (1900), *EE* 51–72.

62 For Blake's "The Mental Traveller" (Blake 483–86; *WWB* 2:31–33), see 384 n9 above, and cf. *AVA* 107 and 271–72 n27.

63 Cf. *AVA* 133: "According to St Chrysostom, John the Baptist was conceived at the Autumnal and Christ at the Spring Equinox, which makes them respectively *primary* and *antithetical* when considered in relation to one another, a mid-summer and a mid-winter child." The Feast of the Nativity of St. John is celebrated on June 24, opposite Christmas; many customs associated with St. John's Day originated as pre-Christian midsummer festivals, as a number of Christmas customs derive from midwinter celebrations. James Grout explains the calendrical traditions: "In correlating the conception of John the Baptist with the birth of Jesus, the author of a fourth-century AD tract erroneously attributed to John Chrysostom (*De Solstitiis et Aequinoctiis*, 'On the Solstices and Equinoxes') calculated that Elizabeth (the mother of John) must have conceived on the Day of Atonement, September 24. . . . John's birth, therefore, was presumed to be June 24 (the eighth Kalends of July) and that of Jesus six months later on December 25. . . . John was understood to be preparing the way for Jesus (cf. John 3:30, "He must increase, but I must decrease"), just as the sun begins to diminish at the summer solstice and eventually increases after the winter solstice. Here, then, the Christian feasts were aligned with the four traditional turning points of the solar year: the birth of Jesus at the winter solstice (December 25), the conception (and death) of Jesus at the vernal equinox (March 25), the birth of John the Baptist at the summer solstice (June 24), and the conception of John at the autumnal equinox (September 24)" (Grout, James, "Sol Invictus," *Encyclopedia Romana*. n.d. Web. 31 Dec. 2013. http://penelope.uchicago.edu/~grout/encyclopaedia_romana/circusmaximus/hippodrome.html).

64 Coventry Kersey Dighton Patmore (1823–96) was an English poet and critic now best known for his narrative poem "The Angel in the House." According to F. A. C. Wilson, WBY was indebted to Coventry Patmore's essay "The Precursor" (*W. B. Yeats and Tradition* [New York: Macmillan, 1958], 67–68). Patmore notes that "the relation of Natural Love to Divine Love is represented by [St John]," who is "'*Precursor*' of Christ, as Natural Love is the precursor of the Divine" (*Religio Poetae, Etc.* [London: George Bell and Sons, 1893], 10–11). Patmore notes of "the great painters of the Renaissance, from Botticelli and earlier downwards" that they associate "the *two* Johns, John the Baptist and John 'the *Divine*,' as companions and co-worshippers of the Child Jesus, their synthesis" (17). Patmore does not mention Dionysus; WBY may be remembering the androgynous, smiling St John the Baptist painted between 1513 and 1516 by Leonardo da Vinci (1452–1519), and the related painting of Bacchus by an unknown follower of Leonardo, which was overpainted from an image of St. John the Baptist, both in the Musée du Louvre, Paris.

65 Plato's major Socratic dialogue *The Republic* concerns justice, government, and the role of philosophy in the ideal state. The Yeats library held two copies. The passage to which WBY refers, about the periods of divine and human births, is 8.546.

66 Alfred Edward Taylor (1869–1945) was a British philosopher and scholar of Plato. The Yeatses owned copies of four of his works, including *Plato: The Man and His Work* (London: Methuen, 1926; YL 2109) and *A Commentary on Plato's Timaeus* (Oxford: Clarendon Press, 1928; YL 2107). The passage to which WBY refers is in the latter work, not the former, in the commentary on *Timaeus* 39d 2–7 (216–19). On March 24, 1929, WBY mentioned in a letter to Sturge Moore that he had been reading this book and one other by Taylor "for a couple of months" (*LTSM* 146). WBY noted "Perfect Number" and "Magnus Annus" in the top margins of these pages.

67 See the entry "Horary Questions" in James Wilson, *A Complete Dictionary of Astrology* (London: William Hughes, 1819; YL 2284):

> The 7th house is that of marriage, love questions, contracts, or speculations in business, war, or travelling about business; of dealings with friends, strangers and women, and their honesty or knavery; encounters with thieves and their success; law-suits, public enemies, and all kinds of litigation. (171)

See also Wilson's entry on "Enemies": "We must here class enmity and friendship together, because they, according to Ptolemy, proceed from the same places" (90).

68 The TS carbon (NLI 36,272/6/1b, leaves 30–32) includes an addition-

al section, appearing between the current sections XVI and XVII: see Appendix II, 280–81.

69 Cf. WBY's notes to Lady Gregory's *Visions and Beliefs in the West of Ireland* (*LE* 268) and *PASL*: "Yet after a time the soul partly frees itself and becomes 'the shape changer' of the legends, and can cast, like the mediaeval magician, what illusions it would" (*LE* 24). See also *LE* 63.

70 On the first-pull Coole proofs (BL Add. 55893) a manuscript correction changes "the present Pope" to "Pope Pius XI." Pope Pius XI, born Ambrogio Damiano Achille Ratti in 1857, was pope from February 6, 1922, until he died on February 10, 1939. His Encyclical *Casti Connubi* of December 31, 1930, took as its focus Christian marriage.

71 Titus Lucretius Carus (d. c. 50 BCE) was an Epicurean poet. His poem *De Natura Rerum* (*On the Nature of Things* or *On the Nature of the Universe*) was translated by the English poet, dramatist, and translator John Dryden (1631–1700). Jeremy Collier (1650–1726), an English bishop and leader of the Nonjurors (clergy who refused to take the Oath of Allegiance to William III and Mary II in 1689, and who set up a schismatic church), wrote a scathing attack on the theater, *Short View of the Immorality and Profaneness of the English Stage* (1698). His attacks provoked a pamphlet war between like-minded Puritans and Restoration dramatists.

The passage in Lucretius to which WBY refers (in Book 4) claims that sexual congress cannot provide spiritual union. In May 1931, WBY talked with the Oxford don John Hanbury Angus Sparrow (1906–92), whose notes recall that

> The finest description of sexual intercourse ever written was in Dryden's translation of Lucretius, and it was justified; it was introduced to illustrate the difficulty of two becoming a unity: "The tragedy of sexual intercourse is the perpetual virginity of the soul." Sexual intercourse is an attempt to solve the eternal antinomy doomed to failure because it takes place only on one side of the gulf. The gulf is that which separates the one and the many, or if you like, God and man.
>
> (Qtd. in Norman Jeffares, *W. B. Yeats: Man and Poet* [2nd ed; London: Routledge & Kegan Paul, 1962], 267)

See also Arkins 148. The TS carbon adds these sentences to the end of the paragraph: "Men and women are still in nature and the resolution must consume circular nature, being that irregular instantaneous lightnigh [*sic*]. Our sigils but commemorate indeed a lingering secondary image cast upon the eyeball not by a past but by a future flash" (NLI 36,272/6/1b, leaf 33).

72 The source of these quotations is indeed in Daisetz Teitaro Suzuki's *Essays in Zen Buddhism* (London: Luzac, 1927; YL 2033), 234 and 242; WBY's wording is considerably altered from that of his source. On August 19, 1927, WBY wrote to Shōtarō Oshima, "I am at present reading with excitement "Zuzuki's [for Susuki's] Essays in Zen Buddhism" (*CL InteLex* 5014). Cf. a draft of *AVB*: "we should discover in this system, in this Unity of Being, not the sphere's messengers but the sphere itself, that which only contradiction can express not 'the lone tower of the absolute self' but its shattering, 'the absolute self' set free, that unknown reality painted or sung by the monks of Zen" (canceled paragraph from "Notes on the Life after Death," NLI 36,272/12, 29, corrected TS). Neil Mann has alerted us also to NLI 36,272/22, 29, where the passage appears (also in a canceled section) and concerns the Purification.

Book III: The Soul in Judgment

1 To one typescript, which may represent the stage prior to the setting typescript (NLI 36,272/21), WBY added the subtitle "Notes Upon Life After Death."

2 Ambroise-Paul-Toussaint-Jules Valéry (1871–1945) was a French Symbolist poet, philosopher, and essayist. Valéry underwent a personal crisis that resulted in a period of nearly twenty years during which he wrote no poetry. WBY mentions this period of silence in a letter to Monk Gibbon in 1932, telling the younger Irish poet about a "second stage of poetic development. Paul Valery seems to have passed through it in its most extreme form. For twenty years he neither wrote nor read poetry, he was finding, through mathematics, convictions" (*CL InteLex* 5613). The Yeatses' library contains five of Valéry's books, two of which are English translations (YL 2184–88). "Le Cimetière Marin," in the volume *Charmes ou poèmes* (1922), is a poem describing the cemetery of Sète, Valery's native town, where he is interred. The Yeatses owned a copy of this volume (*Charmes* [Paris: Gallimard, 1926]; YL 2184).

3 Valéry's (slightly misquoted) line is from the second stanza:

> Quand sur l'abîme un soleil se repose,
> Ouvrages purs d'une éternelle cause,
> Le temps scintille et le songe est savoir. (105)

The erroneous "œuvres" is corrected to "ouvrages" on the first-pull Coole proof (BL Add. 55893, 229), listed in Thomas Mark's notebook, and retained in the 1962 edition.

4 Valéry's lines read:

> Zénon! Cruel Zénon! Zénon d'Êlée!
> M'as-tu percé de cette flèche ailée
> Qui vibre, vole, et qui ne vole pas!
> Le son m'enfante et la flèche me tue!
> Ah! le soleil . . . Quelle ombre de tortue
> Pour l'âme, Achille immobile à grands pas! (112)

Zeno of Elea (c. 490–430 BCE) was a Greek philosopher whose paradoxes oppose commonsense notions with provocative logic, problematising such concepts as time, motion, and multiplicity. Little is known about his life beyond discussion in Plato's dialogue *Parmenides*. One of the most famous of Zeno's paradoxes is about Achilles and the tortoise. Achilles runs a race with a tortoise but gives the tortoise a head start. When he reaches the point where the tortoise began, Achilles is still behind it, although he is swift and the tortoise is slow. He then has to catch up the distance the tortoise traveled since the start, but by the time he gets to any point the tortoise has reached already, the tortoise has traveled beyond it, even by a fractional measure.

5 The philosopher F. H. (Francis Herbert) Bradley (1846–1924), Fellow of Merton College Oxford, was the leading exponent of British Idealism. The Yeatses' library contains a copy of his *Appearance and Reality* (London: George Allen & Unwin, 1925; YL 269). In a letter to Sturge Moore in 1928, WBY characterizes "two great streams of thought" following Kant, "the philosophy of will in Schopenhauer, Hartmann, Bergsen [*sic*], James, and that of knowledge in Hegel, Croce, Gentile, Bradley and the like" (*LTSM* 124). An early version of this passage mentions not only Bradley's book *Appearance and Reality* but also T. S. Eliot, who wrote his undefended 1916 PhD dissertation on Bradley (NLI 36,272/5/2). On the TS carbon, WBY has emended this note in ink, replacing "and was, though an admirable philosopher, a prig" with "an arrogant, sapless man" (NLI 36,272/6/2a, leaf 1).

6 Yeats spent the summer of 1916 in Normandy at the home of Maud Gonne and her daughter Iseult. Iseult wrote to him describing how exhilarating it felt to run along the shore (*Letters to W. B. Yeats and Ezra Pound from Iseult Gonne: A girl that knew all Dante once*, ed. A. Norman Jeffares, Anna MacBride White, and Christina Bridgwater [Basingstoke: Palgrave Macmillan, 2004], 61). WBY wrote to Lady Gregory, "To look at her dancing on the shore at the edge of the sea or coming in with her arms full of flowers you would think her the most joyous of creatures. And yet she is very unhappy—dying of self-analysis" (14 Aug 1916, *CL InteLex* 3017). Cf. two poems from

1912 and 1914, "I. To a Child Dancing in the Wind" and "II. Two Years Later" (*Poems* 121–22).

7 The three states of the soul are described in the Brihadāranyaka Upanishad, one of the oldest of these texts, as well as the Mandukya Upanishad. See "Famous Debates in the Forest (Brihadāranyaka-Upanishad)," Book 10, 127–28, and "At the feet of Master Mandooka (Māndookya-Upanishad)," Book 6, in *The Ten Principal Upanishads*, put into English by Shree Purohit Swāmi and W. B. Yeats, 61.

8 The TS carbon appends a footnote: "'The Religion and Philosophy of the Vedas'" A. B. Keith. Vol:I pp. 568–69" (NLI 36,272/6/2a, leaf 2). WBY's immediate source for this quotation, from the Brihadāranyaka Upanishad, is from the section entitled "The Four States of the Soul" in Chap. 28, "The Philosophy of the Upaniṣads," of Keith's *The Religion and Philosophy of the Veda and Upanishads*, 568. Cf. "Famous Debates in the Forest (Brihadāranyaka-Upanishad)," Book 7, from *The Ten Principal Upanishads*, put into English by Shree Purohit Swāmi and W. B. Yeats: "In dreams he shone by his own light; no horse there, no road, no carriage, but he made it" (149).

9 Porphyry of Tyre (c. 234–305 CE) was a highly learned Neoplatonic philosopher who wrote a number of works in many branches of knowledge although only a small portion of his work is extant. He edited and published the *Enneads*, the work of his teacher Plotinus. In *The Celtic Twilight*, WBY mentions his admiration for "wise Porphyry" and his claim that "all souls come to be born because of water" (*Myth1* 80, *Myth2* 53 and 270 n5). The idea is from Porphyry's *De Antro Nympharum* (*On the Cave of the Nymphs*), an extended allegory based on an episode from *The Odyssey* 13; WBY knew the text in the influential translation by Thomas Taylor, *Select Works of Porphyry* (London: Thomas Rodd, 1823). WBY discusses Porphyry in "The Philosophy of Shelley's Poetry" (*EE* 63–66) and returns to this thought in "Coole Park and Ballylee, 1931": "What's water but the generated soul?" (*Poems* 248). See also "Among School Children" and WBY's note about the phrase "honey of generation," which is from Porphyry (*Poems* 220, 606).

10 WBY had formed a strong interest in Japanese Nō, a highly formal musical drama that has been popular in Japan since the fourteenth century, during the time he stayed at Stone Cottage in Coleman's Hatch, Sussex, with Ezra Pound in the winter of 1913–14. WBY describes several plays in "Swedenborg, Mediums, and the Desolate Places" (*LE* 69–71). See "Certain Noble Plays of Japan" (*EE* 163–73), the essay that originally introduced the Cuala volume *Certain Noble Plays of Japan: From the Manuscripts of Ernest Fenollosa, Chosen and Finished by Ezra Pound, With an Introduction by William Butler Yeats* (Churchtown, Dundrum: Cuala Press 1916).

11 Doneraile (Dún ar Aill) is a town in Co. Cork, Ireland. In 1897, WBY

stayed in Doneraile with Bernard Edward Barnaby FitzPatrick (1848–1937), 2nd Baron Castletown of Upper Ossory, an Irish politician who shared WBY's interests in folklore and Celticism. Lord Castletown's wife, Emily Ursula Clare St. Leger (1853–1927), owned Doneraile Court, which she inherited from her father, Hayes St. Leger, 4th Viscount Doneraile. WBY mentions this tale in "Swedenborg, Mediums, and the Desolate Places," where the informant is identified as a shepherd (*LE* 72). Other tales from Doneraile are mentioned in "The Broken Gates of Death" (1898), *UP* 2:97–98, 106; "Ireland Bewitched" (1899), *UP* 2:182; and *Au* 299. See also *CL* 2:132 nn1, 3, and a brief reference in "A General Introduction for my Work" (*LE* 208).

12 This anecdote is related in *AVA* without mentioning the names of Lady and Sir William Gregory: "A Galway woman told a friend of mine she had met this friend's dead husband in an old torn coat" (197).

13 The "others" may have been fellow members of the Society for Psychical Research. See *AVA* 197.

14 Cf. a description of such funerary objects and their purposes in "Swedenborg, Mediums, and the Desolate Places" (*LE* 72).

15 This practice is described in two articles by R. H. Saunders: "Story of a Christmas Tree; Children of Both Worlds" (*Light* 43.2191 [January 6, 1923]: 7) and "A Christmas Tree in the Spheres" (*Light* 44.2243 [January 5, 1924]: 5). Cf. *AVA* 198.

16 The play is *Nishikigi* by Zeami Motokiyo (c. 1363–c. 1443), one of the foremost practioners of Nō. It is printed in Ernest Fenollosa and Ezra Pound, *"Nō" or Accomplishment: A Study of the Classical Stage of Japan* (London: Macmillan, 1916; YL 1637), 131–49, and in *Certain Noble Plays of Japan*, [1]–16. Cf. "Certain Noble Plays of Japan" (*EE* 171–72). The tale, collected by Lady Gregory, appears in *Visions and Beliefs in the West of Ireland collected and arranged by Lady Gregory: with two Essays and Notes by W. B. Yeats* (Gerrards Cross: Colin Smythe; New York: Oxford University Press, 1970), 79. WBY mentions the two stories together in "Swedenborg, Mediums, and the Desolate Places" (*LE* 70–71).

17 Florence Beatrice Farr Emery (1860–1917) was an English actress, director, composer, writer, activist, and teacher. She acted in several of WBY's plays and performed to the psaltery in experiments with that instrument and the speaking of verse; see "Speaking to the Psaltery" (*EE* 12–19). She was an influential member of the Hermetic Order of the Golden Dawn and an outspoken advocate for the rights of women. In 1912, she moved to Sri Lanka, then known as Ceylon, to become headmistress of a newly formed girls' school. A variant of this anecdote, with the "Indian" specified as a "Brahmin," occurs in *PASL* (*LE* 24) and *AVA* 197. See also *L* 255.

18 *The Tragedy of Hamlet, Prince of Denmark*, a revenge play by Wil-

liam Shakespeare, ends with the death of the titular prince (as well as many other characters).

19 WBY wrote about this event in his essay about the automatic scripts of Elizabeth Radcliffe, a medium whom he consulted in 1912 and 1913. Sister Mary Aloysius Doyle and Sister Mary Helen Ellis served together in the Crimea; later, Sister Mary Aloysius was Mother Superior of a convent in Gort.

As he carried out the request to find information for the spirit of her colleague, WBY wrote to Lady Gregory that he just returned from the British Museum "overwhelmed" at a confirmed spiritualist experience. The medium's hand had written these words, he told her:

> "Sister Mary Ellis, tell her, tell her, Sister Mary Aloysius I have lost her, I have lost her. We were together with Florence Nightingale."
>
> Later in the day I asked the spirit in charge who this was: he said, or rather wrote some words like this: "The spirit in charge this morning has told me that a woman in a dark dress with a deep bonnet asked leave to speak. She was in deep distress. She was looking for someone and seemed to think she could learn of her from you. I think the sister she is looking for is however upon this side. If that is so we will arrange a meeting." He added however that he was not at all sure.
>
> I have spent the morning in the Museum and have just found that Sister Mary Aloysius was one of a group of Irish sisters of Mercy who went with Florence Nightingale to the Crimea. She belonged to Gort Convent and was still living there in 1904. It was no doubt the knowledge that I am Irish and know Gort that made Sister Mary Ellis inquire of me. I forgot to say that Sister Mary Ellis gave 1897 for the date of her death. I want you to have inquiries made at Gort Convent to find if Sister Mary Aloysius is still living and if Sister Mary Ellis ever lived there. (*CL InteLex* 2217)

See George Mills Harper and John S. Kelly, "Preliminary Examination of the Script of E[lizabeth] R[adcliffe]," *YO* 148–49.

20 The Mandukya Upanishad, one of the ten or eleven most important or authentic, is the shortest of the Upanishads, containing twelve verses outlining the philosophy of the mantra OM (AUM) and discussing the *avasthās* or states of consciousness: the waking state (*jāgrat*), the dream state (*svapna*), and deep sleep (*suṣupti*). *Turīya* (meaning "fourth") is a boundless, non-dual consciousness that forms the substrate of the other three. See "At the Feet of Master Mandooka (Māndookya-Upanishad)," Book 6, from *The Ten Principal Upanishads*, put into English by Shree Purohit Swāmi

and W. B. Yeats (London: Faber and Faber, 1937), *59–61*. See also WBY's introduction to Shree Purohit Swāmi's translation of the Mandukya Upanishad, published separately in 1935 (*LE* 156–64). WBY made notes on *turīya* in the back cover of his copy of Woods's edition of *The Yoga-System of Patanjali* (YL 1536; see O'Shea for marginalia). The text on the TS carbon varies from that of the printed edition: "The later Upanishads describe a fourth state, Thuràya or Cathurthu, which resembles dreamless sleep in everything excepth [*sic*] that it is reached in contemplation and remembered. This fourth state, this condition of light so pure that it is almost darkness, seems to be that state wherein the soul, [. . .]" (NLI 36,272/6/2a, leaf 5).

21 The TS carbon (NLI 36,272/6/2a, leaves 5–8) contains a lengthy section of text that in the printed version is replaced by the first five sentences of section V. See Appendix II, 281–83.

22 Sources for the after life states include records of investigations by the Society for Psychical Research, of which WBY was an associate member from 1913 to 1928. See, for example, the monumental posthumous work by Frederic W. H. Myers, one of the founding members and sometime president of the society, *Human Personality and Its Survival of Bodily Death* (1903; rpt., New York: Longmans, Green, 1954). For charts and descriptions, including the relation of these states to the solar months, Faculties, and Principles, see the section "Life and the After Life" in Neil Mann, http://www.yeatsvision.com/After.html#Stages. Cf. the sections describing the relation of the Yeatsian concepts and terminology to two other important sources, Theosophy and Vedantic philosophy: http://www.yeatsvision.com/Theosophy.html and http://www.yeatsvision.com/Vedanta.html.

23 This state, in which "in many death bed visions people see those they have loved as if coming for them," and "they are revived at the moment of death and then left alone," was described in the AS as early as January 1918 (*YVP* 1:312). WBY's note to "The Second Coming" mentions this term: according to the system of "the followers of Kusta-ben-Luka" or the tribe of the Judwalis, subjective man "has a moment of revelation immediately after death, a revelation which they describe as his being carried into the presence of all his dead kindred" (*Poems* 659). WBY made a marginal note "? Vision of the Blood Kindred" beside the following passage in his copy of *On Life After Death* by Gustav Theodor Fechner:

> In the moment of death every one will realize the fact that what his mind received from those who died before him, never ceased to belong to their minds as well, and thus he will enter the third world not like a strange visitor, but like a long expected member of the family, who is welcomed home by all those with whom he was here united in the community of faith, of knowledge, or of love.

(3rd ed., Chicago and London: Open Court, 1914; YL 665), 66–67; Walter Kelly Hood, "'Read Fechner,' the Spirit Said: W. B. Yeats and Gustav Theodor Fechner," *YAACTS* 7 (1989): 95.

24 On "emotion of sanctity," see 134 and 216.

25 The first AS to which WBY refers occurred on January 31, 1918: he was informed that the spirit "meditates only till physical body is buried" and that the burial ceremony "climaxes the meditation" (*YVP* 1:315). The second AS is in fact a sleep from May 31 or June 1, 1920, "Dictated by Dionertes" to GY. The description is accompanied by a drawing, reproduced in *YVP* 3:23 and described also in *AVA* 183–84. The image recalls one of Blake's striking illustrations from 1808 to Robert Blair's *The Grave* entitled *The Soul hovering over the Body reluctantly parting with Life* (available at The William Blake Archive, ed. Morris Eaves, Robert N. Essick, and Joseph Viscomi, http://www.blakearchive.org).

26 Leap Castle, in County Offaly, Ireland, was built under the supervision of the powerful and warring O'Carroll clan and associated with bloodshed and brutality through various battles and power struggles both in it and nearby. It is famously haunted. In 1909, the gothic novelist Mildred Darby, who lived there with her husband Jonathan, wrote an article for the *Occult Review* describing an "Elemental," a terrifying creature, the size of a sheep and reeking like a decomposing corpse, that appeared periodically at the castle. See also Mrs. Darby's correspondence with Mr. R. Carroll about an appearance of the elemental to herself, her husband, and four others (NLI 17,877). WBY's friend Oliver St John Gogarty visited Leap Castle and told WBY about the apparition; see Gogarty, "The Most Haunted House of Them All," *A Weekend in the Middle of the Week and Other Essays on the Bias* (Garden City, NY: Doubleday, 1958), 202–9. According to Gogarty, WBY "listened in silence" then informed Gogarty that the spirit "is not an elemental. . . . It is not even an evil spirit. It is someone who was partially metamorphosized into an animal body and is seeking release" (208). Gogarty mentions that the spirit was female, a detail that WBY has not retained here.

27 This previous sentence replaces a longer section of text, which is present in the TS carbon: "The country-people think that nothing evil can take the form of a sheep because sheep are religious symbols, and I suggest that this spirit which doubtless living shared their conviction, is innocent. Some man who was torn, at the moment of death, between two passions—terror of bodily decay and an abject humility, might precipitate in the common mind just such a nightmare. After centuries the image is still indissoluble, still passed from mind to mind, because in life, as at the moment of death, the link between himself and the general life was broken and is now in a state corresponding to that of the Hunchback" (NLI 36,272/6/2a, leaf 8).

28 WBY noted "Dreaming Back" in the margins of Fechner's *On Life After Death*, 43. Cf. the journey the soul of Robert Gregory is imagined to make in "Shepherd and Goatherd" (*Poems* 145).

29 Dr. Abraham Wallace (1850?–1930), a medical doctor turned psychic and metaphysicist, was a member of the Council of the Society for Psychical Research and an active researcher into psychic phenomena. *The Annual Register: A Review of Public Events at Home and Abroad* was founded in 1758.

30 In *PASL*, this anecdote is attributed to Madame Blavatsky (*LE* 24). Helena Petrovna Blavatsky (1831–91) was the cofounder and leader of the Theosophical Society, of which WBY was a member from 1888–90.

31 W. H. Davies (1871–1940) was a popular Welsh poet and writer, frequently anthologized with the Georgian poets, whose work WBY admired; WBY owned copies of six books by Davies and included seven of his poems in *OBMV*. Davies spent a significant period of time wandering in Great Britain, the United States, and Canada as a drifter or hobo, and his poetry as well as *The Autobiography of a Super Tramp* (1908) reflects these experiences. WBY seems to have liked this aspect of Davies's life, calling him "the tramp Davis" (*CL InteLex* 5347, May 7, 1930). The extract is lines 13–24 of the poem "Body and Spirit," *Collected Poems* (London: A. C. Fifield, 1916; YL 498), 126–27.

32 This footnote was added in ink in WBY's hand on the carbon of the setting copy TS (NLI 36,272/6/2a, leaf 9). WBY refers to the first stanza of the poem.

33 For descriptions of this state in the genetic materials, see *YVP* 1:490, 3:92, and 3:101; cf. Fechner, *On Life After Death*, 36; Hood, "'Read Fechner,'" 95; and *AVA* 185–86, 323 n19.

34 Cf. "A Dialogue of Self and Soul": "I am content to follow to its source / Every event in action or in thought; / Measure the lot; forgive myself the lot!" (*Poems* 240).

35 In the genetic materials, the term "knot" appeared very early (November 22, 1917) as a synonym for a "complex" in psychoanalytic as well as spiritual contexts (*YVP* 1:105; see also *YVP* 2:454 and 3:302). In the record of a sleep dated November 3 [1923], WBY wrote: "In dreaming back after period of dreaming back, comes waking state & in this those who have been part of events that brought about 'knot' now dreamed back display in a kind of 'marionette show' the causes of that knot & event" (*YVP* 3:186). The TS carbon contains a passage of text that has been replaced by the material here beginning at "VI" and continuing to this point. That replaced text reads: "The <u>Spirit</u> has now entered what is called the <u>Return</u> and has for its object the <u>Spirit's</u> separation from nature—"matter"—pleasure and pain, different aspects of *<u>Passionate Body</u>. If the <u>Spirit</u> were completely "in phase"

it would be separate from Passionate Body, but if not completely "in phase" it is drawn backward in to it, compelled to live over and over again the events that had most moved it. There can be no new event because it has left the Wheel of the Faculties, but the old events stand forth in a light which is dim or bright according to the intensity of the conflict or consciousness that was once their accompaniment." The asterisk (*) above points to this note, added in ink in WBY's hand: "Compare the descriptions of the Body of Fate as they affect phases before phase 15. After death the Passionate Body holds back the Spirit, as Body of Fate in those phases held back the Will" (NLI 36,272/6/2a, leaf 10).

36 Extract from *Odyssey* 11.601–4, trans. William Morris, *The Odyssey of Homer* (Vol. 13, *The Collected Works of William Morris* [London: Longmans, Green, 1912; YL 1389]), 169. WBY and GY bought each other the twenty-four-volume *Collected Works of William Morris* as a Christmas gift in 1919. WBY quotes this same passage on 220 and (in a different translation) in the conclusion of "Swedenborg, Mediums and the Desolate Places" (*LE* 73).

Among the figures whom Odysseus relates having seen at the entrance to the Underworld is the ghost of Heracles—not, he says, the great hero himself, who is among the immortal gods. Heracles walks through the night in the passage immediately following the lines quoted above:

> But about him was noise of the dead, as of birds fear-wildered in flight
> About and about; and he wended as the dusk of the midmost night,
> With his bow all bare in his hand and the arrow laid on the string,
> And peering around and about him, as who would loose at a thing. (11:605–8)

Half mortal and half divine, after his death Heracles was raised to join the company of the gods on Mount Olympus. Cf. the figure of Cuchulain striding among the dead who sing "with the throats of birds" in "Cuchulain Comforted" (*Poems* 340).

37 WBY refers to the same comment from Swedenborg on 18. See Swedenborg, *The Spiritual Diary: Being the Record during Twenty Years of his Supernatural Experience*, trans. George Bush and Rev. John H. Smithson (5 vols.; London: James Speirs, 1883–1902; YL 2040–40D), nos. 2436, 4236–37, 4244 (2:248; 3:337, 339). The text immediately following the Homeric quotation differs from that of the TS carbon, which reads: "The Celestial Body lives through events from cause to effect or in their order of occurence, but the Passionate Body in the

order of their intensity and so for the most part through the painful first and then the fainter and happier. But the Passionate Body is not in itself intelligible. Spirit draws from it the concrete image but draws thought and word from the living" (NLI 36,272/6/2a, leaves 10–11). The same footnote as appears here then follows.

38 Eleanor Frances Jourdain (1863–1924) was principal of St. Hugh's Hall, Oxford, from 1915 to 1924; Charlotte Anne Elizabeth Moberly (1846–1937) was principal of St. Hugh's from 1886 to 1915. They co-wrote *An Adventure*, published pseudonymously in 1911 by "Elizabeth Morison and Frances Lamont," and in a fourth edition under their own names in 1931 (London: Faber and Faber; YL 1327), describing their visionary apprehension of the gardens of Versailles and Marie Antoinette (1755–93), queen of France and wife of Louis XVI. Moberly's and Jourdain's papers concerning their experience are held in the Bodleian Library at the University of Oxford. *An Adventure* and its authors appear numerous times in the AS, and WBY mentions it in *AVA* (136, 286–87 n126) and elsewhere. See also *Plays* 722; *LE* 115, 270, 272, 354 n35b, 452 nn36 and 36a, and 360 n10. See *YVP* 1:307, 319, 3:290; *MYV* 1:179, 224–25. In 1912, WBY wrote to Miss Moberly to ask her opinion concerning the appearance of the spirit of her dead father, Bishop George Moberly, to Elizabeth Radcliffe (see WBY's essay about Radcliffe's automatic script, *YO* 141–71). Despite her own experiences, Miss Moberly's reply of March 20, 1918, was cautious: "For the sake of science, I would willingly listen to any so called 'communication' from my Father, but I should try not to surrender my best judgment for any marvel." She noted that her letter was prompted "by your word to us expressing your great anxiety to unravel all the truth" and added that "pure poetical genius and deep thought are as necessary factors in that work as scientific accuracy of observation" (*L* 347–48).

Sutherland (915) suggests that the "similar vision in my own family" may be a reference to a vision seen by WBY's sister Lily in 1914: visiting a house in Glencullen (Gleann Cuilinn, Co. Dublin), she writes that "The moment I got there I felt in touch with some other world—a most pleasant feeling, almost an exalted feeling; but I could get no quiet, and so saw nothing," until she went to bed that night and saw a vision of a scene of the house and "a tall woman in the dress of (I judged) the forties or early fifties," accompanied by a younger man. Further investigations suggested ties between her vision and the house's previous owners (William M. Murphy, "Psychic Daughter, Mystic Son, Sceptic Father," *YO* 17–19). WBY relates accounts of similar visions from Sligo pilots and Galway farmers in *Au* 70–71, *The Celtic Twilight* (*Myth1* 1–141, *Myth2* 5–93), and throughout *Visions and Beliefs in the West of Ireland.*

39 Instead of "they fade into the *Thirteenth Cone*," the TS carbon has "they fade back into the Sphere" (NLI 36,272/6/2a, leaf 11).

40 This note was added in ink in WBY's hand on the TS carbon (NLI 36,272/6/2a, leaf 10). According to Swedenborg in *Heaven and Hell*, the spirit moves through several states after death as it is prepared for eternal life. It also retains its memory (divided into outer and inner, or natural and spiritual), which helps it progress to its final state, but it does not "dream back" per se. See Emanuel Swedenborg, *Heaven and its Wonders, and Hell: From Things Heard & Seen* (London: J. M. Dent & Sons; New York: E. P. Dutton, 1909), esp. "Man in the Other World possesses the Senses, Memory, Thought and Affection which he had in the World, and leaves Nothing behind him except his Earthly Body," 236–46. Cf. "Swedenborg, Mediums, and the Desolate Places" (*LE* 50–51). The quotation is from William Blake: "Swedenborg is the Angel sitting at the tomb; his writings are the linen clothes folded up" (*Marriage of Heaven and Hell*, plate 3; Blake 34; the plate is reproduced in *WWB* 3). See also Luke 24:12 and John 20:5–7.

41 Instead of this sentence, the TS carbon has this text: "Because of its link with the Celestial Body it explores events not in their order of intensity but backward to their source. It is concerned with events and their emotion alone, not with abstract thought in any form. Every event explored is the expression of a concentration of emotion separating a period of time, a portion of being, from the being as a whole and the life as a whole, something knotted, something that has constrained reason, and the dream when the Spirit re-lives it is a smoothing out or an unwinding. It is the punishment and purgation of the soul, and where the soul has great intensity, and where the consequences of the event affected great numbers, it may last with a slowly lessening pain and joy for centuries" (NLI 36,272/6/2a, leaf 13).

42 Robinson Crusoe is the hero and Friday his aboriginal companion and "Man" servant in Daniel Defoe's popular 1719 novel, *The Life and Strange Surprising Adventures of Robinson Crusoe of York, Mariner* (1719). In 1894–95, WBY's father, John Butler Yeats, was commissioned to provide illustrations to an edition of the novel edited by George A. Aitken, as vols. 1–3 in a sixteen-volume series of Defoe's *Romances and Narratives* (London: J. M. Dent, 1895); see *CL* 1:474 n2. See *The Trembling of the Veil*, where WBY writes of Synge, "I have but a vague impression, as of a man trying to look out of a window and blurring all that he sees by breathing upon the window" (*Au* 263).

43 Spiritualist activities often include spirits directing people to books and records. For example, WBY and Lady Gregory sought a codicil to Hugh Lane's will by this method. During the sleeps of 1920 and later, GY and WBY were directed to several works, for example, Freud's *Totem and Taboo* (*YVP* 3:8), Morris's *The Sundering Flood* (*YVP*

3:50), Blake's "The Mental Traveller" (*YVP* 3:57), Percy's *Reliques* (*YVP* 3:64), and Robert Browning's *Poems* (*YVP* 3:185).

44 The Yeatses were informed in a sleep that "During the teachings spirits were in contact with those of 13th cone," information WBY also recorded in his Card File (*YVP* 3:98, 391).

45 From this point to the end of Book III, the TS carbon differs radically from the finalized printed text. See Appendix II, 283–91.

46 See 14. See also WBY's notebook entry about such a smell after the difficult birth of Michael Butler Yeats on August 22, 1921: "The Nurse has noticed the smell of roses in the nursery especially when WM [William Michael, as Michael Butler was named at first] was ill that is to say when George saw the six spirits. Two of the servants smelt them on the stairs since then but thought it seems that we had roses in one bed-room. They know nothing of our work" (*YVP* 3:95–96). *Nursery Life 300 Years Ago: The Story of a Dauphin of France, 1601–10, Taken from the Journal of Dr Jean Héroard, Physician-in-Charge, and from Other Contemporary Sources* (London: George Routledge and Sons, 1929) is by the English author and editor Lucy Crump, whose father, George Birkbeck Norman Hill (1835–1903), was a distinguished editor of Samuel Johnson. She reports that "The use of oil of red roses for new-born infants was a custom centuries old" and that "Héroard only carried on the old tradition . . . ordering a bath for the dauphin with red roses in it 'to make it wholesome'" (20). The "vision of an old Cretan myth" appeared to WBY in 1896. It is described in *Au* 280 and in WBY's note, *Au* 484–87. See also *L* 866; *CL* 2: Appendix "The Vision of the Archer," 658–63; *Mem* 100–104, *LE* 14; and the poems "In the Seven Woods" (*Poems* 77) and "Parnell's Funeral" (*Poems* 285).

47 The Yeatses received a definition in a sleep: "Phantasmagoria is result of Principles foreseeing the future in shiftings Phantasmagoria antithesis of dreamed event as shiftings is of the life. We are not solitary in phantasmagoria—see Japanese story of two lovers, but only meet those who are in dreamed event" (*YVP* 3:187). The term is not used extensively in *AVA* (see 165).

48 Agrippa wrote what is perhaps the most widely read treatise on magic, *De Occulta Philosophia Libri Tres* (YL 24). This section of *AVB* repeats with little variation a passage in "Swedenborg, Mediums, and the Desolate Places" (*LE* 68 and 332 n92). The quotations are from *Three Books of Occult Philosophy*, trans. J. F. [James French] (London: R. W. for Gregory Moule, 1651). See 3.41:

> For as the manners and habits of men are in this life, such affections for the most part follow the soul after death. . . . They [the Poets] called these souls hobgoblins. . . . But they are most cruelly tortured in the irascible faculty with the hatred of an

> imaginary evil, into the perturbations whereof, as also false suspitions, and most horrible Phantasmes they then fall, and there are represented to them sad representations; sometimes of the heaven falling upon their head, sometimes of being consumed by the violence of flames . . . and sometimes of being taken, and tormented by devils. [Such] wicked souls therefore enjoying no good places . . . are called hags, and goblins, inoffensive to them that are good, but hurtfull to the wicked. (479–80)

See also *AVA* 182, 321 n6.

49 This description summarizes the fourteenth-century Nō play *Motomezuka,* which WBY read in Marie C. Stopes and Joji Sakurai, *Plays of Old Japan: The Nō* (London: Heinemann, 1913), 39–52. WBY mentions the play in a note to *The Dreaming of the Bones* (*Plays* 692) and "Swedenborg, Mediums, and the Desolate Places" (*LE* 69–70); see also *AVA* 186.

50 *Shiftings* was one of the first terms for after life states to be developed in the AS (see *AVA* 326–27 n34). Although the ideas are not identical, the state is explained in considerably more detail in *AVA* (189–91).

51 Summarized from the automatic session of June 10, 1918 (*VYP* 1:490–95).

52 "The Impassivity of the Unembodied" is MacKenna's title for the sixth tractate of *Ennead* 3 (Plotinus 2:67–96); Plotinus explains in this discourse that "The purification of the Soul is simply to allow it to be alone; it is pure when it keeps no company; when it looks to nothing without itself; when it entertains no alien thoughts—be the mode or origin of such notions or affections what they may . . . when it no longer sees in the world of image, much less elaborates images into veritable affections" (74).

53 In the AS of June 10, 1918, WBY asked if this after life state were the "ideal form of this life," and the Control Thomas agreed (*YVP* 1:491). The same session revealed that "in shiftings the soul is made free of CB [*Celestial Body*] & spirit becomes indivisible with gost [*sic*] & then becomes complete soul" (*YVP* 1:497, summarized in the Card File, *YVP* 3:245). On February 1, 1918, a session brought the information that "You might call the spirit the intermediary between man & divinity both in life and after"; "Spirit is messenger" (*VYP* 1:321, 325, summarized in the Card File, *VYP* 3:395).

54 For the *Beatitude*, see *AVA* 193–94 and 329 n48. See also the information from the AS that in this state "*All are equal*," meaning that evil souls have ceased to be evil (*YVP* 1:499–500). On the distinction between *Beatitude* and *Beatific Vision*, see Mann, "The *Thirteenth Cone*" (Mann et al. 175).

55 Bardesanes (or Bardaisan, 154–222) was a Syrian Gnostic, scientist, scholar, and poet. The "Hymn of (or on) the Soul," also known as

"The Hymn of the Pearl," is often attributed to Bardesanes; it forms part of the *Acts of Thomas*, one of the New Testament apocrypha. In 1926, WBY wrote to Sturm: "I wonder if you know the works of Bardeasan [*sic*]. He described—they say—a monthly re-creation of all things by a configuration of the [sun symbol] & [moon symbol]. And that excites me especially as he had my doctrine of Mask & Celestial Body—see his Hymn of the Soul—" (*FPS* 90). See also *Plays* 700 and *AVA* 194. According to WBY, his source is F. C. Burkitt's *Early Eastern Christianity* (London: John Murray, 1904, 218–23); see *Au* 284–85 (and *Mem* 126), which also mentions the experience WBY relates in his footnote here (cf. Matthew 1:23). The "Hymn of the Soul" is also mentioned by G. R. S. Mead in *The Hymn of the Robe of Glory* (London and Benares: Theosophical Publishing Society, 1908).

56 An error: "*Mask*" should be "*Passionate Body.*" As Neil Mann notes, "The Passionate Body gives rise to the Mask, and indeed Yeats shows how closely the two were fused in his thinking when he pairs 'the new Husk and Mask,' a slip for Husk and Passionate Body," "The *Mask* of *A Vision*," *YA* 19 [2013]: 186.

57 Quotation untraced. Cf. the "complexities" in "Byzantium," *Poems* 252–53.

58 The AS contains numerous discussions of the motives for the automatic communications. The Yeatses were usually informed that the AS was not primarily for them, that, for example, "my communications are only for a purpose unknown to you & not so much for the matter contained in them" (*YVP* 1:354), though their instructors' objectives were never made clear.

59 Quotation untraced. Cf. "Cuchulain Comforted": "all we do / All must together do" (*Poems* 340).

60 An error: WBY has substituted "Scorpio" for "Virgo" here. See Colin McDowell, "The Six Discarnate States of *A Vision*," *YAACTS* 4 (1986): 95.

61 Sutherland attributes the concept of the "censor" to Freud: "The manner in which the factors of displacement, condensation, and overdetermination play into one another in the formulation of the dream, which is the ruling factor and which the subordinate one, all this will be reserved as the subject of later investigations. For the present, we may state, as a second condition which the elements must satisfy in order to get into the dream, that *they must be withdrawn from the censor of resistance*. From now on we shall take account of dream displacement as an unquestionable fact in the interpretation of dreams" (Sutherland 925; Sigmund Freud, *The Interpretation of Dreams*, 3rd ed., trans. A. A. Brill [New York: Macmillan, 1913], 287–88).

62 William Wordsworth, "The White Doe of Rylstone; or the Fate of the Nortons," lines 274–79, *The Poetical Works*, ed. Edward Dowden (7 vols.; London: George Bell, 1892; YL 2292), 4:13. These lines are

marked in WBY's copy with the words "shape changers" in the margin. See also *LE* 268.

63 The instruction came on November 21, 1917, and again on February 3, 1918 (*VYP* 1:94, 113); cf. *AVA* 19.

64 See a notebook entry from the genetic materials: "The relation of the individual, as daimons, & as Faculties to those others in the state between lives is one of expiation, because in a relation of passion, there is cruelty or deception" (*YVP* 3:113), and cf. a discussion of terminology in the AS on December 14, 1919 (*YVP* 1:511–13). Cf. *AVA* 192.

65 David Herbert Lawrence, an English novelist, essayist, literary critic, poet, and painter (1885–1930), promoted a philosophy of the unconscious and natural love and criticized industrial modernity; he was criticized during his life for his frank depictions of sexuality. *The Rainbow* (1915) is a novel charting the lives and loves of three generations of the Brangwen family in Nottinghamshire. *Women In Love* (1920), the sequel to *The Rainbow*, follows the lives of the Brangwen sisters. WBY was reading Lawrence enthusiastically in the autumn of 1932 and the spring of 1933 (Kelly, *Chronology* 281, 284) and included six poems by Lawrence in *OBMV*.

66 The source of this story is untraced. In Hindu tradition, Krishna is the eighth incarnation of the god Vishnu. Devotion to Krishna as Svayam Bhagavan, "the Lord," developed in the bhakti movement of the sixth to ninth centuries CE and is practiced widely.

67 Expiation and victimage may occur over many lifetimes and in the supernatural states between and beyond them. These concepts are discussed at length in the AS and other documents, and WBY explains them in *AVA* 192–93 and 199–201 (and see *AVA* 328–29 nn42, 43, and 45).

68 St. Simeon Stylites (c. 388–459) was probably the first and is the most famous of the Christian *stylites* or pillar saints, who practiced an extreme form of asceticism: he climbed a pillar in Syria and stayed there until his death over thirty-six years later.

69 See 90.

70 WBY tells this story also in the introduction to *The Holy Mountain* by Bhagwān Shri Hamsa, trans. Shri Purohit Swāmi (*LE* 149).

71 The situation in this untraced story resembles that of the poem "An Image from a Past Life" (*Poems* 180–81). WBY explains the underlying concept of the Over Shadower in his note to that poem (*Poems* 654–56). The reference repeats on 206.

Book IV: The Great Year of the Ancients

1 The textual case of Book IV differs from that of the other revised sections of *A Vision*. The TS carbon (NLI 36,272/6/2b) includes only nine of the eighteen sections of the book; the other leaves appear to

have been lost. There are three other TSs, representing different stages of revision (in working order: NLI 36,272/26, NLI 36,272/28, and NLI 36,272/29). A file contains four miscellaneous revised leaves (MS 36,272/30), perhaps parts of the other TSs at one time. NLI 36,272 /26 contains early versions of all sections of the Macmillan text except X, XII, and XVIII, and it has two sections that would be excised entirely from the final version (see Appendix II, 291–93). None of the other TSs goes beyond the middle of section XI of the published text, although NLI 36,272/30 includes TS for rejected sections XIX and XX (see Appendix II, 292–93). Except that it is incomplete, NLI 36,272/6/2b represents a stage far closer to the published text than do any of the other rewritten parts of *A Vision.*

The astrological Great Year is tied to the phenomenon of the precession of the equinoxes. This is caused by the nutation of the Earth, a "wobble" of the Earth's axis, often compared to a spinning top that is running down. A single cycle of this "wobble" is now known to take about 25,800 years. As the axis of the Earth describes a circle (as the North Pole gyrates and points to different stars at different periods), the points where the plane of the equator of the Earth intersects with that of the apparent motion of the sun (the ecliptic) shift backwards. These two points represent the two equinoxes, and their position is used to fix the position of the "tropical" zodiac (from the Greek *tropoi*, turning points), in contrast with the "sidereal" zodiac used in India (from the Latin *sidera*, stars). At the time when Western astrology and astronomy were being codified in Alexandria, the point of intersection that corresponded to the spring equinox in the Northern Hemisphere was at the start of the constellation of Aries and so came to be called "the first point of Aries" (it retains this name in astronomy and astrology). This point is also the very end (30°) of Pisces, and as time has gone on, the equinox has shifted through the constellation of Pisces, such that the "first point of Aries" has shifted through the constellation of Pisces toward Aquarius. The time taken for the equinoctial point to pass through one twelfth of the circle, corresponding to a sign of the zodiac or a regularized constellation, is some 2,160 years. This is the period adopted by the Yeatses' instructors in their divisions of the historical gyres.

WBY explains the Great Year in the introduction to *The Resurrection*:

> Ptolemy thought the precession of the equinoxes moved at the rate of a degree every hundred years, and that somewhere about the time of Christ and Caesar the equinoctial sun had returned to its original place in the constellations, completing and recommencing the thirty-six thousand years, or three hundred and sixty incarnations of a hundred years apiece, of

> Plato's Man of Ur. Hitherto almost every philosopher had some different measure for the Greatest Year, but this Platonic Year, as it was called, soon displaced all the others; it was a Christian heresy in the twelfth century, and in the East, multiplied by twelve as if it were but a month of a still greater year, it became the Manvantra of 432,000 years, until animated by the Indian jungle it generated new noughts and multiplied itself into Kalpas. (*Plays* 724)

The Great Year has been discussed by any number of commentators in antiquity and into the early modern period (for example, by Marsilio Ficino [1433–99], whose work was translated by GY). The most influential discussion is that by Plato in the *Timaeus* (thus, the concept has often been termed Annus Platonicus). Pierre Duhem's *Le système du monde* is the most comprehensive modern treatment. For a comprehensive list of sources, see Godefroid de Callataÿ, *Annus Platonicus: A Study of World Cycles in Greek, Latin and Arabic Sources* (Louvain-la-Neuve: Université Catholique de Louvain, 1996), Bibliography 1, 269–76. See also 149.

2 The Fourth Eclogue of Publius Vergilius Maro (70–19 BCE) was often called the "Messianic Eclogue" because of Christian interpretations of its enigmatic prophetic verses about a child who would usher in a new golden age. The Yeatses owned two translations of the *Eclogues*, one of which is Samuel Palmer's translation with accompanying etchings (YL 2202, 2203). Cf. *AVA* 125. WBY's sources included an article by Kirby Flower Smith, "Ages of the World (Greek and Roman)," Hastings 1:200. The twelve-volume *Encyclopaedia of Religion and Ethics*, edited by James Hastings, was one of WBY's main sources for information about the Great Year in antiquity; he purchased it using some of the funds from the Nobel Prize. Other sources include an article by W. Warde Fowler about whether this infant referred to a real child or a representative of a coming generation ("Observations on the Fourth Eclogue of Virgil," *Harvard Studies in Classical Philology* 14 [1903], 17–35); and *Virgil and His Meaning to the World of To-Day* by J. W. Mackail (London, Calcutta, and Sydney: George G. Harrap, [n.d.]), as mentioned in *Diary 1930* (*Ex* 336). See also the list of sources WBY used for the Great Year noted in the back flyleaf of his edition of Marcus Tullius Cicero, *Somnium Scipionis* . . . , trans. by L.O. [Levavi Oculos, the Golden Dawn motto of Percy Bullock], Vol. 5 of *Collectanea Hermetica*, ed. W. Wynn Westcott (London: Theosophical Publishing Society, 1894) (YL 387). Liebregts gives a corrected transcription of this list (255).

The god Attis, whose cult was originally associated with Phrygia and Greece, was linked to the Great Mother (Cybele), self-castration, death, and resurrection. In Chap. 34 of *The Golden Bough*, "The

Myth and Ritual of Attis," Sir James Frazer (1854–1941) notes that Attis

> was to Phrygia what Adonis was to Syria. Like Adonis, he appears to have been a god of vegetation, and his death and resurrection were annually mourned and rejoiced over at a festival in spring. The legends and rites of the two gods were so much alike that the ancients themselves sometimes identified them.
> (Part 4, *Adonis Attis Osiris* [2nd ed.; London: Macmillan, 1907; YL 700], 229–30)

Cf. references to Attis in "Vacillation" (*Poems* 254) and *The Resurrection* (1927 version, *VPl* 924). WBY marked passages in his copy of the "Hymn to the Mother of the Gods" by Julian the Apostate having to do with Attis, including the explanation for the festival of Attis taking place at the vernal equinox (Julian the Emperor, *The Works of the Emperor Julian,* trans. Wilmer Cave Wright [3 vols.; Loeb, 1913; YL 1049], 1:471, 473, 479, 489). On the "old lunar year" beginning in March, see n10 below.

3 WBY here substitutes the Roman general and politician Gaius Marius (c. 157–86 BCE) for his great rival Lucius Cornelius Sulla (138–68 BCE) in the complicated military and political upheavals of first-century Rome, but otherwise closely follows his source, Plutarch's *Life of Sulla* (to which WBY refers in a note written into the verso of the title page of his copy of *Somnium Scipionis*). In Chap. 7, Plutarch relates the omens foretelling the disasters in the civil wars following Sulla's march on Rome (88 BCE):

> And when Sulla had set out for his camp on unfinished business, he himself kept at home and contrived that most fatal sedition, which wrought Rome more harm than all her wars together had done, as indeed the heavenly powers foreshowed to them. For fire broke forth of its own accord from the staves which supported the ensigns, and was with difficulty extinguished; and three ravens brought their young forth into the street and devoured them, and then carried the remains back again into their nest; and after mice had gnawed consecrated gold in a temple, the keepers caught one of them, a female, in a trap, and in the very trap she brought forth five young ones and ate up three of them. But most important of all, out of a cloudless and clear air there rang out the voice of a trumpet, prolonging a shrill and dismal note, so that all were amazed and terrified at its loudness. The Tuscan wise men declared that the prodigy foretokened a change of conditions and the advent of a new age. For according to them there are eight ages in all, differ-

ing from one another in the lives and customs of men, and to each of these God has appointed a definite number of times and seasons, which is completed by the circuit of a great year. And whenever this circuit has run out, and another begins, some wonderful sign is sent from earth or heaven, so that it is at once clear to those who have studied such subjects and are versed in them, that men of other habits and modes of life have come into the world, who are either more or less of concern to the gods than their predecessors were. All things, they say, undergo great changes, as one again succeeds another, and especially the art of divination; at one period it rises in esteem and is successful in its predictions, because manifest and genuine signs are sent forth from the Deity; and again, in another age, it is in small repute, being off-hand, for the most part, and seeking to grasp the future by means of faint and blind senses. Such, at any rate, was the tale told by the wisest of the Tuscans, who were thought to know much more about it than the rest.

(Plutarch, *Lives* 4: *Alcibiades and Coriolanus, Lysander and Sulla*, trans. Bernadotte Perrin [Loeb, 1916], 345–49)

Cf. Petrie, *The Revolutions of Civilisation*, 9–10, which quotes part of this extract. The passage occurs on 4:61–62 of North's translation of the *Lives* (YL 1597). Lady Gregory owned a copy of the 1770 translation by John and William Langhorne (we are indebted to James Pethica for information about the library at Coole). The Etruscan civilization, which flourished in central Italy from the eighth to the fifth century BCE, was gradually defeated by Rome by the third century BCE. WBY refers to the "trumpets heard by Etruscan seers" in *On the Boiler* (*LE* 236).

4 From Virgil, *Eclogue* 4.5–14, probably translated by GY: in her copy of *A Vision* (1938; YL 2435), "IVth Ecologue" [*sic*] is written beside the line. The Cumaean Sibyl was the prophetess at the Apollonian oracle at Cumae. Her oracles, the Sibylline Books, were kept in Rome by the *quindecimviri sacris faciundis,* a college of fifteen men who guarded, consulted, and interpreted them in times of crisis. Astraea, the celestial virgin, abandoned the earth during the Iron Age in favor of the heavens where she became the constellation Virgo. A personification of justice, her return would signal a new golden age. Cf. "Two Songs from a Play" (*Poems* 216–17, *Plays* 481–82), *The Resurrection* (*Plays* 487), and *CL* 3:123. The "reign of Saturn" refers to the return of the golden ages associated with one of the oldest gods of Roman religion. Virgil's patron Gaius Asinius Pollio (75 BCE–4 CE) was a Roman soldier, politician, and man of letters.

5 An earlier version of this section is far shorter:

> Why do Caesar and Christ always stand face to face in our imagination? Did not Dante put Judas and Brutus into the mouth of Satan? According to Cicero the official interpreter of oracles had thought of announcing to the Senate House that certain verses of the Sybil proclaimed Caesar that ideal king who would bring the Golden Age, a thought that enraged Cicero the more because "Neither Gods nor men would suffer a king in Rome".[x] ~~Cicero~~ Caesar was killed at the full moon in March—the Ides of March—through coincidence *some old custom of sacrifice* or the derision of his enemies, or—but what do we know of anything? Christ died at a full moon in March, the first full moon after the vernal equinox and upon that day or upon the Sunday nearest we celebrate Easter.

Yeats's note referring back the "x" reads: "I take this from Cudworth's 'Intellectual System of the World' for I have no edition of Cicero's letters near my hand" (NLI 36,272/26, leaves 1–2, text in italics added in manuscript). See n7 below about WBY's revision of this passage in consultation with Cicero's letters.

6 In Dante's *Inferno*, in the ninth circle of Hell, the poet sees and describes Satan, who chews eternally on three traitors partly stuffed into the jaws of his three mouths: Judas Iscariot, who betrays his master Jesus in the gospels; and Marcus Junius Brutus (c. 85–42 BCE) and Gaius Cassius Longinus (d. 42 BCE), leading assassins of Julius Caesar (*Inferno* 34.55–69).

7 Marcus Tullius Cicero (106–43 BCE) was a Roman philosopher, orator, statesman, and writer whose prose style has been of broad influence in Western culture. He wrote a letter to his close friend Titus Pomponius Atticus on July 20 or 21, 45 BCE, alluding in passing to the procession in which Caesar's image was carried amongst those of the gods in the Ludi Victoriae Caesaris as well as the rumor about Cotta (*Letters to Atticus* 13.44). Lucius Aurelius Cotta (who was a member of the quindecimviri) was said to have intended to propose the title of King for Julius Caesar, since it was written that the Parthian Empire could be defeated only by a king. The fuller story is told in Cicero's *De Divinatione* 1.54 (*De Senectute, De Amicitia, De Divinatione*, with trans. by William Armistead Falconer [Loeb, 1923], 494–97). Plutarch also mentions the incidents in his *Life of Caesar* (*Lives* 7: *Demosthenes and Cicero, Alexander and Caesar*, trans. Bernadotte Perrin [Loeb, 1919], 580–83. Many pages in the *Life of Caesar* are uncut in the Yeatses' copy of Plutarch's *Lives* (5:267–349; YL 1597).

This passage was revised while WBY was at Coole staying with the gravely ill Lady Gregory in the autumn of 1931. Putting what he thought were final touches on *A Vision*, he tried and failed to find citations in Cicero's letters for the story of the prophecies connecting

Caesar with a divinely ordained kingship. He enlisted GY for help, as well as Louis Claude Purser (1854–1932), co-editor of Cicero's voluminous correspondence. Purser pointed to an allusion to the letter in a further source: *The True Intellectual System of the Universe*, the magnum opus of the Cambridge Platonist Ralph Cudworth. On October 20, WBY wrote GY asking her to look up a passage for him in one of the two copies in their library (YL 453, 454).

> I enclose a letter of Pursers. Could you look in Cudworths "Intellectual Systems of the World". You will find it under "sibyl" or "sibyllene Oracle" in the Index. Cicero speaks of Ceasar in connection with the great year & uses the words that "neither gods nor men would tolerate a king in Rome". Ceasar had thought of having himself repres[ent]ed as the king fortold by the oracle. We have two copies of Cudworth but the one with an index is in three volumes, an eighteenth century or early nineteenth century edition. If the reference is precise do not trouble Purser but if it is, as I expect, merely to a letter to "Atticus" you might ask his help. There are 3 vols of letters to "Atticus". I don't want the passage I want merely the reference. I am writing to Purser. (*LWBY/GY* 258)

GY's search in the index to the nineteenth-century edition led to the passage in which Cudworth describes Cicero's account (though referring to the fuller description in Cicero's *De Divinatione* and not the letters). Cudworth quotes and translates Cicero extensively, adding a footnote identifying L. Cotta Quindecimvir as the interpreter who, in Cicero's words, "was lately thought to have been about to declare in the senate-house, that if we would be safe, we should acknowledge him for a king who really was so." Cicero's question "If there be any such thing contained in the Sibylline books, then we demand, concerning what man is it spoken, and of what time?" is quoted, as well as Cicero's opinion that "whoever framed those Sibylline verses, he craftily contrived, that whatsoever should come to pass, might seem to have been predicted in them, by taking away all distinction of persons and times." Cudworth reports Cicero writing, "Let us also deal with the Quindecimviri and Interpreters of the Sibylline books, that they would rather produce any thing out of them, than a king" (1.465–66, translating Cicero, *De Divinatione* 1.54).

"The religious party of the Sibyl" is misleading. WBY may have found the phrase in the Loeb edition of the *Epistolae ad Familiares* (Cicero, *The Letters to His Friends*, with translation by W. Glynn Williams [3 vols.; Loeb, 1927]). As translated by Williams, Cicero writes to Publius Lentulus Spinther in August 56 that Ptolemy (XII) might be reinstated as king of Egypt "as the Senate originally decided, and that he will be reinstated 'without a host,' as was the intention (according to the religious party) of the Sibyl" (1:31). Cicero's translated phrase, "quemadmodum homines religiosi Sibyllae placere dixerunt," addresses what the "homines religiosi," possibly the quindecimviri, reported the Sibylline Books to have said about how Ptolemy's restoration was to take place.

8 According to a number of ancient sources, the body of Julius Caesar was partially cremated by a mob of plebians after the reading of his testament and a highly emotional oration by Marcus Antonius (Mark Antony). Members of the crowd snatched brands from the fire to burn down the houses of his assassins. As Suetonius relates,

> The bier on the rostra was carried down into the Forum by magistrates and ex-magistrates; and while some were urging that it be burned in the temple of Jupiter on the Capitol, and others in the Hall of Pompey, on a sudden two beings with swords by their sides and brandishing a pair of darts set fire to it with blazing torches, and at once the throng of bystanders heaped upon it dry branches, the judgment seats with the benches, and whatever else could serve as an offering. Then the musicians and actors tore off their robes, which they had taken from the equipment of his triumphs and put on for the occasion, rent them to bits and threw them into the flames, and the veterans of the legions the arms with which they had adorned themselves for the funeral; many of the women too, offered up the jewels which they wore and the amulets and robes of their children.
>
> (Book 1: The Deified Julius, *The Lives of the Caesars*, trans. J. C. Wolfe [Loeb, 1913], 115)

Later, a man calling himself Amatius erected an altar on the spot where the body had been burnt. He was killed without trial by Antonius, and the altar (as well as a column dedicated to Caesar) was demolished by Dolabella. According to Walter C. A. Ker,

> At the beginning of April an impostor, calling himself a descendant of the great Marius, and therefore of kin to Caesar, but who was, in fact, a horse-doctor called Herophilus or Amatius, appeared in Rome. . . . He now mingled with the crowds that still lingered round the scene of the cremation as a holy spot, fanned the excitement of the mob, and built an altar. . . . At this altar he persuaded the people to pour libations and make sacrifice to Caesar as to a god.
>
> (Cicero, *Philippics*, trans. Walter C. A. Ker [Loeb, 1926], 10–11)

The detail about his profession comes from *Facta et Dicta Memorabilia* by Valerius Maximus; one MS of this work reports him to be a horse doctor [(a)equarius medicus] and another an eye doctor [ocularis medicus] (Valerius Maxiumus, *Memorable Doings and Sayings*, trans. D. R. Shackleton Bailey [Loeb, 2000], 390–91). No sources call Herophilus/Amatius a "cow-doctor," and we have been unable to trace where WBY may have found information about the profession of this minor figure. The events are also described (without this detail) in Charles Merivale, *History of the Romans Under the Empire* (8 vols.; London: Longman, Green, 1865), 2:86–96.

9 Publius Cornelius Dolabella (70–43 BCE) was a Roman general and politician. He had a short-lived marriage to Cicero's daughter Tullia, who died in childbed soon after their divorce. After Caesar's assassination, Cicero wrote him a letter praising him for destroying the altar and pillar erected to Caesar as god and *pater patriae.* In that letter, Cicero compares Dolabella to Brutus, writing that "Nihil est enim, mihi crede, virtute formosius, nihil pulchrius, nihil amabilius" ("There is nothing fairer, nothing more beautiful, nothing more lovable than courageous action"), Cicero, *The Letters to His Friends*, trans. W. Glynn Williams (3 vols.; Loeb, 1928), 9.14, 2:228, 229.

10 The Roman calendar, as described by W. Warde Fowler in Hastings, began "with March, which marks the season when all living things, man included, break into fresh activity, and which bears the name of the deity who represented at once the agricultural and the military activity of the community" [i.e., Mars] ("Roman Religion," 10.822). Julius Caesar revised the Roman calendar in 46 BCE to a new system that was based more closely on a solar or tropical year than the calendar it replaced. The cult of Attis became prominent in Rome after the rise of the empire. According to the entry in Hastings, Attis played a part in a series of Roman festivals occurring in late March. "On March 15 the college of *Cannophori*, or reed-bearers, took part in the ceremonies of the day by carrying reeds in procession—a custom explained as a commemoration of the finding of Attis by the Great Mother on the reedy banks of the river Gallus, but more likely a reminiscence of a primitive phallic procession" (Grant Showerman, "Attis," Hastings 2:217). Fowler describes how "The internal arrangement of each [Roman] month had originally been based on the phases of the moon, and this system was maintained, for convenience of reckoning, long after all relations between these phases and the calendar had been lost. The two chief points in a lunar month are the first appearance of the moon's crescent (*Kalendæ*), and the full moon (*Idus*) (Fowler, "Calendar [Roman]," Hastings 3:134).

11 See James G. Carleton, "Calendar (Christian)": "The primitive Christians all agreed in celebrating Christ's death and resurrection at the season when they actually occurred, that is, at the time of the Jewish

Passover. They also agreed that the Crucifixion took place on a Friday which coincided with the 14th day of the first Jewish (lunar) month Nisan. . . . As Christians made their Paschal anniversaries coincide in season with the Passover, so, for a long period, they were satisfied to accept the Jewish computation of the time of that festival, which should fall on the first full moon after the vernal equinox" (Hastings 3:88–89).

The dating of Easter is a complicated question involving religious principles, solar as well as lunar calculations, and calendars in several Christian and Jewish cultures over many centuries. It has a complex and often tumultuous history. It is not true that the majority of Christendom ever celebrated its major feast on the first full moon after the vernal equinox, as WBY states. Rather, it is generally set on the Sunday after that date. It is unclear where WBY found that some Christians using the Julian calendar (instituted in 46 BCE) celebrated the feast on March 15, an idea that underscores his parallel between Caesar and Christ. See Carleton's description of Quartodecimanism, the practice of celebrating Easter on the fourteenth day of Nisan, regardless of the day of the week (*op. cit.*). Some early Christians seem to have complained that Jewish reckonings varied from community to community, sometimes occurring too soon. The author of *De pascha computus* (243, falsely attributed to St. Cyprian of Carthage and so often referred to as Pseudo-Cyprian) refers to some of his predecessors giving the range of dates for Easter as the Ides of March to the Ides of April (*Patrologia Latina. Patrologiae cursus completus: series Latina*, ed. J. P. Migne et al. [Paris, 1841–1902], 4:942–72, discussed in Alden A. Mosshammer, *The Easter Computus and the Origins of the Christian Era* [Oxford: Oxford University Press, 2008], 125–27). Eusebius quotes Dionysus, bishop of Alexandria (7.20), and Anatolius of Alexandria (7.32), complaining about setting the feast before the equinox through errors in the Jewish calendar (*The Ecclesiastical History of Eusebius Pamphilus*, trans. Christian Frederick Crusé [9th ed.; New York: Stanford & Swords, 1850], 290, 312–14). Since the vernal equinox is an astronomical point, it is not easy to determine. When Julius Caesar reformed the calendar, the vernal equinox was restored to March 25, its date when Numa had made the calendar official rather than truly lunar, but because of the arrangement of leap years, it started drifting "backwards" with the years. It moved back at a rate of about 1 day every 128 years or so, and after a few centuries it was already on March 21.

Another possible source involves the Celtic calendar, probably first made in Gaul at the turn of the fifth century but used in Ireland and Northern England until the mid-7th century. In the Celtic calendar the vernal equinox was set at March 25, so this gave March 26 as the earliest possible date for Easter. Easter calendars using March 21 as the vernal equinox gave March 22 as the earliest possible date for Easter. Thus, in a situation where multiple calendars were in use, as in Merovingian Gaul, the user of the Celtic calendar could criticize the users of the other calendars of celebrating Easter before the vernal equinox. St. Colm Cille (or Columba, 521–97) championed the Celtic calendar and did in fact make this complaint to Pope Gregory the Great in an epistle dated about 600 (see Caitlin Corning, *The Celtic and Roman Traditions: Conflict and Consensus in the Early Medieval Church* [Houndmills: Palgrave Macmillan, 2006], 26ff.).

See WBY's notebook entry from March 26, 1921: "Yesterday morning I was searching through Frazers 'Adonis' to find origin of easter & could not find why it was not always at same date. That evening she [GY] told me how soon after lunch (I had not mentioned my research) she got interested in easter & found in some book, whose name she could not remember, that easter was always at first full moon after easter [*sic*]. . . . I doubt if George's book was real (*YVP* 3:74–75).

12 Christian Matthias Theodor Mommsen (1817–1903), an influential German classical scholar, historian, politician, and jurist, is the author of the *History of Rome* (3 vols.; 1854, 1855, and 1856), which covers the beginnings of Rome to the rule of Julius Caesar (a promised extension into the imperial period was never written). He was awarded the Nobel Prize in Literature in 1902. Mommsen distinguished his profound admiration for Julius Caesar from approval of Caesarism: "From Caesar's time, as the sequel will show and Gibbon has shown long ago, the Roman system had only an external coherence and received only a mechanical extension, while internally it became even with him utterly withered and dead" (*The History of Rome*, trans. William Purdie Dickson [5 vols.; London: Richard Bentley & Son, 1894], 5:326). WBY also mentions Mommsen in the note to *The Resurrection* (*Plays* 726).

13 The passage is from Cicero's *Dream of Scipio* (*Somnium Scipionis*), a deliberate echo of the myth of Er in Plato's *Republic* in an account of a dream vision by Scipio Aemilianus (Scipio Africanus the Younger), which forms the final section of the sixth book of *De re publica* (6.24). It is unclear whose translation is used here (perhaps GY's). The passage is quoted (in French) in Duhem 1:283 and also in Bullock's translation of *Somnium Scipionis* (YL 387); WBY marked it in his copy of the latter (12).

14 The TS carbon here inserts the extra phrase, "an eclipse *perhaps* at some particular place in heaven" (NLI 36,272/6/2b, leaf 4, text in italics added in manuscript).

15 For the Indian Great Year, see WBY's introduction to *The Holy Mountain* (*LE* 153–54) and his note to *The Resurrection* (*Plays* 724), where he cites Duhem, 1:67–68, as a source. For "brightening and

darkening fortnights," cf. *The Ten Principal Upanishads*, translated into English by Shree Purohit Swāmi and W. B. Yeats (London: Faber, 1937), 158. They are also mentioned in *Manusmṛti* 1.66. *Manusmṛti* or *Mānava-Dharmaśāstra*, known in English as The Laws or Code of Manu, is an ancient sacred text in Sanskrit, containing an account of creation and orders in society, as well as an ethical code. Manu, the progenitor of humankind, saved humanity from a great flood and discovered the dharma; the Code of Manu is his response to sages who asked him to declare to them the sacred laws of society (see S. Radhakrishnan, *Indian Philosophy* [2 vols.; London: George Allen & Unwin, 1923, 1927]; YL 1663, 1:515–18). WBY's sources may include Madame Blavatsky, *Isis Unveiled: A Master-Key to the Mysteries of Ancient and Modern Science and Theology* (2 vols.; New York: Bouton; London: Quaritch, 1877), 1:30–35. WBY certainly consulted Sepharial [Walter Gorn Old], *Hebrew Astrology: The Key to the Study of Prophecy* (London: W. Foulsham, 1929), 61; and H. Jacobi's entry "Ages of the World (Indian)" in Hastings 1:200–202. In 1928 or 1929, WBY made extensive entries from Sepharial and Jacobi about the Indian Great Year in Rapallo Notebook D (NLI 13,581). See also Harbans Rai Bachchan, *W. B. Yeats and Occultism* (Dehli, Varanasi, and Patna: Motilal Banarsidass, 1966), 149–57.

16 As WBY notes, this section relies on Pierre Duhem, *Le système du monde*, especially Vol. 1, Chap. 2, Section 10 (on the periodicity of the world according to ancient philosophies, in the context of the Platonic Great Year), 1:69–85; and Chap. 5, sections 6 and 7 (on the Great Year in the works of the Stoics and Neoplatonists), 1:275–95.

17 Anaximander (610–546 BCE) was a Pre-Socratic Greek philosopher. Fragments of his work are the oldest surviving examples of Western philosophy; they suppose an order in the cosmos deriving from *to apeiron*, the boundless. Duhem states, "Anaximandre a . . . professé l'opinion qu'au cours de l'éternité, se succèdent une infinité de mondes dont chacun a une durée limitée," and "nous voyons ici Anaximandre affirmer un double infini: Une étendue infinie, principe de la coexistence d'une infinité de mondes simultanés; une éternité infinie, principe des générations et des destructions périodiques d'une infinité de mondes successifs" (1:70–71). Cf. the summary of Anaximander's system in Burnet 47–55.

18 For alternating destruction by water and fire, see Cicero, *Somnium Scipionis*: "fire and flood, which will inevitably happen at certain fixed periods of time," YL 387, 12 (*De re publica* 6.23). Other sources include those WBY noted in his copy of *Somnium Scipionis* (see n2 above). Quoting from Chap. 18 of *De Die Natali* (238) by the Roman grammarian and philosopher Censorinus (not 17, as WBY's note indicates), Duhem writes,

> Il y a encore l'Année qu'Aristote appelle très grande plutôt que grande, et qui est formée par les révolutions du Soleil, de la Lune et des cinq étoiles errantes, lorsque tous ces astres sont revenus à la fois au point céleste d'où ils étaient partis ensemble. Cette Année a un Grand Hiver appelé par les Grecs κατακλυσμός (inondation) et par les latins *diluvium*; elle a aussi un été que les Grecs nomment ἐκπύρωσις ou incendie du Monde. Le Monde, en effet, doit être, tour à tour inondé ou embrasé à chacune de ces époques. (1:73)

In *Naturales Quaestiones* 3.29 (also noted by WBY in his copy of *Somnium Scipionis*) Lucius Annaeus Seneca (c. 1 BCE–65 CE) relates how the Babylonian historian and astronomer Belosus discusses the day of destruction: "All that the earth inherits will, he assures us, be consigned to flame when the planets, which now move in different orbits, all assemble in Cancer, so arranged in one row that a straight line may pass through their spheres. When the same gathering takes place in Capricorn, then we are in danger of the deluge. Midsummer is at present brought round by the former, midwinter by the latter. They are zodiacal signs of great power seeing that they are the determining influences in the two great changes of the year" (*Physical Science in the Time of Nero: Being a Translation of the* Quaestiones Naturales *of Seneca*, trans. John Clarke [London: Macmillan, 1910], 151).

The phrases "the fire of heaven" and "lunar water" are translated from Duhem (Chap. 2), who discusses the ideas of alternating destruction and re-creation in Heraclitus and Empedocles, called Love and Discord by the latter, then refers to the Pythagorean philosopher and scientist Philolaus (c. 470 to c. 385 BCE), as reported in Pseudo-Plutarch, *De placitis philosophorum*. Duhem quotes: "voici comment s'exprime le Pseudo-Plutarque: 'De quoi se nourrit le Monde—Philolaüs dit que la destruction se produit de deux manières, tantôt parce que le feu du ciel vient à s'écouler, tantòt parce que l'eau lunaire se répand en l'atmosphère aérienne; de ces deux éléments sont formés les aliments gazeux du monde'" (1:77). The "fire [returning] to its seed" is from Duhem (Chap. 5): "Il a plu, en effet, aux philosophes stoïciens que l'Univers se transformât en feu, comme en sa semence (σπέρμα), puis que, de ce feu, se produisît, de nouveau, une disposition toute semblable à celle qui existait auparavant" (1:277). See also *LE* 155.

19 For WBY's interest in Nicholas of Cusa, see 383 n2 and 467 n5. Duhem notes (quoting Empedocles on Love and Discord) that

> ainsi [l'homogène et l'hétérogène] sont sans cesse engendrés; ni à l'un ni à l'autre n'est attribuée l'immuable éternité; mais par là

> que ces alternances n'ont jamais aucune fin, par là même [l'homogène et l'hétérogène] gardent toujours l'immobilité de ce qui est périodique. . . . Par ces vers d'Empédocle, nous entendons, pour la première fois, énoncer une idée que nous retrouverons bien souvent en la Philosophie grecque: Une chose changeante qui se reproduit périodiquement nous présente comme la ressemblance atténuée d'une chose qui demeure éternellement la même (1:75–76)

20 Taken directly from Duhem, quoting Chrysippus the Stoic (1:279). Duhem notes that Empedocles "admettait une période intermédiaire d'immobilité et de repos" (1:76).

21 On the TS carbon, the opening of this sentence reads, "So far the universals had been everything, the individual nothing; *beauty and* truth had mattered, *not* Pericles and Socrates ~~had not~~," (NLI 36,272/6/2b, leaf 6, text in italics added in manuscript).

22 See *Ennead* 5.7.1, which treats the "question whether there exists an ideal archetype of individuals. . . . the individual soul has an existence in the Supreme as well as in his world" (Plotinus 4:69). Cf. WBY's introduction to *The Resurrection*: "Plotinus substituted the archetypes of individual men in all their possible incarnations for a limited number of Platonic Ideas . . . We may come to think that nothing exists but a stream of souls, that all knowledge is biography, and with Plotinus that every soul is unique; that these souls, these eternal archetypes, combine into greater units as days and nights into months, months into years, and at last into the final unit that differs in nothing from that which they were at the beginning" (*Plays* 724–25).

23 On the TS carbon, the beginning of this sentence reads "~~After his pupil Porphyry, the~~ *To the next generation it seemed plain that the* ~~e~~Eternal ~~r~~Return" (NLI 36,272/6/2b, leaf 6, text in italics added in manuscript).

24 The quotation from Proclus's influential *Commentary on Plato's Timaeus* is a direct English version of Duhem's French translation:

> Il semblerait, d'après ce passage, qu'il faille distinguer deux Grandes Années platoniciennes; celle dont il est question au *Timée*, plus petit commun multiple des huit années de révolution des sphères célestes, serait seulement une partie aliquote de l'autre; celle-ci, plus petit commun multiple des périodes de toutes les rotations, de toutes les révolutions visibles ou invisibles qui s'effectuent au sein des cieux, serait celle dont il est question dans la *République*, celle dont le nombre parfait mesure le temps du retour de l'Univers à son état initial. (1:292)

25 The list on the back flyleaf of WBY's copy of Cicero's *Somnium Scipionis* (YL 387) refers to "Adam, Republic / ii.p. 264 ff": that is, the first Appendix to Book 8 in James Adam's edition of *The Republic of Plato* (2 vols.; Cambridge: Cambridge University Press, 1902), 2:264–312. The opening pages of this extensive appendix on "The Number" list, in addition to ancient sources such as Aristotle and Proclus, eleven scholars whose discussions Adam finds "interesting and occasionally suggestive" (264).

26 A. E. Taylor, *A Commentary on Plato's Timaeus* (Oxford: Clarendon Press, 1928; YL 2107), 217–18; in his copy, WBY made several annotations in the sections to do with the Great Year. See 397 n66. For "Plato's Man of Ur," see 392–93 n44 and 413–15 n1.

27 This quotation is also directly rendered from Duhem (1:290). The selections in Duhem are from Ernestus Diehl, ed., *Procli Diadochi In Platonis Timaeum commentaria* (3 vols.; Leipzig: Teubner, 1903), 3:91–94.

28 WBY owned two translations of Hegel, *The Logic of Hegel, Translated from The Encyclopaedia of the Philosophical Sciences* by William Wallace (2nd ed.; Oxford: Clarendon Press, 1892, YL 869) and *Hegel's Logic of World and Idea* by Henry S. Macran (Oxford: Clarendon Press, 1929, YL 868). In the former, WBY marked or turned down a number of pages at passages that argue against perceived separations of, for example, philosophy and religion (5), universal and singular (50–52), identity and difference (224–29), substance and infinity (415–16). In the latter, see Hegel's description of knowledge as a circle, from *Logic* 1:252: "By virtue of the nature of the method just demonstrated, knowledge presents itself as a *circle* returning upon itself, whose mediation carries round its conclusion into its beginning, the simple ground. Moreover, this circle is a *circle of circles*; for each individual link, as animated by the method, is introflection that in returning into the beginning is at the same time the beginning of a new link" (212–13).

29 This quotation follows immediately from the previous selection from Duhem (1:290).

30 According to H. J. Rose, "The Athenian year was supposed to begin with the summer solstice" ("Calendar [Greek]," Hastings 3:107).

31 The article on "Calendar (Persian)" in Hastings, by Louis H. Gray, reports that the first month in the Old Persian calendar was Garmapada ("footstep of heat"), which corresponded to the Hebrew Nisan. "This would make the commencement of the old Persian year harmonize with both the Avesta [later Persian calendar] and the Babylonian systems, as well as with the Hebrew sacred year" (3:128).

32 As WBY states, this passage is from Duhem on the Great Year in the Church fathers (2:451). Duhem quotes Nemesius (fl. 4th cent.), a Christian bishop of Emessa and author of *On the Nature of Man*,

a theological and anthropological text that influenced Byzantine and medieval philosophy significantly. Duhem's citations are from Nemesius Episcopus Emesenus, *De natura hominis*, Patrologiae Cursus Completus, Series Graeca 40 (Paris: J. P. Migne, 1863), Chap. 38, 759–62.

33 Slightly misquoted (WBY has misremembered "Mortality's" for "Immortalities," "furnace-fire" for "funeral pyre") from "From the Night of Forebeing: An Ode After Easter" by the Roman Catholic poet Francis Thompson (1859–1907), *New Poems* (Westminster: Archibald Constable, 1897; YL 2128), 48; *The Collected Poetry* (London: Hodder & Stoughton, 1913; YL 2127), 163. GY changed "Immortalities" to "Mortalities" in her copy of *AVB* (YL 2434). WBY included in *OBMV* Thompson's famous poem *The Hound of Heaven*, a fragment of the long poem *Sister Songs*, and a pair of sonnets. Thompson is mentioned in WBY's introduction to that volume (*LE* 184, 191, 202).

34 This date figures significantly in three plays written during the period when WBY was revising *A Vision*: *The Resurrection* (*Plays* 481–92), *The King in the Great Clock Tower* (*Plays* 493–500), and *A Full Moon in March* (*Plays* 501–8).

35 Plato (speaking as Timaeus) explains the opposite motions of the circles of same and other in *Timaeus* 36b–d; according to A. E. Taylor, these circles refer to the apparent paths of "fixed" stars in the equatorial circle and that of the sun in the ecliptic (Taylor, *Commentary* 148–49). See also Taylor, *Plato: The Man and His Work* (London: Methuen, 1926; YL 2109), 445.

36 Stoicism was a philosophical school from the Hellenistic period, Greek in origin and widely practiced in Rome, which taught detachment from emotions and indifference to all elements of external circumstance. Cicero admired the movement and is an important source of information; no complete work survives by the founder Zeno (344–262 BCE) or his immediate successors Cleanthes (d. 232 BCE) and Chrysippus (d. c. 206 BCE). Although Stoic philosophers were definitely interested in the Great Year, the number 15,000 comes not from any Stoic thinker but Macrobius, who, commenting on this passage, mentions that Cicero began his "world-year" with the hour of the death of Romulus and that the year will be completed 15,000 years later, according to "philosophers" (Macrobius, *Commentary on the Dream of Scipio*, trans. William Harris Stahl [New York and London: Columbia University Press, 1952], 2.11.9–15, 220–22). This value "was to enjoy great success in the Middle Ages and in the Renaissance" (Godefroid de Callataÿ, *Annus Platonicus* 122).

37 See *AVA* 123–25 and Duhem 1:283. Cicero sets a beginning date for a Great Year "when the Soul of Romulus entered into these sacred abodes" in *Somnium Scipionis* (*De re publica* 6.24; Bullock's

translation [YL 387], 12). Mother Shipton, a name linked with apocalyptic prophecies, is the popular name given to Ursula Southeil, the Yorkshire Sibyl, an English prophetess about whom relatively little is actually known, though a variety of pamphlets about her life and prophecies were (and are) widely available. For Cicero's opposition to official interpretations of the Sibylline Books and Virgil's attribution of the prophecy in his fourth Eclogue to that Cumaean Sibyl, see 417 n4 and 418–20 n7.

38 On the TS carbon, both instances of "36,000" in this paragraph were originally typed as "360000," with one of the zeros then struck through (NLI 36,272/6/2b, leaf 11).

39 Duhem's discussion of Hipparchus and Ptolemy on the precession of the equinoxes (2:180–89) underpins this section. As WBY states, this Great or Platonic Year is outlined by Plato and refers to the return of the constellations and planets to their original positions (*Timaeus* 39d). Hipparchus (c. 190–c. 127 BCE) was a Greek mathematician and astronomer who developed trigonometry and has historically been credited with discovering the precession of the equinoxes: according to Duhem, he determined that the rate of precession, i.e., the rate at which the stars move relative to the equinoctial points, is at least 1° per century (see also Adams, *Republic*, 304–5). Claudius Ptolemy (c. 90–c. 168 CE, not third cent.) was an astronomer, mathematician, and geographer from Roman Egypt. His treatise the *Almagest* (*Mathēmatikē Syntaxis*), the earliest extant work of Greek astronomy, was preserved in Arabic and became highly influential on later Christian and Islamic astronomy. Ptolemy used (and arguably misused) Hipparchus. He adopted the figure of 1° per century, which results in a complete cycle of 36,000 years, identifying it with the Platonic Great Year. Duhem treats the question of whether Hipparchus derived knowledge of precession from "astrologues de l'Orient" (i.e., Chaldean), 2:180. See also Alfred Jeremias, "Ages of the World (Babylonian)," Hastings 1:185, one of WBY's trusted sources on the Great Year; and Franz Cumont, *Astrology and Religion Among the Greeks and Romans* (New York and London: G. P. Putnam's Sons, 1912; YL 455), 5, 58.

The precession of the equinoxes actually takes slightly less than 26,000 years, the figure adopted by the Yeatses' Instructors. WBY was not greatly concerned with precise calculations: "because of our modern discovery that the equinox shifts its ground more rapidly than Ptolemy believed, one must, somebody says, invent a new symbolic scheme. No, a thousand times no; I insist that the equinox does shift a degree in a hundred years; anything else would lead to confusion" (*Ex* 396, *Plays* 725). For WBY's symbolic mathematics, see the note by Neil Mann, "Numbers, Accuracy and Precision," http://www.yeatsvision.com/Numbers.html. Cf. *AVA* 122–23 and Bullock, trans., *Somnium Scipionis* (YL 387), 34 n27. See also 150.

40 Aries, the Ram, the first sign in the zodiac, is a fire sign, ruled by the planet Mars (hence "martial"), and associated with masculine energy; in the tropical zodiac, the sun transits the sign between mid-March and mid-April. Capricorn the Goat, the tenth sign, is associated with winter (the sun is in Capricorn from mid-December to mid-January); it is an earth sign, ruled by Saturn, suggesting introversion and tenacity.

41 On the TS carbon, the final lines of this paragraph read "[. . .] cold and wet even if the Goat were lost. And every individual horoscope must preserve the seal set upon it by the position of the planets at their rising, setting and culminating" (NLI 36,272/6/2b, leaf 11).

42 *Ennead* 2.3 ("Are the Stars Causes?") elaborates on the idea that the stars "indicate events to come but without being the cause direct": Plotinus suggests that "we must at once admit signification" but cannot "ascribe to the stars any efficacy except in what concerns the (material) All and in what is of their own function" (Plotinus 2:159, 168).

43 Robin Ernest William Flower (1881–1946) was an Anglo-Saxonist and scholar of the Irish language; he lived on the Blasket Islands for a time and translated *An t-Oileánach* by Tomás Ó Criomhthain (*The Islandman* [Oxford: Clarendon Press, 1951]). The stories told to Lady Gregory and to Robin Flower are untraced, though Flower was visiting Coole in September 1931, when WBY was also staying there.

Cf. an unexplained reference to a "sky-woman" in *The Pot of Broth*, cowritten by WBY and Lady Gregory (*Plays* 117); and a story that contains an inner story about a woman in a cloud, included by Gearóid Ó Crualaoich in his study of the *cailleach* (supernatural old woman) in Irish tradition. The story was collected in the early 1930s from Peig Sayers on the Great Blasket Island (*The Book of the Cailleach: Stories of the Wise-Woman Healer* [Cork: Cork University Press, 2003], 150–52 and 256–57, cited from Kenneth H. Jackson [ed.], *Scéalta ón mBlascaod* [Baile Átha Cliath: An Cumann le Béaloideas Éireann, 1938]).

Time and Western Man (London: Chatto and Windus, 1927) includes an imaginary dialogue between "I" and "You," including this exchange:

> I. "Mr 4.30 or Mr. Eleven o'clock is a truer name than Smith?"
> YOU. "Certainly." (377)

Lewis here satirizes Bergsonian duration rather than the ideas of the British analytic philosopher and mathematician Bertrand Russell (1872–1970) per se, though *Time and Western Man* is an extended critique of notions of time in modern philosophy, including Russell's. On February 12, 1928, WBY wrote to Sturge Moore:

> I have read *Time and Western Man* with gratitude, the last chapters again and again. It has given, what I could not, a coherent voice to my hatred. You are wrong to think Lewis attacks the conclusions of men like Alexander and Russell because he thinks them "uncertain." He thinks them false. To admit uncertainty into philosophy, necessary uncertainty, would seem to him to wrong the sovereignty of intellect, or worse, to accept the hypocritical humility of the scientific propagandists which is, he declares, their "cloak for dogma." (*LTSM* 122)

44 The quotation is from Asclepius 3.35, *Hermetica* (YL 881) 1:329–31.

45 See *AVA* 124–25 and note, and 416–17 n3 above. The source mentioned is Plutarch's *Life of Sulla*; the immediate source is W. M. Flinders Petrie, *The Revolutions of Civilisation* (3rd ed.; London and New York: Harper and Brothers, 1922; YL 1359), 9–10. According to Petrie, the Great Year of the Etruscans is 1,100 years, not 11,000. The TS carbon (NLI 36,272/6/2b) ends here. See 413–14 n1 above.

46 The quotation is from Emmeline M. Plunkett, *Ancient Calendars and Constellations* (London: John Murray, 1903; YL 1596), 17 (this page is turned down in the Yeatses' copy). Georgius Syncellus (George the Syncellus), a Byzantine cleric and scholar who served under the Patriarch Tarasius and died after 810, wrote *Selection of Chronography*, a chronicle of history from the beginning of the world through the reign of the Roman emperor Diocletian. The *Genica* or Genetic books of Hermes (as *Genica* rather than *Genetica* in *AVA* 123 and Plunkett) and the Cyrannid books were theological, historical, and philosophical collections; they contained information about cycles in the computation of time. (Plunkett cites Syncellus, *Chronographia*, 52 [B. G. Niebuhr, ed., *Georgius Syncellus et Nicephorus Cp.*, Corpus Scriptorum Historiae Byzantinae [2 vols.; Bonn: Impensis Ed. Weberi, 1829], 1:97).

47 Duhem notes that Ptolemy posits a ninth sphere beyond the fixed stars in his *Hypothesis of the Planets* (Duhem 2:186). Ptolemy did not calculate the beginning date of the Platonic year.

48 These lines are from *The Resurrection* (*Plays* 482), quoted in WBY's introduction to the play (*Plays* 723) and also printed as one of "Two Songs from a Play" in *The Tower* (*Poems* 216).

49 The material of section X does not appear in NLI 36,272/26, the most complete surviving TS of the latter half of Book IV. See 413–14 n1.

50 See fig. 17 (60).

51 Cf. "The Four Ages of Man," identifying "struggles with the mind" with the third quarter of the wheel (*Poems* 294).

52 Frederick Scott Oliver (1864–1934) was an English historian and biographer, author of *The Endless Adventure* (3 vols.; London: Macmillan, 1931 and 1935). WBY's *Diary 1930* mentions reading this

book and its influence (*Ex* 289). *The Endless Adventure* focuses on the "great administration" of Sir Robert Walpole (1676–1745), after whose fall "there was such an accumulated loss of moral force, of manly independence, of alacrity in national service, that Britain seemed to lie at the mercy of a foreign invader and would-be usurper" (1:3, 16). In the note to *The Words Upon the Window-Pane*, WBY glosses a speech that expresses these opinions by the character John Corbet, noting that Corbet "may have read similar words in Oliver" (*Plays* 708). "Gothic" is here used metonymically to stand for northern European; cf. John Ruskin, "The Nature of Gothic," *The Stones of Venice*, Vol. 2, Chap. 6 (published separately as *The Nature of Gothic* [Hammersmith: Kelmscott Press, 1892]) and 209.

53 Spinoza, Leibniz, and Sir Isaac Newton (1642–1727) are linked with Jansenist monks at the Port Royal monastery in Paris, who took Descartes's notion that animals were machines to extreme and cruel lengths. In an often-quoted remark, a contemporary wrote that solitaries at the monastery, following the theologian Antoine Arnauld (1612–94), "nailed the poor animals up on boards by their four paws to vivisect them to see the circulation of the blood which was a great subject of controversy" (*Mémoires pour servir à l'histoire de Port Royal* [Utrecht, 1736], quoted in Tom Regan, *The Case for Animal Rights* [Berkeley: University of California Press, 1983], 5, quoting Leonora Rosenfield, *From Beast-Machine to Man-Machine* [New York: Columbia, 1968], 54).

54 Vico's theory of history, as elaborated in his *Scienza Nuova*, posits universal stages of historical development, which include a *ricorso* or return to a more primitive stage (though not exactly "the same point").

55 See a draft of this diagram in the first *Vision* notebook, *YVP* 3:172.

56 Petrie divides the "recurrences of civilisation" into eight periods and suggests that the fluctuations he tracks in the civilizations of Egypt and Europe are contemporary, "that is to say, in the same phase at one time" (81).

57 The material in this section does not appear in NLI 36,272/26, the latest surviving TS of the final sections of Book IV. See 413–14 n1. At this point in that TS are two sections that do not appear in the final text: see Appendix II, 292–93.

58 In 1924, WBY read and began to cite from *Origin of Christian Church Art*, trans. O. M. Dalton and H. J. Braunholtz (Oxford: Clarendon Press, 1923; YL 2026), by the Austrian art critic and National Socialist Josef Strzygowski (1862–1941). See *VPl* 80 and *Au* 525, and cf. *AVA* 141 and 289 n138. The parallel section in *AVA* does not link cardinal directions and symbolic civilizations with actual geography. Here, however, "my instructors imply not only the symbolical but the geographical East," and Strzygowski's method, "which I may

describe as research into essential character" (189), became useful, although WBY does not share Strzygowski's overt anti-Semitism. Sections of Strzygowski used include Chap. 7, "The Triumph of Representational Art. Hellenism, Semitism, Mazdaism," discussing geographical influences on levels of naturalistic or conventional representation (155–88), and the section on nonrepresentational European art on 153–54. For WBY's use of Strzygowski, Spengler, and Frobenius, see Matthew Gibson, "'Timeless and Spaceless'?—Yeats's Search for Models of Interpretation in Post-Enlightenment Philosophy, Contemporary Anthropology and Art History, and the Effects of These Theories on 'The Completed Symbol,' 'The Soul in Judgment' and 'The Great Year of the Ancients,'" Mann et al., 123–27.

59 Leo Viktor Frobenius (1873–1938) was a German ethnologist whose cultural theories were supported by fieldwork in Africa and whose work influenced Oswald Spengler. The Yeatses owned a copy of *Paideuma: Umrisse einer Kultur- und Seelenlehre* (Munich: C. H. Beck'sche Verlagsbuchhandlung, 1921; YL 715), which mentions a sense of depth associated with a cavern; the Yeatses' copy has marginalia by Pound, among others. WBY was introduced to Frobenius by Pound; either Pound or GY may have translated the material in *Paideuma*. On April 17, 1929, WBY wrote Sturge Moore that Pound was "sunk in Frobenius, Spengler's German source, and finds him a most interesting person. Frobenius originated the idea that cultures, including arts and sciences, arise out of races, express those races as if they were fruit and leaves in a pre-ordained order, and perish with them; and the two main symbols, that of the Cavern and that of the Boundless. . . . He proves his case all through by African research. I cannot read German and so must get him second-hand" (*LTSM* 153–54). Frobenius is mentioned in *Diary 1930* (*Ex* 313) and the note to *The Words Upon the Window-Pane* (*Plays* 713). WBY did apparently read Frobenius, *The Voice of Africa*, trans. Rudolf Blind (2 vols.; London: Hutchinson & Co, 1913); it is mentioned in the Rapallo Notebook E (NLI 13,582, leaf 1). Frobenius discusses the importance of sixteen directions to the Yoruban (as well as ancient Etruscan) conception of the world (see 252–64), though it is likely that WBY's interpretation of this work as well as *Paideuma* was influenced considerably by Pound.

60 See Frobenius, *Voice of Africa*, 1:260–61.

61 The phrase is a reference to Bergson's concept of duration, criticized by Wyndham Lewis in *Time and Western Man* (op cit., 166–67); cf. n43. Spengler correlates the invention of a clock mechanism, c. 1000 CE, with stirring of the "Faustian" or Western soul, and emphasizes the importance of a fascination with time to Western culture (*The Decline of the West*, 1:14–15). In the Yeatses' copy of this text, a pencil mark highlights the passage, "Observe the significant associ-

ation of time measurement with the edifices of religion" (1:15), and later, "Without exact time-measurement, without a *chronology of becoming* to correspond with his imperative need of archaeology (the preservation, excavation and collection of *things-become*), Western man is unthinkable" (1:124; YL 1975; we are grateful to Wayne K. Chapman for access to his photographs of these volumes). Spengler writes that the idea of "*window as architecture* . . . is peculiar to the Faustian soul and the most significant symbol of its depth-experience. In it can be felt the will to emerge from the interior into the boundless" (1:199).

62 The phrase is from the Brihadāranyaka Upanishad, Book 7, translated as "This knowledge is not born even in a priest" in *The Ten Principal Upanishads*, put into English by Shri Purohit Swāmi and W. B. Yeats (London: Faber and Faber, 1937), 157. This is one of the older of the main Upanishads. WBY's sources such as Arthur Berriedale Keith state that the Upanishads are often believed to be opposed to sacrifice, unlike the Brahmanas (priestly commentaries on the Vedas). However, Keith states, sacrifice is "expressly relegated to an inferior place"; and "sacrifice is least reputed in the Bṛhadāraṇyaka Upanishad where, with a certain insolence, the worship of anything except the self is derided." The theism and doctrine of predestination of the Upanishads represents "a later stage than [the] pantheism and cosmogonism [of the Brāhmaṇas]" (*The Religion and Philosophy of the Veda and Upanishads* [Harvard Oriental Series, vols. 31 and 32; Cambridge, Mass.: Harvard University Press, 1925; YL 1058], 514, 511). See Keith, Chap. 28, "The Philosophy of the Upaniṣads" (489–600). See also S. Radhakrishnan, *Indian Philosophy*, especially Chap. 4, "The Philosophy of the Upaniṣads" (2 vols.; London: George Allen & Unwin, 1923–27; YL 1663), 1:137–267. Radhakrishnan explains that "In the Upaniṣads we find an advance on the Vedic and the Brāhmanical conceptions of future life, though there is not yet any consistent theory about it. It is the idea of rebirth that is the prominent one in the Upaniṣads" (249). See also the *Ten Principal Upanishads*, passim, for details about doctrines such as karma, Self, illusion, and a kingly source mentioned here.

Shankar Gajannan Purohit, who went by the title Shri Purohit Swāmi (1882–1941), was an Indian guru who translated the *Bhagavad Gita* (*The Geeta* [London: Faber, 1935]). WBY met him through Sturge Moore in 1931 and worked with him for several years. WBY wrote to Mario Rossi on February 9, 1932, "I am now helping to correct a curious Autobiography which will I think make a stir. A year ago I met in London an Indian ascetic who has been wandering with a begging bowl for nine years & persuaded him to write all the simple objective facts of his life. The book is full of strange psychical experiences. I am to write the Introduction & describe the books origin. There is no other book of its kind" (*CL InteLex* 5596). WBY contributed introductions to Purohit's spiritual autobiography *An Indian Monk* (London: Macmillan, 1932), his translation of *The Holy Mountain* by his own guru Bhagwān Shri Hamsa (London: Faber, 1934), his translation of the Mandukya Upanishad (*The Criterion* 14 [1935]: 547–58), *The Ten Principal Upanishads*, and his translation of Patañjali's *Aphorisms of Yoga* (London: Faber, 1938), *LE* 130–38, 139–55, 156–64, 171–74, 175–80. WBY also included three translated poems in *OBMV* (223–24). See also *LE* 210, 291.

63 In GY's copy of *A Vision* (1938; YL 2435), there is written in the margin beside this sentence, "X untrue. GY had read Hegel's Philosophy of history."

64 See 7, 10, and 313 n24.

65 Gerald Heard (Henry Fitzgerald Heard, 1889–1971) was a British historian, philosopher, writer about science, and educator, who is best known for his book *The Five Ages of Man* (1963). The Yeatses owned a copy of his book *The Ascent of Humanity: An Essay on The Evolution of Civilization from Group Consciousness through Individuality to Super-Consciousness* (London: Jonathan Cape, 1929; YL 863); for Adams, Petrie, and Spengler see especially 214–29. WBY mentions Heard in *Diary 1930* (*Ex* 314).

WBY owned copies of three works by the American journalist and historian Henry Brooks Adams (1838–1918): his autobiography *The Education of Henry Adams* (Boston: Houghton Mifflin, 1918; YL 17; also YL 18); *Mont-Saint-Michel and Chartres* (Boston: Houghton Mifflin, 1913; YL 19); and *The Degradation of the Democratic Dogma* (New York: Macmillan, 1920; YL 16). The last is a posthumous collection consisting of one letter and two substantial essays, with a biographical essay by Henry's brother Brooks Adams. In January 1923, WBY wrote to the historian H. P. R. Finberg mentioning this book and the last essay, "The Rule of Phase applied to History" (*CL InteLex* 4255). On April 9, 1929, WBY commented to Sturge Moore about Spengler that "There are no doubt errors of historical detail but his vast enlargement of Henry Adams's *History as Phase*, for that is what his work is, is, if it were nothing more, magnificent as a work of imagination" (*LTSM* 150).

66 The quotation is from *The Philosophy of Giambattista Vico* (London: Howard Latimer, 1913; YL 445), 243; this book was given to WBY by GY in August 1924. The French socialist philosopher and syndicalist Georges Sorel (1847–1922) was a follower of Karl Marx who was influential on both Communist and Fascist thought; his book *Réflexions sur la violence* (1908) theorizes the virtue of violence and the importance of myth in the processes of history.

67 Sir John Collings Squire (1884–1958) was a British poet, historian, writer, anthologist, and editor of the *New Statesman* and the *Lon-*

don Mercury, known for his conservative literary and political tastes. WBY included one of his satiric poems in *OBMV*. His essay "The Reader" in the *Spectator* (No. 5,357, February 28, 1931, 304–5) is a reminiscence of seeing Vladimir Lenin (1870–1924) studying in the British Library, including the detail that "His principal study was sociology, economic theory, and the philosophy of history" (305).

68 "The Tendency of History," the first essay of the three collected in *The Degradation of the Democratic Dogma*, was sent as a letter in lieu of the annual address by the president of the American Historical Association (125). Adams describes the risks he sees in advancing his dynamic theory of history, determining that "In whatever direction we look we can see no possibility of converting history into a science without bringing it into hostility toward one or more of the most powerful organizations of the era" (131).

69 See 139 and 384 n9.

70 Most Christian philosophers through St. Augustine were in some sense Platonists. WBY may be recalling Nietzsche, for whom Christianity was fundamentally Platonic. In the preface to *Beyond Good and Evil*, Nietzsche writes that "Christianity is Platonism for the 'people'"; *Beyond Good and Evil*, trans. Judith Norman (Cambridge: Cambridge University Press, 2002). Cf. Nietzsche's remarks in "What I Owe to the Ancients" that Plato was "pre-existently Christian" (2); *Twilight of the Idols*, trans. Walter Kaufmann in *The Portable Nietzsche* (New York: Penguin, 1954). In *On the Genealogy of Morals*, Nietzsche refers to "that Christian faith which was also the faith of Plato" (3.24); London: T. Fisher Unwin, 1899; YL 1443, 207. Peter Liebregts notes that WBY may have found the idea in essays about Nietzsche by Havelock Ellis: "Plato fled from reality into the ideal and was a Christian before his time" (*Selected Essays* [London: J. M. Dent & Sons, 1936], 10; Liebregts 288).

71 Cf. Matthew 22:21.

72 The quotation is from the poem "The Second Coming" (1919), published in *The Dial* and *The Nation* in 1920 and then in the collection *Michael Robartes and the Dancer* (1921).

73 The material in this section does not appear in NLI 36,272/26, the latest surviving TS of the last sections of Book IV. See 413–14 n1.

74 A folder of rejected odd pages (NLI 36,272/30) includes a TS (leaf 28) for two additional sections following what is now the end of the text. See Appendix II, 292–93.

Book V: *Dove or Swan*

1 On March 23, 1935, WBY wrote to Harold Macmillan, "In sending you the script for 'A Vision' I forgot one diagram. At the beginning of Book III 'Dove or Swan' in the old edition of A Vision which you

are partly printing from there is a diagram in black and red called the historical cones. This is to be inserted at the same place in the new edition" (*CL InteLex* 6214).

2 For the story of Leda, see 336 n44. Written September 18, 1923, the poem was first published in the *Dial* (June 1924) as "Leda and the Swan"; this title was also used in its journal publication in *To-morrow* (Dublin, August 1924) and in its book publication in *The Tower* (London and New York: Macmillan, 1928). The immediate visual model for the poem is a plate in Élie Faure, *History of Art*, trans. Walter Path (4 vols.; London: John Lane; New York: Harper, 1921–24; YL 664), Vol. 1, *Ancient Art*, 2, reproducing the Roman copy of a Greek image of Leda and the swan in the British Museum (F. N. Pryce and A. H. Smith, *Catalogue of Greek Sculpture in the British Museum* [3 vols.; London, British Museum Press, 1892], Item 2199). See Charles Madge, "Leda and the Swan," *Times Literary Supplement*, July 20, 1962: 532; Ian Fletcher, "'Leda and the Swan' as Iconic Poem," *YA* 1 (1982): 82–113; and Elizabeth Butler Cullingford, *Gender and History in Yeats's Love Poetry* (Cambridge: Cambridge University Press, 1993), 153. For other literary and visual sources, see Giorgio Melchiori, *The Whole Mystery of Art: Pattern into Poetry in the Work of W. B. Yeats* (London: Routledge and Kegan Paul, 1960), esp. chaps. 2 and 3 as well as Excursus V, Renaissance Paintings of Leda, 280–82.

3 When Agamemnon returned home after the Trojan War, bringing along Cassandra as a part of his war booty, his wife, Clytemnestra (herself in the interval having become the lover of Aegisthus), killed him in his bath as retribution for his sacrificial slaying of their daughter Iphigenia and his unfaithfulness with Cassandra. This story is told in many Greek sources, including Homer, Hesiod, Aeschylus, and Pindar. The "broken wall and tower" are those of Troy, the city destroyed by the war brought on by the abduction of Helen (who was "engender[ed]" by the rape of Leda).

4 According to myth, Aphrodite (*aphros*, "sea-foam") was born of the sea foam near Paphos, Cyprus, after Cronus cut off the genitals of his father, Uranus, and the elder god's blood and semen dropped into the sea. Helen's abduction by Paris is said to have caused the Trojan War.

5 In Greek mythology, Niobe had seven sons and seven daughters; for boasting to Leto about the size of her brood, her children were killed by the children of Leto, Apollo and Artemis. Niobe wept ceaselessly and was transformed by the gods into a weeping stone. On civilization as "a struggle to keep control," see also "Meru" (*Poems* 289).

6 In Greek myth, the peacock derived from a hundred-eyed man, Argus Panoptes, "the all-seeing." Hera set him to guard a cow, the disguised form of the nymph Io, whom Zeus desired and had transformed to protect her from his wife. At Zeus's bidding, Hermes slew Argus,

and Hera put Argus's many eyes into the peacock's tail. The idea that the cry of the peacock produces terror comes from the bestiary tradition: see, for example, the *Aberdeen Bestiary*: "The peacock, as Isidore says, gets its name from the sound of its cry. For when it starts, unexpectedly, to give its cry, it produces sudden fear in its hearers. The peacock is called pavo, therefore, from pavor, fear, since its cry produces fear in those who hear it" (fol. 60v, trans. Colin McLaren; http://www.abdn.ac.uk/bestiary). See also "Meditations in Time of Civil War," sec. 3 ("My Table"), lines 31–32 ("it seemed / Juno's peacock screamed").

7 See Liebregts 280–89.

8 For the eggs of Leda, see 37 and 336 n43.

9 Arnold J. Toynbee (1889–1975) was a British comparative historian whose multivolume work *A Study of History* offered a globalizing theory of the rise and fall of civilizations based on an essentially religious outlook; the Yeatses owned the first three volumes, published in 1934 (2nd ed.; London: Oxford University Press, 1935; YL 2157). Toynbee's survey of Minoan culture stresses the relation between Minoan and later Greek societies, as the "largely monotheistic cult, in which the female form of divinity held the supreme place" of the former and survived as a "ghost of a Minoan universal church which the Hellenic Society succeeded in conjuring up from the tomb" (92–103, quotations from 97, quoting Sir Arthur Evans, and 100).

See Cumont, *Astrology and Religion Among the Greeks and Romans* (New York and London: G. P. Putnam's Sons, 1912; YL 455), for an extended treatment of the "astral 'mathematics'" of Babylonian astrology and its effects on Greek, Roman, and other ancient Middle-Eastern cultures (xvii). The copy of this book in the Yeatses' library belonged to GY, who purchased it in 1913 (Saddlemyer 60). For relations between the Babylonian zodiac and myths of gods, see also Alfred Jeremias, "Ages of the World (Babylonian)," Hastings 1:183–87. That Babylonian astrology spread to Egypt and thence to other cultures is a commonplace; see, for example, the article by Morris Jastrow, *Encyclopaedia Britannica*, 11th ed., s.v. "Astrology," 795–800. See also Burnet 21–22.

10 For Jewish thinking about long life, see such biblical passages as Exodus 20:12, 1 Kings 3:11–14, or Psalms 91:16. The Greek sentiment is common; for an early source, see Menander's fragmentary *The Double Deceiver* and its oft-quoted line, "the man dies young on whom the gods their love bestow" (Menander, *The Principal Fragments*, trans. Francis G. Allison, Loeb, 1921), 345. WBY frequently connected Irish and Greek traditions, as he did in a draft of this passage: "Not only Achilles but our own Cuchulain also, as competent men have thought, coming from that tribal fermentation" (NLI 36,269/4, leaf 1).

11 The "great Empire" of Minoan culture on Crete (c. 3000–1200 BCE) was presumably broken up by invading Greek tribes (2000–1000 BCE), who assimilated elements of Minoan culture. It is difficult to adjust the Yeatses' system to history: while the former would place the Ledean annunciation at roughly 2000 BCE (two millennia before Christ), the latter (to the degree that historians believe that a Trojan War was in fact waged) sets the fall of Troy between 1300 and 1200 (1184 BCE was the traditional date). The system stresses the polytheistic, individualistic nature of Greek religion and thought, in contrast to the subsequent Christian revelation but in accord with the one arriving imminently (see WBY's note to "The Second Coming," *Poems* 658–60).

12 WBY refers here to the so-called Dark Age(s) in Greek history, from the end of Mycenean (Bronze Age) civilization in about 1200–1100 BCE and the series of migrations that resettled Greece during this period, including what nineteenth-century historians called the "Dorian invasion" (associated with the legendary "return of the Heracleides"). The period, which is sometimes called the Homeric Age or the Geometric Age, extended roughly to the ninth century BCE and the formation of city-states (*poleis*).

13 The classical or Phidian period of Greek art (which falls between the Archaic and Hellenistic periods) is named for the Athenian sculptor Phidias (or Pheidias, active c. 465–425 BCE), who probably supervised the carving of the Parthenon frieze and was celebrated especially for his magnificent chryselephantine statues of *Athena Parthenos* (completed 438 BCE) and *Zeus Olympios*. Both were c. 12.75 m (40 ft) tall, and the latter was one of the seven wonders of the ancient world. See Chap. 5, "Phidias," in Faure, *History of Art*, Vol. 1, *Ancient Art*, 149–85. See also the mention of "Phidias' famous ivories" in "Nineteen Hundred and Nineteen," line 7 (*Poems* 210).

14 The Ashmolean Museum of Art and Archaeology at the University of Oxford has in its collection a fifth-century lekythos (a container for oil), with a red-figure image of a Nike suspended in air and plucking a cithara (AN 1888.1401 [V. 312]), which Michael Vickers suggests is the one to which WBY refers (*Ancient Greek Pottery* [Oxford, Ashmolean Museum, 1999], 43). The museum also houses an extensive collection of black-figure pottery, including a number of "certain pots" with images of horses; this technique was used in Greek pottery painting from about 700 BCE until the early fifth century.

15 For the Pre-Socratic Greek philosopher Anaxagoras, supposedly the first philosopher to move to Athens and establish the city as a center for philosophy, see n31 below. The Athenian tragic playwrights Aeschylus (c. 525–455 BCE) and Sophocles (c. 490s–406 BCE) were also fifth-century and thus "Phidian."

16 The cycle of 1,050 years (one-half of the larger wheel, as Yeats explains above) is itself divided into twelve sections, for which in this

Book he uses the term gyres (a term also used for other iterations of the basic symbol elsewhere in *A Vision*). As Neil Mann explains,

> Since they divide up a period of 1050 years, the twelve gyres of "Dove or Swan" are very roughly periods of a century or less. However they show a wide variation in "speed", ranging in practice from 195 years (1680–1875) to 30 years (800–830). The starting dates of the respective gyres were given by the Instructors, and Yeats himself finds a few of the dates rather perplexing, since they do not match his own understanding of either history or the System. He did not feel at liberty to change them, however, so that they stand largely as he was given them in a Sleep in December 1920 . . . ; there are three exceptions, all in the most recent dates, which show correction in the original: for the ninth gyre (19–20–21) Yeats crossed out 1680 in the notebook and put in 1740, but reverted to the first date in *A Vision*, where he also amended 1870 to 1875 and omitted the date for the start of the twelfth gyre (26–27–28), given as 2050.
>
> (http://www.yeatsvision.com/History.html)

On December 9, 1920, "George began diagram" and that night "'Carmichael' [the Control] gave confirmation of classification of devisions [*sic*] of historical cone being devided [*sic*] among phases" (*YVP* 3:60). GY's illustration is reproduced in *YVP* 3:61.

17 Lines 21–24 of "Under the Round Tower" (*Poems* 138), a poem that is a direct outgrowth of an AS (March 20, 1918) at Glendalough, the site of a ruined monastic center containing one of Ireland's famous round towers (*YVP* 1:394–95). This paragraph is slightly changed from the corresponding section in *AVA*, which makes clearer the alchemical and sexual suggestions of the royal dance:

> But one must consider not the movement only from the beginning to the end of the historical cone, but the gyres that touch its sides, the horizontal movement. There is that continual oscillation which I have symbolised elsewhere as a King and Queen, who are Sun and Moon also, and whirl round and round as they mount up through a Round Tower. (*AVA* 152)

18 The distinction between "Ionic elegance" and "Doric vigour" was a standard conception of art history: see Faure, *History of Art*, Vol. 1, *Ancient Art*, 121–38. Ionian art was also associated with the East; the *Encyclopaedia Britannica* calls the spread of its style to the mainland "orientalizing" and mentions that "Ionian painting is unrestrained in character, characterized by a license not foreign to the nature of the

race, and wants the self-control and moderation which belong to Doric art" (11th ed., s.v. "Greek Art," 476, 477). Liebregts suggests that WBY's use of the terms is also endebted to Walter Pater and Nietzsche (284–86).

The Persian Wars, in which Greece repulsed attacks by Darius and Xerxes, empowered the Greeks and created the conditions for the classical period in the fifth century. Cf. "The Statues":

> . . . the men
> That with a mallet or a chisel modelled these
> Calculations that look but casual flesh, put down
> All Asiatic vague immensities,
> And not the banks of oars that swam upon
> The many-headed foam at Salamis.
> Europe put off that foam when Phidias
> Gave women dreams and dreams their looking glass.
> (lines 9–16, *Poems* 345)

19 See *Republic* Books 2 and 3, in which Socrates suggests the necessity in the ideal State of casting out poets who tell immoral tales. (Note that this discussion also suggests banning music in Ionian or Lydian modes, characterized as soft, in opposition to vigorous-sounding Doric or Phrygian harmonies.) The destruction of Ionia resulted from the Ionian revolt against the Persian Empire (499–94 BCE); mainland Greek forces aided the Ionians, thus provoking the Persian Wars between Greece and Persia (c. 498–448 BCE).

20 Cf. Faure, *History of Art*, Vol. 1, *Ancient Art*: "The Dorian spirit and the Ionian spirit—the young countryman bursting with vigor and the woman bedecked, caressing, questionable—met and loved. Attic art, which in its adult age was to be the great classic sculpture, austere and living, was to be born of their union" (137–38). Tiziano Vecellio (1488/90–1576) was the greatest Italian painter of the Venetian school, a virtuoso known both for daring in colour and design and for elegance and simplicity in perception and mood. See similar remarks on Phidias and Callimachus in "Certain Noble Plays of Japan" (*EE* 166).

21 The Greek sculptor Callimachus (fifth century BCE) presumably designed the Corinthian capital based on acanthus leaves growing around a basket on a girl's tomb. See Adolf Furtwängler, *Masterpieces of Greek Sculpture* (ed. Eugénie Sellers [Strong], London: Heinemann, 1895): "In any case, the artist [Callimachus] belonged to the same Ionicizing school, which tended to a wide divergence from the Pheidian style . . ." (450–51). Furtwängler describes the "armchair found in front of the Pronaos of the Parthenon" (441), but he neither says that the chair was marble nor refers to the Persian. Note that in

"Lapis Lazuli" (lines 29ff., *Poems* 301), WBY seems to accept the more usual scholarly view that the chair should not be attributed to Callimachus. Pausanias describes the bronze lamp in *Description of Greece* 1.26.7 (Books 1–2, trans. W. H. S. Jones [London: Heinemann, 1918; YL 1545], 136–37). The lamp also appears in "Lapis Lazuli" (lines 33–34, *Poems* 301). Also see Furtwängler 437.

22 Furtwängler frequently uses the term "archaistic" in references to Callimachus (438–39). Here WBY seems to refer to Nikias, described by Furtwängler as "the head of the conservative party, and personally a man of strictly orthodox belief and timid piety" (432). Furtwängler also asserts that Nikias preferred building the Erechtheion (as representing the "old religion") to the Parthenon; Nikias commissioned a Palladion from Callimachus (438).

23 For this quotation from Heraclitus, see 346 n6.

24 WBY may be thinking of a passage from Longinus quoted by Gibbon in *The History of the Decline and Fall of the Roman Empire*, J. B. Bury, ed. (7 vols.; London: Methuen, 1909–14; YL 746), 1:58, and also by H. G. Wells in *The Outline of History* (London: George Newnes, n.d., 335), although Longinus is a bit late (c. 213–73 CE). See also J. P. Mahaffy, *Social Life in Greece from Homer to Menander* (7th ed. [London: Macmillan, 1907], 433–34), citing Cicero's *De natura deorum* (1.28) and the twenty-first oration of Dio Chrysostom.

25 The Greek comic dramatist Aristophanes (c. 448–380 BCE), known for biting satire and bold wit, raised comedy to the highest levels of artistic expression.

26 Aristotle (384–322 BCE) and his teacher Plato are considered to mark the beginning of organized ethical and epistemological Greek thought. See Burnet, for example, who writes that Pre-Socratic philosophy is visual and tactile rather than conceptual: "When, therefore we seek to understand these systems, what we have to do is not to think them by means of rational concepts, but to picture them in our minds by means of images" (27–28). Cf. "The Coming of Wisdom with Time" (line 4, *Poems* 93): "Now I may wither into the truth."

27 Platonic dualism is interpreted as promoting a kind of asceticism, in that devaluing the physical world presumably leads to profound dismissals like Stoicism and the practices of Christian hermits in the Egyptian deserts. Suicide was permitted in Stoicism. In the third century, the Egyptian Desert Fathers developed forms of spirituality that encouraged physical privation; their ways of life led to Christian monasticism (see n38 below).

28 Alexander III of Macedon (356–323 BCE), known as Alexander the Great, conquered the Persian Empire, including Anatolia, Syria, Phoenicia, Gaza, Egypt, Bactria, and Mesopotamia, and extended the boundaries of his own empire (which had originally included only the unified city-states of ancient Greece) as far as the Punjab. Following

the Asian campaign, Alexander turned back westward, possibly intending to conquer Arabia and then perhaps Carthage, Sicily, and Italy (although his intentions have long been disputed). After his death, his empire was divided among his officers, marking the beginning of the Hellenistic period, when Greek culture spread among and was changed by the non-Greek peoples conquered by Alexander.

29 The word "adore" suggests Byzantine emperor worship. WBY had learned of this in such works as W. G. Holmes, *The Age of Justinian and Theodora: A History of the Sixth Century A.D.* (2nd ed., 2 vols.; London: G. Bell, 1912; YL 903). See also Gibbon: "The mode of *adoration*, of falling prostrate on the ground and kissing the feet of the emperor, was borrowed by Diocletian from Persian servitude; but it was continued and aggravated till the last age of the Greek monarchy" (6:83).

30 On the taurobolium, or ritual bull-sacrifice, see Frazer, *The Golden Bough*, Part 4, *Adonis Attis Osiris* (2nd ed.; London: Macmillan, 1907; YL 700), 229–30; Grant Showerman, "Taurobolium," *Encyclopaedia Britannica* (11th ed., s.v. "Taurobolium," 26:455); and Franz Cumont, *The Oriental Religions in Roman Paganism* (trans. Grant Showerman [Chicago: Open Court, 1911]). Cumont twice uses the metaphor of the shower-bath (on 71–72 and 208); see also Wells, *The Outline of History* 337.

31 Stoicism and Epicureanism have often been pitted against each other in popular thinking, the former associated with the denial of pleasure and the latter with hedonism. The school of thought founded by Epicurus (341–270 BCE), an atomist and materialist, emphasized simple pleasure and friendship. The reference to the Greek philosopher Anaxagoras (c. 500–c. 428 BCE) may derive from translated passages about his theory of *Nous* ("mind" or "reason") in Burnet 282–85; Burnet also quotes from Plato's *Phaedo* (sec. 97) in which Socrates remarks, "I once heard a man reading a book, as he said, of Anaxagoras', and saying that it was Mind that ordered the world and was the cause of all things" (292).

32 Eugénie Sellers Strong, in *Apotheosis and After Life: Three Lectures on Certain Phases of Art and Religion in the Roman Empire*, addresses the "apocalyptic-messianic character that centred about Alexander looked upon as the 'Prince of Peace' who was to return and unite all mankind under his rule in a brotherhood of love" and the influence of "his portraiture, idealised into a type" upon "the plastic conception of the Christian God" (London: Constable, 1915, 280–81). GY purchased a copy of this book in early 1916 (Saddlemyer 83; YL 2015). On Strong's influence, see Murphy, Russell Elliott, "'Old Rocky Face, look forth': W. B. Yeats, the Christ Pantokrator, and the Soul's History (The Photographic Record)," *YAACTS* 14 (1996): 82–85.

33 For an almost identical passage written in 1902, see *Myth1* 43; *Myth2* 28.

34 The often-depicted biblical story of the death of John the Baptist at the behest of Salome is told in Mark 6:14–29. WBY's description echoes popular treatments of Salome in the nineteenth century, she is an exotic femme fatale in the work of Surrealist and Decadent writers and artists such as Aubrey Beardsley, Joris-Karl Huysmans, Stephane Mallarmé, Gustave Moreau, and Oscar Wilde.

35 In GY's copy of *A Vision* (1938; YL 2435), she has written beside this line, "Diary 1930." See *Diary 1930*: "Where did I pick up that story of the Byzantine bishop and the singer of Antioch, where learn that to anoint your body with the fat of a lion ensured the favour of a king?" (*Ex* 291). Concerning the depiction of Roman emperors, see Strong's *Apotheosis and After Life*, which is particularly concerned with their deification and the relationship between these depictions and artistic portraits of Christ. Strong mentions a lead medallion with images of "Diocletian and his colleague, who, with their solar nimbi, resemble two enthroned apostles" (96–97, also 103; see also *YVP* 3:89). See also Cumont, *Astrology and Religion Among the Greeks and Romans*, 53–56.

36 See also *Au* 346: "In Christianity what was philosophy in Eastern Asia became life, biography and drama."

37 These dates comprise a cycle: 1,050 years is also half the larger cycle, to end in 2100 with the coming of the New Messiah. The manuscript at this point is headed "AD 1 to AD 100" (NLI 36,269/1, leaf 4).

38 Scopas (or Skopas, fl. 4th cent. BCE) was a Greek sculptor of the late classical period. The Thebaid is a region near Thebes in ancient Egypt, associated with early Christian monasticism such as that of St. Anthony. Among WBY's sources are James O. Hannay's *The Spirit and Origin of Christian Monasticism* (London: Methuen, 1903) and *The Wisdom of the Desert* (London: Methuen, 1904); Gustave Flaubert's *The Temptation of St. Anthony* (trans. D. F. Hannigan [London: H. S. Nichols, 1895]); and Gibbon (Chap. 37). WBY mentions the Thebaid in the poem "Demon and Beast," especially lines 43–50 (*Poems* 188–89); see also *Ex* 301 and *Au* 238, 242.

39 See O. M. Dalton, *Byzantine Art and Archaeology* (Oxford: Clarendon, 1911; YL 461): "The Emperor Marcus Aurelius expressed one truth when he said that everything which is beautiful is beautiful in itself and terminates in itself. But to the artists of the Middle Ages, whether in East or West, this was false doctrine. To them the individual was nothing, the immanent idea or *eidos* was both a type and an ensample" (37).

40 Duhem and Burnet outline Greek discoveries. See Burnet's account of Diogenes of Apollonia: "The earth itself is round, that is to say, it is a disc: for the language of the doxographers does not point to the spherical form" (365). The theory of the plurality of worlds also appears in Burnet's accounts of Anaximander (64), Anaximenes (82),

Anaxagoras (295), and Leukippos (358). Duhem notes that Aristarchus of Samothrace endorsed the heliocentric theory (1:418–23).

41 See *LE* 136–37: "Our moral indignation, our uniform law, perhaps even our public spirit, may come from the Christian conviction that the soul has but one life to find or lose salvation in: the Asiatic courtesy from the conviction that there are many lives."

42 Greek daimons were intermediaries between the gods and humans, like the Christian angel (from Greek *angelos*, "messenger"); however, unlike angels, Greek daimons could be spirits of human beings, especially heroes. Cf. *AVA* 239 n62.

43 The AS frequently contrasts love (*antithetical*) and pity (*primary*). The distinction is most forceful in a discussion of Judas and Christ (26 Jan 1918, *YVP* 1:290–92). The contrast is also important to the play *Calvary*: Christ's pity is "an objective realisation of a collective despair"; Judas, "the C[reative] G[enius] only," does not pity (*YVP* 1:291; see *Plays* 695–97).

44 Jesus' parable of the Good Samaritan appears in Luke 10:29–37.

45 This date is close to Gibbon's (248 CE) for the turning-point for the worse in Roman history (Gibbon, Chap. 7). The manuscript at this point identifies "Phases 2 to 7 AD. 100 to AD 300" (NLI 36,269/1, leaf 8).

46 Eugénie Strong writes that Roman art "only becomes of paramount importance in the historic chain in the second century after Christ" (*Roman Sculpture from Augustus to Constantine* [London: Duckworth, 1907], 10). A long entry in one of the notebooks containing records of Sleeps from April 6 [1921] cites Strong's book. Concerning Phase 27 ("always the union with external strength"), WBY observed: "I do not feel that my old people were creative—I have seen something like them though less kindness in roman faces in the procession, perhaps of the altar of peace in Mrs Strongs book—but their culture is subjective. Will the second master (from 16, 17 or 18) find among such his deciples?, & use their objective method as christ when he personified himself in Judas used the subjective classical method" (*YVP* 3:87–88). On the "altar of peace," see Strong, *Roman Sculpture* 39–58.

47 See Strong, *Roman Sculpture* 347–76.

48 In *Discoveries*, WBY refers to "the young horsemen on the Parthenon, that seem happier than our boyhood ever was" (*EE* 212). And he had surely read Walter Pater's comment in the essay on "Winckelmann" in *The Renaissance*: "If a single product only of Hellenic art were to be saved in the wreck of all beside, one might choose perhaps from the 'beautiful multitude' of the Panathenaic frieze, that line of youths on horseback, with their level glances, their proud, patient lips, their chastened reins, their whole bodies in exquisite service" (London: Macmillan, 1935; YL 1539), 203–4.

49 See Faure, *History of Art*, Vol. 1, *Ancient Art*: "Sarcophagi and statues were made in advance: the orator dressed in his toga, the general in his cuirass, the tribune, the quaestor, the consul, the senator, or the imperator, could be supplied at any time. The body was interchangeable. The head was screwed on to the shoulders" (284–85).

50 Cf. "The Statues," lines 20–22 (*Poems* 345). After this point, the manuscript has a header, "Phases 8 & 9. AD 300 to 450" (NLI 36,269/1, leaf 12). In the typescript derived from it, which has several variations in dates, the subtitle reads "Phase 8. A D 325 to 395" (NLI 36,269/4, leaf 12).

51 Blake, "The Mental Traveller," line 95 (Blake 486; *WWB* 2:33). See also 80, where WBY quotes this line slightly differently.

52 The Yeatses were more interested in the mental than the physical phenomena of spiritualism, but they were widely read on the topic and had both attended séances in which the medium communicated with the dead using methods including trance or "direct voice" speaking and rapping on or tipping tables.

53 See Gibbon: "In the Byzantine palace, the emperor was the first slave of . . . the rigid forms which . . . besieged him in the palace. . . . The legislative and executive power were centered in the person of the monarch" (6:89–90). See also Holmes, *The Age of Justinian and Theodora*, concerning the Roman Empire under Anastasius:

> In earlier times a Roman proconsul in his spacious province was almost an independent potentate during his term of office, the head alike of the civil and military power. But in the new dispensation no man was intrusted with such plenary authority. . . . a shift of authority was made, and the reins of government were delivered into fewer hands, until, at the head of the system, the source of all power, stood the Emperor himself. (1:332)

54 See Gibbon:

> Since the time of the Peloponnesian and Punic wars, the sphere of action had not been enlarged; and the science of naval architecture appears to have declined. . . . The principles of maritime tactics had not undergone any change since the time of Thucydides; a squadron of galleys still advanced in a crescent. . . . Steel and iron were still the common instruments of destruction and safety; and the helmets, cuirasses, and shields of the tenth century did not, either in form or substance, essentially differ from those which had covered the companions of Alexander or Achilles. (6:92–94)

55 Thaumaturgy, or wonder-working (from Gr. *thauma*, wonder or marvel, and *ergon*, work), was associated with holy men and women

in Christian times; it was first used in English by Dr. Dee (1570), who also gave it the associations with magic it now carries.

56 Ammonius Saccas (first half of the third century CE), the Alexandrian self-taught philosopher and teacher of Plotinus and Origen, is usually considered the founder of Neoplatonism, although he left no writings; his second name literally indicates that he had been a sack-carrier in his youth.

57 In GY's copy of *A Vision* (1938; YL 2435), this last phrase is underlined, and a note in the margin reads, "+ re-read in Sept. 1913 at the Prelude, Coleman's Hatch GY."

58 Origen (Oregenes Adamantius, c. 185–c. 254) was the most learned theologian and biblical scholar of the early Greek church. He studied with Clement of Alexandria, and Porphyry attests to his having attended lectures given by Ammonius Saccas. His deep knowledge of Neoplatonism made him suspect to late Church Fathers, but it probably explains his attractiveness to WBY and GY. GY studied Origen in 1913 (Saddlemyer 48); in 1928, WBY wrote that Origen was the only "Father of the Church . . . I have read or rather dipped into" (*L* 734).

59 Constantine I (Flavius Valerius Aurelius Constantinus, 272–337) defeated Maxentius, one of his many rivals for the imperial throne, at the battle of the Milvian Bridge near Rome (312). According to H. B. Workman in Hastings, Constantine "was warned in a dream on the night before the battle to draw the monogram of Christ [the labarum or Chi Rho] upon the shields of his soldiers." Workman's essay also discusses the complex topic of Constantine's relation with Christianity, including his deathbed baptism, and the story of "The return of his aged mother Helena from her pilgrimage to Palestine . . . with two nails from the Cross, one of which he turned into the bit of his war-horse" (4:77–78). Having placed his capital at Constantinople, Constantine established Christianity as the state religion in 324.

Gibbon tells the famous story and analyzes the vision of the cross (2:299–305). He also stresses that Constantine's conversion was both genuine and political: "In an age of religious fervour, the most artful statesmen are observed to feel some part of the enthusiasm which they inspire" (2:305–6).

60 The comment comes from a prophecy attributed to the pagan philosopher Antoninus as recounted by Eunapius in his *Lives of the Philosophers*, in the section usually called "Life of Maximus." WBY is likely to have found it in an article or in a lecture by William Ralph Inge, dean of St. Paul's Cathedral (1860–1954). In his article "Neo-Platonism" in Hastings, Dean Inge notes, "The real objection felt against Christianity was that it was the religion of 'barbarians.' One of the 4th cent. Neo-Platonists, Antoninus, predicted plaintively that 'a fabulous and formless darkness is about to tyrannize over all that is beautiful on earth'" (Hastings 9:317). In his Gifford lectures,

Dean Inge remarks further that "Modern historians too, lamenting the wreck of the ancient culture and the destruction of its treasures in the stormy night of the Dark Ages, have felt a thrill of sympathy with the melancholy prophecy of Antoninus, son of Eustathius, that soon 'a fabulous and formless darkness shall tyrannise over the fairest things on the earth'" (*The Philosophy of Plotinus, The Gifford Lectures at St. Andrews, 1917–18* [2 vols.; London: Longmans, Green, 1918; YL 954], 26). GY's copy of this book contains marginalia referring to *A Vision*. The text can be found in Eusebius, *Lives of the Philosophers and Sophists*, in Philostratus and Eunapius, *The Lives of the Sophists* (ed. and trans. Wilmer Cave Wright [Loeb, 1922], 417). The passage is also quoted by E. R. Dodds, *Select Passages Illustrating Neoplatonism* (London: Society for Promoting Christian Knowledge, 1923), 8. In his autobiography, Dodds assumes credit for having introduced WBY to the phrase (*Missing Persons* [Oxford: Oxford University Press, 1977]), 60. The phrase also appears in WBY's note to *Fighting the Waves* (*Plays* 706) and is alluded to in the opening song from *The Resurrection* (*Plays* 482), also published as one of "Two Songs from a Play" (line 16, *Poems* 217). We are grateful to Neil Mann for his assistance: see Mann, "*A Vision* [1925]: A Review Essay," *YA* 18 (2013), 282.

61 WBY's primary sources for Byzantine history include Holmes, *The Age of Justinian and Theodora* (YL 903); Dalton, *Byzantine Art and Archaeology* (YL 461); Strong, *Apotheosis and After Life* (YL 2015); Gibbon; the *Encyclopaedia Britannica*; and the *Cambridge Mediaeval History* (see Jeffares, *New Commentary on the Collected Poems* 212).

62 The manuscript, much revised in this section, identifies "Phases 10 11 12 13.14.15.16" with "AD 450. to 600" (NLI 36,269/1, leaf 13).

63 The book of Revelation (sometimes called the Apocalypse after its Greek title, taken from the first word of the text) is the last book of the New Testament. The writer, who identifies himself as John, offers a prophetic vision of the new Jerusalem (21:1–22:5).

64 Justinian I (Flavius Petrus Sabbatius Justinianus, 483–565) was emperor of Byzantium from 527 until his death. He closed the Academy of Plato in Athens in 529 and opened the domed basilica of Hagia Sophia, rebuilt under his direction into the greatest cathedral of its time, in 537.

65 This idea echoes a famous passage from Gregory of Nyssa's "Oratio de deitate Filii et Spiritus Sancti":

> This city [Constantinople] . . . is full of mechanics and slaves, who are all of them profound theologians, and preach in the shops and in the streets. If you desire a man to change a piece of silver, he informs you wherein the Son differs from the Father;

> if you ask the price of a loaf, you are told, by way of reply, that the Son is inferior to the Father; and if you inquire whether the bath is ready, the answer is, that the Son was made out of nothing.

This passage is quoted in Gibbon (3:142–43), in Holmes (1:280n), and in G. W. F. Hegel's *The Philosophy of History* (3.3.3; trans. J. Sibree [1858; rev. ed., New York: The Colonial Press, 1899], 339).

66 Cf. O. M. Dalton, *Byzantine Art and Archaeology*:

> Suppose a Venice, suddenly enriched and without individual tradition, opening her gates not to one or two foreign artists, but to a host, a *colluvies pictorum*, from any quarter where a vigorous art flourished, and you have some parallel to the position of Constantinople in the fourth century. . . . by Justinian's reign the capital had attained a full self-consciousness; it had assumed to itself a directive power; and this epoch has been justly described as the First Golden Age of Byzantine Art. (10)

67 Satan as "the half-divine Serpent" suggests the myth of Eden, in which a serpent tempts Eve (Genesis 3), rather than representations of Satan as a devil (Revelation 12:9 and 20:22 conflate the two depictions, "that old serpent" and "the Devil"). The most common image of Satan in eastern Christian art occurs in iconic images of St. George killing the dragon (although the earliest images are from the twelfth century, later than the period WBY describes here), paralleling imagery of St. Michael and Satan in later art (often only the wings of Michael make it possible to differentiate). Cf. "Michael Robartes and the Dancer," *Poems* 177–78.

68 As articles on asceticism in the *Encyclopaedia Britannica* and Hastings explain, the word "ascetic" derives from the Greek *askesis*, meaning practice or exercise, and once referred to the discipline of the Greek athlete. See James O. Hannay, *The Spirit and Origin of Christian Monasticism*, who notes that in Eusebius "there is mention of Apphianus, an 'athlete of piety' . . . that is to say, an ascetic. This metaphorical use of the word athlete to denote an ascetic striver after perfection probably had its origin in St Paul's writings. It is common in the accounts of the fourth-century Egyptian hermits" (81). See also Hannay, *The Wisdom of the Desert* (London: Methuen, 1904), 21 and 143. In a passage cited by Aquinas and widely known, Origen uses this metaphor: "Many are strengthened in the flesh, and their bodies become more powerful. But an athlete of God should become more powerful in spirit" (*Homilies on Luke, Fragments on Luke*, ed. Joseph T. Lienhard, S.J. [Washington, D.C.: Catholic University of America Press,

1996], 11.3, 45). As Neil Mann notes, translations of Origen's homily available to WBY use the term "wrestler" rather than "athlete," but a passage in Eusebius, which mentions Alexandria, is suggestive:

> When Severus began to persecute the churches, glorious testimonies were given everywhere by the athletes of religion. This was especially the case in Alexandria, to which city, as to a most prominent theater, athletes of God were brought from Egypt and all Thebais according to their merit, and won crowns from God through their great patience under many tortures and every mode of death. Among these was Leonides, who was called the father of Origen, and who was beheaded while his son was still young.
>
> (Eusebius, *Church History*, 6.1, trans. A. C. McGiffert, in *A Select Library of Nicene and Post-Nicene Fathers of the Christian Church*, 2nd Series, ed. P. Schaff and H. Wace [London: Parker & Co., 1890], 1:249)

69 Cf. 18, 211, and 319 n47 in this edition.

70 The Greek *hagios* means both "holy" as an adjective and "saint" when combined with a name, and *sophia* means "wisdom"; the cathedral in Constantinople is literally both St. Sophia and "holy wisdom" (see also *LE* 133).

71 In *AVA*, the mosaics were "of Rome and Sicily" (159). In January and February 1925, the Yeatses traveled in Italy, visiting Sicily, Naples, Capri, and Rome. WBY's interest in Byzantine mosaics may have begun with his visit to Ravenna and Venice in 1907 (Foster 2:279, 1:367–69). On the details of WBY's visual encounters with Byzantine mosaics, see Murphy, "'Old Rocky Face, look forth'," 69–117; and Melchiori, *The Whole Mystery of Art*. See "Sailing to Byzantium" (*Poems* 197–98).

72 Faure follows this narrative, describing Greco-Roman art, in which "at the contact of Roman energy the Greek element recovered a certain dignity" and later Greco-Egyptian faces "with their faces of enigma and their shadowy eyes in which a light trembles" (*History of Art*, Vol. 1, *Ancient Art*, 214 and 228, figure on 226. Palmyra, an ancient city in central Syria, is famous for its archaeological sites including a necropolis featuring "sculptured portraits of the dead" (*Encyclopaedia Britannica*, 11th ed., s.v. "Palmyra," 20.652). On Fayyum mummy portraits, see W. M. Flinders Petrie, *Roman Portraits and Memphis (IV)* (London: School of Archaeology in Egypt and Bernard Quaritch, 1911). On conventional vs. realistic images of human forms, see Chap. 7 of Josef Strzygowski's *Origin of Christian Church Art*. See also Chap. 13 of O. M. Dalton's *Byzantine Art and Archaeology*. On the motif of the vine, see Strzygowski, 150–51 and Dalton 700–703.

73 See Strzygowski's *Origin of Christian Church Art*, Chap. 6, "Non-Representational Church Art, and the Subsequent Anti-Representational Movement." According to Strzygowski, the earliest Christian art was nonrepresentational, influenced by groups of people from east and north of Rome. He mentions that conflicts over the issue of representation occurred in tandem with the Council of Chalcedon (451), which insisted on the two natures of Christ (as God and man), 133–34. See also his discussion of the symbol of the cross (149). WBY presented these differing views of Christ's nature in *The Resurrection*, begun in 1925.

74 The opening of Hagia Sophia in 537 precedes the date 560 for the "climax" that is the midpoint Phase 15 on the diagram "The Historical Cones," fig. 22 (193).

75 In the Yeatses' system, the Age of Phidias, the Age of Justinian, and the Renaissance are parallel as fifteenth phases of millennial eras.

76 Leo III (c. 680–741), emperor from 717 to his death, issued a series of edicts in 726–29 prohibiting the worship of holy images. The source for this information is an entry in Hastings by Adrian Fortescue, who mentions that a "Jacobite bishop, Xenaias of Hierapolis, was a forerunner of the Iconclasts; and, when this party succeeded in getting the ear of the Emperor, the Iconclast persecution began" ("Iconoclasm," Hastings 7:78). Xenaias or Philoxenus was bishop (late fifth century–523) of Mabbug (Arabic *Manbij*) or Hierapolis Bambyce in what is now Eastern Turkey. He was an outspoken advocate of miaphysitism, a doctrine that holds that Christ has a single nature that is both divine and human, rather than two separate natures in one person. Miaphysitism (an orthodox position in Eastern Orthodox churches) is often identified with monophysitism, which claims that Christ has a single nature, the divine having dissolved the human (a doctrine declared heretical by the Fourth Ecumenical Council, held in Chalcedon in 451). At this point, the manuscript has the heading "Phases 16 to 25. A D 600 to 900" (NLI 36,269/1, leaf 19); in the revised typescript it has been changed to "Phase 22. AD. 630 to 900." 36,269/4, leaf 17).

77 Explaining the Iconoclast movement, Fortescue writes that "Undoubtedly in the 8th cent. the worship of images in the East had arrived at an extreme point. When we read of people who chose, not a living man but some special icon (εἰκών), to be the godfather of their child, and who ground an image to powder, mixed this with water, and drank it as a magic medicine, it is not dfficult to understand that a reaction would come" ("Iconoclasm," Hastings 7:78).

78 Born and educated in Ireland, Johannes Scotus Erigena or Eriugena (c. 815–77) went to the court of Charlemagne about 847, translated Pseudo-Dionysius the Areopagite from Greek into Latin, and wrote, as WBY put it in the manuscript, "an exposition of the orders of the

angels according to the vision of Dionysius" (i.e., *The Celestial Hierarchy*).

79 Phase 22 occurs in one cycle around 323 BCE, with the death of Alexander and the dissolution of his empire, and in another at between roughly 830 to 900 CE, a period that saw the Carolingian empire divided at the death of Charlemagne and contested thereafter; the various wars over succession ended in 843 with the Treaty of Verdun.

80 One draft of this passage in the manuscript has the heading "Phases 26. 27. 28. AD 900 to A D 1000," with "or 1100" crossed out (NLI 36,269/1, leaf 20); the next draft is headed "Phases 25 26. 27 AD 900 to 1000" (NLI 36,269/1, leaf 21).

81 Identification of "some book" and "another book" is problematic, perhaps because these are rhetorical tags and not references to any particular books. This period was often defined by historians in terms of "anarchy" (Christopher Dawson, *Progress and Religion: An Historical Enquiry* [London: Sheed and Ward, 1929], 165; *The Making of Europe: An Introduction to the History of European Unity* [London: Sheed & Ward, 1932], 266); WBY quotes from Dawson in Rapallo Notebook D (NLI 13,581, leaf 2). See also Faure, *History of Art*, Vol. 2, *Medieval Art*. Of this period, Faure remarks, "The Crusaders, from the end of the eleventh century onward, were hurling Europe upon the Orient in troubled torrents. . . . Europe breaks down the rampart that protects her from Asia" (227); "The religious communities had remained, up to the Crusades, the only isles of light in darkened Europe" (266).

82 Sydenham chorea (also known as St. Vitus Dance) is a neurological disorder characterized by brief, irregular contractions that appear to flow from one muscle to the next.

83 This passage may be influenced by Strzygowski's discussion of Northern and Eastern influence on Romanesque design. Strzygowski traces East Iranian motifs on one church—"the vinescroll with enclosed animals"—and suggests that comparison "reveals that fusion of Iranian and Greek art which succeeded the displacement of the latter in late Roman times, and led gradually to the development of Byzantine art on the Mediterranean, of 'Romanesque' in the West, and to the complete triumph of Iranian art in the world of Islam" (*Origins of Christian Church Art* 112–14). Romanesque art, sculpture, painting, and manuscript illumination flourished in France, Italy, Britain, and German lands from about 1000 until about 1150; the Romanesque period was succeeded by the Gothic.

84 Cf. 175.

85 See Gibbon:

> The influence of two sister prostitutes, Marozia and Theodora, was founded on their wealth and beauty, their political and am-

> orous intrigues: the most strenuous of their lovers were rewarded with the Roman mitre, and their reign may have suggested to the darker ages the fable of a female pope. The bastard son, the grandson, and the great-grandson of Marozia, a rare genealogy, were seated in the chair of St Peter; and it was at the age of nineteen years that the second of these became the head of the Latin Church. (5:297–98)

H. G. Wells notes of Theodora and Marozia, noblewomen of Rome whose histories are complex, that "these two women were as bold, unscrupulous, and dissolute as any male prince of the time could have been, and they are abused by historians as though they were ten times worse" (*The Outline of History* 448).

86 The Norman cathedrals at Cefalù (begun 1131) and Monreale (founded 1174) in Sicily are Byzantine in aesthetic. See Dalton, *Byzantine Art and Archaeology*, 410–12, and cf. *Diary 1930*, which mentions "a terrible Christ like that in the apse at Cefalù" (*Ex* 317). The Yeatses visited both Cefalù and Monreale in early 1925 during their travels in southern Italy with the Pounds. See Murphy, "'Old Rocky Face, look forth'," 69–117. On Phidias's *Zeus Olympios*, see Pausanias, 5.11.1 (*Description of Greece*, Books 2–5, trans. W. H. S. Jones [Loeb, 1926], 436–37), and note 688 above. For Byzantine images of Christ, see, for example, Christ Pantokrator, Dalton 409, 671; of the Virgin, Dalton 320, 402.

87 The source is "The Life of St. Pelagia." The tale is widespread, found in such collections as the *Legenda Aurea* (compiled by Jacobus de Voraigne, trans. William Caxton, ed. F. S. Ellis [London: Temple Classics, 1900], Vol. 5, 235; http://www.fordham.edu/halsall/basis/goldenlegend/GoldenLegend-Volume5.asp#Pelagienne. WBY demonstrated familiarity with a similar tale in *The Celtic Twilight* (*Myth1* 49, *Myth2* 32). See also a diary entry in *Diary 1930* (*Ex* 291).

88 From "The Tale of the Girl Heart's-Miracle, Lieutenant of the Birds" in *The Book of the Thousand Nights and One Night*; compiled and trans. J. C. Mardrus, ed. and rendered into English by E. Powys Mathers (2nd ed., 4 vols.; London: Casanova Society, 1923); YL 251 (Vol. 1), 4:495.

89 This passage draws not from the late twelfth-century poet Chrétien de Troyes but, as William O'Donnell notes, from William Wells Newell, *King Arthur and the Table Round. Tales chiefly after the Old French of Chrestien of Troyes, with an account of Arthurian romance, and notes* (2 vols.; London: A. P. Watt; Boston and New York: Houghton Mifflin, 1897), 2:137–39. See also *LE* 56, 163, and 384 n28.

90 See *Parzival: A Knightly Epic* by the German knight and poet Wolfram von Eschenbach (c. 1170–c. 1220), trans. Jessie L. Weston (2 vols.; London: David Nutt, 1894). Weston's notes suggest,

> It is very curious that, constantly as Baptism is insisted upon as essential to salvation, the equal necessity for the Second Great Sacrament of the Faith is passed over. It is perfectly true that Wolfram's knights attend Mass, and that Mass is apparently celebrated with regularity, but here their obligation seems to end; never once do we hear of one of his knights communicating, even Gamuret, when dying, though he receives absolution, does not receive the viaticum. (2:196)

At one point, Kunnewaare's squire comes upon Parzival and sees "A helmet all battle-dinted, and a shield which yet traces bore / Of many a bitter conflict that was foughten for lady fair" (1:161, lines 70–71). See also *IDM* 30, 103; *Au* 138.

91 The *locus classicus* of Gothic freedom is "The Nature of Gothic" in John Ruskin's *The Stones of Venice* (3 vols.; London: J. M. Dent, n.d., 2:138–212), which was published separately in 1892 in an ornamental edition by William Morris at the Kelmscott Press. Blake (in many places) and William Morris (in *Gothic Architecture*) similarly suggest that Gothic architecture allowed the workmen to cooperate yet express their individual views freely. St. Bernard of Clairvaux (1090–1153), the founder of the Cistercian order, explains his opposition to the wealthy Benedictine monks at Cluny in his *Apology* to Abbot William of St. Thierry (trans. Michael Casey, n.p.: Cistercian Publishers, 1970). In Chap. 12, he decries the Romanesque features of the wealthy abbey in Cluny as unworthy of monks; Faure cites it for its detailed descriptions of Romanesque architecture and sculpture (*History of Art*, Vol. 2, *Medieval Art* [YL 664], 336).

92 The thirteenth-century French architect Villard de Honnecourt's book of drawings (published Paris, 1858) contains sketches of machines, architecture, monuments, human figures, animals, and important Gothic churches in process. WBY visited Maud Gonne in Normandy in May 1910, and together they saw Mont Saint-Michel, home to the unusual Benedictine Abbey and steepled church (built between the eleventh and sixteenth centuries); see *Mem* 249–50, *EE* 245–46, and Foster 1:421. About Mont Saint-Michel WBY wrote,

> Yet at Mont-Saint-Michel I have been seeing a different art, a marvellous powerful living thing created by a community working for hundreds of years and allowing only a very little place for the individual. Are there not groups which obtain, through powerful emotion, organic vitality? How do they differ from the mob of casual men who are the enemies of all that has fineness? Why is it that the general thought is our enemy in the towns of Ireland, and would be our friend in the country if we had the same symbols? (*Mem* 250)

WBY had also read Henry Adams's *Mont-Saint-Michel and Chartres* (1904; Boston: Houghton Mifflin, 1913; YL 19): "I have read all Adams and find an exact agreement even to dates with my own 'law of history'" (*L* 666).

93 In GY's copy of *A Vision* (1938; YL 2435), "grown transparent" is underlined, and a note in the margin reads "Justinian & Theodora."

94 The Dominican order was founded by St. Dominic in 1216. Dominic wanted to bring the dedication and systematic education of the older monastic orders (like the Benedictines) to bear on the religious problems of the burgeoning city populations.

95 A chronology at the end of one of the notebooks shows that WBY's source was Adams: for the years 1180 to 1250, WBY wrote "(5.6.7) 1150 to 1250 given by Henry Adams as time when man most felt his unity in a unified world. He seeks its expression in 'Amiens Cathedral & the Works of Thomas Aquinas[']" (*YVP* 3:70). See *The Education of Henry Adams: An Autobiography* (Boston: Houghton Mifflin, 1918), 435.

96 This passage is also indebted to Adams. In the same note, WBY wrote: "325 to 400 AD (8) Constantine (Constantinople founded 324 (Gibbon) Henry Adams takes 310 as significant date 'Cross took the place of the Legions' (? coming of unification by Church)" (*YVP* 3:70). Compare with Adams: ". . . the nearest approach to the revolution of 1900 was that of 310, when Constantine set up the Cross" (*Education* 383). Gibbon devotes Chap. 17 to the establishment of Constantinople, which he dates to 324 or 326 (2:140). Another section of the chronology in WBY's notebook is pertinent: "1250 to 1300. Aparently struggles to establish Kingly Powers. Note C[haucer]'[s] allusion to King Arthur" (*YVP* 3:70). According to an entry for December 20, 1920, WBY had confirmation of his theory about this period from one of his Controls: "Was looking through some books of history to find why 1250 is the start of 50 years attributed to phase 8 & wondered if St Clovis consolidation of his power was typical of period when George heard a voice say 'Percys Reliques Vol III poem 5'[.] This proved to be a ballad about Arthurs struggle with his barons & so confirmed the opinion" (*YVP* 3:64). The poem cited is "The Legend of King Arthur" in Thomas Percy's *Reliques of Ancient English Poetry* (1765).

97 See WBY's essay "A People's Theatre" (1919):

> Dante in that passage in the *Convito* which is, I think, the first passage of poignant autobiography in literary history, for there is nothing in S. Augustine not formal and abstract beside it, in describing his poverty and his exile counts as his chief misfortune that he has had to show himself to all Italy and so publish his human frailties that men who honoured him unknown honour him no more. Lacking means he had lacked seclusion,

> and he explains that men such as he should have but few and intimate friends. (*IDM* 128)

The first treatise of the *Convito* laments the poet's exile and the consequent need to explain his work; see 1.3 and 4 (14–21).

98 Italian painters Giotto di Bondone (1267–1337) and Fra Angelico (Il Beato Fra Giovanni Angelico da Fiesole, 1395–1455) join French chronicler Jean Froissart (c. 1337–c. 1405).

99 References here are to Italian painter Masaccio (Tommaso di Ser Giovanni di Mone Cassai, 1401–28), English poet Geoffrey Chaucer (c. 1343–1400), and French poet François Villon (c. 1431–c. 1474).

100 Masaccio is usually said to have lived one more year than he is here allowed; WBY's friend Beardsley lived from 1872 to 1898.

101 This passage refers to three of Masaccio's paintings in the Brancacci Chapel (Florence): *The Baptism of the Neophytes*, *The Rendering of the Tribute Money*, and *The Expulsion of Adam and Eve.*

102 After a life of crime and several narrow escapes from death sentences, François Villon disappeared, leaving his partly serious, partly humorous *Testament*. See *L* 583 and *Au* 217, 240.

103 Casts of sculpture and architectural features from classical Greece and Rome and also from later periods in European art were part of the collection of the Victoria and Albert Museum from its establishment in 1852. Acquisitions from the 1860s to the 1880s especially emphasized the medieval and Renaissance periods, and after the Architectural or Cast courts opened in 1873, the large exhibit space allowed for considerable expansion of an already extensive collection. In 1916, the cast collection of the Architectural Museum, which was particularly strong in examples of Gothic architectural ornament, was brought permanently to the museum. The collection of casts of post-classical European statuary at the V & A is still perhaps the most comprehensive in the world.

104 The sculptor Donatello (Donato di Niccolò di Betto Bardi, c. 1386–1466); Michelangelo; the sculptor Jacopo della Quercia (c. 1374–1438); and the painter, draughtsman, and architect Raphael (Raffaelo Sanzio, 1483–1520) are all associated with the Italian Renaissance. The Greek sculptor Myron of Eleutherai (c. 470–c. 440 BCE) was a leading early classical bronze sculptor of the Attic school. There may be an echo here of Furtwängler, who observes of Myron that "the ancient orators name him among the last masters of the severe style" (*Masterpieces of Greek Sculpture* 182).

105 The Platonic Academy of Cosimo de' Medici, headed by Marsilio Ficino, was a fifteenth-century intellectual group loosely based on the Academy of Plato; members included Pico della Mirandola and Angelo Ambrogini (Poliziano).

106 The phrase "vestibule of Christianity" was a fairly common expres-

sion for periods leading into the Christian era. See, for instance, the title of Johann Joseph Ignaz von Döllinger's *Heidenthum und Judenthum, Vorhalle des Christenthums* (Regensburg: Verlag von G. Joseph Manz, 1857). See also F. X. Kraus in "Medicean Rome" (Vol. 2 of *The Cambridge Modern History*, ed. A. W. Ward et al. [Cambridge: Cambridge University Press, 1902–11], 2:61; YL 14). After describing the work of Julius II (1443–1513, pope from 1503–13), Kraus adds: "Not only Judaism, but also Graeco-Roman paganism, is an antechamber to Christianity . . ." (2:61). The German painter, draughtsman, and printmaker Albrecht Dürer (1471–1528) made two trips to Venice, in 1494–95 and 1505–7, during which he secured the commission for an altarpiece in San Bartolomeo, the church of the German community. The finished piece paid tribute to the aesthetics of Venetian painting of the time. On the "perfectly proportioned human body," see 353 n37 and 188.

107 See 203–4 and n68 above. This epoch takes its distinctive image from the roof of the Sistine Chapel: see "Under Ben Bulben" (*Poems* 333–36, lines 45–52) and "Long-legged Fly" (*Poems* 347, lines 21–22).

108 *The National Gallery Illustrated General Catalogue* (London, 1973) translates the inscription to Botticelli's *Mystic Nativity* (1500) discussed in WBY's note: "I Sandro painted this picture at the end of the year 1500 (?) in the troubles of Italy in the half time according to the 11th chapter of S. John in the second woe of the Apocalypse in the loosing of the devil for three and a half years then he will be chained in the 12th chapter and we shall see clearly (?) [damage] as in this picture" (62; insertions are from the *Catalogue*).

The Yeatses visited Capri in 1925, and as Murphy notes, WBY in the note refers to the natural Grotta di Matermania, transformed during Roman times into a nymphaeum, which has frequently, as in WBY's Baedeker (1912), been wrongly associated with Mithra. See Karl Baedeker, *Handbook for Travelers: Southern Italy and Sicily* (17th rev. ed. [Leipzig: Karl Baedeker, 1912], 187), and Murphy, "'Old Rocky Face, look forth,'" 70. On the linking of the Mithraic cave with the Christian manger, see Murphy, "'Old Rocky Face, look forth,'" 104–6.

109 Italian Renaissance painters Carlo Crivelli (1435–95) and Andrea Mantegna (c. 1431–1506), like Botticelli and Da Vinci, are of the generation following Masaccio, who is usually considered the first of the great quattrocento painters.

110 The quotation is from Baldassare Castiglione, *The Book of the Courtier*, trans. Sir Thomas Hoby (London: David Nutt, 1900; YL 351): "Therefore Beautie is the true monument and spoile of the victory of the soule, when she with heavenly influence beareth rule over martiall and grosse nature, and with her light overcometh the darkenesse of the bodie" (311). See *Mem* 157.

111 Roughly here in the manuscript, WBY marked the next division, then crossed out the following: "1500 to—Phases 16, 17, & 18." The terminal date was to have been 1640, the start of the next division, which extended to "?1880" (NLI 36,269/1, leaves 29, 32). Cf. *Au* 227–28.

112 A new generation of artists exemplifies the waning moon that begins after the phase of "complete beauty" that "knows nothing of desire, for desire implies effort" (101). See "Under Ben Bulben," lines 45–52 (*Poems* 334). Cf. the theory of eugenics WBY developed in *On the Boiler* (*LE* 220–51).

113 Pope Julius II directed the decoration of these rooms in the Vatican palace. In 1508–12, Michelangelo decorated the ceiling of the Sistine Chapel (the pope's private chapel and the site of conclaves for the election of popes), alternating Hebrew prophets and pagan sibyls in seated positions around the lower curved part of the barrel-vaulted room. Raphael painted the Stanza della Segnatura (1508–11), where the pope signed bulls and briefs. The long wall opposite the entry to the Stanza holds the *Disputa*, or "Disputation of the Holy Sacrament," a discussion about the Eucharist but also a glorification of Roman Catholicism. Opposite it is the *School of Athens*, showing the triumph of philosophy and a balance to the triumph of theology.

114 John Milton's "On the Morning of Christ's Nativity" (1629) stresses that the coming of Christ silenced the pagan oracles (*The Poems of John Milton*, ed. John Carey and Alastair Fowler [London and Harlow: Longmans, Green, 1968], 109). The Yeatses' library contains a copy of the poem with illustrations by William Blake (Cambridge: Cambridge University Press, 1923; YL 1320).

115 On the diagram of historical cones, Phases 16–18 are dated 1550, and the next gyre (Phases 19–21) has a date of 1680. In 1603, Elizabeth I died, and James VI of Scotland (1567–1625) assumed the throne of England as James I of England. The Jacobean Age, like the Elizabethan, is known for its flourishing literary culture. The English poets Abraham Cowley (1618–67) and John Dryden (1631–1700) wrote during the latter part of the seventeenth century.

116 The Flemish painter Sir Anthony van Dyck (1599–1641) became an important portrait painter in the English court of Charles I. The description of art from the Low Countries suggests the genre painting of Pieter Bruegel (Brueghel) the Elder (1525–69), as well as that of his sons Pieter Brueghel the Younger (1564/65–1636) and Jan Brueghel the Elder (1568–1625).

117 The English philosopher, statesman, and essayist Sir Francis Bacon (1561–1626) is known for establishing an inductive methodology for scientific inquiry. The Italian sculptor Gian Lorenzo Bernini (1598–1680) designed and created a bronze baroque canopy, 29 meters in height, that acts as a baldachin over the high altar of St. Peter's Ba-

silica in Rome. The plinths beneath the columns of this baldachin are decorated with images of a woman's face, contorted as if in pain.

118 WBY refers to the eighteenth-century poets Alexander Pope (1688–1744) and Thomas Gray (1716–71), the man of letters Samuel Johnson (1709–84), and the philosopher Jean Jacques Rousseau (1712–78).

119 In *Religio Medici* (1643), Sir Thomas Browne (1605–82) declares his belief in witches: "I could believe that Spirits use with man the act of carnality, and that in both sexes; I conceive they may assume, steal, or contrive a body, wherein there may be action enough to content decrepit lust, or passion to satisfie more active veneries . . ." (1.30). WBY quotes the same passage in *LE* 72; see also *Myth1* 267, *Myth2* 177. He owned copies of three editions of this work (YL 289–91).

120 See 381 n210.

121 The quotation is a paraphrase from the second stanza of "Claire de lune" by Verlaine (1844–96): "Ils n'ont pas l'air de croire à leur bonheur / Et leur chanson se mêle au clair de lune . . ." (*Fêtes galantes* [1869; nouvelle édition, Paris: Léon Vanier, 1891, 5). This well-known poem (inspiring music by Gabriel Fauré and Claude Debussy) and its collection *Fêtes galantes* are indebted to the painting of the French rococo painter Jean-Antoine Watteau (1684–1721). Faure considers Thomas Gainsborough the best of English eighteenth-century painters and finds in his portraits of society women a resonance from ancient mythology: "If those ethereal robes were torn, if the dulled tones of the crossed neckloths, the high, powdered coiffures, the laces, the blue ribbons, and the scarfs of pink pearl were to mingle their impalpable dust with the ashes of the airy harmonies which always accompany them, we should doubtless see, appearing for a second and instantly fleeing beneath the trees, tall, chaste huntresses who would not reappear" (*History of Art*, Vol. 4, *Modern Art*, 266). Egyptian sculptors worked in wood but often in more durable materials. The most famous face of an Egyptian princess is the beautifully preserved polychrome limestone bust of Nefertiti, wife of the Egyptian pharaoh Akhenaton (Amenhotep IV), now in the Altes Museum, Berlin.

122 The British painter Sir Joshua Reynolds (1723–92), whose stay in Rome (1749–52) emphasized study of Raphael and Michelangelo, was among the founding members and the first president of the Royal Academy of Arts. Like Blake, who published adverse marginal comments on Reynolds's *Discourses* (Erdman 635–62), and like the Pre-Raphaelite Brotherhood, WBY rejected Reynolds's aesthetic and epistemological theories. Faure is equally dismissive: "In the course of his travels on the Continent, Reynolds was not able to see, in Rembrandt, whom he pillages, and in the Venetians, whom he treats loftily in his Discourses, anything but a creamy and triturated paste, melting

tones, and lights with warm shadows. . . . He treats his admirable gifts as a painter like frippery to crumble with the tips of the fingers" (*History of Art*, Vol. 4, *Modern Art*, 263–64). In practice as well, as Bernadette McCarthy points out, WBY disliked Reynolds's advocacy of copying Old Masters as a principal method for training artists. WBY's courses at the Dublin Metropolitan School of Art and the Royal Hibernian Academy were based on ideas propounded by Reynolds (Bernadette McCarthy, Chap. 6, "Yeats and the Dublin Art Colleges," in "The 'lidless eye': W. B. Yeats, Visual Practice, and Modernism," PhD dissertation, University College Cork, 2011, 53–68).

123 The "village providence" apparently refers to the eighteenth-century idea of benevolence. Compare *LE* 44: "To Balzac indeed it [the solution of the social question] was but personal charity, the village providence of the eighteenth century . . ." cf. *EAR* 247. The claim is that the Faust of part 2 (written in Goethe's elder years) expresses a good-hearted eighteenth-century desire, as did the hero of Samuel Richardson's novel *Sir Charles Grandison* (1753). Similarly, in his later years, Voltaire defended religious freedom. Cf. *Mem* 158: "Faust in the end was only able to reclaim land like some officer of the Agricultural Board."

124 WBY told Lady Gregory that he had enjoyed reading the novels of English novelist Jane Austen (1775–1817) during the American tour that he and GY took in the spring of 1920 (Foster 2:168).

125 The English writers Blake and Arnold are compared with the Belgian poet Émile Verhaeren (1855–1916).

126 The French painter Louis Gustave Ricard (1823–73) was best known for his still lives and portraits in the classical manner. See *EE* 174. According to the *Grove Dictionary of Art*, Ricard, a "reclusive, studious aesthete," "worked for long periods of time on his portraits without his sitters being present. When his task seemed almost complete, he would recall them and was quoted as saying that he took pleasure in seeing how they resembled the portraits he had made of them" (s.v. "Ricard, [Louis-]Gustave"). The English painter and writer Charles Ricketts (1866–1931) founded the Vale Press and, with the English painter and lithographer Charles Shannon (1863–1937), edited *The Dial* (1897–99). His effect on WBY is clear from letters and from *Self-Portrait Taken from the Letters and Journals of Charles Ricketts, R. A.*, collected and compiled by T. Sturge Moore, ed. Cecil Lewis (London: Peter Davies, 1939). WBY owned a number of Ricketts's books (YL 1727, 1745–49). Ricketts illustrated the first edition of Oscar Wilde's poem "The Sphinx" (1894). WBY included "the Charles Ricketts of *The Danaides*, and of the earlier illustrations of *The Sphinx*," among "the great myth-makers and mask-makers" (*Au* 403–4). Ricketts created three wood engravings for T. Sturge Moore's *Danae: A Poem* (London: Hacon and Ricketts, 1903).

127 The first major novel of Charles Dickens (1812–70) was *The Posthumous Papers of the Pickwick Club*, better known as *The Pickwick Papers* (1836). See WBY's remarks at the opening meeting of the Dublin University Philosophical Society, as reported in "The Modern Novel" (*Irish Times*, November 9, 1923):

> Sometime in the middle of the eighteenth century there came into the faces of women, as painted by the great painters, an exquisite subtlety which they called a mark of high breeding. They got it in Gainsborough and one or two painters before him, and they got it in the first volume of "Sir Charles Grandison." Then he [WBY] found the same thing in the novels of Jane Austen. These novels were simply a description, an elaboration, of the pursuit of good breeding—that was to say, a quality which only a few happily nurtured people ever found. Then he did not find that pursuit again until they got to the writings of Henry James.
>
> He discovered, about five years ago, the particular devil that spoiled that celebrated quality in literature. "Pickwick" was the devil. In "Pickwick" the qualities celebrated were qualities any man could possess: good humour, a certain amount of openness of heart, kindness—qualities which everyman might hope to possess; they were democratic qualities. It gave them the kind of sculpture they saw in Dublin, like Tom Moore and the statue in Leinster Lawn. That smile of vacuous benevolence came out of "Pickwick."
>
> (Quoted in Torchiana, *W. B. Yeats and Georgian Ireland* [Evanston, Ill.: Northwestern University Press, 1966], 212)

See also Lady Gregory's journal entry for November 11, 1925: "Talking of novels, Yeats said Jane Austen and Richardson had written only of the upper classes. 'Dickens changed all that'" (*Lady Gregory's Journals 1916–1930,* ed. Lennox Robinson (London: Putnam, 1946), 262.

128 In addition to Blake, Nietzsche, and Spencer, this list includes the English poet and critic Coventry Patmore, the English novelist Samuel Richardson (1689–1781), the Russian novelist Leo Tolstoy, and the English political philosopher Thomas Hobbes (1588–1679). In *AVA*, the last cluster also includes the English philosopher and political economist John Stuart Mill.

129 The idea of Eternal Return, that one's life might recur in exactly the same way, requires the "highest formulation of affirmation that is at all attainable" (EH 3:Z-1) and is an important concept in Nietzsche's work. In 1902, WBY wrote excitedly to Lady Gregory about his discovery of Nietzsche, "that strong enchanter": "I have read him so much that I have made my eyes bad again. . . . Nietzsche completes Blake and has the same roots" (*L* 379).

130 See 309–10 n14.
131 The references are to the novels *War and Peace* (1865–69) by Tolstoy and *La tentation de Saint Antoine* (*The Temptation of Saint Anthony*) by Flaubert.
132 The "recent mathematical research" recalls *The Education of Henry Adams*, Chap. 31, in which the work of various modern scientists and mathematicians ("since Bacon and Newton") suggest to Adams that "Chaos was the law of nature; Order was the dream of man" (451); the older scientific view had transitioned to a scientific relativism where—as Poincaré had said—Euclidean geometry is not more true but more convenient than non-Euclidean types (455). In the reference to "a new dimension," there may be an echo of the discussion of "The Limited Universe" in Lyndon Bolton's *Introduction to the Theory of Relativity*: "The curvature of space, or of the aether, leads to the conclusion that any region, if sufficiently extended, may eventually bend round into itself, and thus that the universe of experience may be limited" (London: Methuen, 1921; YL 240, 170–71). The new dimension is time.
133 At this point, *AVA* continues with explanation and prophecy of the recent past and near future. With the manuscript of the new material, WBY gave instructions to the compositors:

> After the words "possibility of science["] in "Dove or Swan" – "A Vision" page 210— put a row of dots and then the words "finished at Capri. February 1925."
>
> Omit all from "possibility of science" to the end of page 215 and insert instead what follows, under the heading "1931 to the end of the cycle". (NLI 36,272/6/2c, leaf 10)

134 Several extant drafts (from 1932) discuss the contemporary period, including political and artistic figures and movements. A letter to Olivia Shakespear of July 23, 1933, mentions being introduced to General O'Duffy of the Fascist Blueshirt movement; WBY writes, "I was ready, for I had just re-written for the seventh time the part of *A Vision* that deals with the future" (*L* 812). See Foster's account of the meeting between two men "on different levels," as GY put it (2:474). However, WBY finally trusted his own admission that (in the words of one draft) "No more can perhaps be said" and omitted most analysis and prophecy from his conclusion (NLI 36,272/4/2).

A heavily corrected nine-page typescript entitled "Michael Robartes Foretells" is probably one of the discarded versions of the ending of *A Vision* (published in *YO* 219–24 and separately in Hazard Adams, *Blake and Yeats: The Contrary Vision* [Ithaca: Cornell University Press, 1955], 301–5). This section of the text was reworked many times. See, for instance, NLI 36,272/31 (dated "Oct 16, 1931") and

36,272/32, which is substantially different. One TS, dated September 1932 and preserved with the TS carbon, represents a radically different conception of this section from that printed in 1937: see Appendix II.

135 Balzac had a famous infatuation (which ended badly) with Claire Clémence Henriette Claudine de Maillé de La Tour-Landry, the Duchesse de Castries (1796–1861). See the story "L'Illustre Gaudissart" ("Gaudissart the Great"), which opens *Parisians in the Country*, trans. James Waring (one volume of the Temple reprint of the J. M. Dent complete *Comédie Humaine* [New York: Macmillan, 1901]; YL 99). Dedicated "To Madame la Duchesse de Castries," it begins:

> Is not the commercial traveller—a being unknown in earlier times—one of the most curious types produced by the manners and customs of this age? And is it not his peculiar function to carry out in a certain class of things the immense transition which connects the age of material development with that of intellectual development? Our epoch will be the link between the age of isolated forces rich in original creativeness, and that of the uniform but levelling force which gives monotony to its products, casting them in masses, and following out a unifying idea—the ultimate expression of social communities. After the Saturnalia of intellectual communism, after the struggles of many civilisations concentrating all the treasures of the world on a single spot, must not the darkness of barbarism invariably supervene? (1)

WBY refers to the idea of "history as a personal experience" expressed by "Balzac in his letter to the Duchess de Castries" in the "Private Thoughts" section of *On the Boiler* (*Ex* 429–30). Cf. Warwick Gould, "The 'myth [in] . . . reply to a myth'—Yeats, Balzac, and Joachim of Fiore," *YA 5* (Houndmills, Basingstoke: Macmillan, 1987), 238–51.

136 See *Au* 130–39 for WBY's recollection of gatherings at the "old stable beside Kelmscott House, William Morris's house at Hammersmith," the "debates held there upon Sunday evenings by the Socialist League" and "the little group who had supper with Morris afterwards" (*Au* 130). See also Philip Henderson, *William Morris: His Life, Work, and Friends* (New York: McGraw-Hill, 1967), 301–2.

137 Toyohiko Kagawa (1888–1960) was a Japanese Christian peace activist, labor organizer, and writer, especially honored by Protestants in the United States; he was twice nominated for a Nobel Prize and is venerated by the Episcopal Church (USA) and the Evangelical Lu-

theran Church in America. On August 19, 1927, WBY mentioned in a letter to the Japanese scholar Shōtarō Oshima that he had been reading "Toyohiko Kagawa's Novel which is translated into English under the title 'before the Dawn', and find it about the most moving account of a modern saint that I have met, a Tolstoyan saint which is probably all wrong for Japan, but very exciting to an European" (*CL InteLex* 5014). See also a diary entry in *Diary 1930*, *Ex* 326–29. We have not identified the "Galway clergyman."

138 Captain J. R. White (1879–1946), born in County Antrim, was an officer in the British Army before resigning his commission and returning to Ireland, working for Home Rule, the workers movement, and leftist republican politics. He cofounded the Irish Citizens Army with James Larkin. Chap. 16 of his memoir *Misfit* (London and Toronto: Jonathan Cape, 1930) describes his experience in Whiteway Colony, a communist experimental community in the Cotswold Hills, including his encounter with Francis Sedlak, "the only man I have ever met who claimed to have mastered and digested Hegel's logic."

> He had written a book called *A Holiday with a Hegelian*, which no one on earth but himself could understand. I, as little as any; but I could understand that Francis understood. He had entered a world of pure thought with the key of Hegel's logic that suited him. He retained his giant's body, but he lived in his mind. He was no longer a groundling, but on the road to become a god. He declared he had found a key to the movements of the heavenly bodies in the fifty-two movements of thought in Hegel's logic and could make thereby slight corrections in astronomical calendars. (147)

Sedlak's appearance is described by Nellie Shaw ("the lady to whom he once described himself as 'married but not legally, my wife objecting to chattel slavery'" [146]) in her own words:

> In those days we was pure Communists. . . . Well, as I was sayin', we was eating our lunch one day when I looked up, and there was the queerest sight comin' along the road ever I seen in all my life; a great 'airy giant of a man as naked as 'is mother made 'im to the waist, and nothing but a pair of running-drawers, and sandals below that. (149–50)

139 WBY refers here to the *fascio*, a bundle of sticks bound together with an axe, borrowed from Roman iconography and used in Fascist Italy as a symbol of the state.

140 These two lines vary only slightly from those of WBY's poem "Conjunctions," from the sequence "Supernatural Songs" (*Poems* 294). In

a letter to Olivia Shakespear, August 25, 1934, WBY frames a full quotation of the poem: "I was told, you may remember, that my two children would be Mars conjunctive Venus, Saturn conjunctive Jupiter respectively; and so they were—Anne the Mars-Venus personality. Then I was told that they would develop so that I could study in them the alternating dispensations, the Christian or objective, then the Antithetical or subjective. The Christian is Mars-Venus—it is democratic. The Jupiter-Saturn civilization is born free among the most cultivated, out of tradition, out of rule" (*L* 827–28).

141 See 407 n36.

All Souls' Night

1 Written in November 1920 and published in March 1921 (in *The New Republic* and *The London Mercury*), the poem would later appear as the close of *The Tower* (London and New York: Macmillan, 1928). In the Roman Catholic Church, All Souls' Day (usually November 2) is the feast on which the earthly church prays for the souls of the faithful departed suffering in Purgatory. It is also "the night before the Irish *Samhain*," which "was the proper time for prophecy and the unveiling of mysteries" (John Rhys, *Lectures on the Origin and Growth of Religion as Illustrated by Celtic Heathendom*, 2nd ed. [London: William and Norgate, 1892; YL 1741], 514). See also Frazer, *The Golden Bough*, 6:51–83 and cf. 10:224; and *IDM* 10.

2 Like the other two friends whose ghosts are summoned in the poem, William Thomas Horton (1864–1919) was a fellow member of the Hermetic Order of the Golden Dawn. He was a visionary artist; WBY wrote the introduction for his *A Book of Images* (London: The Unicorn Press, 1898; YL 918, Wade 255). Horton's ecstatic Platonic love for the historian Amy Audrey Locke (who died in 1916) left him inconsolable. After her death, according to WBY, Horton "saw her in apparition & he believed, & held communion with her . . . & attained through her certain of the traditional experiences of the saints" (qtd. in George Mills Harper, *W. B. Yeats and W. T. Horton: The Record of An Occult Friendship* [London: Macmillan, 1980], 2).

3 For Florence Farr Emery, see 402 n17.

4 For "Chance and Choice," cf. "Solomon and the Witch," lines 20–32 (*Poems* 179); on how a soul might "sink into its own delight," cf. "A Prayer for My Daughter," lines 65–72 (*Poems* 192). These existential polarities are related to the distinctions between Destiny and Fate, which depend upon the *Daimon*. See 64, 101–2, and 139 in this edition, and cf. *PASL*: "I think that all religious men believe that there is a hand not ours in the events of life, and that, as somebody says in *Wilhelm Meister*, accident is destiny; and I think it was Heraclitus who said: the Daemon is our destiny" (*LE* 11).

5 For WBY's reminiscences of Samuel Liddell (MacGregor) Mathers (1854–1918), the founding chief of the Golden Dawn, see *Au* 159–62. Yeats dedicated *AVA* to Moina (Bergson) Mathers, MacGregor's wife, who was the sister of Henri Bergson (liii–lvi).

Appendix I

1 In Alspach, the mark "see table" has been replaced by the language from the table.
2 See n1 above.
3 In Alspach, this correction is made properly, to "*Cimitière Marin.*"
4 On the first-pull Coole proofs, right-hand headings are written in to correlate with the section of *A Vision* ("A Packet for Ezra Pound," "Michael Robartes and his Friends," etc.). These headings are printed on the second-pull proofs.
5 In the bound unmarked proofs for signature P, the text reads: Wheel [upper-case].
6 Again, in the bound unmarked proofs for signature P, the text reads: Wheel [upper-case].
7 In the bound unmarked proofs for signature P, the text reads: jelly fish [no hyphen].
8 In the bound unmarked proofs for signature P, the text reads: November, and, [with comma].
9 In the bound unmarked proofs for signature P, the text reads: I or West [no commas].
10 In the bound unmarked proofs for signature P, the text reads: wheel [lower-case].
11 On the second-pull proof, this section of the word is printed upside down.

Appendix II

1 WBY refers to *Enneads* 3.4, titled in MacKenna's translation "Our Tutelary Spirit" (Plotinus 2:46–53).
2 WBY quotes the same comment in "J. M. Synge and the Ireland of his Time," sec. 9 (*EE* 238). Synge wrote in a notebook of 1895–98: "Lyrics can be written by people who are immature, drama cannot. There is little great lyrical poetry. Dramatic literature is relatively more mature. . . . Lyrical art is the art of national adolescence" (*Collected Works: Prose*, ed. Robin Skelton [Gerrards Cross, Bucks: Colin Smythe; Washington, D.C.: Catholic University of America Press, 1982], 350).
3 WBY refers to specific poems from *Personae*. The poems of *Cathay* (London: Elkin Mathews, 1915; Gallup A9) are translations from

Chinese poetry, and "Homage to Sextus Propertius" appeared in *Quia Pauper Amavi* (London: The Egoist, 1919; Gallup A17).

4 This quotation that concludes the Cuala version of the passage is the first three of four lines of Pound's short poem "Ité," first published in *Poetry* in November 1913 and then in *Lustra* (1916). WBY leaves off the last line, "And take your wounds from it gladly" (*Personae* 95).

5 WBY seems to draw the idea that "in eternity opposites coincide" from Nicholas of Cusa, who in *De Possest* (1460) writes that in God all opposites coincide. See 425–26 n19 above.

6 WBY's note here about Blake's "Mental Traveller" also appears in the text on 139.

7 At this point in the TS, an "x" refers readers to a note the same as WBY's note to 146.

8 At this point in the TS, an "x" refers readers to a note corresponding to WBY's second note on 162.

9 William Lilly (1602–81), practitioner of horary astrology, was considered England's leading astrologer during the period of the Civil War: he predicted the defeat of Charles I at Naseby, advised many politicians and soldiers, and predicted the Great Fire fourteen years in advance. His library is preserved in the Ashmolean collection at Oxford.

10 The marked version of this text includes the following text, struck through: "and certain young men not all affected by Marxian Russia who in criticising literature repudiate as bourgeois all individual characterisation and commend let us say the second act of O'Caey's [*sic*] Silver Tassie because man is there described in the mass. Have not similar though finer susceptibilities exalted Ulysses and the Waste Land where character and detail however clearly seen lead the mind away into some undefined immensity, into sacred books. I think of Pirandello whose dramatis personae feel their own charact [sheet cut off] parasites who create by some carefully selected vice or crime or eccentricity an artificial character" (leaves 2–3).

11 WBY refers to Seán O'Casey's four-act play *The Silver Tassie* (1927–28), which WBY had rejected for the Abbey Theatre.

12 In addition to James Joyce's *Ulysses*, WBY refers here to T. S. Eliot's poem *The Waste Land* (1922).

13 The marked version of this text includes the following text, struck through: "These artificial characters are invented not out of any personal bias but from the mere pleasure of inventing; they claim no such authority as the Hunchback claims; they are technical tricks learned from the environment; there [*sic*] object is not permanence but plasticity; they are that 23rd phase which is symbolised by a juggler and by a man who beats his shadow with a whip. Phase24 [*sic*] must come with the acceptance of an external code, an ideal in life fixed by public opinion. One foresees an exagerration [*sic*] of everything that makes

the good as the mass of men understand perceive it, the general standard. Somebody has pointed out that civilisations in their final phase abandon in their practical life difficult or unattainable ideas, delight in some form of mass production whether of thoughts commodities or populations. One can expect some self-conscious" (leaf 5).

INDEX